oks

Insights

R FOR WRITERS

W9-CXU-850

Edited by PAUL ESCHHOLZ
and ALFRED ROSA
University of Vermont

Outlooks
and Insights

A READER FOR WRITERS

St. Martin's Press / New York

Library of Congress Catalog Card Number: 82-06-463
Copyright © 1983 by St. Martin's Press, Inc.
All Rights Reserved.
Manufactured in the United States of America.

76543
fedcba

For information, write St. Martin's Press, Inc.
175 Fifth Avenue, New York, NY 10010

ISBN: 0-312-59164-0

Interior design and photo research: BETTY BINNS GRAPHICS
Cover design and photography: DARBY DOWNEY

Part Opening Photographs

Private Lives: Harvey Stein
Family and Friends: Burt Glinn/Magnum
Thinking and Learning: Burk Uzzle/Magnum
An Awareness of Language: Cary Wolinsky/Stock, Boston
The Quality of Life: Burk Uzzle/Magnum
The Lively Arts: Ira Berger/Woodfin Camp
Pastimes: Erich Hartmann/Magnum
The State of the Union: Bohdan Hrynewch/Stock, Boston
Ultimates: Jill Freedman/Archive Pictures

Acknowledgments

Gordon Allport, "The Language of Prejudice." Reprinted from *The Nature of Prejudice* by Gordon Allport. Copyright © 1979, 1958, 1954 by permission of Addison-Wesley Publishing Co., Reading, MA.

Julia Alvarez, "El Doctor." Copyright © 1982 by Julia Alvarez. First published in *Revista Chicano-Riqueña* and reprinted by permission of the author.

Acknowledgments and copyrights continue at the back of the book on pages 752–757, which constitute an extension of the copyright page.

Preface

Outlooks and Insights is a new solution to an old problem: how best to use readings to help students improve their writing. Most teachers of writing, and indeed most writers, would agree that reading supports writing in many ways. A fine essay can serve as an example of masterful writing, and also of mature thought and insight; such examples can give inexperienced writers a sense of what is possible and inspire them to aim high. An essay can also provide students with information and ideas for use in their writing, or it may stimulate them to pursue new lines of inquiry and to write on new topics of their own. And of course an essay can illustrate rhetorical strategies and techniques in effective use. The readings collected here will serve all of these familiar purposes. But *Outlooks and Insights* has an additional dimension: It provides students with explicit guidance, through discussion, examples, and exercises, in reading well and in using their reading in their writing.

This guidance is provided, first of all, in an introductory chapter, "On Reading." Here we offer well-grounded, sympathetic, and practical instruction to students on how to become more active and accurate readers and how to turn what they read to effective use in their compositions. We acknowledge that different people respond differently to the same text, and also that one reader may use different reading strategies at different times according to the particular purpose. But we also insist that any interpretation of a text should be supported by evidence drawn from the words on the page, so that diverse readers can find common ground for discussion and agreement. To this end we offer criteria and a set of heuristic questions designed to help students respond fully to what they read and to help them distinguish between a purely personal response and reasoned understanding.

Many students simply do not know what to do when they are required to write about something they have read. To help them understand what is expected of them, "On Reading" offers not only advice but full-length examples of three different kinds of papers that composition students are frequently required to write: the paper that analyzes a reading, the expository or argumentative essay on a topic derived from the reading, and the personal experience essay. All three examples were written in response to the same selection, George Orwell's "A Hanging." The first analyzes some aspects of Orwell's rhetoric, showing how he uses certain details to support his thesis. The second argues in support of capital punishment, engaging Orwell's topic but taking an independent position on it. The third recounts a personal experience in which the student writer discovered her own aptitude for thoughtless cruelty. Taken together, these compositions suggest the wide range of original responses that are possible in college writing assignments.

The heart of any anthology is, of course, the selections it contains. The readings in *Outlooks and Insights* are both numerous and fresh, more than half of them appearing in a freshman reader for the first time. We have chosen 76 essays, 10 short stories, and 20 poems, offering instructors a large variety of options for making individual assignments and for organizing the course. The readings are grouped in nine thematic sections, beginning with themes of personal experiences and relationships, continuing with such aspects of our lives as education, life styles, pastimes, and the arts, and finally arriving at considerations of contemporary social issues and of universal religious and ethical questions. Each reading has been chosen to be challenging but not baffling, and we have sought not only to appeal to students' interests and concerns but to broaden them.

The selections are a mixture of the new and the familiar—familiar to composition teachers, that is, for few freshmen will have read even such durable pieces as E. B. White's "Once More to the Lake," Virginia Woolf's "The Death of the Moth," and George Orwell's "Politics and the English Language," essays that have earned their places in the small canon of essential readings for composition courses. We have hunted out unknown pieces by well-known authors and have discovered some writers new to us and, we expect, to many other teachers as well. Most of the essays were written in the last decade or two, but we have seasoned them with a few selections from classic authors—Montaigne, Jefferson, Swift, Thoreau, Abraham Lincoln, the apostle Matthew. In each section we have also included a few poems and a story or two which we think can be used effectively in a composition course; any writer can learn from the meticulously sustained irony of Auden's "The Unknown Citizen" as well as from Swift's "A Modest Proposal," from the controlled and modulated prose style of a Cheever or Oates story as well as from that of a White or Didion essay. The questions and writing suggestions for the stories and poems are much like those supplied for the essays, with minimal attention to questions of literary form, but at the end of "On Reading" we do alert students to some important generic differences, so that they will not read stories and poems in exactly the same way they read essays.

The questions and assignments supplied for each selection further develop and exploit the advice and instruction given in "On Reading." The study questions about each essay, story, and poem, like the general heuristic questions in the introduction, help students to test and increase their understanding of what they have read, and may also help them gather material for analytical papers. The assignments, which are called "Explorations," suggest a few ways that students may use a reading to start them on their own lines of thought, and are designed to elicit results ranging from autobiographical essays to research papers. After working with these questions for a while and using what they have learned from "On Reading," many students will be able to devise their own analytical questions and find their own avenues of exploration.

Each thematic section begins with a picture, a handful of epigraphs, and a few paragraphs that establish the range of its theme. These materials, particularly the epigraphs, may find use in their own right as objects of discussion and as sources of writing assignments. Each selection is provided with a biographical headnote, somewhat less terse and impersonal than is usual in composition readers, which sets the piece in the context of the author's work and where necessary supplies information about the author's original audience and purpose. To make *Outlooks and Insights* still more flexible and useful there is a rhetorical index that classifies the selections by type and by principle of organization, as well as a glossary that will help students understand rhetorical and literary terms in the questions without having to refer to other sources.

In working on *Outlooks and Insights* we have benefitted inestimably from the observations and suggestions of our fellow teachers. In particular we thank Miriam Dow, George Washington University; James A. W. Heffernan, Dartmouth College; Michael Hennessy, Southwest Texas State

University; Francis A. Hubbard, University of Wisconsin—Milwaukee; Wayne Losano, University of Florida; James H. Pickering, University of Houston; Alan C. Purves, University of Illinois at Urbana-Champaigne; and Edward M. White, California State College at San Bernardino, for their close reading and constructive criticism of parts of the manuscript. Our colleagues at the University of Vermont helped us by assigning George Orwell's "A Hanging" to their composition classes and providing us with student papers for the introduction, "On Reading," and Daniel P. Daley made especially useful suggestions concerning the selection of poems. We would also like to express our appreciation of our helpers at St. Martin's Press, especially John W. N. Francis, our editor, and Marilyn Moller, who oversaw the copy-editing and production of the manuscript. For the typing of the manuscript, we would like to thank Judy Cota, our secretary. Of our many other debts, more than there is space to repay, we want particularly to acknowledge the contribution of our students, who teach us something new every day.

Contents

2. *Family and Friends*   111

3. *Thinking and Learning* 187

4. *An Awareness of Language*   247

5. The Quality of Life

6. *The Lively Arts*   415

7. *Pastimes* 493

8. *The State of the Union* 571

9. *Ultimates*   651

Introduction: On Reading

PEOPLE read for many different reasons, and they read in different ways as well. They may read for enjoyment, or to improve themselves, or to gather information, or to obtain an education or do a job; sometimes their reading benefits them in several ways at once, and in ways they did not expect. Sometimes they read with painstaking care, while at other times they may skip and skim, or even begin reading in the middle or at the end, all depending on what they are reading and what they want from it. But whatever the reason and whatever the method, reading is most rewarding when it is done actively, in a thoughtful spirit and with an inquiring mind.

Many believe that the right way to read is passively, taking in what they read and storing it away for later use, as if on recording tape. But this kind of reading is seldom either fulfilling or useful. Unless you bring to bear on your reading what you know and believe, testing what you read and allowing it to test you, you will seldom find the experience particularly rewarding, and you may have some trouble even remembering much of what you have read. Active reading is less like tape recording than like conversation: You give as well as take. You examine and question the

1

author's claims, you remember and ponder ideas and information that relate to your reading, you even laugh at the jokes—at least the good ones. By responding so fully, you are taking possession of what you read, making it your own and getting it ready for use—in discussions with your friends, classmates, and teachers, for example, or in writing of your own.

Unquestionably, one of the benefits of active reading is that it can help you become a better writer. Reading can provide you with information and ideas for use in your writing, and often with subjects to write about. More, it can provide you with examples to learn from. Writing is a skill that can be learned, a skill like playing tennis or playing the piano, and one of the best ways to improve your writing skills is by observing how accomplished writers get their results. As you read you can see for yourself what a writer's strategies are, analyze how they work, and then adapt them to your own writing purposes. By picking up ideas and techniques from many different writers and incorporating them into your writing, you can increase your mastery and develop your own personal style.

Outlooks and Insights is a reader for writers, as the subtitle says. The selections in this book can entertain you, inform you, and even contribute to your self-awareness and understanding of the world around you, but above all they have been chosen and presented so as to aid your efforts to become a better writer. The writers included here are among the most skillful of their time, many of them well known and widely published. From their work you can learn important and useful writing strategies and skills. Most are contemporary, writing on issues of our own day for readers like us, but some great writers of the past are here as well. The idealism of a Henry David Thoreau, the moral indignation of a Jonathan Swift, the noble vision of an Abraham Lincoln continue to move readers despite the intervening years.

Outlooks and Insights is an anthology of writings arranged according to their subjects and themes. The first of its nine sections includes narratives and discussions of personal experiences and relationships, while the following sections broaden to increasingly wide frames of reference, finally arriving at themes concerning our society and, ultimately, all humanity. Each section begins with several aphorisms that can serve as topics for thought, discussion, and writing, and with a brief essay that defines and explores the section's theme. Within each section, every piece has its own brief introduction providing information about the author and often about the selection's original purpose and audience. After each piece there come two series of questions. The first set, called "About the Essay" (or poem, or story), is an aid to active reading. These questions ask you to analyze what you have just read in order to discover, or rediscover, important points about its content and its writing. The second set, "Explorations," offers a few ways to use the piece as a starting point for your own thoughts, for class discussion, or for writing. You will find that many of these questions have no single correct answer but rather ask you to state your own views. That is because all readers are different, and therefore respond to the same piece in different ways.

Different Readers, Different Responses

Each of us is unique, with our own experiences, tastes, views of the world, and so we respond in different ways to what we read. That is because the words on the page refer to experience, and if we are reading actively, engaging our whole minds and hearts, the words will evoke different experiences for each of us. The word *love* has dictionary meanings we may all agree upon, but it also has much stronger personal meanings growing out of the love each of us has felt and known. Should you suppress those personal meanings? Absolutely not! It may not be possible to tell exactly what love meant to the author but it was certainly not the flat, consensus definition given in the dictionaries. Indeed, authors themselves recognize and accept their readers' individuality. Ralph Waldo Emerson once wrote: "What can we see, read, acquire, but ourselves? Take the book, my friend, and read your eyes out, you will never find there what I find."

Yet the book, or the essay, story, or poem, presents the same words in the same order to those who read it. If the text leaves each of us much room for individual response, it also has an essential, core meaning of its own that different readers can agree on—if it did not, all writing and indeed all language would be futile. So while all of your responses to a text may be important to you personally, only some of them are relevant to the core meaning of the piece and contribute to your understanding of it. During your first reading you may not want to censor the thoughts and feelings as they come flooding in, for to do so might be to suppress something valuable. But sooner or later you must focus closely on the meaning of the text, trying to discover as fully and accurately as possible what it is trying to tell you.

For writers—and in one way or another we are all writers—there is a special reason to cultivate the habits and skills of close, critical reading. For everything we write we are our own first readers and critics. How well we read our own drafts will powerfully affect how well we revise them, and revising well is crucial to writing well. So reading others' writings carefully is an important practical exercise.

Understanding What You Read

What does it mean, to understand a piece of writing—an essay, for example? It means, of course, that you comprehend all the words in it. It also means that you have enough background knowledge to grasp its subject matter; a discussion of Brownian motion would mean little to someone who knew no physics, nor would an analysis of Elizabethan metrics enlighten someone unfamiliar with sixteenth-century English poetry. But there's more: You have only understood the essay if you have grasped it as a whole, so that you can summarize and explain its chief points in your own words and show what each part contributes to the whole.

As you read, you absorb the essay part by part. You cannot "read" the whole all at once, as you can take in a building or a face, but must hold most of the essay in your memory and form your impression of it bit by bit as you read. How this works—what the mind does—is not fully understood, and different readers may well have different ways of doing it. That could be yet another reason why a single piece can evoke so many diverse responses. But there are some guidelines that can help you achieve an understanding of what you read.

UNDERSTANDING THE PARTS

As you progress through an essay, word by word and sentence by sentence, keep the following guidelines in mind:

• Make sure you understand what each word means. If a word is new to you and the context does not make its meaning clear, don't guess—look it up.

• Stay sensitive to connotations, the associations words carry with them. The words *falsehood* and *fib* mean about the same thing, but they convey quite different attitudes and feelings.

• Watch for allusions and try to interpret them. If the author refers to "the patience of Job," you don't really understand the passage unless you know how patient Job was. If you don't understand the allusion, check standard reference works such as dictionaries, encyclopedias, and books of quotations, or ask someone you think might know the answer.

• Be on the alert for key words and ideas. The two often go together. One key word in this introduction, for example, is *different*; its repetition points up the key idea that individuals respond in diverse ways to what they read. A key idea within an essay is normally developed at some length in one or more paragraphs, and it may be stated directly at the beginning or end of a paragraph.

• Use your knowledge and your critical sense to test what you read. Is each "fact" true, as far as you know (or can find out)? Is the author's reasoning logical?

• Interpret figures of speech. When George Orwell speaks of a writer who "turns as it were instinctively to long words and exhausted idioms, like a cuttlefish squirting out ink," you must not only know or find out what a cuttlefish is but also find out how and why it squirts ink and consider how the image expresses the author's idea.

• Pay attention to where you are in the essay. Note where the introduction ends and the body of the essay begins, and where the body gives way to the conclusion. Note where the author turns, let us say, from personal narrative to a series of arguments, or where those arguments are succeeded by refutation of other people's views. And be on the alert for the point at which you discover what the essay is really about—the point where it "makes its move," like a chess player going on the attack or a basketball forward streaking toward the basket. Often the essay's purpose and main idea are clear from the beginning, but sometimes the author withholds or even conceals them until much later.

UNDERSTANDING THE WHOLE

As you read, you are constantly creating and recreating your idea of the essay as a whole. At the end you will have reached some conclusions about it. Here, again, are some points to keep in mind while reading:

• Look for the main idea of the essay—what is often called the *thesis*. Sometimes the main idea is directly stated, either in the introduction or later on; sometimes it is not stated but can be inferred from the essay as a whole. Define the thesis of an essay as narrowly and specifically as you can while still taking the whole of the essay into account.

Sometimes the author may be writing *ironically*, pretending to support a thesis that he or she actually opposes. Your clue that irony is at work may be that the main idea is so inhuman or ridiculous that nobody would advance it seriously—as for example in Jonathan Swift's "A Modest Proposal" (page 695). Gilbert Highet's analysis of Swift's piece (page 432) can help you understand irony better.

• Determine the author's purpose. Is it to persuade you to a point of view? to explain a subject to you? The author may directly state his or her purpose, or it may be clearly implied by the thesis.

• Consider the relation between the whole and its parts. How does the main idea of each paragraph relate to the thesis? Does the information supplied in the body of the essay support the thesis—make it more persuasive or easier to understand? Does the author ever seem to get away from the main point, and if so why?

• Look for omissions. Has the author left out any information that you think might be relevant to the thesis? Does he or she fail to consider any important views—including perhaps your own view? Does the author assume anything without supporting the assumption or even stating it? How important are these omissions—do they lessen the clarity or the persuasiveness of the essay?

• Look for implications. Information and ideas can have significance that an author does not discuss, and may not even realize. For example, John Kenneth Galbraith's proposals to deal with poverty (page 602) imply a massive redistribution of income from the haves to the have-nots, which in turn implies a substantial reduction in selfishness among the haves. This might lead a reader to conclude that Galbraith's solutions, however logical and humane, are not likely to be adopted at all soon.

• Evaluate the essay. Whether or not you like the essay or agree with it is important, but don't stop there; ask yourself why. Test its reasoning for errors and omissions. Test its explanations for clarity and completeness. Consider the author's style, whether it is suitable to the subject, agreeable or powerful in itself, and consistently maintained. In short, assess all the strengths and weaknesses.

Some Reading Tips and Techniques

Each essay offers its own distinctive challenges and rewards, but there are some reading techniques that you can use successfully with all of them in your quest for understanding. Here are some tips on reading.

Prepare Yourself. Before you plunge into reading the essay itself, form some expectations of it. Ponder the title: What does it tell you about the essay's subject matter? About its tone? Think about the author: Have you read anything else by him or her? If so, what do you know about the author's attitudes and style that may help prepare you now? If any materials accompany the essay, like the introductions in *Outlooks and Insights*, read them. These preparations will help you put yourself into an alert, ready frame of mind.

Read and Reread. You should read the selection at least twice, no matter how long or short it is. Very few essays yield their full meaning on first reading, and their full meaning is what you should be aiming to extract.

The first reading is for getting acquainted with the essay and forming your first impressions of it. The essay will offer you information, ideas, and arguments you did not expect, and as you read you will find yourself continually modifying your sense of its purpose, its strategy, and sometimes even what it is about or what point it is intended to make. (This is especially true when the author delays stating the thesis—or makes no thesis statement at all.) Only when you have finished your first reading can you be confident that you have then really begun to understand the piece as a whole.

The second reading is quite different from the first one. You will know what the essay is about, where it is going and how it gets there; now you can relate the parts more accurately to the whole. You can work at the difficult passages to make sure you fully understand what they mean. You can test your first impressions against the words on the page, developing and deepening your sense of the essay's core meaning—or possibly changing your mind about it. And as a writer, you can now pay special attention to the author's purpose and means of achieving that purpose, looking for features of organization and style that you can learn from and adapt to your own work.

Now why not read the essay a third time? If you do, you will find that you can now move through it rapidly yet with your appreciation of it heightened by what you discovered about it during that second, close, critical reading. And often you will find still more that is new, things that strike you as they did not during your previous readings. Try a third reading of a selection you especially like—you'll almost certainly be surprised at how much more you get out of it.

Ask Yourself Questions. As you probe the essay, focus your attention by asking yourself some basic questions about it. Here are some you may find useful:

1. Do I like the essay or not? What, for me, are the most interesting parts of it? What parts do I find least interesting or hardest to understand?

2. What is the essay's main idea? What are the chief supporting ideas, and how do they relate to the main idea?

3. What is the author's attitude toward the essay's subject? (Consider the possibility of irony.) What is the author's purpose? What readers was the author apparently writing for, and what is his or her attitude toward them? How am I part of the intended audience—if I am?

4. How is the essay structured? How does its organization relate to its main idea, and to the author's purpose?

5. Can I follow the essay's line of reasoning? Is its logic valid, however complex, or are there mistakes and fallacies? If the reasoning is flawed, how much damage does this do to the essay's effect?

6. Does the author supply enough information to support the essay's ideas, and enough details to make its descriptions precise? Is all of the information relevant and, as far as I know, accurate? Are all of

the details convincing? What does the author leave out, and how do these omissions affect my response to the essay?

7. What are the essay's basic, underlying assumptions? Which are stated and which are left unspoken? Are they acceptable, or do I challenge them? If I do, and I am right, how does this affect the essay's main idea?

8. What are the most important implications of the essay's ideas and the information it presents? Does the author acknowledge those implications and discuss them adequately? How do the implications affect my response to the essay's main idea?

9. Do all the elements of the essay relate, directly or indirectly, to its main idea? Can I explain how they relate? If any do not, what other purposes do they serve, if any?

10. Where do I place this essay in the context of my other reading? In the context of my life and thought? What further thoughts, and further reading, does it incite me to? Would I recommend it to anyone else to read? To whom, and why?

Each selection in *Outlooks and Insights* is followed by five or six questions, similar to the ones just suggested but usually more specific, which should help you in your effort to understand the piece. All of these questions work best when you try to answer them as fully as you can, remembering and considering many details from the selection to support your answers. Most of the questions are variations on these three basic ones: "What's going on here?" and "Why?" and "How do I feel about it?"

Make Notes. Keep a pencil in hand and use it. Some readers like to write in their books, putting notes and signals to themselves in the margins and underlining key passages; others keep notebooks and jot their responses down there.

There is no all-purpose, universal method for annotating a text; what you write will depend on the details of the work at hand and how you respond. But you may find these tips useful:

• Keep track of your responses. Jot down ideas that come to mind whether or not they seem directly relevant to what you are reading. If you think of a fact or example that supports the author's ideas, or disproves them, make a note. If a passage impresses or amuses you, set it off with an exclamation point in the margin. Converse with the text. Write *yes* or *no* or *why?* or *so what?* in response to the author's ideas and arguments.

• Mark words or passages you don't understand at first reading. A question mark in the margin may do the job, or you may want to circle words or phrases in the text. During the second reading you can look up the words and allusions and puzzle out the more difficult passages.

• Mark key points. Underline or star the main idea, or write it down in your notebook. Mark off the selection into its main sections, such as the introduction, body, and conclusion.

When annotating a text, don't be timid. Mark up the book as much as you please—provided, of course, that you own it! Above all, don't let annotating become burdensome; it's an aid, not a chore. A word or phrase will often serve as well as a sentence. You may want to delay much of your annotating until your second reading, so that the first reading can be fast and free.

Case Study: George Orwell's "A Hanging"

Some writers, and some essays, become classics—people continue to read them for decades or centuries. Such a writer is George Orwell, the English author best known for his novel, *1984*, a vivid and terrifying evocation of life in a totalitarian state. But that was his last major work. One of his first works was an essay, "A Hanging," which he wrote in 1931 (he was then twenty-eight) about one of his experiences as a police official in Burma, where he had served from 1922 to 1927. "A Hanging" was published in *The Adelphi*, a socialist literary magazine whose readers would have been sympathetic to Orwell's attitudes.

As you read "A Hanging," note your own questions and responses in the margins or in your notebook. At the end of the essay you will find one reader's notes to which you can compare your responses.

A Hanging

GEORGE ORWELL

It was in Burma, a sodden morning of the rains. A sickly light, like yellow tinfoil, was slanting over the high walls into the jail yard. We were waiting outside the condemned cells, a row of sheds fronted with double bars, like small animal cages. Each cell measured about ten feet by ten and was quite bare within except for a plank bed and a pot for drinking water. In some of them brown silent men were squatting at the inner bars, with their blankets draped around them. These were the condemned men, due to be hanged within the next week or two.

1

One prisoner had been brought out of his cell. He was a Hindu, a puny wisp of a man, with a shaven head and vague liquid eyes. He had a thick, sprouting moustache, absurdly too big for his body, rather like the moustache of a comic man on the films. Six tall Indian warders were guarding him and getting him ready for the gallows. Two of them stood by with rifles and fixed bayonets, while the others handcuffed him, passed a chain through his handcuffs and fixed it to their belts, and lashed his arms tight to his sides. They crowded very close about him, with their hands always on him in a careful, caressing grip as though all the while feeling him to make sure he was there. It was like men handling a fish which is still alive and may jump back into the water. But he stood quite unresisting, yielding his arms limply to the ropes, as though he hardly noticed what was happening. 2

Eight o'clock struck and a bugle call, desolately thin in the wet air, floated from the distant barracks. The superintendent of the jail, who was standing apart from the rest of us, moodily prodding the gravel with his stick, raised his head at the sound. He was an army doctor, with a gray toothbrush moustache and a gruff voice. "For God's sake hurry up, Francis," he said irritably. "The man ought to have been dead by this time. Aren't you ready yet?" 3

Francis, the head jailer, a fat Dravidian in a white drill suit and gold spectacles, waved his black hand. "Yes sir, yes sir," he bubbled. "All iss satisfactorily prepared. The hangman iss waiting. We shall proceed." 4

"Well, quick march, then. The prisoners can't get their breakfast till this job's over." 5

We set out for the gallows. Two warders marched on either side of the prisoner, with their rifles at the slope; two others marched close against him, gripping him by arm and shoulder, as though at once pushing and supporting him. The rest of us, magistrates and the like, followed behind. Suddenly, when we had gone ten yards, the procession stopped short without any order or warning. A dreadful thing had happened—a dog, come goodness knows whence, had appeared in the yard. It came bounding among us with a loud volley of barks, and leapt round us wagging its whole body, wild with glee at finding so many human beings together. It was a large woolly dog, half Airedale, half pariah. For a moment it pranced round us, and then, before anyone could stop it, it had made a dash for the prisoner and, jumping up, tried to lick his face. Everyone stood aghast, too taken aback even to grab at the dog. 6

"Who let that bloody brute in here?" said the superintendent angrily. "Catch it, someone!" 7

A warder, detached from the escort, charged clumsily after the dog, but it danced and gamboled just out of his reach, taking everything as part of the game. A young Eurasian jailer picked up a handful of gravel and tried to stone the dog away, but it dodged the stones and came after us again. Its yaps echoed from the jail walls. The prisoner, 8 in the grasp of the two warders, looked on incuriously, as though this was another formality of the hanging. It was several minutes before someone managed to catch the dog. Then we put my handkerchief through its collar and moved off once more, with the dog still straining and whimpering.

It was about forty yards to the gallows. I watched the bare brown back of the prisoner marching in front of me. He walked clumsily with his bound arms, but quite steadily, with that bobbing gait of the Indian who never straightens his knees. At each step his muscles slid neatly into place, the lock of hair on his scalp danced up and down, his feet printed themselves on the wet gravel. And once, in spite of the men who gripped him by each shoulder, he stepped slightly aside to avoid a puddle on the path.

It is curious, but till that moment I had never realized what it means to destroy a healthy, conscious man. When I saw the prisoner step aside to avoid the puddle I saw the mystery, the unspeakable wrongness, of cutting a life short when it is in full tide. This man was not dying, he was alive just as we are alive. All the organs of his body were working—bowels digesting food, skin renewing itself, nails grow-ing, tissues forming—all toiling away in solemn foolery. His nails would still be growing when he stood on the drop, when he was falling through the air with a tenth of a second to live. His eyes saw the yellow gravel and the gray walls, and his brain still remembered, fore-saw, reasoned—reasoned even about puddles. He and we were a party of men walking together, seeing, hearing, feeling, understanding the same world; and in two minutes, with a sudden snap, one of us would be gone—one mind less, one world less.

The gallows stood in a small yard, separate from the main grounds of the prison, and overgrown with tall prickly weeds. It was a brick erection like three sides of a shed, with planking on top, and above that two beams and a crossbar with the rope dangling. The hangman, a gray-haired convict in the white uniform of the prison, was waiting beside his machine. He greeted us with a servile crouch as we entered. At a word from Francis the two warders, gripping the prisoner more closely than ever, half led half pushed him to the gallows and helped him clumsily up the ladder. Then the hangman climbed up and fixed the rope round the prisoner's neck.

We stood waiting, five yards away. The warders had formed in a rough circle round the gallows. And then, when the noose was fixed, the prisoner began crying out to his god. It was a high, reiterated cry of "Ram! Ram! Ram! Ram!"[1] not urgent and fearful like a prayer or cry for help, but steady, rhythmical, almost like the tolling of a bell. The dog answered the sound with a whine. The hangman, still stand-ing on the gallows, produced a small cotton bag like a flour bag and drew it down over the prisoner's face. But the sound, muffled by the

---

[1] In the Hindu religion, Rama is the incarnation of the god Vishnu.

cloth, still persisted, over and over again: "Ram! Ram! Ram! Ram! Ram!"

The hangman climbed down and stood ready, holding the lever. 13
Minutes seemed to pass. The steady, muffled crying from the prisoner went on and on, "Ram! Ram! Ram!" never faltering for an instant. The superintendent, his head on his chest, was slowly poking the ground with his stick; perhaps he was counting the cries, allowing the prisoner a fixed number—fifty, perhaps, or a hundred. Everyone had changed color. The Indians had gone gray like bad coffee, and one or two of the bayonets were wavering. We looked at the lashed, hooded man on the drop, and listened to his cries—each cry another second of life; the same thought was in all our minds: oh, kill him quickly, get it over, stop that abominable noise!

Suddenly the superintendent made up his mind. Throwing up 14
his head he made a swift motion with his stick. "Chalo!"[2] he shouted almost fiercely.

There was a clanking noise, and then dead silence. The prisoner 15
had vanished, and the rope was twisting on itself. I let go of the dog, and it galloped immediately to the back of the gallows; but when it got there it stopped short, barked, and then retreated into a corner of the yard, where it stood among the weeds, looking timorously out at us. We went round the gallows to inspect the prisoner's body. He was dangling with his toes pointed straight downward, very slowly revolving, as dead as a stone.

The superintendent reached out with his stick and poked the 16
bare brown body: it oscillated slightly. "*He's* all right," said the superintendent. He backed out from under the gallows, and blew out a deep breath. The moody look had gone out of his face quite suddenly. He glanced at his wrist watch. "Eight minutes past eight. Well, that's all for this morning, thank God."

The warders unfixed bayonets and marched away. The dog, so- 17
bered and conscious of having misbehaved itself, slipped after them. We walked out of the gallows yard, past the condemned cells with their waiting prisoners, into the big central yard of the prison. The convicts, under the command of warders armed with lathis,[3] were already receiving their breakfast. They squatted in long rows, each man holding a tin pannikin, while two warders with buckets marched round ladling out rice; it seemed quite a homely, jolly scene, after the hanging. An enormous relief had come upon us now that the job was done. One felt an impulse to sing, to break into a run, to snigger. All at once everyone began chattering gaily.

The Eurasian boy walking beside me nodded toward the way we 18
had come, with a knowing smile: "Do you know, sir, our friend [he meant the dead man] when he heard his appeal had been dismissed,

---

[2]*"Let go,"* in Hindi.
[3]Wooden batons.

he pissed on the floor of his cell. From fright. Kindly take one of my cigaréttes, sir. Do you not admire my new silver case, sir? From the boxwalah, two rupees eight annas.[4] Classy European style."

Several people laughed—at what, nobody seemed certain.   19

Francis was walking by the superintendent, talking garrulously: 20 "Well, sir, all hass passed off with the utmost satisfactoriness. It was all finished—flick! like that. It iss not always so—oah, no! I have known cases where the doctor wass obliged to go beneath the gallows and pull the prissoner's legs to ensure decease. Most disagreeable!"

"Wriggling about, eh? That's bad," said the superintendent.   21

"Ach, sir, it iss worse when they become refractory! One man,   22 I recall, clung to the bars of hiss cage when we went to take him out. You will scarcely credit, sir, that it took six warders to dislodge him, three pulling at each leg. We reasoned with him. 'My dear fellow,' we said, 'think of all the pain and trouble you are causing to us!' But no, he would not listen! Ach, he wass very troublesome!"

I found that I was laughing quite loudly. Everyone was laughing.   23 Even the superintendent grinned in a tolerant way. "You'd better all come out and have a drink," he said quite genially. "I've got a bottle of whisky in the car. We could do with it."

We went through the big double gates of the prison into the   24 road. "Pulling at his legs!" exclaimed a Burmese magistrate suddenly, and burst into a loud chuckling. We all began laughing again. At that moment Francis' anecdote seemed extraordinarily funny. We all had a drink together, native and European alike, quite amicably. The dead man was a hundred yards away.

One Reader's Notes

Here are the notes one reader made in his notebook during and after his first reading of "A Hanging." They include personal comments, queries concerning the meaning of words and details, and some reflections on the piece and its subject. The numbers in parentheses indicate which paragraphs the notes refer to.

NOTES MADE DURING THE READING

(2) puny prisoner, 6 tall guards, handcuffs, rope, chains. handled "like a fish"—cells like animal cages. suggests prisoner thought less than human.

(4) natives do dirty work, Brits stand around supervising. what's a Dravidian?

---

[4]Indian currency worth less than 50 cents. *Boxwalah:* in Hindi, a seller of boxes.

(6) dog—half Airedale, half pariah, like prison staff a mixture of Brits and natives. prisoner its favorite person. why? pet?

(10) main idea (?): "I saw the mystery, the unspeakable wrongness, of cutting a life short when it is in full tide."

But what was the man's crime? might have been a murderer or terrorist. Does O. mean that *all* cap. pun. is wrong?

Dog incident—dog recog. prisoner's humanity, behaves naturally, O. claims the execution is unnatural.

(11) hangman a convict, not an official. yard overgrown—significance?

(12) what god is Ram? prisoner a Hindu.

(13) why everyone transfixed? more than surprise? "kill him quickly"—selfish.

(15) the dog again. what was O. doing there anyway? all he does is hold dog. observer from P.D.?

(17) what's a lathi? or lathis? dog "conscious of having misbehaved"—how does O. know?

(18) prisoner afraid before, found courage to face death—humanizes him. what's a boxwalah?

Anticlimax from here on. prisoners impassive, officials near hysteria. again, why such a big deal, if they do executions often (other condemned men there). take O's word that this time was different. laughing it off, life goes on, etc.

(24) Euros and natives on same side, against prisoners. still nothing about dead man's crime, but can't have been so bad given everyone's reactions—? nobody says it's what he deserved.

NOTES MADE AFTER FINISHING THE READING

did this really happen? seems too pat, with dog and all, and O. hanging around doing nothing instead of whatever he usually did. Could have happened, maybe that's enough.

no argument against cap. pun., just personal insight from personal experience. can't make laws that way. no reasons pro or con except O. thinks it unnatural, with dog's behavior as the proof.

form—chron. narration, no gaps or flashbacks. intro para 1, sets scene. climax: the hanging. conclusion starts para 17 (?), winds story down. style clear, direct, not fancy, strong words, lots of detail and color, etc. good writing obviously, but he doesn't persuade me about cap. pun.

Looking over this reader's shoulder, you can see that he gets increasingly skeptical about Orwell's thesis statement, and you may guess that he himself supports capital punishment—or at least sees some point in it.

The reader has noted a good deal of what Orwell put into the essay, such as who does what at the prison; perhaps on the second reading he will get more out of the essay's concluding paragraphs, which are skimmed over in his notes. And the reader has also noticed some of the things Orwell left out, such as the nature of the prisoner's offense. He has begun to find relations between the details and the whole, notably by thinking about the significance of the dog's behavior. All in all, he has made a good beginning at understanding "A Hanging."

From Reading to Writing

In many college courses you will be required to discuss your reading in some writing of your own. In composition courses, such writing assignments often take these forms:

1. An analysis of the reading's content, form, or both.
2. An original composition on the topic of the reading, or on a related topic.
3. An original composition on a topic of your choice, inspired in some way by the reading but not bound by its subject matter.

Which kind of paper you write may be specified by your instructor, or the choice may be left to you.

In the following pages you will find papers of all three types, each a response to Orwell's "A Hanging" and each typical of how students write for their composition courses.

An Analytical Paper: "The Disgrace of Man"

When you write an analysis of something you have read, your purpose is to show that you have understood the work and to help your readers increase their understanding of it too. You do this by drawing attention to aspects of its meaning, structure, and style that are important but not obvious. Such an analysis grows directly out of your reading, and more specifically out of the notes you made during your first and subsequent readings of the text.

When planning your analytical paper, start by considering what point you most want to make—what your thesis will be. If you can think of several possible theses for your paper, and you often will be able to, select the one that seems to you the most important—and that you think you can support and defend most strongly and effectively using evidence from the piece you are writing about. Many different theses would be possible for an analytical paper about Orwell's "A Hanging." Here are a few:

In "A Hanging," George Orwell carefully selects details in order to persuade us that capital punishment is wrong.

"A Hanging" reveals how thoroughly the British had imposed their laws, customs, and values on colonial Burma.

Though "A Hanging" appeals powerfully to the emotions, it does not make a reasoned argument against capital punishment.

In "A Hanging," George Orwell employs metaphor, personification, and dialogue to express man's inhumanity to other men.

This last is the thesis of the student paper that follows, "The Disgrace of Man."

Think, too, about your audience. Who will read your paper? Will they know the work you are analyzing? If not, then you need to supply enough information about the work so that your readers can understand you—as Gilbert Highet does in his essay, "On Swift's 'A Modest Proposal' " (page 432), and as Eudora Welty does in " 'Is Phoenix Jackson's Grandson Really Dead?' " (page 428). But if you expect your essay to be read by your instructor and classmates, and if it is about an assigned reading, you can usually assume that they know the work and need no summary of it, though they may need clear reminders of specific details and passages that you analyze closely and that may have escaped their attention.

Students writing papers for their courses have a special problem: What can they say that their readers, especially their instructors, do not already know? This is a problem all writers face, including instructors themselves when writing professional articles, and the answer is always the same: Write honestly about what you see in the work and what you think about it. Since all readers respond differently to the same text, any one of them—including you—may notice details or draw conclusions that others miss. Teachers may be experienced, knowledgeable readers, but they do not know everything. Some might not have noticed that Orwell excludes from "A Hanging" any hint of the prisoner's crime, yet this omission is important because it reinforces Orwell's main point: Capital punishment is always wrong, no matter what the circumstances. And even if you think you have no such discoveries to offer, your individual point of view and response to the text will lend your writing originality and interest. As the poet James Stephens once wrote, "Originality does not consist in saying what no one has ever said before, but in saying exactly what you think yourself."

The following student essay, "The Disgrace of Man," is original in Stephens' sense, and the student has also discovered something in "A Hanging" that other readers might well have missed, something about Orwell's way of telling his story that contributes, subtly but significantly, to its effect.

The Disgrace of Man

George Orwell's "A Hanging" graphically depicts the execution of a prisoner in a way that expresses a universal tragedy. He artfully employs metaphor, personification, and dialogue to indicate man's inhumanity toward other men, and to prompt the reader's sympathy and self-examination.

Orwell uses simile and metaphor to show that the prisoner is treated more like an animal than like a human being. The cells of the condemned men, "a row of sheds . . . quite bare within," are "like small animal cages." The warders grip the prisoner "like men handling a fish." Though they refer to the prisoner as "the man" or "our friend," the other characters view him as less than human. Even his cry resounds like the "tolling of a bell" rather than a human "prayer or cry for help," and after he is dead the superintendent pokes at the body with a stick. These details direct the reader's attention to the lack of human concern for the condemned prisoner.

In contrast, Orwell emphasizes the "wrongness of cutting a life short" by representing the parts of the prisoner's body as taking on human behavior. He describes the lock of hair "dancing" on the man's scalp, his feet "printing themselves" on the gravel, all his organs "toiling away" like a team of laborers at some collective project. In personifying these bodily features, Orwell forces the reader to see the prisoner's vitality, his humanity. The reader, in turn, associates each bodily part with himself; he becomes highly aware of the frailty of life. As the author focuses on how easily these actions can be stopped, in any human being, "with a sudden snap," the reader feels the "wrongness" of the hanging as if his own life were threatened.

In addition to creating this sense of unmistakable life, Orwell uses the dog as a standard for evaluating the characters' appreciation of human life. The dog loves people—he is "wild with glee to find so many human beings together"—and the person he loves the most is the prisoner, who has been treated as less than human by the jail attendants. When the prisoner starts to pray, the other people are silent, but the dog answers "with a whine." Even after the hanging, the dog runs directly to the gallows to see the prisoner again. The reader is forced to reflect on his own reaction: Which is more shocking, the dog's actions or the observers' cold response?

Finally, Orwell refers to the characters' nationalities to stress that

this insensitivity extends to all nationalities and races. The hanging
takes place in Burma, in a jail run by a European army doctor and a
native of southern India. The warders are also Indians, and the hangman is actually a fellow prisoner. The author calls attention to each of
these participants, and implies that each one of them might have halted
the brutal proceedings. He was there too and could have intervened
when he suddenly realized that killing the prisoner would be wrong.
Yet the "formality of the hanging" goes on.

As he reflects on the meaning of suddenly destroying human
life, Orwell emphasizes the similarities among all men, regardless of
nationality. Before the hanging, they are "seeing, hearing, feeling,
understanding the same world," and afterward there would be "one
mind less, one world less." Such feelings do not affect the other characters, who think of the hanging not as killing but as a job to be
done, a job made unpleasant by those reminders (the incident of the
dog, the prisoner's praying) that they are dealing with a human being.
Orwell uses dialogue to show how selfish and callous the observers are.
Though they have different accents—the superintendent's "for God's
sake hurry up," the Dravidian's "It wass all finished"—they think and
feel the same. Their words, such as *"He's* all right," show that they
are more concerned about their own lives than the one they are destroying.

Although George Orwell sets his story in Burma, his point is
universal; although he deals with capital punishment, he implies other
questions of life and death. We are all faced with issues such as capital
punishment, abortion, and euthanasia, and sometimes we find ourselves directly involved, as Orwell did. "A Hanging" urges us to examine ourselves and to take very seriously the value of a human life.

Most teachers would consider "The Disgrace of Man" a fine student
essay. It is well organized, stating its thesis early, supporting it effectively,
and sticking to the point. The discussion is clear and coherent, and it is
firmly based on Orwell's text—the student author has understood the core
meaning of "A Hanging." She has also noticed many details that express
Orwell's attitude toward the hanging and toward his imperial colleagues,
and she has interpreted them so that her readers can plainly see how those
details contribute to the total effect of "A Hanging." How many would
have observed that Orwell actually personifies the parts of the prisoner's
body? How many, having noticed it, would have grasped the relation of
this detail to Orwell's point? That's accurate, active reading.

An Argumentative Essay: "For Capital Punishment"

Perhaps you recall the annotations of "A Hanging" on pages 13–14.
The writer of those notes was attentive to the meaning of the text, but
as he read he found himself disagreeing with Orwell's view that taking

human life is always unspeakably wrong. He might have gone on to analyze "A Hanging," as he was obviously capable of doing, but he did not.
Instead, given the opportunity to choose his own topic, he decided to
present his own views on Orwell's subject: capital punishment.

The writer began by exploring the topic, jotting down notes on
what he knew and believed. He also went to the library to look up recent
research into the effects of capital punishment, but found that authorities
still cannot agree on whether the death penalty deters crime or protects
society, so his efforts led only to a few sentences in his first paragraph.
Why go to so much trouble for a short writing assignment? Evidently the
writer cared enough about his topic to want to do it justice, not just for
the assignment's sake but for his own. As the English philosopher John
Stuart Mill wrote, "If the cultivation of the understanding consists in one
thing more than in another, it is surely in learning the grounds of one's
own opinions." The author of "For Capital Punishment" knew what he
believed, and he used the occasion of a writing assignment to work out a
rationale for that belief.

For Capital Punishment

The debate on capital punishment goes on and on. Does the
death penalty deter people from committing murder? Does it protect us
from criminals who would murder again if they were returned to society? These questions have not yet been answered beyond any doubt,
and maybe they never will be. But is the death penalty cruel and unnatural? This is a different kind of question, having to do with the
nature of the punishment itself, and it can be answered. I think the
answer is no, and that capital punishment has a place in a civilized
society. I also feel that it should be imposed as the penalty for the worst
crimes.

In the United States this is a constitutional issue, because the
Bill of Rights does not allow cruel and unusual punishment. The Supreme Court has interpreted these words not to include capital punishment, and there is a basis in the Constitution for their decision: The
fifth amendment says that "no person shall . . . be deprived of life,
liberty, or property, without due process of law," which means that a
person can be deprived of life if due process has been observed. The
Court did find some years ago that the death penalty was being imposed
much more often on poor black people than on any others, and suspended capital punishment throughout the nation because due process
was obviously *not* being observed, but when the Court considered that
that situation had been corrected it permitted executions to resume in
1977 with the death of Gary Gilmore.

But beyond the constitutionality of capital punishment there is
the deeper question of whether it is morally wrong. We accept some

punishments as just, while others seem barbaric. The difference, I think, has to do with what the condemned man is made to suffer. The lightest punishments take away some of his money or restrict his freedom of movement in society; some examples are fines, probation, and work-release programs. Then there are punishments that remove the criminal from society, such as imprisonment and deportation. The kind of punishment we do not accept, though it is still used in some countries, is the kind that is meant to do physical harm: beating, maiming, torture. The death penalty is a special case. It removes criminals from society permanently and economically, but it also involves physical harm. It is in the balance between these two effects, I think, that we can find out whether capital punishment is morally acceptable.

If we condemned people to death because we wanted them to suffer, you would expect that methods of execution would have been made more painful and frightening over the years. Instead, the opposite has happened. Traitors used to be tortured to death before screaming mobs, but now the condemned man dies in private as painlessly as possible; Texas now uses chemical injections that are apparently almost painless. It must be, then, that the reason for execution is not physical harm but removal from society, which is a widely accepted purpose for judicial punishment.

But why, then, would not life imprisonment serve the same purpose just as well? There are two main reasons why it does not. First, "life imprisonment" does not mean what it says; most lifers are considered for parole after fifteen years or less, even monsters like Charles Manson and Sirhan Sirhan. It's true that these two have not been released, but they might be at any time their California parole board changes its mind. So life imprisonment does not insure that the worst criminals will be removed from society permanently. Second, as long as a criminal stays in prison he is a burden on the very society he has offended against, costing society tens of thousands of dollars each year to keep him secure and healthy. There is also a real question in my mind whether caging a prisoner for life, if it actually *is* for life, is any more merciful than putting him to death. The conditions in American prisons, where the inmates are often brutalized and degraded by each other and even by their guards, must often seem a "fate worse than death."

Most nations of the world, and most states in the United States, have legalized capital punishment and used it for many years. They—we—are not bloodthirsty monsters, but ordinary people seeking safety and justice under the law. Maybe the time will come when the death penalty is no longer needed or wanted, and then it will be abolished. But that time is not yet here.

The writer of "For Capital Punishment" has taken on a large subject, on which many books have been and many more will be written. When discussing a controversial topic of wide interest, many people tend to parrot back uncritically the opinions they have read and heard, which is easy to do but does not add much to what everyone knows. This writer has escaped that temptation and thought his subject through, in the process working out reasoned and partly original arguments of his own to support his view. His discussion is clear and well-organized; he states his thesis at the end of the first paragraph and supports it with evidence and reasoning throughout the paper. Of course many reasonable people will disagree with his support of capital punishment, just as he disagrees with Orwell's opposition to it. But most composition teachers, even those who do not share this writer's views, would consider "For Capital Punishment" a good student paper.

A Personal Essay: "Killing for Fun"

In "A Hanging," George Orwell writes about an incident that brought him to an important insight. The author of the following essay did the same. Reading Orwell brought back to mind a childhood experience which had made her aware of the potential for thoughtless violence that lies within us all. Part of Orwell's influence on her is revealed by her choice of subject—the heedless killing of three helpless nestlings. But she also follows Orwell in her choice of a writing strategy; like him she narrates a personal experience that illustrates a general moral principle.

Killing for Fun

Every summer my family returns to our ancestral home, which is in a community where the same families have lived generation after generation. There are tennis courts, a golf course, boats, and other occupations to help pass the long, hot days. This all sounds very enjoyable, and it usually was, but sometimes it got very boring. Spending every summer with the same gang and doing the same things, under the same grown-ups' noses, began to seem dull, and by the time I was thirteen I was ready to experience the thrill of the forbidden.

One afternoon in July, I was supposed to sail in some races with my best friend Mitchell, but the air was so thick and heavy that we decided not to go. We sat around his house all day, waiting for his brother to bring back the family power boat so that we could water ski. Thinking back to that summer, I remember how frustrated and irritable we were, our pent-up energy ready to explode. We roamed his house searching for something—anything—to do, but we only succeeded in making one mess after another and angering his mother. Finally we hit on something. We were eating lunch on Mitchell's back porch when we both noticed his father's rifle propped in a corner.

Now Mitchell's father had often warned all of us that his rifle was strictly off limits. The rifle itself was not very dangerous, as it was only an air gun that shot small pellets, but he was afraid of its being misused and hurting someone. He himself used it to scare off stray dogs and was usually very careful to put it away, but for some reason on that particular day he had forgotten. We decided that it would be fun to take the rifle out in the nearby woods and shoot at whatever we found there.

We had to be very careful not to be seen by the borough residents as they all knew us. For most parents, kids heading for the woods meant trouble. So Mitchell and I sneaked out of his house with the gun and went slinking through some old horse stables on our way to the woods. By the time we arrived at the edge of the woods we felt like spies. There was a caretaker's cottage there, and the caretaker was forever on the lookout for what he thought were troublesome kids. When we successfully passed the cottage our spirits were high, as we had gotten safely through the danger zone on the way to our forbidden project.

As we went into the woods we began to find some animals and birds to use as targets, but try as we might, we could not hit anything. Our pellets seemed to disappear in flight, not even giving us the satisfaction of hitting a tree and making a noise. Our mission was not succeeding, and we decided to look for an easier target.

Finally we startled a mother bird, who flew away leaving her nest behind. We thought the nest would make a fine target, stationary as it was and with live creatures inside. We took turns shooting at it in an attempt to knock it out of the tree, intoxicated with our power and carried away by the thrill of it all. Mitchell was the one to knock it down. It tottered, and after a little rustling a small object fell out, and the nest followed, landing upside down.

Mitchell ran up and excitedly turned it over. The sight was horribly repulsive. Underneath lay three naked pink corpses, staring up at us silently with wide dark eyes and wide, underdeveloped, faintly yellow beaks. They looked as if they had been savagely strangled one by one, except for the small pellet holes in each tiny body. A few feet away a slight movement caught my eye. The object that had fallen first was a fourth baby bird. It had survived the shooting and the fall and was flopping around, mutilated as it was. I poked Mitchell, who was staring at the massacre underneath the nest, and directed his attention to the desperately flapping pink lump a few feet away.

I could see that Mitchell was repulsed by the sight, but being a thirteen-year-old boy he refused to show it. He made an attempt to maintain a hunter's attitude, and fiercely drove pellet after pellet into the injured bird. We tried to joke about it, and as soon as we were out of sight of the nest we broke into hysterically uncontrollable laughter, trying to avoid thinking about what we had done. On the way home we avoided talking about it, and I felt relieved to part company with Mitchell when we got home.

That incident shocked me into thinking about the results of my actions. Mitchell and I were not inhuman monsters, determined to massacre baby birds; we were just bored kids looking for an adventure and not thinking about the consequences. I wonder how much unhappiness and even crime comes from young people acting selfishly and thoughtlessly, out for a thrill. If they had to see the suffering they cause, they would surely think harder before they act.

The author of "Killing for Fun" tells her story well. She describes her experience vividly, with much closely observed detail, and builds suspense to hold her readers' attention. What makes "Killing for Fun" not just a story but a personal essay is the last paragraph, where she turns her experience to an observation about life. The observation may not be brand new, but then it needn't be—few important truths are. George Orwell was certainly not the first to oppose capital punishment. In both essays it is the author's personal experience, honestly and precisely recounted, that gives their general observations force.

These three essays, each different from the other two and from Orwell's, illustrate but a few of the many ways different people can respond to their reading and use their responses in their writing. Each paper also shows how a student, working under the limitations of an assigned reading and a specific writing assignment, can create an interesting and original piece of writing by analyzing the reading carefully, or exploring his or her own beliefs, or drawing upon personal experience. Each of the selections in *Outlooks and Insights* provides you with opportunities to do the same.

Some Notes on Fiction and Poetry

The poems and short stories in *Outlooks and Insights* explore many of the same themes the essays do, and can serve your writing purposes in similar ways. A story or a poem may give you ideas for your writing or topics to write about, and even though you may never write poetry or fiction you can still learn much about structure and style from reading literature. These selections will be most useful to you, however, if you know something about the basic elements of fiction and poetry, and so the following pages provide a brief, highly selective introduction to some of their most important qualities and forms.

READING SHORT STORIES

Short stories look much like essays, and the two forms are similar in other ways as well. Both are written in prose; some essays, like nearly all stories, are narratives; both may contain dialogue. And certainly a reader can learn from fiction as well as from nonfiction about the ways other people think, feel, and behave, and how they deal with ethical problems. But stories also differ from essays in fundamental respects, and call for different expectations and responses from their readers.

Though a short story may incorporate materials from real life, including places and even characters and incidents, it is essentially the product of the author's imagination. Eudora Welty says that she got the idea for her short story "A Worn Path" (page 102) from watching an old woman walking slowly across a winter country landscape, but that the rest of the story was pure invention. (See Eudora Welty, " 'Is Phoenix Jackson's Grandson Really Dead?' " page 428.) In an essay, on the other hand, we expect the events and characters to be rendered accurately from real life. Part of the force of George Orwell's "A Hanging" comes from our belief that he is reporting a personal experience—that he did indeed attend a hanging at which the events he narrates actually took place.

Both essays and stories can make points about life, but each type does so differently. An essay normally states its main idea or *thesis* openly and explains or argues that idea at length in a direct and orderly way. A story, however, does not tell—it shows. Its main idea, called its *theme*, is not so much discussed as embodied in the characters and action, and is seldom presented openly—each reader has to discover a story's theme for himself or herself. As Eudora Welty puts it, "A narrative line is in its deeper sense . . . the tracing out of a meaning"—which is the story's theme (page 430). Theme is not the same as subject. The subject of "A Worn Path" is an old woman's long, wearying trip to town to get medicine for her ill grandson—a trip which she has made many times before and will make again. The story's theme, however, is the general observation it illustrates and embodies. Different readers may put the theme of "A Worn Path" into different words. Welty says it this way: "The habit of love cuts through confusion and stumbles or contrives its way out of difficulty, it remembers the way even when it forgets, for a dumbfounded moment, its reason for being." This is the story's true meaning and encompasses all of its details, right down to the path itself, worn by the old woman's often-repeated errand of love. As this suggests, a story's theme reveals the unity of the whole work—or can even be said to give the work its unity.

Most short stories have other elements in common which are seldom found in nonfiction writing. The action in a short story, called its *plot*, typically unfolds in a pattern consisting of a series of stages that can be diagrammed in this way:

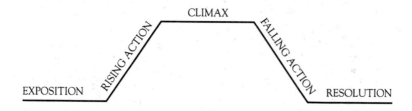

The *exposition* sets the scene, describes the situation, and begins to introduce some of the characters. The *rising action* (sometimes called the *complication*) sets the characters into conflict—with each other or within themselves—and the conflict rises in tension and complexity. At the *climax* the tension and complexity reach their peak, and the central character takes an action or undergoes an experience that is the turning point of the story. After the climax comes the *falling action*, in which the tension slackens and the story moves toward its conclusion. The end of the story is the *resolution*, in which the conflict of the plot gives way to a new stability. "A Worn Path" follows this pattern. Its exposition consists of the first two paragraphs. The rising action, beginning in paragraph 3, builds to a climax when Phoenix meets the hunter. After the falling action, in which she makes her way into town, the resolution begins in paragraph 70 when she arrives at the doctor's office. These conventions of plot have served countless writers for more than two thousand years with no loss in effectiveness and vitality, and still provide the structure for novels, short stories, plays—even movies and television dramas.

How we take in the events of the plot is determined by the author's use of a narrative *point of view*. Sometimes the story is told by one of the characters, as in Sherwood Anderson's "The Egg" (page 405), or even by the main character, as in Isaac Bashevis Singer's "Gimpel the Fool" (page 723). This is called *first person point of view* because the narrator often uses the first person pronoun *I*. When the story is told by a narrator standing somewhere outside the events of the story, this is called *third person point of view* because the narrator uses the third person pronoun *he*, *she*, and *they*. "A Worn Path" is told from the third person point of view; the narrator, like a movie camera's eye, tracks old Phoenix Jackson all the way to town, reporting on her doings from outside the story.

The third person point of view has two main forms: *omniscient* and *limited.* If the narrator tells us what all the characters are doing, wherever they are, and even what they are thinking and feeling, the author is using the third person omniscient point of view. An example is John Updike's "A Sense of Shelter" (page 90), in which we learn a great deal about William Young's unspoken thoughts and attitudes—things that only Young himself, and the omniscient narrator, could possibly know. In "A Worn Path," on the other hand, the narrator tells us only what Phoenix Jackson does, says, hears, and sees; we can only infer what the characters are thinking from what they say and do.

READING POEMS

Almost anything can be subject matter for poetry, and the range of poetic styles and forms is enormous: W. B. Yeats's "The Lake Isle of Innisfree" (page 403), for example, uses special poetic devices such as rhyme, while William Carlos Williams's "The Red Wheelbarrow" (page 517) seems as plain as prose. But even the plainest poetry should never be read merely to understand its message, for that would be to ignore the special delights and the special kinds of meaning which only poetry can convey.

Let's look at one poem as an active reader would, trying to respond not only to its literal meaning but also to its special qualities as a poem. The poem is by William Shakespeare:

That time of year thou may'st in me behold
When yellow leaves, or none, or few, do hang
Upon those boughs which shake against the cold,
Bare ruined choirs where late the sweet birds sang.
In me thou seest the twilight of such day   5
As after sunset fadeth in the west,
Which by and by black night doth take away,
Death's second self that seals up all in rest.
In me thou seest the glowing of such fire
That on the ashes of his youth doth lie,   10
As the deathbed whereon it must expire,
Consumed with that which it was nourished by.
  This thou perceiv'st, which makes thy love more strong,
  To love that well which thou must leave ere long.

One of the first things a reader would notice about this poem is that it conveys its meaning in a special way. The speaker of the poem says, in effect, that he is old, but he only tells us so indirectly. He compares his time of life with a season, a time of day, and a stage in the life of a fire, and these three images evoke our own experience so that we understand what he means. In autumn the days grow shorter and colder, at twilight the day's heat and light are going fast, and the embers of a dying fire grow dimmer and cooler with every minute; so too with advancing age, when the vigor and passions of earlier years have faded and death is soon to come. The images also reinforce each other, each describing a natural process that cannot be avoided or stopped and evoking the same progression from warmth to cold, from light to dark. And there is a progression from one image to the next: Autumn, a span of months and days, is succeeded by twilight, a matter of an hour or less, and last comes fire, which can rise and go out in a few minutes. This speeding up of time prepares for the last line's suggestion that death will come "ere long." Images such as these, which occur only occasionally in prose, can often be a poem's chief means of conveying its meaning.

Another resource which prose writers use sparingly but which is vital to poetry is the *sound* of the language—its vowels and consonants, and the rhythms of words and phrases. Tradition has it that poetry began as song, and poets often choose their words not only to convey meaning but to make a kind of music through planned patterns of verbal sounds. To hear and appreciate that music to the fullest, it's a good idea to read a poem aloud, listening for those patterns. And even if you can't read aloud (for example, if you are in a library reading room or on the bus), try to "hear" the poem in your imagination.

Even on first reading "That Time of Year" you probably noticed that Shakespeare has written his poem with not only its sense but its sound in mind. The rhythm is regular, as each of the fourteen lines has exactly ten syllables, and those syllables alternate regularly between weak and strong stress: "That *time* of *year* thou *may'st* in *me* be*hold.*" Shakespeare's skill is such that to achieve this musical effect he never needs to sacrifice clarity, and indeed he rarely departs from natural phrasing. There is evidence, too, that Shakespeare has coordinated the vowel and consonant sounds of his poem. For one thing, he rhymes his lines in a complex but regular pattern. For another, two particular consonants, *l* and *s*, recur throughout the poem. They are most conspicuous in phrases like "second self that seals" (line 8) and "leave ere long" (line 14), which are examples of alliteration, but on closer examination you will find that one or both sounds appear, usually more than once, in each line of the poem, and help to give it its special music.

Shakespeare's use of rhyme deserves special attention, because it fits perfectly the meaning and even the grammar of his poem. Each of the three images is expressed in a single sentence that takes up four lines, and those lines are rhymed in an interlocking pattern that makes the image, and the sentence, seem all the more self-contained. The arrival of a new image brings the beginning not only of a new sentence but also of a new and different set of rhymes. The last two lines of the poem are not an image but a direct statement, and they have a rhyme pattern of their own using *strong* and *long.* Some readers may even notice in this last rhyme a distant echo of *hang* and *sang* from the beginning of the poem.

Shakespeare's rhyme scheme fits the meaning of his poem so closely that you might think he had invented both as part of the same creative act. In fact this is not so. He wrote 153 other poems in exactly the same form, which is sometimes called the Shakespearean sonnet in his honor. Moreover, Shakespeare did not invent the form, which had existed for forty years and been used by many poets before he took it up. Here we have a strange thing: Maybe the form itself gave Shakespeare ideas for poems, or at least set him challenges that heated rather than cooled his imagination. How versatile the sonnet form was in Shakespeare's hands you can see from the following, which has exactly the same structure as "That Time of Year" but a very different theme:

My mistress' eyes are nothing like the sun;
Coral is far more red than her lips' red;
If snow be white, why then her breasts are dun;
If hairs be wires, black wires grow on her head.
I have seen roses demasked, red and white,
But no such roses see I in her cheeks;
And in some perfumes is there more delight
Than in the breath that from my mistress reeks.
I love to hear her speak; yet well I know
That music hath a far more pleasing sound:
I grant I never saw a goddess go;
My mistress, when she walks, treads on the ground.
   And yet, by heaven, I think my love as rare
   As any she belied with false compare.

1 Private Lives

Know thyself.

Know thyself! A maxim as pernicious as it is ugly. Whoever observes himself arrests his own development. A caterpillar who wanted to know itself would never become a butterfly.
ANDRÉ GIDE

The life which is unexamined is not worth living.
SOCRATES

Our entire life, with our fine moral code and our precious freedom, consists ultimately in accepting ourselves as we are.
JEAN ANOUILH

That favorite subject, Myself.
JAMES BOSWELL

THERE is perhaps no subject more fascinating to each of us than ourselves. No question is more absorbing, or more difficult to answer, than this: "Who am I?" The answer is well worth seeking, because self-knowledge can help us to make better decisions about how to live. Those who struggle to perceive their own true character may not always be pleased with what they find. But only those who pursue self-knowledge, and who live by what they have learned, can lead what Socrates would have called an "examined" life.

We come to self-understanding in many ways. We may approach it directly by looking inward, observing our actions and motives, our thoughts and emotions. We may also look outward, observing how other people live their lives and how their behavior relates to their views of themselves. Reading can be a great aid in the quest for self-understanding, and so can writing. By reading about people—their successes and failures, their joys and fears—we can share their experiences and perceptions, and by comparing them with our own we can come to a fuller sense of ourselves. And writing can be a penetrating way to look inward. In the process of trying to write something that is both significant and honest, our minds often cut deeper than we expect, and bring forth much that would otherwise have gone undiscovered.

Each of the following essays, poems, and stories has some bearing on the search for self. Some of the authors write of their personal experiences, while others inquire into experience in general. Each of them touches on some aspect of our inner, private lives.

JOAN DIDION

Essayist, novelist, and journalist, Joan Didion was born in Sacramento in 1934 and educated at the University of California at Berkeley. She often writes on aspects of life in California and in the West. She has written for a wide spectrum of magazines, from *Mademoiselle* to the *National Review,* and her essays have been collected in *Slouching Towards Bethlehem* (1969) and *The White Album* (1979). Her novels include *Run River* (1963), *Play It As It Lays* (1971), and *A Book of Common Prayer* (1977).

"On Self-Respect" was first published in *Vogue* in 1961. As in many of Didion's other writings, this piece is concerned with some aspect of herself and with what it means to seek self-knowledge. In another essay from *Slouching Towards Bethlehem,* she gives a very good reason for the desire to know oneself, saying: "I think we are well advised to keep on nodding terms with the people we used to be, whether we find them attractive company or not. Otherwise they turn up unannounced and surprise us, come hammering on the mind's door at 4 A.M. of a bad night. . . ."

On Self-Respect

Once, in a dry season, I wrote in large letters across two pages of   1
a notebook that innocence ends when one is stripped of the delusion that one likes oneself. Although now, some years later, I marvel that a mind on the outs with itself should have nonetheless made painstaking record of its every tremor, I recall with embarrassing clarity the flavor of those particular ashes. It was a matter of misplaced self-respect.

I had not been elected to Phi Beta Kappa. This failure could scarcely   2
have been more predictable or less ambiguous (I simply did not have the grades), but I was unnerved by it; I had somehow thought myself a kind of academic Raskolnikov, curiously exempt from the cause-effect relationships which hampered others.[1] Although even the humorless nineteen-year-old that I was must have recognized that the situation lacked real tragic stature, the day that I did not make Phi Beta Kappa nonetheless marked the end of something, and innocence may well be the word for it. I lost the conviction that lights would always turn green for me, the pleasant certainty that those rather passive virtues which had won me approval as a child automatically guaranteed me not only Phi

---

[1]Raskolnikov is the central character in *Crime and Punishment,* a novel by Fyodor Dostoevsky. Raskolnikov had committed two murders, but his guilt was not discovered until he confessed.

33

Beta Kappa keys but happiness, honor, and the love of a good man; lost a certain touching faith in the totem power of good manners, clean hair, and proven competence on the Stanford-Binet scale.[2] To such doubtful amulets had my self-respect been pinned, and I faced myself that day with the nonplused apprehension of someone who has come across a vampire and has no crucifix at hand.

Although to be driven back upon oneself is an uneasy affair at best,   3 rather like trying to cross a border with borrowed credentials, it seems to me now the one condition necessary to the beginnings of real self-respect. Most of our platitudes notwithstanding, self-deception remains the most difficult deception. The tricks that work on others count for nothing in that very well-lit back alley where one keeps assignations with oneself: no winning smiles will do here, no prettily drawn lists of good intentions. One shuffles flashily but in vain through one's marked cards—the kindness done for the wrong reason, the apparent triumph which involved no real effort, the seemingly heroic act into which one had been shamed. The dismal fact is that self-respect has nothing to do with the approval of others—who are, after all, deceived easily enough; has nothing to do with reputation, which, as Rhett Butler told Scarlett O'Hara, is something people with courage can do without.

To do without self-respect, on the other hand, is to be an unwilling   4 audience of one to an interminable documentary that details one's failings, both real and imagined, with fresh footage spliced in for every screening. *There's the glass you broke in anger, there's the hurt on X's face; watch now, this next scene, the night Y came back from Houston, see how you muff this one.* To live without self-respect is to lie awake some night, beyond the reach of warm milk, phenobarbital, and the sleeping hand on the coverlet, counting up the sins of commission and omission, the trusts betrayed, the promises subtly broken, the gifts irrevocably wasted through sloth or cowardice or carelessness. However long we postpone it, we eventually lie down alone in that notoriously uncomfortable bed, the one we make ourselves. Whether or not we sleep in it depends, of course, on whether or not we respect ourselves.

To protest that some fairly improbable people, some people who   5 *could not possibly respect themselves,* seem to sleep easily enough is to miss the point entirely, as surely as those people miss it who think that self-respect has necessarily to do with not having safety pins in one's underwear. There is a common superstition that "self-respect" is a kind of charm against snakes, something that keeps those who have it locked in some unblighted Eden, out of strange beds, ambivalent conversations,

---

[2] A system for ranking children by their mental potential, based on standardized tests.

and trouble in general. It does not at all. It has nothing to do with the face of things, but concerns instead a separate peace, a private reconciliation. Although the careless, suicidal Julian English in *Appointment in Samarra* and the careless, incurably dishonest Jordan Baker in *The Great Gatsby* seem equally improbable candidates for self-respect, Jordan Baker had it, Julian English did not.[3] With that genius for accommodation more often seen in women than in men, Jordan took her own measure, made her own peace, avoided threats to that peace: "I hate careless people," she told Nick Carraway. "It takes two to make an accident."

Like Jordan Baker, people with self-respect have the courage of   6
their mistakes. They know the price of things. If they choose to commit adultery, they do not then go running, in an access of bad conscience, to receive absolution from the wronged parties; nor do they complain unduly of the unfairness, the undeserved embarrassment, of being named co-respondent. In brief, people with self-respect exhibit a certain toughness, a kind of moral nerve; they display what was once called *character*, a quality which, although approved in the abstract, sometimes loses ground to other, more instantly negotiable virtues. The measure of its slipping prestige is that one tends to think of it only in connection with homely children and United States senators who have been defeated, preferably in the primary, for reelection. Nonetheless, character—the willingness to accept responsibility for one's own life—is the source from which self-respect springs.

Self-respect is something that our grandparents, whether or not   7
they had it, knew all about. They had instilled in them, young, a certain discipline, the sense that one lives by doing things one does not particularly want to do, by putting fears and doubts to one side, by weighing immediate comforts against the possibility of larger, even intangible, comforts. It seemed to the nineteenth century admirable, but not remarkable, that Chinese Gordon put on a clean white suit and held Khartoum against the Mahdi; it did not seem unjust that the way to free land in California involved death and difficulty and dirt.[4] In a diary kept during the winter of 1846, an emigrating twelve-year-old named Narcissa Cornwall noted coolly: "Father was busy reading and did not notice that

---

[3] *Appointment in Samarra* is a novel by John O'Hara; *The Great Gatsby* is a novel by F. Scott Fitzgerald.

[4] Chinese Gordon was Charles George Gordon, the British general who, with no military support from his superiors, organized the defense of the Sudanese city of Khartoum against Moslem forces led by Mohammed Ahmed, who called himself the Mahdi, or messiah. At the end of a ten-month siege Khartoum fell and Gordon was killed.

the house was being filled with strange Indians until Mother spoke about it." Even lacking any clue as to what Mother said, one can scarcely fail to be impressed by the entire incident: the father reading, the Indians filing in, the mother choosing the words that would not alarm, the child duly recording the event and noting further that those particular Indians were not, "fortunately for us," hostile. Indians were simply part of the *donnée.*[5]

In one guise or another, Indians always are. Again, it is a question of recognizing that anything worth having has its price. People who respect themselves are willing to accept the risk that the Indians will be hostile, that the venture will go bankrupt, that the liaison may not turn out to be one in which *every day is a holiday because you're married to me.* They are willing to invest something of themselves; they may not play at all, but when they do play, they know the odds.

That kind of self-respect is a discipline, a habit of mind that can never be faked but can be developed, trained, coaxed forth. It was once suggested to me that, as an antidote to crying, I put my head in a paper bag. As it happens, there is a sound physiological reason, something to do with oxygen, for doing exactly that, but the psychological effect alone is incalculable: it is difficult in the extreme to continue fancying oneself Cathy in *Wuthering Heights* with one's head in a Food Fair bag.[6] There is a similar case for all the small disciplines, unimportant in themselves; imagine maintaining any kind of swoon, commiserative or carnal, in a cold shower.

But those small disciplines are valuable only insofar as they represent larger ones. To say that Waterloo was won on the playing fields of Eton is not to say that Napoleon might have been saved by a crash program in cricket; to give formal dinners in the rain forest would be pointless did not the candlelight flickering on the liana call forth deeper, stronger disciplines, values instilled long before.[7] It is a kind of ritual, helping us to remember who and what we are. In order to remember it, one must have known it.

To have that sense of one's intrinsic worth which constitutes self-respect is potentially to have everything: the ability to discriminate, to

[5]Literally, "given"; that which is taken for granted.

[6]*Wuthering Heights* is a romantic English novel by Emily Brontë. Cathy is its much abused heroine.

[7]Napoleon was defeated at Waterloo in 1812 chiefly by British armies under the command of officers who, as members of the upper class, had been educated at Eton, a prestigious boarding school. Sports such as cricket were part of an educational system intended to build character.

love and to remain indifferent. To lack it is to be locked within oneself, paradoxically incapable of either love or indifference. If we do not respect ourselves, we are on the one hand forced to despise those who have so few resources as to consort with us, so little perception as to remain blind to our fatal weaknesses. On the other, we are peculiarly in thrall to everyone we see, curiously determined to live out—since our self-image is untenable—their false notions of us. We flatter ourselves by thinking this compulsion to please others an attractive trait: a gist for imaginative empathy, evidence of our willingness to give. *Of course* I will play Francesca to your Paolo, Helen Keller to anyone's Annie Sullivan: no expectation is too misplaced, no role too ludicrous.[8] At the mercy of those we cannot but hold in contempt, we play roles doomed to failure before they are begun, each defeat generating fresh despair at the urgency of divining and meeting the next demand made upon us.

It is the phenomenon sometimes called "alienation from self." In its advanced stages, we no longer answer the telephone, because someone might want something; that we could say *no* without drowning in self-reproach is an idea alien to this game. Every encounter demands too much, tears the nerves, drains the will, and the specter of something as small as an unanswered letter arouses such disproportionate guilt that answering it becomes out of the question. To assign unanswered letters their proper weight, to free us from the expectations of others, to give us back to ourselves—there lies the great, the singular power of self-respect. Without it, one eventually discovers the final turn of the screw: one runs away to find oneself, and finds no one at home.

12

About the Essay

1. Explain what Didion means when she says that her reaction to not being elected to Phi Beta Kappa "was a matter of misplaced self-respect."

2. What, according to Didion, is self-respect? What is its relationship to character?

3. According to Didion, what makes self-respect so important? What does she say it enables you to do?

4. Didion makes a number of allusions to works of literature and to historical events. Identify one or two of these allusions, and consider their effect on the essay as a whole. What is the value of making such allusions?

---

[8]Francesca da Rimini and Paolo are star-crossed, adulterous lovers in an Italian romance. Helen Keller, struck blind and deaf by illness soon after birth, was taught to speak and write by her inspiring and resourceful tutor Annie Sullivan.

5. Didion uses the characters in Narcissa Cornwall's diary as examples of a certain aspect of self-respect. What is that aspect? Can you suggest any modern-day examples of the same aspect?

6. Didion's writing style in this essay varies between formal and informal. Find examples of each in the essay, and comment on their use. Can you generalize about when she is formal and when she becomes informal?

Explorations

1. Recall an event in which you have gained an increased awareness of yourself. Write a brief account of that experience and what it means to you.

2. Didion defines character as "the willingness to accept responsibility for one's own life." Is that what character means to you? If so, develop the definition into an essay of your own. If not, write an essay explaining what you think character really is.

3. To have self-respect, one must not deceive oneself, as Didion says. How and why do people deceive themselves? Why is self-deception so difficult to overcome?

DICK GREGORY

Being a comedian carries the risk of not being taken seriously, yet comedy can sometimes make it possible to tell unpalatable truths. Dick Gregory was one of the new, angry black comics who emerged at the beginning of the 1960s who, as entertainers, could speak with anger of racial injustice to audiences that would not listen to other black leaders. A contemporary of Martin Luther King, Jr., and Malcolm X, Gregory played a significant part in the civil rights movement of the sixties with his comedy, his political advocacy, and his writing. His books include *From the Back of the Bus* (1962) and *nigger* (1964).

Gregory's childhood was hard. He was born in the Depression year of 1932 in the segregated state of Missouri, and grew up burdened by deprivations of all kinds. The following excerpt from his autobiography, *nigger*, gives a hint of what his early years were like, describing a childhood experience that made him aware of how others saw him—and of the meaning of shame.

Shame

I never learned hate at home, or shame. I had to go to school for   1
that. I was about seven years old when I got my first big lesson. I was in love with a little girl named Helene Tucker, a light-complected little girl with pigtails and nice manners. She was always clean and she was smart in school. I think I went to school then mostly to look at her. I brushed my hair and even got me a little old handkerchief. It was a lady's handkerchief, but I didn't want Helene to see me wipe my nose on my hand. The pipes were frozen again, there was no water in the house, but I washed my socks and shirt every night. I'd get a pot, and go over to Mister Ben's grocery store, and stick my pot down into his soda machine. Scoop out some chopped ice. By evening the ice melted to water for washing. I got sick a lot that winter because the fire would go out at night before the clothes were dry. In the morning I'd put them on, wet or dry, because they were the only clothes I had.

Everybody's got a Helene Tucker, a symbol of everything you want.   2
I loved her for her goodness, her cleanness, her popularity. She'd walk down my street and my brothers and sisters would yell, "Here comes Helene," and I'd rub my tennis sneakers on the back of my pants and wish my hair wasn't so nappy and the white folks' shirt fit me better. I'd run out on the street. If I knew my place and didn't come too close, she'd wink at me and say hello. That was a good feeling. Sometimes I'd

follow her all the way home, and shovel the snow off her walk and try to make friends with her Momma and her aunts. I'd drop money on her stoop late at night on my way back from shining shoes in the taverns. And she had a Daddy, and he had a good job. He was a paper hanger.

I guess I would have gotten over Helene by summertime, but something happened in that classroom that made her face hang in front of me for the next twenty-two years. When I played the drums in high school it was for Helene and when I broke track records in college it was for Helene and when I started standing behind microphones and heard applause I wished Helene could hear it, too. It wasn't until I was twenty-nine years old and married and making money that I finally got her out of my system. Helene was sitting in that classroom when I learned to be ashamed of myself.

It was on a Thursday. I was sitting in the back of the room, in a seat with a chalk circle drawn around it. The idiot's seat, the troublemaker's seat.

The teacher thought I was stupid. Couldn't spell, couldn't read, couldn't do arithmetic. Just stupid. Teachers were never interested in finding out that you couldn't concentrate because you were so hungry, because you hadn't had any breakfast. All you could think about was noontime, would it ever come? Maybe you could sneak into the cloakroom and steal a bite of some kid's lunch out of a coat pocket. A bite of something. Paste. You can't really make a meal of paste, or put it on bread for a sandwich, but sometimes I'd scoop a few spoonfuls out of the big paste jar in the back of the room. Pregnant people get strange tastes. I was pregnant with poverty. Pregnant with dirt and pregnant with smells that made people turn away, pregnant with cold and pregnant with shoes that were never bought for me, pregnant with five other people in my bed and no Daddy in the next room, and pregnant with hunger. Paste doesn't taste too bad when you're hungry.

The teacher thought I was a troublemaker. All she saw from the front of the room was a little black boy who squirmed in his idiot's seat and made noises and poked the kids around him. I guess she couldn't see a kid who made noises because he wanted someone to know he was there.

It was on a Thursday, the day before the Negro payday. The eagle always flew on Friday. The teacher was asking each student how much his father would give to the Community Chest. On Friday night, each kid would get the money from his father, and on Monday he would bring it to the school. I decided I was going to buy a Daddy right then. I had money in my pocket from shining shoes and selling papers, and whatever Helene Tucker pledged for her Daddy I was going to top it. And I'd hand the money right in. I wasn't going to wait until Monday to buy me a Daddy.

I was shaking, scared to death. The teacher opened her book and started calling out names alphabetically.

"Helene Tucker?"

"My Daddy said he'd give two dollars and fifty cents."

"That's very nice, Helene. Very, very nice indeed."

That made me feel pretty good. It wouldn't take too much to top that. I had almost three dollars in dimes and quarters in my pocket. I stuck my hand in my pocket and held onto the money, waiting for her to call my name. But the teacher closed her book after she called everybody else in the class.

I stood up and raised my hand.

"What is it now?"

"You forgot me?"

She turned toward the blackboard. "I don't have time to be playing with you, Richard."

"My Daddy said he'd . . ."

"Sit down, Richard, you're disturbing the class."

"My Daddy said he'd give . . . fifteen dollars."

She turned around and looked mad. "We are collecting this money for you and your kind, Richard Gregory. If your Daddy can give fifteen dollars you have no business being on relief."

"I got it right now, I got it right now, my Daddy gave it to me to turn in today, my Daddy said . . ."

"And furthermore," she said, looking right at me, her nostrils getting big and her lips getting thin and her eyes opening wide. "We know you don't have a Daddy."

Helene Tucker turned around, her eyes full of tears. She felt sorry for me. Then I couldn't see her too well because I was crying, too.

"Sit down, Richard."

And I always thought the teacher kind of liked me. She always picked me to wash the blackboard on Friday, after school. That was a big thrill, it made me feel important. If I didn't wash it, come Monday the school might not function right.

"Where are you going, Richard?"

I walked out of school that day, and for a long time I didn't go back very often. There was shame there.

Now there was shame everywhere. It seemed like the whole world had been inside that classroom, everyone had heard what the teacher had said, everyone had turned around and felt sorry for me. There was shame in going to the Worthy Boys Annual Christmas Dinner for you and your kind, because everybody knew what a worthy boy was. Why couldn't they just call it the Boys Annual Dinner, why'd they have to give it a name? There was shame in wearing the brown and orange and white plaid mackinaw the welfare gave to 3,000 boys. Why'd it have to be the same for everybody so when you walked down the street the people could see you were on relief? It was a nice warm mackinaw and it had a hood, and my Momma beat me and called me a little rat when she found out I stuffed it in the bottom of a pail full of garbage way over on Cottage Street. There was shame in running over to Mister Ben's at the end of the day and asking for his rotten peaches, there was shame in asking Mrs. Simmons for a spoonful of sugar, there was shame in running out to meet the relief truck. I hated that truck, full of food for you and your kind. I ran into the house and hid when it came. And then I started to sneak through alleys, to take the long way home so the people going into White's Eat Shop wouldn't see me. Yeah, the whole world heard the teacher that day, we all know you don't have a Daddy.

It lasted for a while, this kind of numbness. I spent a lot of time feeling sorry for myself. And then one day I met this wino in a restaurant. I'd been out hustling all day, shining shoes, selling newspapers, and I had googobs of money in my pocket. Bought me a bowl of chili for fifteen cents, and a cheeseburger for fifteen cents, and a Pepsi for five cents, and a piece of chocolate cake for ten cents. That was a good meal. I was eating when this old wino came in. I love winos because they never hurt anyone but themselves. [29]

The old wino sat down at the counter and ordered twenty-six cents worth of food. He ate it like he really enjoyed it. When the owner, Mister Williams, asked him to pay the check, the old wino didn't lie or go through his pocket like he suddenly found a hole. [30]

He just said: "Don't have no money." [31]

The owner yelled: "Why in hell you come in here and eat my food if you don't have no money? That food cost me money." [32]

Mister Williams jumped over the counter and knocked the wino off his stool and beat him over the head with a pop bottle. Then he stepped back and watched the wino bleed. Then he kicked him. And he kicked him again. [33]

I looked at the wino with blood all over his face and I went over. "Leave him alone, Mister Williams. I'll pay the twenty-six cents." [34]

The wino got up, slowly, pulling himself up to the stool, then up to the counter, holding on for a minute until his legs stopped shaking so bad. He looked at me with pure hate. "Keep your twenty-six cents. You don't have to pay, not now. I just finished paying for it." [35]

He started to walk out, and as he passed me, he reached down and   36
touched my shoulder. "Thanks, sonny, but it's too late now. Why didn't
you pay it before?"

I was pretty sick about that. I waited too long to help another man.   37

About the Essay

1. What does Gregory mean by shame? What precisely was he ashamed of,
and what in particular did he learn from the incident at school?

2. What is the teacher's attitude toward Gregory? Cite her own words and
actions as well as Gregory's opinion.

3. What role does money play in Gregory's narrative? How does it relate to
his sense of shame?

4. Gregory's use of details—his description of Helene Tucker's manners or
his plaid mackinaw, for example—does more than merely make his narrative
vivid and interesting. Cite several other specific details he gives, and consider
the effect each has on your understanding of the story.

5. What effect does Gregory's repetition of the word *shame* have on you?
Does Gregory pointedly repeat any other words or phrases, and with what
effect?

Explorations

1. Describe an event in your life that made you sharply aware of how other
people see you. How did you feel—surprised, ashamed, angry, proud, or
something else? Why? Do you still feel the same way?

2. Social institutions and organizations help to shape our self-esteem, as they
did with Dick Gregory. Discuss the effect one such institution or organization
has had on you. How did it influence you? Did it help or hinder you in
developing a positive image of yourself?

3. Read Joan Didion's "On Self-Respect" (pages 33–37) and compare it to
"Shame." How does Gregory's experience relate to Didion's discussion?

JAMES HERRIOT

Born James Alfred Wight in 1916 in Scotland, James Herriot is known the world over for his memoirs about his life as a veterinarian in Yorkshire, England. Thus far he has published four volumes: *All Creatures Great and Small* (1972), *All Things Bright and Beautiful* (1974), *All Things Wise and Wonderful* (1977), and *The Lord God Made Them All* (1981)—together, the titles form the first verse of a well-known Anglican hymn. Through these books and through the television series based on them, millions have come to appreciate Herriot's warm personality and to enjoy his sometimes ironic wit. This episode from *The Lord God Made Them All* is typical of Herriot; called on to treat a pet cat, he proves a sharp observer of its owner as well.

The Junkman and His Cat

When Walt Barnett asked me to see his cat, I was surprised. He had employed other veterinary surgeons ever since [my colleague] Siegfried had mortally offended him by charging him ten pounds for castrating a horse, and that had been a long time ago. I was surprised, too, that a man like him should concern himself with the ailments of a cat.

A lot of people said Walt Barnett was the richest man in Darrowby—rolling in brass which he made from his many and diverse enterprises. He was mainly a scrap merchant, but he had a haulage business, too, and he was a dealer in second-hand cars, furniture, anything, in fact, that came his way. I knew he kept some livestock and horses around his big house outside the town, but there was money in these things, and money was the ruling passion of his life. There was no profit in cat keeping.

Another thing that puzzled me as I drove to his office was that owning a pet indicated some warmth of character, a vein of sentiment, however small. It just didn't fit into his nature.

I picked my way through the litter of the scrap yard to the wooden shed in the corner from which the empire was run. Walt Barnett was sitting behind a cheap desk and he was exactly as I remembered him, the massive body stretching the seams of the shiny, navy-blue suit, the cigarette dangling from his lips, even the brown trilby hat perched on the back of his head. Unchanged, too, was the beefy red face with its arrogant expression and hostile eyes.

"Over there," he said, glowering at me and poking a finger at a black and white cat sitting among the papers on the desk.

It was a typical greeting. I hadn't expected him to say, "Good   6
morning," or anything like that, and he never smiled. I reached across
the desk and tickled the animal's cheek, rewarded by a rich purring and
an arching of the back against my hand. He was a big tom, long-haired
and attractively marked, with a white breast and white paws, and though
I have always had a predilection for tabbies, I took an immediate liking
to this cat. He exuded friendliness.

"Nice cat," I said. "What's the trouble?"   7

"It's 'is leg. There's summat[1] wrong with that 'un there. Must've   8
cut 'isself."

I felt among the fluffy hair, and the little creature flinched as I   9
reached a point halfway up the limb. I took out my scissors and clipped
a clear area. I could see a transverse wound, quite deep, and discharging
a thin, serous fluid. "Yes . . . this could be a cut. But there's something
unusual about it. I can't see how he's done it. Does he go out in the yard
much?"

The big man nodded. "Aye, wanders around a bit."   10

"Ah, well, he may have caught it on some sharp object. I'll give   11
him a penicillin injection and leave you a tube of ointment to squeeze
into the wound night and morning."

Some cats object strongly to hypodermics, and since their ar-   12
moury includes claws as well as teeth, they can be difficult, but this one
never moved. In fact, the purring increased in volume as I inserted the
needle.

"He really is good-natured," I said. "What do you call him?"   13

"Fred." Walt Barnett looked at me expressionlessly. There didn't   14
appear to be anything particularly apposite about the name, but the man's
face discouraged further comment.

I produced the ointment from my bag and placed it on the desk.   15
"Right, let me know if he doesn't improve."

I received no reply, neither acknowledgment nor goodbye, and I   16
took my leave feeling the same prickle of resentment as when I had first
encountered his boorishness.

But as I walked across the yard, I forgot my annoyance in my   17
preoccupation with the case. There was something very peculiar about
that wound. It didn't look like an accidental laceration. It was neat and
deep, as though somebody had drawn a razor blade across the flesh. I
listened as I had listened so often before to that little inner voice—the
voice that said things were not as they seemed.

A touch on my arm brought me out of my musings. One of the   18

---

[1]Yorkshire dialect for "something."

men who had been working among the scrap was looking at me con-
spiratorially. "You've been in to see t'big boss?"

"Yes."   19

"Funny thing, t'awd[2] bugger botherin' about a cat, eh?"   20

"I suppose so. How long has he had it?"   21

"Oh, about two years now. It was a stray. Ran into 'is office one   22
day, and, knowin' him, I thought he'd 'ave booted it straight out, but 'e
didn't. Adopted it, instead. Ah can't reckon it up. It sits there all day
on 'is desk."

"He must like it," I said.   23

"Him? He doesn't like anythin' or anybody. He's a . . ."   24

A bellow from the office doorway cut him short.   25

"Hey, you! Get on with your bloody work!" Walt Barnett, huge   26
and menacing, brandished a fist, and the man, after one terrified glance,
scuttled away.

As I got into my car, the thought stayed with me that this was how   27
Walt Barnett lived—surrounded by fear and hate. His ruthlessness was a
byword in the town, and though no doubt it had made him rich, I didn't
envy him.

I heard his voice on the phone two days later. "Get out 'ere sharpish 28
and see that cat."

"Isn't the wound any better?"   29

"Naw, it's wuss, so don't be long."   30

Fred was in his usual place on the desk, and he purred as I went   31
up and stroked him, but the leg was certainly more painful. It was disappointing, but what really baffled me was that the wound was bigger
instead of smaller. It was still the same narrow slit in the skin, but it had
undoubtedly lengthened. It was as though it was trying to creep its way
round the leg.

I had brought some extra instruments with me, and I passed a metal   32
probe gently into the depths of the cut. I could feel something down
there, something which caught the end of the probe and sprang away. I
followed with long forceps and gripped the unknown object before it
could escape. When I brought it to the surface and saw the narrow brown
strand, all became suddenly clear.

"He's got an elastic band round his leg," I said. I snipped the thing 33
through, withdrew it and dropped it on the desk. "There it is. He'll be
all right now."

Walt Barnett jerked himself upright in his chair. "Elastic band!   34
Why the 'ell didn't you find it fust time?"

---

[2]The old.

He had me there. Why the hell hadn't I? In those days my eyesight   35
was perfect, but on that first visit all I had seen was a little break in the
skin.

"I'm sorry, Mr. Barnett," I said. "The elastic was embedded in the   36
flesh, out of sight." It was true, but I didn't feel proud.

He puffed rapidly at the ever-present cigarette. "And 'ow did it get   37
there?"

"Somebody put it on his leg, without a doubt."   38

"Put it on . . . wot for?"   39

"Oh, people do that to cats. I've heard of cases like this but never   40
actually seen one. There are some cruel folk around."

"One o' them fellers in the yard, ah'll wager."   41

"Not necessarily. Fred goes out in the street, doesn't he?"   42

"Oh, aye, often."   43

"Well, it could have been anybody."   44

There was a long silence as the big man sat scowling, his eyes half-   45
closed. I wondered if he was going over the list of his enemies. That
would take some time.

"Anyway," I said. "The leg will heal very quickly now. That's the   46
main thing."

Walt Barnett reached across the desk and slowly rubbed the cat's   47
side with a sausagelike forefinger. I had seen him do this several times
during my previous visit. It was an odd, unsmiling gesture, but probably
the nearest he could get to a caress.

On my way back to the surgery I slumped low in the car seat, hardly   48
daring to think of what would have happened if I hadn't found that
elastic. Arrest of circulation, gangrene, loss of the foot or even death. I
broke into a sweat at the thought.

Walt Barnett was on the phone three weeks later, and I felt a twinge   49
of apprehension at the sound of the familiar voice. Maybe I wasn't out
of the wood yet.

"Is his leg still troubling him?" I asked.   50

"Naw, that's 'ealed up. There's summat matter with 'is head."   51

"His head?"   52

"Aye, keeps cockin' it from side to side. Come and see 'im."   53

This sounded to me like canker, and, in fact, when I saw the cat   54
sitting on the desk twisting his head around uneasily, I was sure that was
it, but the ears were clean and painless.

This amiable cat seemed to like being examined, and the purring   55
rose to a crescendo as I made a close inspection of his teeth, mouth, eyes
and nostrils. Nothing. Yet something up there was causing a lot of discomfort.

I began to work my way through the black hair, and suddenly the   56
purring was interrupted by a sharp "miaow" as my fingers came upon a
painful spot on his neck.

"Something here," I murmured. I took out my scissors and began   57
to clip. And as the hair fell away and the skin showed through, a wave
of disbelief swept through me. I was looking down at a neat little transverse slit, the identical twin of the one I had seen before.

My God, surely not on the neck. I went into the wound with probe   58
and forceps, and within seconds I had brought the familiar brown band
to the surface. A quick snip and I pulled it clear.

"More elastic," I said dully.   59

"Round 'is neck!"   60

"Afraid so. Somebody really meant business this time."   61

He drew his enormous forefinger along the furry flank, and the cat   62
rubbed delightedly against him. "Who's doin' this?"

I shrugged. "No way of telling. The police are always on the lookout   63
for cruelty, but they would have to catch a person actually in the act."

I knew he was wondering when the next attempt would come, and   64
so was I, but there were no more elastic bands for Fred. The neck healed
rapidly, and I didn't see the cat for nearly a year till one morning [my
wife] Helen met me as I was coming in from my round.

"Mr. Barnett's just been on the phone, Jim. Would you please go   65
at once? He thinks his cat has been poisoned."

Another attack on this nice little animal, and after all this time.   66
It didn't make sense, and my mind was a jumble as I hurried into Walt
Barnett's office.

I found a vastly different Fred this time. The cat was not in his old   67
place on the desk but was crouched on the floor among a litter of newspapers. He did not look up, but as I went over to him, he retched and
vomited a yellow fluid onto the paper. More vomit lay around among
pools of diarrhea which had the same yellowish hue.

Walt Barnett, overflowing the chair behind the desk, spoke past   68
the dangling cigarette. "He's poisoned, isn't 'e? Somebody's given 'im
summat."

"It's possible. . . ." I watched the cat move slowly to a saucer of   69
milk and sit over it in the same crouching attitude. He did not drink
but sat looking down with a curious immobility. There was a sad familiarity in the little animal's appearance. This could be something worse
even than poison.

"Well, it is, isn't it?" the big man went on. "Somebody's tried to   70
kill 'im again."

"I'm not sure." As I took the cat's temperature, there was none of   71
the purring or outgoing friendliness I had known before. He was sunk in
a profound lethargy.

The temperature was 105°F. I palpated the abdomen, feeling the   72
doughy consistency of the bowels, the lack of muscular tone.

"Well, if it's not that, what is it?"   73

"It's feline enteritis. I'm nearly certain."   74

He looked at me blankly.   75

"Some people call it cat distemper," I said. "There's an outbreak   76
in Darrowby just now. I've seen several cases lately, and Fred's symptoms
are typical."

The big man heaved his bulk from behind the desk, went over to   77
the cat and rubbed his forefinger along the unheeding back. "Well, if it's
that, can you cure 'im?"

"I'll do my best, Mr. Barnett, but the mortality rate is very high."   78

"You mean, most of 'em die?"   79

"I'm afraid so."   80

"How can that be? I thought you fellers had all them wonderful   81
new medicines now."

"Yes, but this is a virus, and viruses are resistant to antibiotics."   82

"Awright, then." Wheezing, he drew himself upright and returned   83
to his chair. "What are you goin' to do?"

"I'm going to start right now," I said. I injected electrolytic fluid   84
to combat the dehydration. I gave antibiotics against the secondary bac-
teria and finished with a sedative to control the vomiting. But I knew
that everything I had done was merely supportive. I had never had much
luck with feline enteritis.

I visited Fred each morning, and the very sight of him made me   85
unhappy. He was either hunched over the saucer or he was curled up on
the desk in a little basket. He had no interest in the world around him.

He never moved when I gave him his injections. It was like pushing   86
a needle into a lifeless animal, and on the fourth morning I could see
that he was sinking rapidly.

"I'll call in tomorrow," I said, and Walt Barnett nodded without   87
speaking. He had shown no emotion throughout the cat's illness.

Next day, when I entered the office, I found the usual scene—the   88
huge figure in his chair, brown trilby on the back of his head and cigarette
hanging from his lips, the cat in the basket on the desk.

Fred was very still and as I approached, I saw with a dull feeling of   89
inevitability that he was not breathing. I put my stethoscope over his
heart for a few moments, then looked up.

"I'm afraid he's dead, Mr. Barnett."   90

The big man did not change expression. He reached slowly across   91
and rubbed his forefinger against the dark fur in that familiar gesture.
Then he put his elbows on the desk and covered his face with his hands.

I did not know what to say; I watched helplessly as his shoulders   92
began to shake and tears welled between the thick fingers. He stayed like
that for some time, then he spoke.

"He was my friend," he said.   93

I still could find no words, and the silence was heavy in the room   94
until he suddenly pulled his hands from his face.

He glared at me defiantly. "Aye, ah know what you're thinkin'.   95
This is that big, tough bugger, Walt Barnett, cryin' his eyes out over a
cat. What a joke! I reckon you'll have a bloody good laugh later on."

Evidently he was sure that what he considered a display of weakness   96
would lower my opinion of him, and yet he was so wrong. I have liked
him better ever since.

About the Essay

1. What is Herriot's impression of Walt Barnett at the beginning of the selection? At the end of the selection? On the basis of his behavior in the selection, how would you characterize Barnett?

2. This story includes three different kinds of language: the Yorkshire speech of Barnett, the standard English of the narrator, and the medical terms used by Herriot. What do these different varieties of speech illustrate in the story?

3. What view does Barnett hold of himself? Do you think he is comfortable with that image? Can you cite any textual evidence in support of your answer?

4. Aside from Herriot himself, there are three "characters" in this selection. Who are they? How does Herriot depict their personalities? What sort of "personality" does the cat have? And what of Herriot's own personality—how does it come through his narrative?

Explorations

1. Barnett's feelings toward his cat reveal a side of his personality that he does not want people to see. Do you know of someone like that—a parent, a friend, a character in a story or drama? Describe that person and explain as best you can why he or she chooses to disguise or hide his or her true feelings.

2. Why do people keep pets? If you have owned a pet, what did the experience mean to you, and do for you?

3. Herriot believes that "owning a pet indicate[s] some warmth of character, a vein of sentiment." In the next selection, "What You See Is the Real You" (pages 52–54), Willard Gaylin argues that a person's actual behavior is all that really matters. How do you think Gaylin would assess Barnett's character? Do you agree?

What is the true measure of character—our inward feelings and motives, or what we actually do? According to Willard Gaylin, a distinguished psychiatrist and teacher, our actions are what count. Born in Cleveland in 1925, Gaylin is professor of clinical psychiatry at Columbia University and president of the Institute of Society, Ethics, and Life Sciences. As this latter position suggests, he is deeply concerned with moral issues in human behavior, a concern reflected in his books—among them, *In Service of Their Country: War Resistors in Prison* (1970), *Partial Justice: A Study of Bias in Sentencing* (1974), and *Feelings: Our Vital Signs* (1979). Gaylin's views on the inner and outer person affect not only his social attitudes but also his conception of the self. His notion of what might be called the "integrated self" has a bearing on important questions of social policy.

What You See Is the Real You

It was, I believe, the distinguished Nebraska financier Father Edward J. Flanagan who professed to having "never met a bad boy."[1] Having, myself, met a remarkable number of bad boys, it might seem that either our experiences were drastically different or we were using the word "bad" differently. I suspect neither is true, but rather that the Father was appraising the "inner man," while I, in fact, do not acknowledge the existence of inner people.   1

Since we psychoanalysts have unwittingly contributed to this confusion, let one, at least, attempt a small rectifying effort. Psychoanalytic data—which should be viewed as supplementary information—is, unfortunately, often viewed as alternative (and superior) explanation. This has led to the prevalent tendency to think of the "inner" man as the real man and the outer man as an illusion or pretender.   2

While psychoanalysis supplies us with an incredibly useful tool for explaining the motives and purposes underlying human behavior, most of this has little bearing on the moral nature of that behavior.   3

Like roentgenology, psychoanalysis is a fascinating, but relatively new, means of illuminating the person. But few of us are prepared to substitute an X-ray of Grandfather's head for the portrait that hangs in the parlor. The inside of the man represents another view, not a truer one. A man may not always be what he appears to be, but what he   4

---

[1]Father Flanagan founded Boys Town, a village for homeless boys. He also created an enormous and highly successful fund-raising system to support the town.

appears to be is always a significant part of what he is. A man is the sum total of *all* his behavior. To probe for unconscious determinants of behavior and then define *him* in their terms exclusively, ignoring his overt behavior altogether, is a greater distortion than ignoring the unconscious completely.

Kurt Vonnegut has said, "You are what you pretend to be," which is simply another way of saying, you are what we (all of us) perceive you to be, not what you think you are.

Consider for a moment the case of the ninety-year-old man on his deathbed (surely the Talmud[2] must deal with this?) joyous and relieved over the success of his deception. For ninety years he has shielded his evil nature from public observation. For ninety years he has affected courtesy, kindness, and generosity—suppressing all the malice he knew was within him while he calculatedly and artificially substituted grace and charity. All his life he had been fooling the world into believing he was a good man. This "evil" man will, I predict, be welcomed into the Kingdom of Heaven.

Similarly, I will not be told that the young man who earns his pocket money by mugging old ladies is "really" a good boy. Even my generous and expansive definition of goodness will not accommodate that particular form of self-advancement.

It does not count that beneath the rough exterior he has a heart—or, for that matter, an entire innards—of purest gold, locked away from human perception. You are for the most part what you seem to be, not what you would wish to be, nor, indeed, what you believe yourself to be.

Spare me, therefore, your good intentions, your inner sensitivities, your unarticulated and unexpressed love. And spare me also those tedious psychohistories which—by exposing the goodness inside the bad man, and the evil in the good—invariably establish a vulgar and perverse egalitarianism, as if the arrangement of what is outside and what inside makes no moral difference.

Saint Francis may, in his unconscious, indeed have been compensating for, and denying, destructive, unconscious Oedipal impulses identical to those which Attila projected and acted on.[3] But the similarity

[2]An ancient collection of Jewish law and commentaries by sages on the written and oral traditions of the Jews.

[3]Saint Francis, founder of the Franciscan order of begging friars, was born into a wealthy family but took vows of poverty. Oedipal impulses, in psychoanalysis, refer to complex emotions resulting from a child's sexual attraction to a parent of the opposite sex and a view of the same-sex parent as a rival to be destroyed. Attila led the Huns, a Germanic tribe, in a brutal conquest of ancient Rome.

of the unconscious constellations in the two men matters precious little, if it does not distinguish between them.

I do not care to learn that Hitler's heart was in the right place. A knowledge of the unconscious life of the man may be an adjunct to understanding his behavior. It is *not* a substitute for his behavior in describing him.   11

The inner man is a fantasy. If it helps you to identify with one, by all means, do so; preserve it, cherish it, embrace it, but do not present it to others for evaluation or consideration, for excuse or exculpation, or, for that matter, for punishment or disapproval.   12

Like any fantasy, it serves your purposes alone. It has no standing in the real world which we share with each other. Those character traits, those attitudes, that behavior—that strange and alien stuff sticking out all over you—*that's the real you!*   13

About the Essay

1. What is Gaylin's fullest statement of his thesis? How does he defend it? What counterarguments does he answer? From your point of view, are his answers adequate? Why, or why not?

2. Why does Gaylin feel that we need to think more carefully than we have about the inner and outer person? What is mistaken in the prevailing view, according to him?

3. Toward the end, Gaylin says that "The inner man is a fantasy." Why does he say that? Are there statements or concerns in the essay that imply a contradiction? Explain your answer.

4. In paragraphs 10 and 11 Gaylin refers to famous historical figures as examples. For the purpose of his argument, what are the advantages of doing this? What are the disadvantages?

5. What analogy does Gaylin use to support his statement that "the inside of the man represents another view, not a truer one"? Why do you think he chose that analogy? What are its strong and weak points?

6. Gaylin opens his essay by quoting Father Flanagan. What purpose do Flanagan's thoughts serve in the essay? Why do you think Gaylin chooses to place them at the very beginning of the essay?

Explorations

1. Everyone makes mistakes, and probably all of us have at one time or another tried to excuse ourselves by saying we didn't *mean* to do wrong. Gaylin seems to say that intentions do not matter, that they have no standing

in the real world which we share with each other. Do you agree or disagree with Gaylin's view?

2. What implications might Gaylin's views have for social policies and institutions? You might choose an area of society in which you are particularly interested—for example, business, politics, community activities, or criminal justice.

LEWIS THOMAS

A distinguished physician, medical researcher, and teacher, Lewis
Thomas heads the Memorial Sloan-Kettering Cancer Center in New York. He
is, however, probably most widely known for the brief essays he has been
writing since 1971 for *The New England Journal of Medicine,* many of them
collected in *The Lives of a Cell* (1974) and *The Medusa and the Snail* (1979).
Born in New York in 1913, Thomas attended Princeton University and
Harvard Medical School before embarking on a medical career that has
included affiliations with medical centers and schools in Minneapolis, New
York, and New Haven. Though he refers to these pieces as "notes of a biology
watcher," Thomas actually writes on a wide variety of subjects—from the
reform of the premedical curriculum to the delights of reading Montaigne, to
the use of magic in medicine. In "The Selves," from *The Medusa and the Snail,*
Thomas reflects on his own multiple personalities.

The Selves

There are psychiatric patients who are said to be incapacitated by   1
having more than one self. One of these, an attractive, intelligent young
woman in distress, turned up on a television talk show a while back,
sponsored to reveal her selves and their disputes. She possessed, she said,
or was possessed by, no fewer than eight other separate women, all different, with different names, arguing and elbowing their way into control
of the enterprise, causing unending confusion and embarrassment. She
(they) wished to be rid of all of them (her), except of course herself
(themselves).

People like this are called hysterics by the professionals, or maybe   2
schizophrenics, and there is, I am told, nothing much that can be done.
Having more than one self is supposed to be deeply pathological in itself,
and there is no known way to evict trespassers.

I am not sure that the number of different selves is in itself all that   3
pathological; I hope not. Eight strikes me personally as a reasonably small
and easily manageable number. It is the simultaneity of their appearance
that is the real problem, and I should think psychiatry would do better
by simply persuading them to queue up and wait their turn, as happens
in the normal rest of us. Couldn't they be conditioned some way, by
offering rewards or holding out gently threatening sanctions? "How *do*
you do, I'm absolutely delighted to see you here and I have exactly fifty-
five minutes, after which I very much regret to say someone else will be
dropping in, but could I see you again tomorrow at this same time, do

have a chocolate mint and let's just talk, just the two of us." That sort of thing might help at least to get them lined up in some kind of order.

Actually, it would embarrass me to be told that more than a single self is a kind of disease. I've had, in my time, more than I could possibly count or keep track of. The great difference, which keeps me feeling normal, is that mine (ours) have turned up one after the other, on an orderly schedule. Five years ago I was another person, juvenile, doing and saying things I couldn't possibly agree with now. Ten years ago I was a stranger. Twenty—forty years ago . . . I've forgotten. The only thing close to what you might call illness, in my experience, was in the gaps in the queue when one had finished and left the place before the next one was ready to start, and there was nobody around at all. Luckily, that has happened only three or four times that I can recall, once when I'd become a very old child and my adolescent hadn't appeared, and a couple of times later on when there seemed to be some confusion about who was next up. The rest of the time they have waited turns and emerged on cue ready to take over, sometimes breathless and needing last-minute briefing but nonetheless steady enough to go on. The surprising thing has always been how little background information they seemed to need, considering how the times changed. I cannot remember who it was five years ago. He was reading linguistics and had just discovered philology, as I recall, but he left before getting anything much done.

To be truthful there have been a few times when they were all there at once, like those girls on television, clamoring for attention, whole committees of them, a House Committee, a Budget Committee, a Grievance Committee, even a Committee on Membership, although I don't know how any of them ever got in. No chairman, ever, certainly not me. At the most I'm a sort of administrative assistant. There's never an agenda. At the end I bring in the refreshments.

What do we meet about? It is hard to say. The door bangs open and in they come, calling for the meeting to start, and then they all talk at once. Odd to say, it is not just a jumble of talk; they tend to space what they're saying so that words and phrases from one will fit into short spaces left in silence by the others. At good times it has the feel of an intensely complicated conversation, but at others the sounds are more like something overheard in a crowded station. At worse times the silences get out of synchrony, interrupting each other; it is as though all the papers had suddenly blown off the table.

We never get anything settled. In recent years I've sensed an increase in their impatience with me, whoever they think I am, and with the fix they're in. They don't come right out and say so, but what they are beginning to want more than anything else is a chairman.

The worst times of all have been when I've wanted to be just one. 8
Try walking out on the ocean beach at night, looking at stars, thinking,
Be one, be one. Doesn't work, ever. Just when you feel ascension, turning, wheeling, and that whirring sound like a mantel clock getting ready
to strike, the other selves begin talking. Whatever you're thinking, they
say, it's not like that at all.

The only way to quiet them down, get them to stop, is to play 9
music. That does it. Bach stops them every time, in their tracks, almost
as though that's what they've been waiting for.

About the Essay

1. How does Thomas differentiate between a normal person, such as himself,
and someone who is "incapacitated by having more than one self"?

2. What does Thomas mean when he speaks of his many selves? What is his
thesis? How do you know?

3. What analogy does Thomas use in discussing his multiple selves? What
are the advantages of this analogy? What are its limitations?

4. What do you think Thomas's purpose was in writing this essay?

5. What does the final paragraph tell us about Thomas and his selves?

6. Throughout this essay, Thomas uses a lightly ironic tone. How does he
achieve this tone? Why is it appropriate to his subject?

Explorations

1. To use Thomas's image, do you feel that you are one self or made up of
many selves—either in succession, at the same time, or both? Identify your
self or selves and describe each one briefly. If you have several selves "meeting" regularly, which is the "chairman"? Which would you appoint as chairman if you could, and how would you run the meetings?

2. In his essay "Why Montaigne Is Not a Bore," Lewis Thomas quotes from
Montaigne's essay, "On Inconsistency" (pages 65–70). Read Montaigne's essay, and consider whether Thomas's "The Selves" essentially paraphrases and
updates Montaigne or whether it has its own distinctive message. How does
Thomas's way of thinking and writing differ from Montaigne's?

JEANNE WAKATSUKI HOUSTON

An American of Japanese descent, Jeanne Wakatsuki Houston is
married to the writer James Houston. Like many other Japanese-Americans,
Houston and her family were relocated from their southern California home
during World War II, and they spent three and a half years in an internment
camp at Manzanar, near Death Valley. In collaboration with her husband, she
has written about that experience in *Farewell to Manzanar* (1973). Here, she
reflects on growing up in California after the war, and on the mixture of
Japanese and *Hakujin* ("all-American") traits in her own personality.

Living in Two Cultures

The memories surrounding my awareness of being female fall into   1
two categories: those of the period before World War II, when the family
made up my life, and those after the war, when I entered puberty and
my world expanded to include the ways and values of my Caucasian
peers. I did not think about my Asian-ness and how it influenced my
self-image as a female until I married.

In remembering myself as a small child, I find it hard to separate   2
myself from the entity of the family. I was too young to be given "duties"
according to my sex, and I was unaware that this was the organizational
basis for operating the family. I took it for granted that everyone just did
what had to be done to keep things running smoothly. My five older
sisters helped my mother with domestic duties. My four older brothers
helped my father in the fishing business. What I vaguely recall about the
sensibility surrounding our sex differences was that my sisters and I all
liked to please our brothers. More so, we tried to attract positive attention
from Papa. A smile or affectionate pat from him was like a gift from
heaven. Somehow, we never felt this way about Mama. We took her
love for granted. But there was something special about Papa.

I never identified this specialness as being one of the blessings of   3
maleness. After all, I played with my brother Kiyo, two years older than
myself, and I never felt there was anything special about him. I could
even make him cry. My older brothers were fun-loving, boisterous and
very kind to me, especially when I made them laugh with my imitations
of Carmen Miranda dancing or of Bonnie Baker singing "Oh, Johnny."
But Papa was different. His specialness came not from being male, but
from being the authority.

After the war and the closing of the camps, my world drastically   4
changed. The family had disintegrated; my father was no longer godlike,
despite my mother's attempt to sustain that pre-war image of him. I was
spending most of my time with my new Caucasian friends and learning
new values that clashed with those of my parents. It was also time that
I assumed the duties girls were supposed to do, like cooking, cleaning
the house, washing and ironing clothes. I remember washing and ironing
my brothers' shirts, being careful to press the collars correctly, trying not
to displease them. I cannot ever remember my brothers performing domestic chores while I lived at home. Yet, even though they may not
have been working "out there," as the men were supposed to do, I did
not resent it. It would have embarrassed me to see my brothers doing
the dishes. Their reciprocation came in a different way. They were very
protective of me and made me feel good and important for being a female.
If my brother Ray had extra money, he would sometimes buy me a sexy
sweater like my Caucasian friends wore, which Mama wouldn't buy for
me. My brothers taught me to ride a bicycle and to drive a car, took me
to my first dance, and proudly introduced me to their friends.

Although the family had changed, my identity as a female within   5
it did not differ much from my older sisters who grew up before the war.
The males and females supported each other but for different reasons.
No longer was the survival of the family as a group our primary objective;
we cooperated to help each other survive "out there" in the complicated
world that had weakened Papa.

We were living in Long Beach then. My brothers encouraged me   6
to run for school office, to try out for majorette and song leader, and to
run for queen of various festivities. They were proud that I was breaking
social barriers still closed to them. It was acceptable for an Oriental male
to excel academically and in sports. But to gain recognition socially in
a society that had been fed the stereotyped model of the Asian male as
cook, houseboy or crazed kamikaze pilot was almost impossible. The more
alluring myth of mystery and exotica that surrounds the Oriental female
made it easier, though no less inwardly painful, for me.

Whenever I succeeded in the *Hakujin* world, my brothers were   7
supportive, whereas Papa would be disdainful, undermined by my obvious
capitulation to the ways of the West. I wanted to be like my Caucasian
friends. Not only did I want to look like them, I wanted to act like them.
I tried hard to be outgoing and socially aggressive and to act confidently,
like my girlfriends. At home I was careful not to show these personality
traits to my father. For him it was bad enough that I did not even look
very Japanese: I was too big, and I walked too assertively. My breasts
were large, and besides that I showed them off with those sweaters the

Hakujin girls wore! My behavior at home was never calm and serene, but around my father I still tried to be as Japanese as I could.

As I passed puberty and grew more interested in boys, I soon became 8 aware that an Oriental female evoked a certain kind of interest from males. I was still too young to understand how or why an Oriental female fascinated Caucasian men, and of course, far too young to see then that it was a form of "not seeing." My brothers would warn me, "Don't trust the *Hakujin* boys. They only want one thing. They'll treat you like a servant and expect you to wait on them hand and foot. They don't know how to be nice to you." My brothers never dated Caucasian girls. In fact, I never really dated Caucasian boys until I went to college. In high school, I used to sneak out to dances and parties where I would meet them. I wouldn't even dare to think what Papa would do if he knew.

What my brothers were saying was that I should not act toward 9 Caucasian males as I did toward them. I must not "wait on them" or allow them to think I would, because they wouldn't understand. In other words, be a Japanese female around Japanese men and act *Hakujin* around Caucasian men. This double identity within a "double standard" resulted not only in a confusion for me of my role or roles as female, but also in who or what I was racially. With the admonitions of my brothers lurking deep in my consciousness, I would try to be aggressive, assertive and "come on strong" toward Caucasian men. I mustn't let them think I was submissive, passive and all-giving like Madame Butterfly.[1] With Asian males I would tone down my natural enthusiasm and settle into patterns instilled in me through the models of my mother and my sisters. I was not comfortable in either role.

Although I was attracted to males who looked like someone in a 10 Coca-Cola ad, I yearned for the expressions of their potency to be like that of Japanese men, like that of my father: unpredictable, dominant, and brilliant—yet sensitive and poetic. I wanted a blond samurai.

When I met my blond samurai, during those college years in San 11 Jose, I was surprised to see how readily my mother accepted the idea of our getting married. My father had passed away, but I was still concerned about her reaction. All of my married brothers and sisters had married Japanese-American mates. I would be the first to marry a Caucasian. "He's a strong man and will protect you. I'm all for it," she said. Her main concern for me was survival. Knowing that my world was the world of the *Hakujin*, she wanted me to be protected, even if it meant marriage

---

[1]The heroine of an American play and an Italian opera, Madame Butterfly married an American navy lieutenant for love, then committed ritual suicide when he left her to marry an American woman.

to one of them. It was 1957, and interracial couples were a rare sight to
see. She felt that my husband-to-be was strong because he was acting
against the norms of his culture, perhaps even against his parent's wishes.
From her vantage point, where family and group opinion outweighed the
individual's, this willingness to oppose them was truly a show of strength.

When we first married I wondered if I should lay out his socks and   12
underwear every morning like my mother used to do for my father. But
my brothers' warning would float up from the past: don't be subservient
to Caucasian men or they will take advantage. So I compromised and
laid them out sporadically, whenever I thought to do it . . . which grew
less and less often as the years passed. (Now my husband is lucky if he
can even find a clean pair of socks in the house!) His first reaction to
this wifely gesture was to be uncomfortably pleased. Then he was puzzled
by its sporadic occurrence, which did not seem to coincide as an act of
apology or because I wanted something. On the days when I felt I should
be a good Japanese wife, I did it. On other days, when I felt American
and assertive, I did not.

When my mother visited us, as she often did when she was alive,   13
I had to be on good behavior, much to my husband's pleasure and surprise. I would jump up from the table to fill his empty water glass (if she
hadn't beat me to it) or butter his roll. If I didn't notice that his plate
needed refilling, she would kick me under the table and reprimand me
with a disapproving look. Needless to say, we never had mother-in-law
problems. He would often ask, with hope in his voice, "when is your
mother coming to visit?"

My mother had dutifully served my father throughout their mar-   14
riage, but I never felt she resented it. I served my brothers and father
and did not resent it. I was made to feel not only important for performing
duties of my role, but absolutely integral for the functioning of the family.
I realized a very basic difference in attitude between Japanese and American cultures toward serving another. In my family, to serve another could
be uplifting, a gracious gesture that elevated oneself. For many white
Americans, it seems that serving another is degrading, an indication of
dependency or weakness in character, or a low place in the social ladder.
To be ardently considerate is to be "self-effacing" or apologetic.

My father used to say, "Serving humanity is the greatest virtue.   15
Giving service of yourself is more worthy than selling the service or goods
of another." He would prefer that we be maids in someone's home,
serving someone well, than be salesgirls where our function would be to
exchange someone else's goods, handling money. Perhaps it was his way
of rationalizing and giving pride to the occupations open to us as Ori-
entals. Nevertheless, his words have stayed with me, giving me spiritual

sustenance at times when I perceived that my willingness to give was misconstrued as a need to be liked or an act of manipulation to get something.

My husband and I often joke that the reason we have stayed married   16
for so long is that we continually mystify each other with responses and attitudes that are plainly due to our different backgrounds. For years I frustrated him with unpredictable silences and accusing looks. I felt a great reluctance to tell him what I wanted or what needed to be done in the home. I was inwardly furious that I was being put into the position of having to *tell* him what to do. I felt my femaleness, in the Japanese sense, was being degraded. I did not want to be the authority. That would be humiliating for him and for me. He, on the other hand, considering the home to be under my dominion, in the American sense, did not dare to impose on me what he thought I wanted. He wanted me to tell him or make a list, like his parents did in his home.

Entertaining socially was also confusing. Up to recent times, I still   17
hesitated to sit at one head of our rectangular dining table when my husband sat at the other end. It seemed right to be seated next to him, helping him serve the food. Sometimes I did it anyway, but only with our close friends who didn't misread my physical placement as psychological subservience.

At dinner parties I always served the men first, until I noticed the   18
women glaring at me. I became self-conscious about it and would try to remember to serve the women first. Sometimes I would forget and automatically turn to a man. I would catch myself abruptly, dropping a bowl of soup all over him. Then I would have to serve him first anyway, as a gesture of apology. My unconscious Japanese instinct still managed to get what it wanted.

Now I just entertain according to how I feel that day. If my Japanese   19
sensibility is stronger, I act accordingly and feel comfortable. If I feel like going all-American, I can do that, too, and feel comfortable. I have come to accept the cultural hybridness of my personality, to recognize it as a strength and not weakness. Because I am culturally neither pure Japanese nor pure American does not mean I am less of a person. It means I have been enriched with the heritage of both.

How my present attitudes will affect my children in later years   20
remains to be seen. My world is radically different from my mother's world, and all indications point to an even wider difference between our world and our children's. Whereas my family's and part of my struggle was racially based, I do not foresee a similar struggle for our children. Their biracialism is, indeed, a factor in their identity and self-image, but I feel their struggle will be more to sustain human dignity in a world

rapidly dehumanizing itself with mechanization and technology. My hope is they have inherited a strong will to survive, that essential trait ethnic minorities in this country have so sharply honed.

About the Essay

1. What caused Houston to start thinking about her self-image as a female? When in her life did this happen?

2. Brought up in a Japanese-American family, Houston sees *Hakujin* attitudes and ways from a special perspective. What does she seem to consider most distinctive about *Hakujin* culture? Do any of her observations surprise you?

3. Houston often describes her own attitudes and behavior in relation to certain roles. What roles does she mention, and how does she characterize them?

4. By the end of the essay, do you believe that Houston has found her own identity? Is she still struggling to conform to each of her two cultures? How much is she her own woman? Do you find paragraph 19 convincing?

Explorations

1. Houston explores her identity almost completely in terms of family roles, first as a daughter and sister and then as a wife. What roles in your life have the most influence on what you do and how you see yourself? Do you ever feel torn between various roles?

2. Is there ever a reason to assume conventional roles, or do you think they are always an obstacle to happiness? Is an "unexamined" life necessarily incomplete?

MICHEL DE MONTAIGNE

Said by some to have invented the essay, Montaigne not only gave this literary form much of its distinctive form and character, but he also gave it its name. He called his own writings—short explorations of his own thoughts on a variety of topics—*essais* (French for "attempts" or "experiments") to reflect their personal and tentative quality. Born in 1533 to a prosperous noble family in Périgord, France, Montaigne was educated as a lawyer. After thirteen years of practicing law, however, he retired at thirty-eight to manage the family estate and to write. Except for the years from 1581 to 1585, when he served as mayor of Bordeaux, his essays were to be his main occupation until his death in 1592.

Even in Donald Frame's excellent translation, Montaigne can seem to modern readers an odd mixture of the archaic and the strikingly contemporary. Educated in an earlier age, he often alludes to and quotes from the ancient Greeks and Romans. But his subject is not ancient lore; it is himself. Montaigne explores and records his own nature with honesty and good humor, and we discover to our surprise that this sixteenth-century Frenchman is much like us. In this essay, written about 1572, Montaigne takes up the inconsistency of people's actions and attitudes and observes ruefully that "there is as much difference between us and ourselves as between us and others."

On Inconsistency

Those who make a practice of comparing human actions are never   1
so perplexed as when they try to see them as a whole and in the same light; for they commonly contradict each other so strangely that it seems impossible that they have come from the same shop. One moment young Marius is a son of Mars, another moment a son of Venus.[1] Pope Boniface VIII, they say, entered office like a fox, behaved in it like a lion, and died like a dog. And who would believe that it was Nero, that living image of cruelty, who said, when they brought him in customary fashion the sentence of a condemned criminal to sign: "Would to God I had never learned to write!" So much his heart was wrung at condemning a man to death!

Everything is so full of such examples—each man, in fact, can   2
supply himself with so many—that I find it strange to see intelligent men sometimes going to great pains to match these pieces; seeing that irres-

---

[1]Mars and Venus are the Roman gods of war and love.

olution seems to me the most common and apparent defect of our nature, as witness that famous line of Publilius, the farce writer:

Bad is the plan that never can be changed.[2]

There is some justification for basing a judgment of a man on the most ordinary acts of his life; but in view of the natural instability of our conduct and opinions, it has often seemed to me that even good authors are wrong to insist on fashioning a consistent and solid fabric out of us. They choose one general characteristic, and go and arrange and interpret all a man's actions to fit their picture; and if they cannot twist them enough, they go and set them down to dissimulation. Augustus has escaped them; for there is in this man throughout the course of his life such an obvious, abrupt, and continual variety of actions that even the boldest judges have had to let him go, intact and unsolved.[3] Nothing is harder for me than to believe in men's consistency, nothing easier than to believe in their inconsistency. He who would judge them in detail would more often hit upon the truth.

In all antiquity it is hard to pick out a dozen men who set their lives to a certain and constant course, which is the principal goal of wisdom. For, to comprise all wisdom in a word, says an ancient, and to embrace all the rules of our life in one, it is "always to will the same things, and always to oppose the same things."[4] I would not deign, he says, to add "provided the will is just"; for if it is not just, it cannot always be whole.

In truth, I once learned that vice is only unruliness and lack of moderation, and that consequently consistency cannot be attributed to it. It is a maxim of Demosthenes, they say, that the beginning of all virtue is consultation and deliberation; and the end and perfection, consistency. If it were by reasoning that we settled on a particular course of action, we would choose the fairest course—but no one has thought of that:

He spurns that thing he sought, and seeks anew
What he just spurned; he seethes, his life's askew.[5]

Our ordinary practice is to follow the inclinations of our appetite, to the left, to the right, uphill and down, as the wind of circumstance

---

[2]Quoted from Aulus Gellius, *Attic Nights*, XVII, 14.

[3]Adopted son and heir of Julius Caesar, Augustus was the most powerful of the ancient Roman emperors.

[4]Seneca, *Epistles*, XX, 5.

[5]Horace, *Epistles*, I, i, 98–9.

carries us. We think of what we want only at the moment we want it, and we change like that animal which takes the color of the place you set it on. What we have just now planned, we presently change, and presently again we retrace our steps: nothing but oscillation and inconsistency:

> Like puppets we are moved by outside strings.[6]

We do not go; we are carried away, like floating objects, now gently, now violently, according as the water is angry or calm:

> Do we not see all humans unaware,
> Of what they want, and always searching everywhere,
> And changing place, as if to drop the load they bear?[7]

Every day a new fancy, and our humors shift with the shifts in the weather:

> Such are the minds of men, as is the fertile light
> That Father Jove himself sends down to make earth bright.[8]

If any man could prescribe and establish definite laws and a definite organization in his head, we should see shining throughout his life an evenness of habits, an order, and an infallible relation between his principles and his practice. This man would be easy to understand, as is shown by the example of the younger Cato: he who has touched one chord of him has touched all; he is a harmony of perfectly concordant sounds, which cannot conflict.[9] With us, it is the opposite: for so many actions, we need so many individual judgments. The surest thing, in my opinion, would be to trace our actions to the neighboring circumstances, without getting into any further research and without drawing from them any other conclusions.

During the disorders of our poor country,[10] I was told that a girl, living near where I then was, had thrown herself out of a high window to avoid the violence of a knavish soldier quartered in her house. Not killed by the fall, she reasserted her purpose by trying to cut her throat with a knife. From this she was prevented, but only after wounding herself

---

[6]Horace, *Satires*, II, vii, 82.

[7]Lucretius, *Of the Nature of Things*, III, 1057–9.

[8]Homer, *Odyssey*, XVIII, 136–7.

[9]Cato was a Roman philosopher and holder of various public offices in the time of Julius Caesar.

[10]Refers to a series of wars between French Catholics and Protestants that began in 1562 and were to continue until 1594.

gravely. She herself confessed that the soldier had as yet pressed her only with requests, solicitations, and gifts; but she had been afraid, she said, that he would finally resort to force. And all this with such words, such expressions, not to mention the blood that testified to her virtue, as would have become another Lucrece.[11] Now, I learned that as a matter of fact, both before and since, she was a wench not so hard to come to terms with. As the story says: Handsome and gentlemanly as you may be, when you have had no luck, do not promptly conclude that your mistress is inviolably chaste; this does not prove that the mule driver may not have his chance with her.

Antigonus, having taken a liking to one of his soldiers for his virtue   9
and valor, ordered his physicians to treat the man for a persistent internal malady that had long tormented him. After his cure, his master noticed that he was going about his business much less warmly, and asked him what had changed him so and made him such a coward. "You yourself, Sire," he answered, "by delivering me from the ills that made my life indifferent to me." A soldier of Lucullus who had been robbed of everything by the enemy made a bold attack on them to get revenge. When he had retrieved his loss, Lucullus, having formed a good opinion of him, urged him to some dangerous exploit with all the fine expostulations he could think of,

> With words that might have stirred a coward's heart.[12]

"Urge some poor soldier who has been robbed to do it," he replied;

> Though but a rustic lout,
> "That man will go who's lost his money," he called out;[13]

and resolutely refused to go.

That man whom you saw so adventurous yesterday, do not think   10
it strange to find him just as cowardly today: either anger, or necessity, or company, or wine, or the sound of a trumpet, had put his heart in his belly. His was a courage formed not by reason, but by one of these circumstances; it is no wonder if he has now been made different by other, contrary circumstances.

Not only does the wind of accident move me at will, but, besides,   11
I am moved and disturbed as a result merely of my own unstable posture;

---

[11]The virtuous Roman matron who, raped by her husband's son, ended her dishonor by committing suicide.

[12]Horace, *Epistles,* II, ii, 36.

[13]Horace, *Epistles,* II, ii, 39–40.

and anyone who observes carefully can hardly find himself twice in the same state. I give my soul now one face, now another, according to which direction I turn it. If I speak of myself in different ways, that is because I look at myself in different ways. All contradictions may be found in me by some twist and in some fashion. Bashful, insolent; talk-ative, taciturn; tough, delicate; clever, stupid; surly, affable; lying, truth-ful; all this I see in myself to some extent according to how I turn; and whoever studies himself really attentively finds in himself, yes, even in his judgment, this gyration and discord. I have nothing to say about myself absolutely, simply, and solidly, without confusion and without mixture, or in one word. *Distinguo*[14] is the most universal member of my logic.

Although I am always minded to say good of what is good, and inclined to interpret favorably anything that can be so interpreted, still it is true that the strangeness of our condition makes it happen that we are often driven to do good by vice itself—were it not that doing good is judged by intention alone. 12

Therefore one courageous deed must not be taken to prove a man valiant; a man who was really valiant would be so always and on all occasions. If valor were a habit of virtue, and not a sally, it would make a man equally resolute in any contingency, the same alone as in com-pany, the same in single combat as in battle; for, whatever they say, there is not one valor for the pavement and another for the camp. As bravely would he bear an illness in his bed as a wound in camp, and he would fear death no more in his home than in an assault. We would not see the same man charging into the breach with brave assurance, and later tormenting himself, like a woman, over the loss of a lawsuit or a son. 13

There is no more extreme valor of its kind than Alexander's;[15] but it is only of one kind, and not complete and universal enough; which is why we see him worry so frantically when he conceives the slightest suspicion that his men are plotting against his life, and why he behaves in such matters with such violent and indiscriminate injustice and with a fear that subverts his natural reason. Also superstition, with which he was so strongly tainted, bears some stamp of pusillanimity. 14

Our actions are nothing but a patchwork, and we want to gain honor under false colors. Virtue will not be followed except for her own sake; and if we sometimes borrow her mask for some other purpose, she 15

[14]I distinguish, I make distinctions.

[15]Alexander the Great, conqueror of Greece, Persia, Egypt, and India in the third century B.C..

promptly snatches it from our face. It is a strong and vivid dye, once the soul is steeped in it, and will not go without taking the fabric with it. That is why, to judge a man, we must follow his traces long and carefully. If he does not maintain consistency for its own sake, if changing circumstances make him change his pace (I mean his path, for his pace may be hastened or slowed), let him go: that man goes before the wind, as the motto of our Talbot[16] says.

It is no wonder, says an ancient, that chance has so much power over us, since we live by chance.[17] A man who has not directed his life as a whole toward a definite goal cannot possibly set his particular actions in order. A man who does not have a picture of the whole in his head cannot possibly arrange the pieces. What good does it do a man to lay in a supply of paints if he does not know what he is to paint? No one makes a definite plan of his life; we think about it only piecemeal. The archer must first know what he is aiming at, and then set his hand, his bow, his string, his arrow, and his movements for that goal. Our plans go astray because they have no direction and no aim. No wind works for the man who has no port of destination.

We are all patchwork, and so shapeless and diverse in composition that each bit, each moment, plays its own game. And there is as much difference between us and ourselves as between us and others. Ambition can teach men valor, and temperance, and liberality, and even justice. Greed can implant in the heart of a shop apprentice, brought up in obscurity and idleness, the confidence to cast himself far from hearth and home, in a frail boat at the mercy of the waves and angry Neptune;[18] it also teaches discretion and wisdom. Venus herself supplies resolution and boldness to boys still subject to discipline and the rod, and arms the tender hearts of virgins who are still in their mothers' laps:

Furtively passing sleeping guards, with Love as guide,
Alone by night the girl comes to the young man's side.[19]

In view of this, a sound intellect will refuse to judge men simply by their outward actions; we must probe the inside and discover what springs set men in motion. But since this is an arduous and hazardous undertaking, I wish fewer people would meddle with it.

---

[16]English earl and general, Talbot was well-liked in the region where Montaigne lived, where he was killed in battle in 1453. There is still a Château Talbot in France.

[17]Seneca, in *Epistles*, lxxi, 3.

[18]The Roman god of the sea.

[19]Tibullus, *Elegies*, II, i, 75–6.

About the Essay

1. What is Montaigne's central thesis? Where in his essay does he state it? How does he qualify it?

2. Montaigne is presenting a particular viewpoint. How does he support it?

3. Why does Montaigne say ". . . authors are wrong to insist on fashioning a consistent and solid fabric out of us"? What, basically, is he complaining of here?

4. At different points in his essay, Montaigne is somewhat satirical, as in his account of the young woman who threw herself from a window. At what other times does he seem mocking or ironic?

5. Montaigne often uses figures of speech, as when he says: "We do not go; we are carried away, like floating objects. . . ." Cite several other figures of speech that appear in Montaigne's essay. What does each mean? What purpose does each one serve?

6. Does Montaigne believe that people should be judged on the basis of their behavior alone? How does he support his position?

7. Interestingly, Montaigne's essay can be read as favoring two opposing views. One is the view that consistency is a high ideal we should all strive for. The other is that inconsistency is perfectly natural and should be accepted. What statements in the essay support each position? Which position do you think reflects Montaigne's own view? (Take into account your answer to question 1.)

Explorations

1. Write an essay on the consistency or inconsistency of your own actions. Do you believe, as Montaigne does, that consistency is a virtue and inconsistency a failing?

2. On the subject of bravery, Montaigne says, "A man who was really valiant would be so always and on all occasions." On the other hand, Ralph Waldo Emerson observes that "A hero is no braver than an ordinary man, but he is brave five minutes longer." What are your views on courage? If you like, go beyond your own experience and opinions to consult the works of psychologists and psychiatrists.

WILLIAM F. BUCKLEY, JR.

William F. Buckley, Jr., is best known as an articulate spokesman for the political right. He was born in New York City in 1925 and graduated from Yale in 1950; while there he wrote his first book, *God and Man at Yale* (1951). For thirty years he has edited the *National Review*, America's leading conservative magazine, and is published three times weekly in a widely syndicated newspaper column. Television viewers can also see him in action on his interview program "Firing Line," as well as quadrennially during network telecasts of presidential nominating conventions when he does battle with his friend and liberal opponent, John Kenneth Galbraith (pages 602–608). Buckley also writes on a variety of subjects, ranging from political analysis (*Up from Liberalism*, 1959) to sailing (*Airborne*, 1978) and spy novels (*Marco Polo, If You Can*, 1982). In the following selection, one of the newspaper columns collected in his book *A Hymnal: The Controversial Arts* (1978), Buckley tells the story of a self on the brink of its own destruction and of one man's success in saving himself.

Up from Misery

A friend of long standing who has never asked me to devote this 1 space to advertising any enthusiasm of his has now, diffidently, made the exception. He does not want to do anything less that what he can do, through his own efforts and those of his friends, to pass along the word that, within walking distance of the great majority of Americans, there is help waiting which can lead them out of the darkness, as indisputably as an eye surgeon, restoring sight, can lead someone into the sunlight.

Kenneth (we'll call him) is a cocky feller, something of a sport, 2 tough-talking, an ace in his individualistic profession, who remembers getting drunk at college in the late '20's on the night he won an important boxing match, but at no other time during his college career. Emerging from college into the professional world, he revved up slowly, hitting in his late 30's his cruising speed: two or three martinis per day. These he was dearly attached to, but not apparently dominated by: He would not, gladly, go a day without his martinis, but neither, after the third, did he require a fourth.

Then in the spring of 1972 his gentle, devoted (teetotaling) wife 3 had a mastectomy, the prognosis optimistic; but with a shade of uncertainty. So, to beef up his morale, he increased the dosage just a little. When, later that year, the doctor called to tell him the worst, he walked straightaway to the nearest bar. After she died, he began buying a fifth each of bourbon and gin on Saturdays, a week's supply to eke out the several martinis he had been drinking at and after lunch. Fascinated, he watched himself casually making minor alterations: "Make that quarts" was the modest beginning. Then the resupplying would come on Friday; then Thursday. In due course it was a quart a day.

In the morning he would begin; one, then up to five snorts before   4
leaving for the office—later and later in the morning. Before reaching the door he would rinse out his mouth. But always—this fascinated him, as gradually he comprehended the totality of his servitude—he would, on turning the door handle, go back: for just one more.

At night he would prepare himself dinner, then lie down for a little   5
nap, wake hours later, go to the kitchen to eat dinner—only to find he had already eaten it. Once he returned to a restaurant three hours after having eaten his dinner: he forgot he had been there. Blackouts, he called the experiences.

On the crucial day it was nothing special. He walked home from   6
the office, full of gin, and vomited in the street (this often happened), struggling to do this with aplomb in the posh backdrop of the East 60's. On reaching his apartment he lurched gratefully for the bottle, sipped from the glass . . . and was clapped by the hand of Providence as un-mistakably as any piece of breast was ever struck by a lance.

He heard his own voice say, as if directed by an outside force,   7
"What the hell am I doing to myself?" He poured his martini into the sink, emptied the gin bottle, then emptied the bourbon bottle, then went to the telephone and, never in his life having given a second's conscious thought to the organization, fumbled through the directory and dialed the number for Alcoholics Anonymous.

One must suppose that whoever answered that telephone call was   8
as surprised as a fireman excitedly advised that a house was ablaze. Ken-neth would like to . . . inquire—but perhaps AA was too busy tonight, perhaps next week sometime? . . . What? Come today? How about to-morrow? Do you have a meeting every week? You have 800 *meetings in New York a week?* . . . Scores every night? . . . Okay. Tomorrow.

Tomorrow would be the first of 250 meetings in ninety days with   9
Alcoholics Anonymous. AA advises at least ninety meetings in the first ninety days. Kenneth had assumed he would be mixing with hoi polloi. Always objective, he advises now that "on a scale of 1–10"—incorpo-rating intelligence, education, success, articulateness—"I would rank around six or seven." He made friends. And he made instant progress during those first weeks, quickly losing the compulsion for the morning drinks. But for the late afternoon martinis he thirsted, and he hungered, and he lusted. He dove into a despair mitigated only by his thrice-daily contacts

with AA. His banked-up grief for his wife raged now, and every moment, every long afternoon and evening without her, and without alcohol, were endless bouts with the haunting question: What is the point in living at all?

And then, suddenly, as suddenly as on the day he poured the booze   10
into the sink, twenty-seven weeks later, he had been inveigled into going
to a party. Intending to stay one dutiful hour, he stayed five. On returning, he was exhilarated. He had developed anew the capacity to talk
with people, other than in the prescribed ritualisms of his profession, or
in the boozy idiom of the tippler. He was so excited, so pleased, so elated,
he could not sleep until early morning for pleasure at re-experiencing
life.

That was two months ago, and every day he rejoiced at his liber-   11
ation, and prays that others who suffer will find the hand of Alcoholics
Anonymous. And—one might presumptuously add—the hand of the Prime
Mover, Who was there in that little kitchen on the day the impulse came
to him; and Who, surely, is the wellspring of the faith of Alcoholics
Anonymous, as of so many other spirits united to help their fellow man.

About the Essay

1. What was Buckley's purpose in writing about Kenneth? How do you know?

2. What is alcoholism? What details from Buckley's essay can you use in arriving at your definition?

3. Did you find Buckley's description of Kenneth's recovery from alcoholism believable? Why, or why not?

4. In paragraph 11, what does Buckley mean by the "Prime Mover"? How does the final sentence of that paragraph relate to the rest of the essay? How does it affect your response to the essay?

5. How would you describe Buckley's prose style in this essay? Would you say it is formal, informal, breezy, severe? What effect does the style have on you? Is the style consistently maintained, or are there words and phrases that con-trast with the overall style? If so, what effect do those words and phrases have?

Explorations

1. Why can it be so difficult to seek the help of others? Consider examples from your experience and from what you have seen and read about other people.

2. Alcoholism is a form of addiction. There are other addictions as well—to drugs, cigarettes, computer games, even food. Describe the characteristics of one of these addictions and the difficulties in overcoming it.

3. Alcoholism is a major problem today not only for individuals but for American society. Choose an aspect of the problem and consider its causes, its effects, and possible solutions.

GEORGE ORWELL

George Orwell (1903–1950) was one of the most brilliant social critics of our times. He was born in Bengal, India, of British parents in the imperial civil service, but he grew up in England and received a traditional education at the prestigious school of Eton, an experience Orwell disliked intensely. Instead of going on to a university, he joined the civil service himself and was sent to Burma at nineteen as an assistant superintendent of police. Two incidents from his five years in the Far East are recounted in two essays included in this volume, "A Hanging" and "Shooting an Elephant." Disillusioned with British imperialism, Orwell resigned in 1929 and began a decade of studying social and political issues first-hand and then writing about them in such works as *Down and Out in Paris and London* (1933) and *The Road to Wigan Pier* (1937). His most famous books are *Animal Farm* (1945), a satire on the Russian Revolution, and *1984* (1949), a chilling novel set in an imagined totalitarian state of the future.

"Shooting an Elephant" was published in the British magazine *New Writing* in 1936. Hitler, Mussolini, and Stalin were in power, building the "younger empires" Orwell refers to in his second paragraph, and the old British Empire was soon to decline, as Orwell predicted. In this essay, Orwell tells of a man in authority who finds himself compelled to act against his convictions.

Shooting an Elephant

In Moulmein, in lower Burma, I was hated by large numbers of people—the only time in my life that I have been important enough for this to happen to me. I was sub-divisional police officer of the town, and in an aimless, petty kind of way anti-European feeling was very bitter. No one had the guts to raise a riot, but if a European woman went through the bazaars alone somebody would probably spit betel juice over her dress. As a police officer I was an obvious target and was baited whenever it seemed safe to do so. When a nimble Burman tripped me up on the football field and the referee (another Burman) looked the other way, the crowd yelled with hideous laughter. This happened more than once. In the end the sneering yellow faces of young men that met me everywhere, the insults hooted after me when I was at a safe distance, got badly on my nerves. The young Buddhist priests were the worst of all. There were several thousands of them in the town and none of them seemed to have anything to do except stand on street corners and jeer at Europeans.

All this was perplexing and upsetting. For at that time I had already   2
made up my mind that imperialism was an evil thing and the sooner I
chucked up my job and got out of it the better. Theoretically—and
secretly, of course—I was all for the Burmese and all against their oppressors, the British. As for the job I was doing, I hated it more bitterly
than I can perhaps make clear. In a job like that you see the dirty work
of Empire at close quarters. The wretched prisoners huddling in the
stinking cages of the lock-ups, the gray, cowed faces of the long-term
convicts, the scarred buttocks of the men who had been flogged with
bamboos—all these oppressed me with an intolerable sense of guilt. But
I could get nothing into perspective. I was young and ill educated and I
had had to think out my problems in the utter silence that is imposed
on every Englishman in the East. I did not even know that the British
Empire is dying, still less did I know that it is a great deal better than
the younger empires that are going to supplant it. All I knew was that I
was stuck between my hatred of the empire I served and my rage against
the evil-spirited little beasts who tried to make my job impossible. With
one part of my mind I thought of the British Raj as an unbreakable
tyranny, as something clamped down, in *saecula saeculorum,* upon the
will of prostrate peoples; with another part I thought that the greatest
joy in the world would be to drive a bayonet into a Buddhist priest's
guts.[1] Feelings like these are the normal by-products of imperialism; ask
any Anglo-Indian official, if you can catch him off duty.

One day something happened which in a roundabout way was en-   3
lightening. It was a tiny incident in itself, but it gave me a better glimpse
than I had had before of the real nature of imperialism—the real motives
for which despotic governments act. Early one morning the sub-inspector
at a police station the other end of the town rang me up on the 'phone
and said that an elephant was ravaging the bazaar. Would I please come
and do something about it? I did not know what I could do, but I wanted
to see what was happening and I got on a pony and started out. I took
my rifle, an old .44 Winchester and much too small to kill an elephant,
but I thought the noise might be useful *in terrorem*. Various Burmans
stopped me on the way and told me about the elephant's doings. It was
not, of course, a wild elephant, but a tame one which had gone "must."[2]
It had been chained up, as tame elephants always are when their attack
of "must" is due, but on the previous night it had broken its chain and
escaped. Its mahout, the only person who could manage it when it was
in that state, had set out in pursuit, but had taken the wrong direction

---

[1]Raj: rule, especially in India. *Saecula saeculorum:* from time immemorial.
[2]That is, gone into an uncontrollable frenzy.

and was now twelve hours' journey away, and in the morning the elephant had suddenly reappeared in the town. The Burmese population had no weapons and were quite helpless against it. It had already destroyed somebody's bamboo hut, killed a cow and raided some fruit-stalls and devoured the stock; also it had met the municipal rubbish van and, when the driver jumped out and took to his heels, had turned the van over and inflicted violences upon it.

The Burmese sub-inspector and some Indian constables were waiting for me in the quarter where the elephant had been seen. It was a very poor quarter, a labyrinth of squalid bamboo huts, thatched with palm-leaf, winding all over a steep hillside. I remember that it was a cloudy, stuffy morning at the beginning of the rains. We began questioning the people as to where the elephant had gone and, as usual, failed to get any definite information. That is invariably the case in the East; a story always sounds clear enough at a distance, but the nearer you get to the scene of events the vaguer it becomes. Some of the people said that the elephant had gone in one direction, some said that he had gone in another, some professed not even to have heard of any elephant. I had almost made up my mind that the whole story was a pack of lies, when we heard yells a little distance away. There was a loud, scandalized cry of "Go away, child! Go away this instant!" and an old woman with a switch in her hand came round the corner of a hut, violently shooing away a crowd of naked children. Some more women followed, clicking their tongues and exclaiming; evidently there was something that the children ought not to have seen. I rounded the hut and saw a man's dead body sprawling in the mud. He was an Indian, a black Dravidian coolie, almost naked, and he could not have been dead many minutes. The people said that the elephant had come suddenly upon him round the corner of the hut, caught him with its trunk, put its foot on his back and ground him into the earth. This was the rainy season and the ground was soft, and his face had scored a trench a foot deep and a couple of yards long. He was lying on his belly with arms crucified and head sharply twisted to one side. His face was coated with mud, the eyes wide open, the teeth bared and grinning with an expression of unendurable agony. (Never tell me, by the way, that the dead look peaceful. Most of the corpses I have seen looked devilish.) The friction of the great beast's foot had stripped the skin from his back as neatly as one skins a rabbit. As soon as I saw the dead man I sent an orderly to a friend's house nearby to borrow an elephant rifle. I had already sent back the pony, not wanting it to go mad with fright and throw me if it smelt the elephant.

The orderly came back in a few minutes with a rifle and five cartridges, and meanwhile some Burmans had arrived and told us that the elephant was in the paddy fields below, only a few hundred yards away. As I started forward practically the whole population of the quarter flocked out of the houses and followed me. They had seen the rifle and were all shouting excitedly that I was going to shoot the elephant. They had not shown much interest in the elephant when he was merely ravaging their homes, but it was different now that he was going to be shot. It was a bit of fun to them, as it would be to an English crowd; besides they wanted the meat. It made me vaguely uneasy. I had no intention of shooting the elephant—I had merely sent for the rifle to defend myself if necessary—and it is always unnerving to have a crowd following you. I marched down the hill, looking and feeling a fool, with the rifle over my shoulder and an ever-growing army of people jostling at my heels. At the bottom, when you got away from the huts, there was a metalled road and beyond that a miry waste of paddy fields a thousand yards across, not yet ploughed but soggy from the first rains and dotted with coarse grass. The elephant was standing eight yards from the road, his left side toward us. He took not the slightest notice of the crowd's approach. He was tearing up bunches of grass, beating them against his knees to clean them, and stuffing them into his mouth.

I had halted on the road. As soon as I saw the elephant I knew with perfect certainty that I ought not to shoot him. It is a serious matter to shoot a working elephant—it is comparable to destroying a huge and costly piece of machinery—and obviously one ought not to do it if it can possibly be avoided. And at that distance, peacefully eating, the elephant looked no more dangerous than a cow. I thought then and I think now that his attack of "must" was already passing off; in which case he would merely wander harmlessly about until the mahout came back and caught him. Moreover, I did not in the least want to shoot him. I decided that I would watch him for a little while to make sure that he did not turn savage again, and then go home.

But at that moment I glanced round at the crowd that had followed me. It was an immense crowd, two thousand at the least and growing every minute. It blocked the road for a long distance on either side. I looked at the sea of yellow faces above the garish clothes—faces all happy and excited over this bit of fun, all certain that the elephant was going to be shot. They were watching me as they would watch a conjurer about to perform a trick. They did not like me, but with the magical rifle in my hands I was momentarily worth watching. And suddenly I realized that I should have to shoot the elephant after all. The people expected it of me and I had got to do it; I could feel their two thousand wills pressing me forward, irresistibly. And it was at this moment, as I stood there with the rifle in my hands, that I first grasped the hollowness, the futility of the white man's dominion in the East. Here was I, the white man with his gun, standing in front of the unarmed native crowd—seemingly the leading actor of the piece; but in reality I was only an absurd puppet pushed to and fro by the will of those yellow faces behind. I perceived in this moment that when the white man turns tyrant it is his own freedom that he destroys. He becomes a sort of hollow, posing dummy, the conventionalized figure of a sahib. For it is the condition of his rule that he shall spend his life in trying to impress the "natives," and so in every crisis he has got to do what the "natives" expect of him. He wears a mask, and his face grows to fit it. I had got to shoot the elephant. I had committed myself to doing it when I sent for the rifle. A sahib has got to act like a sahib; he has got to appear resolute, to know his own mind and do definite things. To come all that way, rifle in hand, with two thousand people marching at my heels, and then to trail feebly away, having done nothing—no, that was impossible. The crowd would laugh at me. And my whole life, every white man's life in the East, was one long struggle not to be laughed at.

But I did not want to shoot the elephant. I watched him beating his bunch of grass against his knees with that preoccupied grandmotherly air that elephants have. It seemed to me that it would be murder to shoot him. At that age I was not squeamish about killing animals, but I had never shot an elephant and never wanted to. (Somehow it always seems worse to kill a *large* animal.) Besides, there was the beast's owner to be considered. Alive, the elephant was worth at least a hundred pounds; dead, he would only be worth the value of his tusks, five pounds, possibly.[3] But I had got to act quickly. I turned to some experienced-looking Burmans who had been there when we arrived, and asked them how the elephant had been behaving. They all said the same thing: he took no notice of you if you left him alone, but he might charge if you went too close to him.

It was perfectly clear to me what I ought to do. I ought to walk up to within, say, twenty-five yards of the elephant and test his behavior. If he charged, I could shoot; if he took no notice of me, it would be safe to leave him until the mahout came back. But also I knew that I was going to do no such thing. I was a poor shot with a rifle and the ground was soft mud into which one would sink at every step. If the elephant charged and I missed him, I should have about as much chance as a toad under a steam-roller. But even then I was not thinking particularly of my own skin, only of the watchful yellow faces behind. For at that moment, with the crowd watching me, I was not afraid in the ordinary

[3]The British pound would have been worth $5.00 at the time.

sense, as I would have been if I had been alone. A white man mustn't be frightened in front of "natives"; and so, in general, he isn't frightened. The sole thought in my mind was that if anything went wrong those two thousand Burmans would see me pursued, caught, trampled on, and reduced to a grinning corpse like that Indian up the hill. And if that happened it was quite probable that some of them would laugh. That would never do. There was only one alternative. I shoved the cartridges into the magazine and lay down on the road to get a better aim.

The crowd grew very still, and a deep, low, happy sigh, as of people who see the theater curtain go up at last, breathed from innumerable throats. They were going to have their bit of fun after all. The rifle was a beautiful German thing with cross-hair sights. I did not then know that in shooting an elephant one would shoot to cut an imaginary bar running from ear-hole to ear-hole. I ought, therefore, as the elephant was sideways on, to have aimed straight at his ear-hole; actually I aimed several inches in front of this, thinking the brain would be further forward. 10

When I pulled the trigger I did not hear the bang or feel the kick— one never does when a shot goes home—but I heard the devilish roar of glee that went up from the crowd. In that instant, in too short a time, one would have thought, even for the bullet to get there, a mysterious, terrible change had come over the elephant. He neither stirred nor fell, but every line of his body had altered. He looked suddenly stricken, shrunken, immensely old, as though the frightful impact of the bullet had paralyzed him without knocking him down. At last, after what seemed a long time—it might have been five seconds, I dare say—he sagged flabbily to his knees. His mouth slobbered. An enormous senility seemed to have settled upon him. One could have imagined him thousands of years old. I fired again into the same spot. At the second shot he did not collapse but climbed with desperate slowness to his feet and stood weakly upright, with legs sagging and head drooping. I fired a third time. That was the shot that did for him. You could see the agony of it jolt his whole body and knock the last remnant of strength from his legs. But in falling he seemed for a moment to rise, for as his hind legs collapsed beneath him he seemed to tower upward like a huge rock toppling, his trunk reaching skyward like a tree. He trumpeted, for the first and only time. And then down he came, his belly toward me, with a crash that seemed to shake the ground even where I lay. 11

I got up. The Burmans were already racing past me across the mud. It was obvious that the elephant would never rise again, but he was not dead. He was breathing very rhythmically with long rattling gasps, his great mound of a side painfully rising and falling. His mouth was wide open—I could see far down into caverns of pale pink throat. I waited a 12 long time for him to die, but his breathing did not weaken. Finally I fired my two remaining shots into the spot where I thought his heart must be. The thick blood welled out of him like red velvet, but still he did not die. His body did not even jerk when the shots hit him, the tortured breathing continued without a pause. He was dying, very slowly and in great agony, but in some world remote from me where not even a bullet could damage him further. I felt that I had got to put an end to that dreadful noise. It seemed dreadful to see the great beast lying there, powerless to move and yet powerless to die, and not even to be able to finish him. I sent back for my small rifle and poured shot after shot into his heart and down his throat. They seemed to make no impression. The tortured gasps continued as steadily as the ticking of a clock.

In the end I could not stand it any longer and went away. I heard   13
later that it took him half an hour to die. Burmans were bringing dahs[4] and baskets even before I left, and I was told they had stripped his body almost to the bones by the afternoon.

Afterward, of course, there were endless discussions about the shooting   14
of the elephant. The owner was furious, but he was only an Indian and could do nothing. Besides, legally I had done the right thing, for a mad elephant has to be killed, like a mad dog, if its owner fails to control it. Among the Europeans opinion was divided. The older men said I was right, the younger men said it was a damn shame to shoot an elephant for killing a coolie, because an elephant was worth more than any damn Coringhee coolie. And afterwards I was very glad that the coolie had been killed; it put me legally in the right and it gave me a sufficient pretext for shooting the elephant. I often wondered whether any of the others grasped that I had done it solely to avoid looking a fool.

About the Essay

1. Why is the setting of this narrative significant? What is imperialism, and what does Orwell's essay say about it?

2. Why, according to Orwell, did he shoot the elephant? Do you find his interpretation convincing? Why, or why not?

3. What do you think was Orwell's purpose in telling this story? Cite evidence from the essay that indicates to you that purpose. Does he accomplish his purpose?

4. What part of the essay struck you most strongly? The shooting itself? Orwell's feelings? The descriptions of the Burmans and their behavior? Or

---

[4]Heavy knives.

something else? Can you identify anything about Orwell's prose that enhances the impact of that passage? Explain.

5. "Shooting an Elephant" was written ten years or more after the incident it describes. What passages reveal that perspective? What did Orwell know when he wrote the essay that he did not know when the incident occurred?

6. What is Orwell doing in the final paragraph? How does that paragraph affect your response to the whole essay?

Explorations

1. Consider situations in which you have been a leader, like Orwell, or part of a crowd, like the Burmans. As a leader, what was your attitude toward your followers? As a follower, what did you feel toward your leader? From these experiences, what conclusions can you draw about the relationship between leaders and followers?

2. Tell of a situation in which you felt compelled to act against your convictions. What arguments can justify your action? How much freedom of choice did you actually have, and what were the limits on your freedom? On what basis can you refuse to subordinate your convictions to others', or to society's?

3. Orwell has shown one of the ironies of imperialism, that colonial officers are ruled by those they govern, or, to put it another way, that the rulers are ruled by the ruled. What are some other criticisms of imperialism? Using library sources, write an essay on the differing views of imperialism, from the perspective of the imperial power and from that of the people subject to the power.

STEVIE SMITH

Florence Margaret Smith was born in the English city of Hull in 1902. Because she was small, she was nicknamed "Stevie" after a famous English jockey. When she was three, her family moved to a suburb of London, and there she remained, in the same house, for the rest of her life. Her closest companion was the indomitable aunt whom Stevie called Auntie Lion; their life together is the subject of the play and film *Stevie*, with Glenda Jackson as Stevie. Stevie Smith died in 1971.

Though her poems often have a childlike quality, with simple words and situations borrowed from children's stories and nursery rhymes, they are anything but naive. In the poem reprinted here, she uses the fairy tale of the prince transformed into a frog. In this tale a princess drops a golden ball into a well. The ball is retrieved by a frog after the princess promises to play with him, kiss him, and sleep with him. Once she has the ball, however, she runs away from the frog, breaking her promise. Later the frog appears at the palace and the king forces the princess to fulfill her promise. When she kisses the frog, he turns into a prince . . . and the two live happily ever after. In Smith's poem, the frog talks about himself and uses certain words in a way that suggests that the poet is offering more than a playful variation on a children's story.

The Frog Prince

I am a frog
I live under a spell
I live at the bottom
Of a green well

And here I must wait   5
Until a maiden places me
On her royal pillow
And kisses me
In her father's palace.

The story is familiar   10
Everybody knows it well
But do other enchanted people feel as nervous
As I do? The stories do not tell,

Ask if they will be happier
When the changes come   15
As already they are fairly happy
In a frog's doom?

I have been a frog now
For a hundred years
And in all this time   20
I have not shed many tears,

I am happy, I like the life,
Can swim for many a mile
(When I have hopped to the river)
And am forever agile.   25

And the quietness,
Yes, I like to be quiet
I am habituated
To a quiet life,

But always when I think these thoughts   30
As I sit in my well
Another thought comes to me and says:
It is part of the spell

To be happy
To work up contentment   35
To make much of being a frog
To fear disenchantment

Says, It will be *heavenly*
To be set free,
Cries, *Heavenly* the girl who disenchants   40
And the royal times, *heavenly*,
And I think it will be.

Come then, royal girl and royal times,
Come quickly,
I can be happy until you come   45
But I cannot be heavenly,
Only disenchanted people
Can be heavenly.

About the Poem

1. Can you understand the poem without knowing the fairy tale? In what way does the poem differ from the story line of the fairy tale?

2. Consider the poet's use of two words: *enchanted* and *disenchanted*. What do they seem to mean in the context of the poem? Each of these words has other possible meanings. What effect do the multiple meanings have on your response to the poem?

3. Do you believe, as the headnote suggests, that the poem is more than a variation on a fairy tale? If so, what do you think its symbolic meaning is? What in the poem supports your interpretation?

4. What is the poet saying in the poem's last six lines?

Explorations

1. What fairy tale, or legend, or myth do you like best? Why do you like it? How does it relate to your view of life?

2. The frog prince is torn between his present quiet way of life and a more glamorous and possibly more rewarding one. Do you wish for a more exciting life, or for a calmer one? Or are you content as you are? What pleases you most about the way you live? What pleases you least about it?

3. Compare the frog's situation, waiting for the princess to "disenchant" him, with that of William Young in John Updike's story, "A Sense of Shelter" (pages 90–100). How do the themes of the two works compare?

W. H. AUDEN

Wystan Hugh Auden was born in York, England, in 1907, and was educated at Oxford University. While a student at Christ Church College there, he began to write the poems that brought him attention as an original, modern voice in English letters. During the 1930s Auden developed his special kind of direct, often political poetry and also wrote plays, a movie script, and books that grew out of journeys to Iceland and China with such friends and fellow writers as Louis MacNeice and Christopher Isherwood. In 1937 he went to Spain to work for the government forces opposing the fascist revolution led by Francisco Franco, and was put to work broadcasting propaganda. At the end of the thirties, however, he left England for the United States, later to become an American citizen. As he grew older, his poetry became more introspective, less "public" and political. He died in 1973. Many countries have monuments dedicated to their "unknown soldier," a soldier killed on the battlefield who symbolizes the ideals of national service and sacrifice. "The Unknown Citizen" suggests what might be written on a monument for a symbolic civilian, who represents his society's peacetime values.

The Unknown Citizen

(To JS/07/M/378
This Marble Monument
Is Erected by the State)

He was found by the Bureau of Statistics to be
One against whom there was no official complaint,
And all the reports on his conduct agree
That, in the modern sense of an old-fashioned word, he was a saint,
For in everything he did he served the Greater Community.   5
Except for the War till the day he retired
He worked in a factory and never got fired,
But satisfied his employers, Fudge Motors Inc.
Yet he wasn't a scab or odd in his views,
For his Union reports that he paid his dues,   10
(Our report on his Union shows it was sound)
And our Social Psychology workers found
That he was popular with his mates and liked a drink.
The Press are convinced that he bought a paper every day

And that his reactions to advertisements were normal in every way.   15
Policies taken out in his name prove that he was fully insured,
And his Health-card shows he was once in hospital but left it cured.
Both Producers Research and High-Grade Living declare
He was fully sensible to the advantages of the Instalment Plan
And had everything necessary to the Modern Man,   20
A phonograph, a radio, a car and a frigidaire.
Our researchers into Public Opinion are content
That he held the proper opinions for the time of year;
When there was peace, he was for peace; when there was war, he
    went.
He was married and added five children to the population,   25
Which our Eugenist says was the right number for a parent of his
    generation,
And our teachers report that he never interfered with their education.
Was he free? Was he happy? The question is absurd:
Had anything been wrong, we should certainly have heard.

About the Poem

1. Do the words in this poem literally express Auden's own views? What makes you think so? If not, whose views are they meant to express?

2. Why do you think Auden presents this poem as an inscription on a public monument? What is the advantage of this choice? Why would a society erect a monument to its "unknown citizen"?

3. What does the poem tell us about the unknown citizen? What doesn't it tell us? What do its inclusions and omissions reveal about the state's official attitudes and values? How do these attitudes and values compare with Auden's? How do you know?

4. Look at the inscription following the title. What can you say about its content and style? How does it affect your understanding of the poem?

5. Comment on Auden's use of capitalization, citing examples from the poem. How does it affect the poem's meaning?

6. How do you think Auden meant readers to respond to this poem? Cite evidence from the poem to support your answer. How do you respond to it? Why do you respond that way?

Explorations

1. Auden wrote his poem in 1939. Using whatever information you think relevant, describe the "unknown citizen" of the 1980s.

2. Suppose that in the year 2000 the state were to erect a monument to you,

and that you could write the inscription yourself, within a limit of 300 words. What would you want your monument to say? If you could design it yourself, what would it look like?

3. The United States government relies heavily on statistical information about its citizens, information that depersonalizes them in various ways. What sort of information does the government collect? What are the advantages and uses of having such information? What are the disadvantages and abuses?

JOHN UPDIKE

John Updike was born in 1932 and grew up in Shillington, Pennsylvania, a small town where his father taught high school. His childhood, described in a sketch called "The Dogwood Tree" (1965), was much like that of millions of other middle-class Americans, and these are typically the characters of his short stories and novels. Like the young man in the following story, Updike carried a rubber-lined bookbag, which was from time to time stolen by girls, and he loved "deeply, but ineffectually" one of those girls. Updike went to Harvard, where he became editor of its undergraduate humor magazine *The Lampoon*. Since graduation he has published many short stories as well as poems, plays, and ten novels. Three of his best known novels are about Harry "Rabbit" Angstrom: *Rabbit, Run* (1961), *Rabbit Redux* (1971), and *Rabbit Is Rich* (1981). "A Sense of Shelter" is from the short story collection *Pigeon Feathers* (1960).

A Sense of Shelter

Snow fell against the high school all day, wet big-flaked snow that did not accumulate well. Sharpening two pencils, William looked down on a parking lot that was a blackboard in reverse; car tires had cut smooth arcs of black into its white, and where the school buses had backed around, there were handsome pairs of arabesque V's. The snow, though at moments it whirled opaquely, could not quite bleach these scars away. The temperature must be exactly 32°. The window was open a crack, and a canted pane of glass lifted outdoor air into his face, coating the cedarwood smell of pencil shavings with the transparent odor of the wet window sill. With each revolution of the handle his knuckles came within a fraction of an inch of the tilted glass, and the faint chill this proximity breathed on them sharpened his already acute sense of shelter.

The sky behind the shreds of snow was stone-colored. The murk inside the high classroom gave the air a solidity that limited the overhead radiance to its own vessels; six globes of dull incandescence floated on the top of a thin sea. The feeling the gloom gave him was not gloomy, it was joyous: he felt they were all sealed in, safe; the colors of cloth were dyed deeper, the sound of whispers was made more distinct, the smells of tablet paper and wet shoes and varnish and face powder pierced him with a vivid sense of possession. These were his classmates sealed in, his, the stupid as well as the clever, the plain as well as the lovely, his enemies as well as his friends, his. He felt like a king and seemed to

90

move to his seat between the bowed heads of subjects that loved him less than he loved them. His seat was sanctioned by tradition; for twelve years he had sat at the rear of classrooms, William Young, flanked by Marsha Wyckoff and Andy Zimmerman. Once there had been two Zimmermans, but one went to work in his father's greenhouse, and in some classes—Latin and Trig—there were none, and William sat at the edge of the class as if on the lip of a cliff, and Marsha Wyckoff became Marvin Wolf or Sandra Wade, but it was always the same desk, whose surface altered from hour to hour but from whose blue-stained ink-hole his mind could extract, like a chain of magician's handkerchiefs, a continuity of years. As a senior he was a kind of king, and as a teacher's pet another kind, a puppet king, who had gathered in appointive posts and even, when the moron vote split between two football heroes, some elective ones. He was not popular, he had never had a girl, his intense friends of childhood had drifted off into teams and gangs, and in large groups—when the whole school, for instance, went in the fall to the beautiful, dung-and-cotton-candy-smelling county fair—he was always an odd man, without a seat on the bus home. But exclusion is itself a form of inclusion. He even had a nickname: Mip, because he stuttered. Taunts no longer much frightened him; he had come late into his inheritance of size, but this summer it had arrived, and he at last stood equal with his enormous, boisterous parents, and had to unbutton his shirt cuffs to get his wrists through them, and discovered he could pick up a basketball with one hand. So, his long legs blocking two aisles, he felt regal even in size and, almost trembling with happiness under the high globes of light beyond whose lunar glow invisible snowflakes were drowning on the gravel roof of his castle, believed that the long delay of unpopularity had been merely a consolation, that he was at last strong enough to make his move. Today he must tell Mary Landis he loved her.

He had loved her since, a fat-faced toughie with freckles and green eyes, she deftly stole his rubber-lined schoolbag on the walk back from second grade along Jewett Street and outran him—simply had better legs. The superior speed a boy was supposed to have failed to come; his kidneys burned with panic. In front of the grocery store next to her home she stopped and turned. She was willing to have him catch up. This humiliation on top of the rest was too much to bear. Tears broke in his throat; he spun around and ran home and threw himself on the floor of the front parlor, where his grandfather, feet twiddling, perused the newspaper and soliloquized all morning. In time the letter slot rustled, and the doorbell rang, and his mother and Mary exchanged the schoolbag and polite apologies. Their gentle voices had been to him, lying there on the carpet with his head wrapped in his arms, indistinguishable. Mother had always liked Mary. From when she had been a tiny girl dancing along the hedge on the end of an older sister's arm, Mother had liked her. Out of all the children that flocked, similar as pigeons, around the neighborhood, Mother's heart had reached out with claws and fastened on Mary. He never took the schoolbag to school again, had refused to touch it. He supposed it was still in the attic, still faintly smelling of pink rubber.

The buzzer sounded the two-minute signal. In the middle of the classroom Mary Landis stood up, a Monitor badge pinned to her belt. She wore a lavender sweater with the sleeves pushed up to expose her forearms, a delicately cheap effect. Wild stories were told about her; perhaps it was merely his knowledge of these that put the hardness in her face. Her eyes in their shape seemed braced for squinting and their green was frosted. Her freckles had faded. William thought she laughed less this year; now that she was in the Secretarial Course and he in the College Preparatory, he saw her in only one class a day, this one, English. She stood a second, eclipsed at the thighs by Jack Stephens' shoulders, looking back at the room with a stiff glance, as if she had seen the same faces too many times before. Her habit of perfect posture emphasized the angularity she had grown into; there was a nervous edge, a boxiness in her bones, that must have been waiting all along under the childish fat. Her eye sockets were deeply indented and her chin had a prim square set that seemed defiant to him. Her brown skirt was snug and straight; she had less hips than bosom, and thin, athletic legs. Her pronged chest poised, she sauntered up the aisle and encountered a leg thrown in her path. She stared down until it withdrew; she was used to such attentions. As she went out the door, somebody she saw in the hall made her smile, a wide smile full of warmth and short white teeth, and love scooped at his heart. He would tell her.

In another minute, the second bell rasped. Shuffling through the perfumed crowds to his next class, he crooned to himself, in the slow, over-enunciated manner of the Negro vocalist who had brought the song back this year,

> Lah-vender blue, dilly dilly,
> Lavendih green-een;
> *Eef* I were king, dilly dilly,
> You would: be queen.

The song gave him an exultant sliding sensation that intertwined with the pleasures of his day. He knew all the answers, he had done all the work, the teachers called upon him only to rebuke the ignorance of the others. In Trig and Soc Sci both it was this way. In gym, the fourth hour of the morning, he, who was always picked near the last, startled his side by excelling at volleyball, leaping like a madman, shouting like a bully. The ball felt light as a feather against his big bones. His hair wet from the shower, he walked in the icy air to Luke's Luncheonette, where he ate three hamburgers in a booth with three juniors. There was Barry Kruppman, a tall, thyroid-eyed boy who came on the school bus from the country town of Bowsville and was an amateur hypnotist and occultist; he told them about a Portland, Oregon, businessman who under hypnosis had been taken back through sixteen reincarnations to the condition of an Egyptian concubine in the household of a high priest of Isis.[1] There was his friend Lionel Griffin, a pudgy simp whose blond hair stood out above his ears in two slick waxed wings. He was supposed to be a fairy, and in fact did seem most excited by the transvestite aspect of the soul's transmigration. And there was Lionel's girl, Virginia, a drab little mystery who chain-smoked Herbert Tareytons and never said anything. She had sallow skin, and Lionel kept jabbing her and shrieking. William would rather have sat with members of his own class, who filled the other booths, but he would have had to force himself on them. These juniors admired him and welcomed his company. He asked, "Wuh-well, was he ever a c-c-c-cockroach, like Archy?"[2]

Kruppman's face grew intense; his furry lids dropped down over the bulge of his eyes, and when they drew back, his pupils were as small and hard as BBs. "That's the really interesting thing. There was this gap, see, between his being a knight under Charlemagne and then a sailor on a ship putting out from Macedonia—that's where Yugoslavia is now—in the time of Nero;[3] there was this gap when the only thing the guy would do was walk around the office snarling and growling, see, like this." Kruppman worked his blotched ferret face up into a snarl and Griffin shrieked. "He tried to bite one of the assistants and they think that for six hundred years"—the uncanny, unhealthy seriousness of his whisper hushed Griffin momentarily—"for six hundred years he just was a series of wolves. Probably in the German forests. You see, when he was in Macedonia"—his whisper barely audible—"he murdered a woman."

Griffin squealed with pleasure and cried, "Oh, Kruppman! Kruppman, how you do go on!" and jabbed Virginia in the arm so hard a

7

8

---

[1] People with a thyroid condition often have bulging eyes. Isis was the supreme goddess of ancient Egypt.

[2] Refers to *archy and mehitabel* (1927) by Don Marquis. Archy the cockroach is the purported author. William has gotten it wrong: it was mehitabel the cat who was a reincarnation of ancient Egyptian queens.

[3] Kruppman is moving backward in time, from the eighth century and its chivalrous knights to the first century reign of the dissolute Roman emperor Nero.

Herbert Tareyton jumped from her hand and bobbled across the Formica table.

The crowd at the soda bar had thinned and when the door to the outside opened he saw Mary come in and stand there for a second where the smoke inside and the snow outside swirled together. The mixture made a kind of—Kruppman's ridiculous story had put the phrase in his head—wolf-weather, and she was just a gray shadow against it. She bought a pack of cigarettes from Luke and went out again, a kerchief around her head, the pneumatic thing above the door hissing behind her. For a long time, always in fact, she had been at the center of whatever gang was the best one: in the second grade the one that walked home up Jewett Street together, and in the sixth grade the one that went bicycling as far away as the quarry and the Rentschler estate and played touch football Saturday afternoons, and in the ninth grade the one that went roller-skating at Candlebridge Park with the tenth-grade boys, and in the eleventh grade the one that held parties lasting past midnight and that on Sundays drove in caravans as far as Philadelphia and back. And all the while there had been a succession of boy friends, first Jack Stephens and Fritz March in their class and then boys a grade ahead and then Barrel Lord, who was a senior when they were sophomores and whose name was in the newspapers all football season, and then this last summer someone out of the school altogether, a man she met while working as a waitress in the city of Alton. So this year her weekends were taken up, and the party gang carried on as if she had never existed, and nobody saw her much except in school and when she stopped by in Luke's to buy a pack of cigarettes. Her silhouette against the big window had looked wan, her head hooded, her face nibbled by light, her fingers fiddling on the glassy counter with her coins. He yearned to reach out, to comfort her, but he was wedged deep in the shrill booths, between the jingling guts of the pinball machine and the hillbilly joy of the jukebox. The impulse left him with a disagreeable feeling. He had loved her too long to want to pity her; it endangered the investment of worship on which he had not yet realized any return.

The two hours of the school afternoon held Latin and a study hall. In study hall, while the five people at the table with him played tick-tacktoe and sucked cough drops and yawned, he did all his homework for the next day. He prepared thirty lines of Vergil, Aeneas in the Underworld. The study hall was a huge low room in the basement of the building; its coziness crept into Tartarus.[4] On the other side of the fudge-

---

[4]The Underworld, where all mortal souls were sent after death, according to the ancient Roman religion. William's Latin homework is a translation of a famous passage from Vergil's epic poem, the *Aeneid*.

colored wall the circular saw in the woodworking shop whined and gasped
and then whined again; it bit off pieces of wood with a rising, terrorized
inflection—*bzzzzzup!* He solved ten problems in trigonometry. His mind
cut neatly through their knots and separated them, neat stiff squares of
correctness, one by one from the long but finite plank of problems that
connected Plane with Solid Geometry. Lastly, as the snow on a ragged
slant drifted down into the cement pits outside the steel-mullioned windows, he read a short story by Edgar Allan Poe. He closed the book softly
on the pleasing sonority of its final note of horror, gazed at the red, wet,
menthol-scented inner membrane of Judy Whipple's yawn, rimmed with
flaking pink lipstick, and yielded his conscience to the snug sense of his
work done, of the snow falling, of the warm minutes that walked through
their shelter so slowly. The perforated acoustic tiling above his head
seemed the lining of a long tube that would go all the way: high school
merging into college, college into graduate school, graduate school into
teaching at a college—section man, assistant, associate, *full* professor,
possessor of a dozen languages and a thousand books, a man brilliant in
his forties, wise in his fifties, renowned in his sixties, revered in his
seventies, and then retired, sitting in a study lined with acoustical books
until the time for the last transition from silence to silence, and he would
die, like Tennyson, with a copy of "Cymbeline" beside him on the moon-
drenched bed.[5]

     After school he had to go to Room 101 and cut a sports cartoon
into a stencil for the school paper. He liked the building best when it
was nearly empty. Then the janitors went down the halls sowing seeds
of red wax and making an immaculate harvest with broad brooms, gathering all the fluff and hairpins and wrappers and powder that the animals
had dropped that day. The basketball team thumped in the hollow gym-
nasium; the cheerleaders rehearsed behind drawn curtains on the stage.
In Room 101 two giggly typists with stripes bleached into their hair
banged away between mistakes. At her desk Mrs. Gregory, the faculty
sponsor, wearily passed her pencil through misspelled news copy. William
took the shadow box from the top of the filing cabinet and the styluses
and shaders from their drawer and the typed stencils from the closet
where they hung, like fragile blue scarves, on hooks. "B-BALLERS BOW,
57-42," was the headline. He drew a tall b-baller bowing to a stumpy
pagan idol, labeled "W" for victorious Weiserton High, and traced it in
the soft blue wax with a fine loop stylus. His careful breath grazed his
fingers. His eyebrows frowned while his heart throbbed happily on the
giddy prattle of the typists. The shadow box was simply a plastic frame

[5]Alfred, Lord Tennyson was the most respected and honored English poet of the late
nineteenth century. *Cymbeline* is one of Shakespeare's lesser-known plays.

holding a pane of glass and lifted at one end by two legs so the light bulb, fitted in a tin tray, could slide under; it was like a primitive lean-to sheltering a fire. As he worked, his eyes smarting, he mixed himself up with the light bulb, felt himself burning under a slanting roof upon which a huge hand scratched. The glass grew hot; the danger in the job was pulling the softened wax with your damp hand, distorting or tearing the typed letters. Sometimes the center of an o stuck to your skin like a bit of blue confetti. But he was expert and cautious. He returned the things to their places feeling airily tall, heightened by Mrs. Gregory's appreciation, which she expressed by keeping her back turned, in effect saying that other staff members were undependable but William did not need to be watched.

In the hall outside Room 101 only the shouts of a basketball scrim-   12
mage reverberated; the chant of the cheerleaders had been silenced. Though he had done everything, he felt reluctant to leave. Neither of his parents would be home yet. Since the death of his grandfather, both worked in Alton, and this building was as much his home. He knew all its nooks. On the second floor of the annex, beyond the art room, there was a strange, narrow boys' lavatory that no one ever seemed to use. It was here one time that Barry Kruppman tried to hypnotize him and thus cure his stuttering. Kruppman's voice purred and his irises turned tiny in the bulging whites, and for a moment William felt himself lean backward involuntarily, but he was distracted by the bits of bloodshot pink in the corners of these portentous eyes, the folly of giving up his will to an intellectual inferior occurred to him; he refused to let go and go under, and perhaps therefore his stuttering had continued.

The frosted window at the end of the long room cast a watery light   13
on the green floor and made the porcelain urinals shine like slices of moon. The semiopacity of this window gave great denseness to the room's feeling of secrecy. William washed his hands with close attention, en-joying the lavish amount of powdered soap provided for him in this castle. He studied his face in the mirror, making infinitesimal adjustments to attain the absolutely most flattering angle, and then put his hands below his throat to get their strong, long-fingered beauty into the picture. As he walked toward the door he sang, closing his eyes and gasping as if he were a real Negro whose entire career depended upon this recording.

> Who—told me so, dilly dilly,
> Who told me soho?
> *Aii* told myself, dilly dilly,
> I told: me so.

When he emerged into the hall it was not empty: one girl walked   14 down its varnished perspective toward him, Mary Landis, in a heavy brown coat, with a scarf on her head and books in her arms. Her locker was up here, on the second floor of the annex. His own was in the annex basement. A ticking sensation that existed neither in the medium of sound nor of light crowded against his throat. She flipped the scarf back from her hair and in a conversational voice that carried well down the clean planes of the hall said, "Hi, Billy." The name came from way back, when they were both children, and made him feel small but brave.

"Hi. How are you?"   15

"Fine." Her smile broadened.   16

What was so funny? Was she really, as it seemed, pleased to see   17
him? "Du-did you just get through cheer-cheer-cheerleading?"

"Yes. Thank God. *Oh* she's so awful. She makes us do the same   18
stupid locomotives for every cheer; I told her, no wonder nobody cheers
any more."

"This is M-M-Miss Potter?" He blushed, feeling that he made an   19
ugly face in getting past the "M." When he got caught in the middle of
a sentence the constriction was somehow worse. He admired the way
words poured up her throat, distinct and petulant.

"Yes, Potbottom Potter," she said. "She's just aching for a man and   20
takes it out on us. I wish she would get one. Honestly, Billy, I have half
a mind to quit. I'll be so glad when June comes, I'll never set foot in
this idiotic building again."

Her lips, pale with the lipstick worn off, crinkled bitterly. Her face,   21
foreshortened from the height of his eyes, looked cross as a cat's. He was
a little shocked that poor Miss Potter and this kind, warm school stirred
her to what he had to take as actual anger; this grittiness in her was the
first abrasive texture he had struck today. Couldn't she see around teachers, into their fatigue, their poverty, their fear? It had been so long since
he had spoken to her, he didn't know how insensitive she had become.
"Don't quit," he brought out of his mouth at last. "It'd be n-n-nuh—
it'd be nothing without you."

He pushed open the door at the end of the hall for her and as   22
she passed under his arm she looked up and said, "Why, aren't you
sweet."

The stair well, all asphalt and iron, smelled of galoshes. It felt more   23
private than the hall, more specially theirs; there was something magical
in its shifting multiplicity of planes as they descended that lifted the spell
on his tongue, so that words came as quickly as his feet pattered on the
steps.

"No I mean it," he said, "you're really a beautiful cheerleader. But   24
then you're beautiful period."

"I have skinny legs." 25
"Who told you that?" 26
"Somebody." 27
"Well, *he* wasn't very sweet." 28
"No." 29
"Why do you hate this poor old school?" 30
"Now, Billy. You know you don't care about this junky place any 31
more than I do."
"I love it. It breaks my heart to hear you say you want to get out, 32
because then I'll never see you again."
"You don't care, do you?" 33
"Why *sure* I care you *know*"—their feet stopped; they had reached 34
bottom, the first-floor landing, two brass-barred doors and a grimy radia-
tor—"I've always li-loved you."
"You don't mean that." 35
"I do too. It's ridiculous but there it is. I wanted to tell you today 36
and now I have."
He expected her to go out of the door in derision but instead she 37
showed a willingness to discuss this awkward matter. He should have
realized before this that women enjoy being talked to. "It's a very silly
thing to say," she asserted tentatively.
"I don't see why," he said, fairly bold now that he couldn't seem 38
more ridiculous, and yet picking his words with a certain strategic care.
"It's not *that* silly to love somebody, I mean what the hell. Probably
what's silly is not to do anything about it for umpteen years but then I
never had an opportunity, I thought."
He set his books down on the radiator and she set hers down beside 39
his. "What kind of opportunity were you waiting for?"
"Well, see, that's it; I didn't know." He wished, in a way, she'd go 40
out the door. But she had propped herself against the wall and plainly
expected him to keep talking. "Yuh-you were such a queen and I was
such a nothing and I just didn't really want to presume." It wasn't very
interesting; he was puzzled that she seemed to be interested. Her face
had grown quite stern, the mouth very small and thoughtful, and he
made a gesture with his hands intended to release her from the bother of
thinking about it; after all, it was just a disposition of his heart, nothing
permanent or expensive; maybe it was just his mother's idea anyway.
Half in impatience to close the account, he asked, "Will you marry
me?"
"You don't want to marry me," she said. "You're going to go on 41
and be a great man."

He blushed in pleasure; is this how she saw him, is this how they   42
all saw him, as worthless now but in time a great man? "No, I'm not,"
he said, "but anyway, you're great now. You're so pretty, Mary."

"Oh, Billy," she said, "if you were me for just one day you'd hate   43
it."

She said this rather blankly, watching his eyes; he wished her voice   44
had shown more misery. In his world of closed surfaces a panel, carelessly
pushed, had opened, and he hung in this openness paralyzed, unable to
think what to say. Nothing he could think of quite fitted the abruptly
immense context. The radiator cleared its throat; its heat made, in the
intimate volume just on this side of the doors on whose windows the
snow beat limply, a provocative snugness; he supposed he should try,
and stepped forward, his hands lifting toward her shoulders. Mary side-
stepped between him and the radiator and put the scarf back on, lifting
the cloth like a broad plaid halo above her head and then wrapping it
around her chin and knotting it so she looked, in her red galoshes and
bulky coat, like a peasant woman in a European movie. With her thick
hair swathed, her face seemed pale and chunky, and when she recradled
the books in her arms her back bent humbly under the point of the
kerchief. "It's too hot in here," she said. "I have to wait for somebody."
The disconnectedness of the two statements seemed natural in the fragmented atmosphere his stops and starts had produced. She bucked the
brass bar with her shoulder and the door slammed open; he followed her
into the weather.

"For the person who thinks your legs are too skinny?"   45

"Uh-huh." As she looked up at him a snowflake caught on the   46
lashes of one eye. She jerkily rubbed that cheek on the shoulder of her
coat and stamped a foot, splashing slush. Cold water gathered on the
back of his shirt. He put his hands in his pockets and pressed his arms
against his sides to keep from shivering.

"Thuh-then you wo-wo-won't marry me?" His wise instinct told   47
him the only way back was by going forward, through absurdity.

"We don't know each other," she said.   48

"My God," he said. "Why not? I've known you since I was two."   49

"What do you know about me?"   50

This awful seriousness of hers; he must dissolve it. "That you're not   51
a virgin." But instead of making her laugh, this made her face go dead
and turned it away. Like beginning to kiss her, it had been a mistake;
in part, he felt grateful for his mistakes. They were like loyal friends,
who are nevertheless embarrassing. "What do you know about *me*?" he
asked, setting himself up for a finishing insult but dreading it. He hated

the stiff feel of his smile between his cheeks; glimpsed, as if the snow were a mirror, how hateful he looked.

"That you're basically very nice."   52

Her returning good for evil blinded him to his physical discomfort,   53
set him burning with regret. "Listen," he said, "I did love you. Let's at
least get that straight."

"You never loved anybody," she said. "You don't know what it is."   54

"O.K.," he said. "Pardon me."   55

"You're excused."   56

"You better wait in the school," he said. "He's-eez-eez going to be   57
a long time."

She didn't answer and walked a little distance, toeing out in the   58
childish way common to the women of the county, along the slack cable
that divided the parking lot from the softball field. One bicycle, rusted
as if it had been there for years, leaned in the rack, its fenders supporting
thin crescents of white.

The warmth inside the door felt heavy, like a steamed towel laid   59
against his face. William picked up his books and ran his pencil along
the black ribs of the radiator before going down the stairs to his locker
in the annex basement. The shadows were thick at the foot of the steps;
suddenly it felt late, he must hurry and get home. He had the irrational
fear they were going to lock him in. The cloistered odors of paper, sweat,
and, from the woodshop at the far end of the basement hall, sawdust
were no longer delightful to him. The tall green double lockers appeared
to study him through the three air slits near their tops. When he opened
his locker, and put his books on his shelf, below Marvin Wolf's, and
removed his coat from his hook, his self seemed to crawl into the long
dark space thus made vacant, the ugly, humiliated, educable self. In
answer to a flick of his great hand the steel door weightlessly slammed
shut, and through the length of his body he felt so clean and free he
smiled. Between now and the happy future predicted for him he had
nothing, almost literally nothing to do.

About the Story

1. How does William see himself—what kind of person does he think he is?
What kind of person do you think he is? Use specific details from the story
to support your answers.

2. What kind of person is Mary Landis? Is she as William sees her? What is
it about Mary that attracts him to her? Why does William feel that he must
tell her he loves her?

3. Look back at the conversation between Mary and William. What is each

thinking at each point in the conversation? How do you know? Are there any points where you cannot interpret their thoughts?

4. Updike tells his story from William's point of view, but in the third person. What is the advantage of this narrative strategy? Could Updike have used a different strategy as effectively, for example, from the first person point of view? Why, or why not?

5. Consider the story's title, "A Sense of Shelter." How does it fit the story? Who is being sheltered, by what, and from what?

6. In the last paragraph we are given William's response to his conversation with Mary. What is his response?

Explorations

1. For William Young, his attitude toward his school embodies his attitude toward life and his plans for the future. How do your feelings toward school and your classmates relate to your ambitions and your view of life?

2. What is love? Use whatever examples you like in your definition, whether from your own experience, from psychology, literature, or some other field.

3. The years of adolescence are a crucial period in the development of one's personality, and they have been much studied by psychologists. Consulting a textbook in the psychology of adolescence, if you like, choose an aspect of the subject that interests you, and investigate what psychologists have to say about it.

EUDORA WELTY

The American South has brought forth more than its share of fine writers, and Eudora Welty holds an honored place among them. She was born in 1909 in Jackson, Mississippi, and that is where she has lived for most of her life. Her father was president of an insurance company, and she was able to go away to the University of Wisconsin and then to take a postgraduate course in advertising at Columbia University's business school. By then the Great Depression had set in, and jobs in advertising were scarce, so she returned home to Jackson and began to write. Her published works include many short stories, now available as her *Collected Stories* (1980), and five novels: *The Robber Bridegroom* (1944), *Delta Wedding* (1946), *The Ponder Heart* (1954), *Losing Battles* (1970), and *The Optimist's Daughter* (1972). A collection of her essays has been published as *The Eye of the Story* (1975). In "A Worn Path" we meet one of Welty's memorable characters, old Phoenix Jackson, on her way to town on a vital errand. The story is discussed by Welty in the essay "Is Phoenix Jackson's Grandson Really Dead?" (pages 428–430).

A Worn Path

It was December—a bright frozen day in the early morning. Far out   1
in the country there was an old Negro woman with her head tied in a red rag, coming along a path through the pinewoods. Her name was Phoenix Jackson. She was very old and small and she walked slowly in the dark pine shadows, moving a little from side to side in her steps, with the balanced heaviness and lightness of a pendulum in a grandfather clock. She carried a thin, small cane made from an umbrella, and with this she kept tapping the frozen earth in front of her. This made a grave and persistent noise in the still air, that seemed meditative like the chirping of a solitary little bird.

She wore a dark striped dress reaching down to her shoe tops, and   2
an equally long apron of bleached sugar sacks, with a full pocket: all neat and tidy, but every time she took a step she might have fallen over her shoelaces, which dragged from her unlaced shoes. She looked straight ahead. Her eyes were blue with age. Her skin had a pattern all its own of numberless branching wrinkles and as though a whole little tree stood in the middle of her forehead, but a golden color ran underneath, and the two knobs of her cheeks were illumined by a yellow burning under the dark. Under the red rag her hair came down on her neck in the frailest of ringlets, still black, and with an odor like copper.

Now and then there was a quivering in the thicket. Old Phoenix   3
said, "Out of my way, all you foxes, owls, beetles, jack rabbits, coons
and wild animals! . . . Keep out from under these feet, little bob-whites.
. . . Keep the big wild hogs out of my path. Don't let none of those
come running my direction. I got a long way." Under her small black-
freckled hand her cane, limber as a buggy whip, would switch at the
brush as if to rouse up any hiding things.

On she went. The woods were deep and still. The sun made the   4
pine needles almost too bright to look at, up where the wind rocked.
The cones dropped as light as feathers. Down in the hollow was the
mourning dove—it was not too late for him.

The path ran up a hill. "Seem like there is chains about my feet,   5
time I get this far,' she said, in the voice of argument old people keep
to use with themselves. "Something always take a hold of me on this
hill—pleads I should stay."

After she got to the top she turned and gave a full, severe look   6
behind her where she had come. "Up through pines," she said at length.
"Now down through oaks."

Her eyes opened their widest, and she started down gently. But   7
before she got to the bottom of the hill a bush caught her dress.

Her fingers were busy and intent, but her skirts were full and long,   8
so that before she could pull them free in one place they were caught in
another. It was not possible to allow the dress to tear. "I in the thorny
bush," she said. "Thorns, you doing your appointed work. Never want
to let folks pass, no sir. Old eyes thought you was a pretty little *green*
bush."

Finally, trembling all over, she stood free, and after a moment dared   9
to stoop for her cane.

"Sun so high!" she cried, leaning back and looking, while the thick   10
tears went over her eyes. "The time getting all gone here."

At the foot of this hill was a place where a log was laid across the   11
creek.

"Now comes the trial," said Phoenix.   12

Putting her right foot out, she mounted the log and shut her eyes.   13
Lifting her skirt, leveling her cane fiercely before her, like a festival figure
in some parade, she began to march across. Then she opened her eyes
and she was safe on the other side.

"I wasn't as old as I thought," she said.   14

But she sat down to rest. She spread her skirts on the bank around   15
her and folded her hands over her knees. Up above her was a tree in a
pearly cloud of mistletoe. She did not dare to close her eyes, and when
a little boy brought her a plate with a slice of marble-cake on it she spoke

to him. "That would be acceptable," she said. But when she went to take it there was just her own hand in the air.

So she left that tree, and had to go through a barbed-wire fence. 16 There she had to creep and crawl, spreading her knees and stretching her fingers like a baby trying to climb the steps. But she talked loudly to herself: she could not let her dress be torn now, so late in the day, and she could not pay for having her arm or her leg sawed off if she got caught fast where she was.

At last she was safe through the fence and risen up out in the 17 clearing. Big dead trees, like black men with one arm, were standing in the purple stalks of the withered cotton field. There sat a buzzard.

"Who you watching?" 18

In the furrow she made her way along. 19

"Glad this not the season for bulls," she said, looking sideways, 20 "and the good Lord made his snakes to curl up and sleep in the winter. A pleasure I don't see no two-headed snake coming around that tree, where it come once. It took a while to get by him, back in the summer."

She passed through the old cotton and went into a field of dead 21 corn. It whispered and shook and was taller than her head. "Through the maze now," she said, for there was no path.

Then there was something tall, black, and skinny there, moving 22 before her.

At first she took it for a man. It could have been a man dancing 23 in the field. But she stood still and listened, and it did not make a sound. It was as silent as a ghost.

"Ghost," she said sharply, "who be you the ghost of? For I have 24 heard of nary death close by."

But there was no answer—only the ragged dancing in the wind. 25

She shut her eyes, reached out her hand, and touched a sleeve. 26 She found a coat and inside that an emptiness, cold as ice.

"You scarecrow," she said. Her face lighted. "I ought to be shut up 27 for good," she said with laughter. "My senses is gone. I too old. I the oldest people I ever know. Dance, old scarecrow," she said, "while I dancing with you."

She kicked her foot over the furrow, and with mouth drawn down, 28 shook her head once or twice in a little strutting way. Some husks blew down and whirled in streamers about her skirts.

Then she went on, parting her way from side to side with the cane, 29 through the whispering field. At last she came to the end, to a wagon track where the silver grass blew between the red ruts. The quail were walking around like pullets, seeming all dainty and unseen.

"Walk pretty," she said. "This the easy place. This the easy going." 30

She followed the track, swaying through the quiet bare fields, through 31
the little strings of trees silver in their dead leaves, past cabins silver
from weather, with the doors and windows boarded shut, all like old
women under a spell sitting there. "I walking in their sleep," she said,
nodding her head vigorously.

In a ravine she went where a spring was silently flowing through a 32
hollow log. Old Phoenix bent and drank. "Sweetgum makes the water
sweet," she said, and drank more. "Nobody know who made this well,
for it was here when I was born."

The track crossed a swampy part where the moss hung as white as 33
lace from every limb. "Sleep on, alligators, and blow your bubbles." Then
the track went into the road.

Deep, deep the road went down between the high green-colored 34
banks. Overhead the live-oaks met, and it was as dark as a cave.

A black dog with a lolling tongue came up out of the weeds by the 35
ditch. She was meditating, and not ready, and when he came at her she
only hit him a little with her cane. Over she went in the ditch, like a
little puff of milkweed.

Down there, her senses drifted away. A dream visited her, and she 36
reached her hand up, but nothing reached down and gave her a pull. So
she lay there and presently went to talking. "Old woman," she said to
herself, "that black dog come up out of the weeds to stall you off, and
now there he sitting on his fine tail, smiling at you."

A white man finally came along and found her—a hunter, a young 37
man, with his dog on a chain.

"Well, Granny!" he laughed. "What are you doing there?" 38

"Lying on my back like a June-bug waiting to be turned over, 39
mister," she said, reaching up her hand.

He lifted her up, gave her a swing in the air, and set her down. 40
"Anything broken, Granny?"

"No sir, them old dead weeds is springy enough," said Phoenix, 41
when she had got her breath. "I thank you for your trouble."

"Where do you live, Granny?" he asked, while the two dogs were 42
growling at each other.

"Away back yonder, sir, behind the ridge. You can't even see it 43
from here."

"On your way home?" 44

"No sir, I going to town." 45

"Why, that's too far! That's as far as I walked when I come out 46
myself, and I get something for my trouble." He patted the stuffed bag

he carried, and there hung down a little closed claw. It was one of the
bob-whites, with its beak hooked bitterly to show it was dead. "Now you
go on home, Granny!"

"I bound to go to town, mister," said Phoenix. "The time come
around." 47

He gave another laugh, filling the whole landscape. "I know you
old colored people! Wouldn't miss going to town to see Santa Claus!" 48

But something held old Phoenix very still. The deep lines in her
face went into a fierce and different radiation. Without warning, she had
seen with her own eyes a flashing nickel fall out of the man's pocket
onto the ground. 49

"How old are you, Granny?" he was saying. 50

"There is no telling, mister," she said, "no telling." 51

Then she gave a little cry and clapped her hands and said, "Git on
away from here, dog! Look! Look at that dog!" She laughed as if in
admiration. "He ain't scared of nobody. He a big black dog." She whispered, "Sic him!" 52

"Watch me get rid of that cur," said the man. "Sic him, Pete! Sic
him!" 53

Phoenix heard the dogs fighting, and heard the man running and
throwing sticks. She even heard a gunshot. But she was slowly bending
forward by that time, further and further forward, the lids stretched down
over her eyes, as if she were doing this in her sleep. Her chin was
lowered almost to her knees. The yellow palm of her hand came out
from the fold of her apron. Her fingers slid down and along the ground
under the piece of money with the grace and care they would have in
lifting an egg from under a setting hen. Then she slowly straightened
up, she stood erect, and the nickel was in her apron pocket. A bird
flew by. Her lips moved. "God watching me the whole time. I come to
stealing." 54

The man came back, and his own dog panted about them. "Well,
I scared him off that time," he said, and then he laughed and lifted his
gun and pointed it at Phoenix. 55

She stood straight and faced him. 56

"Doesn't the gun scare you?" he said, still pointing it. 57

"No, sir, I seen plenty go off closer by, in my day, and for less than
what I done," she said, holding utterly still. 58

He smiled, and shouldered the gun. "Well, Granny," he said, "you
must be a hundred years old, and scared of nothing. I'd give you a dime
if I had any money with me. But you take my advice and stay home,
and nothing will happen to you." 59

"I bound to go on my way, mister," said Phoenix. She inclined her 60 head in the red rag. Then they went in different directions, but she could hear the gun shooting again and again over the hill.

She walked on. The shadows hung from the oak trees to the road 61
like curtains. Then she smelled wood-smoke, and smelled the river, and she saw a steeple and the cabins on their steep steps. Dozens of little black children whirled around her. There ahead was Natchez shining. Bells were ringing. She walked on.

In the paved city it was Christmas time. There were red and green 62
electric lights strung and crisscrossed everywhere, and all turned on in the daytime. Old Phoenix would have been lost if she had not distrusted her eyesight and depended on her feet to know where to take her.

She paused quietly on the sidewalk where people were passing by. 63
A lady came along in the crowd, carrying an armful of red-, green- and silver-wrapped presents; she gave off perfume like the red roses in hot summer, and Phoenix stopped her.

"Please, missy, will you lace up my shoe?" She held up her foot. 64

"What do you want, Grandma?" 65

"See my shoe," said Phoenix. "Do all right for out in the country, 66
but wouldn't look right to go in a big building."

"Stand still then, Grandma," said the lady. She put her pack- 67
ages down on the sidewalk beside her and laced and tied both shoes tightly.

"Can't lace 'em with a cane," said Phoenix. "Thank you, missy. I 68
doesn't mind asking a nice lady to tie up my shoe, when I gets out on the street."

Moving slowly and from side to side, she went into the big building, 69
and into a tower of steps, where she walked up and around and around until her feet knew to stop.

She entered a door, and there she saw nailed up on the wall the 70
document that had been stamped with the gold seal and framed in the gold frame, which matched the dream that was hung up in her head.

"Here I be," she said. There was a fixed and ceremonial stiffness 71
over her body.

"A charity case, I suppose," said an attendant who sat at the desk 72
before her.

But Phoenix only looked above her head. There was sweat on her 73
face, the wrinkles in her skin shone like a bright net.

"Speak up, Grandma," the woman said. "What's your name? We 74
must have your history, you know. Have you been here before? What seems to be the trouble with you?"

Old Phoenix only gave a twitch to her face as if a fly were bothering 75
her.

"Are you deaf?" cried the attendant.   76

But then the nurse came in.   77

"Oh, that's just old Aunt Phoenix," she said. "She doesn't come   78
for herself—she has a little grandson. She makes these trips just as regular
as clockwork. She lives away back off the Old Natchez Trace." She bent
down. "Well, Aunt Phoenix, why don't you just take a seat? We won't
keep you standing after your long trip." She pointed.

The old woman sat down, bolt upright in the chair.   79

"Now, how is the boy?" asked the nurse.   80

Old Phoenix did not speak.   81

"I said, how is the boy?"   82

But Phoenix only waited and stared straight ahead, her face very   83
solemn and withdrawn into rigidity.

"Is his throat any better?" asked the nurse. "Aunt Phoenix, don't   84
you hear me? Is your grandson's throat any better since the last time you
came for the medicine?"

With her hands on her knees, the old woman waited, silent, erect,   85
and motionless, just as if she were in armor.

"You mustn't take up our time this way, Aunt Phoenix," the nurse   86
said. "Tell us quickly about your grandson, and get it over. He isn't dead,
is he?"

At last there came a flicker and then a flame of comprehension   87
across her face, and she spoke.

"My grandson. It was my memory had left me. There I sat and   88
forgot why I made my long trip."

"Forgot?" The nurse frowned. "After you came so far?"   89

Then Phoenix was like an old woman begging a dignified forgive-   90
ness for waking up frightened in the night. "I never did go to school, I
was too old at the Surrender," she said in a soft voice. "I'm an old woman
without an education. It was my memory fail me. My little grandson, he
is just the same, and I forgot it in the coming."

"Throat never heals, does it?" said the nurse, speaking in a loud,   91
sure voice to old Phoenix. By now she had a card with something written
on it, a little list. "Yes. Swallowed lye. When was it?—January—two-
three years ago—"

Phoenix spoke unasked now. "No, missy, he not dead, he just the   92
same. Every little while his throat begin to close up again, and he not
able to swallow. He not get his breath. He not able to help himself. So
the time come around, and I go on another trip for the soothing medicine."

"All right. The doctor said as long as you came to get it, you could   93
have it," said the nurse. "But it's an obstinate case."

"My little grandson, he sit up there in the house all wrapped up, waiting by himself," Phoenix went on. "We is the only two left in the world. He suffer and it don't seem to put him back at all. He got a sweet look. He going to last. He wear a little patch quilt and peep out holding his mouth open like a little bird. I remembers so plain now. I not going to forget him again, no, the whole enduring time. I could tell him from all the others in creation." 94

"All right." The nurse was trying to hush her now. She brought her a bottle of medicine. "Charity," she said, making a check mark in a book. 95

Old Phoenix held the bottle close to her eyes, and then carefully put it into her pocket. 96

"I thank you," she said. 97

"It's Christmas time, Grandma," said the attendant. "Could I give you a few pennies out of my purse?" 98

"Five pennies is a nickel," said Phoenix stiffly. 99

"Here's a nickel," said the attendant. 100

Phoenix rose carefully and held out her hand. She received the nickel and then fished the other nickel out of her pocket and laid it beside the new one. She stared at her palm closely, with her head on one side. 101

Then she gave a tap with her cane on the floor. 102

"This is what come to me to do," she said. "I going to the store and buy my child a little windmill they sells, made out of paper. He going to find it hard to believe there such a thing in the world. I'll march myself back where he waiting, holding it straight up in this hand." 103

She lifted her free hand, gave a little nod, turned around, and walked out of the doctor's office. Then her slow step began on the stairs, going down. 104

About the Story

1. Why is Old Phoenix going to Natchez? Is she eager to tell why she is making her journey? Who does she tell, and why?

2. What obstacles does Phoenix meet on the way? How, emotionally, does she cope with those obstacles? What does this reveal about her character?

3. How does Phoenix get the money she plans to spend at the end of the story? What will she be bringing home to her grandson? What is the significance of this gift?

4. In paragraph 90 Phoenix says, "I never did go to school, I was too old at the Surrender." What does this mean?

5. Welty uses many figurative comparisons in this story—for example, "Over she went in the ditch, like a little puff of milkweed." Collect some other examples of metaphor and simile, and explain what each means. Do all of them have something in common? If so, what significance do you find in that?

6. What does the title of the story mean to you? Does it have any metaphorical meaning? Explain.

Explorations

1. Write a character sketch of an old person you know well. If you like, you can organize your sketch by showing your subject engaged in some typical activity.

2. Family obligations can be tiresome chores, or willing acts of love, or even both. What family obligations do you have—or do others have toward you? How do you feel about these obligations?

3. Though brought up in a time and place where racial discrimination and hatred were widespread, Eudora Welty writes of Phoenix Jackson with understanding and love. Is this typical of her? Read some of her other works—perhaps the story "Powerhouse" or the essay "A Pageant of Birds"—to assess the image of black people in her work.

Without a family, man, alone in the world, trembles with the cold.
ANDRÉ MAUROIS

Fond as we are of our loved ones, there comes at times during their absence an unexplainable peace.
ANNE SHAW

If we judge of love by its results, it resembles hatred more than friendship.
FRANÇOIS DE LA ROCHEFOUCAULD

Wishing to be friends is quick work, but friendship is a slow-ripening fruit.
ARISTOTLE

The reward of friendship is itself. The man who hopes for anything else does not understand what true friendship is.
SAINT AILRED OF RIEVAULX

THE strongest and most significant relationships most of us have are with our families and friends. Usually these are the people who have the greatest influence on our lives, and we depend on them for the fulfillment of some of our deepest needs. At best, family and friends offer us companionship, the sharing of joys and sorrows, the security of knowing that we are not alone, that we are wanted and loved. But these rich benefits also entail responsibilities and risks. To be a member of a family, to be a friend, is to offer not only love but also support and protection, sometimes at considerable sacrifice. And to expose our most private thoughts and feelings can make us vulnerable, for those closest to us have great power to do harm as well as good.

Our earliest contacts are with family, and often our last ones as well. At first we make many demands on our parents, and in time we come to accept those that they make on us. As children we compete vigorously with brothers and sisters for attention and possessions, but in time we may come to see them as friends and allies. We delight in our grandparents' affection, but we share in the responsibility of

113

caring for them in old age and infirmity. If we marry, we may find that new relationship more difficult and complex than we had imagined, for it can often depend at least as much on understanding and tolerance as on love. The family is the school in which we first learn to surrender some of our egotism and to grant other people the same consideration we want from them.

While we have no choice as to the family we are born into, we are free to choose the people we want as friends—and they to choose us. When does an acquaintance become a friend? The change is often gradual, but it probably begins when two people start to seek each other out for no reason other than the pleasure they get from being together, doing things together, or talking about whatever happens to be on their minds. Friendships can be of many kinds and on many levels of intimacy, from temporary relationships that satisfy immediate or special needs to enduring bonds that survive separation and the passage of time. All are valuable in their different ways, and all fill strong human needs.

The selections that follow are concerned in various ways with relationships within families and among friends. Some of these relationships are seen under great stress. A severely retarded child, a senile grandparent, a very old-fashioned father pose rigorous tests of familial love and understanding. And the troubles of friends, especially when we cannot help them, can cause tension and unhappiness. But, as you will see, such difficulties sometimes reveal to people strengths they did not know they had and values they might otherwise never have imagined. And this is what ultimately makes human relationships both trying and rewarding.

S. I. HAYAKAWA

He has been president of San Francisco State College and a United States Senator, but Samuel Ichiyé Hayakawa has been most influential as a scholar and teacher of general semantics, the role and influence of words and their meanings in our lives. Born in Vancouver, Canada, in 1906, Hayakawa attended the University of Manitoba, McGill University, and the University of Wisconsin before beginning a career as a professor of English. Since then he has written several books, including *Language in Thought and Action* (1941), which has been widely used as a textbook in writing and philosophy courses. Hayakawa has also written many articles on a wide range of social and personal issues, making frequent reference to the use of general semantics in everyday life. Some of these have been collected in *Through the Communication Barrier* (1979).

This is one of those articles. It was written for *McCall's* magazine, which is read mainly by women, many of them mothers—some of them no doubt faced with the same dilemma as the Hayakawas, whose son Mark was born with Down's syndrome, a form of retardation. What happened next, and why, is the subject of "Our Son Mark."

Our Son Mark

It was a terrible blow for us to discover that we had brought a 1
retarded child into the world. My wife and I had had no previous acquaintance with the problems of retardation—not even with the words
to discuss it. Only such words as imbecile, idiot, and moron came to
mind. And the prevailing opinion was that such a child must be "put
away," to live out his life in an institution.

Mark was born with Down's syndrome, popularly known as mon- 2
golism. The prognosis for his ever reaching anything approaching nor-
mality was hopeless. Medical authorities advised us that he would show
some mental development, but the progress would be painfully slow and
he would never reach an adolescent's mental age. We could do nothing
about it, they said. They sympathetically but firmly advised us to find a
private institution that would take him. To get him into a public institution, they said, would require a waiting period of five years. To keep
him at home for this length of time, they warned, would have a disastrous
effect on our family.

That was twenty-seven years ago. In that time, Mark has never 3
been "put away." He has lived at home. The only institution he sees
regularly is the workshop he attends, a special workshop for retarded

115

adults. He is as much a part of the family as his mother, his older brother, his younger sister, his father, or our longtime housekeeper and friend, Daisy Rosebourgh.

Mark has contributed to our stability and serenity. His retardation has brought us grief, but we did not go on dwelling on what might have been, and we have been rewarded by finding much good in things the way they are. From the beginning, we have enjoyed Mark for his delightful self. He has never seemed like a burden. He was an "easy" baby, quiet, friendly, and passive; but he needed a baby's care for a long time. It was easy to be patient with him, although I must say that some of his stages, such as his love of making chaos, as we called it, by pulling all the books he could reach off the shelves, lasted much longer than normal children's. 4

Mark seems more capable of accepting things as they are than his immediate relatives; his mental limitation has given him a capacity for contentment, a focus on the present moment, which is often enviable. His world may be circumscribed, but it is a happy and bright one. His enjoyment of simple experiences—swimming, food, birthday candles, sports-car rides, and cuddly cats—has that directness and intensity so many philosophers recommend to all of us. 5

Mark's contentment has been a happy contribution to our family, and the challenge of communicating with him, of doing things we can all enjoy, has drawn the family together. And seeing Mark's communicative processes develop in slow motion has taught me much about the process in all children. 6

Fortunately Mark was born at a time when a whole generation of parents of retarded children had begun to question the accepted dogmas about retardation. Whatever they were told by their physicians about their children, parents began to ask: "Is that so? Let's see." For what is meant by "retarded child"? There are different kinds of retardation. Retarded child No. 1 is not retarded child No. 2, or 3, or 4. Down's syndrome is one condition, while brain damage is something else. There are different degrees of retardation, just as there are different kinds of brain damage. No two retarded children are exactly alike in all respects. Institutional care *does* turn out to be the best answer for some kinds of retarded children or some family situations. The point is that one observes and reacts to the *specific* case and circumstances rather than to the generalization. 7

This sort of attitude has helped public understanding of the nature and problems of retardation to become much deeper and more widespread. It's hard to believe now that it was "definitely known" twenty years ago that institutionalization was the "only way." We were told that 8 a retarded child could not be kept at home because "it would not be fair to the other children." The family would not be able to stand the stress. "Everybody" believed these things and repeated them, to comfort and guide the parents of the retarded.

We did not, of course, lightly disregard the well-meant advice of university neurologists and their social-worker teams, for they had had much experience and we were new at this shattering experience. But our general semantics, or our parental feelings, made us aware that their reaction to Mark was to a generalization, while to us he was an individual. They might have a valid generalization about statistical stresses on statistical families, but they knew virtually nothing about our particular family and its evaluative processes. 9

Mark was eight months old before we were told he was retarded. Of course we had known that he was slower than the average child in smiling, in sitting up, in responding to others around him. Having had one child who was extraordinarily ahead of such schedules, we simply thought that Mark was at the other end of the average range. 10

In the course of his baby checkups, at home and while traveling, we had seen three different pediatricians. None of them gave us the slightest indication that all was not well. Perhaps they were made uncertain by the fact that Mark, with his part Japanese parentage, had a right to have "mongolian" features. Or perhaps this news is as hard for a pediatrician to tell as it is for parents to hear, and they kept putting off the job of telling us. Finally, Mark's doctor did suggest a neurologist, indicating what his fears were, and made an appointment. 11

It was Marge who bore the brunt of the first diagnosis and accompanying advice, given at the university hospital at a time when I had to be out of town. Stunned and crushed, she was told: "Your husband is a professional man. You can't keep a child like this at home." 12

"But he lives on love," she protested. 13

"Don't your other children live on love, too?" the social worker asked. 14

Grief-stricken as she was, my wife was still able to recognize a non sequitur. One does not lessen the love for one's children by dividing it among several. 15

"What can I read to find out more about his condition and how to take care of him?" Marge asked. 16

"You can't get help from a book," answered the social worker. "You must put him away." 17

Today this sounds like dialogue from the Dark Ages. And it *was* the Dark Ages. Today professional advice runs generally in the opposite direction: "Keep your retarded child at home if it's at all possible." 18

It was parents who led the way: They organized into parents' groups; 19
they pointed out the need for preschools, schools, diagnostic centers,
work-training centers, and sheltered workshops to serve the children who
were being cared for at home; they worked to get these services, which
are now being provided in increasing numbers. But the needs are a long
way from being fully met.

Yet even now the cost in money—not to mention the cost in 20
human terms—is much less if the child is kept at home than if he is sent
to the institutions in which children are put away. And many of the
retarded are living useful and independent lives, which would never have
been thought possible for them.

But for us at that time, as for other parents who were unknowingly 21
pioneering new ways for the retarded, it was a matter of going along from
day to day, learning, observing, and saying, "Let's see."

There was one more frightening hurdle for our family to get over. 22
On that traumatic day Marge got the diagnosis, the doctor told her that
it was too risky for us to have any more children, that there was a fifty
percent chance of our having another mongoloid child. In those days,
nothing was known of the cause of mongolism. There were many theories. Now, at least, it is known to be caused by the presence of an extra
chromosome, a fault of cell division. But the question "Why does it
happen?" had not yet been answered.

Today, genetic counseling is available to guide parents as to the 23
probabilities of recurrence on a scientific basis. We were flying blind.
With the help of a doctor friend, we plunged into medical books and
discovered that the doctor who gave us the advice was flying just as blind
as we were. No evidence could be found for the fifty percent odds. Although there did seem to be some danger of recurrence, we estimated
that the probabilities were with us. We took the risk and won.

Our daughter, Wynne, is now twenty-five. She started as Mark's 24
baby sister, soon passed him in every way, and really helped bring him
up. The fact that she had a retarded brother must have contributed at
least something to the fact that she is at once delightfully playful and
mature, observant, and understanding. She has a fine relationship with
her two brothers.

Both Wynne and Alan, Mark's older brother, have participated, 25
with patience and delight, in Mark's development. They have shown
remarkable ingenuity in instructing and amusing him. On one occasion,
when Mark was not drinking his milk, Alan called him to his place at
the table and said, "I'm a service station. What kind of car are you?"
Mark, quickly entering into the make-believe, said, "Pord."

Alan: "Shall I fill her up?"   26

Mark: "Yes."   27

Alan: "Ethyl or regular?"   28

Mark: "Reg'lar."   29

Alan (bringing the glass to Mark's mouth): "Here you are."   30

When Mark finished his glass of milk, Alan asked him, "Do you   31
want your windshield cleaned?" Then, taking a napkin, he rubbed it
briskly across Mark's face, while Mark grinned with delight. This routine
became a regular game for many weeks.

Alan and Wynne interpret and explain Mark to their friends, but   32
never once have I heard them apologize for him or deprecate him. It is
almost as if they judge the quality of other people by how they react to
Mark. They think he is "great," and expect their friends to think so too.

Their affection and understanding were shown when Wynne flew   33
to Oregon with Mark to visit Alan and his wife, Cynthea, who went to
college there. Wynne described the whole reunion as "tremendous" and
especially enjoyed Mark's delight in the trip."

"He was great on the plane," she recalls. "He didn't cause any   34
trouble except that he rang the bell for the stewardess a couple of times
when he didn't need anything. He was so great that I was going to send
him back on the plane alone. He would have enjoyed that." But she
didn't, finally, because she didn't trust others to be able to understand
his speech or to know how to treat him without her there to give them
clues.

Mark looks reasonably normal. He is small for his age (about five   35
feet tall) and childlike. Anyone who is aware of these matters would
recognize in him some of the characteristic symptomatic features, but
they are not extreme. His almost incomprehensible speech, which few
besides his family and teachers can understand, is his most obvious sign
of retardation.

Mark fortunately does not notice any stares of curiosity he may   36
attract. To imagine how one looks in the eyes of others takes a level of
awareness that appears to be beyond him. Hence he is extremely direct
and totally without self-consciousness.

I have seen him come into our living room, walk up to a woman   37
he has never seen before, and kiss her in response to a genuinely friendly
greeting. Since few of us are accustomed to such directness of expression—especially the expression of affection—the people to whom this
has happened are deeply moved.

Like other children, Mark responds to the evaluations of others. In   38
our family, he is accepted just as he is. Because others have always treated

him as an individual, a valued individual, he feels good about himself, and, consequently, he is good to live with. In every situation between parent and child or between children, evaluations are involved—and these interact on each other. Certainly, having Mark at home has helped us be more aware and be more flexible in our evaluations.

This kind of sensitivity must have carried over into relations between the two normal children, because I cannot remember a single real fight or a really nasty incident between Alan and Wynne. It's as if their readiness to try to understand Mark extended into a general method of dealing with people. And I think Marge and I found the same thing happening to us, so that we became more understanding with Alan and Wynne than we might otherwise have been. If we had time and patience for Mark, why not for the children who were quick and able? We knew we could do serious damage to Mark by expecting too much of him and being disappointed. But how easy it is to expect too much of bright children and how quickly they feel your disappointment! Seeing Mark's slow, slow progress certainly gave us real appreciation of the marvelous perception and quick learning processes of the other two, so that all we had to do was open our eyes and our ears, and listen and enjoy them. 39

I don't want to sound as if we were never impatient or obtuse as parents. We were, of course. But parents need to be accepted as they are, too. And I think our children—bless their hearts—were reasonably able to do so. 40

With Mark, it was easy to feel surprise and delight at any of his accomplishments. He cannot read and will never be able to. But he can pick out on request almost any record from his huge collection—Fleetwood Mac, or the Rolling Stones, or Christmas carols—because he knows so well what each record looks like. Once we were discussing the forthcoming marriage of some friends of ours, and Mark disappeared into his playroom to bring out, a few minutes later, a record with the song "A House, a Car, and a Wedding Ring." 41

His love of music enables him to figure out how to operate almost any record changer or hi-fi set. He never tries to force a piece of machinery because he cannot figure out how it works, as brighter people often do. And in a strange hotel room, with a TV set of unknown make, it is Mark—not Marge or I—who figures out how to turn it on and get a clear picture. As Alan once remarked: "Mark may be retarded, but he's not stupid!" 42

Of course, it has not all been easy—but when has easiness been the test of the value of anything? To us, the difficult problems that must be faced in the future only emphasize the value of Mark as a person. 43

What does that future hold for Mark?   44

He will never be able to be independent; he will always have to   45
live in a protected environment. His below-50 IQ reflects the fact that
he cannot cope with unfamiliar situations.

Like most parents of the retarded, we are concentrating on provid-   46
ing financial security for Mark in the future, and fortunately we expect
to be able to achieve this. Alan and his wife and Wynne have all offered
to be guardians for Mark. It is wonderful to know they feel this way. But
we hope that Mark can find a happy place in one of the new residence
homes for the retarded.

The residence home is something new and promising and it fills an   47
enormous need. It is somewhat like a club, or a family, with a house-
mother or manager. The residents share the work around the house, go
out to work if they can, share in recreation and companionship. Away
from their families, who may be overprotective and not aware of how
much the retarded can do for themselves (are we not guilty of this, too!),
they are able to live more fully as adults.

An indication that there is still much need for public education   48
about the retarded here in California is that there has been difficulty in
renting decent houses for this kind of home. Prospective neighbors have
objected. In some ways the Dark Ages are still with us; there are still
fear and hostility where the retarded are concerned.

Is Mark able to work? Perhaps. He thrives on routine and enjoys   49
things others despise, like clearing the table and loading the dishwasher.
To Mark, it's fun. It has been hard to develop in him the idea of work,
which to so many of us is "doing what you don't want to do because you
have to." We don't know yet if he could work in a restaurant loading a
dishwasher. In school, he learned jobs like sorting and stacking scrap
wood and operating a delightful machine that swoops the string around
and ties up a bundle of wood to be sold in the supermarket. That's fun,
too.

He is now in a sheltered workshop where he can get the kind—   50
the one kind—of pleasure he doesn't have much chance for. That's the
pleasure of contributing something productive and useful to the outside
world. He does various kinds of assembling jobs, packaging, sorting, and
simple machine operations. He enjoys getting a paycheck and cashing it
at the bank. He cannot count, but he takes pride in reaching for the
check in a restaurant and pulling out his wallet. And when we thank
him for dinner, he glows with pleasure.

It's a strange thing to say, and I am a little startled to find myself   51
saying it, but often I feel that I wouldn't have had Mark any different.

About the Essay

1. The Hayakawas were warned that Mark, if kept at home, would have a "disastrous effect" on the family. Why? What effect did Mark actually have on his parents, his brother, and his sister?

2. What do you believe was Hayakawa's purpose in writing this essay? Apart from what the essay says about Mark, and about Down's syndrome, what important point does it make?

3. How did the Hayakawas' sensitivity to the uses and misuses of language affect their responses to professional advice about Mark?

4. Several times Hayakawa refers to the Dark Ages. What were the Dark Ages? Why are they relevant to Hayakawa's account?

5. Does the essay ever suggest that the Hayakawas may at times have found Mark's behavior irritating, or worse? How does this affect your response to the essay?

Explorations

1. Sometimes it is wise to accept and follow expert advice. At other times it may be necessary to disregard such advice and make one's own decision. Have you ever deliberately gone against an authoritative opinion? Recount the episode, and say whether on reflection you still think your decision was a good one.

2. What is now known about Down's syndrome—its cause, its treatment, its risks?

3. According to many books, magazine articles, and television documentaries, the American family is "in trouble." Do you agree? What exactly does such a statement mean to you? Is it a meaningful statement at all?

JULIA ALVAREZ

Julia Alvarez was born in New York City in 1950 but spent her early childhood in the Dominican Republic, the homeland of both her parents. Bilingual from her early years, she returned to New York at the age of ten and later attended Abbot Academy, Middlebury College, and Syracuse University. Her poetry and short fiction have been published in such small magazines and anthologies as the *American Poetry Review, Poetry Magazine, Revista Chicano-Riqueña,* and the *Cincinnati Review.* In the following selection Alvarez draws a loving and detailed portrait of her father, El Doctor, an intriguing gentleman who seems to be of both the old world and the new.

El Doctor

"Lights! At this hour?" my father asks, looking up from his empty dinner plate at the glowing lamp my mother has just turned on above the table. "Are we in Plato's cave, Mother?" He winks at me; as the two readers in the family we show off by making allusions my mother and sisters don't understand. He leans his chair back and picks up the hem of the curtain. A dim gray light falls into the room. "See, Mother. It's still light out there!"

"*Ya, ya!*" she snaps, and flips the switch off.

"Your mother is a wonder," he announces, then he adds, "El Doctor is ready for bed." Dinner is over; every night my father brings the meal to a close with a third-person goodnight before he leaves the room.

Tonight he lingers, watching her. She says nothing, head bent, intent on her mashed plantains with oil and onions. "Yessir," he elaborates, "El Doctor—" The rest is garbled, for he's balled up his napkin and rubbed his lips violently as if he meant to erase them from his face. Perhaps he shouldn't have spoken up? She is jabbing at the few bites of beefsteak on her plate. Perhaps he should have just let the issue drop like water down his chest or whatever it is the Americans say. He scrapes his chair back.

Her scowl deepens. "Eduardo, please." And then, because he already knows better, she adds only, "The wax finish."

"*Por supuesto,*"[1] he says, his voice full of false concern as he examines her spotless kitchen floor for damages. Then, carefully, he lifts

---

[1] Of course.

his chair up and tucks it back in its place. "This old man is ready for bed." He leans over and kisses the scowl off her face. "Mother, this country agrees with you. You look more beautiful every day. Doesn't she, girls?" And with a wink of encouragement to each of us, he leaves us in the dark.

I remember my mother mornings, slapping around in her comfortable slippers, polishing her windows into blinding panes of light. But I remember him mostly at night, moving down the dark halls, undressing as he climbed the dark stairs to bed.   7

I want to say there were as many buttons on his vest as stairs up to the bedroom: it seemed he unbuttoned a button on each step so that by the time he reached the landing, his vest was off. His armor, I thought, secretly pleased with all I believed I understood about him. But his vest couldn't have had more than six buttons, and the stairs were long and narrow. Of course, I couldn't see well in the dark he insisted on.   8

"I'm going to take this dollar," he showed me, holding a bill in one hand and a flickering lighter in the other, "and I'm going to set fire to it." He never actually did. He spoke in parables, he complained in metaphor because he had never learned to say things directly. I already knew what he meant, but I had my part to play.   9

"Why would you want to do something like that?" I asked.   10

"Exactly! Why burn up my money with all these lights in the house!"   11

As we grew up, confirmed in our pyromania, he did not bother to teach us to economize, but went through the house, turning off lights in every room, not noticing many times that we were there, reading or writing a letter, and leaving us in the dark, hurt that he had overlooked us.   12

At the bedroom door he loosened his tie and, craning his neck, undid the top button of his shirt. Then he sat at the edge of the bed and turned on his bedside lamp. Not always; if a little reflected sun dappled the room with shadowy light, if it was late spring or early fall or summertime, he waited until the last moment to turn on the lamp, sometimes reading in the dark until we came in and turned it on for him. "Papi, you're going to ruin your eyes," we scolded.   13

Once I worked it out for him with the pamphlet the electric company sent me. Were he to leave his bedside light, say, burning for the rest of his evenings—and I allowed him a generous four decades ("I won't need it for that long," he protested; I insisted.)—the cost (side by side we multiplied, added, carried over to the next column) would be far less than if he lost his eyesight, was forced to give up his practice, and had to spend the next four decades—   14

"Like your friend Milton," he said, pleased with the inspired pos- 15
sibilities of blindness.[2] Now that I was turning out to be the family poet,
all the greats were my personal friends. " 'When I consider how my light
is spent,' " he began. He loved to recite, racing me through poems to
see who would be the first one to finish.

" 'How my light is spent,' " I echoed and took the lead. " 'Ere half 16
my days, in this dark world and wide . . .' "

Just as I was rounding the linebreak to the last line, he interjected 17
it, " 'They also serve who only stand and wait.' "

I scowled. How dare he clap the last line on after I had gone 18
through all the trouble of reciting the poem! "Not every blind man
is a Milton," I said, and I gave him the smirk I wore all through adolescence.

"Nutrition," he said mysteriously. 19

"What about nutrition?" 20

"Good nutrition. We're starting to see the effects: children grow 21
taller; they have better teeth, better bones, better minds than their elders." And he reached for his book on the bedside table.

Actually, the reading came later. First there is the scene that labels 22
him immigrant and shows why I could never call him, sweetly, playfully,
Daddy. He took from his back pocket a wad of bills so big his hand could
not close over it. And he began to count. If at this point we disturbed
him, he waved us away. If we called from downstairs, he did not answer.
All over the bed he shared with my mother were piles of bills: I do not
know the system; no one ever did. Perhaps all the fives were together,
all the tens? Perhaps each pile was a specific amount? But this was the
one private moment he insisted on. Not even catching him undressing,
which I never did, seems as intimate a glimpse of him.

After the counting came the binding and marking: each pile was 23
held together with rubber bands he saved up from the rolled-up *New
York Times,* and the top bill was scribbled on. He marked them as a
reminder of how much was in each pile, I'm sure, but I can't help thinking it was also his way of owning what he had earned, much as ranchers
brand their cattle. The Secretary of the Treasury had signed this twenty;
there was Andrew Jackson's picture; he had to add his hand to it to make
it his—to try to convince himself that it was his, for he never totally
believed it was. Even after he was a successful doctor in New York with
a house in the suburbs and lands at "home," his daughters in boarding

---

[2]John Milton (1608–1674) was an English poet who became blind in his early forties
and in 1655 wrote the sonnet from which the Alvarezes quote.

schools and summer camps, a second car with enough gadgets to keep him busy in bad traffic, he was turning off lights, frequenting thrift shops for finds in ties, taking the 59th Street bridge even if it was out of his way to avoid paying a toll to cross the river.

He could not afford the good life, he could only pass it on. And he did. Beneath the surface pennypinching, his extravagance might have led him to bankruptcy several times had mother not been there to remind him that the weather was apt to change. "Save for a snowy day," she advised him. 24

"Julie! Isn't it rainy day?" he enlisted me. He was always happy to catch his wife at an error since she spoke English so much better than he did. "Save it for a rainy day?" 25

Eager to be an authority on anything, I considered Arbiter of Clichés a compliment to my literary talent. "Save it for a rainy day," I agreed. 26

"See, Mother." 27

She defended herself. "Snow is much worse than rain. For one thing, you need to own more clothes in the winter . . ." 28

Out from his pocket came a ten when we needed small change for the subway. Away at college I opened the envelope, empty but for the money order for fifty, a hundred; typed out in the blank beside *for* was his memo: "Get yourself a little something in my name." It was the sixties and parental money was under heavy suspicion; my friends needed me as a third world person to be a good example of poverty and oppression by the capitalist, military-industrial complex. I put my little somethings quietly in the bank. By the time I graduated from college, I had a small corrupt fortune. 29

But my rich father lived in the dark, saving string, going the long way. I've analyzed it with my economist friends. Perhaps since his fortune came from the same work which in his country had never earned him enough, he could never believe that his being well-to-do wasn't an I.R.S. oversight. My psychologist friends claim that it is significant that he was the youngest of twenty-five children. Coming after so many, he would always fear that the good things would run out. And indeed he had a taste for leftovers, which made his compliments come a day or two after a special meal. Whenever we had chicken, he insisted on the wings and the neck bone because those had been the portions left by the time the platter got to him, the baby. He liked the pale, bitter center of the lettuce. ("The leaves were gone when I got the salad bowl.") And when we had soup, he was surprised to find a piece of meat bobbing at the surface. "Someone missed this one." 30

Unlike mother, he saved for a sunny day. Extravaganza! On his birthday, on Christmas, on his saint's day which was never celebrated 31 for anyone else, his presents multiplied before us. Beside the ones we had bought for him, there were always other glossy packages, ribboned boxes which dwarfed ours. The cards were forged: "To my dearest father from his loving daughter." "Which of you gave me this?" he asked with mock surprise and real delight. Cordelias all, we shook our heads as he unwrapped a silk lounging jacket or a genuine leather passport case.[3] I wish he had allowed someone to give him something.

Perhaps we did on those evenings after the money was counted and put away, and he was ready for company. With an instinct for his rituals, we knew when it was time to come into the bedroom. We heard the bathroom door click shut; he was undressing, putting on his pajamas. The hamper lid clapped on its felt lip. We heard steps. The bed creaked. We found him in the darkening room with a book. "Papi, you're ruining your eyes!" and we turned on the bedside lamp for him since he could not give himself the luxury of that light. "Oh my God, it's gotten dark already," he almost thanked us.

He wanted company, not conversation. He had us turn on the television so we could learn our English. This after years here, after his money had paid for the good private schools which unrolled our r's and softened our accents; after American boyfriends had whispered sweet colloquialisms in our ears. As the television's cowboys and beauty queens and ladies with disappointing stains in their wash droned on in their native English, he read the usual: a history book in Spanish. We sat at the edge of the king-size bed and wondered what he wanted from us. He wanted presences: Walter Cronkite, his children, his wife, the great gods of the past, Napoleon, Caesar, Maximilian.[4] If one of us, bored with his idea of company, got up to leave, he lowered his book. "Did you know that in the campaign of 1808, Napoleon left his General behind to cut off the enemy from the rear, and the two divisions totally missed each other?" That was the only way he knew to ask us to stay, appealing to history and defeat, to wintry campaigns, bloody frost-bitten feet, a field strewn with war dead.

I taste the mints that he gave us, one each. He kept a stash of them in a drawer next to his bed like a schoolboy and ate exactly one each night and gave away four. That was the other way he kept us there if we got up to go after Napoleon's troops had been annihilated. "Don't you want a mint?" He didn't mean right then and there. It was a promise

32

33

34

---

[3]Cordelia is the faithful daughter of Shakespeare's *King Lear*, who refuses to compete with his other daughters in making exaggerated claims of love for him.

[4]The emperors of France (1805–1814), ancient Rome (31 B.C. to 14 A.D.), and Mexico (1864–1867).

we had to wait for, perhaps until the chapter ended or the Roman empire fell or he was sure we had given up on the evening and decided to stay, talking in code with each other about school, our friends, our wild (for that room) adventures.

We were not fooled into rash confessions there, for at the merest 35 hint of misadventure, the book came down like a coffin lid on Caesar or Claudius.[5] Oh, we confessed, we were just exaggerating! Of course we didn't raid the dorm kitchen at midnight, our friends did. "Tell me who your friends are," he said in Spanish, "and I'll tell you who *you* are." No, we hadn't gotten help on our math. "The man who reaches the summit following another's trail will not find his way back to his own valley." If he caught us, hurrying, scurrying, here, there, he stopped us mid-flight to tell us what Napoleon had said to his valet, "Dress me slowly, I'm in a hurry."

But why look beyond one's own blood for good examples? "You 36 come from good stock," he bragged when I came home from boarding school, my pride wounded. I'd been called ugly names by some great great granddaughters of the American Revolution. "You tell them your great grandfather was the son of a count." He had paid a lot of money on a trip to Barcelona to find that out from a man who claimed he was licensed to do family trees. The elaborate chart, magnificently framed in curlicued wood, hung in the waiting room of his office in Spanish Brooklyn along with his medical degrees. His patients, I suppose, were meant to be reassured that their ailments would be treated, not only by the valedictorian of the faculty of medicine of La Universidad de Santo Domingo, but also by the descendant of a count. "We were in this hemisphere before they were. In fact, the first group of Puritans—"

"You don't understand, you don't understand," I wailed, hot tears 37 welling in my eyes. And I closed the door of my room, forbidding anyone to enter.

"What's she doing in there, Mother?" I heard him ask her. 38

"I don't know. Writing poetry or something." 39

"Are you sure? You think she's all right?" 40

I had been reading Sylvia Plath and my talk was spiked with sui- 41 cide.[6]

"These girls are going to drive us crazy!" My mother said. "That's 42 what I'm sure of. One of them has to have straight hair. Straight hair, at this stage of the game! Another wants to spend the weekend at a boy's school. All the other girls get to! This one wants to die young and

---

[5]Claudius was another emperor of ancient Rome (41–54 A.D.).
[6]Sylvia Plath was an American poet (1932–1963) who killed herself.

miserable!" Then she yelled at father. "I'm going to end up in Bellevue![7] And then you're all going to be very sorry!" I heard the rushed steps down the stairs, the bang of the screen door, finally the patter of the hose as she watered the obedient grass in the growing dark.

He knocked first. "Hello?" he asked tentatively, the door ajar. 43 "Hello, hello, Edgar Allan Poe," he teased, entering. He sat at the foot of my bed and told me the story of his life.

"The point is," he concluded, " '*La vida es sueño y los sueños, sueños* 44 *son.*' " He stood by the window and watched mother watering her fussy bushes as if she could flush roses out of them. "My father," he turned to me, "used to say that to my mother: Life is a dream, Mauran, and dreams are dreams."

He came across the shadowy room as if he did not want anyone to 45 overhear. It was getting late. In the darkening garden she would be winding the hose into drooping coils. "Always, always," he said. "I always wanted to be a poet. '*La vida es sueño.*' 'They also serve who only stand and wait.' 'To be or not to be.'[8] Can you imagine! To say such things! My God! Everyone gets a little something." He cupped his hands towards me. I nodded, too stunned at his flood of words to ask him what he meant. "And some make a building," he made a building with a wave of his hand. "Some," he rubbed his thumb and index finger together, "make money. Some make friends, connections, you know. But some, some make something that can change the thinking of mankind! Oh my God!" He smacked his forehead with his palm in disbelief. "Think of the Bible. Think of your friend Edgar Allan Poe. But then," he mused, "then you grow older, you discover . . ." He looked down at me. I don't know what he saw in my eyes, perhaps how young I still was, perhaps his eyes duplicated in my face. He stopped himself.

"You discover?" I said. 46

But he was already half way across the room. "Papi?" I tried to call 47 him back.

"Your mother," he explained, letting himself out of the room and 48 the revelation. "I think she is calling for me."

A few days later as I sat in his bedroom after supper, waiting for 49 him to fall asleep, I tried to get him to finish his sentence. He couldn't remember what he was about to say, he said, but speaking of discoveries, "We're descended from the conquistadores, you know? Your grandfather

---

[7]Bellevue Hospital is New York City's main receiving center for the insane.

[8]Literary allusions. *La vida es sueño* (*Life Is a Dream*) is a play by the Spanish playwright Pedro Calderón de la Barca (1600–1681); "To be or not to be" is part of the famous soliloquy from Shakespeare's *Hamlet*.

traveled the whole north coast on horseback![9] Now there was a great man!" The supporting evidence was slim. "He looked like an Irishman. Ah, he was big and pink-tinted—what is that word, Julie? *Rowdy?*"

"You mean *ruddy?*" I said, knowing Don Jose de Jesus was probably   50
ruddy with drink and rowdy with women. He had sired twenty-five children, widowed once, and kept four or five mistresses who raised the figure to thirty-five children. Of course, father never told us that; mother did when she explained how one of our uncles could be born within two months of father's birthday. She cautioned us never ever to mention to father what she had told us.

The youngest did, pretending ignorance, practicing addition. If   51
Teolinda, the first wife, had ten children, and Mauran, the second one, had fifteen, and four of the kids had already died, then how come there were still thirty uncles and aunts left? "They were not hijos de padre y madre,"[10] he explained. "You know where that term came from? *Hijos de padre y madre?* When the Spaniards—"

"Where did the extra uncles and aunts come from?" She was not   52
one to be diverted by a red herring twitching in the sun when a skeleton was rattling in the closet.

So, so, he said. The time had come. The uncles and aunts were   53
half brothers and sisters. The mothers *were* wives, yes, in the eyes of God, where it really mattered.

When we raised our eyebrows and pressed the smile out of our lips,   54
he would have none of it. Customs changed. Our grandfather was a patriotic man. There had been a terrible epidemic, the island was underpopulated, the birthrate was low, the best men did what what they had to do. "So," he looked pointedly at each of us. "There's a good *ejemplo*[11] for you. Always put in that extra little bit in whatever you do," he said, lifting up the history of Constantinople or Machu Picchu or Rome.

His mother? He sighed. Don't talk to him about his mother! A saint!   55
Sweet, very religious, patience personified, always smiling. They didn't make them like that anymore, with a few exceptions, he winked at me.

But since Mauran knew about the half children, and being very   56
religious, she must have believed her husband and she would spend eternity separated, I imagined her as a dour and dowdy woman alternately saying her rosary when her husband transgressed or having his children when he didn't.

---

[9]Refers to the north coast of the Caribbean island of Hispaniola.
[10]Children of father and mother.
[11]Example.

"Does mother remind you of her?" I asked, thinking that leading questions might help him remember what he had been about to say in my room a few nights ago.

"Your mother is a wonder," he said. A good woman, so devoted, so thorough, a little nervous, so giving, a little forceful, a good companion, a little too used to her own way, so generous. "Every garland needs a few thorns," he added.

"I heard that," she said, coming into the room. "What was that about too used to my own way?"

"Did I say that, girls?" father turned to us. "No, Mami, you misheard."

"Then what did you say?"

"What did I say, girls?"

We shrugged, leaving him wide open.

"I said, Mother," he said, unwrapping a rare second mint and putting it in his mouth to buy time. "I said: so used to giving to others. Mother, you're too generous!"

"Ay, put gravy on the chicken." She waved him off, terribly pleased as father winked at our knowing looks.

A few nights later, still on the track of his secret self, I asked him, "Papi, how do you see yourself?" Only I, who had achieved a mild reputation as a deep thinker, could get away with such questions.

"You ask deep questions," he mused, interrupting Napoleon's advance across the Russian steppes. "I like that."

He offered me my mint and unwrapped his. "I am the rock," he said, nodding.

"Ay, Papi, that's too impersonal. How do you perceive yourself? What kind of man are you?" I was young and thought such definitions could be given and trusted. I was young and ready to tear loose, but making it harder for myself by trying to understand those I was about to wound.

"I am a rock," he repeated, liking his analogy. "Mother, you girls, my sisters, everyone needs my support. I am the strong one!"

That admission put a mermaid on the rock, luring me back with a delicate song about loss and youth's folly and the loneliness of the father. "But, Papi," I whispered as I moved from the armchair to the foot of his bed, "you don't always have to be strong."

That was my mistake. The conversation was over. He hated touching scenes; they confused him. Perhaps as the last child of an older, disappointed woman, he was used to diffuse attention, not intimacy. To take hold of a hand, to graze a cheek and whisper an endearment were beyond him. Tenderness had to be mothered by necessity: he was a good doctor. Under the cover of Hippocrates' oath, with the stethoscope around his neck and the bright examination light flushing out the personal and making any interchange terribly professional, he was amazingly delicate: tapping a bone as if it were the fontenelle of a baby, easing a patient back on a pillow like a lover his sleeping beloved, stroking hair away from a feverish forehead. But now he turned away.

He fell asleep secretly in that room full of presences, my mother   73
beside him. No one knew exactly when it happened. We looked to him during a commercial or when a slip had implicated us in some forbidden adventure, and the book had collapsed like a card house on his chest and his glasses rode the bridge of his nose like a schoolmarm's. Though if we got up to leave and one of us reached for his glasses he woke with a start. "I'm not asleep!" he lied. "Don't go yet, it's early."

He fell asleep in the middle of the Hundred Days while Napoleon   74
marched towards Waterloo or, defeated, was shipped off to St. Helena. We stifled our giggles at his comic-book snores, the sheets pulled over his head, his nose poking out like a periscope. Very quietly, widening our eyes at each other as if that might stop any noise, we rose. One turned off the set and threw a kiss at mother, who put her finger to her lips from her far side of the bed. Another and another kiss traveled across the hushed room. A scolding wave from mother hurried my sisters out.

I liked to be the one who stayed, bending over the bedside table   75
strewn with candy wrappers, slipping a hand under the tassled shade. I turned the switch over, once. The room burst into brighter light, the tassels swung madly, mother signaled to me, crossly, Out! Out at once! I shrugged apologies. Her scowl deepened. Father groaned. I bent closer. I turned again. The room went back into economical dark.

About the Essay

1. How does the author regard her father? Does she understand him? What tone does her description of him take? Show examples from the text.

2. What contrasts in her father's character does Alvarez reveal? How do you account for his simultaneous frugality and extravagance? What do you make of his constantly turning off the lights?

3. The author and her father make use of a number of literary and historical allusions in their conversations. Why do you think they use so many allusions? What do the allusions add to our understanding of their relationship?

4. Alvarez presents a detailed picture of her father, yet gives very few physical details. Do you think she does so successfully? If so, how? How might more physical description have changed the effect of her portrait?

5. In "El Doctor" Alvarez has written about her family, an extremely personal subject which could cause her to become sentimental. Has she done so? If so, where?

Explorations

1. What did you learn about the family and family life by reading "El Doctor"? Is this family like yours in its interrelationships, in the way its members communicate with each other, in what they talk about and keep secret, in the roles they play? Describe the similarities and the differences.

2. Write a detailed sketch of your father or mother. Like Alvarez does, you should try to portray his or her ways of dress, talk, and action, as well as the ways that he or she relates to you.

ANTHONY BRANDT

Anthony Brandt was born in Cranford, New Jersey, in 1936 and studied at Princeton and Columbia. After a brief career in business, he became a freelance writer and has contributed essays and poems to such magazines as the *Atlantic Monthly, Prairie Schooner,* and the *New York Quarterly.* He published *Reality Police: The Experience of Insanity in America* in 1975 and is presently at work on a book about the American dream, which he says will attempt to define that dream and trace its origins and development.

As a young boy, Brandt was forced to watch his beloved grandmother slowly lose her grip on reality and gradually slide into senility. Thirty years later his mother, too, has had to be consigned to a nursing home, no longer able to take care of herself. In the following memoir, first published in the *Atlantic Monthly,* Brandt describes the two cases and what they have meant to him.

Rite of Passage: A Memoir

Some things that happen to us can't be borne, with the paradoxical result that we carry them on out backs the rest of our lives. I have been half obsessed for almost thirty years with the death of my grandmother. I should say with her dying: with the long and terrible changes that came at the worst time for a boy of twelve and thirteen, going through his own difficult changes. It felt like and perhaps was the equivalent of a puberty rite: dark, frightening, aboriginal, an obscure emotional exchange between old and young. It has become part of my character. 1

I grew up in New Jersey in a suburban town where my brother still lives and practices law. One might best describe it as quiet, protected, and green; it was no preparation for death. Tall, graceful elm trees lined both sides of the street where we lived. My father's brother-in-law, a contractor, built our house; we moved into it a year after I was born. My grandmother and grandfather (my mother's parents; they were the only grandparents who mattered) lived up the street "on the hill"; it wasn't much of a hill, the terrain in that part of New Jersey being what it is, but we could ride our sleds down the street after it snowed, and that was hilly enough. 2

Our family lived, or seemed to a young boy to live, in very stable, very ordinary patterns. My father commuted to New York every day, taking the Jersey Central Railroad, riding in cars that had windows you could open, getting off the train in Jersey City and taking a ferry to Manhattan. He held the same job in the same company for more than 3 thirty years. The son of Swedish immigrants, he was a funny man who could wiggle his ears without raising his eyebrows and made up the most dreadful puns. When he wasn't being funny he was quiet, the newspaper his shield and companion, or the *Saturday Evening Post,* which he brought home without fail every Wednesday evening, or *Life,* which he brought home Fridays. It was hard to break through the quiet and the humor, and after he died my mother said, as much puzzled as disturbed, that she hardly knew him at all.

She, the backbone of the family, was fierce, stern, the kind of person who can cow you with a glance. My brother and I, and my cousins, were all a little in awe of her. The ruling passion in her life was to protect her family; she lived in a set of concentric circles, sons and husband the closest, then nieces, nephews, brothers, parents, then more distant relatives, and outside that a few friends, very few. No one and nothing else existed for her; she had no interest in politics, art, history, or even the price of eggs. "Fierce" is the best word for her, or single-minded. In those days (I was born in 1936) polio was every parent's bugbear; she, to keep my brother and me away from places where the disease was supposed to be communicated, particularly swimming pools, took us every summer for the entire summer to the Jersey shore, first to her parents' cottage, later to a little cottage she and my father bought. She did that even though it meant being separated from my father for nearly three months, having nobody to talk to, having to handle my brother and me on her own. She hated it, she told us years later, but she did it: fiercely. Or there's the story of one of my cousins who got pregnant when she was sixteen or seventeen; my mother took her into our house, managed somehow to hide her condition from the neighbors, then, after the birth, arranged privately to have the child adopted by a family the doctor recommended, all this being done without consulting the proper authorities, and for the rest of her life never told a single person how she made these arrangements or where she had placed the child. She was a genuine primitive, like some tough old peasant woman. Yet her name was Grace, her nickname Bunny; if you saw through the fierceness, you understood that it was a version of love.

Her mother, my grandmother, seemed anything but fierce. One of our weekly routines was Sunday dinner at their house on the hill, some five or six houses from ours. When I was very young, before World War II, the house had a mansard roof, a barn in the back, lots of yard space, lots of rooms inside, and a cherry tree. I thought it was a palace. Actually it was rather small, and became smaller when my grandmother insisted on tearing down the mansard roof and replacing it with a conventional peaked roof; the house lost three attic rooms in the process. Sunday dinner was invariably roast beef or chicken or leg of lamb with mashed potatoes and vegetables, standard American fare but cooked by my grand-parents' Polish maid, Josephine, not by my grandmother. Josephine made wonderful pies in an old cast-iron coal stove and used to let me tie her with string to the kitchen sink. My grandfather was a gentle man who smoked a pipe, had a bristly reddish moustache, and always seemed to wind up paying everybody else's debts in the family; my mother wor-shipped him. There were usually lots of uncles at these meals, and they were a playful bunch. I have a very early memory of two of them tossing me back and forth between them, and another of the youngest, whose name was Don, carrying me on his shoulders into the surf. I also remem-ber my grandmother presiding at these meals. She was gray-haired and benign.

Later they sold that house. My benign grandmother, I've been told since, was in fact a restless, unsatisfied woman; changing the roof line, moving from house to house, were her ways of expressing that dissatis-faction. In the next house, I think it was, my grandfather died; my grandmother moved again, then again, and then to a house down the street, at the bottom of the hill this time, and there I got to know her better. I was nine or ten years old. She let me throw a tennis ball against the side of the house for hours at a time; the noise must have been terribly aggravating. She cooked lunch for me and used to make pancakes the size of dinner plates, and corn fritters. She also made me a whole set of yarn figures a few inches long, rolling yarn around her hand, taking the roll and tying off arms, legs, and a head, then sewing a face onto the head with black thread. I played with these and an odd assortment of hand-me-down toy soldiers for long afternoons, setting up wars, foot-ball games, contests of all kinds, and designating particular yarn figures as customary heroes. Together we played a spelling game: I'd be on the floor playing with the yarn figures, she'd be writing a letter and ask me how to spell "appreciate" (it was always that word), and I'd spell it for her while she pretended to be impressed with my spelling ability and I pretended that she hadn't asked me to spell that same word a dozen times before. I was good, too, at helping her find her glasses.

One scene at this house stands out. My uncle Bob came home from the war and the whole family, his young wife, other uncles, my mother and father and brother and I, gathered at the house to meet him, and he came in wearing his captain's uniform and looking to me, I swear it, like a handsome young god. In fact he was an ordinary man who spent the rest of his life selling insurance. He had been in New Guinea, a ground officer in the Air Corps, and the story I remember is of the native who came into his tent one day and took a great deal of interest in the scissors my uncle was using. The native asked in pidgin English what my uncle would require for the scissors in trade, and he jokingly said, well, how about a tentful of bananas. Sure enough, several days later two or three hundred natives came out of the jungle, huge bunches of bananas on their shoulders, and filled my uncle's tent.

Things went on this way for I don't know how long, maybe two years, maybe three. I don't want to describe it as idyllic. Youth has its problems. But this old woman who could never find her glasses was wonderful to me, a grandmother in the true likeness of one, and I couldn't understand the changes when they came. She moved again, against all advice, this time to a big, bare apartment on the other side of town. She was gradually becoming irritable and difficult, not much fun to be around. There were no more spelling games; she stopped writing letters. Because she moved I saw her less often, and her home could no longer be a haven for me. She neglected it, too; it grew dirtier and dirtier, until my mother eventually had to do her cleaning for her. [8]

Then she began to see things that weren't there. A branch in the back yard became a woman, I remember, who apparently wasn't fully clothed, and a man was doing something to her, something unspeakable. She developed diabetes and my mother learned to give her insulin shots, but she wouldn't stop eating candy, the worst thing for her, and the diabetes got worse. Her face began to change, to slacken, to lose its shape and character. I didn't understand these things; arteriosclerosis, hardening of the arteries, whatever the explanation, it was only words. What I noticed was that her white hair was getting thinner and harder to control, that she herself seemed to be shrinking even as I grew, that when she looked at me I wasn't sure it was me she was seeing anymore. [9]

After a few months of this, we brought her to live with us. My mother was determined to take care of her, and certain family pressures were brought to bear too. That private man my father didn't like the idea at all, but he said nothing, which was his way. And she was put in my brother's bedroom over the garage, my brother moving in with me. It was a small house, six rooms and a basement, much too small for what we had to face. [10]

What we had to face was a rapid deterioration into senile dementia and the rise from beneath the surface of this smiling, kindly, white-haired old lady of something truly ugly. Whenever she was awake she called for attention, calling, calling a hundred times a day. Restless as always, she picked the bedclothes off, tore holes in sheets and pillows, took off her nightclothes and sat naked talking to herself. She hallucinated more and [11] more frequently, addressing her dead husband, a dead brother, scolding, shouting at their apparitions. She became incontinent and smeared feces on herself, the furniture, the walls. And always calling—"Bunny, where are you? Bunny, I want you!"—scolding, demanding; she could seldom remember what she wanted when my mother came. It became an important event when she fell asleep; to make sure she stayed asleep the radio was kept off, the four of us tiptoed around the house, and when I went out to close the garage door, directly under her window (it was an overhead door and had to be pulled down), I did it so slowly and carefully, half an inch at a time, that it sometimes took me a full fifteen minutes to get it down.

That my mother endured this for six months is a testimony to her   12
strength and determination, but it was really beyond her and almost destroyed her health. My grandmother didn't often sleep through the night; she would wake up, yell, cry, a creature of disorder, a living *memento mori*,[1] and my mother would have to tend to her. The house began to smell in spite of all my mother's efforts to keep my grandmother's room clean. My father, his peace gone, brooded in his chair behind his newspaper. My brother and I fought for *Lebensraum*,[2] each of us trying to grow up in his own way. People avoided us. My uncles were living elsewhere—Miami, Cleveland, Delaware. My grandmother's two surviving sisters, who lived about ten blocks away, never came to see her. Everybody seemed to sense that something obscene was happening, and stayed away. Terrified, I stayed away, too. I heard my grandmother constantly, but in the six months she lived with us I think I went into her room only once. That was as my mother wished it. She was a nightmare, naked and filthy without warning.

After six months, at my father's insistence, after a night nurse had   13
been hired and left, after my mother had reached her limits and beyond, my parents started looking for a nursing home, anyplace they could put her. It became a family scandal; the two sisters were outraged that my mother would consider putting her own mother in a home, there were telephone calls back and forth between them and my uncles, but of course the sisters had never come to see her themselves, and my mother never forgave them. One of my uncles finally came from Cleveland, saw what was happening, and that day they put my grandmother in a car and drove her off to the nearest state mental hospital. They brought her back the same day; desperate as they were, they couldn't leave her in hell. At

---

[1]A remembrance of death, usually a work of art with symbols of death or mortality, such as a skull.

[2]Living space, room for growth, development, or the like.

last, when it had come time to go to the shore, they found a nursing home in the middle of the Pine Barrens, miles from anywhere, and kept her there for a while. That, too, proving unsatisfactory, they put her in a small nursing home in western New Jersey, about two hours away by car. We made the drive every Sunday for the next six months, until my grandmother finally died. I always waited in the car while my mother visited her. At the funeral I refused to go into the room for one last look at the body. I was afraid of her still. The whole thing had been a subtle act of violence, a violation of the sensibilities, made all the worse by the fact that I knew it wasn't really her fault, that she was a victim of biology, of life itself. Hard knowledge for a boy just turned fourteen. She became the color of all my expectations.

Life is savage, then, and even character is insecure. Call no man 14 happy until he be dead, said the Greek lawgiver Solon. But what would a wise man say to this? In that same town in New Jersey, that town I have long since abandoned as too flat and too good to be true, my mother, thirty year older now, weighing in at ninety-two pounds, incontinent, her white hair wild about her head, sits strapped into a chair in another nursing home talking incoherently to her fellow patients and working her hands at the figures she thinks she sees moving around on the floor. It's enough to make stones weep to see this fierce, strong woman, who paid her dues, surely, ten times over, reduced to this.

Yet she is *cheerful.* This son comes to see her and she quite literally 15 babbles with delight, introduces him (as her father, her husband—the connections are burnt out) to the aides, tells him endless stories that don't make any sense at all, and *shines,* shines with a clear light that must be her soul. Care and bitterness vanish in her presence. Helpless, the victim of numerous tiny strokes—"shower strokes," the doctors call them—that are gradually destroying her brain, she has somehow achieved a radiant serenity that accepts everything that happens and incorporates and transforms it.

Is there a lesson in this? Is some pattern larger than life working 16 itself out; is this some kind of poetic justice on display, a mother balancing a grandmother, gods demonstrating reasons beyond our comprehension? It was a bitter thing to put her into that place, reeking of disinfectant, full of senile, dying old people, and I used to hate to visit her there, but as she has deteriorated she has also by sheer force of example managed to change my attitude. If she can be reconciled to all this, why can't I? It doesn't last very long, but after I've seen her, talked to her for half an hour, helped feed her, stroked her hair, I walk away amazed, as if I had been witness to a miracle.

About the Essay

1. What, for Brandt, is the meaning of his experiences with his grandmother and mother? How have those experiences affected his attitude toward life? What meaning does the essay have for you?

2. A "rite of passage" is a ritual associated with an important change in one's life. Brandt finds an analogy between his experiences with his grandmother and the frightening ritual in primitive societies by which the elders formally initiate the young into adulthood. How are Brandt's experiences like an initiation? How do they differ?

3. How much time passes between the onset of the grandmother's senility and her death? How does Brandt indicate this passage of time? As you read, did you feel that events were moving more quickly or slowly than that? If so, why?

4. Are there any other "rites of passage" (besides Brandt's own) in the essay? Who changes, and how? What rituals, if any, are involved?

5. What part of this essay struck you most forcefully? Examine the writing of that passage. Can you identify any specific elements that seem to affect the total impact of the passage?

6. Brandt writes in paragraph 13, "The whole thing had been a subtle act of violence, a violation of the sensibilities." What does he mean?

Explorations

1. Does this essay bring to mind any "rite of passage" you yourself have gone through? Describe your experience, and tell about the effects it has had on you.

2. What is senility? Are its causes and its nature known? Can senility be treated? Look up the condition in library sources to find the answers.

3. Old age may be a time of great achievement, as in the cases of the cellist Pablo Casals or the artist Georgia O'Keeffe, or it may bring senility, as with Anthony Brandt's grandmother. What is your conception of old age? Describe the people you know, or know about, who are examples of that conception.

N. SCOTT MOMADAY

For many Americans, the search for roots leads over the sea to Europe or Africa. For Native Americans like Natachee Scott Momaday, a Kiowa Indian, the ancestral lands are right here, beneath our feet. In the 1960s he set out on a pilgrimage to retrace the Kiowas' great migration to Oklahoma, where he was born in 1934. Momaday grew up and attended school on Navaho, Apache, and Pueblo reservations before earning degrees at the University of New Mexico and Stanford University. He has taught English and comparative literature at the University of California at Berkeley and now teaches at Stanford. His novel *House Made of Dawn* (1968) was awarded the Pulitzer Prize for Fiction. His best-known work, however, may be the collection of Kiowa tales and personal reminiscences published first as *The Journey of Tai-me* (1967) and then, in revised form, as *The Way to Rainy Mountain* (1969). The following selection is the introduction to that book. Momaday begins his essay where the Kiowa migration ended, at Rainy Mountain in Oklahoma, where his grandmother is buried. Thinking back, he remembers her as both a strong, mysterious woman and the embodiment of his tribe's history and culture.

The Way to Rainy Mountain

A single knoll rises out of the plain in Oklahoma, north and west of the Wichita Range. For my people, the Kiowas, it is an old landmark, and they gave it the name Rainy Mountain. The hardest weather in the world is there. Winter brings blizzards, hot tornadic winds arise in the spring, and in summer the prairie is an anvil's edge. The grass turns brittle and brown, and it cracks beneath your feet. There are green belts along the rivers and creeks, linear groves of hickory and pecan, willow and witch hazel. At a distance in July or August the steaming foliage seems almost to writhe in fire. Great green and yellow grasshoppers are everywhere in the tall grass, popping up like corn to sting the flesh, and tortoises crawl about on the red earth, going nowhere in the plenty of time. Loneliness is an aspect of the land. All things in the plain are isolate; there is no confusion of objects in the eye, but *one* hill or *one* tree or *one* man. To look upon that landscape in the early morning, with the sun at your back, is to lose the sense of proportion. Your imagination comes to life, and this, you think, is where Creation was begun.

I returned to Rainy Mountain in July. My grandmother had died in the spring, and I wanted to be at her grave. She had lived to be very old and at last infirm. Her only living daughter was with her when she died, and I was told that in death her face was that of a child.

I like to think of her as a child. When she was born, the Kiowas   3
were living the last great moment of their history. For more than a
hundred years they had controlled the open range from the Smoky Hill
River to the Red, from the headwaters of the Canadian to the fork of
the Arkansas and Cimarron. In alliance with the Comanches, they had
ruled the whole of the southern Plains. War was their sacred business,
and they were among the finest horsemen the world has ever known.
But warfare for the Kiowas was preeminently a matter of disposition rather
than of survival, and they never understood the grim, unrelenting advance of the U.S. Cavalry. When at last, divided and ill-provisioned,
they were driven onto the Staked Plains in the cold rains of autumn,
they fell into panic. In Palo Duro Canyon they abandoned their crucial
stores to pillage and had nothing then but their lives. In order to save
themselves, they surrendered to the soldiers at Fort Sill and were imprisoned in the old stone corral that now stands as a military museum.
My grandmother was spared the humiliation of those high gray walls by
eight or ten years, but she must have known from birth the affliction of
defeat, the dark brooding of old warriors.

Her name was Aho, and she belonged to the last culture to evolve   4
in North America. Her forebears came down from the high country in
western Montana nearly three centuries ago. They were a mountain people, a mysterious tribe of hunters whose language has never been positively classified in any major group. In the late seventeenth century they
began a long migration to the south and east. It was a journey toward
the dawn, and it led to a golden age. Along the way the Kiowas were
befriended by the Crows, who gave them the culture and religion of the
Plains. They acquired horses, and their ancient nomadic spirit was suddenly free of the ground. They acquired Tai-me, the sacred Sun Dance
doll, from that moment the object and symbol of their worship, and so
shared in the divinity of the sun. Not least, they acquired the sense of
destiny, therefore courage and pride. When they entered upon the southern Plains they had been transformed. No longer were they slaves to the
simple necessity of survival; they were a lordly and dangerous society of
fighters and thieves, hunters and priests of the sun. According to their
origin myth, they entered the world through a hollow log. From one
point of view, their migration was the fruit of an old prophecy, for indeed
they emerged from a sunless world.

Although my grandmother lived out her long life in the shadow of   5
Rainy Mountain, the immense landscape of the continental interior lay
like memory in her blood. She could tell of the Crows, whom she had
never seen, and of the Black Hills, where she had never been. I wanted

to see in reality what she had seen more perfectly in the mind's eye, and traveled fifteen hundred miles to begin my pilgrimage.

Yellowstone, it seemed to me, was the top of the world, a region 6 of deep lakes and dark timber, canyons and waterfalls. But, beautiful as it is, one might have the sense of confinement there. The skyline in all directions is close at hand, the high wall of the woods and deep cleavages of shade. There is a perfect freedom in the mountains, but it belongs to the eagle and the elk, the badger and the bear. The Kiowas reckoned their stature by the distance they could see, and they were bent and blind in the wilderness.

Descending eastward, the highland meadows are a stairway to the 7 plain. In July the inland slope of the Rockies is luxuriant with flax and buckwheat, stonecrop and larkspur. The earth unfolds and the limit of the land recedes. Clusters of trees, and animals grazing far in the distance, cause the vision to reach away and wonder to build upon the mind. The sun follows a longer course in the day, and the sky is immense beyond all comparison. The great billowing clouds that sail upon it are shadows that move upon the grain like water, dividing light. Farther down, in the land of the Crows and Blackfeet, the plain is yellow. Sweet clover takes hold of the hills and bends upon itself to cover and seal the soil. There the Kiowas paused on their way; they had come to the place where they must change their lives. The sun is at home on the plains. Precisely there does it have the certain character of a god. When the Kiowas came to the land of the Crows, they could see the dark lees of the hills at dawn across the Bighorn River, the profusion of light on the grain shelves, the oldest deity ranging after the solstices. Not yet would they veer southward to the caldron of the land that lay below; they must wean their blood from the northern winter and hold the mountains a while longer in their view. They bore Tai-me in procession to the east.

A dark mist lay over the Black Hills, and the land was like iron. 8 At the top of a ridge I caught sight of Devil's Tower upthrust against the gray sky as if in the birth of time the core of the earth had broken through its crust and the motion of the world was begun. There are things in nature that engender an awful quiet in the heart of man; Devil's Tower is one of them. Two centuries ago, because they could not do otherwise, the Kiowas made a legend at the base of the rock. My grandmother said:

> Eight children were there at play, seven sisters and their brother. Suddenly the boy was struck dumb; he trembled and began to run upon his hands and feet. His fingers became claws, and his body was covered with fur. Directly there was a bear where the boy had been. The sisters were terrified; they ran, and the bear after them. They came to the stump of a great tree,

and the tree spoke to them. It bade them climb upon it, and as they did so it began to rise into the air. The bear came to kill them, but they were just beyond its reach. It reared against the tree and scored the bark all around with its claws. The seven sisters were borne into the sky, and they became the stars of the Big Dipper.

From that moment, and so long as the legend lives, the Kiowas have kinsmen in the night sky. Whatever they were in the mountains, they could be no more. However tenuous their well-being, however much they had suffered and would suffer again, they had found a way out of the wilderness.

My grandmother had a reverence for the sun, a holy regard that now is all but gone out of mankind. There was a wariness in her, and an ancient awe. She was a Christian in her later years, but she had come a long way about, and she never forgot her birthright. As a child she had been to the Sun Dances; she had taken part in those annual rites, and by them she had learned the restoration of her people in the presence of Tai-me. She was about seven when the last Kiowa Sun Dance was held in 1887 on the Washita River above Rainy Mountain Creek. The buffalo were gone. In order to consummate the ancient sacrifice—to impale the head of a buffalo bull upon the medicine tree—a delegation of old men journeyed into Texas, there to beg and barter for an animal from the Goodnight herd. She was ten when the Kiowas came together for the last time as a living Sun Dance culture. They could find no buffalo; they had to hang an old hide from the sacred tree. Before the dance could begin, a company of soldiers rode out from Fort Sill under orders to disperse the tribe. Forbidden without cause the essential act of their faith, having seen the wild herds slaughtered and left to rot upon the ground, the Kiowas backed away forever from the medicine tree. That was July 20, 1890, at the great bend of the Washita. My grandmother was there. Without bitterness, and for as long as she lived, she bore a vision of deicide.

Now that I can have her only in memory, I see my grandmother in the several postures that were peculiar to her: standing at the wood stove on a winter morning and turning meat in a great iron skillet; sitting at the south window, bent above her beadwork, and afterwards, when her vision failed, looking down for a long time into the fold of her hands; going out upon a cane, very slowly as she did when the weight of age came upon her; praying. I remember her most often at prayer. She made long, rambling prayers out of suffering and hope, having seen many things. I was never sure that I had the right to hear, so exclusive were they of all mere custom and company. The last time I saw her she prayed standing by the side of her bed at night, naked to the waist, the light of a kerosene lamp moving upon her dark skin. Her long, black hair, always drawn and braided in the day, lay upon her shoulders and against her breasts like a shawl. I do not speak Kiowa, and I never understood her prayers, but there was something inherently sad in the sound, some merest hesitation upon the syllables of sorrow. She began in a high and descending pitch, exhausting her breath to silence; then again and again—and always the same intensity of effort, of something that is, and is not, like urgency in the human voice. Transported so in the dancing light among the shadows of her room, she seemed beyond the reach of time. But that was illusion; I think I knew then that I should not see her again.

Houses are like sentinels in the plain, old keepers of the weather watch. There, in a very little while, wood takes on the appearance of great age. All colors wear soon away in the wind and rain, and then the wood is burned gray and the grain appears and the nails turn red with rust. The windowpanes are black and opaque; you imagine there is nothing within, and indeed there are many ghosts, bones given up to the land. They stand here and there against the sky, and you approach them for a longer time than you expect. They belong in the distance; it is their domain. 11

Once there was a lot of sound in my grandmother's house, a lot of coming and going, feasting and talk. The summers there were full of excitement and reunion. The Kiowas are a summer people; they abide the cold and keep to themselves, but when the season turns and the land becomes warm and vital they cannot hold still; an old love of going returns upon them. The aged visitors who came to my grandmother's house when I was a child were made of lean and leather, and they bore themselves upright. They wore great black hats and bright ample shirts that shook in the wind. They rubbed fat upon their hair and wound their braids with strips of colored cloth. Some of them painted their faces and carried the scars of old and cherished enmities. They were an old council of warlords, come to remind and be reminded of who they were. Their wives and daughters served them well. The women might indulge themselves; gossip was at once the mark and compensation of their servitude. They made loud and elaborate talk among themselves, full of jest and gesture, fright and false alarm. They went abroad in fringed and flowered shawls, bright beadwork and German silver. They were at home in the kitchen, and they prepared meals that were banquets. 12

There were frequent prayer meetings, and great nocturnal feasts. When I was a child I played with my cousins outside, where the lamplight fell upon the ground and the singing of the old people rose up around us and carried away into the darkness. There were a lot of good things to eat, a lot of laughter and surprise. And afterwards, when the quiet re- 13 turned, I lay down with my grandmother and could hear the frogs away by the river and feel the motion of the air.

Now there is funeral silence in the rooms, the endless wake of some 14 final word. The walls have closed in upon my grandmother's house. When I returned to it in mourning, I saw for the first time in my life how small it was. It was late at night, and there was a white moon, nearly full. I sat for a long time on the stone steps by the kitchen door. From there I could see out across the land; I could see the long row of trees by the creek, the low light upon the rolling plains, and the stars of the Big Dipper. Once I looked at the moon and caught sight of a strange thing. A cricket had perched upon the handrail, only a few inches away from me. My line of vision was such that the creature filled the moon like a fossil. It had gone there, I thought, to live and die, for there, of all places, was its small definition made whole and eternal. A warm wind rose up and purled like the longing within me.

The next morning I awoke at dawn and went out on the dirt road 15 to Rainy Mountain. It was already hot, and the grasshoppers began to fill the air. Still, it was early in the morning, and the birds sang out of the shadows. The long yellow grass on the mountain shone in the bright light, and a scissortail hied above the land. There, where it ought to be, at the end of a long and legendary way, was my grandmother's grave. Here and there on the dark stones were ancestral names. Looking back once, I saw the mountain and came away.

About the Essay

1. Why does Momaday return to his grandmother's house and visit her grave? What is the significance of the title he gives his account?

2. How would you describe the relationship between Momaday and his grandmother while she was alive? After she died?

3. What is Momaday's attitude toward the land, his people, and their myths?

4. What does the legend of Devil's Tower reveal about the ways of the Kiowas?

5. At one point, Momaday refers to his grandmother's use of the Kiowa language. What significance can you find in that episode?

6. At times, Momaday appears to choose certain words partly because of the way they sound. For example, in paragraph 6 he refers to "the eagle and the elk, the badger and the bear." Can you find any other passages where he is evidently doing this? Why do you think he does it, and what is the effect on you?

7. Momaday uses many images throughout his essay. Choose one or two that are particularly appealing to you. What are the qualities in the image or images that you find effective?

Explorations

1. Momaday remembers his grandmother as an ageless, austere presence; Anthony Brandt (in "Rite of Passage," pages 134–139) describes his as an elderly, loving, playful companion. What have your grandparents been to you? What do you think a grandparent's role should be?

2. Consider the Kiowa myths that Momaday tells us about in his essay. What part do they play in his culture? What myths, if any, does the culture you belong to rely upon? What do those myths tell you about that culture?

3. In paragraph 9, the U.S. Cavalry makes its appearance in a characteristic role. What was the American government's policy toward Native Americans in the period from 1860 to 1890? How does knowledge of that policy affect your view of the tribal history Momaday provides?

SUSAN JACOBY

When Susan Jacoby became a newspaper reporter in 1963, at the age of seventeen, she had no intention of writing about "women's subjects." "To write about women was to write about trivia: charity balls, cake sales, and the like," she recalls. "I would have laughed at anyone who tried to tell me that one day I would believe the members of my own sex were important enough to write about." But times have changed. Although the old female stereotypes have not completely disappeared, many people have come to regard them as unfair and unacceptable. And Jacoby has, in fact, written extensively about women's subjects, often in *The New York Times* and *McCall's*. Many of these pieces have been collected in her book *The Possible She* (1979). In the following essay, originally published in the "Hers" column of the *Times* in 1978, Jacoby tells of two experiences when she felt mistreated because she was a woman and describes how she dealt with each situation.

Unfair Game

My friend and I, two women obviously engrossed in conversation, are sitting at a corner table in the crowded Oak Room of the Plaza at ten o'clock on a Tuesday night. A man materializes and interrupts us with the snappy opening line, "A good woman is hard to find."

We say nothing, hoping he will disappear back into his bottle. But he fancies himself as our genie and asks, "Are you visiting?" Still we say nothing. Finally my friend looks up and says, "We live here." She and I look at each other, the thread of our conversation snapped, our thoughts focused on how to get rid of this intruder. In a minute, if something isn't done, he will scrunch down next to me on the banquette and start offering to buy us drinks.

"Would you leave us alone, please," I say in a loud but reasonably polite voice. He looks slightly offended but goes on with his bright social patter. I become more explicit. "We don't want to talk to you, we didn't ask you over here, and we want to be alone. Go away." This time he directs his full attention to me—and he is mad. "All right, all right, *excuse me.*" He pushes up the corners of his mouth in a Howdy Doody smile. "You ought to try smiling. You might even be pretty if you smiled once in a while."

At last the man leaves. He goes back to his buddy at the bar. I watch them out of the corner of my eye, and he gestures angrily at me for at least fifteen minutes. When he passes our table on the way out of the room, this well-dressed, obviously affluent man mutters, "Good-bye, bitch," under his breath.

Why is this man calling me names? Because I have asserted my   5
right to sit at a table in a public place without being drawn into a sexual flirtation. Because he has been told, in no uncertain terms, that two attractive women prefer each other's company to his.

This sort of experience is an old story to any woman who travels,   6
eats, or drinks—for business or pleasure—without a male escort. In Holiday Inns and at the Plaza, on buses and airplanes, in tourist and first class, a woman is always thought to be looking for a man in addition to whatever else she may be doing. The man who barged in on us at the bar would never have broken into the conversation of two men, and it goes without saying that he wouldn't have imposed himself on a man and a woman who were having a drink. But two women at a table are an entirely different matter. Fair game.

This might be viewed as a relatively small flaw in the order of the   7
universe—something in a class with an airline losing luggage or a computer fouling up a bank statement. Except a computer doesn't foul up your bank account every month and an airline doesn't lose your suitcase every time you fly. But if you are an independent woman, you have to spend a certain amount of energy, day in and day out, in order to go about your business without being bothered by strange men.

On airplanes, I am a close-mouthed traveler. As soon as the "No   8
Smoking" sign is turned off, I usually pull some papers out of my briefcase and start working. Work helps me forget that I am scared of flying. When I am sitting next to a woman, she quickly realizes from my monosyllabic replies that I don't want to chat during the flight. Most men, though, are not content to be ignored.

Once I was flying from New York to San Antonio on a plane that   9
was scheduled to stop in Dallas. My seatmate was an advertising executive who kept questioning me about what I was doing and who remained undiscouraged by my terse replies until I ostentatiously covered myself with a blanket and shut my eyes. When the plane started its descent into Dallas, he made his move.

"You don't really have to get to San Antonio today, do you?"   10
"Yes."   11
"Come on, change your ticket. Spend the evening with me here.   12
I'm staying at a wonderful hotel, with a pool, we could go dancing . . ."
"No."   13
"Well, you can't blame a man for trying."   14
I do blame a man for trying in this situation—for suggesting that a   15

woman change her work and travel plans to spend a night with a perfect stranger in whom she had displayed no personal interest. The "no personal interest" is crucial; I wouldn't have blamed the man for trying if I had been stroking his cheek and complaining about my dull social life.

There is a nice postscript to this story. Several months later, I was   16
walking my dog in Carl Schurz Park when I ran into my erstwhile seatmate, who was taking a stroll with his wife and children. He recognized me, all right, and was trying to avoid me when I went over and courteously reintroduced myself. I reminded him that we had been on the same flight to Dallas. "Oh yes," he said. "As I recall you were going on to somewhere else." "San Antonio," I said. "I was in a hurry that day."

The code of feminine politeness, instilled in girlhood, is no help   17
in dealing with the unwanted approaches of strange men. Our mothers didn't teach us to tell a man to get lost; they told us to smile and hint that we'd be just delighted to spend time with the gentleman if we didn't have other commitments. The man in the Oak Room bar would not be put off by a demure lowering of eyelids; he had to be told, roughly and loudly, that his presence was a nuisance.

Not that I am necessarily against men and women picking each   18
other up in public places. In most instances, a modicum of sensitivity will tell a woman or a man whether someone is open to approaches.

Mistakes can easily be corrected by the kind of courtesy so many   19
people have abandoned since the "sexual revolution." One summer evening, I was whiling away a half hour in the outdoor bar of the Stanhope Hotel. I was alone, dressed up, having a drink before going on to meet someone in a restaurant. A man at the next table asked, "If you're not busy, would you like to have a drink with me?" I told him I was sorry but I would be leaving shortly. "Excuse me for disturbing you," he said, turning back to his own drink. Simple courtesy. No insults and no hurt feelings.

One friend suggested that I might have avoided the incident in the   20
Oak Room by going to the Palm Court instead. It's true that the Palm Court is a traditional meeting place for unescorted ladies. But I don't like violins when I want to talk. And I wanted to sit in a large, comfortable leather chair. Why should I have to hide among the potted palms to avoid men who think I'm looking for something else?

About the Essay

1. What is the main point of Jacoby's essay? Where is it stated most directly? What was her purpose in writing this piece?

2. What solutions, if any, does Jacoby suggest for dealing with the problem she describes?

3. Jacoby complains about the code of feminine politeness. What exactly is this "code"? Does she seem constrained by it?

4. In paragraph 16, why does Jacoby say as her parting shot, "I was in a hurry that day."?

5. What is Jacoby's tone in this essay? How does she achieve this tone? Give several examples from the essay.

Explorations

1. Jacoby has written that this article drew a larger response than anything she has ever published. What kinds of responses do you imagine it drew from women? From men? How do you respond to this article? Compose a response as if you were going to send it to *The New York Times* or to Jacoby herself.

2. In one respect, the situations Jacoby describes have mainly to do with courtesy, with good and bad manners. From your own experience, and your knowledge of personal and professional social interaction, what do you think courtesy is? What purpose does it serve? Should people be expected always to show consideration for others, or should they be free to say and do whatever they please? Why

3. Why do people go on dates? What do people gain from dining together, or going to a movie together? How has dating changed in the last ten years? How should one arrange a date with a stranger?

ANAÏS NIN

Anaïs Nin was born in Paris in 1903 and came to the United States when she was nine. She wrote fiction and literary criticism but is best known for her diaries, which she began at a very early age as letters to her father, the Spanish composer Joaquin Nin. In the sixty-five diaries that she composed during her lifetime she writes intimately of her impressions of the world around her, carrying on what she called a dialogue with herself. Her fiction includes the novels *Winter of Artifice* (1939) and *A Spy in the House of Love* (1954), and the short story collection *Ladders to Fire* (1946). She also published *The Novel of the Future* (1970), a study of avant-garde fiction. She died in 1977. In "My Turkish Grandmother" Nin tells us about four stranded travelers who in befriending one another at an Athens airport are reminded of the larger human family.

My Turkish Grandmother

I was travelling on Air France to New York via Paris when the plane ran into a flock of sea gulls and we had to stop at Athens. At first we sat around and waited for information, looking out now and then at the airplane. Vague news filtered out. Some passengers became anxious, fearing they would miss their connections. Air France treated us to dinner and wine. But after that there was a shortage of seats, so I sat on the floor like a gypsy, together with a charming hippie couple with whom I had made friends during the trip. He was a musician and she was a painter. They were hitchhiking through Europe with backpacks. She was slender and frail-looking, and I was not surprised when he complained that her knapsack was full of vitamins. As we sat talking about books, films, music, a very old lady approached us. She looked like my Spanish grandmother. Dressed completely in black, old but not bent, with a face that seemed carved of wood through which the wrinkles appeared more like veins of the wood. She handed me a letter she carried around her neck in a Turkish cloth bag. It was written in exquisite French. It was a request from her daughter to help her Turkish mother in every way possible. The daughter was receiving her doctorate in medicine at the Sorbonne[1] and could not come to fetch her mother for the ceremony, so she had entrusted her to the care of Air France. I read the letter and translated it for my hippie friends. Although we could not talk to the

---

[1]The great university in Paris.

old woman, it was evident that a strong, warm sympathy existed among the four of us. She wanted to sit with us. We made room for her, and she gave me her old wrinkled hand to hold. She was anxious. She did not know what had happened. She realized she would be late for her rendezvous in Paris. We looked for a Turkish passenger who would translate and explain the delay. There was none, but we found an Air France hostess who spoke a little Turkish. We thought the old lady would choose to stay with the hostess, but once the message was conveyed to her, she returned to sit with us. She adopted us. Hours passed. We were told that the plane could not be repaired, that the airline offered us a few hours of sleep in a hotel not too far away, and to be ready for an early flight on another plane. So the four of us were placed in a taxi, which caused my Turkish grandmother such anxiety that she would not let go of my hand; but her anxiety would always recede when, she looked at the delicate features and soft eyes of the young woman painter, at the smile and gentleness of the musician's face, at my reassuring words in French, which she did not understand. At the hotel, she would not go into her bedroom alone, so I left our connecting doors open and explained I was right there next to her. She studied this for a while and then finally consented to lie in her bed. A few hours later, we were called and taken to our plane. Because I was changing planes in Paris, I could not take her to the home of her daughter. I had to find someone who would. Questioning the passengers, I found a woman who promised to take her in a taxi to the address in the letter. She held on to my hand until the last minute. Then she kissed me ceremoniously, kissed my hippie friends, and went on her way. Having been in her fishermen's village, I could imagine the little stone house she came from, her fisherman husband, her daughter sent to Paris to study medicine and now achieving the high status of doctor. Did she arrive in time for a ceremony which had to be translated to her? I know she arrived safely. Guarded by universal grandchildren, Turkish grandmothers always travel safely.

About the Essay

1. In what way is the old Turkish woman Nin's "grandmother"? How did she "adopt" Nin and the hippie couple?

2. What does Nin mean in the last sentence by the expression "universal grandchildren"?

3. As you read, did you find the situation described in the essay easy or hard to accept? What, if anything, did you find unbelievable? Would the situation have been more or less plausible in another setting—say, in a store or a city park?

4. Perhaps because she was writing in her diary, Nin tells her story in one long paragraph. Did the lack of paragraphs affect your reading? How? How would you have divided the piece into paragraphs if you had been its author?

5. What point do you think the essay makes about relationships, particularly family relationships? Does Nin state that point directly?

Explorations

1. Nin and the hippie couple were not obliged to accept responsibility for the old Turkish woman, but they did so almost automatically. What attitude toward social responsibility does this little incident express? Do you agree with that attitude, or do you have a different sense of social responsibility? Explain.

2. Travel almost always brings us into contact with strangers and often results in new relationships. Has this happened to you? What were the circumstances, what relationships were formed, and what forms did they take? Do such relationships have the same strength and last as long as those formed in other settings—in school, in the neighborhood, and the like?

JUDITH VIORST

The American philosopher George Santayana once wrote, "Friendship is almost always the union of a part of one mind with a part of another; people are friends in spots." Judith Viorst would agree. In fact, in this essay, she goes further, mapping the different kinds of spots where her mind achieves union with her friends'. A professional writer, Viorst was born in 1936 and has marked off the periods of her life with books of light verse: *It's Hard to Be Hip over Thirty and Other Tragedies of Married Life* (1970); *How Did I Get to Be Forty and Other Atrocities* (1976). She also writes books for children, has collaborated with her husband on a guide to the restaurants of Washington, D.C., and is a contributing editor of *Redbook*. As you read this essay, which first appeared in her regular column in *Redbook*, see whether your own friends fit into Viorst's categories.

Friends, Good Friends —and Such Good Friends

Women are friends, I once would have said, when they totally love   1
and support and trust each other, and bare to each other the secrets of their souls, and run—no questions asked—to help each other, and tell harsh truths to each other (no, you can't wear that dress unless you lose ten pounds first) when harsh truths must be told.

Women are friends, I once would have said, when they share the   2
same affection for Ingmar Bergman, plus train rides, cats, warm rain, charades, Camus, and hate with equal ardor Newark and Brussels sprouts and Lawrence Welk and camping.

In other words, I once would have said that a friend is a friend all   3
the way, but now I believe that's a narrow point of view. For the friend-ships I have and the friendships I see are conducted at many levels of intensity, serve many different functions, meet different needs and range from those as all-the-way as the friendship of the soul sisters mentioned above to that of the most nonchalant and casual playmates.

Consider these varieties of friendship: 4

1. Convenience friends. These are women with whom, if our paths   5
weren't crossing all the time, we'd have no particular reason to be friends: a next-door neighbor, a woman in our car pool, the mother of one of our children's closest friends or maybe some mommy with whom we serve juice and cookies each week at the Glenwood Co-op Nursery.

155

Convenience friends are convenient indeed. They'll lend us their cups and silverware for a party. They'll drive our kids to soccer when we're sick. They'll take us to pick up our car when we need a lift to the garage. They'll even take our cats when we go on vacation. As we will for them.

6

But we don't, with convenience friends, ever come too close or tell too much; we maintain our public face and emotional distance. "Which means," says Elaine, "that I'll talk about being overweight but not about being depressed. Which means I'll admit being mad but not blind with rage. Which means that I might say that we're pinched this month but never that I'm worried sick over money."

7

But which doesn't mean that there isn't sufficient value to be found in these friendships of mutual aid, in convenience friends.

8

2. Special-interest friends. These friendships aren't intimate, and they needn't involve kids or silverware or cats. Their value lies in some interest jointly shared. And so we may have an office friend or a yoga friend or a tennis friend or a friend from the Women's Democratic Club.

9

"I've got one woman friend," says Joyce, "who likes, as I do, to take psychology courses. Which makes it nice for me—and nice for her. It's fun to go with someone you know and it's fun to discuss what you've learned, driving back from the classes." And for the most part, she says, that's all they discuss.

10

"I'd say that what we're doing is *doing* together, not being together," Suzanne says of her Tuesday-doubles friends. "It's mainly a tennis relationship, but we play together well. And I guess we all need to have a couple of playmates."

11

I agree.

12

My playmate is a shopping friend, a woman of marvelous taste, a woman who knows exactly *where* to buy *what*, and furthermore is a woman who always knows beyond a doubt what one ought to be buying. I don't have the time to keep up with what's new in eyeshadow, hemlines and shoes and whether the smock look is in or finished already. But since (oh, shame!) I care a lot about eyeshadows, hemlines and shoes, and since I don't *want* to wear smocks if the smock look is finished, I'm very glad to have a shopping friend.

13

3. Historical friends. We all have a friend who knew us when . . . maybe way back in Miss Meltzer's second grade, when our family lived in that three-room flat in Brooklyn, when our dad was out of work for seven months, when our brother Allie got in that fight where they had to call the police, when our sister married the endodontist from Yonkers and when, the morning after we lost our virginity, she was the first, the only, friend we told.

14

The years have gone by and we've gone separate ways and we've 15 little in common now, but we're still an intimate part of each other's past. And so whenever we go to Detroit we always go to visit this friend of our girlhood. Who knows how we looked before our teeth were straightened. Who knows how we talked before our voice got un-Brooklyned. Who knows what we ate before we learned about artichokes. And who, by her presence, puts us in touch with an earlier part of ourself, a part of ourself it's important never to lose.

"What this friend means to me and what I mean to her," says 16 Grace, "is having a sister without sibling rivalry. We know the texture of each other's lives. She remembers my grandmother's cabbage soup. I remember the way her uncle played the piano. There's simply no other friend who remembers those things."

4. Crossroads friends. Like historical friends, our crossroads friends 17 are important for *what was*—for the friendship we shared at a crucial, now past, time of life. A time, perhaps, when we roomed in college together; or worked as eager young singles in the Big City together; or went together, as my friend Elizabeth and I did, through pregnancy, birth and that scary first year of new motherhood.

Crossroads friends forge powerful links, links strong enough to en- 18 dure with not much more contact than once-a-year letters at Christmas. And out of respect for those crossroads years, for those dramas and dreams we once shared, we will always be friends.

5. Cross-generational friends. Historical friends and crossroads friends 19 seem to maintain a special kind of intimacy—dormant but always ready to be revived—and though we may rarely meet, whenever we do connect, it's personal and intense. Another kind of intimacy exists in the friendships that form across generations in what one woman calls her daughter-mother and her mother-daughter relationships.

Evelyn's friend is her mother's age—"but I share so much more 20 than I ever could with my mother"—a woman she talks to of music, of books and of life. "What I get from her is the benefit of her experience. What she gets—and enjoys—from me is a youthful perspective. It's a pleasure for both of us."

I have in my own life a precious friend, a woman of 65 who has 21 lived very hard, who is wise, who listens well; who has been where I am and can help me understand it; and who represents not only an ultimate ideal mother to me but also the person I'd like to be when I grow up.

In our daughter role we tend to do more than our share of self- 22 revelation; in our mother role we tend to receive what's revealed. It's another kind of pleasure—playing wise mother to a questing younger person. It's another very lovely kind of friendship.

6. Part-of-a-couple friends. Some of the women we call our friends   23
we never see alone—we see them as part of a couple at couples' parties.
And though we share interests in many things and respect each other's
views, we aren't moved to deepen the relationship. Whatever the reason,
a lack of time or—and this is more likely—a lack of chemistry, our
friendship remains in the context of a group. But the fact that our feeling
on seeing each other is always, "I'm *so* glad she's here" and the fact that
we spend half the evening talking together says that this too, in its own
way, counts as a friendship.

(Other part-of-a-couple friends are the friends that came with the   24
marriage, and some of these are friends we could live without. But sometimes, alas, she married our husband's best friend; and sometimes, alas,
she *is* our husband's best friend. And so we find ourselves dealing with
her, somewhat against our will, in a spirit of what I'll call *reluctant* friendship.)

7. Men who are friends. I wanted to write just of women friends,   25
but the women I've talked to won't let me—they say I must mention
man-woman friendships too. For these friendships can be just as close
and as dear as those that we form with women. Listen to Lucy's description of one such friendship:

"We've found we have things to talk about that are different from   26
what he talks about with my husband and different from what I talk
about with his wife. So sometimes we call on the phone or meet for
lunch. There are similar intellectual interests—we always pass on to each
other the book that we love—but there's also something tender and
caring too."

In a couple of crises, Lucy says, "he offered himself for talking and   27
for helping. And when someone died in his family he wanted me there.
The sexual, flirty part of our friendship is very small—but *some*—just
enough to make it fun and different." She thinks—and I agree—that the
sexual part, though small, is always *some*, is always there when a man
and a woman are friends.

It's only in the past few years that I've made friends with men, in   28
the sense of a friendship that's *mine*, not just part of two couples. And
achieving with them the ease and the trust I've found with women friends
has value indeed. Under the dryer at home last week, putting on mascara
and rouge, I comfortably sat and talked with a fellow named Peter. Peter,
I finally decided, could handle the shock of me minus mascara under the
dryer. Because we care for each other. Because we're friends.

There are medium friends, and pretty good friends, and very good   29
friends indeed, and these friendships are defined by their level of intimacy. And what we'll reveal at each of these levels of intimacy is cali-

brated with care. We might tell a medium friend, for example, that yesterday we had a fight with our husband. And we might tell a pretty good friend that this fight with our husband made us so mad that we slept on the couch. And we might tell a very good friend that the reason we got so mad in that fight that we slept on the couch had something to do with that girl who works in his office. But it's only to our very best friends that we're willing to tell all, to tell what's going on with that girl in his office.

The best of friends, I still believe, totally love and support and trust each other, and bare to each other the secrets of their souls, and run—no questions asked—to help each other, and tell harsh truths to each other when they must be told. [30]

But we needn't agree about everything (only 12-year-old girl friends agree about *everything*) to tolerate each other's point of view. To accept without judgment. To give and to take without ever keeping score. And to *be* there, as I am for them and as they are for me, to comfort our sorrows, to celebrate our joys. [31]

About the Essay

1. In the opening paragraphs Viorst explains how she once would have defined friendship. What definition might she have given? Why does she now think differently?

2. What is Viorst's purpose in this essay? How does her extended list of categories serve that purpose?

3. The readership of *Redbook*, where this essay first appeared, consists largely of women between the ages of twenty-five and thirty-five. If Viorst had been writing for an audience of young men, how might her categories have been different? How might her examples have been different?

4. How does Viorst use quotation in her essay? Are her quotations appropriate and credible?

5. Throughout the essay Viorst often uses the word *we*. Why do you think she does this? Does it cause problems? If so, where?

6. What is the tone of this essay? Cite passages that show how Viorst creates the tone.

Explorations

1. Some people would say that all the relationships Viorst describes are forms of friendship. Others may feel that most are mere acquaintances, and that true friendship is something different. What is your idea of friendship? Illustrate your definition with examples from your experience or your reading.

2. American society holds a much broader notion of friendship than many other societies do, and Americans are quite quick to address each other familiarly—using first names and not using titles, for example. Those who have traveled or lived abroad invariably notice this, as do foreigners visiting the United States. What do you think are the advantages of such "easy" friendship and informality? What might the disadvantages be?

3. In paragraph 2 Viorst lists some of her favorite and least favorite things. What would you include if you were to make such a list? Which of your loves and hates can you share, and which do you have to nourish by yourself? Does sharing your enthusiasms make any difference in how you feel about them?

ANDREA LEE

Andrea Lee and her husband Tom were graduate students at Harvard when they traveled to the Soviet Union in 1978 as part of a government-sponsored exchange of scholars. During their stay Andrea kept a journal which was later published as *Russian Journal* (1981). Because they were both young and Tom was fluent in Russian, she was able to capture an unusual and refreshingly candid view of life in contemporary Russia. In her words, "each entry presents a small piece of Russian reality as seen by an American whose vision, if not refined by study, was at least not much distorted by prejudice for or against Communism." The following journal entry, dated September 24, 1978, tells of the Lees' Russian friend Seryozha and his troubles with his wife and her family.

Russian Friends

I should write this down while it is still fresh. We have just come back home, tired. It's not weariness brought on by physical exertion, it's the gutless exhaustion that follows shock. Early this morning—a beautiful, hazy autumn morning—we set off for the apartment of our friend Seryozha. We three planned to visit the monastery at Zagorsk, a town about forty-five miles outside Moscow, and make a day of it; Tom was carrying a bottle of cognac and six *pirozhki* (meat dumplings), still warm in their paper wrapping. Now, barely two hours later, we're back, and we don't know when we can see Seryozha again. When we left his apartment, he told us that after everything was over he would send us a letter giving only a date and a time for a meeting. The place we would already know; it would be a Metro station where we had met before. After Seryozha said this, he told us to run, not walk, away from his apartment, avoiding anyone we might see. The danger, of course, was to him, not to us, but I still felt panicky. We dashed down the stairs and out of the place, the bag of food banging absurdly against Tom's legs, and then walked rapidly until we reached a bus stop around a corner. There we stood, catching our breath. Both of us felt a little sick.

We had known very little about Seryozha's troubles at first. American friends had introduced us. He is a thin young man with the mobile face and the expressive body of an actor or a mime. He has curly blond hair, which he wears long, and hazel eyes, which reveal a lively and ironic wit. Seryozha works as a chemical researcher, but, like so many Russians, he is in a profession that has little to do with his real interests: art, literature, music, and anything concerning the West. (Strange that

161

so many scientists we've met here are passionately devoted to the arts. In the past month, I've met three or four young poets and novelists whose nominal calling is chemistry or physics.)

The first time we visited Seryozha, he met us at a Metro stop near   3
Arbat Street, and we took a trolley to his apartment.[1] He was with his friend, Anya, an attractive dark-haired young art student. Tom and I were both struck by their stylish Western clothes: Seryozha wore jeans and an English tweed cap, Anya, a subtly striped sweater dress and heavy silver bracelets. In Moscow, such clothing is a mark of high status, of black-market connections, or of a devotion to taste and quality extreme enough to sustain days and weeks of combing the barren stores. In any case, it is a statement of nonconformity. I was also impressed by Seryozha's apartment. It was closer than anything else I have seen in the Soviet Union to the apartment of a student or a young professional in the United States. Most of the apartments I've visited here combine sheer bleakness with depressingly gaudy attempts at modishness; this one was not only spacious and comfortable but tastefully, even imaginatively, furnished. The kitchen, where we spent most of our time, was a snug place decorated with English and American photographs and posters; there were plants, an old brass lamp, and an elegant china tea set. The bathroom, in true student fashion, was lined with metal signs stolen from construction sites. In Seryozha's bedroom, a wall of books faced a wall covered with photographs of poets and other writers.

That night, we drank tea and then vodka with lemon peel steeped   4
in it. The four of us talked in Russian and English about mutual friends and American railroads and the Rolling Stones. Seryozha loves the Stones, and his face grew wistful as we spoke about their recent album, "Some Girls." He played a tape of "Let It Bleed" over and over, until we could translate some difficult phrases for him; after that, he came out with the phrases at intervals during the evening, in a pretty decent imitation of Jagger's Cockney snarl. He was an adroit and oddly formal host, inconspicuously filling our teacups and politely urging us to eat bread and cheese and chocolate. While he talked to us, he teased Anya, calling her "Piglet," and she shook back her bangs and glowered at him. It was clear that theirs was a fiery relationship. After a while, we talked about ourselves. Anya told us about painting and printmaking, and about how hard it was to buy supplies in Moscow. There had been something angry in her dark face since the beginning of the evening; I thought at first that it meant she didn't like Americans, but now I realized that it was constant, barely suppressed rage at her own situation. Imagine being a

---

[1] The Metro is the Moscow subway.

painter, she said, and having only four colors of acrylics to choose from, and being unable to buy canvas. A little later, I mentioned the Louvre.[2] Anya gave a sardonic smile. "Oh, *Paris!*" she said, and her voice was full of bitter humor.

She left the room for a moment, and Seryozha told us that her deepest desire was to travel. "She's ready to do anything," he said. "But it's no good—she won't be allowed." He explained that Anya's father, a Pole living in Moscow, had been sent to a labor camp in the late fifties. The sentence had left a mark on the entire family, and it was unlikely that Anya would ever get to Paris.

"And what about you?" Tom asked.

Seryozha said, "I have some problems of my own." He put his slim hands on the table, looked down, and then hesitated. "I'll tell you about them later," he said. "Not now—the next time."

He took us into his bedroom to see his collection of photographs: heads of Pasternak and Mandelstam; Akhmatova leaning backward in black draperies.[3] Among these was a small sepia portrait of several children in identical sailor suits under a tree.

We asked who they were.

"This is my grandmother, sitting with her brothers and sisters," said Seryozha, pointing to a girl with a long blond braid. "And this is their village," he added, pointing to another old picture. From his intonation, and from the look of the children, it was clear that this was not a village that they inhabited but one that they owned. Seryozha explained to us that his family had for generations been noble landowners in the Volga region. He told us his mother's maiden name, and we recognized it. The family has a long tradition of literary and artistic achievement. One ancestor of Seryozha's was a distinguished minor poet of the eighteen-twenties, and his maternal grandmother is well known as a woman of letters, a friend of Pasternak and other writers. Seryozha showed us two daguerreotypes—one a portrait of a beautiful young woman in a riding habit and the other a formal shot of an officer with sharply pointed mustaches. "Two of my great-grandparents," he said. The family, he told us, was listed in the General Armorial of Noble Families of the Russian Empire, Imperial Russia's oldest and most distinguished book of heraldry.

Seryozha had given us all this information in a flat, half-mocking voice. Now he flashed his wrist at us and gave the same sardonic smile Anya had given. "We say in Russia, 'blue, blue blood,' " he said.

5

6

7

8

9

10

11

---

[2] The great art museum in Paris.

[3] These are three of the greatest modern Russian poets, all of them at one time or another victims of the Soviet government's official disfavor.

"But how in the world did your family manage to survive the Revolution?" I asked.

Seryozha shrugged. "They managed." A little later, he explained that his grandparents on both sides had quietly decided to go along with the new regime. His father joined the Party in the early thirties and has remained active in it ever since. This membership eventually placed the once noble family in a position of privilege under Soviet rule. But Seryozha hates the Party, and feels that his father's devotion to Communism springs from willful blindness. "My grandfather—my father's own father—was shot down in the street during the purges," he said. "And my father pretends that it was an accident—that his dear Party could not have deliberately killed an innocent man. The rest of my family think differently." Seryozha's refusal to be active in the Komsomol[4] has become a focal point of tension between father and son, in much the same way that draft resistance did in American families ten years ago. In fact, listening to Seryozha talk about his father made me think of endless conversations I'd heard in the late sixties. "We can go for a drive together and not agree on one single thing," he said. "My father hates the Rolling Stones, my books, my foreign friends, my long hair." Seryozha prefers his grandparents, who carry on the genteel family tradition of literary and artistic involvement. Often, he talks to his grandmothers for hours about their life before the Revolution. It's interesting to me that one way in which the minor sixties-type rebellion taking place in Russia manifests itself is in a devotion to all things pre-Revolutionary. Many of my student friends pointedly call Leningrad St. Petersburg or "Piter."[5]

Seryozha doesn't entirely condemn his father, however. "In the thirties, the family had no money, and my grandmother was sick," he said. The entire family was starving in the big old town house they'd been allowed to retain. (The place, torn down in the early sixties, was a crumbling wooden mansion like many that still cluster in the formerly aristocratic neighborhood around Arbat Street. Seryozha was born in the house. He remembers it as a series of big, dark rooms full of old people and enormous stoves.) Seryozha showed us a picture of his father, a dour-faced man in his late fifties. He glanced at the picture himself, and began to whistle through his teeth; the tune was the Stones' "Ruby Tuesday." He was leaning against the bookcase, looking very slim in his jeans and sweater. "My father had to do it, I know," he said. "But he started to believe in it, and that was his great mistake."

---

[4]The Komsomol is the Soviet communist youth organization.

[5]As the city was known until 1914. St. Petersburg was the capital of Russia from 1712 to 1917. After the Revolution it was renamed Leningrad.

On the Metro going home, I said to Tom, "I think it shows." 15

"What shows?" said Tom. 16

"The blue, blue blood." 17

Tom laughed, and said that I was in love with anything that had 18
to do with fallen fortunes. "If you hadn't heard that story, you would
think he was an ordinary Russian," he said.

I disagreed. I thought I recognized in Seryozha a courtesy so in- 19
grained that it operated by reflex, an instinctive delicacy of wit. There
was something else, too—a peculiar frailty. I think that most Russians
are tougher, physically and spiritually, than anything we can imagine in
America. But Seryozha was not tough. I thought of this as the train
crossed the Moskva River and we looked out at Moscow. The huge city
was well lit in the cold fall night; with the gigantic Stalin Gothic towers
poking up at intervals, it looked a little like a sinister Oz.[6] In this context,
the apartment we had just left seemed like a refuge, a shelter for a very
fragile way of life. I wished suddenly and intensely that Seryozha lived
in any other city in the world.

The following Sunday, we visited Seryozha again, arriving half an 20
hour later than we had agreed. (The end of a visit with Russian friends
is always occupied with elaborate arrangements for the next meeting—
time, place. No one likes to use the phone in Moscow.) After we knocked,
we heard quiet footsteps coming toward the door. They stopped, and
there was a long pause. We knocked again. There was another pause,
and finally two heavy bolts were shot back. Seryozha's face appeared
through a crack in the door. "Come in, come in," he said rapidly. Once
we were inside, he berated us for being late. "You see, when you come
to visit me you have to be on time," he said. "Exactly. I will unlock my
door for you and only you."

This was our first glimpse of what we took to be Seryozha's paranoia. 21
We learned that there was a reason for it after he made us tea and
sandwiches. He put on a Rod Stewart tape, and then sat down and looked
at us gravely. There was a pause, which I could not help thinking was a
little stagy; like many of my Russian friends, Seryozha has an exaggerated
sense of the moment, the grand gesture. "I'll tell you my story now," he
said, in his stilted English. Then he laughed. "I sound like a novel. But
it's a very dirty story."

It was a very dirty story, and one that unfortunately seems not at 22
all out of the ordinary in this country. Here it is, briefly: Seryozha is
married, and he and his wife are separated. Like many of our friends

---

[6]Refers to the exaggerated, monumental style of Joseph Stalin's urban renewal projects
of the 1930s and 1940s.

here, he married very young; Masha, the wife he chose, was a young Siberian woman. She didn't share his high education or his cultural interests; her parents, Party members in Irkutsk, were conservative, and thought their aristocratic son-in-law a bad bargain, with his interest in literature and Western music, and his disdain for the Party. After a few years, Seryozha and Masha separated amicably, leading independent lives in a way that seems common in this country. (Many young Russians we know seem to have a shadowy spouse, even a child, off somewhere—perhaps in another province, perhaps across town.) All fine. But Masha's family, as families will, intervened, pressing their daughter to get a divorce until she finally agreed. They also wanted to make trouble for Seryozha; the most effective method of accomplishing this was to denounce him to the K.G.B. (Strange, incidentally, to hear these letters whispered against rock music in a kitchen. The power of their mere sound to awaken nervousness in Russians is incredible. Tom once casually mentioned the K.G.B. as he sat with a Russian friend in a remote corner of a park. She shivered, and stopped him from saying the name again. "It makes me very nervous to hear that," she said.) Seryozha's small desk, which he kept locked, was broken into and searched—he described this to us with a peculiar wincing delicacy, as if he were talking about the loss of a limb. Inside were copies of "The Gulag Archipelago" and Mikhail Bulgakov's "The Master and Margarita," a modern classic novel banned by the government. There was also a picture of Czar Nicholas II.[7] ("I used to light candles to it," Seryozha said ironically.) These possessions, along with his aristocratic background, a reputation for associating with foreigners, and his dislike of the Party, were enough to compromise him thoroughly.

What was behind this ugly action was the most commonplace of Russian personal motives. From far away in Siberia, Seryozha's parents-in-law had long had their eye on Seryozha's gem of an apartment—and on the alluring possibility of life in the capital. A Moscow *propiska*, or residence permit, is extremely difficult to obtain; one major requirement, as they well knew, is the existence of an available apartment. The denunciation of their son-in-law might mean that he must forfeit the apartment to Masha in a divorce settlement. Seryozha sighed as he told us this, and I thought of the nightmarish housing shortage in Moscow. The loss of a good apartment is a very serious thing. But the other consequences of the denunciation are more serious. One of them was that Seryozha would certainly forfeit any chance of fulfilling his dream of travel outside the Soviet Union. Moreover, his father might be demoted

23

---

[7]The last Russian czar, deposed in 1917 and executed the next year.

from his rather high position in the Party. This was what Seryozha feared most of all. Anonymous letters concerning Seryozha had already been sent to his father's superiors. "Russian families have strong ties," he told us, "but this would create a rift nothing could bridge."

For the next month, Tom and I visited Seryozha twice a week. It was a period of limbo for him. The divorce hearing was set for the indefinite future; the outcome of the denunciation was uncertain. Although we thought that meeting with foreigners at this time might compromise him further, he insisted on inviting us over. He acted with a strange mixture of recklessness and paranoia. We spent one amazing afternoon with him and Anya at the sixteenth-century Novo-Devichy Convent. Seryozha showed us how to slip through a wooden reconstruction barricade and climb to the forbidden top of the ramparts. He laughed as hard as any of us as he led us running around the top of the convent walls, ducking to avoid being seen by guards or tourists. In a taxi going home, however, he forbade us to speak any English—too dangerous for him, he said. At home, he would often lecture us on our naïveté about the Soviet Union. "You are not critical enough," he said. He told us about hidden cameras and listening devices. Often, as he spoke, he would get up and turn the tape player up louder. He told us about a friend of his who had been reading a forbidden book while riding on the Metro and had been spotted by a K.G.B. agent. The agent hustled his friend off the train and threatened to turn him in. But Seryozha's friend had the presence of mind to offer a bribe of forty rubles, and the agent went away after only issuing a warning. "The danger always exists," Seryozha said, drumming his fingers on the table. "But it is not often the kind of danger you envision. For most of us, it is an ugly, petty danger. The long arm ends in greedy little men."

When we saw Seryozha in the middle of last week, he was uneasy. He had heard rumors that his wife's parents were now in Moscow; this meant they were planning some decisive move. But he promised to visit the monastery at Zagorsk with us on Sunday morning—today. When we knocked on the door this morning, we heard the usual footsteps, then silence, then the rattling of the locks. Seryozha finally opened the door and pulled us inside. The apartment was unlit. Seryozha wore jeans and a shrunken black sweater that made his slim body look theatrically thin. He was very pale, and his mouth wore a trembling smile. He hurried us into the kitchen, putting a finger to his lips until he had shut the kitchen door. He said, "I'll explain to you very quickly, and then you have to go."

He told us that his wife's family had pulled some strings to advance the date of the hearing, that it was set for noon on Monday, and that until then he was being watched constantly—by his wife's family, by his own family, and by the K.G.B. His lawyer had told him that the denunciation was uncontestable; it was almost certain that he would lose his apartment and that his father would suffer as well. Our presence there was dangerous to him: if he should be seen with Americans right now, it would make his case far worse. As he told us this, there was a loud knock at the front door. We froze. The knock was repeated. We heard a slight commotion of voices in the hall, and the sound of someone trying the lock. Seryozha crept out of the kitchen to listen through the door, and then returned to us. "They're all there," he said. "My wife's family—the vultures! But they can't come in. I've changed the locks. They'll leave for a while, and when they do you must go quickly. Run down the stairs, don't walk." He said this last in English; then he added, still in English. "It's a very dirty thing. Very dirty."

The knocking and rattling went on for a few minutes while the three of us sat in the dim little kitchen. The knocking disturbed me very much. It was not loud, but it seemed to be breaking through something inside me, a membrane of privacy I hadn't known existed. I saw Seryozha wincing, and I thought of the purges, of Anya's father—times past when a knock on the door meant the breaking apart of lives.

The knocking stopped, and there was silence. The three of us took several deep breaths. Seryozha grabbed our arms and hurried us out of the kitchen. He set his ear against the door. Then he thrust our coats at us. "All right, go, go!" he said. "Wait. I'll see you sometime when this is over." And he made the arrangements for getting in touch with us which I have described. As he shook our hands and said goodbye, I took a good look at him. I thought that in the States he would have been a student friend of mine: well-mannered, idle, artistic, mildly radical—in short, someone to frequent a coffeehouse in Harvard Square, not to head a list of political victims. Then I thought of the family who had just left his door. He had got entangled in this shabby web of denunciation not through the operation of some gigantic, all-seeing machine but through the greed and petty vindictiveness of those near to him. Seryozha's life was not shattered—it had only been disrupted in a particularly degrading way. I remembered his story of his friend's encounter with the K.G.B. agent on the Metro. This, it seemed to me, showed the same theme, which is one I've run into constantly since I've been in the Soviet Union: that the evil of the system is aided less by a desire to uphold that system than by some of the nastier personal motives that drive human nature. The greedy little men are everywhere.

All this went through my mind in a rush, confused by fear. For a few seconds, Tom and I stood in the hall, looking at Seryozha across the barrier that misfortune erects around a friend. There was nothing to say except "Good luck" and "We will think of you." He opened the door and gave us a slight push. "Go, go! he whispered, with his trembling smile. I gave him a kiss, and then we bolted down the stairs.

About the Essay

1. What does Seryozha say lies at the bottom of his difficulties with his wife's family? What does this suggest about life in the Soviet Union today? Are there any similar problems in the United States?

2. How does Seryozha regard his father? The rest of his family?

3. What is there in Seryozha's behavior that makes him suspect and vulnerable in Soviet society? Does he seem unreasonably paranoid?

4. How would you characterize the friendship that exists between the author, her husband, and Seryozha?

5. How has Lee organized her narrative? Why do you suppose she begins it where she does? What would have been gained or lost if she had started it at another point?

Explorations

1. At the end of her essay, Andrea Lee writes that Seryozha's troubles showed the same theme that she had constantly encountered since she had been in the Soviet Union. Discuss what she means when she writes that "the evil of the system is aided less by a desire to uphold that system than by some of the nastier personal motives that drive human nature. The greedy little men are everywhere." Is Lee's observation true only of Soviet society?

2. If you have traveled or lived abroad, what struck you as strange and different about the country or countries you visited? What was surprisingly familiar? How would you go about giving someone who had never been there a sense of what it was really like?

3. Seryozha is much attached to some of the cultural features of the United States. Do you know anyone here who has a similar fascination with a foreign country? If so, describe that person. If not, select a country that interests you and describe those aspects that attract your interest.

ISAAC BASHEVIS SINGER

In his formal speech accepting the 1978 Nobel Prize for literature, Isaac Bashevis Singer mentioned his "cronies in the cafeteria near the *Jewish Daily Forward* in New York." The reference is typical of him, for Singer has never sought to forget or overlook the humble, mundane parts of his life. Born in the small Polish town of Bilgoray in 1904, he grew up in the Jewish ghetto in Warsaw. His father was a rabbi of the mystical Hasidic sect, and Singer himself studied to become a rabbi. Instead he began a career as a writer with Warsaw's Yiddish newspaper, meanwhile writing short stories, novellas, and his first novel, *Satan in Goray* (1935). In 1935 he emigrated to New York, four years before Hitler invaded Poland and razed the Warsaw ghetto. Though fluent in English, he has continued to write his fiction in Yiddish, saying: "In a figurative way, Yiddish is the wise and humble language of us all, the idiom of frightened and hopeful humanity." The following selection comes from the autobiographical *A Day of Pleasure* (1969). In it Singer remembers his childhood, poor in means but rich in tradition and imagination, and his childhood friend Shosha, the little girl who lived down the hall.

Shosha

In the days when we used to live at 10 Krochmalna Street, I mostly stayed home at night. Our courtyard was dark and the small kerosene lamps in the hallway gave more smoke than light. The stories my parents told about devils, demons, and werewolves made me afraid to go out, so I would remain indoors and read.

In those days, we had a neighbor called Basha, who had three daughters: Shosha, who was nine; Ippa, five; and Teibele, two. Basha owned a store that stayed open until late in the evening.

In the summertime the nights are short, but in winter they are very long. The only place I could go at night was Shosha's apartment, but to get there I had to pass through a dark corridor. It took only a minute, yet that minute was filled with terror. Luckily, Shosha would almost always hear me coming, running and breathing heavily, and would quickly open the door. At the sight of her, I lost all fear. Shosha, though she was a year older than I, was more childish. She was fair, with blond braids and blue eyes. We were drawn to each other because we loved to tell each other stories, and we also loved to play together.

The moment I entered the apartment, Shosha took out "the things." Her toys consisted of articles discarded by grown-ups: buttons from old coats, a teakettle handle, a wooden spool with no thread left, tinfoil

170

from a package of tea, and other such objects. With my colored pencils, I often drew people and animals for Shosha. Shosha and her sister Ippa admired my artwork.

There was a tile stove in Shosha's apartment behind which there lived a cricket. It chirped the nights through all winter long. I imagined that the cricket was telling a story that would never end. But who can understand the language of crickets? Shosha believed that a house imp also made its home behind the stove. A house imp never does anyone any harm. Sometimes it even helps the household. Just the same, one is afraid of it.   5

Shosha's house imp liked to play little tricks. When Shosha took off her shoes and stockings before she went to sleep and placed them near her bed, she'd find them on the table in the morning. The house imp had put them there. Several times when Shosha went to bed with her hair unbraided, the house imp braided it while she was asleep. Once when Shosha was playing at casting goat shadows on the wall with her fingers, the shadow goat jumped off the wall and butted her on the forehead. This, too, was a trick of the house imp. Another time Shosha's mother sent her to the baker to buy fresh rolls and gave her a silver gulden to pay for them. Shosha lost the gulden in the gutter and came home frightened and crying. Suddenly she felt a coin in her hand. The house imp tweaked her left braid and whispered into her ear: "Schlemiel."   6

I had heard these stories many times, but they never failed to make me shiver with excitement. I myself liked to invent things. I told the girls that my father had a treasure that was hidden in a cave in the forest. I boasted that my grandfather was the King of Bilgoray. I assured Shosha that I knew a magic word that could destroy the world if spoken. "Please, Itchele, please don't say it," she would beg me.   7

The trip home was even more frightening than getting to Shosha's. My fear grew with the stories we told each other. It seemed to me that the dark hall was full of evil spirits. I had once read a story about a boy who had been forced by the demons to marry one of their she-devils. I was afraid that it might happen to me. According to the story, the couple lived somewhere in the desert near Mount Seir.[1] Their children were half human and half demon. As I ran through the dark corridor, I kept repeating words that would guard me against the creatures of the night: 8

"Thou shalt not permit a witch to live—
A witch to live thou shalt not permit."

When we moved to 12 Krochmalna Street, there was no question   9

---

[1]Mountain range in the ancient Palestinian land of Edom, now part of Jordan.

of visiting Shosha at night. Also, it was not fitting for a Hasidic boy, a student of the Talmud, to play with girls.[2] I missed Shosha. I hoped we'd meet on the street sometime, but months and years passed and we did not see each other.

In time Shosha became for me an image of the past. I often thought about her during the day and dreamed about her at night. In my dreams Shosha was as beautiful as a princess. Several times I dreamed that she had married the house imp and lived with him in a dark cellar. He brought her food but never let her go out. I saw her sitting on a chair, to which she had been tied with rope, while the house imp fed her jam with a tiny spoon. He had the head of a dog and the wings of a bat.

After the First World War, I left my family in Bilgoray and returned to Warsaw. I began to write and my stories appeared in newspapers and magazines. I also wrote a novel called *Satan in Goray* in which I described the devils and demons of olden times. I was married and had a son. I applied for a passport and a visa to emigrate to the United States, and one day they arrived. I was about to leave Warsaw forever.

A few days before I left, my feet led me to Krochmalna Street. I hadn't been there for years and I wanted once again to see the street where I grew up.

Few changes had taken place, though the buildings were older and even shabbier. I peered into some courtyards: huge trash cans; barefoot, half-naked children. The boys played tag, hide-and-seek, cops-and-robbers, just as we had twenty-five years ago. The girls occupied themselves with hopscotch. Suddenly it occurred to me that I might be able to find Shosha. I made my way to the building where we used to live. God in heaven, everything was the same—the peeling walls, the refuse. I reached the corridor that led to Shosha's apartment, and it was just as dark as in the old days. I lit a match and found the door. As I did so, I realized how foolish I was being. Shosha would be over thirty now. It was most unlikely that the family would still be living in the same place. And even if her parents were still alive and living there, Shosha would surely have married and moved away. But some power I cannot explain forced me to knock on the door.

There was no reply. I drew the latch (as I had sometimes done in the old days) and the door opened. I entered a kitchen that looked exactly like Basha's kitchen of twenty-five years before. I recognized the mortar and pestle, the table, the chairs. Was I dreaming? Could it be true?

---

[2]The Talmud is an ancient collection of Jewish law and of commentaries by sages on the written and oral traditions of the Jews.

Then I noticed a girl of about eight or nine. My God, it was Shosha! 15
The same fair face, the same blond hair braided with red ribbons, the
same longish neck. The girl stared at me in surprise, but she didn't seem
alarmed.

"Who are you looking for?" she asked, and it was Shosha's voice. 16

"What is your name?" I said. 17

"Me? Basha." 18

"And your mother's name?" 19

"Shosha," the girl replied. 20

"Where is your mother?" 21

"In the store." 22

"I once lived here," I explained. "I used to play with your mother 23
when she was a little girl."

Basha looked at me with large eyes and inquired, "Are you Itchele?" 24

"How do you know about Itchele?" I said. A lump stuck in my 25
throat. I could barely speak.

"My mother told me about him." 26

"Yes, I am Itchele." 27

"My mother told me everything. Your father had a cave in the 28
forest full of gold and diamonds. You knew a word that could set the
whole world on fire. Do you still know it?"

"No, not any more." 29

"What happened to the gold in the cave?" 30

"Somebody stole it," I said. 31

"And is your grandfather still a king?" 32

"No, Basha, he is not a king any more." 33

For a while we were both silent. Then I asked, "Did your mother 34
tell you about the house imp?"

"Yes, we used to have a house imp, but he's gone." 35

"What happened to him?" 36

"I don't know." 37

"And the cricket?" 38

"The cricket is still here, but it chirps mostly at night." 39

I went down to the candy store—the one where Shosha and I used 40
to buy candy—and bought cookies, chocolate, and halvah. Then I went
back upstairs and gave them to Basha.

"Would you like to hear a story?" I asked her. 41

"Yes, very much." 42

I told Basha a story about a beautiful blond girl whom a demon had 43
carried away to the desert, to Mount Seir, and had forced to marry him,
and about the children that were born of the marriage, who were half
human, half demon.

Basha's eyes grew pensive. "And she stayed there?"   44

"No, Basha, a saintly man called Rabbi Leib learned about her   45
misfortune. He traveled to the desert and rescued her."

"How?"   46

"An angel helped him."   47

"And what happened to her children?"   48

"The children became completely human and went with their mother.   49
The angel carried them to safety on his wings."

"And the demon?"   50

"He remained in the desert."   51

"And he never married again?"   52

"Yes, Basha, he did. He married a she-demon, one of his own   53
kind."

We were both silent again, and suddenly I heard the familiar chirp- 54
ing of a cricket. Could it be the cricket of my childhood? Certainly not.
Perhaps her great-great-great-granddaughter. But she was telling the same
story, as ancient as time, as puzzling as the world, and as long as the
dark winter nights of Warsaw.

About the Essay

1. What seems to be the point of Singer's narrative? Why do you think he
tells the story?

2. Characterize the friendship between the young Singer and his neighbor
Shosha. Why did they think of their friendship as something special?

3. What draws Singer back to his old neighborhood? What has changed and
what remains the same?

4. Why do you think he tells Basha a demon story like the one he used to
tell Shosha? How has he changed the story? Why do you think he changed
it?

5. How important is the setting in Singer's narrative? What is the significance of the cricket?

6. The child Basha has the same name as her grandmother, looks and sounds
like her mother, Shosha, and knows the childhood stories told by Itchele.
How do these correspondences relate to the point of the story?

Explorations

1. Think back to your strongest childhood friendships. What were they like?
What needs do you think they fulfilled? Do they differ in any way from the
friendships you now have? If so, how?

2. The Warsaw ghetto came to an end in 1939, when it was razed by the Nazis. Consulting historical sources, describe the violent destruction of the Warsaw ghetto, and tell what happened to the many Jews who had lived there.

3. The Singer family was poor, and so was Dick Gregory's family (see "Shame," in Section 1). How did the two families and their circumstances differ? From what you can infer from the two pieces included here, how have these differences affected Gregory's and Singer's memories of their childhood?

ROBERT HAYDEN

The black experience is the source of some of Robert Hayden's best poetry, from his dramatic evocation of the slave trade in "Middle Passage" to his elegy for Malcolm X in "El-Hajj Malik El-Shabazz." Alongside these, however, are many other poems about his own particular roots, "Pennsylvania gothic, Kentucky homespun, Virginia baroque," and a great-grandmother who was "a Virginia freedman's Indian bride," as he says in "Beginnings." Hayden was born in Detroit in 1913 and went to college there at Wayne State University, which was then Detroit City College. He taught English at Fisk University in Nashville from 1946 to 1969 and then returned to his native state, where he taught at the University of Michigan until his death in 1980. In his last years he was named Consultant in Poetry to the Library of Congress, the only public position by which the United States can honor its leading poets. His own selection of his best poems was published in 1975 as *Angle of Ascent*.

One of Hayden's first published poems, "Obituary," was about his father. Twenty years later, when he was nearly fifty and was himself a parent, he reflected once again on his father in "Those Winter Sundays." One hears often of labors of love; here, Hayden tells of a love that could express itself only through labor.

Those Winter Sundays

Sundays too my father got up early
and put his clothes in the blueblack cold,
then with cracked hands that ached
from labor in the weekday weather made
banked fires blaze. No one ever thanked him.   5

I'd wake and hear the cold splintering, breaking.
When the rooms were warm, he'd call,
and slowly I would rise and dress,
fearing the chronic angers of that house,

Speaking indifferently to him,   10
who had driven out the cold
and polished my good shoes as well.
What did I know, what did I know
of love's austere and lonely offices?

About the Poem

1. What does the speaker of the poem now realize about his father that he did not realize at an earlier age? Why do those "winter Sundays" stand out in his memory?

2. What might Hayden mean when he refers to "the chronic angers of that house?"

3. Does the poem suggest something about the relationship that often exists between parents and children? If so, what?

4. How does the speaker of the poem now view his behavior as a child? How does he feel about it? What lines indicate his feeling?

5. What is the tone of the poem? How would you describe Hayden's diction? What effect does it create?

6. What does Hayden mean by "love's austere and lonely offices"? State the meaning of the phrase in your own words, and explain how it applies to the rest of the poem.

Explorations

1. In the last line of the poem, Hayden writes of "love's austere and lonely offices." How can one know that an action is motivated by love, if it is not done in a clearly loving way? Or do actions really speak louder than words? Call on your own experience to support your answer.

2. Hayden refers to "chronic angers" in the household in which he grew up. What are some of the effects such a situation has on children? Besides your own experience and that of people you know, you may want to consult sources in psychiatry or developmental psychology.

THEODORE ROETHKE

Theodore Roethke is known among readers and critics as one of the finest American poets of his generation. Among poets, he is also remembered as an inspiring teacher of creative writing, especially during his fourteen years at the University of Washington. He was born in Michigan in 1908 and educated at the University of Michigan; later he had his first teaching job there and also served as the university's public relations director and tennis coach. A complex man, swinging between extremes of egoistic boastfulness and severe depression, he could be both formidable and vulnerable in the classroom, sometimes in the same hour. In 1959 he received the Bollingen Prize for the body of his poetic work, which was published after his death in 1963 as his *Collected Poems* (1966). "Elegy for Jane" presents both Roethke the skillful, sensitive poet and Roethke the loving teacher, one who could be both mentor and friend.

Elegy for Jane

My Student, Thrown by a Horse

I remember the neckcurls, limp and damp as tendrils;
And her quick look, a sidelong pickerel smile;
And how, once startled into talk, the light syllables leaped for her,
And she balanced in the delight of her thought,
A wren, happy, tail into the wind,   5
Her song trembling the twigs and small branches.
The shade sang with her;
The leaves, their whispers turned to kissing;
And the mold sang in the bleached valleys under the rose.

Oh, when she was sad, she cast herself down into such a pure depth,   10
Even a father could not find her;
Scraping her cheek against straw;
Stirring the clearest water.

My sparrow, you are not here,
Waiting like a fern, making a spiny shadow.   15
The sides of wet stones cannot console me,
Nor the moss, wound with the last light.

If only I could nudge you from this sleep,
My maimed darling, my skittery pigeon.
Over this damp grave I speak the words of my love: 20
I, with no rights in this matter,
Neither father nor lover.

About the Poem

1. What is the setting of the poem?

2. How is the poem organized? How does the emphasis shift from stanza to stanza? In what way does the poet lead you gradually to the death that is lamented in the final stanza?

3. Roethke compares Jane with many things through similes and metaphors. Identify several of these. What do these comparisons have in common? What does each contribute to our knowledge of Jane?

4. What do lines 10–14 mean?

5. What is the quality of the speaker's feeling toward Jane? How would you characterize their relationship? Do you agree with the speaker that he has "no rights in this matter"?

Explorations

1. Think of the teacher you believe has taught you the most, and the teacher you have liked the best. Were they the same person? Describe each teacher's qualities, as a person and as a teacher.

2. Have you experienced the death of a loved one or close friend? How did you feel at the news of this death? On reflection, how does this experience affect your understanding of Roethke's poem?

KATHERINE ANNE PORTER

Born in 1890 in Texas, and a resident of Mexico for several years, Katherine Anne Porter knew first-hand the sunburnt, wide-open land in which her short story "Rope" is set. She also knew first-hand the tensions of marriage, which the story depicts in convincing detail. Educated in convent schools, she eloped from one of them at sixteen and between 1933 and 1942 was twice married and twice divorced. As she put it, her problem was that writing came before everything else. Even so, her collected short fiction consists of only twenty-seven stories and novellas, and she wrote only one full-length novel, *Ship of Fools* (1962). Her last book, reflecting her continuing concern with politics and social issues, is a remembrance of the Sacco-Vanzetti trial of the 1920s (*The Never-Ending Wrong*, 1977). She died in 1980.

"Rope" comes from Porter's first collection of short stories, *Flowering Judas* (1930). Without making grand statements, she uses a short, sharp quarrel between a husband and wife to reveal something of the risks and rewards of marriage.

Rope

On the third day after they moved to the country he came walking back from the village carrying a basket of groceries and a twenty-four-yard coil of rope. She came out to meet him, wiping her hands on her green smock. Her hair was tumbled, her nose was scarlet with sunburn; he told her that already she looked like a born country woman. His gray flannel shirt stuck to him, his heavy shoes were dusty. She assured him he looked like a rural character in a play.

Had he brought the coffee? She had been waiting all day long for coffee. They had forgot it when they ordered at the store the first day.

Gosh, no, he hadn't. Lord, now he'd have to go back. Yes, he would if it killed him. He thought, though, he had everything else. She reminded him it was only because he didn't drink coffee himself. If he did he would remember it quick enough. Suppose they ran out of cigarettes? Then she saw the rope. What was that for? Well, he thought it might do to hang clothes on, or something. Naturally she asked him if he thought they were going to run a laundry? They already had a fifty-foot line hanging right before his eyes? Why, hadn't he noticed it, really? It was a blot on the landscape to her.

He thought there were a lot of things a rope might come in handy for. She wanted to know what, for instance. He thought a few seconds,

180

but nothing occurred. They could wait and see, couldn't they? You need all sorts of strange odds and ends around a place in the country. She said, yes, that was so; but she thought just at that time when every penny counted, it seemed funny to buy more rope. That was all. She hadn't meant anything else. She hadn't just seen, not at first, why he felt it was necessary.

Well, thunder, he had bought it because he wanted to, and that was all there was to it. She thought that was reason enough, and couldn't understand why he hadn't said so, at first. Undoubtedly it would be useful, twenty-four yards of rope, there were hundreds of things, she couldn't think of any at the moment, but it would come in. Of course. As he had said, things always did in the country.

But she was a little disappointed about the coffee, and oh, look, look, look at the eggs! Oh, my, they're all running! What had he put on top of them? Hadn't he known eggs mustn't be squeezed? Squeezed, who had squeezed them, he wanted to know. What a silly thing to say. He had simply brought them along in the basket with the other things. If they got broke it was the grocer's fault. He should know better than to put heavy things on top of eggs.

She believed it was the rope. That was the heaviest thing in the pack, she saw him plainly when he came in from the road, the rope was a big package on top of everything. He desired the whole wide world to witness that this was not a fact. He had carried the rope in one hand and the basket in the other, and what was the use of her having eyes if that was the best they could do for her?

Well, anyhow, she could see one thing plain: no eggs for breakfast. They'd have to scramble them now, for supper. It was too damned bad. She had planned to have steak for supper. No ice, meat wouldn't keep. He wanted to know why she couldn't finish breaking the eggs in a bowl and set them in a cool place.

Cool place! if he could find one for her, she'd be glad to set them there. Well, then, it seemed to him they might very well cook the meat at the same time they cooked the eggs and then warm up the meat for tomorrow. The idea simply choked her. Warmed-over meat, when they might as well have had it fresh. Second best and scraps and makeshifts, even to the meat! He rubbed her shoulder a little. It doesn't really matter so much, does it, darling? Sometimes when they were playful, he would rub her shoulder and she would arch and purr. This time she hissed and almost clawed. He was getting ready to say that they could surely manage somehow when she turned on him and said, if he told her they could manage somehow she would certainly slap his face.

He swallowed the words red hot, his face burned. He picked up the   10
rope and started to put it on the top shelf. She would not have it on the
top shelf, the jars and tins belonged there; positively she would not have
the top shelf cluttered up with a lot of rope. She had borne all the clutter
she meant to bear in the flat in town, there was space here at least and
she meant to keep things in order.

Well, in that case, he wanted to know what the hammer and nails   11
were doing up there? And why had she put them there when she knew
very well he needed that hammer and those nails upstairs to fix the
window sashes? She simply slowed down everything and made double
work on the place with her insane habit of changing things around and
hiding them.

She was sure she begged his pardon, and if she had had any reason   12
to believe he was going to fix the sashes this summer she would have left
the hammer and nails right where he put them; in the middle of the
bedroom floor where they could step on them in the dark. And now if
he didn't clear the whole mess out of there she would throw them down
the well.

Oh, all right, all right—could he put them in the closet? Naturally   13
not, there were brooms and mops and dustpans in the closet, and why
couldn't he find a place for his rope outside her kitchen? Had he stopped
to consider there were seven God-forsaken rooms in the house, and only
one kitchen?

He wanted to know what of it? And did she realize she was making   14
a complete fool of herself? And what did she take him for, a three-year-
old idiot? The whole trouble with her was she needed something weaker
than she was to heckle and tyrannize over. He wished to God now they
had a couple of children she could take it out on. Maybe he'd get some
rest.

Her face changed at this, she reminded him he had forgot the coffee   15
and had bought a worthless piece of rope. And when she thought of all
the things they actually needed to make the place even decently fit to
live in, well, she could cry, that was all. She looked so forlorn, so lost
and despairing he couldn't believe it was only a piece of rope that was
causing all the racket. What *was* the matter, for God's sake?

Oh, would he please hush and go away, and *stay* away, if he could,   16
for five minutes? By all means, yes, he would. He'd stay away indefinitely
if she wished. Lord, yes, there was nothing he'd like better than to clear
out and never come back. She couldn't for the life of her see what was
holding him, then. It was a swell time. Here she was, stuck, miles from
a railroad, with a half-empty house on her hands, and not a penny in
her pocket, and everything on earth to do; it seemed the God-sent mo-

ment for him to get out from under. She was surprised he hadn't stayed in town as it was until she had come out and done the work and got things straightened out. It was his usual trick.

It appeared to him that this was going a little far. Just a touch out of bounds, if she didn't mind his saying so. Why the hell had he stayed in town the summer before? To do a half-dozen extra jobs to get the money he had sent her. That was it. She knew perfectly well they couldn't have done it otherwise. She had agreed with him at the time. And that was the only time so help him he had ever left her to do anything by herself.   17

Oh, he could tell that to his great-grandmother. She had her notion of what had kept him in town. Considerably more than a notion, if he wanted to know. So, she was going to bring all that up again, was she? Well, she could just think what she pleased. He was tired of explaining. It may have looked funny but he had simply got hooked in, and what could he do? It was impossible to believe that she was going to take it seriously. Yes, yes, she knew how it was with a man: if he was left by himself a minute, some woman was certain to kidnap him. And naturally he couldn't hurt her feelings by refusing!   18

Well, what was she raving about? Did she forget she had told him those two weeks alone in the country were the happiest she had known for four years? And how long had they been married when she said that? All right, shut up! If she thought that hadn't stuck in his craw.   19

She hadn't meant she was happy because she was away from him. She meant she was happy getting the devilish house nice and ready for him. That was what she had meant, and now look! Bringing up something she had said a year ago simply to justify himself for forgetting her coffee and breaking the eggs and buying a wretched piece of rope they couldn't afford. She really thought it was time to drop the subject, and now she wanted only two things in the world. She wanted him to get that rope from underfoot, and go back to the village and get her coffee, and if he could remember it, he might bring a metal mitt for the skillets, and two more curtain rods, and if there were any rubber gloves in the village, her hands were simply raw, and a bottle of milk of magnesia from the drugstore.   20

He looked out at the dark blue afternoon sweltering on the slopes, and mopped his forehead and sighed heavily and said, if only she could wait a minute for *anything*, he was going back. He had said so, hadn't he, the very instant they found he had overlooked it?   21

Oh, yes, well . . . run along. She was going to wash windows. The country was so beautiful! She doubted they'd have a moment to enjoy it. He meant to go, but he could not until he had said that if she wasn't   22 such a hopeless melancholiac she might see that this was only for a few days. Couldn't she remember anything pleasant about the other summers? Hadn't they ever had any fun? She hadn't time to talk about it, and now would he please not leave that rope lying around for her to trip on? He picked it up, somehow it had toppled off the table, and walked out with it under his arm.

Was he going this minute? He certainly was. She thought so. Some- 23 times it seemed to her he had second sight about the precisely perfect moment to leave her ditched. She had meant to put the mattresses out to sun, if they put them out this minute they would get at least three hours, he must have heard her say that morning she meant to put them out. So of course he would walk off and leave her to it. She supposed he thought the exercise would do her good.

Well, he was merely going to get her coffee. A four-mile walk for 24 two pounds of coffee was ridiculous, but he was perfectly willing to do it. The habit was making a wreck of her, but if she wanted to wreck herself there was nothing he could do about it. If he thought it was coffee that was making a wreck of her, she congratulated him: he must have a damned easy conscience.

Conscience or no conscience, he didn't see why the mattresses 25 couldn't very well wait until tomorrow. And anyhow, for God's sake, were they living *in* the house, or were they going to let the house ride them to death? She paled at this, her face grew livid about the mouth, she looked quite dangerous, and reminded him that housekeeping was no more her work than it was his: she had other work to do as well, and when did he think she was going to find time to do it at this rate?

Was she going to start on that again? She knew as well as he did 26 that his work brought in the regular money, hers was only occasional, if they depended on what *she* made—and she might as well get straight on this question once for all!

That was positively not the point. The question was, when both 27 of them were working on their own time, was there going to be a division of the housework, or wasn't there? She merely wanted to know, she had to make her plans. Why, he thought that was all arranged. It was under- stood that he was to help. Hadn't he always, in summers?

Hadn't he, though? Oh, just hadn't he? And when, and where, 28 and doing what? Lord, what an uproarious joke!

It was such a very uproarious joke that her face turned slightly 29 purple, and she screamed with laughter. She laughed so hard she had to sit down, and finally a rush of tears spurted from her eyes and poured down into the lifted corners of her mouth. He dashed towards her and dragged her up to her feet and tried to pour water on her head. The dipper hung by a string on a nail and he broke it loose. Then he tried to pump water with one hand while she struggled in the other. So he gave it up and shook her instead.

She wrenched away, crying for him to take his rope and go to hell, 30 she had simply given him up: and ran. He heard her high-heeled bedroom slippers clattering and stumbling on the stairs.

He went out around the house into the lane; he suddenly realized 31 he had a blister on his heel and his shirt felt as if it were on fire. Things broke so suddenly you didn't know where you were. She could work herself into a fury about simply nothing. She was terrible, damn it: not an ounce of reason. You might as well talk to a sieve as that woman when she got going. Damned if he'd spend his life humoring her! Well, what to do now? He would take back the rope and exchange it for something else. Things accumulated, things were mountainous, you couldn't move them or sort them out or get rid of them. They just lay and rotted around. He'd take it back. Hell, why should he? He wanted it. What was it anyhow? A piece of rope. Imagine anybody caring more about a piece of rope than about a man's feelings. What earthly right had she to say a word about it? He remembered all the useless, meaningless things she bought for herself: Why? because I wanted it; that's why! He stopped and selected a large stone by the road. He would put the rope behind it. He would put it in the tool-box when he got back. He'd heard enough about it to last him a life-time.

When he came back she was leaning against the post box beside 32 the road waiting. It was pretty late, the smell of broiled steak floated nose high in the cooling air. Her face was young and smooth and fresh-looking. Her unmanageable funny black hair was all on end. She waved to him from a distance, and he speeded up. She called out that supper was ready and waiting, was he starved?

You bet he was starved. Here was the coffee. He waved it at her. 33 She looked at his other hand. What was that he had there?

Well, it was the rope again. He stopped short. He had meant to 34 exchange it but forgot. She wanted to know why he should exchange it, if it was something he really wanted. Wasn't the air sweet now, and wasn't it fine to be here?

She walked beside him with one hand hooked into his leather belt. 35 She pulled and jostled him a little as he walked, and leaned against him. He put his arm clear around her and patted her stomach. They exchanged wary smiles. Coffee, coffee for the Ootsum-Wootsums! He felt as if he were bringing her a beautiful present.

He was a love, she firmly believed, and if she had had her coffee 36 in the morning, she wouldn't have behaved so funny . . . There was a whippoorwill still coming back, imagine, clear out of season, sitting in the crab-apple tree calling all by himself. Maybe his girl stood him up. Maybe she did. She hoped to hear him once more, she loved whippoorwills . . . He knew how she was, didn't he?

Sure, he knew how she was. 37

About the Story

1. Discuss the circumstances of the couple's move to the country. Why are they so disorganized?

2. How would you characterize the man and woman in this story? What exactly do they seem to be quarreling about? What do you think is the underlying cause of their disagreement? Why does the man offer to go back to town?

3. The story is told by an impersonal third-person narrator. How would it be different if told from the wife's point of view? From the husband's point of view?

4. Though most of the story consists of conversation, Porter has chosen not to use any dialogue. What is the advantage of presenting the quarrel indirectly, instead of making the characters speak directly for themselves? How do you account for the large number of questions in the story?

5. At several points in the story the tone changes. Locate the places where this occurs. How do the changes in tone affect the development of the story?

6. Why do you think Porter introduces the whippoorwill in the concluding scene?

7. What is the significance of the story's title?

Explorations

1. Married people, like the couple in Porter's story, do often get into quarrels over seemingly trivial matters. From your own experience and observation, what can such quarrels do to a marital relationship? What can they signify? When are they destructive, and when are they constructive?

2. Like the man in the story, do you sometimes buy things without any immediate plan to use them—or possibly without any particular idea of how? Is your closet full of forgotten objects you never use? What is the charm of buying such things? Why is it so hard to get rid of them?

3 Thinking and Learning

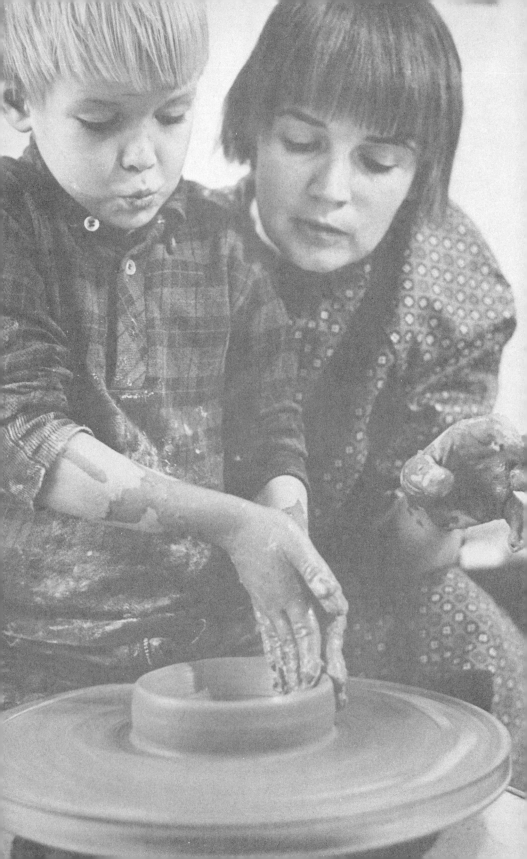

I think, therefore I am.
RENÉ DESCARTES

*Thought is not a gift to man but a laborious, precarious and
volatile acquisition.*
JOSÉ ORTEGA Y GASSET

The great difficulty in education is to get experience out of ideas.
GEORGE SANTAYANA

*Knowledge is of two kinds; we know a subject ourselves, or we
know where we can find information upon it.*
SAMUEL JOHNSON

*There may be a tendency to mistake data for wisdom, just as there
has always been a tendency to confuse logic with values, and
intelligence with insight.*
NORMAN COUSINS

Only the educated are free.
EPICTETUS

THERE is no mistaking the fact that we have entered the computer age. Indeed, we live in the decade when the computer not only continued to transform the office and assembly line but finally followed America home from work—and stayed to play, as well as to help with homework, keep the tax records, and turn off the lights. It has been estimated that by 1990 there will be a computer in one out of three American homes. In our schools, the talk is of a new kind of literacy—"computer literacy"—and some colleges have begun to require all entering students to have personal computers along with their textbooks. So equipped, these students not only can use ready-made programs to perform calculations, practice foreign languages, and revise and proofread term papers, but they also can gain direct electronic access, day or night, to numerous "data bases" located both off the campus and in the college library. Whether we are at work, at home, or at school, the amount of information we can have at—

189

literally—our fingertips and the speed with which we can summon that information are almost beyond comprehension.

Are we, therefore, wiser? Is our judgment getting better? No doubt the computer has made certain kinds of instruction easier, but is education really improving in the decade of the data base? Perhaps there has never been a more appropriate time to ask under what conditions we are justified in calling our information *knowledge,* our acquisition of it *learning,* and our manipulation of it *thinking.*

Such questions as these are raised, seriously but not always solemnly, in the readings that follow. Some examine the ways people think, whether logical or otherwise; others discuss aspects of American education in the past, present, and future. Taken together, they offer diverse and sometimes surprising perspectives on what it means to think and to learn.

WILLIAM GOLDING

Among his hobbies, the British novelist William Golding counts sailing, archaeology, classical Greek—and thinking. Thinking as a hobby? In his essay on the subject it soon becomes clear that Golding is referring to thinking of certain kinds and for certain purposes. Born in 1911, Golding attended Marlborough Grammar School and Brasenose College, Oxford, the settings of the essay. He has worked as a school teacher and has also written, acted, and directed for small theater companies. He is best known for his novel *Lord of the Flies* (1954), in which a group of young boys, stranded on a tropical island, quickly revert to savagery. His other writings confirm his view that civilization is a precarious state, easily lost. "Thinking as a Hobby" first appeared in *Holiday* magazine. In it Golding describes grade-three, grade-two, and grade-one thinking and tells how he became the kind of thinker he is.

Thinking as a Hobby

While I was still a boy, I came to the conclusion that there were three grades of thinking; and since I was later to claim thinking as my hobby, I came to an even stranger conclusion—namely, that I myself could not think at all.

I must have been an unsatisfactory child for grownups to deal with. I remember how incomprehensible they appeared to me at first, but not, of course, how I appeared to them. It was the headmaster of my grammar school who first brought the subject of thinking before me—though neither in the way, nor with the result he intended. He had some statuettes in his study. They stood on a high cupboard behind his desk. One was a lady wearing nothing but a bath towel. She seemed frozen in an eternal panic lest the bath towel slip down any farther; and since she had no arms, she was in an unfortunate position to pull the towel up again. Next to her, crouched the statuette of a leopard, ready to spring down at the top drawer of a filing cabinet labeled A-AH. My innocence interpreted this as the victim's last, despairing cry. Beyond the leopard was a naked, muscular gentleman, who sat, looking down, with his chin on his fist and his elbow on his knee. He seemed utterly miserable.

Some time later, I learned about these statuettes. The headmaster had placed them where they would face delinquent children, because they symbolized to him the whole of life. The naked lady was the Venus of Milo. She was Love. She was not worried about the towel. She was just busy being beautiful. The leopard was Nature, and he was being natural. The naked, muscular gentleman was not miserable. He was Rodin's Thinker, an image of pure thought. It is easy to buy small plaster models of what you think life is like.

I had better explain that I was a frequent visitor to the headmaster's   4
study, because of the latest thing I had done or left undone. As we now say, I was not integrated. I was, if anything, disintegrated; and I was puzzled. Grownups never made sense. Whenever I found myself in a penal position before the headmaster's desk, with the statuettes glimmering whitely above him, I would sink my head, clasp my hands behind my back and writhe one shoe over the other.

The headmaster would look opaquely at me through flashing spec-   5
tacles.

"What are we going to do with you?"   6

Well, what *were* they going to do with me? I would writhe my shoe   7
some more and stare down at the worn rug.

"Look up, boy! Can't you look up?"   8

Then I would look up at the cupboard, where the naked lady was   9
frozen in her panic and the muscular gentleman contemplated the hind-quarters of the leopard in endless gloom. I had nothing to say to the headmaster. His spectacles caught the light so that you could see nothing human behind them. There was no possibility of communication.

"Don't you ever think at all?"   10

No, I didn't think, wasn't thinking, couldn't think—I was simply   11
waiting in anguish for the interview to stop.

"Then you'd better learn—hadn't you?"   12

On one occasion the headmaster leaped to his feet, reached up and   13
plonked Rodin's masterpiece on the desk before me.

"That's what a man looks like when he's really thinking."   14

I surveyed the gentleman without interest or comprehension.   15

"Go back to your class."   16

Clearly there was something missing in me. Nature had endowed   17
the rest of the human race with a sixth sense and left me out. This must be so, I mused, on my way back to the class, since whether I had broken a window, or failed to remember Boyle's Law, or been late for school, my teachers produced me one, adult answer: "Why can't you think?"

As I saw the case, I had broken the window because I had tried to   18
hit Jack Arney with a cricket ball and missed him; I could not remember Boyle's Law because I had never bothered to learn it; and I was late for school because I preferred looking over the bridge into the river. In fact, I was wicked. Were my teachers, perhaps, so good that they could not understand the depths of my depravity? Were they clear, untormented people who could direct their every action by this mysterious business of thinking? The whole thing was incomprehensible. In my earlier years, I

found even the statuette of the Thinker confusing. I did not believe any of my teachers were naked, ever. Like someone born deaf, but bitterly determined to find out about sound, I watched my teachers to find out about thought.

There was Mr. Houghton. He was always telling me to think. With a modest satisfaction, he would tell me that he had thought a bit himself. Then why did he spend so much time drinking? Or was there more sense in drinking than there appeared to be? But if not, and if drinking were in fact ruinous to health—and Mr. Houghton was ruined, there was no doubt about that—why was he always talking about the clean life and the virtues of fresh air? He would spread his arms wide with the action of a man who habitually spent his time striding along mountain ridges.   19

"Open air does me good, boys—I know it!"   20

Sometimes, exalted by his own oratory, he would leap from his desk and hustle us outside into a hideous wind.   21

"Now, boys! Deep breaths! Feel it right down inside you—huge draughts of God's good air!"   22

He would stand before us, rejoicing in his perfect health, an open-air man. He would put his hands on his waist and take a tremendous breath. You could hear the wind, trapped in the cavern of his chest and struggling with all the unnatural impediments. His body would reel with shock and his ruined face go white at the unaccustomed visitation. He would stagger back to his desk and collapse there, useless for the rest of the morning.   23

Mr. Houghton was given to high-minded monologues about the good life, sexless and full of duty. Yet in the middle of one of these monologues, if a girl passed the window, tapping along on her neat little feet, he would interrupt his discourse, his neck would turn of itself and he would watch her out of sight. In this instance, he seemed to me ruled not by thought but by an invisible and irresistible spring in his nape.   24

His neck was an object of great interest to me. Normally it bulged a bit over his collar. But Mr. Houghton had fought in the First World War alongside both Americans and French, and had come—by who knows what illogic?—to a settled detestation of both countries. If either country happened to be prominent in current affairs, no argument could make Mr. Houghton think well of it. He would bang the desk, his neck would bulge still further and go red. "You can say what you like," he would cry, "but I've thought about this—and I know what I think!"   25

Mr. Houghton thought with his neck.   26

There was Miss Parsons. She assured us that her dearest wish was our welfare, but I knew even then, with the mysterious clairvoyance of   27 childhood, that what she wanted most was the husband she never got. There was Mr. Hands—and so on.

I have dealt at length with my teachers because this was my intro-   28
duction to the nature of what is commonly called thought. Through them I discovered that thought is often full of unconscious prejudice, ignorance and hypocrisy. It will lecture on disinterested purity while its neck is being remorselessly twisted toward a skirt. Technically, it is about as proficient as most businessmen's golf, as honest as most politicians' in-tentions, or—to come near my own preoccupation—as coherent as most books that get written. It is what I came to call grade-three thinking, though more properly, it is feeling, rather than thought.

True, often there is a kind of innocence in prejudices, but in those   29
days I viewed grade-three thinking with an intolerant contempt and an incautious mockery. I delighted to confront a pious lady who hated the Germans with the proposition that we should love our enemies. She taught me a great truth in dealing with grade-three thinkers; because of her, I no longer dismiss lightly a mental process which for nine-tenths of the population is the nearest they will ever get to thought. They have immense solidarity. We had better respect them, for we are outnumbered and surrounded. A crowd of grade-three thinkers, all shouting the same thing, all warming their hands at the fire of their own prejudices, will not thank you for pointing out the contradictions in their beliefs. Man is a gregarious animal, and enjoys agreement as cows will graze all the same way on the side of a hill.

Grade-two thinking is the detection of contradictions. I reached   30
grade two when I trapped the poor, pious lady. Grade-two thinkers do not stampede easily, though often they fall into the other fault and lag behind. Grade-two thinking is a withdrawal, with eyes and ears open. It became my hobby and brought satisfaction and loneliness in either hand. For grade-two thinking destroys without having the power to create. It set me watching the crowds cheering His Majesty the King and asking myself what all the fuss was about, without giving me anything positive to put in the place of that heady patriotism. But there were compensa-tions. To hear people justify their habit of hunting foxes and tearing them to pieces by claiming that the foxes liked it. To hear our Prime Minister talk about the great benefit we conferred on India by jailing people like Pandit Nehru and Gandhi.[1] To hear American politicians talk about peace in one sentence and refuse to join the League of Nations in the next. Yes, there were moments of delight.

---

[1]Mohandas Gandhi and Jawaharlal Nehru were leaders of the movement that brought independence to India in 1947. Nehru was India's first prime minister.

But I was growing toward adolescence and had to admit that Mr. 31
Houghton was not the only one with an irresistible spring in his neck.
I, too, felt the compulsive hand of nature and began to find that pointing
out contradictions could be costly as well as fun. There was Ruth, for
example, a serious and attractive girl. I was an atheist at the time. Grade-
two thinking is a menace to religion and knocks down sects like skittles.
I put myself in a position to be converted by her with an hypocrisy worthy
of grade three. She was a Methodist—or at least, her parents were, and
Ruth had to follow suit. But, alas, instead of relying on the Holy Spirit
to convert me, Ruth was foolish enough to open her pretty mouth in
argument. She claimed that the Bible (King James Version) was literally
inspired. I countered by saying that the Catholics believed in the literal
inspiration of Saint Jerome's *Vulgate*, [2] and the two books were different.
Argument flagged.

At last she remarked that there were an awful lot of Methodists, 32
and they couldn't be wrong, could they—not all those millions? That
was too easy, said I restively (for the nearer you were to Ruth, the nicer
she was to be near to) since there were more Roman Catholics than
Methodists anyway; and they couldn't be wrong, could they—not all
those hundreds of millions? An awful flicker of doubt appeared in her
eyes. I slid my arm around her waist and murmured breathlessly that if
we were counting heads, the Buddhists were the boys for my money. But
Ruth had *really* wanted to do me good, because I was so nice. She fled.
The combination of my arm and those countless Buddhists was too much
for her.

That night her father visited my father and left, red-cheeked and 33
indignant. I was given the third degree to find out what had happened.
It was lucky we were both of us only fourteen. I lost Ruth and gained an
undeserved reputation as a potential libertine.

So grade-two thinking could be dangerous. It was in this knowledge, 34
at the age of fifteen, that I remember making a comment from the heights
of grade two, on the limitations of grade three. One evening I found
myself alone in the school hall, preparing it for a party. The door of the
headmaster's study was open. I went in. The headmaster had ceased to
thump Rodin's Thinker down on the desk as an example to the young.
Perhaps he had not found any more candidates, but the statuettes were
still there, glimmering and gathering dust on top of the cupboard. I stood
on a chair and rearranged them. I stood Venus in her bath towel on the
filing cabinet, so that now the top drawer caught its breath in a gasp of
sexy excitement. "A-ah!" The portentous Thinker I placed on the edge

---

[2]The Latin Bible, whose text is the definitive basis for Roman Catholic doctrine.

of the cupboard so that he looked down at the bath towel and waited for it to slip.

Grade-two thinking, though it filled life with fun and excitement,   35
did not make for content. To find out the deficiencies of our elders bolsters the young ego but does not make for personal security. I found that grade two was not only the power to point out contradictions. It took the swimmer some distance from the shore and left him there, out of his depth. I decided that Pontius Pilate was a typical grade-two thinker. "What is truth?" he said, a very common grade-two thought, but one that is used always as the end of an argument instead of the beginning.[3] There is still a higher grade of thought which says, "What is truth?" and sets out to find it.

But these grade-one thinkers were few and far between. They did   36
not visit my grammar school in the flesh though they were there in books. I aspired to them, partly because I was ambitious and partly because I now saw my hobby as an unsatisfactory thing if it went no further. If you set out to climb a mountain, however high you climb, you have failed if your cannot reach the top.

I *did* meet an undeniably grade-one thinker in my first year at Ox-   37
ford. I was looking over a small bridge in Magdalen Deer Park, and a tiny mustached and hatted figure came and stood by my side. He was a German who had just fled from the Nazis to Oxford as a temporary refuge. His name was Einstein.

But Professor Einstein knew no English at that time and I knew   38
only two words of German. I beamed at him, trying wordlessly to convey by my bearing all the affection and respect that the English felt for him. It is possible—and I have to make the admission—that I felt here were two grade-one thinkers standing side by side; yet I doubt if my face conveyed more than a formless awe. I would have given my Greek and Latin and French and a good slice of my English for enough German to communicate. But we were divided; he was as inscrutable as my head-master. For perhaps five minutes we stood together on the bridge, un-deniable grade-one thinker and breathless aspirant. With true greatness, Professor Einstein realized that any contact was better than none. He pointed to a trout wavering in midstream.

He spoke: "*Fisch.*"   39

My brain reeled. Here I was, mingling with the great, and yet   40
helpless as the veriest grade-three thinker. Desperately I sought for some

---

[3]In response to Jesus's statement, "For this I was born, and for this I have come into the world, to bear witness to the truth. Everyone who is of the truth hears my voice." Pilate was the Roman administrator of Judea who tried Jesus and turned him over for crucifixion.

sign by which I might convey that I, too, revered pure reason. I nodded vehemently. In a brilliant flash I used up half of my German vocabulary.

"*Fisch. Ja Ja.*"   41

For perhaps another five minutes we stood side by side. Then Pro-   42
fessor Einstein, his whole figure still conveying good will and amiability, drifted away out of sight.

I, too, would be a grade-one thinker. I was irreverent at the best   43
of times. Political and religious systems, social customs, loyalties and traditions, they all came tumbling down like so many rotten apples off a tree. This was a fine hobby and a sensible substitute for cricket, since you could play it all the year round. I came up in the end with what must always remain the justification for grade-one thinking, its sign, seal and charter. I devised a coherent system for living. It was a moral system, which was wholly logical. Of course, as I readily admitted, conversion of the world to my way of thinking might be difficult, since my system did away with a number of trifles, such as big business, centralized government, armies, marriage. . . .

It was Ruth all over again. I had some very good friends who stood   44
by me, and still do. But my acquaintances vanished, taking the girls with them. Young women seemed oddly contented with the world as it was. They valued the meaningless ceremony with a ring. Young men, while willing to concede the chaining sordidness of marriage, were hesitant about abandoning the organizations which they hoped would give them a career. A young man on the first rung of the Royal Navy, while perfectly agreeable to doing away with big business and marriage, got as rednecked as Mr. Houghton when I proposed a world without any battleships in it.

Had the game gone too far? Was it a game any longer? In those   45
prewar days, I stood to lose a great deal, for the sake of a hobby.

Now you are expecting me to describe how I saw the folly of my   46
ways and came back to the warm nest, where prejudices are so often called loyalties, where pointless actions are hallowed into custom by repetition, where we are content to say we think when all we do is feel.

But you would be wrong. I dropped my hobby and turned profes-   47
sional.

If I were to go back to the headmaster's study and find the dusty   48
statuettes still there, I would arrange them differently. I would dust Venus and put her aside, for I have come to love her and know her for the fair thing she is. But I would put the Thinker, sunk in his desperate thought, where there were shadows before him—and at his back, I would put the leopard, crouched and ready to spring.

About the Essay

1. Briefly describe each of the three categories into which Golding classifies thinkers. Can you suggest any categories that Golding does not mention?

2. According to Golding, why do people become grade-three and grade-two thinkers? What does he say is wrong with each type? What sacrifices does grade-one thinking require?

3. How does Golding explain grade-one thinking? Does he succeed in making the concept clear to you? Why, or why not?

4. What does each of the headmaster's statuettes symbolize? Why did Golding rearrange them as he describes in paragraph 34? Why would he now rearrange them as he describes in the last paragraph?

5. What is Golding's tone in this essay? Citing examples from the text, show how it expresses his attitude toward his teachers, his subject, and himself.

6. Why does Golding say that thinking was his hobby? What does he mean by saying that he dropped his hobby and turned professional?

Explorations

1. What practical value do you find in Golding's classification of grades of thinking? Does it clarify the nature of thought for you? How would you classify different kinds of thought?

2. Using Golding's system of classification, describe a person you know who fits into one of his categories, providing enough details and anecdotes to support your categorization. Or apply Golding's system to another selection in this book, showing which grade of thinking it represents and why.

ALEXANDER CALANDRA

Tests in school and college are usually designed so that each question has only one correct answer, especially in disciplines such as the natural sciences. Yet many important discoveries have been made by individuals who have reached beyond the obvious and "known" answers—take Galileo, Columbus, and Einstein, for example. Alexander Calandra, a professor of physics at Washington University in St. Louis, once came across a college student who insisted on giving every answer but the expected one to a physics exam question. In this essay, originally published in *Saturday Review*, he tells what happened.

Angels on a Pin

Some time ago, I received a call from a colleague who asked if I would be the referee on the grading of an examination question. He was about to give a student a zero for his answer to a physics question, while the student claimed he should receive a perfect score and would if the system were not set up against the student. The instructor and the student agreed to submit this to an impartial arbiter, and I was selected.

I went to my colleague's office and read the examination question: "Show how it is possible to determine the height of a tall building with the aid of a barometer."

The student had answered: "Take the barometer to the top of the building, attach a long rope to it, lower the barometer to the street, and then bring it up, measuring the length of the rope. The length of the rope is the height of the building."

I pointed out that the student really had a strong case for full credit, since he had answered the question completely and correctly. On the other hand, if full credit were given, it could well contribute to a high grade for the student in his physics course. A high grade is supposed to certify competence in physics, but the answer did not confirm this. I suggested that the student have another try at answering the question. I was not surprised that my colleague agreed, but I was surprised that the student did.

I gave the student six minutes to answer the question, with the warning that his answer should show some knowledge of physics. At the end of five minutes, he had not written anything. I asked if he wished to give up, but he said no. He had many answers to this problem; he was just thinking of the best one. I excused myself for interrupting him,

199

and asked him to please go on. In the next minute, he dashed off his answer, which read:

"Take the barometer to the top of the building and lean over the edge of the roof. Drop the barometer, timing its fall with a stopwatch. Then, using the formula $S = \frac{1}{2}at^2$, calculate the height of the building." 6

At this point, I asked my colleague if *he* would give up. He conceded, and I gave the student almost full credit. 7

In leaving my colleague's office, I recalled that the student had said he had other answers to the problem, so I asked him what they were. "Oh, yes," said the student. "There are many ways of getting the height of a tall building with the aid of a barometer. For example, you could take the barometer out on a sunny day and measure the height of the barometer, the length of its shadow, and the length of the shadow of the building, and by the use of a simple proportion, determine the height of the building." 8

"Fine," I said. "And the others?" 9

"Yes," said the student. "There is a very basic measurement method that you will like. In this method, you take the barometer and begin to walk up the stairs. As you climb the stairs, you mark off the length of the barometer along the wall. You then count the number of marks, and this will give you the height of the building in barometer units. A very direct method. 10

"Of course, if you want a more sophisticated method, you can tie the barometer to the end of a string, swing it as a pendulum, and determine the value of 'g' at the street level and at the top of the building. From the difference between the two values of 'g,' the height of the building can, in principle, be calculated." 11

Finally he concluded, there are many other ways of solving the problem. "Probably the best," he said, "is to take the barometer to the basement and knock on the superintendent's door. When the superintendent answers, you speak to him as follows: 'Mr. Superintendent, here I have a fine barometer. If you will tell me the height of this building, I will give you this barometer.'" 12

At this point, I asked the student if he really did not know the conventional answer to this question. He admitted that he did, but said that he was fed up with high school and college instructors trying to teach him how to think, to use the "scientific method," and to explore the deep inner logic of the subject in a pedantic way, as is often done in the new mathematics, rather than teaching him the structure of the subject. With this in mind, he decided to revive scholasticism as an academic lark to challenge the Sputnik-panicked classrooms of America. 13

About the Essay

1. What is the point of this essay? What makes the narrative more than a humorous story about a student and his physics exam?

2. What was the exam question supposed to test? Why did the question fail? How might the actual wording have caused this failure? How would you re-write the question so that it would do what it was meant to do?

3. Why do you think the student gave the answer in paragraph 6 as the best one? Do you agree? What motivated him to avoid the conventional answer?

4. Why do you think the teacher accepted the answer in paragraph 6 but did not give the student full credit? Was he right to do so?

5. What relevant information does Calandra leave out of the essay? Why do you think he does this?

6. The scholastic philosophers of the Middle Ages used to debate theological questions that seem pointless to us today, such as how many angels could dance on the head of a pin. In this context, what do you think is meant by the reference to scholasticism in the last sentence of the essay? What does the title contribute to the essay?

7. How would you characterize all of the student's answers? Granting their imaginativeness, what other quality did they all possess?

Explorations

1. History and everyday life are full of examples of what Edward de Bono calls "lateral thinking," going outside the conventional limits of a problem to find an unexpected but effective answer. The student in Calandra's essay is obviously an imaginative lateral thinker. What examples of lateral thinking can you find in your own experience, or from other sources? How can one set about thinking laterally?

2. What are tests and exams normally used for? What should they be used for? How can you tell a good examination question from a bad one?

NEIL POSTMAN

In his book *Crazy Talk, Stupid Talk* (1976), Neil Postman defines "stupid talk" as language that is used inappropriately in a situation and which thus reveals muddled or superficial thinking. Such issues concern Postman both personally and professionally as a teacher of communications at New York University. He was born in New York City in 1931, and after graduating from the State University of New York at Fredonia and Columbia University he taught for several years in elementary and secondary schools. One outcome of that experience was the book he wrote with Charles Weingartner, *Teaching as a Subversive Activity* (1967), which has influenced many other teachers to adopt more flexible teaching techniques and to encourage students to be more independent of mind. In the following chapter from *Crazy Talk, Stupid Talk*, Postman shows how our thoughts and actions are often shaped by hidden, almost unconscious prejudgments built into the language we use.

Silent Questions

I cannot vouch for the story, but I have been told that once upon a time, in a village in what is now Lithuania, there arose a most unusual problem. A curious disease afflicted many of the townspeople. It was mostly fatal (although not always), and its onset was signaled by the victim's lapsing into a deathlike coma. Medical science not being quite so advanced as it is now, there was no definite way of knowing if the victim was actually dead when it appeared seemly to bury him. As a result, the townspeople feared that several of their relatives had already been buried alive and that a similar fate might await them—a terrifying prospect, and not only in Lithuania. How to overcome this uncertainty was their dilemma.

One group of people suggested that the coffins be well stocked with water and food and that a small air vent be drilled into them just in case one of the "dead" happened to be alive. This was expensive to do, but seemed more than worth the trouble. A second group, however, came up with an inexpensive and more efficient idea. Each coffin would have a twelve-inch stake affixed to the inside of the coffin lid, exactly at the level of the heart. Then, when the coffin was closed, all uncertainty would cease.

There is no record as to which solution was chosen, but for my purposes, whichever it was is irrelevant. What is mostly important here is that the two different solutions were generated by two different questions. The first solution was an answer to the question, How can we

202

make sure that we do not bury people who are still alive? The second was an answer to the question, How can we make sure that everyone we bury is dead?

The point is that all the answers we ever get are responses to ques- 4
tions. The questions may not be evident to us, especially in everyday affairs, but they are there nonetheless, doing their work. Their work, of course, is to design the form that our knowledge will take and therefore to determine the direction of our actions. A great deal of stupid and/or crazy talk is produced by bad, unacknowledged questions which inevitably produce bad and all-too-visible answers.

As far as I can determine, there are at least four important reasons 5
why question-asking language causes us problems. The first is that our questions are sometimes formed at such a high level of abstraction that we cannot answer them at all. "Why am I a failure?" and "What is the meaning of life?" are typical examples. . . . The key words in the ques-tions are so vague that it is a mystery to know where to begin looking for answers. For example, in trying to respond helpfully to a troubled questioner who asks, Why am I a failure?, a sensible person would have to ask several more pointed questions to get within answering range: What do you mean by "failure"? What specifically have you "failed" at? When have these "failures" taken place? In what circumstances? What do you mean by "success," when and where have you experienced it, and how many "successes" have you had? What needs to be done with such questions is to "operationalize" them, to restate them in forms that will allow for concrete, reality-oriented answers. In the process of doing this, one may discover that the question being asked was not so much, "Why am I a failure?" but, "Why did my marriage end in divorce?" "Why did I lose my job?" or even something as relatively simple as, "Why did I fail advanced calculus?"

I do not say that questions about one's dead marriage or lost job 6
are easy ones; only that they are more approachable than loose-ended questions that imply one's nature is marred by some nondefinable afflic-tion called *failure*.

It is characteristic of the talk of troubled people that they will resist 7
bringing their questions down to a level of answerability. If fanaticism is falling in love with an irrefutable answer, then a neurosis is falling in love with an unanswerable question. "Why are people always trying to cheat me?" or "When will the breaks start to come my way?" is the sort of question that can be treacherously endearing. As it stands, there is no answer to it, and perhaps that is why some people choose to ask it and ask it repeatedly. It is, in fact, not so much a question as a kind of assertion that the responsibility for one's life lies entirely outside oneself.

But because it has the *form* of a question, one may well be deceived into trying to answer it, which will lead to continuous frustration and demoralization.

Of course, questions of this type are not confined to one's personal relationship to the cosmos but are also used, unfortunately, as an instrument for discovering "facts." And they produce the same unsatisfying results. "Who is the best President that America has ever had?" is the sort of commonplace, completely unanswerable question which results in no knowledge at all. The conversation between Stupid Talk and Sensible Talk usually goes something like this:

Stupid Talk:	Who's the best President we ever had?
Sensible Talk:	What do you mean by "best"?
Stupid Talk:	What do you mean "What do I mean?"? Best means "the best," "the most excellent," "tops."
Sensible Talk:	"Tops" in what respect? Most votes? Least criticized? Most well-read? Richest?
Stupid Talk:	What do those things have to do with it? I mean "the best"—all around.
Sensible Talk:	Using what criteria for which aspects of his performance?
Stupid Talk:	Why are you making this so complicated? You mean to tell me you don't know what "best" means?
Sensible Talk:	Right.
Stupid Talk:	Jeez!

Now, it is possible I am being unfair to Stupid Talk here, in that he may have asked the question only in order to get some diversion at a rather dull party. If that was his intention, then you should reverse the names of the characters in my scene. Sensible Talk is simply being obnoxious or has misunderstood the purpose of the semantic environment he is in. But if the question was asked to start a serious conversation, resulting in the development and expression of informed opinion, then the names of my characters must stand as they are. The question as originally posed will not produce a discussable answer. . . .

The first problem, then, in question-asking language may be stated in this way: The type of words used in a question will determine the type of words used in the answer. In particular, question-words that are vague, subjective, and not rooted in any verifiable reality will produce their own kind in the answer.

A second problem arises from certain structural characteristics, or grammatical properties, of sentences. For example, many questions seem almost naturally to imply either-or alternatives. "Is that good?" (as against "bad"), "Is she smart?" (as against "dumb"), "Is he rich?" (as against "poor"), and so on. The English language is heavily biased toward "either-or-ness," which is to say that it encourages us to talk about the world in polarities. We are inclined to think of things in terms of their singular opposites rather than as part of a continuum of multiple alternatives. *Black* makes us think of *white*, *rich* of *poor*, *smart* of *dumb*, *fast* of *slow*, and so on. Naturally, when questions are put in either-or terms, they will tend to call forth an either-or answer. "This is bad," "She's dumb," "He's poor," etc. There are many situations in which such an emphatic answer is all that is necessary, since the questioner is merely seeking some handy label, to get a "fix" on someone, so to speak. But, surprisingly and unfortunately, this form of question is also used in situations where one would expect a more serious and comprehensive approach to a subject. For example, in Edwin Newman's popular book, *Strictly Speaking*, he asks in his subtitle, "Will America Be the Death of English?" The form of the question demands either a *yes* or a *no* for its answer. (Newman, by the way, says yes, and for no particular reason, so far as I could tell.) Had the question been phrased as, "To what extent will English be harmed (impoverished, diminished, etc.) by Americans?" you would have had a very boring subtitle but, in my opinion, a much more serious book, or at least the possibility of one. Questions which ask, "To what extent" or "In what manner" invite a more detailed, qualified look at a problem than questions which ask, "Is it this or that?" The latter divide the universe into two possibilities; the former allow one to consider the multiple possibilities inherent in a problem. "Is America an imperial power?" "Have we lost our faith in democracy?" "Are our taxes too high?"—these are some questions which insinuate that a position must be taken; they do not ask that thought be given.

A similar structural problem in our questions is that we are apt to use singular forms instead of plural ones. What is the cause of . . . ? What is the reason for . . . ? What is the result of . . . ? As with either-or questions, the form of these questions limits our search for answers and therefore impoverishes our perceptions. We are not looking for causes, reasons, or results, but for *the* cause, *the* reason, and *the* result. The idea of multiple causality is certainly not unfamiliar, and yet the form in which we habitually ask some of our most important questions tends to discourage our thinking about it: What is the reason we don't get along? What is the cause of your overeating? What will be the effect of school integration? What is the problem that we face? I do not say that a question of this sort rules out the possibility of our widening our inquiries. But to the extent that we allow the form of such questions to go un-

12

challenged, we are in danger of producing shallow and unnecessarily restricted answers.

This is equally true of the third source of problems in question-asking language, namely, the assumptions that underlie it. Unless we are paying very close attention, we can be led into accepting as fact the most precarious and even preposterous ideas. Perhaps the two most famous assumption-riddled questions are, Have you stopped beating your wife? and How many angels can dance on the head of a pin? But in almost every question, there lurks at least one assumption which may slip by if we are not accustomed to looking for it. By an assumption, I mean a belief that is not subject to scrutiny because it is so deeply embedded in the question that we are hardly even aware of its presence. Consider, for instance, such questions as these, which I have recently heard discussed on television: Why is America losing its moral direction? When will we achieve equality of opportunity? How does the white power structure operate? The first question assumes that there is such a thing as a "moral direction," that a country can have one, that America once did, and, of course, that we are presently losing it. I do not say that these assumptions are untenable, but each one of them is surely worth inquiring into before proceeding to the question. In fact, once you start discussing these assumptions, you may never get back to the original question, and may even find it has disappeared, to everyone's relief.

The second question assumes that there is such a thing as equality of opportunity; that it is, in some sense, "achievable" by society; that it is worth achieving; and that some effort is being made to achieve it— all extremely arguable assumptions in my opinion. I have, for example, long suspected that the phrase "equality of opportunity" is a kind of semantic fiction, not unlike the legal term "a reasonable and prudent man"; that is to say, one is free to give it almost any meaning that suits one's purpose in a given situation. In any case, I should want the term carefully defined before listening to a discussion of when "it" will be achieved.

The third question, of course, assumes the existence of a white power structure, as well as mechanisms through which it operates. Given the rather bumbling, haphazard ways of American business and government, I am inclined to be at least suspicious of this assumption, although I would like to hear it defended.

The point is that if you proceed to answer questions without reviewing the assumptions implicit in them, you may end up in never-never land without quite knowing how you got there. My favorite invitation to never-never land, incidentally, was extended to me by a young woman who asked, "Why do you think the extraterrestrials are coming in such large numbers to Earth?" You might expect that a person who would ask such a question also would have an answer to it—which was, you will be happy to know, "to help Earth people develop an effective World Organization."

The fourth source of difficulty in question-asking language is that two people in the same semantic environment may ask different questions about a situation, but without knowing it. For example, in a classroom, the teacher may be asking himself, "How can I get the students to learn this?" But it is almost certain that the students are asking, "How can I get a good grade in this course?" Naturally, two different questions will generate two different approaches to the situation and may be the source of great frustration for everyone concerned. There are many situations where it is well understood that different "roles" are required to ask different questions, and this in itself is not necessarily a source of trouble. In business transactions, for instance, buyers and sellers are almost always asking different questions. That is inherent in their situation. I have never heard of a buyer, for example, who has asked himself, "How can I make sure this man makes the largest possible profit from this sale?" (The reason, incidentally, that used-car salesmen have such low credibility is that they are inclined to pretend that they are asking the same question as the potential car buyer, namely, "How can I get this car at the lowest possible price?" Since the buyer knows that the dealer cannot possibly be interested in this question, he is rightfully suspicious.) But in situations where it is assumed that different people will be asking roughly the same question—and they are not—we are faced with problems that are sometimes hard to discern. I have recently heard of a situation where a family vacation was marred because, without their knowing it, wife and husband were seeking answers to two quite different questions. The wife was asking, "How can we have a good time?" The husband was asking, "How can we get through this without spending too much money?" Two administrators who were trying to avoid bankruptcy provide another example: The first was asking, "How can we cut our staff?" The second, "How can we increase our income?" Naturally, their solutions moved in different directions. Finally, a pregnant woman and her obstetrician: The woman is asking, "How can I have my baby safely and with no unnecessary pain?" The doctor is asking, "How can this baby get born in time for me to have a full two-week vacation?"

I do not say that different questions are always incompatible in such situations. But they do have considerable potential for confusion if we are ignorant of their existence.

17

18

About the Essay

1. In your own words, how would you summarize Postman's thesis in this essay?

2. What are the four kinds of questions Postman says cause difficulties? Give examples of your own for each.

3. Comment on the appropriateness of the anecdote Postman tells at the opening of his essay. Which of the four kinds of problem questions does the story illustrate?

4. What is wrong with the questions "Have you stopped beating your wife?" and "How many angels can dance on the head of a pin?"

5. Postman has organized his essay so that the four kinds of silent questions are discussed in a particular order. What is that order, and why do you think he chose it? What if this order were reversed, for example—would the essay be more or less effective? Explain.

6. According to Postman, what is the function of the questions we ask? How does his explanation influence your understanding of the essay?

7. What is the significance of the title, "Silent Questions"? Do you think it appropriate or inappropriate to the essay? Explain your answer.

Explorations

1. Do you sometimes pose questions, for yourself or others, that, as Postman says, are "at such a high level of abstraction that we cannot answer them at all"? How might you restate those questions so that they can be answered?

2. In education, how important do you think it is to find good answers to other people's questions, and how important to learn how to ask good questions yourself? Where has the emphasis been in your education so far? Can good question-asking be taught and learned? If so, how? If not, why not?

RUSSELL BAKER

A newspaper columnist's task is to fill a specified amount of space several times a week, and each time to offer something both current and provocative. That is Russell Baker's job for the *New York Times*, which he has performed so well that he was in 1979 awarded the Pulitzer Prize, journalism's highest award. Born in Virginia in 1925, Baker graduated from Johns Hopkins University in 1947 and began his career as a newspaperman with the *Baltimore Sun*. He joined the *Times* in 1954, and after eight years with its Washington bureau covering national politics, he began writing his syndicated "Observer" column, which is now published four times a week. His most recent columns, including this selection, have been collected in *So This Is Depravity* (1980). A memoir of his youth, *Growing Up*, was published in 1982.

School vs. Education

By the age of six the average child will have completed the basic American education and be ready to enter school. If the child has been attentive in these pre-school years, he or she will already have mastered many skills.

From television, the child will have learned how to pick a lock, commit a fairly elaborate bank holdup, prevent wetness all day long, get the laundry twice as white and kill people with a variety of sophisticated armaments.

From watching his parents, the child, in many cases, will already know how to smoke, how much soda to mix with whiskey, what kind of language to use when angry and how to violate the speed laws without being caught.

At this point, the child is ready for the second stage of education, which occurs in school. There, a variety of lessons may be learned in the very first days.

The teacher may illustrate the economic importance of belonging to a strong union by closing down the school before the child arrives. Fathers and mothers may demonstrate to the child the social cohesion that can be built on shared hatred by demonstrating their dislike for children whose pigmentation displeases them. In the latter event, the child may receive visual instruction in techniques of stoning buses, cracking skulls with a nightstick and subduing mobs with tear gas. Formal education has begun.

During formal education, the child learns that life is for testing.

209

This stage lasts twelve years, a period during which the child learns that success comes from telling testers what they want to hear.

Early in this stage, the child learns that he is either dumb or smart. 7 If the teacher puts intelligent demands upon the child, the child learns he is smart. If the teacher expects little of the child, the child learns he is dumb and soon quits bothering to tell the testers what they want to hear.

At this point, education becomes more subtle. The child taught by 8 school that he is dumb observes that neither he, she, nor any of the many children who are even dumber, ever fails to be promoted to the next grade. From this, the child learns that while everybody talks a lot about the virtue of being smart, there is very little incentive to stop being dumb.

What is the point of school, besides attendance? the child wonders. 9 As the end of the first formal stage of education approaches, school answers this question. The point is to equip the child to enter college.

Children who have been taught they are smart have no difficulty. 10 They have been happily telling testers what they want to hear for twelve years. Being artists at telling testers what they want to hear, they are admitted to college joyously, where they promptly learn that they are the hope of America.

Children whose education has been limited to adjusting themselves 11 to their schools' low estimates of them are admitted to less joyous colleges which, in some cases, may teach them to read.

At this stage of education, a fresh question arises for everyone. If 12 the point of lower education was to get into college, what is the point of college? The answer is soon learned. The point of college is to prepare the student—no longer a child now—to get into graduate school. In college, the student learns that it is no longer enough simply to tell the testers what they want to hear. Many are tested for graduate school; few are admitted.

Those excluded may be denied valuable certificates to prosper in 13 medicine, at the bar, in the corporate boardroom. The student learns that the race is to the cunning and often, alas, to the unprincipled.

Thus, the student learns the importance of destroying competitors 14 and emerges richly prepared to play his role in the great simmering melodrama of American life.

Afterward, the former student's destiny fulfilled, his life rich with 15 Oriental carpets, rare porcelain and full bank accounts, he may one day find himself with the leisure and the inclination to open a book with a curious mind, and start to become educated.

About the Essay

1. What is the main idea in Baker's essay? Is it stated explicitly or implicitly?

2. What does Baker mean by "education"? Does the word hold the same meaning throughout the essay?

3. What does Baker find wrong with the American school system? How does he substantiate his criticisms? Do you agree with him? If so, why? If not, why not?

4. What is the implication of the essay's title?

5. What is Baker's tone in this essay? How does he achieve that tone? Is the tone suitable to his subject, point of view, and intended audience? Why?

6. Aside from tone, what are the features of Baker's satirical style?

7. In addition to criticizing American education, Baker is critical of American life in general. What aspects of life in the United States is he criticizing? What opposite values are implicit in his criticism?

Explorations

1. From your own experience, how true is it that success in school comes from "telling testers what they want to hear"? What else does success depend on? How often have your teachers encouraged you to "open a book with a curious mind"?

2. Educational psychologists such as John Holt have studied the relation between what teachers expect of specific students and how well those students do in school. Consult some of Holt's studies, and consider his findings. Summarize his conclusions, and comment on them, referring to your own experience.

3. Can you identify one feature of your own education that has done the most for you? What would that feature be, and why do you consider it so valuable? Has there been anything in your education that you feel has held you back? If so, what?

First as a student and now as a professor, Joel Seligman has concerned himself with how law is taught and why it is taught that way. He was born in 1950 in New York City, and graduated in the mid-1970s from Harvard Law School. He then joined the Corporate Accountability Research Group organized by Ralph Nader, another Harvard Law graduate, and with Nader and Mark Green he wrote *Taming the Giant Corporation* (1976). While still a Nader associate, he returned to Harvard to study and evaluate his alma mater's law curriculum, its methods, and its philosophy. The product of this research is *The High Citadel* (1978), from which the following selection is taken. Seligman now teaches at Northeastern University Law School.

At Harvard Law School students don't use textbooks; they read actual legal cases. And the professors generally don't lecture but instead question students in class on the day's assigned cases. This is called the Socratic method, after the Greek philosopher Socrates, who taught exclusively by asking his students leading questions. Here we sit in with Seligman to audit a first-year class in contract law.

Learning to Think Like a Lawyer

When a client or an acquaintance admires a lawyer, the lawyer is often praised for his or her reasoning ability. "Lawyers," it is said, "cut through to the heart of the matter . . . They ask the right questions . . . They know how to solve problems." 1

One of the most proficient teachers of legal reasoning at Harvard Law School is Clark Byse. Like many of his colleagues, Byse relies on the distinctive interrogative approach popularly known as the Socratic method to question students on their understanding of actual law cases. 2

Before class, seated in his book-lined Langdell Hall office, Byse often seems to possess a languid air. Slightly hunched behind his massive wooden desk, the sixty-six-year-old professor regards visitors with doleful eyes. "Well, Mr. _____ ," he begins answers to questions almost shyly, warming to his subject as he speaks. A similar change comes over Byse as the time for a class session draws near. Visibly his posture stiffens as he reviews his notes. "I can't see you now," he says firmly. "I've got a class in ten minutes." Slipping on an impeccably tailored dark suitjacket, Byse impatiently flicks lint off it. By the time he arrives in his cavernous Langdell North classroom, there is a buoyancy to his manner. He chats whimsically with a number of students near the lectern, his eyes playful now, his manner exuberant. A firm hand reaches out and grasps a stu- 3 dent's shoulder, an unmistakable gesture of friendship or support. Moments later, Byse grins and mischievously pats a second student on the cheek. But this is prelude. Forcefully he plants his book and seating chart on the standing lectern.

At precisely 10:10 A.M., virtually every student is in an assigned   4
seat, notebook out, casebook open, pen poised. Clark Byse at this point is unmistakably *Professor Byse*: mercurial; authoritarian; his jests biting now; his energy like that of a coiled spring.

Above the professor's Langdell Hall office desk is a gift from an   5
earlier class, a papier-mâché rabbit popping out of a papier-mâché hat. The figure has a single-word caption: "Why?" In Professor Byse's classroom this word is seldom spoken; it is usually roared. "Why, Mr. _____ ?" or "Why, Miss _____ ?" Byse starts hundreds of questions during a school year. Sometimes the vehemence of Byse's "Why" causes him to rise up on his toes like a carnival-goer trying to gain leverage before slamming the weighted hammer down and ringing the far-off bell. "Why" is the concept that trails the students home after class; "Why" surfaces in their minds as they read cases alone; and as examinations approach, "Why" nags at their sleep. In Professor Byse's control, "Why" is the essence of legal reasoning, the force that pushes a class from comprehending law as particular rules applied to particular facts to a glimpse of an entire social order. "Why" is skepticism, "Why" is argument, "Why" is doubt, and ultimately "Why" is the basis of courtroom logic: comparison and generalization.

"Miss _____ ," Byse begins this session, "what was the promise in   6
Hamer versus *Sidway*?"

Like many cases in first-year law casebooks, the facts in *Hamer* v.   7
Sidway seem slightly ridiculous. At a family gathering in 1869, an uncle promised his nephew that if he refrained from drinking, using tobacco, swearing, and playing cards or billiards for money until he turned twenty-one the uncle would pay him $5000. The nephew agreed and six years later wrote to his uncle that he had lived up to his promise. "Dear Nephew," the uncle replied, "I have no doubt but you have, for which you shall have $5000, as I promised you." But before the nephew collected the money, the uncle died. The almost comic-opera question of the lawsuit was: Can the virtuous nephew collect the $5000 from the recalcitrant executor of his uncle's estate? The case is included in virtually every modern American contracts casebook because it illustrates some of the most fundamental principles of contracts law.

Miss _____ answers Professor Byse's question, "An uncle promised   8
his nephew $5000 if he wouldn't commit any vices until he was twenty-one."

"Well Miss _____ ," Byse retorts, "the imagination runs rampant. State the facts clearly. Why editorialize?"   9

She does so.   10

"How old was the nephew?"   11

"Hmmm . . ."   12

"Anybody know?"   13

A second student shouts, "Fifteen or sixteen."   14

"Was the contract enforced?"   15

"Yes, the court did."   16

It comes out softly this time, "Why?"   17

The student doesn't answer.   18

Byse offers, "Because it was supported by consideration." Miss   19
_____ starts to nod as Byse ridicules his own answer, "Or do we say there was consideration because it was enforced?" A brief pause. Like a referee in a sporting event, Byse construes part of his task to keep the game alive yet limited to a specific field. After thirty-three years of teaching law, he is a master at this. He tosses out a fresh question. "What was the argument of the defendant?"

Miss _____ answers, "There was no benefit to the uncle."   20

"What did the plaintiff argue was the benefit to the uncle?'   21

Miss _____ sees the trap. "He didn't," and correctly circumvents   22
it. "The plaintiff argued that the consideration was the detriment he suffered by not drinking, smoking, and so on."

Now the game has picked up. Byse plays with the student's answer.   23
"How could it be a detriment not to indulge in bad habits? That is no detriment, is it?"

The student stumbles. "Some people will think it is," and another   24
student, startled, loudly exclaims, "Huh!"

Byse slaps that down. "Is someone here a moose hunter?" Then   25
quickly reiterates the question, "How could this be a detriment?"

"Because the plaintiff had a legal right to drink, smoke, swear, and   26
play cards."

Byse holds up the answer so everyone in the class will precisely   27
understand it. "Recall the editor's note on the meanings of the word 'right.' *Plaintiff was legally privileged to drink and smoke. That is a right.*" He briefly pauses for dramatic effect. "All right then," Byse continues, reading from a page he has just picked up from the lectern, "I promise you $5000 if you do not (a) commit murder, (b) commit suicide, (c) get arrested, (d) drive faster than the legal speed limit, (e) bother me, or (f) refuse to accept a gift of $5000 from me. Consideration in all of these cases?"

A new student answers, "None except bothering. Other cases in- 28
volve illegal activities or gross disparity."

Shrilly in Professor Byse's mind a cacophonic alarm goes off. Red 29
flags wave. His body visibly stiffens. "Gross disparity," he roars with
painful disdain. "What is gross disparity?" The student isn't expected to
respond. With six thunderous words of formal legal logic, Clark Byse has
eviscerated two words of frothy layperson fudge talk. Somewhere in the
back of the room the phrase "gross disparity" collapses to the floor. The
two words have been annihilated. They are absolutely dead. Briskly Byse
presses on, "Miss _____ just said a detriment was a sufficient consideration. Now, murder is wrong—there is no privilege to murder, therefore
no detriment. The same with suicide. But not get arrested. What about
that?"

Ten years ago, a student would have argued at this point that there 30
was a legal privilege to commit civil disobedience if one was willing to
accept the consequences. References might have been made to Martin
Luther King, Jr., and Gandhi, or draft resisters. There would have been
a heated student debate; a useful release from the tension of trying to
phrase every argument in the language of formal legal doctrines.

But this class occurred in January 1977, and no one was quite sure 31
why Byse had asked the question.

A student responded dully, "There is no legal right to be arrested." 32

Byse's forehead furrowed slightly, "Anybody disagree?" 33

Another student answers, "No law makes it illegal to get arrested?" 34

The class is thoroughly confused; someone hisses. 35

"Is it consideration?" 36

"I am not sure." 37

Byse struggles with the hypothetical question and a related one for 38
ten minutes until yet another student stammers to silence. He then starts
the reasoning process over again. "We have an eminent killer shooting
people. He says to the uncle: 'Give me $5000 and I won't shoot people.'
Better yet, $50,000—make it worth his while. Is there consideration?"

Mr. _____ answers, "There is no legal right, but look at the legal 39
benefit . . ."

"The killer wasn't going to shoot the uncle." 40

"But other people . . ." 41

Byse cuts in sharply, "You can't do this by magic. You can't justify 42
everything by a vague notion of public policy. We are trying to develop
an organized society, one in which there will be a general rule that the
full power of the state will only be invoked to enforce certain contracts
. . ." And for a full forty-eight minutes the colloquy concerning a trivial

one-and-one-half-page 1891 case goes on, with Byse rapidly shifting hypothetical variations on the case, prodding students to vocalize alternative legal arguments and debate directly with each other, and, at one
point, chewing out the class for not seeing obvious relationships between
his hypothetical questions and earlier cases the class had discussed. Only
in the very last few minutes of the class, when Byse had moved on to
another case, does a student vocalize what the doctrine of legal consideration is really about.

"The courts don't want to turn gifts into enforceable promises."   43

"Aha!" exclaimed Byse. "The courts do not enforce gift promises.   44
Gifts are one category of promises different from others. But why?" And
this "Why," though not a roar, felt like one. For weeks the class had
been absorbing the notion that contracts was the category of law that
made a market economy possible. By allowing persons to enforce their
private bargains with each other, theoretically the most efficient allo-
cation of resources will be realized. But to make this possible, proclaimed
a prominently situated case holding in the students' text, "the law will
not enter into an inquiry as to the adequacy of the consideration." Now
the rug was being pulled out from under the absoluteness of this principle.
Plainly the law sometimes will inquire.

"Why?" Byse asks. "What are the functions this doctrine performs?"   45

With astonishing coolness, a student raises his hand and answers,   46
"Cautionary and evidentiary. It is easier to prove a contract if there is
evidence of it. Parties are less likely to enter contracts lightly if each
must give up something."

For Byse, the answer is almost too good to be true. To highlight   47
its importance, he writes on the blackboard, "Form and Substance."
Pointing to the word "Form," he writes, "Form—evidence of a contract."
Pointing to the word "Substance," he explains, "Substantive Rule: Parties are discouraged from making rash enforceable promises. You should
see page 118 where Von Mehren summarizes these ideas for you." He
continues for a few minutes relating this point to the next case, but the
dénouement has been reached. For Byse, a successful class hour has been
taught.

About the Essay

1. What is the central issue in Byse's questioning? Why is it so difficult for
students to arrive at an answer? Why doesn't Byse simply *tell* them the answer?

2. In paragraph 9, Byse says, "the imagination runs rampant. State the facts
clearly. Why editorialize?" What exactly does he mean by this?

3. Seligman describes the phrase "gross disparity" as "frothy layperson fudge talk" (paragraph 29). What does "gross disparity" mean? Why does it not fit into the class discussion?

4. Summarize the way Byse leads the class through discussion of *Hamer v. Sidway.* What do you think makes him "one of the most proficient teachers of legal reasoning"? What is the function of the hypothetical situations he proposes?

5. Seligman gives us many descriptive details about Professor Byse—his appearance, his manners, his interactions with students. What do these details contribute to our sense of Byse as a teacher? As a person?

Explorations

1. Who has been your best teacher—or your worst? How would you describe that person's character and teaching style?

2. How is thinking like a lawyer different from other ways of thinking—such as your own? Support your answer with examples and analyses from this selection and from other sources available to you. (Consider, for example, Byse's comment: "You can't do this by magic. You can't justify everything by a vague notion of public policy. . . .")

ARTHUR C. CLARKE

Imagining the future is Arthur C. Clarke's business, but it was not always so. He was born in 1917 in Somerset, England, and first worked as an accountant in the British government. In the Royal Air Force during the Second World War, he served as an instructor of radar, then a new invention, and, in 1945, was the first to propose using artificial satellites for communications. After the war, he went to King's College in London to study physics and mathematics. It was in the early 1950s that Clarke began writing the books of science fiction and fact for which he is best known. Perhaps his most famous novel is *Childhood's End* (1953), although he is even better known for writing the screenplay for Stanley Kubrick's movie, *2001: A Space Odyssey* (1968). Since 1954 he has lived in Sri Lanka, engaged in writing and in underwater exploration and photography.

"Electronic Tutors" was written for *Omni*, a magazine for general readers of science and science fiction, and was published in 1980. Clarke's exuberant, personal view of how computers may affect education appears to be more than an informed guess. Some of his 1980 predictions have, in fact, already begun to come true.

Electronic Tutors

We are now witnessing one of the swiftest and most momentous revolutions in the entire history of technology. For more than a century the slide rule was the essential tool of engineers, scientists, and anyone else whose work involved extensive calculations. Then, just a decade ago, the invention of the pocket calculator made the slide rule obsolete almost overnight, and with it whole libraries of logarithmic and trigonometric tables. 1

There has never been so stupendous an advance in so short a time. Simply no comparison can be made between the two devices. The pocket calculator is millions of times more accurate and scores of times swifter than the slide rule, and it now actually costs less. It's as if we'd jumped overnight from bullock carts to the Concorde—and Concorde were cheaper! No wonder the slide rule manufacturers have gone out of business. If you have a good slide rule, leave it in your will. It will someday be a valuable antique. 2

Pocket calculators are already having a profound effect on the teaching of mathematics, even at the level of elementary arithmetic. But they are about to be succeeded by devices of much greater power and sophistication—machines that may change the very nature of the educational system. 3

The great development in our near future is the portable electronic   4
library—a library not only of books, but of films and music. It will be
about the size of an average book and will probably open in the same
way. One half will be the screen, with high-definition, full-color display.
The other will be a keyboard, much like one of today's computer consoles, with the full alphabet, digits, basic mathematical functions, and a
large number of special keys—perhaps 100 keys in all. It won't be as
small as some of today's midget calculators, which have to be operated
with toothpicks.

In theory, such a device could have enough memory to hold all the   5
books in the world. But we may settle for something more modest, like
the *Encyclopaedia Britannica*, the *Oxford English Dictionary*, and *Roget's
Thesaurus*.[1] (Incidentally, Peter Mark Roget was the inventor of the log-
log slide rule.) Whole additional libraries, stored in small, plug-in memory
modules, could be inserted into the portable library when necessary. All
this technology has already been developed, though for other uses. Oddly
enough, the most skilled practitioners of this new art are the designers
of video games.

Reading material may be displayed as a fixed page or else "scrolled"   6
so that it rolls upward at a comfortable reading rate. Pictures could appear
as in an ordinary book, but they may eventually be displayed as three-
dimensional holographic images. Text and imagery, of course, will be
accompanied by sound. Today's tape recorders can reproduce an entire
symphony on a cassette. The electronic library may be able to play back
the complete works of Beethoven while displaying the scores on its screen.

And how nice to be able to summon up Lord Clark's *Civilisation* or   7
Jacob Bronowski's *Ascent of Man* whenever or wherever you felt like it!
(Yes, I know that these tapes currently cost about $2,000 apiece, unless
you are lucky or wicked enough to have a pirated copy. But one day the
BBC will get its money back, and thereafter the price will be peanuts.)

I still haven't touched on the real potential of this technology, the   8
opportunity to cure one of the great failings in conventional education,
especially in large classes. Genuine education requires feedback—interaction between pupil and teacher. At the very least, this allows the
student to clear up points he does not understand. Ideally, it provides
inspiration as well. Yet I recently met a Turkish engineer who said that
all he had ever seen of his professor was the tiny figure up on the platform,
above a sea of heads. It is a predicament shared by all too many students.

The electronic tutor will go a long way toward solving this problem.   9
Some computer programs already allow the student to carry on a dialogue

---

[1]About 42,000 pages in all.

with the computer, asking it questions and answering the questions it asks. "Computer-aided instruction"—CAI, not to be confused with CIA—can be extremely effective. At best, the pupil may refuse to believe that he is dealing with a computer program and not with another human being.

Technology's influence on education is nothing new. There's an old saying that the best educational setup consists of a log with teacher at one end and pupil at the other. Our modern world is not only woefully short of teachers, it's running out of logs. But there has always been a shortage of teachers, and technology has always been used to ameliorate this—a fact that many people tend to forget.

The first great technological aid to education was the book. You don't have to clone teachers to multiply them. The printing press did just that, and the mightiest of all educational machines is the library. Yet this potent resource is now about to be surpassed by an even more remarkable one, a depository of knowledge as astonishing to most of us today as books were to our remote ancestors.

I can still recall my own amazement when at a NASA conference less than ten years ago, I saw my first "electronic slide rule." It was a prototype of the HP 35, demonstrated to us by Dr. Bernard Oliver, vice-president of Hewlett-Packard. Though I was impressed, even awed, I did not fully realize that something revolutionary had come into the world.

It is quite impossible for even the most farsighted prophet to visualize all the effects of a really major technological development. The telephone and the automobile produced quantum jumps in communication and transportation. They gave ordinary men a mastery over space that not even kings and emperors had possessed in the past. They changed not only the patterns of everyday life, but the physical structure of the world—the shapes of our cities, the uses of the land. This all happened in what is historically a moment of time, and the process is still accelerating. Look how the transistor radio swept across the planet within a single generation.

Though they are not yet as important as books, audiovisual aids such as film strips, 16-millimeter projectors, and videotape machines are rapidly penetrating the educational field. Most of these aids are still far too expensive for developing countries, however, and I'm not sure they are really worth the cost of producing them.

Perhaps the most influential device of all is the ordinary television set, whether intended for education or not. I'd be interested to know what impact *Sesame Street* has on the relatively few children of a totally different culture who see it here in Sri Lanka. Still, every TV program has some educational content; the cathode-ray tube is a window on the world—indeed, on many worlds. Often it's a very murky window, with a limited view, but I've slowly come to the conclusion that on balance even bad TV is preferable to no TV.

The power of television lies in its ability to show current events, often as they are happening. But for basic educational purposes, the video recorder is much more valuable. Its pretaped programs can be repeated at any convenient time. Unfortunately, the chaos of competing systems has prevented standardization and cheap mass production.   16

Videotape machines, however, are far too complicated, they can never be really cheap or long-lived. Video discs, which are just coming on the market, will be much cheaper. Yet I am sure that they, too, represent only a transitional stage. Eventually we will have completely solid-state memory and storage devices, with no moving parts except laser beams or electric fields. After all, the human brain doesn't have any moving parts, and it can hold an enormous amount of information. The electronic memories I'm talking about will be even more compact than the brain—and very cheap. They should be ready soon.   17

Consider the very brief history of the computer. The first models were clumsy giants filling whole rooms, consuming kilowatts of power, and costing millions of dollars. Today, only 35 years later, far greater storage and processing capacity can be packed into a microchip measuring 1.625 square centimeters. That's miracle number one. Miracle number two is the cost of that chip: not a couple of million dollars, but about $10.   18

The change has already begun. Computer-aided instruction is now available in many American colleges and high schools. Consoles with typewriter keyboards allow the student to "talk" to a central computer at any time of day, going through any subject when he feels like doing so, at the rate that suits him. The computer, of course, can talk to hundreds of students simultaneously, giving each the illusion that he is the center of attention. It's infinitely patient, unlike most teachers, and it's never rude or sarcastic. What a boon to slow or handicapped students!   19

Today's CAI consoles are big, expensive, fixed units, usually wired into the college computer. They could be portable. Already businessmen are traveling the world with attaché case-sized consoles they can plug into the telephone to talk with their office computer thousands of kilometers away. But it is the completely portable and self-contained electronic tutor that will be the next full step beyond today's pocket calculators.   20

Its prototype is already here, in the nurseries of the affluent West. The first computer toys, many of them looking as if they'd flown off the screen during a showing of *Star Wars*, invaded the shops last Christmas.   21

They play tick-tack-toe, challenge you to repeat simple melodies, ask questions, present elementary calculations, and await the answer—making rude noises if you get it wrong. Children love them, when they're able to wrestle them away from their parents. In 1978 they cost $50; now they're half that. Soon they'll be given away as prizes in cereal boxes.

These are toys, but they represent the wave of the future. Much more sophisticated are the pocket electronic translators that first came on the market in 1979, at about the cost of calculators five years earlier. When you type words and phrases into a little alphabetical keyboard, the translation appears on a small screen. You change languages simply by plugging in a different module. The latest models of these machines have even learned to speak. Soon they may become superb language teachers. They could listen to your pronunciation, match it with theirs and correct you until they are satisfied.

Such devices would be specialized versions of the general-purpose pocket tutor, which will be the student's universal tool by the end of the century. It is hard to think of a single subject that could not be programmed into these devices at all levels of complexity. You'll be able to change subjects or update courses merely by plugging in different memory modules or cassettes, exactly as you can in today's programmable pocket computers.

Where does this leave the human teacher? Well, let me quote this dictum: Any teacher who can be replaced by a machine should be!

During the Middle Ages many scholars regarded printed books with apprehension. They felt that books would destroy their monopoly on knowledge. Worse still, books would permit the unwashed masses to improve their position in society, perhaps even to learn the most cherished secret of all—that no man is better than any other. And they were correct. Those of you who have seen the splendid television series *Roots*, which I hope comes to Sri Lanka someday, will recall that the slaves were strictly forbidden to learn reading and had to pretend that they were illiterate if they had secretly acquired this skill. Societies based on ignorance or repression cannot tolerate general education.

Yet the teaching profession has survived the invention of books. It should welcome the development of the electronic tutor, which will take over the sheer drudgery, the tedious repetition, that are unavoidable in so much basic education. By removing the tedium from the teacher's work and making learning more like play, electronic tutors will paradoxically humanize education. If a teacher feels threatened by them, he's surely in the wrong profession.

We need mass education to drag this world out of the Stone Age, and any technology, any machine, that can help do that is to be welcomed, not feared. The electronic tutor will spread across the planet as swiftly as the transistor radio, with even more momentous consequences. No social or political system, no philosophy, no culture, no religion can withstand a technology whose time has come—however much one may deplore such unfortunate side effects as the blaring tape recorders being carried by pilgrims up the sacred mountain Sri Pada. We must take the good with the bad.

When electronic tutors reach technological maturity around the 28 end of the century, they will be produced not in the millions but in the hundreds of millions and cost no more than today's pocket calculators. Equally important, they will last for years. (No properly designed solid-state device need ever wear out. I'm still using the HP 35 Dr. Oliver gave me in 1970.) So their amortized cost will be negligible; they may even be given away, with users paying only for the programs plugged into them. Even the poorest countries could afford them—especially when the reforms and improved productivity that widespread education will stimulate help those countries to pull themselves out of poverty.

Just where does this leave the schools? Already telecommunication 29 is making these ancient institutions independent of space. *Sunrise Semester* and *University of the Air* can be heard far from their "campuses." The pocket tutor will complete this process, giving the student complete freedom of choice in study time as well as in work location.

We will probably still need schools to teach younger children the 30 social skills and discipline they will need as adults. But remember that educational toys are such fun that their young operators sometimes have to be dragged kicking and screaming away from their self-imposed classes.

At the other end of the spectrum, we'll still need universities for 31 many functions. You can't teach chemistry, physics, or engineering without labs, for obvious reasons. And though we'll see more and more global classes, even at the graduate level, electronics can never completely convey all the nuances of personal interaction with a capable teacher.

There will be myriads of "invisible colleges" operating through the 32 global communications networks. I remarked earlier that any teacher who could be replaced by a machine should be. Perhaps the same verdict should apply to any university, however ivy-covered its walls, if it can be replaced by a global electronic network of computers and satellite links.

But there will also be nexuses where campuses still exist. In the 33 year 2000 many thousands of students and instructors will still meet in person, as they have done ever since the days of Plato's Academy 23 centuries ago.

About the Essay

1. What, according to Clarke, are the capabilities that electronic tutors will one day have? What will their limitations be? Do you agree with Clarke's predictions? Explain.

2. Clarke suggests in paragraph 5 that a portable electronic library might come with three particular books in its standard memory. Why do you think he chose those books? Would you choose others instead? Why?

3. At one point Clarke says that "even bad TV is preferable to no TV" (paragraph 15). Why does he think so? Do you agree or disagree? Explain your answer.

4. "Any teacher who can be replaced by a machine should be," says Clarke in paragraph 24. How does he support this claim? What teaching functions does he say would still have to be performed by human beings? Do you agree?

5. What is Clarke's tone in this essay? Refer to the essay to show how he achieves this tone.

6. How does Clarke develop his points and support his generalizations? Can you cite evidence to contradict any of his statements? Explain.

Explorations

1. Clarke's essay is full of implications about the nature and purpose of education. Do his views agree with common opinions about education today? with what you think it should be in the future?

2. In the past twenty years computers have begun what Clarke calls "one of the swiftest and most momentous revolutions in the entire history of technology." How has this affected your life? Try to make your own educated guess as to how they will affect the future.

RICHARD WILBUR

Richard Wilbur was born in New York City in 1921, but has lived for most of his life in New England. He graduated from Amherst College in 1942 and served in the Army in World War II. Since 1957 he has taught at Wesleyan University; he is also Poet-in-Residence at Smith College. Wilbur has won every award for poetry that America offers, including the Pulitzer Prize and the National Book Award. His choice of his best work is collected in *The Poems of Richard Wilbur* (1963), and his more recent poems may be found in *Walking to Sleep* (1969) and *The Mind-Reader* (1976). He has also done valuable work for the stage, ranging from his polished translations of the classical French dramatists Molière and Racine to his witty lyrics for Leonard Bernstein's Broadway musical *Candide* (1956). In "Mind," from *Things of This World* (1956), Wilbur offers a surprising comparison that helps to illuminate human thought.

Mind

Mind in its purest play is like some bat
That beats about in caverns all alone,
Contriving by a kind of senseless wit
Not to conclude against a wall of stone.

It has no need to falter or explore;   5
Darkly it knows what obstacles are there,
And so may weave and flitter, dip and soar
In perfect courses through the blackest air.

And has this simile a like perfection?
The mind is like a bat. Precisely. Save   10
That in the very happiest intellection
A graceful error may correct the cave.

About the Poem

1. How did you respond at first to the poem's comparison between a mind and a bat? Has Wilbur succeeded in convincing you that his comparison is just?

2. Wilbur writes in the first line of "mind in its purest play." What do you think he means by that? Is the poem playful or serious? Why do you think so?

3. Trace the points of Wilbur's comparison. How does each detail fit in? For example, what would "a wall of stone" signify in the play of the mind?

4. What meaning or meanings of the following words fit the sense of Wilbur's poem? Look these words up in a dictionary, paying special attention to the information in the etymologies about their origins. Do you think Wilbur had any of these etymologies in mind when he chose his words? In which cases and to what effect?

    a. wit (line 3)
    b. conclude (line 4)
    c. falter (line 5)
    d. darkly (line 6)
    e. weave (line 7)
    f. courses (line 8)
    g. graceful (12)
    h. error (12)

Explorations

1. How does your mind "play" when you explore an idea or a topic for writing? Can you describe the process, either directly or by means of comparisons such as the one in Wilbur's poem?

2. Wilbur compares the human mind at work to a bat in flight. In the same way, love has been compared to fire, red roses, and summer days. Consider one human concern—perhaps work or children or death—and think of three appropriate images for comparison. Compose a short poem using one of these images.

LANGSTON HUGHES

One reason why the Roaring Twenties roared was that a new generation of black artists was finally recognized by a nationwide, even a worldwide, audience. People flocked to Harlem to hear Duke Ellington and Louis Armstrong, and the Harlem Renaissance literary movement brought black writing to a wide public.

Langston Hughes was a prominent figure in that movement. He was born in 1902 in Joplin, Missouri, and though he began writing poetry at an early age, he was at first unable to get his work published and supported himself by traveling about the country, doing whatever work he could find. He was working as a busboy when his poetry was discovered in 1925 by Vachel Lindsay, a famous poet of the time. A year later Hughes published his first book of poems, *The Weary Blues*, and entered Lincoln University in Pennsylvania. He graduated in 1929 and set about making his way as a writer. Hughes's work focuses on American Negro life, often incorporating dialect and jazz rhythms. His writings include novels, plays, and a popular series of newspaper sketches, but his reputation rests most solidly on his poems. Much of his finest poetry has been collected as *Selected Poems* (1959). He died in 1967.

The speaker of "Theme for English B" is a student at Columbia University, where Hughes had enrolled for a year in 1921. The poem, though quite short, embodies the two great themes of Hughes's work and indeed of the Harlem Renaissance: the celebration of black culture and the demand for equal treatment and respect.

Theme for English B

The instructor said,

> Go home and write
> a page tonight.
> And let that page come out of you—
> Then, it will be true.   5

I wonder if it's that simple?
I am twenty-two, colored, born in Winston-Salem.
I went to school there, then Durham, then here
to this college on the hill above Harlem.[1]
I am the only colored student in my class.   10

---

[1]Refers to Columbia University, which is located next to Harlem.

The steps from the hill lead down into Harlem,
through a park, then I cross St. Nicholas,
Eighth Avenue, Seventh, and I come to the Y,
the Harlem Branch Y, where I take the elevator
up to my room, sit down, and write this page: 15

It's not easy to know what is true for you or me
at twenty-two, my age. But I guess I'm what
I feel and see and hear, Harlem, I hear you:
hear you, hear me—we two—you, me, talk on this page.
(I hear New York, too.) Me—who?   20

Well, I like to eat, sleep, drink, and be in love.
I like to work, read, learn, and understand life.
I like a pipe for a Christmas present,
or records—Bessie,[2] bop, or Bach.
I guess being colored doesn't make me *not* like   25
the same things other folks like who are other races.
So will my page be colored that I write?
Being me, it will not be white.
But it will be
a part of you, instructor.   30
You are white—
yet a part of me, as I am a part of you.
That's American.
Sometimes perhaps you don't want to be a part of me.
Nor do I often want to be a part of you.   35
But we are, that's true!
As I learn from you,
I guess you learn from me—
although you're older—and white—
and somewhat more free.   40

This is my page for English B.

---

[2]Bessie Smith [1898?–1937], American blues singer, considered by many critics to be
the greatest jazz singer of her time.

About the Poem

1. What does the instructor mean when he tells the student that the writing should "come out of you"? Why would it then be "true"?

2. Is the student in the poem Hughes himself? Why, or why not?

3. What is the significance of the student's speaking of Columbia as "on the hill above Harlem"?

4. The student says that he is a part of his instructor, and that his instructor is a part of him. What does he mean? Are we all part of each other? If so, in what way? If not, why not?

5. The student ends by saying, "This is my page for English B." Is the "page" what the instructor asked for or wanted? Why, or why not?

Explorations

1. The poem says, "As I learn from you, / I guess you learn from me." What do you think teachers learn from their students, if anything? What should they learn?

2. Imagine yourself a college instructor. Think up one or two essay assignments for your class, keeping in mind the purpose of your imagined course and your students' backgrounds and interests. Why do you think each of them is a good assignment?

JOYCE CAROL OATES

Like many a writer, Joyce Carol Oates draws on her own observations and experiences for her fiction. Born in 1938 to a Roman Catholic family in Lockport, New York, she earned a bachelor's degree from Syracuse University and a master of arts degree in English from the University of Wisconsin. She has taught English, first at the University of Detroit, and since 1967 at the University of Windsor in Ontario, Canada. A prodigious and versatile writer, Oates has published thirteen novels, including *Them* (1969), *Bellefleur* (1980), and *Angel of Light* (1981); dozens of short stories; eight books of poems; six plays; and four volumes of literary criticism. "In the Region of Ice" is from her third collection of stories, *The Wheel of Love* (1971). In it Sister Irene, a nun and a professor of literature at a Jesuit university, struggles to be true to her vocation when she is confronted by a searching and troubled student.

In the Region of Ice

Sister Irene was a tall, deft woman in her early thirties. What one   1
could see of her face made a striking impression—serious, hard gray eyes, a long slender nose, a face waxen with thought. Seen at the right time, from the right angle, she was almost handsome. In her past teaching positions she had drawn a little upon the fact of her being young and brilliant and also a nun, but she was beginning to grow out of that.

This was a new university and an entirely new world. She had   2
heard—of course it was true—that the Jesuit administration of this school had hired her at the last moment to save money and to head off the appointment of a man of dubious religious commitment. She had prayed for the necessary energy to get her through this first semester. She had no trouble with teaching itself; once she stood before a classroom she felt herself capable of anything. It was the world immediately outside the classroom that confused and alarmed her, though she let none of this show—the cynicism of her colleagues, the indifference of many of the students, and, above all, the looks she got that told her nothing much would be expected of her because she was a nun. This took energy, strength. At times she had the idea that she was on trial and that the excuses she made to herself about her discomfort were only the common excuses made by guilty people. But in front of a class she had no time to worry about herself or the conflicts in her mind. She became, once and for all, a figure existing only for the benefit of others, an instrument by which facts were communicated.

230

About two weeks after the semester began, Sister Irene noticed a   3
new student in her class. He was slight and fair-haired, and his face was
blank, but not blank by accident, blank on purpose, suppressed and
restricted into a dumbness that looked hysterical. She was prepared for
him before he raised his hand, and when she saw his arm jerk, as if he
had at last lost control of it, she nodded to him without hesitation.

"Sister, how can this be reconciled with Shakespeare's vision in   4
Hamlet? How can these opposing views be in the same mind?"

Students glanced at him, mildly surprised. He did not belong in   5
the class, and this was mysterious, but his manner was urgent and blind.

"There is no need to reconcile opposing views," Sister Irene said,   6
leaning forward against the podium. "In one play Shakespeare suggests
one vision, in another play another; the plays are not simultaneous crea-
tions, and even if they were, we never demand a logical—"

"We must demand a logical consistency," the young man said. "The   7
idea of education is itself predicated upon consistency, order, sanity—"

He had interrupted her, and she hardened her face against him—   8
for his sake, not her own, since she did not really care. But he noticed
nothing. "Please see me after class," she said.

After class the young man hurried up to her.   9

"Sister Irene, I hope you didn't mind my visiting today. I'd heard   10
some things, interesting things," he said. He stared at her, and something
in her face allowed him to smile. "I . . . could we talk in your office?
Do you have time?"

They walked down to her office. Sister Irene sat at her desk, and   11
the young man sat facing her; for a moment they were self-conscious and
silent.

"Well, I suppose you know—I'm a Jew," he said.   12

Sister Irene stared at him. "Yes?" she said.   13

"What am I doing at a Catholic university, huh?" He grinned.   14
"That's what you want to know."

She made a vague movement of her hand to show that she had no   15
thoughts on this, nothing at all, but he seemed not to catch it. He was
sitting on the edge of the straight-backed chair. She saw that he was
young but did not really look young. There were harsh lines on either
side of his mouth, as if he had misused that youthful mouth somehow.
His skin was almost as pale as hers, his eyes were dark and not quite in
focus. He looked at her and through her and around her, as his voice
surrounded them both. His voice was a little shrill at times.

"Listen, I did the right thing today—visiting your class! God, what   16
a lucky accident it was; some jerk mentioned you, said you were a good
teacher—I thought, what a laugh! These people know about good teach-

ers here? But yes, listen, yes, I'm not kidding—you are good. I mean that."

Sister Irene frowned. "I don't quite understand what all this means."   17

He smiled and waved aside her formality, as if he knew better.   18
"Listen, I got my B.A. at Columbia, then I came back here to this crappy
city. I mean, I did it on purpose, I wanted to come back. I wanted to.
I have my reasons for doing things. I'm on a three-thousand-dollar fellowship," he said, and waited for that to impress her. "You know, I could
have gone almost anywhere with that fellowship, and I came back home
here—my home's in the city—and enrolled here. This was last year. This
is my second year. I'm working on a thesis, I mean I was, my master's
thesis—but the hell with that. What I want to ask you is this: Can I
enroll in your class, is it too late? We have to get special permission if
we're late."

Sister Irene felt something nudging her, some uneasiness in him   19
that was pleading with her not to be offended by his abrupt, familiar
manner. He seemed to be promising another self, a better self, as if his
fair, childish, almost cherubic face were doing tricks to distract her from
what his words said.

"Are you in English studies?" she asked.   20

"I was in history. Listen," he said, and his mouth did something   21
odd, drawing itself down into a smile that made the lines about it deepen
like knives, "listen, they kicked me out."

He sat back, watching her. He crossed his legs. He took out a   22
package of cigarettes and offered her one. Sister Irene shook her head,
staring at his hands. They were small and stubby and might have belonged to a ten-year-old, and the nails were a strange near-violet color.
It took him awhile to extract a cigarette.

"Yeah, kicked me out. What do you think of that?"   23

"I don't understand."   24

"My master's thesis was coming along beautifully, and then this   25
bastard—I mean, excuse me, this professor, I won't pollute your office
with his name—he started making criticisms, he said some things were
unacceptable, he—" The boy leaned forward and hunched his narrow
shoulders in a parody of secrecy. "We had an argument. I told him some
frank things, things only a broad-minded person could hear about himself. That takes courage, right? He didn't have it! He kicked me out of
the master's program, so now I'm coming into English. Literature is greater
than history; European history is one big pile of garbage. Sky-high. Filth
and rotting corpses, right? Aristotle says that poetry is higher than history; he's right; in your class today I suddenly realized that this is my
field, Shakespeare, only Shakespeare is—"

Sister Irene guessed that he was going to say that only Shakespeare was equal to him, and she caught the moment of recognition and hesitation, the half-raised arm, the keen, frowning forehead, the narrowed eyes; then he thought better of it and did not end the sentence. "The students in your class are mainly negligible, I can tell you that. You're new here, and I've been here a year—I would have finished my studies last year but my father got sick, he was hospitalized, I couldn't take exams and it was a mess—but I'll make it through English in one year or drop dead. I can do it, I can do anything. I'll take six courses at once—" He broke off, breathless. Sister Irene tried to smile. "All right then, it's settled? You'll let me in? Have I missed anything so far?"

He had no idea of the rudeness of his question. Sister Irene, feeling suddenly exhausted, said, "I'll give you a syllabus of the course."

"Fine! Wonderful!"

He got to his feet eagerly. He looked through the schedule, muttering to himself, making favorable noises. It struck Sister Irene that she was making a mistake to let him in. There were these moments when one had to make an intelligent decision. . . . But she was sympathetic with him, yes. She was sympathetic with something about him.

She found out his name the next day: Allen Weinstein.

After this she came to her Shakespeare class with a sense of excitement. It became clear to her at once that Weinstein was the most intelligent student in the class. Until he had enrolled, she had not understood what was lacking, a mind that could appreciate her own. Within a week his jagged, protean mind had alienated the other students, and though he sat in the center of the class, he seemed totally alone, encased by a miniature world of his own. When he spoke of the "frenetic humanism of the High Renaissance," Sister Irene dreaded the raised eyebrows and mocking smiles of the other students, who no longer bothered to look at Weinstein. She wanted to defend him, but she never did, because there was something rude and dismal about his knowledge; he used it like a weapon, talking passionately of Nietzsche and Goethe and Freud until Sister Irene would be forced to close discussion.

In meditation, alone, she often thought of him. When she tried to talk about him to a young nun, Sister Carlotta, everything sounded gross. "But no, he's an excellent student," she insisted. "I'm very grateful to have him in class. It's just that . . . he thinks ideas are real." Sister Carlotta, who loved literature also, had been forced to teach grade-school arithmetic for the last four years. That might have been why she said, a little sharply, "You don't think ideas are real?"

Sister Irene acquiesced with a smile, but of course she did not think 33
so: only reality is real.

When Weinstein did not show up for class on the day the first 34
paper was due, Sister Irene's heart sank, and the sensation was somehow
a familiar one. She began to lecture and kept waiting for the door to
open and for him to hurry noisily back to his seat, grinning an apology
toward her—but nothing happened.

If she had been deceived by him, she made herself think angrily, 35
it was as a teacher and not as a woman. He had promised her nothing.

Weinstein appeared the next day near the steps of the liberal arts 36
building. She heard someone running behind her, a breathless exclamation: "Sister Irene!" She turned and saw him, panting and grinning
in embarrassment. He wore a dark-blue suit with a necktie, and he looked,
despite his childish face, like a little old man; there was something oddly
precarious and fragile about him. "Sister Irene, I owe you an apology,
right?" He raised his eyebrows and smiled a sad, forlorn, yet irritatingly
conspiratorial smile. "The first paper—not in on time, and I know what
your rules are. . . . You won't accept late papers, I know—that's good
discipline, I'll do that when I teach too. But, unavoidably, I was unable
to come to school yesterday. There are many—many—" He gulped for
breath, and Sister Irene had the startling sense of seeing the real Weinstein stare out at her, a terrified prisoner behind the confident voice.
"There are many complications in family life. Perhaps you are unaware—
I mean—"

She did not like him, but she felt this sympathy, something tugging 37
and nagging at her the way her parents had competed for her love so
many years before. They had been whining, weak people, and out of
their wet need for affection, the girl she had been (her name was Yvonne)
had emerged stronger than either of them, contemptuous of tears because
she had seen so many. But Weinstein was different; he was not simply
weak—perhaps he was not weak at all—but his strength was confused
and hysterical. She felt her customary rigidity as a teacher begin to falter.
"You may turn your paper in today if you have it," she said, frowning.

Weinstein's mouth jerked into an incredulous grin. "Wonderful! 38
Marvelous!" he said. "You are very understanding, Sister Irene, I must
say. I must say . . . I didn't expect, really . . ." He was fumbling in a
shabby old briefcase for the paper. Sister Irene waited. She was prepared
for another of his excuses, certain that he did not have the paper, when
he suddenly straightened up and handed her something. "Here! I took
the liberty of writing thirty pages instead of just fifteen," he said. He was
obviously quite excited; his cheeks were mottled pink and white. "You
may disagree violently with my interpretation—I expect you to, in fact

I'm counting on it—but let me warn you, I have the exact proof, right here in the play itself!" He was thumping at a book, his voice growing louder and shriller. Sister Irene, startled, wanted to put her hand over his mouth and soothe him.

"Look," he said breathlessly, "may I talk with you? I have a class now I hate, I loathe, I can't bear to sit through! Can I talk with you instead?"   39

Because she was nervous, she stared at the title page of the paper: 40
"Erotic Melodies in *Romeo and Juliet*' by Allen Weinstein, Jr."

"All right?" he said. "Can we walk around here? Is it all right? I've   41
been anxious to talk with you about some things you said in class."

She was reluctant, but he seemed not to notice. They walked slowly   42
along the shaped campus paths. Weinstein did all the talking, of course, and Sister Irene recognized nothing in his cascade of words that she had mentioned in class. "The humanist must be committed to the totality of life," he said passionately. "This is the failing one finds everywhere in the academic world! I found it in New York and I found it here and I'm no ingénu, I don't go around with my mouth hanging open—I'm experienced, look, I've been to Europe, I've lived in Rome! I went everywhere in Europe except Germany, I don't talk about Germany . . . Sister Irene, think of the significant men in the last century, the men who've changed the world! Jews, right? Marx, Freud, Einstein! Not that I believe Marx, Marx is a madman . . . and Freud, no, my sympathies are with spiritual humanism. I believe that the Jewish race is the exclusive . . . the exclusive, what's the word, the exclusive means by which humanism will be extended . . . Humanism begins by excluding the Jew, and now," he said with a high, surprised laugh, "the Jew will perfect it. After the Nazis, only the Jew is authorized to understand humanism, its limitations and its possibilities. So, I say that the humanist is committed to life in its totality and not just to his profession! The religious person is totally religious, he is his religion! What else? I recognize in you a humanist and a religious person—"

But he did not seem to be talking to her or even looking at her.   43

"Here, read this," he said. "I wrote it last night." It was a long   44
free-verse poem, typed on a typewriter whose ribbon was worn out.

"There's this trouble with my father, a wonderful man, a lovely   45
man, but his health—his strength is fading, do you see? What must it be to him to see his son growing up? I mean, I'm a man now, he's getting old, weak, his health is bad—it's hell, right? I sympathize with him. I'd do anything for him, I'd cut open my veins, anything for a father—right? That's why I wasn't in school yesterday," he said, and his voice dropped for the last sentence, as if he had been dragged back to earth by a fact.

Sister Irene tried to read the poem, then pretended to read it. A   46
jumble of words dealing with "life" and "death" and "darkness" and
"love." "What do you think?" Weinstein said nervously, trying to read
it over her shoulder and crowding against her.

"It's very . . . passionate," Sister Irene said.   47

This was the right comment; he took the poem back from her in   48
silence, his face flushed with excitement. "Here, at this school, I have
few people to talk with. I haven't shown anyone else that poem." He
looked at her with his dark, intense eyes, and Sister Irene felt them focus
upon her. She was terrified at what he was trying to do—he was trying
to force her into a human relationship.

"Thank you for your paper," she said, turning away.   49

When he came the next day, ten minutes late, he was haughty and   50
disdainful. He had nothing to say and sat with his arms folded. Sister
Irene took back with her to the convent a feeling of betrayal and confusion. She had been hurt. It was absurd, and yet—She spent too much
time thinking about him, as if he were somehow a kind of crystallization
of her own loneliness; but she had no right to think so much of him.
She did not want to think of him or of her loneliness. But Weinstein
did so much more than think of his predicament: he embodied it, he
acted it out, and that was perhaps why he fascinated her. It was as if he
were doing a dance for her, a dance of shame and agony and delight,
and so long as he did it, she was safe. She felt embarrassment for him,
but also anxiety; she wanted to protect him. When the dean of the
graduate school questioned her about Weinstein's work, she insisted that
he was an "excellent" student, though she knew the dean had not wanted
to hear that.

She prayed for guidance, she spent hours on her devotions, she was   51
closer to her vocation than she had been for some years. Life at the
convent became tinged with unreality, a misty distortion that took its
tone from the glowering skies of the city at night, identical smokestacks
ranged against the clouds and giving to the sky the excrement of the
populated and successful earth. This city was not her city, this world was
not her world. She felt no pride in knowing this, it was a fact. The little
convent was not like an island in the center of this noisy world, but
rather a kind of hole or crevice the world did not bother with, something
of no interest. The convent's rhythm of life had nothing to do with the
world's rhythm, it did not violate or alarm it in any way. Sister Irene
tried to draw together the fragments of her life and synthesize them
somehow in her vocation as a nun: she was a nun, she was recognized
as a nun and had given herself happily to that life, she had a name, a

place, she had dedicated her superior intelligence to the Church, she worked without pay and without expecting gratitude, she had given up pride, she did not think of herself but only of her work and her vocation, she did not think of anything external to these, she saturated herself daily in the knowledge that she was involved in the mystery of Christianity.

A daily terror attended this knowledge, however, for she sensed 52 herself being drawn by that student, that Jewish boy, into a relationship she was not ready for. She wanted to cry out in fear that she was being forced into the role of a Christian, and what did that mean? What could her studies tell her? What could the other nuns tell her? She was alone, no one could help; he was making her into a Christian, and to her that was a mystery, a thing of terror, something others slipped on the way they slipped on their clothes, casually and thoughtlessly, but to her a magnificent and terrifying wonder.

For days she carried Weinstein's paper, marked A, around with her; 53 he did not come to class. One day she checked with the graduate office and was told that Weinstein had called in to say his father was ill and that he would not be able to attend classes for a while. "He's strange, I remember him," the secretary said. "He missed all his exams last spring and made a lot of trouble. He was in and out of here every day."

So there was no more of Weinstein for a while, and Sister Irene 54 stopped expecting him to hurry into class. Then, one morning, she found a letter from him in her mailbox.

He had printed it in black ink, very carefully, as if he had not 55 trusted handwriting. The return address was in bold letters that, like his voice, tried to grab onto her: Birchcrest Manor. Somewhere north of the city. "Dear Sister Irene," the block letters said, "I am doing well here and have time for reading and relaxing. The Manor is delightful. My doctor here is an excellent, intelligent man who has time for me, unlike my former doctor. If you have time, you might drop in on my father, who worries about me too much I think, and explain to him what my condition is. He doesn't seem to understand. I feel about this new life the way that boy, what's his name, in *Measure for Measure*, feels about the prospects of a different life; you remember what he says to his sister when she visits him in prison, how he is looking forward to an escape into another world. Perhaps you could *explain* this to my father and he would stop worrying." The letter ended with his father's name and address, in letters that were just a little too big. Sister Irene, walking slowly down the corridor as she read the letter, felt her eyes cloud over with tears. She was cold with fear, it was something she had never experienced before. She knew what Weinstein was trying to tell her, and the desperation of his attempt made it all the more pathetic; he did not deserve this, why did God allow him to suffer so?

She read through Claudio's speech to his sister, in *Measure for Measure:*

> Ay, but to die, and go we know not where;
> To lie in cold obstruction and to rot;
> This sensible warm motion to become
> A kneaded clod; and the delighted spirit
> To bathe in fiery floods, or to reside
> In thrilling region of thick-ribbed ice,
> To be imprison'd in the viewless winds
> And blown with restless violence round about
> The pendent world; or to be worse than worst
> Of those that lawless and incertain thought
> Imagines howling! 'Tis too horrible!
> The weariest and most loathed worldly life
> That age, ache, penury, and imprisonment
> Can lay on nature is a paradise
> To what we fear of death.

Sister Irene called the father's number that day. "Allen Weinstein residence, who may I say is calling?" a woman said, bored. "May I speak to Mr. Weinstein? It's urgent—about his son," Sister Irene said. There was a pause at the other end. "You want to talk to his mother, maybe?" the woman said. "His mother? Yes, his mother, then. Please. It's very important."

She talked with this strange, unsuspected woman, a disembodied voice that suggested absolutely no face, and insisted upon going over that afternoon. The woman was nervous, but Sister Irene, who was a university professor, after all, knew enough to hide her own nervousness. She kept waiting for the woman to say, "Yes, Allen has mentioned you . . ." but nothing happened.

She persuaded Sister Carlotta to ride over with her. This urgency of hers was something they were all amazed by. They hadn't suspected that the set of her gray eyes could change to this blurred, distracted alarm, this sense of mission that seemed to have come to her from nowhere. Sister Irene drove across the city in the late afternoon traffic, with the high whining noises from residential streets where trees were being sawed down in pieces. She understood now the secret, sweet wildness that Christ must have felt, giving himself for man, dying for the billions of men who would never know of him and never understand the sacrifice. For the first time she approached the realization of that great act. In her troubled mind the city traffic was jumbled and yet oddly coherent, an image of the world that was always out of joint with what was happening in it, its inner history struggling with its external spectacle. This sacrifice of Christ's, so mysterious and legendary now, almost lost in time—it was that by which Christ transcended both God and man at one moment, more than man because of his fate to do what no other man could do, and more than God because no god could suffer as he did. She felt a flicker of something close to madness.

She drove nervously, uncertainly, afraid of missing the street and afraid of finding it too, for while one part of her rushed forward to confront these people who had betrayed their son, another part of her would have liked nothing so much as to be waiting as usual for the summons to dinner, safe in her room. . . . When she found the street and turned onto it, she was in a state of breathless excitement. Here lawns were bright green and marred with only a few leaves, magically clean, and the houses were enormous and pompous, a mixture of styles: ranch houses, colonial houses, French country houses, white-bricked wonders with curving glass and clumps of birch trees somehow encircled by white concrete. Sister Irene stared as if she had blundered into another world. This was a kind of heaven, and she was too shabby for it.

The Weinsteins' house was the strangest one of all: it looked like a small Alpine lodge, with an inverted-V-shaped front entrance. Sister Irene drove up the black-topped driveway and let the car slow to a stop; she told Sister Carlotta she would not be long.

At the door she was met by Weinstein's mother, a small, nervous woman with hands like her son's. "Come in, come in," the woman said. She had once been beautiful, that was clear, but now in missing beauty she was not handsome or even attractive but looked ruined and perplexed, the misshapen swelling of her white-blond professionally set hair like a cap lifting up from her surprised face. "He'll be right in. Allen?" she called, "our visitor is here." They went into the living room. There was a grand piano at one end and an organ at the other. In between were scatterings of brilliant modern furniture in conversational groups, and several puffed-up white rugs on the polished floor. Sister Irene could not stop shivering.

"Professor, it's so strange, but let me say when the phone rang I had a feeling—I had a feeling," the woman said, with damp eyes. Sister Irene sat, and the woman hovered about her. "Should I call you Professor? We don't . . . you know . . . we don't understand the technicalities that go with—Allen, my son, wanted to go here to the Catholic school; I told my husband why not? Why fight? It's the thing these days, they do anything they want for knowledge. And he had to come home, you know. He couldn't take care of himself in New York, that was the beginning of the trouble. . . . Should I call you Professor?"

"You can call me Sister Irene." 64

"Sister Irene?" the woman said, touching her throat in awe, as if 65
something intimate and unexpected had happened.

Then Weinstein's father appeared, hurrying. He took long, impa- 66
tient strides. Sister Irene stared at him and in that instant doubted everything—he was in his fifties, a tall, sharply handsome man, heavy but not
fat, holding his shoulders back with what looked like an effort, but holding them back just the same. He wore a dark suit and his face was flushed,
as if he had run a long distance.

"Now," he said, coming to Sister Irene and with a precise wave of 67
his hand motioning his wife off, "now, let's straighten this out. A lot of
confusion over that kid, eh?" He pulled a chair over, scraping it across
a rug and pulling one corner over, so that it's brown underside was
exposed. "I came home early just for this, Libby phoned me. Sister, you
got a letter from him, right?"

The wife looked at Sister Irene over her husband's head as if trying 68
somehow to coach her, knowing that this man was so loud and impatient
that no one could remember anything in his presence.

"A letter—yes—today—" 69

"He says what in it? You got the letter, eh? Can I see it?" 70

She gave it to him and wanted to explain, but he silenced her with 71
a flick of his hand. He read through the letter so quickly that Sister Irene
thought perhaps he was trying to impress her with his skill at reading.
"So?" he said, raising his eyes, smiling, "so what is this? He's happy out
there, he says. He doesn't communicate with us any more, but he writes
to you and says he's happy—what's that? I mean, what the hell is that?"

"But he isn't happy. He wants to come home," Sister Irene said. 72
It was so important that she make him understand that she could not
trust her voice; goaded by this man, it might suddenly turn shrill, as his
son's did. "Someone must read their letters before they're mailed, so he
tried to tell me something by making an allusion to—"

"What?" 73

"—an allusion to a play, so that I would know. He may be thinking 74
suicide, he must be very unhappy—"

She ran out of breath. Weinstein's mother had begun to cry, but 75
the father was shaking his head jerkily back and forth. "Forgive me,
Sister, but it's a lot of crap, he needs the hospital, he needs help—right?
It costs me fifty a day out there, and they've got the best place in the
state, I figure it's worth it. He needs help, that kid, what do I care if
he's unhappy? He's unbalanced!" he said angrily. "You want us to get

him out again? We argued with the judge for two hours to get him in, an acquaintance of mine. Look, he can't control himself—he was smashing things here, he was hysterical. They need help, lady, and you do something about it fast! You do something! We made up our minds to do something and we did it! This letter—what the hell is this letter? He never talked like that to us!"

"But he means the opposite of what he says—" 76

"Then he's crazy! I'm the first to admit it." He was perspiring and 77
his face had darkened. "I've got no pride left this late. He's a little bastard, you want to know? He calls me names, he's filthy, got a filthy mouth—that's being smart, huh? They give him a big scholarship for his filthy mouth? I went to college too, and I got out and knew something, and I for Christ's sake did something with it; my wife is an intelligent woman, a learned woman, would you guess she does book reviews for the little newspaper out here? Intelligent isn't crazy—crazy isn't intelligent. Maybe for you at the school he writes nice papers and gets an A, but out here, around the house, he can't control himself, and we got him committed!"

"But—" 78

"We're fixing him up, don't worry about it!" He turned to his wife. 79
"Libby, get out of here, I mean it. I'm sorry, but get out of here, you're making a fool of yourself, go stand in the kitchen or something, you and the goddamn maid can cry on each other's shoulders. That one in the kitchen is nuts too, they're all nuts. Sister," he said, his voice lowering, "I thank you immensely for coming out here. This is wonderful, your interest in my son. And I see he admires you—that letter there. But what about that letter? If he did want to get out, which I don't admit— he was willing to be committed, in the end he said okay himself—if he wanted out I wouldn't do it. Why? So what if he wants to come back? The next day he wants something else, what then? He's a sick kid, and I'm the first to admit it."

Sister Irene felt that sickness spread to her. She stood. The room 80
was so big it seemed it must be a public place; there had been nothing personal or private about their conversation. Weinstein's mother was standing by the fireplace, sobbing. The father jumped to his feet and wiped his forehead in a gesture that was meant to help Sister Irene on her way out. "God, what a day," he said, his eyes snatching at hers for understanding, "you know—one of those days all day long? Sister, I thank you a lot. There should be more people in the world who care about others, like you. I mean that."

On the way back to the convent, the man's words returned to her, 81
and she could not get control of them; she could not even feel anger.

She had been pressed down, forced back, what could she do? Weinstein might have been watching her somehow from a barred window, and he surely would have understood. The strange idea she had had on the way over, something about understanding Christ, came back to her now and sickened her. But the sickness was small. It could be contained.

About a month after her visit to his father, Weinstein himself showed up. He was dressed in a suit as before, even the necktie was the same. He came right into her office as if he had been pushed and could not stop.   82

"Sister," he said, and shook her hand. He must have seen fear in her because he smiled ironically. "Look, I'm released. I'm let out of the nut house. Can I sit down?"   83

He sat. Sister Irene was breathing quickly, as if in the presence of an enemy who does not know he is an enemy.   84

"So, they finally let me out. I heard what you did. You talked with him, that was all I wanted. You're the only one who gave a damn. Because you're a humanist and a religious person, you respect . . . the individual. Listen," he said, whispering, "it was hell out there! Hell Birchcrest Manor! All fixed up with fancy chairs and *Life* magazines lying around—and what do they do to you? They locked me up, they gave me shock treatments! Shock treatments, how do you like that, it's discredited by everybody now—they're crazy out there themselves, sadists. They locked me up, they gave me hypodermic shots, they didn't treat me like a human being! Do you know what that is," Weinstein demanded savagely, "not to be treated like a human being? They made me an animal— for fifty dollars a day! Dirty filthy swine! Now I'm an outpatient because I stopped swearing at them. I found somebody's bobby pin, and when I wanted to scream I pressed it under my fingernail and it stopped me— the screaming went inside and not out—so they gave me good reports, those sick bastards. Now I'm an outpatient and I can walk along the street and breathe in the same filthy exhaust from the buses like all you normal people! Christ," he said, and threw himself back against the chair.   85

Sister Irene stared at him. She wanted to take his hand, to make some gesture that would close the aching distance between them. "Mr. Weinstein—"   86

"Call me Allen!" he said sharply.   87

"I'm very sorry—I'm terribly sorry—"   88

"My own parents committed me, but of course they didn't know what it was like. It was hell," he said thickly, "and there isn't any hell except what other people do to you. The psychiatrist out there, the main shrink, he hates Jews too, some of us were positive of that, and he's got   89 a bigger nose than I do, a real beak." He made a noise of disgust. "A dirty bastard, a sick, dirty, pathetic bastard—all of them. Anyway, I'm getting out of here, and I came to ask you a favor."

"What do you mean?" 90

"I'm getting out. I'm leaving. I'm going up to Canada and lose 91 myself. I'll get a job, I'll forget everything, I'll kill myself maybe—what's the difference? Look, can you lend me some money?"

"Money?" 92

"Just a little! I have to get to the border, I'm going to take a 93 bus."

"But I don't have any money—" 94

"No money?" He stared at her. "You mean—you don't have any? 95 Sure you have some!"

She stared at him as if he had asked her to do something obscene. 96 Everything was splotched and uncertain before her eyes.

"You must . . . you must go back," she said, "you're making a—" 97

"I'll pay it back. Look, I'll pay it back, can you go to where you 98 live or something and get it? I'm in a hurry. My friends are sons of bitches: one of them pretended he didn't see me yesterday—I stood right in the middle of the sidewalk and yelled at him, I called him some appropriate names! So he didn't see me, huh? You're the only one who understands me, you understand me like a poet, you—"

"I can't help you, I'm sorry—I . . ." 99

He looked to one side of her and flashed his gaze back, as if he 100 could control it. He seemed to be trying to clear his vision.

"You have the soul of a poet," he whispered, "you're the only one. 101 Everybody else is rotten! Can't you lend me some money, ten dollars maybe? I have three thousand in the bank, and I can't touch it! They take everything away from me, they make me into an animal. . . . You know I'm not an animal, don't you? Don't you?"

"Of course," Sister Irene whispered. 102

"You could get money. Help me. Give me your hand or something, 103 touch me, help me—please. . . ." He reached for her hand and she drew back. He stared at her and his face seemed about to crumble, like a child's. "I want something from you, but I don't know what—I want something!" he cried. "Something real! I want you to look at me like I was a human being, is that too much to ask? I have a brain, I'm alive, I'm suffering—what does that mean? Does that mean nothing? I want something real and not this phony Christian love garbage—it's all in the books, it isn't personal—I want something real—look. . . ."

He tried to take her hand again, and this time she jerked away. 104 She got to her feet. "Mr. Weinstein," she said, "please—"

"You! You nun!" he said scornfully, his mouth twisted into a mock   105
grin. "You nun! There's nothing under that ugly outfit, right? And you're
not particularly smart even though you think you are; my father has more
brains in his foot than you—"

He got to his feet and kicked the chair.   106

"You bitch!" he cried.   107

She shrank back against her desk as if she thought he might hit   108
her, but he only ran out of the office.

Weinstein: the name was to become disembodied from the figure,   109
as time went on. The semester passed, the autumn drizzle turned into
snow, Sister Irene rode to school in the morning and left in the afternoon, four days a week, anonymous in her black winter cloak, quiet and
stunned. University teaching was an anonymous task, each day disso-
ciated from the rest, with no necessary sense of unity among the teachers:
they came and went separately and might for a year just miss a colleague
who left his office five minutes before they arrived, and it did not matter.

She heard of Weinstein's death, his suicide by drowning, from the   110
English Department secretary, a handsome white-haired woman who kept
a transistor radio on her desk. Sister Irene was not surprised; she had
been thinking of him as dead for months. "They identified him by some
special television way they have now," the secretary said. "They're shipping the body back. It was up in Quebec. . . ."

Sister Irene could feel a part of herself drifting off, lured by the   111
plains of white snow to the north, the quiet, the emptiness, the sweep
of the Great Lakes up to the silence of Canada. But she called that part
of herself back. She could only be one person in her lifetime. That was
the ugly truth, she thought, that she could not really regret Weinstein's
suffering and death; she had only one life and had already given it to
someone else. He had come too late to her. Fifteen years ago, perhaps,
but not now.

She was only one person, she thought, walking down the corridor   112
in a dream. Was she safe in this single person, or was she trapped? She
had only one identity. She could make only one choice. What she had
done or hadn't done was the result of that choice, and how was she
guilty? If she could have felt guilt, she thought, she might at least have
been able to feel something.

About the Story

1. How does Sister Irene view her responsibilities as a teacher? As a nun? In
paragraph 51, she refers to her vocation; what exactly is this vocation?

2. What profession is Allen preparing for? What does he say that suggests

why he might be attracted to that profession? Does he seem suited for it? Why, or why not?

3. Does Oates make it clear whether or not Allen is really insane? If so, where? How does this affect your reading of the story?

4. What do you learn about Allen and the source of his disturbance from Sister Irene's visit to his family? How does what we know of Sister Irene's own upbringing help to explain her attitudes and behavior?

5. Why does Sister Irene think that Allen is "making her into a Christian"? Why is it a "terrifying wonder" for her to assume the role of a Christian?

6. Where does Oates draw the title of the story from? What does the title contribute to your understanding of the story?

7. What is the meaning of the last paragraph of the story?

Explorations

1. Sister Irene believes that teachers exist "only for the benefit of others" and that she is "an instrument by which facts [are] communicated." Allen, on the other hand, claims that humanists, including academics, must be "committed to life in its totality and not just to [their] profession." What can you say in support of each view? Can the two views be reconciled?

2. Sister Irene says of Allen that he thinks ideas are real, but she thinks that only reality is real. What is the issue here? For example, what does it mean to speak of *ideas* that change the world?

4 An Awareness of Language

The limits of my language stand for the limits of my world.
LUDWIG WITTGENSTEIN

If language be not in accordance with the truth of things, affairs cannot be carried on to success.
CONFUCIUS

You can tell the ideals of a nation by its advertisements.
NORMAN DOUGLAS

A thing is not necessarily true because badly uttered, nor false because spoken magnificently.
ST. AUGUSTINE

Originality does not consist in saying what no one has ever said before, but in saying exactly what you think yourself.
JAMES STEPHENS

LANGUAGE is our birthright. In every nation, tribe, and family you will find people communicating with each other in one or more of humanity's 3,000 living languages. And every child, unless severely handicapped or somehow isolated from society during the formative years, learns to speak by the age of four and without much formal instruction. We therefore tend to accept language much as we accept the air we breathe: We cannot do without it, and we seldom think very much about it. Yet language has great potential for both good and evil. We are in countless ways the beneficiaries of language, but we can also become its victims when it is used to manipulate and mislead us.

Clearly, language is a powerful instrument. We use it for giving and getting information, for teaching and learning, for seeking and offering help. More than that, philosophers argue that language is essential to human thought; without words many of our fundamental ideas would quite literally be unthinkable. And language artfully used has the ability to reach deep within us, moving us to laughter, tears,

249

or anger, and even stirring us to action. But the power of language, like any other power, carries with it the temptation to abuse. Political propaganda, with its emotionally loaded words and phrases, can persuade us to act against our own best interests. People with something to sell or something to hide can use language to dress up their claims or cover up their misdeeds. To see through what George Orwell has called the "swindles and perversions" of language, and to speak and write scrupulously and well ourselves, we must develop a lively awareness of language, both its pitfalls and its possibilities.

Some of the selections that follow analyze ways that language can be used to exploit or harm us. Others suggest ways in which we may use language responsibly and well. And a few invite us simply to enjoy the play of language and the amusements and pleasures it can afford.

RICHARD RODRIGUEZ

Speaking and writing English well is difficult enough for those brought up in the language, but for those who were not, it can be a complicated and even wounding experience. Like millions of Americans, Richard Rodriguez learned English as his second language. He was born in 1944 in San Francisco, but his parents were from Mexico, and Spanish was the language spoken at home. As a child, Rodriguez had undertaken a successful if often painful struggle to master what he calls his "public" language. As an adult, he went on to Stanford and Columbia and did graduate work at the Warburg Institute in London and the University of California at Berkeley. A writer and lecturer who has returned to San Francisco to live, Rodriguez has written of his experiences in *Hunger of Memory: The Education of Richard Rodriguez* (1981).

"An Education in Language" is an earlier version of a chapter in *Hunger of Memory*, and was first published in 1980. From the title, you might expect Rodriguez to focus on his actual efforts to learn English, but he does not. Instead, he tells what English meant to his family and himself, and how his success in school affected his relationship with his family.

An Education in Language

Some educationists have recently told me that I received a very bad education. They are proponents of bilingual schooling, that remarkable innovation—the latest scheme—to improve education. They think it is a shame, a disgrace, that my earliest teachers never encouraged me to speak Spanish, "my family language," when I entered the classroom.

Those educators who tell me such things, however, do not understand very much about the nature of classroom language. Nor do they understand the kind of dilemma I faced when I started my schooling. A socially disadvantaged child, I desperately needed to be taught that I had the obligation—the right—to speak *public* language. (Until I was nearly seven years old, I had been almost always surrounded by the sounds of my family's Spanish, which kept me safely at home and made me a stranger in public.) In school, I was initially terrified by the language of *gringos*. Silent, waiting for the bell to go home, dazed, diffident, I couldn't believe that English concerned me. The teacher in the (Catholic) school I attended kept calling out my name, anglicizing it as *Rich-heard Road-ree-guess*, telling me with her sounds that I had a public identity. But I couldn't believe her. I wouldn't respond.

251

Classroom words were used in ways very different from family words;   3
they were directed to a general audience. (The nun remarked in a friendly,
but oddly theatrical voice, "Speak up, Richard. And tell it to the entire
class, not just to me.") Classroom words, moreover, meant just what
they said. (*Grammar* school.) The teacher quizzed: Why do we use that
word in this sentence? Could I think of a better word to use there? Would
the sentence change its meaning if the words were differently arranged?
And wasn't there a much better way of saying the same thing?

I couldn't say.   4

Eventually my teachers connected my silence with the difficult   5
progress my older brother and sister were making. All three of us were
directed to daily tutoring sessions. I was the "slow learner" who needed
a year and a half of special attention. I also needed my teachers to keep
my attention from straying in class by calling out, "Richard!" And most
of all I needed to hear my parents speak English at home—as my teachers
had urged them to do.

The scene was inevitable: one Saturday morning, when I entered   6
a room where my mother and father were talking, I did not realize that
they were speaking in Spanish until the moment they saw me they abruptly started speaking English. The *gringo* sounds they uttered (had previously spoken only to strangers) startled me, pushed me away. In that
moment of trivial misunderstanding and profound insight I felt my throat
twisted by a grief I didn't sound as I left the room. But I had no place
to escape to with Spanish. (My brothers were speaking English in another
part of the house.) Again and again in the weeks following, increasingly
angry, I would hear my parents uniting to urge, "Speak to us now, *en
inglés.*" Only then did it happen, my teachers' achievement, my greatest
academic success: I raised my hand in the classroom and volunteered an
answer and did not think it remarkable that the entire class understood.
That day I moved very far from the disadvantaged child I had been only
weeks before.

But this great public success was measured at home by a feeling of   7
loss. We remained a loving family—enormously different. No longer were
we as close as we had earlier been. (No longer so desperate for the
consolation of intimacy.) My brothers and I didn't rush home after school.
Even our parents grew easier in public, following the Americanization of
their children. My mother started referring to neighbors by name. My
father continued to speak about *gringos*, but the word was no longer
charged with bitterness and suspicion. Hearing it sometimes, I wasn't
even sure if my father was saying the Spanish word, *gringo*, or saying,
gringo, in English.

Our house was no longer noisy. And for that I blamed my mother 8
and father, since they had encouraged our classroom success. I flaunted
my second-grade knowledge as a kind of punishment. ("Two negatives
make a positive!") But this anger was spent after several months, replaced
by a feeling of guilt as school became more and more important to me.
Increasingly successful in class, I would come home a troubled son, aware
that education was making me different from my parents. Sadly I would
listen as my mother or father tried unsuccessfully (laughing self-con-
sciously) to help my brothers with homework assignments.

My teachers became the new figures of authority in my life. I began 9
imitating their accents. I trusted their every direction. Each book they
told me to read, I read and then waited for them to tell me which books
I enjoyed. Their most casual opinions I adopted. I stayed after school
"to help"—to get their attention. It was their encouragement that mattered to me. Memory caressed each word of their praise so that compliments teachers paid me in grammar school classes come quickly to mind
even today.

Withheld from my parents was any mention of what happened at 10
school. In late afternoon, in the midst of preparing our dinner, my mother
would come up behind me while I read. Her head just above mine, her
breath scented with food, she'd ask, "What are you reading?" Or: "Tell
me about all your new courses." I would just barely respond. "Just the
usual things, ma." (Silence, Silence! Instead of the intimate sounds which
had once flowed between us, there was this silence.) After dinner, I
would rush off to a bedroom with papers and books. As often as possible,
I resisted parental pleas to "save lights" by staying in the kitchen to
work. I kept so much, so often to myself. Nights when relatives visited
and the front room was warmed by familiar Spanish sounds, I slipped out
of the house.

I was a fourth-grade student when my mother asked me one day for 11
a "nice" book to read. ("Something not too hard which you think I
might like.") Carefully, I chose Willa Cather's My Ántonia.[1] When,
several days later, I happened to see it next to her bed, unread except
for the first several pages, I felt a surge of sorrow, a need for my mother's
embrace. That feeling passed by the time I had taken the novel back to
my room.

"Your parents must be so proud of you. . . ." People began to say 12

---

[1]A novel written in 1918 about the life of an immigrant from Bohemia who lives on
the western frontier of the United States, and whose strength of character sees her
through many hardships.

that to me about the time I was in sixth grade. I'd smile shyly, never betraying my sense of the irony.

"Why didn't you tell me about the award?" my mother scolded— 13
although her face was softened by pride. At the grammar school ceremony, several days later, I heard my father speak to a teacher and felt
ashamed of his accent. Then guilty for the shame. My teacher's words
were edged sharp and clean. I admired her until I sensed that she was
condescending to them. I grew resentful. Protective. I tried to move my
parents away. "You both must be so proud of him," she said. They quickly
responded. (They were proud.) "We are proud of all our children." Then
this afterthought: "They sure didn't get their brains from us." They laughed.

Always I knew my parents wanted for my brothers and me the 14
chances they had never had. It saddened my mother to learn of relatives
who forced their children to start working right after high school. To *her*
children she would say, "Get all the education you can." In schooling
she recognized the key to job advancement. As a girl, new to America,
she had been awarded a high school diploma by teachers too careless or
busy to notice that she hardly spoke English. On her own, she determined
to learn how to type. That skill got her clean office jobs in "letter shops"
and nurtured her optimism about the possibility of advancement. (Each
morning, when her sisters put on uniforms, she chose a bright-colored
dress.) The years of young womanhood passed and her typing speed increased. Also, she became an excellent speller of words she mispro-
nounced. ("And I've never been to college," she would say, smiling when
her children asked her to spell a word they didn't want to look up in a
dictionary.)

After her youngest child began high school, my mother once more 15
got an office job. She worked for the (California) state government in
civil service positions, numbered and secured by examinations. The old
ambition of her youth was still bright then. Regularly she consulted
bulletin boards for news of openings, further advancements. Until one
day she saw mentioned something about an "anti-poverty agency." A
typing job—part of the governor's staff. ("A knowledge of Spanish required.") Without hesitation she applied, and grew nervous only when
the job was suddenly hers.

"Everyone comes to work all dressed up," she reported at night. 16
And didn't need to say more than that her co-workers would not let her
answer the phones. She was, after all, only a typist, though a very fast
typist. And an excellent speller. One day there was a letter to be sent
to a Washington cabinet officer. On the dictating tape there was reference to urban guerillas. My mother typed (the wrong word, correctly):
"gorillas." The mistake horrified the anti-poverty bureaucrats. They re-

turned her to her previous job. She would go no further. So she willed her ambition to her children.

"Get all the education you can," she would repeatedly say. "With education you can do anything." When I was a freshman in high school, I admitted to her one day that I planned to become a teacher. And that pleased her. Though I never explained that it was not the occupation of teaching I yearned for as much as something more elusive and indefinite: I wanted to know what my teachers knew; to possess their authority and their confidence. 17

In contrast to my mother, my father never openly encouraged the academic success of his children. Nor did he praise us. The only thing he regularly said to me was that school work wasn't *real* work. Those times when I claimed to be tired by writing and reading, he would laugh, not scornful so much as bemused. "You'll never know what real work is," he would say smiling, unsmiling. Whereas my mother saw in education the opportunity for job advancement, for my father education implied an even more startling possibility: escape from the workaday world. (After I introduced him to some of my high school friends he remarked that their hands were soft.) 18

His hands were calloused by a lifetime of work. In Mexico, he was orphaned when he was eight. At eight (my age when I achieved my first academic success) my father had to leave school to work for his uncle. Eighteen years later, in frustration, he left for America. There survive photos of him, in his first American years, dressed in a dandy's wardrobe. My mother remembers how he used to spend a week's salary then at the San Francisco opera on Saturday nights. And how they used to watch polo matches on Sundays. 19

He had great expectations of becoming an engineer. He knew a Catholic priest who had promised money to enable him to study full-time for a high school diploma. But the promises came to nothing. Instead, there was a dark succession of warehouse, factory, and cannery jobs. Nights, he went to school with my mother. A year, two passed. Nothing much changed, except that fatigue worked its way into the bone. And then suddenly everything was different. He gave away his fancy clothes. He didn't go to the opera. And he stayed outside, on the steps of the night school, while my mother went inside. 20

In almost my earliest memories of him, my father seems old. (He has never grown old gradually like my mother.) From boyhood to manhood, I have remembered him most powerfully in a single image: seated, asleep, on the sofa, his head thrown back in a hideous grin, the evening newspaper spread out before him. ("You'll never know what real work is. . . .") 21

It was my father who became angry when watching on television a Miss America contestant tell the announcer that she was going to college. ("Majoring in fine arts.") "College!" he snarled. He despised the trivialization of higher education, the inflated grades and cheapened diplomas, the half-education that increasingly passed for mass education in my generation. It was also my father who wondered why I didn't display my awards in my bedroom. He said that he liked to go to doctors' offices and see their certificates on the wall. My awards from school got left at home in closets and drawers. My father found my high school diploma as it was about to be thrown out with the trash. Without telling me, he put it away with his own things for safekeeping. ("We are proud of all our children.")   22

The separation which slowly unraveled (so long) between my parents and me was not the much-discussed "generation gap" caused by the tension of youth and experience. Age figured in our separation, but in a very odd way. Year after year, advancing in my studies, I would notice that my parents had not changed as much as I. They oddly measured my progress. Often I realized that my command of English was improving, for example, because at home I would hear myself simplify my diction and syntax when addressing my parents.   23

Too deeply troubled, I did not join my brothers when, as high school students, they toyed with our parents' opinions, devastating them frequently with superior logic and factual information. My mother and father would usually submit with sudden silence, although there were times when my mother complained that our "big ideas" were going to our heads. More acute was her complaint that the family wasn't as close as some of our relatives. It was toward me that she most often would glance when she mimicked the "yes" and "no" answers she got in response to her questions. (My father never asked.) Why was everyone "so secret," she wondered. (I never said.)   24

When the time came to go to college, I was the first in the family who asked to leave home. My departure only made physically apparent the separation that had occurred long before. But it was too stark a reminder. In the months preceding my departure, I heard the question my mother never asked except indirectly. In the hot kitchen, tired at the end of the workday, she demanded to know, "Why aren't the colleges around here good enough for you? They were for your brother and sister." Another time, in the car, never turning to face me, she wondered, "Why do you need to go so far away?" Late one night ironing, she said with disgust, "Why do you have to put us through this big expense? You know your scholarship will never cover it all." But when September came,   25 there was a rush to get everything ready. In a bedroom that last night, I packed the brown valise. My mother sat nearby sewing my initials onto the clothes I would take. And she said nothing more about my leaving.

About the Essay

1. Rodriguez distinguishes between "classroom words" (or "public language") and "family words." What differences does he see? What differences do you find between the way you talk or write for school and the way you talk at home or among friends?

2. Summarize Rodriguez' changing attitude toward his parents as reflected in his essay. Why, according to him, had his family once been so close? Why did this change? Was the change inevitable? Why?

3. Rodriguez tells of his mother's experience as a typist in the California civil service. Why does he tell this story? How does it relate to the point of Rodriguez' essay?

4. Why does Rodriguez call his essay "An Education in Language"?

5. It is ironic that Rodriguez, now obviously an accomplished writer in English, was once a "slow learner" of the language after starting late. What other situations, events, or remarks in the essay are ironic?

6. Look back at the incident recounted in paragraph 11. How would you interpret that incident? Why does Rodriguez recount it?

Explorations

1. Think back to your early experiences with language. Did you have problems learning English? What were they? Do you find that you now have greater facility with language? In what way do you use language to show what kind of person you are and to control difficult situations?

2. "Classroom English" is not just English, it is standard English, or "educated" English, or simply "good" English, the kind that college writing courses teach. Yet linguists say that all kinds (or dialects) of English are equally "good"— that is, equally understandable, lively, and deserving of respect. Why, then, do you think so many people, not just teachers, insist that standard English is best? Do you agree? Give your reasons.

3. In paragraph 23, Rodriguez says: "Year after year, advancing in my studies, I would notice that my parents had not changed as much as I. They oddly measured my progress." Have you noticed this in your own family? How do you account for it? How has it affected your relations with others in your family?

GORDON ALLPORT

When Gordon Allport was writing *The Nature of Prejudice,* the influential book from which the following essay is taken, much of the United States was still racially segregated and Senator Joseph McCarthy was at the height of his sensational career, chasing suspected communists and subversives from the national government. Allport's book appeared in 1954, the year in which things began to change. McCarthy's influence was finally ended by Senate censure. That same year the Supreme Court ruled against racial segregation in public schools, and Martin Luther King, Jr., led the boycott against Montgomery's segregated bus system that began the modern civil rights movement.

Allport himself was not one to join the picket lines. He was born in 1897 in Montezuma, Indiana, attended Harvard University, and ultimately returned there as a professor of psychology; he retired in 1962 and died five years later. His articles and books on personality established him as a leading authority in his field. *The Nature of Prejudice* remains his most widely-read book, however, as readable and relevant today as it was when first published. In this selection, Allport identifies and discusses some of the ways in which language itself, often very subtly, can express prejudice and even cause it.

The Language of Prejudice

Without words we should scarcely be able to form categories at all. 1
A dog perhaps forms rudimentary generalizations, such as small-boys-are-to-be-avoided—but this concept runs its course on the conditioned reflex level, and does not become the object of thought as such. In order to hold a generalization in mind for reflection and recall, for identification and for action, we need to fix it in words. Without words our world would be, as William James said, an "empirical sand-heap."

Nouns That Cut Slices

In the empirical world of human beings there are some [four] billion 2
grains of sand corresponding to our category "the human race." We cannot possibly deal with so many separate entities in our thought, nor can we individualize even among the hundreds whom we encounter in our daily round. We must group them, form clusters. We welcome, therefore, the names that help us to perform the clustering.

258

The most important property of a noun is that it brings many grains   3
of sand into a single pail, disregarding the fact that the same grains might
have fitted just as appropriately into another pail. To state the matter
technically, a noun *abstracts* from a concrete reality some one feature and
assembles different concrete realities only with respect to this one feature.
The very act of classifying forces us to overlook all other features, many
of which might offer a sounder basis than the rubric we select. Irving Lee
gives the following example:

> I knew a man who had lost the use of both eyes. He was called a "blind
> man." He could also be called an expert typist, a conscientious worker, a
> good student, a careful listener, a man who wanted a job. But he couldn't
> get a job in the department store order room where employees sat and typed
> orders which came over the telephone. The personnel man was impatient
> to get the interview over. "But you're a blind man," he kept saying, and
> one could almost feel his silent assumption that somehow the incapacity in
> one aspect made the man incapable in every other. So blinded by the label
> was the interviewer that he could not be persuaded to look beyond it.

Some labels, such as "blind man," are exceedingly salient and pow-   4
erful. They tend to prevent alternative classification, or even cross-clas-
sification. Ethnic labels are often of this type, particularly if they refer to
some highly visible feature, e.g., Negro, Oriental. They resemble the
labels that point to some outstanding incapacity—*feeble-minded, cripple,
blind man.* Let us call such symbols "labels of primary potency." These
symbols act like shrieking sirens, deafening us to all finer discriminations
that we might otherwise perceive. Even though the blindness of one man
and the darkness of pigmentation of another may be defining attributes
for some purposes, they are irrelevant and "noisy" for others.

Most people are unaware of this basic law of language—that every   5
label applied to a given person refers properly only to one aspect of his
nature. You may correctly say that a certain man is *human, a philanthropist,
a Chinese, a physician, an athlete.* A given person may be all of these; but
the chances are that *Chinese* stands out in your mind as the symbol of
primary potency. Yet neither this nor any other classificatory label can
refer to the whole of a man's nature. (Only his proper name can do so.)

Thus each label we use, especially those of primary potency, dis-   6
tracts our attention from concrete reality. The living, breathing, complex
individual—the ultimate unit of human nature—is lost to sight. As in
Figure 1, the label magnifies one attribute out of all proportion to its true
significance, and masks other important attributes of the individual. . . .

A category, once formed with the aid of a symbol of primary po-   7
tency, tends to attract more attributes than it should. The category labeled *Chinese* comes to signify not only ethnic membership but also reti-

cence, impassivity, poverty, treachery. To be sure, . . . there may be
genuine ethnic-linked traits, making for a certain *probability* that the
member of an ethnic stock may have these attributes. But our cognitive
process is not cautious. The labeled category, as we have seen, includes
indiscriminately the defining attribute, probable attributes, and wholly
fanciful, nonexistent attributes.

Even proper names—which ought to invite us to look at the indi- 8
vidual person—may act like symbols of primary potency, especially if they
arouse ethnic associations. Mr. Greenberg is a person, but since his name
is Jewish, it activates in the hearer his entire category of Jews-as-a-whole.
An ingenious experiment performed by Razran shows this point clearly,
and at the same time demonstrates how a proper name, acting like an
ethnic symbol, may bring with it an avalanche of stereotypes.

> Thirty photographs of college girls were shown on a screen to 150 students.
> The subjects rated the girls on a scale from one to five for *beauty, intelli-
> gence, character, ambition, general likability.* Two months later the same sub-
> jects were asked to rate the same photographs (and fifteen additional ones
> introduced to complicate the memory factor). This time five of the original
> photographs were given Jewish surnames (Cohen, Kantor, etc.), five Ital-
> ian (Valenti, etc.), and five Irish (O'Brien, etc.); and the remaining girls
> were given names chosen from the signers of the Declaration of Independ-
> ence and from the Social Register (Davis, Adams, Clark, etc.).
>
> When Jewish names were attached to photographs there occurred
> the following changes in ratings:
> decrease in liking
> decrease in character
> decrease in beauty
> increase in intelligence
> increase in ambition
> For those photographs given Italian names there occurred:
> decrease in liking
> decrease in character
> decrease in beauty
> decrease in intelligence
> Thus a mere proper name leads to prejudgments of personal attributes.
> The individual is fitted to the prejudice ethnic category, and not judged in
> his own right.
>
> While the Irish names also brought about depreciated judgment, the
> depreciation was not as great as in the case of the Jews and Italians. The
> falling of likability of the "Jewish girls" was twice as great as for "Italians"
> and five times as great as for "Irish." We note, however, that the "Jewish"
> photographs caused higher ratings in *intelligence* and in *ambition.* Not all
> stereotypes of out-groups are unfavorable.

The anthropologist, Margaret Mead, has suggested that labels of   9
primary potency lose some of their force when they are changed from
nouns into adjectives. To speak of a Negro soldier, a Catholic teacher, or
a Jewish artist calls attention to the fact that some other group classifica-
tions are just as legitimate as the racial or religious. If George Johnson is
spoken of not only as a Negro but also as a *soldier*, we have at least two
attributes to know him by, and two are more accurate than one. To depict
him truly as an individual, of course, we should have to name many more
attributes. It is a useful suggestion that we designate ethnic and religious
membership where possible with *adjectives* rather than with *nouns*.

Emotionally Toned Labels

Many categories have two kinds of labels—one less emotional and   10
one more emotional. Ask yourself how you feel, and what thoughts you
have, when you read the words *school teacher*, and then *school marm*.
Certainly the second phrase calls up something more strict, more ridiculous, more disagreeable than the former. Here are four innocent letters:
m-a-r-m. But they make us shudder a bit, laugh a bit, and scorn a bit.
They call up an image of a spare, humorless, irritable old maid. They do
not tell us that she is an individual human being with sorrows and troubles of her own. They force her instantly into a rejective category.

In the ethnic sphere even plain labels such as Negro, Italian, Jew,   11
Catholic, Irish-American, French-Canadian may have emotional tone
for a reason that we shall soon explain. But they all have their higher key
equivalents: nigger, wop, kike, papist, harp, canuck. When these labels
are employed we can be almost certain that the speaker *intends* not only
to characterize the person's membership, but also to disparage and reject
him.

Quite apart from the insulting intent that lies behind the use of   12
certain labels, there is also an inherent ("physiognomic") handicap in
many terms designating ethnic membership. For example, the proper names

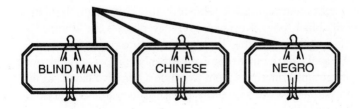

characteristic of certain ethnic memberships strike us as absurd. (We compare them, of course, with what is familiar and therefore "right.") Chinese names are short and silly; Polish names intrinsically difficult and outlandish. Unfamiliar dialects strike us as ludicrous. Foreign dress (which, of course, is a visual ethnic symbol) seems unnecessarily queer.

But of all these "physiognomic" handicaps the reference to color, 13 clearly implied in certain symbols, is the greatest. The word Negro comes from the Latin *niger* meaning black. In point of fact, no Negro has a black complexion, but by comparison with other blonder stocks, he has come to be known as a "black man." Unfortunately *black* in the English language is a word having a preponderance of sinister connotations: the outlook is black, blackball, blackguard, blackhearted, black death, blacklist, blackmail, Black Hand. In his novel *Moby Dick,* Herman Melville considers at length the remarkably morbid connotations of black and the remarkably virtuous connotations of white.

Nor is the ominous flavor of black confined to the English language. 14 A cross-cultural study reveals that the semantic significance of black is more or less universally the same. Among certain Siberian tribes, members of a privileged clan call themselves "white bones," and refer to all others as "black bones." Even among Uganda Negroes there is some evidence for a white god at the apex of the theocratic hierarchy; certain it is that a white cloth, signifying purity, is used to ward off evil spirits and disease.

There is thus an implied value-judgment in the very concept of 15 *white race* and *black race.* One might also study the numerous unpleasant connotations of *yellow,* and their possible bearing on our conception of the people of the Orient.

Such reasoning should not be carried too far, since there are un- 16 doubtedly, in various contexts, pleasant associations with both black and yellow. Black velvet is agreeable; so too are chocolate and coffee. Yellow tulips are well liked; the sun and moon are radiantly yellow. Yet it is true that "color" words are used with chauvinistic overtones more than most people realize. There is certainly condescension indicated in many familiar phrases: dark as a nigger's pocket, darktown strutters, white hope (a term originated when a white contender was sought against the Negro heavyweight champion, Jack Johnson), the white man's burden, the yellow peril, black boy. Scores of everyday phrases are stamped with the flavor of prejudice, whether the user knows it or not.

We spoke of the fact that even the most proper and sedate labels for 17 minority groups sometimes seem to exude a negative flavor. In many contexts and situations the very terms *French-Canadian, Mexican,* or *Jew,* correct and nonmalicious though they are, sound a bit opprobrious. The reason is that they are labels of social deviants. Especially in a culture where uniformity is prized, the name of *any* deviant carries with it *ipso facto* a negative value-judgment. Words like *insane, alcoholic, pervert* are presumably neutral designations of a human condition, but they are more: they are finger-pointings at deviance. Minority groups are deviants, and for this reason, from the very outset, the most innocent labels in many situations imply a shading of disrepute. When we wish to highlight the deviance and denigrate it still further we use words of a higher emotional key: crackpot, soak, pansy, greaser, Okie, nigger, harp, kike.

Members of minority groups are often understandably sensitive to   18
names given them. Not only do they object to deliberately insulting epithets, but sometimes see evil intent where none exists. Often the word Negro is spelled with a small *n*, occasionally as a studied insult, more often from ignorance. (The term is not cognate with white, which is not capitalized, but rather with Caucasian, which is.) Terms like "mulatto," or "octoroon" cause hard feeling because of the condescension with which they have often been used in the past. Sex differentiations are objectionable, since they seem doubly to emphasize ethnic difference: why speak of Jewess and not of Protestantess, or of Negress and not of whitess? Similar overemphasis is implied in the terms like Chinaman or Scotchman; why not American man? Grounds for misunderstanding lie in the fact that minority group members are sensitive to such shadings, while majority members may employ them unthinkingly.

The Communist Label

Until we label an out-group it does not clearly exist in our minds.   19
Take the curiously vague situation that we often meet when a person wishes to locate responsibility on the shoulders of some out-group whose nature he cannot specify. In such a case he usually employs the pronoun "they" without an antecedent. "Why don't they make these sidewalks wider?" "I hear they are going to build a factory in this town and hire a lot of foreigners." "I won't pay this tax bill; they can just whistle for their money." If asked "who?" the speaker is likely to grow confused and embarrassed. The common use of the orphaned pronoun *they* teaches us that people often want and need to designate out-groups (usually for the purpose of venting hostility) even when they have no clear conception of the out-group in question. And so long as the target of wrath remains

vague and ill-defined specific prejudice cannot crystallize around it. To have enemies we need labels.

Until relatively recently—strange as it may seem—there was no agreed-upon symbol for *communist*. The word, of course, existed but it had no special emotional connotation, and did not designate a public enemy. Even when, after World War I, there was a growing feeling of economic and social menace in this country, there was no agreement as to the actual source of the menace.

A content analysis of the *Boston Herald* for the year 1920 turned up the following list of labels. Each was used in a context implying some threat. Hysteria had overspread the country, as it did after World War II. Someone must be responsible for the postwar malaise, rising prices, uncertainty. There must be a villain. But in 1920 the villain was impartially designated by reporters and editorial writers with the following symbols:

> alien, agitator, anarchist, apostle of bomb and torch, Bolshevik, communist, communist laborite, conspirator, emissary of false promise, extremist, foreigner, hyphenated-American, incendiary, IWW, parlor anarchist, parlor pink, parlor socialist, plotter, radical, red, revolutionary, Russian agitator, socialist, Soviet, syndicalist, traitor, undesirable.[1]

From this excited array we note that the *need* for an enemy (someone to serve as a focus for discontent and jitters) was considerably more apparent than the precise *identity* of the enemy. At any rate, there was no clearly agreed upon label. Perhaps partly for this reason the hysteria abated. Since no clear category of "communism" existed there was no true focus for the hostility.

But following World War II this collection of vaguely interchangeable labels became fewer in number and more commonly agreed upon. The out-group menace came to be designated almost always as *communist* or *red.* In 1920 the threat, lacking a clear label, was vague; after 1945 both symbol and thing became more definite. Not that people knew precisely what they meant when they said "communist," but with the aid of the term they were at least able to point consistently to *something* that inspired fear. The term developed the power of signifying menace and led to various repressive measures against anyone to whom the label was rightly or wrongly attached.

Logically, the label should apply to specifiable defining attributes, such as members of the Communist Party, or people whose allegiance is

---

[1]The IWW, or Industrial Workers of the World, was a radical labor organization that advocated violence. Syndicalism advocated that labor unions take over the government and industry.

with the Russian system, or followers, historically, of Karl Marx. But the label came in for far more extensive use.

What seems to have happened is approximately as follows. Having suffered through a period of war and being acutely aware of devastating revolutions abroad, it is natural that most people should be upset, dreading to lose their possessions, annoyed by high taxes, seeing customary moral and religious values threatened, and dreading worse disasters to come. Seeking an explanation for this unrest, a single identifiable enemy is wanted. It is not enough to designate "Russia" or some other distant land. Nor is it satisfactory to fix blame on "changing social conditions." What is needed is a human agent near at hand: someone in Washington, someone in our schools, in our factories, in our neighborhood. If we *feel* an immediate threat, we reason, there must be a near-lying danger. It is, we conclude, communism, not only in Russia but also in America, at our doorstep, in our government, in our churches, in our colleges, in our neighborhood.

Are we saying that hostility toward communism is prejudice? Not necessarily. There are certainly phases of the dispute wherein realistic social conflict is involved. American values (e.g., respect for the person) and totalitarian values as represented in Soviet practice are intrinsically at odds. A realistic opposition in some form will occur. Prejudice enters only when the defining attributes of "communist" grow imprecise, when anyone who favors any form of social change is called a communist. People who fear social change are the ones most likely to affix the label to any persons or practices that seem to them threatening.

For them the category is undifferentiated. It includes books, movies, preachers, teachers who utter what for them are uncongenial thoughts. If evil befalls—perhaps forest fires or a factory explosion—it is due to communist saboteurs. The category becomes monopolistic, covering almost anything that is uncongenial. On the floor of the House of Representatives in 1946, Representative Rankin called James Roosevelt a communist. Congressman Outland replied with psychological acumen, "Apparently everyone who disagrees with Mr. Rankin is a communist."

When differentiated thinking is at a low ebb—as it is in times of social crises—there is a magnification of two-valued logic. Things are perceived as either inside or outside a moral order. What is outside is likely to be called "communist." Correspondingly—and here is where damage is done—whatever is called communist (however erroneously) is immediately cast outside the moral order.

This associative mechanism places enormous power in the hands of a demagogue. For several years Senator McCarthy managed to discredit many citizens who thought differently from himself by the simple device of calling them communist. Few people were able to see through this trick and many reputations were ruined. But the famous senator has no monopoly on the device. As reported in the *Boston Herald* on November 1, 1946, Representative Joseph Martin, Republican leader in the House, ended his election campaign against his Democratic opponent by saying, "The people will vote tomorrow between chaos, confusion, bankruptcy, state socialism or communism, and the preservation of our American life, with all its freedom and its opportunities." Such an array of emotional labels placed his opponent outside the accepted moral order. Martin was re-elected. . . .

Not everyone, of course, is taken in. Demagogy, when it goes too far, meets with ridicule. Elizabeth Dilling's book, *The Red Network*, was so exaggerated in its two-valued logic that it was shrugged off by many people with a smile. One reader remarked, "Apparently if you step off the sidewalk with your left foot you're a communist." But it is not easy in times of social strain and hysteria to keep one's balance, and to resist the tendency of a verbal symbol to manufacture large and fanciful categories of prejudiced thinking.

Verbal Realism and Symbol Phobia

Most individuals rebel at being labeled, especially if the label is uncomplimentary. Very few are willing to be called *fascistic, socialistic,* or *anti-Semitic.* Unsavory labels may apply to others, but not to us.

An illustration of the craving that people have to attach favorable symbols to themselves is seen in the community where white people banded together to force out a Negro family that had moved in. They called themselves "Neighborly Endeavor" and chose as their motto the Golden Rule.[2] One of the first acts of this symbol-sanctified band was to sue the man who sold property to Negroes. They then flooded the house which another Negro couple planned to occupy. Such were the acts performed under the banner of the Golden Rule.

Studies made by Stagner and Hartmann show that a person's political attitudes may in fact entitle him to be called a fascist or a socialist, and yet he will emphatically repudiate the unsavory label, and fail to endorse any movement or candidate that overtly accepts them. In short, there is a *symbol phobia* that corresponds to *verbal realism*. We are more inclined to the former when we ourselves are concerned, though we are

---

[2] "Do unto others as you would have others do unto you."

much less critical when epithets of "fascist," "communist," "blind man," "school marm" are applied to others.

When symbols provoke strong emotions they are sometimes re-   34
garded no longer as symbols, but as actual things. The expressions "son of a bitch" and "liar" are in our culture frequently regarded as "fighting words." Softer and more subtle expressions of contempt may be accepted. But in these particular cases, the epithet itself must be "taken back." We certainly do not change our opponent's attitude by making him take back a word, but it seems somehow important that he word itself be eradi-cated.

Such verbal realism may reach extreme length.   35

> The City Council of Cambridge, Massachusetts, unanimously passed a res-olution (December, 1939) making it illegal "to possess, harbor, sequester, introduce or transport, within the city limits, any book, map, magazine, newspaper, pamphlet, handbill or circular containing the words Lenin or Leningrad."

Such naiveté in confusing language with reality is hard to comprehend unless we recall that word-magic plays an appreciable part in human thinking. The following examples, like the one preceding, are taken from Hayakawa.[3]

> The Malagasy soldier must eschew kidneys, because in the Malagasy lan-guage the word for kidney is the same as that for "shot"; so shot he would certainly be if he ate a kidney.
> In May, 1937, a state senator of New York bitterly opposed a bill for the control of syphilis because "the innocence of children might be corrupted by a widespread use of the term. . . . This particular word creates a shudder in every decent woman and decent man."

This tendency to reify words underscores the close cohesion that   36
exists between category and symbol. Just the mention of "communist," "Negro," "Jew," "England," "Democrats," will send some people into a panic of fear or a frenzy of anger. Who can say whether it is the word or the thing that annoys them? The label is an intrinsic part of any monopolistic category. Hence to liberate a person from ethnic or political prejudice it is necessary at the same time to liberate him from *word fetishism*. This fact is well known to students of general semantics who tell us that prejudice is due in large part to verbal realism and to symbol phobia. Therefore any program for the reduction of prejudice must in-clude a large measure of semantic therapy.

---

[3]S.I. Hayakawa, author of *Language in Thought and Action*.

About the Essay

1. Where does Allport state his main point? How does he support and develop that point in this essay?

2. Names and nouns are essential if we are to make sense of the world, as Allport suggests in his opening paragraph, yet he goes on to say that nouns are inherently unfair. Why is this so?

3. Why are "labels of primary potency" so important? Should we always avoid the use of such labels? Does Allport suggest any ways in which the force of these labels can be diminished? If so, what are they?

4. In paragraphs 10–18, Allport observes that different words with approximately the same literal meaning often express different attitudes. What about this passage had the greatest impact on you? Did any of it seem no longer valid? Why? What does the passage, and your response to it, suggest about the relation between language and prejudice?

5. Paragraphs 19–30 deal with an attitude that was widespread in the early 1950s but is much rarer now. Is Allport's point nonetheless still relevant? Why? If so, what present-day examples would you give to make its relevance plain?

6. What does Allport mean by "symbol phobia" and "verbal realism"? Give your own examples of each.

Explorations

1. Everyone belongs to various categories according to sex, race, religion, cultural background, and even appearance. How would you categorize yourself? What is your own image of the categories to which you belong? How do outsiders view these categories? In what ways has language been used to stigmatize you or the categories to which you belong? How do you feel about it?

2. In recent years, members of various groups have sought to have new labels applied to themselves, labels that express their own views rather than those of outsiders. Two prominent examples are women and blacks. Choose a group and trace how it has named itself and how this has influenced the labels others use. What conclusions can you draw from that history?

GEORGE ORWELL

In the totalitarian state of George Orwell's novel *1984* (1949), the government has imposed on its subjects a simplified language, Newspeak, which is continually revised to give them fewer and fewer words with which to express themselves. Words like *terrible, abhorrent,* and *evil,* for example, have all been replaced by the single expression, *double-plus-ungood.* The way people use language, Orwell maintained, is both a result of the way they think and an important influence on their thought as well. This is also the point of his classic essay, "Politics and the English Language." Though published in 1946, the essay is as accurate and relevant now as it was then. Indeed, during the war in Vietnam various American officials were still using euphemisms such as "pacification" and "transfer of population," as if Orwell hadn't long since exposed those phrases as doubletalk. But Orwell goes beyond exposé. He not only holds up to public view and ridicule some choice examples of political language at its worst, but also offers a few short, simple, and effective rules for writers who want to do better. (For biographical information about Orwell, see page 76.)

Politics and the English Language

Most people who bother with the matter at all would admit that the English language is in a bad way, but it is generally assumed that we cannot by conscious action do anything about it. Our civilization is decadent and our language—so the argument runs—must inevitably share in the general collapse. It follows that any struggle against the abuse of language is a sentimental archaism, like preferring candles to electric light or hansom cabs to aeroplanes. Underneath this lies the half-conscious belief that language is a natural growth and not an instrument which we shape for our own purposes.

Now, it is clear that the decline of a language must ultimately have political and economic causes: it is not due simply to the bad influence of this or that individual writer. But an effect can become a cause, reinforcing the original cause and producing the same effect in an intensified form, and so on indefinitely. A man may take to drink because he feels himself to be a failure, and then fail all the more completely because he drinks. It is rather the same thing that is happening to the English language. It becomes ugly and inaccurate because our thoughts are foolish, but the slovenliness of our language makes it easier for us to have foolish thoughts. The point is that the process is reversible. Modern English, especially written English, is full of bad habits which spread by

269

imitation and which can be avoided if one is willing to take the necessary trouble. If one gets rid of these habits one can think more clearly, and to think clearly is a necessary first step toward political regeneration: so that the fight against bad English is not frivolous and is not the exclusive concern of professional writers. I will come back to this presently, and I hope that by that time the meaning of what I have said here will have become clearer. Meanwhile, here are five specimens of the English language as it is now habitually written.

These five passages have not been picked out because they are especially bad—I could have quoted far worse if I had chosen—but because they illustrate various of the mental vices from which we now suffer. They are a little below the average, but are fairly representative samples. I number them so that I can refer back to them when necessary:

> (1) I am not, indeed, sure whether it is not true to say that the Milton who once seemed not unlike a seventeenth-century Shelley had not become, out of an experience even more bitter in each year, more alien [sic] to the founder of that Jesuit sect which nothing could induce him to tolerate.
>
> Professor Harold Laski (Essay in *Freedom of Expression*)

> (2) Above all, we cannot play ducks and drakes with[1] a native battery of idioms which prescribes such egregious collocations of vocables as the Basic *put up with* for *tolerate* or *put at a loss* for *bewilder*.
>
> Professor Lancelot Hogben (*Interglossa*)

> (3) On the one side we have the free personality: by definition it is not neurotic, for it has neither conflict nor dream. Its desires, such as they are, are transparent, for they are just what institutional approval keeps in the forefront of consciousness; another institutional pattern would alter their number and intensity; there is little in them that is natural, irreducible, or culturally dangerous. But *on the other side*, the social bond itself is nothing but the mutual reflection of these self-secure integrities. Recall the definition of love. Is not this the very picture of a small academic? Where is there a place in this hall of mirrors for either personality or fraternity?
>
> Essay on psychology in *Politics* (New York)

> (4) All the "best people" from the gentlemen's clubs, and all the frantic fascist captains, united in common hatred of Socialism and bestial horror of the rising tide of the mass revolutionary movement, have turned to acts of provocation, to foul incendiarism, to medieval legends of poisoned wells, to legalize their own destruction of proletarian organizations, and rouse the agitated petty-bourgeoisie to chauvinistic fervor on behalf of the fight against the revolutionary way out of the crisis.
>
> Communist pamphlet

[1]Squander.

(5) If a new spirit *is* to be infused into this old country, there is one thorny and contentious reform which must be tackled, and that is the humanization and galvanization of the B.B.C.[2] Timidity here will bespeak canker and atrophy of the soul. The heart of Britain may be sound and of strong beat, for instance, but the British lion's roar at present is like that of Bottom in Shakespeare's *Midsummer Night's Dream*—as gentle as any sucking dove. A virile new Britain cannot continue indefinitely to be traduced in the eyes or rather ears, of the world by the effete languors of Langham Place, brazenly masquerading as "standard English." When the Voice of Britain is heard at nine o'clock, better far and infinitely less ludicrous to hear aitches honestly dropped than the present priggish, inflated, inhibited, school-ma'amish arch braying of blameless bashful mewing maidens!

Letter in *Tribune*

Each of these passages has faults of its own, but, quite apart from avoidable ugliness, two qualities are common to all of them. The first is staleness of imagery; the other is lack of precision. The writer either has a meaning and cannot express it, or he inadvertently says something else, or he is almost indifferent as to whether his words mean anything or not. This mixture of vagueness and sheer incompetence is the most marked characteristic of modern English prose, and especially of any kind of political writing. As soon as certain topics are raised, the concrete melts into the abstract and no one seems able to think of turns of speech that are not hackneyed: prose consists less and less of *words* chosen for the sake of their meaning, and more and more of *phrases* tacked together like the sections of a prefabricated henhouse. I list below, with notes and examples, various of the tricks by means of which the work of prose-construction is habitually dodged:

DYING METAPHORS

A newly invented metaphor assists thought by evoking a visual image, while on the other hand a metaphor which is technically "dead" (e.g., *iron resolution*) has in effect reverted to being an ordinary word and can generally be used without loss of vividness. But in between these two classes there is a huge dump of worn-out metaphors which have lost all evocative power and are merely used because they save people the trouble of inventing phrases for themselves. Examples are: *Ring the changes on, take up the cudgels for, toe the line, ride roughshod over, stand shoulder to shoulder with, play into the hands of, no axe to grind, grist to the mill, fishing in troubled waters, on the order of the day, Achilles' heel, swan song,*

---

[2]British Broadcasting Corporation, the government-run radio and television network. "B.B.C. English" is meant to reflect standard pronunciation in England.

hotbed. Many of these are used without knowledge of their meaning (what is a "rift," for instance?), and incompatible metaphors are frequently mixed, a sure sign that the writer is not interested in what he is saying. Some metaphors now current have been twisted out of their original meaning without those who use them even being aware of the fact. For example, *toe the line* is sometimes written *tow the line.* Another example is *the hammer and the anvil,* now always used with the implication that the anvil gets the worst of it. In real life it is always the anvil that breaks the hammer, never the other way about: a writer who stopped to think what he was saying would be aware of this, and would avoid perverting the original phrase.

OPERATORS OR VERBAL FALSE LIMBS

These save the trouble of picking out appropriate verbs and nouns,   6
and at the same time pad each sentence with extra syllables which give it an appearance of symmetry. Characteristic phrases are *render inoperative, militate against, make contact with, be subjected to, give rise to, give grounds for, have the effect of, play a leading part (role) in, make itself felt, take effect, exhibit a tendency to, serve the purpose of,* etc., etc. The keynote is the elimination of simple verbs. Instead of being a single word, such as *break, stop, spoil, mend, kill,* a verb becomes a *phrase,* made up of a noun or adjective tacked on to some general-purpose verb such as *prove, serve, form, play, render.* In addition, the passive voice is wherever possible used in preference to the active, and noun constructions are used instead of gerunds (*by examination of* instead of *by examining*). The range of verbs is further cut down by means of the *-ize* and *de-* formations, and the banal statements are given an appearance of profundity by means of the *not un-* formation. Simple conjunctions and prepositions are replaced by such phrases as *with respect to, having regard to, the fact that, by dint of, in view of, in the interests of, on the hypothesis that;* and the ends of sentences are saved from anticlimax by such resounding commonplaces as *greatly to be desired, cannot be left out of account, a development to be expected in the near future, deserving of serious consideration, brought to a satisfactory conclusion,* and so on and so forth.

PRETENTIOUS DICTION

Words like *phenomenon, element, individual* (as noun), *objective, cate-*   7
gorical, effective, virtual, basic, primary, promote, constitute, exhibit, exploit, utilize, eliminate, liquidate, are used to dress up simple statement and give an air of scientific impartiality to biased judgments. Adjectives like *epoch-*

making, epic, historic, unforgettable, triumphant, age-old, inevitable, inexorable, veritable, are used to dignify the sordid processes of international politics, while writing that aims at glorifying war usually takes on an archaic color, its characteristic words being: *realm, throne, chariot, mailed fist, trident, sword, shield, buckler, banner, jackboot, clarion.* Foreign words and expressions such as *cul de sac, ancien régime, deus ex machina, mutatis mutandis, status quo, gleichschaltung, weltanschauung,* are used to give an air of culture and elegance. Except for the useful abbreviations *i.e., e.g.,* and *etc.,* there is no real need for any of the hundreds of foreign phrases now current in English. Bad writers, and especially scientific, political, and sociological writers, are nearly always haunted by the notion that Latin or Greek words are grander than Saxon ones, and unnecessary words like *expedite, ameliorate, predict, extraneous, deracinated, clandestine, subaqueous,* and hundreds of others constantly gain ground from their Anglo-Saxon opposite numbers.[3] The jargon peculiar to Marxist writing (*hyena, hangman, cannibal, petty bourgeois, these gentry, lackey, flunkey, mad dog, White Guard,* etc.) consists largely of words and phrases translated from Russian, German, or French; but the normal way of coining a new word is to use a Latin or Greek root with the appropriate affix and, where necessary, the size formation. It is often easier to make up words of this kind (*deregionalize, impermissible, extramarital, nonfragmentary* and so forth) than to think up the English words that will cover one's meaning. The result, in general, is an increase in slovenliness and vagueness.

MEANINGLESS WORDS

In certain kinds of writing, particularly in art criticism and literary criticism, it is normal to come across long passages which are almost completely lacking in meaning.[4] Words like *romantic, plastic, values, human, dead, sentimental, natural, vitality,* as used in art criticism, are strictly

8

---

[3]An interesting illustration of this is the way in which the English flower names which were in use till very recently are being ousted by Greek ones, *snapdragon* becoming *antirrhinum, forget-me-not* becoming *myosotis,* etc. It is hard to see any practical reason for this change of fashion: it is probably due to an instinctive turning away from the more homely word and a vague feeling that the Greek word is scientific. [Orwell's note]

[4]Example: "[Alex] Comfort's catholicity of perception and image, strangely Whitmanesque in range, almost the exact opposite in aesthetic compulsion, continues to evoke that trembling atmospheric accumulative hinting at a cruel, an inexorably serene timelessness. . . . Wrey Gardiner scores by aiming at simple bull's-eyes with precision. Only they are not so simple, and through this contented sadness runs more than the surface bittersweet of resignation." (*Poetry Quarterly.*) [Orwell's note]

meaningless, in the sense that they not only do not point to any discoverable object, but are hardly ever expected to do so by the reader. When one critic writes, "The outstanding feature of Mr. X's work is its living quality," while another writes, "The immediately striking thing about Mr. X's work is its peculiar deadness," the reader accepts this as a simple difference of opinion. If words like *black* and *white* were involved, instead of the jargon words *dead* and *living*, he would see at once that language was being used in an improper way. Many political words are similarly abused. The word *Fascism* has now no meaning except in so far as it signifies "something not desirable." The words *democracy, socialism, freedom, patriotic, realistic, justice*, have each of them several different meanings which cannot be reconciled with one another. In the case of a word like *democracy*, not only is there no agreed definition, but the attempt to make one is resisted from all sides. It is almost universally felt that when we call a country democratic we are praising it: consequently the defenders of every kind of régime claim that it is a democracy, and fear that they might have to stop using the word if it were tied down to any one meaning. Words of this kind are often used in a consciously dishonest way. That is, the person who uses them has his own private definition, but allows his hearer to think he means something quite different. Statements like *Marshal Pétain was a true patriot*,[5] *The Soviet press is the freest in the world, The Catholic Church is opposed to persecution*, are almost always made with intent to deceive. Other words used in variable meanings, in most cases more or less dishonestly, are: *class, totalitarian, science, progressive, reactionary, bourgeois, equality*.

Now that I have made this catalogue of swindles and perversions, let me give another example of the kind of writing that they lead to. This time it must of its nature be an imaginary one. I am going to translate a passage of good English into modern English of the worst sort. Here is a well-known verse from *Ecclesiastes*:

9

> I returned and saw under the sun, that the race is not to the swift, nor the battle to the strong, neither yet bread to the wise, nor yet riches to men of understanding, nor yet favour to men of skill; but time and chance happeneth to them all.

Here it is in modern English:

> Objective considerations of contemporary phenomena compels the conclusion that success or failure in competitive activities exhibits no tendency to be commensurate with innate capacity, but that a considerable element of the unpredictable must invariably be taken into account.

---

[5]In fact, Pétain was the Nazi-supported ruler of much of France from 1940 to 1944, and was convicted of treason in 1945.

This is a parody, but not a very gross one. Exhibit (3), above, for 10 instance, contains several patches of the same kind of English. It will be seen that I have not made a full translation. The beginning and ending of the sentence follow the original meaning fairly closely, but in the middle the concrete illustrations—race, battle, bread—dissolve into the vague phrase "success or failure in competitive activities." This had to be so, because no modern writer of the kind I am discussing—no one capable of using phrases like "objective consideration of contemporary phenomena"—would ever tabulate his thoughts in that precise and detailed way. The whole tendency of modern prose is away from concreteness. Now analyze these two sentences a little more closely. The first contains forty-nine words but only sixty syllables, and all its words are those of everyday life. The second contains thirty-eight words of ninety syllables: eighteen of its words are from Latin roots, and one from Greek. The first sentence contains six vivid images, and only one phrase ("time and chance") that could be called vague. The second contains not a single fresh, arresting phrase, and in spite of its ninety syllables it gives only a shortened version of the meaning contained in the first. Yet without a doubt it is the second kind of sentence that is gaining ground in modern English. I do not want to exaggerate. This kind of writing is not yet universal, and outcrops of simplicity will occur here and there in the worst-written page. Still, if you or I were told to write a few lines on the uncertainty of human fortunes, we should probably come much nearer to my imaginary sentence than to the one from *Ecclesiastes.*

As I have tried to show, modern writing at its worst does not consist 11 in picking out words for the sake of their meaning and inventing images in order to make the meaning clearer. It consists in gumming together long strips of words which have already been set in order by someone else, and making the results presentable by sheer humbug. The attraction of this way of writing is that it is easy. It is easier—even quicker, once you have the habit—to say *In my opinion it is not an unjustifiable assumption that* than to say *I think.* If you use ready-made phrases, you not only don't have to hunt about for words; you also don't have to bother with the rhythms of your sentences, since these phrases are generally so arranged as to be more or less euphonious. When you are composing in a hurry— when you are dictating to a stenographer, for instance, or making a public speech—it is natural to fall into a pretentious, Latinized style. Tags like *a consideration which we should do well to bear in mind* or *a conclusion to which all of us would readily assent* will save many a sentence from coming down with a bump. By using stale metaphors, similes, and idioms, you save much mental effort, at the cost of leaving your meaning vague, not only for your reader but for yourself. This is the significance of mixed metaphors. The sole aim of a metaphor is to call up a visual image. When these images clash—as in *The Fascist octopus has sung its swan song, the jackboot is thrown into the melting pot*—it can be taken as certain that the writer is not seeing a mental image of the objects he is naming; in other words he is not really thinking. Look again at the examples I gave at the beginning of this essay. Professor Laski (1) uses five negatives in fifty-three words. One of these is superfluous, making nonsense of the whole passage, and in addition there is the slip—*alien* for akin—making further nonsense, and several avoidable pieces of clumsiness which increase the general vagueness. Professor Hogben (2) plays ducks and drakes with a battery which is able to write prescriptions, and, while disapproving of the everyday phrase *put up with*, is unwilling to look *egregious* up in the dictionary and see what it means; (3), if one takes an uncharitable attitude towards it, is simply meaningless: probably one could work out its intended meaning by reading the whole of the article in which it occurs. In (4), the writer knows more or less what he wants to say, but an accumulation of stale phrases chokes him like tea leaves blocking a sink. In (5), words and meaning have almost parted company. People who write in this manner usually have a general emotional meaning— they dislike one thing and want to express solidarity with another—but they are not interested in the detail of what they are saying. A scrupulous writer, in every sentence that he writes, will ask himself at least four questions, thus: What am I trying to say? What words will express it? What image or idiom will make it clearer? Is this image fresh enough to have an effect? And he will probably ask himself two more: Could I put it more shortly? Have I said anything that is avoidably ugly? But you are not obliged to go to all this trouble. You can shirk it by simply throwing your mind open and letting the ready-made phrases come crowding in. They will construct your sentences for you—even think your thoughts for you, to a certain extent—and at need they will perform the important service of partially concealing your meaning even from yourself. It is at this point that the special connection between politics and the debasement of language becomes clear.

In our time it is broadly true that political writing is bad writing. Where it is not true, it will generally be found that the writer is some kind of rebel, expressing his private opinions and not a "party line." Orthodoxy, of whatever color, seems to demand a lifeless, imitative style. The political dialects to be found in pamphlets, leading articles, manifestoes, White Papers and the speeches of undersecretaries do, of course, vary from party to party, but they are all alike in that one almost never finds in them a fresh, vivid, homemade turn of speech. When one watches some tired hack on the platform mechanically repeating the familiar phrases—*bestial atrocities, iron heel, bloodstained tyranny, free peoples of the world, stand shoulder to shoulder*—one often has a curious feeling that one is not watching a live human being but some kind of dummy: a feeling which suddenly becomes stronger at moments when the light catches the speaker's spectacles and turns them into blank discs which seem to have no eyes behind them. And this is not altogether fanciful. A speaker who uses that kind of phraseology has gone some distance toward turning himself into a machine. The appropriate noises are coming out of his larynx, but his brain is not involved as it would be if he were choosing his words for himself. If the speech he is making is one that he is accustomed to make over and over again, he may be almost unconscious of what he is saying, as one is when one utters the responses in church. And this reduced state of consciousness, if not indispensable, is at any rate favorable to political conformity.

In our time, political speech and writing are largely the defense of 13 the indefensible. Things like the continuance of British rule in India, the Russian purges and deportations, the dropping of the atom bombs on Japan, can indeed be defended, but only by arguments which are too brutal for most people to face, and which do not square with the professed aims of political parties. Thus political language has to consist largely of euphemism, question-begging and sheer cloudy vagueness. Defenseless villages are bombarded from the air, the inhabitants driven out into the countryside, the cattle machine-gunned, the huts set on fire with incendiary bullets: this is called *pacification*. Millions of peasants are robbed of their farms and sent trudging along the roads with no more than they can carry: this is called *transfer of population* or *rectification of frontiers*. People are imprisoned for years without trial, or shot in the back of the neck or sent to die of scurvy in Arctic lumber camps: this is called *elimination of unreliable elements*. Such phraseology is needed if one wants to name things without calling up mental pictures of them. Consider for instance some comfortable English professor defending Russian totalitarianism. He cannot say outright, "I believe in killing your opponents when you can get good results by doing so." Probably, therefore, he will say something like this:

"While freely conceding that the Soviet régime exhibits certain 14 features which the humanitarian may be inclined to deplore, we must, I think, agree that a certain curtailment of the right to political opposition is an unavoidable concomitant of transitional periods, and that the rigors which the Russian people have been called upon to undergo have been amply justified in the sphere of concrete achievement."

The inflated style is itself a kind of euphemism. A mass of Latin 15 words falls upon the facts like soft snow, blurring the outlines and covering up all the details. The great enemy of clear language is insincerity. When there is a gap between one's real and one's declared aims, one turns as it were instinctively to long words and exhausted idioms, like a cuttlefish squirting out ink. In our age there is no such thing as "keeping out of politics." All issues are political issues, and politics itself is a mass of lies, evasions, folly, hatred, and schizophrenia. When the general atmosphere is bad, language must suffer. I should expect to find—this is a guess which I have not sufficient knowledge to verify—that the German, Russian and Italian languages have all deteriorated in the last ten or fifteen years, as a result of dictatorship.

But if thought corrupts language, language can also corrupt thought. 16
A bad usage can spread by tradition and imitation, even among people who should and do know better. The debased language that I have been discussing is in some ways very convenient. Phrases like *a not unjustifiable assumption, leaves much to be desired, would serve no good purpose, a consideration which we should do well to bear in mind,* are a continuous temptation, a packet of aspirins always at one's elbow. Look back through this essay, and for certain you will find that I have again and again committed the very faults I am protesting against. By this morning's post I have received a pamphlet dealing with conditions in Germany. The author tells me that he "felt impelled" to write it. I open it at random, and here is almost the first sentence that I see: "[The Allies] have an opportunity not only of achieving a radical transformation of Germany's social and political structure in such a way as to avoid a nationalistic reaction in Germany itself, but at the same time of laying the foundations of a co-operative and unified Europe." You see, he "feels impelled" to write—feels, presumably, that he has something new to say—and yet his words, like cavalry horses answering the bugle, group themselves automatically into the familiar dreary pattern. This invasion of one's mind by ready-made phrases (*lay the foundations, achieve a radical transformation*) can only be prevented if one is constantly on guard against them, and every such phrase anaesthetizes a portion of one's brain.

I said earlier that the decadence of our language is probably curable. 17
Those who deny this would argue, if they produced an argument at all, that language merely reflects existing social conditions, and that we cannot influence its development by any direct tinkering with words and constructions. So far as the general tone or spirit of a language goes, this may be true, but it is not true in detail. Silly words and expressions have often disappeared, not through any evolutionary process but owing to the conscious action of a minority. Two recent examples were *explore every avenue* and *leave no stone unturned,* which were killed by the jeers of a few journalists. There is a long list of flyblown metaphors which

could similarly be got rid of if enough people would interest themselves in the job; and it should also be possible to laugh the *not un-* formation out of existence,[6] to reduce the amount of Latin and Greek in the average sentence, to drive out foreign phrases and strayed scientific words, and, in general, to make pretentiousness unfashionable. But all these are minor points. The defense of the English language implies more than this, and perhaps it is best to start by saying what it does *not* imply.

To begin with it has nothing to do with archaism, with the salvaging of obsolete words and turns of speech, or with the setting up of a "standard English" which must never be departed from. On the contrary, it is especially concerned with the scrapping of every word or idiom which has outworn its usefulness. It has nothing to do with correct grammar and syntax, which are of no importance so long as one makes one's meaning clear, or with the avoidance of Americanisms, or with having what is called a "good prose style." On the other hand it is not concerned with fake simplicity and the attempt to make written English colloquial. Nor does it even imply in every case preferring the Saxon word to the Latin one, though it does imply using the fewest and shortest words that will cover one's meaning. What is above all needed is to let the meaning choose the word, and not the other way about. In prose, the worst thing one can do with words is to surrender to them. When you think of a concrete object, you think wordlessly, and then, if you want to describe the thing you have been visualizing you probably hunt about till you find the exact words that seem to fit it. When you think of something abstract you are more inclined to use words from the start, and unless you make a conscious effort to prevent it, the existing dialect will come rushing in and do the job for you, at the expense of blurring or even changing your meaning. Probably it is better to put off using words as long as possible and get one's meaning as clear as one can through pictures or sensations. Afterward one can choose—not simply *accept*—the phrases that will best cover the meaning, and then switch round and decide what impression one's words are likely to make on another person. This last effort of the mind cuts out all stale or mixed images, all prefabricated phrases, needless repetitions, and humbug and vagueness generally. But one can often be in doubt about the effect of a word or a phrase, and one needs rules that one can rely on when instinct fails. I think the following rules will cover most cases:

(i) Never use a metaphor, simile, or other figure of speech which you are used to seeing in print.

---

[6]One can cure oneself of the *not un-* formation by memorizing this sentence: A *not unblack dog was chasing a not unsmall rabbit across a not ungreen field.*

(ii) Never use a long word where a short one will do.

(iii) If it is possible to cut a word out, always cut it out.

(iv) Never use the passive where you can use the active.

(v) Never use a foreign phrase, a scientific word, or a jargon word if you can think of an everyday English equivalent.

(vi) Break any of these rules sooner than say anything outright barbarous.

These rules sound elementary, and so they are, but they demand a deep change of attitude in anyone who has grown used to writing in the style now fashionable. One could keep all of them and still write bad English, but one could not write the kind of stuff that I quoted in those five specimens at the beginning of this article.

I have not here been considering the literary use of language, but merely language as an instrument for expressing and not for concealing or preventing thought. Stuart Chase and others have come near to claiming that all abstract words are meaningless, and have used this as a pretext for advocating a kind of political quietism. Since you don't know what Fascism is, how can you struggle against Fascism? One need not swallow such absurdities as this, but one ought to recognize that the present political chaos is connected with the decay of language, and that one can probably bring about some improvement by starting at the verbal end. If you simplify your English, you are freed from the worst follies of orthodoxy. You cannot speak any of the necessary dialects, and when you make a stupid remark its stupidity will be obvious, even to yourself. Political language—and with variations this is true of all political parties, from Conservatives to Anarchists—is designed to make lies sound truthful and murder respectable, and to give an appearance of solidity to pure wind. One cannot change this all in a moment, but one can at least change one's own habits, and from time to time one can even, if one jeers loudly enough, send some worn-out and useless phrase—some *jack-boot, Achilles' heel, hotbed, melting pot, acid test, veritable inferno*, or other lump of verbal refuse—into the dustbin where it belongs.

About the Essay

1. In your own words, explain the relationship Orwell sees between politics and the English language. Do you agree with him? Why or why not?

2. What terms and concepts does Orwell define in his essay? What is his purpose in defining them? How does he go about it?

3. Our world is becoming increasingly prefabricated. In what way does the

concept of prefabrication relate to Orwell's observations about the prevalence of habitual and trite phrases?

4. Orwell uses the following comparisons in his essay. How does each of them reinforce or clarify his meaning?

a. "But in between these two classes there is a huge dump of worn-out metaphors which have lost all evocative power. . . ." (paragraph 5)

b. "The writer knows more or less what he wants to say, but an accumulation of stale phrases chokes him like tea leaves blocking a sink. . . ." (paragraph 11)

c. "A mass of Latin words falls upon the facts like soft snow, blurring the outlines and covering up all the details." (paragraph 15)

d. "When there is a gap between one's real and one's declared aims, one turns as it were instinctively to long words and exhausted idioms, like a cuttlefish squirting out ink." (paragraph 15)

e. "He 'feels impelled' to write—feels, presumably, that he has something new to say—and yet his words, like cavalry horses answering the bugle, group themselves automatically into the familiar dreary pattern." (paragraph 16)

5. Orwell confesses that he himself is guilty, in this essay, of some of the errors he is pointing out. Can you detect any of them? What is the effect on you of these "errors," and of Orwell's confession?

6. The last of Orwell's six rules for better English reads, "Break any of these rules sooner than say anything outright barbarous." What do you think he means by this?

Explorations

1. As some of Orwell's examples suggest, language is sometimes used not to express our meanings but to conceal them. Is this true only of politics? Can you think of any situations in which you, or others you know, have been under pressure to say something yet had nothing you were ready or willing to say? What happened? How can one handle such situations honestly?

2. Gather five examples of recent American political English that you consider, in Orwell's words, "ugly and inaccurate." Can you analyze them using Orwell's terms? If not, what new terms would you invent to classify them?

3. Read Orwell's discussion of Newspeak in *1984*. What is the relation between politics and language in Oceania? How does it connect with Orwell's views in "Politics and the English Language"?

DONNA WOOLFOLK CROSS

Most people are opposed to propaganda in principle, but few know exactly what it is and how it works. Donna Woolfolk Cross has looked closely at the subject, and her observations have been published in the widely read *Word Abuse: How the Words We Use, Use Us* (1979). She was born in New York City in 1947, and graduated from the University of Pennsylvania and UCLA. She now teaches at Onondaga Community College in New York State. For several years prior to teaching she worked in publishing and advertising, practicing as well as observing some of the techniques she writes about in her book *Mediaspeak* (1981). Her most recent book, written in collaboration with her father, is *Daddy's Little Girl: The Unspoken Bargain Between Fathers and Their Daughters* (1982).

Propaganda is a Latin term meaning "that which is to be made known" and is basically a means of persuasion. As such, it can be used "for good causes as well as bad." In the following essay, adapted by the author from *Word Abuse*, she discusses thirteen fallacies that propagandists can use to trick and mislead us and offers advice on how we can avoid being misled or manipulated by the propaganda that is part of our everyday lives.

Propaganda: How Not to Be Bamboozled

Propaganda. If an opinion poll were taken tomorrow, we can be sure that nearly everyone would be against it because it *sounds* so bad. When we say, "Oh, that's just propaganda," it means, to most people, "That's a pack of lies." But really, propaganda is simply a means of persuasion and so it can be put to work for good causes as well as bad— to persuade people to give to charity, for example, or to love their neighbors, or to stop polluting the environment.

For good or evil, propaganda pervades our daily lives, helping to shape our attitudes on a thousand subjects. Propaganda probably determines the brand of toothpaste you use, the movies you see, the candidates you elect when you get to the polls. Propaganda works by tricking us, by momentarily distracting the eye while the rabbit pops out from beneath the cloth. Propaganda works best with an uncritical audience. Joseph Goebbels, Propaganda Minister in Nazi Germany, once defined his work as "the conquest of the masses." The masses would not have been conquered, however, if they had known how to challenge and to question, how to make distinctions between propaganda and reasonable argument.

People are bamboozled mainly because they don't recognize propaganda when they see it. They need to be informed about the various

282

devices that can be used to mislead and deceive—about the propagandist's overflowing bag of tricks. The following, then, are some common pitfalls for the unwary.

1. Name-Calling

As its title suggests, this device consists of labeling people or ideas 4
with words of bad connotation, literally, "calling them names." Here the propagandist tries to arouse our contempt so we will dismiss the "bad name" person or idea without examining its merits.

Bad names have played a tremendously important role in the history 5
of the world. They have ruined reputations and ended lives, sent people to prison and to war, and just generally made us mad at each other for centuries.

Name-calling can be used against policies, practices, beliefs and ideals, 6
as well as against individuals, groups, races, nations. Name-calling is at work when we hear a candidate for office described as a "foolish idealist" or a "two-faced liar" or when an incumbent's policies are denounced as "reckless," "reactionary," or just plain "stupid." Some of the most effective names a public figure can be called are ones that may not denote anything specific: "Congresswoman Jane Doe is a *bleeding heart!*" (Did she vote for funds to help paraplegics?) or "The Senator is a *tool of Washington!*" (Did he happen to agree with the President?) Senator Yakalot uses name-calling when he denounces his opponent's "radical policies" and calls them (and him) "socialist," "pinko," and part of a "heartless plot." He also uses it when he calls small cars "puddle-jumpers," "canopeners," and "motorized baby buggies."

The point here is that when the propagandist uses name-calling, he 7
doesn't want us to think—merely to react, blindly, unquestioningly. So the best defense against being taken in by name-calling is to stop and ask, "Forgetting the bad name attached to it, what are the merits of the idea itself? What does this name really mean, anyway?"

2. Glittering Generalities

Glittering generalities are really name-calling in reverse. Name-calling 8
uses words with bad connotations; glittering generalities are words with good connotations—"virtue words," as the Institute for Propaganda Analysis has called them. The Institute explains that while name-calling tries to get us to *reject* and *condemn* someone or something without examining the

evidence, glittering generalities try to get us to *accept* and *agree* without examining the evidence.

We believe in, fight for, live by "virtue words" which we feel deeply   9
about: "justice," "motherhood," "the American way," "our Constitutional rights," "our Christian heritage." These sound good, but when we examine them closely, they turn out to have no specific, definable meaning. They just make us feel good. Senator Yakalot uses glittering generalities when he says, "I stand for all that is good in America, for our American way and our American birthright." But what exactly *is* "good for America"? How can we define our "American birthright"? Just what parts of the American society and culture does "our American way" refer to?

We often make the mistake of assuming we are personally unaf-   10
fected by glittering generalities. The next time you find yourself assuming that, listen to a political candidate's speech on TV and see how often the use of glittering generalities elicits cheers and applause. That's the danger of propaganda; it *works*. Once again, our defense against it is to ask questions: Forgetting the virtue words attached to it, what are the merits of the idea itself? What does "Americanism" (or "freedom" or "truth") really *mean* here? . . .

Both name-calling and glittering generalities work by stirring our   11
emotions in the hope that this will cloud our thinking. Another approach that propaganda uses is to create a distraction, a "red herring," that will make people forget or ignore the real issues. There are several different kinds of "red herrings" that can be used to distract attention.

3. Plain Folks Appeal

"Plain folks" is the device by which a speaker tries to win our con-   12
fidence and support by appearing to be a person like ourselves—"just one of the plain folks." The plain-folks appeal is at work when candidates go around shaking hands with factory workers, kissing babies in supermarkets, and sampling pasta with Italians, fried chicken with Southerners, bagels and blintzes with Jews. "Now I'm a businessman like yourselves" is a plain-folks appeal, as is "I've been a farm boy all my life." Senator Yakalot tries the plain-folks appeal when he says, "I'm just a small-town boy like you fine people." The use of such expressions once prompted Lyndon Johnson to quip, "Whenever I hear someone say, 'I'm just an old country lawyer,' the first thing I reach for is my wallet to make sure it's still there."

The irrelevancy of the plain-folks appeal is obvious: even if the man   13
is "one of us" (which may not be true at all), that doesn't mean his ideas

and programs are sound—or even that he honestly has our best interests at heart. As with glittering generalities, the danger here is that we may mistakenly assume we are immune to this appeal. But propagandists wouldn't use it unless it had been proved to work. You can protect yourself by asking, "Aside from his 'nice guy next door' image, what does this man stand for? Are his ideas and his past record really supportive of my best interests?"

4. *Argumentum ad Populum (Stroking)*

Argumentum ad populum means "argument to the people" or "telling   14
the people what they want to hear." The colloquial term from the Watergate era is "stroking," which conjures up pictures of small animals or children being stroked or soothed with compliments until they come to like the person doing the complimenting—and, by extension, his or her ideas.

We all like to hear nice things about ourselves and the group we   15
belong to—we like to be liked—so it stands to reason that we will respond warmly to a person who tells us we are "hard-working taxpayers" or "the most generous, free-spirited nation in the world." Politicians tell farmers they are the "backbone of the American economy" and college students that they are the "leaders and policy makers of tomorrow." Commercial advertisers use stroking more insidiously by asking a question which invites a flattering answer: "What kind of a man reads *Playboy*?" (Does he really drive a Porsche and own $10,000 worth of sound equipment?) Senator Yakalot is stroking his audience when he calls them the "decent law-abiding citizens that are the great pulsing heart and the life blood of this, our beloved country," and when he repeatedly refers to them as "you fine people," "you wonderful folks."

Obviously, the intent here is to sidetrack us from thinking critically   16
about the man and his ideas. Our own good qualities have nothing to do with the issue at hand. Ask yourself, "Apart from the nice things he has to say about me (and my church, my nation, my ethnic group, my neighbors), what does the candidate stand for? Are his or her ideas in my best interests?"

5. *Argumentum ad Hominem*

Argumentum ad hominem means "argument to the man" and that's   17
exactly what it is. When a propagandist uses *argumentum ad hominem*, he

wants to distract our attention from the issue under consideration with personal attacks on the people involved. For example, when Lincoln issued the Emancipation Proclamation, some people responded by calling him the "baboon." But Lincoln's long arms and awkward carriage had nothing to do with the merits of the Proclamation or the question of whether or not slavery should be abolished.

Today *argumentum ad hominem* is still widely used and very effective. You may or may not support the Equal Rights Amendment, but you should be sure your judgment is based on the merits of the idea itself, and not the result of someone's denunciation of the people who support the ERA as "fanatics" or "lesbians" or "frustrated old maids." Senator Yakalot is using *argumentum ad hominem* when he dismisses the idea of using smaller automobiles with a reference to the personal appearance of one of its supporters, Congresswoman Doris Schlepp. Refuse to be waylaid by *argumentum ad hominem* and ask, "Do the personal qualities of the person being discussed have anything to do with the issues at hand? Leaving him or her aside, how good is the idea itself?"   18

6. Transfer (Guilt or Glory by Association)

In *argumentum ad hominem,* an attempt is made to associate negative aspects of a person's character or personal appearance with an issue or idea he supports. The transfer device uses this same process of association to make us accept or condemn a given person or idea.   19

A better name for the transfer device is guilt (or glory) by association. In glory by association, the propagandist tries to transfer the positive feelings of something we love and respect to the group or idea he wants us to accept. "This bill for a new dam is in the best tradition of this country, the land of Lincoln, Jefferson, and Washington," is glory by association at work. Lincoln, Jefferson, and Washington were great leaders that most of us revere and respect, but they have no logical connection to the proposal under consideration—the bill to build a new dam. Senator Yakalot uses glory by association when he says full-sized cars "have always been as American as Mom's apple pie or a Sunday drive in the country."   20

The process works equally well in reverse, when guilt by association is used to transfer our dislike or disapproval of one idea or group to some other idea or group that the propagandist wants us to reject and condemn. "John Doe says we need to make some changes in the way our government operates; well, that's exactly what the Ku Klux Klan has said, so there's a meeting of great minds!" That's guilt by association for you;   21 there's no logical connection between John Doe and the Ku Klux Klan apart from the one the propagandist is trying to create in our minds. He wants to distract our attention from John Doe and get us thinking (and worrying) about the Ku Klux Klan and its politics of violence. (Of course, there are sometimes legitimate associations between the two things; if John Doe had been a *member* of the Ku Klux Klan, it would be reasonable and fair to draw a connection between the man and his group.) Senator Yakalot tries to trick his audience with guilt by association when he re-marks that "the words 'Community' and 'Communism' look an awful lot alike!" He does it again when he mentions that Mr. Stu Pott "sports a Fidel Castro beard."

How can we learn to spot the transfer device and distinguish be- 22
tween fair and unfair associations? We can teach ourselves to *suspend judgment* until we have answered these questions: "Is there any legitimate connection between the idea under discussion and the thing it is associated with? Leaving the transfer device out of the picture, what are the merits of the idea by itself?"

7. Bandwagon

Ever hear of the small, ratlike animal called the lemming? Lem- 23
mings are arctic rodents with a very odd habit: periodically, for reasons no one entirely knows, they mass together in a large herd and commit suicide by rushing into deep water and drowning themselves. They all run in together, blindly, and not one of them ever seems to stop and ask, "*Why* am I doing this? Is this really what I want to do?" and thus save itself from destruction. Obviously, lemmings are driven to perform their strange mass suicide rites by common instinct. People choose to "follow the herd" for more complex reasons, yet we are still all too often the unwitting victims of the bandwagon appeal.

Essentially, the bandwagon urges us to support an action or an opin- 24
ion because it is popular—because "everyone else is doing it." This call to "get on the bandwagon" appeals to the strong desire in most of us to be one of the crowd, not to be left out or alone. Advertising makes ex-tensive use of the bandwagon appeal ("join the Pepsi people"), but so do politicians ("Let us join together in this great cause"). Senator Yakalot uses the bandwagon appeal when he says that "More and more citizens are rallying to my cause every day," and asks his audience to "join them—and me—in our fight for America."

One of the ways we can see the bandwagon appeal at work is in the 25
overwhelming success of various fashions and trends which capture the

interest (and the money) of thousands of people for a short time, then disappear suddenly and completely. For a year or two in the fifties, every child in North America wanted a coonskin cap so they could be like Davy Crockett; no one wanted to be left out. After that there was the hula-hoop craze that helped to dislocate the hips of thousands of Americans. More recently, what made millions of people rush out to buy their very own "pet rocks"?

The problem here is obvious: just because everyone's doing it doesn't   26 mean that *we* should too. Group approval does not prove that something is true or is worth doing. Large numbers of people have supported actions we now condemn. Just a generation ago, Hitler and Mussolini rose to absolute and catastrophically repressive rule in two of the most sophisticated and cultured countries of Europe. When they came into power they were welled up by massive popular support from millions of people who didn't want to be "left out" at a great historical moment.

Once the mass begins to move—on the bandwagon—it becomes   27 harder and harder to perceive the leader *riding* the bandwagon. So don't be a lemming, rushing blindly on to destruction because "everyone else is doing it." Stop and ask, "Where is this bandwagon headed? Never mind about everybody else, is this what is best for *me*?" . . .

As we have seen, propaganda can appeal to us by arousing our   28 emotions or distracting our attention from the real issues at hand. But there's a third way that propaganda can be put to work against us—by the use of faulty logic. This approach is really more insidious than the other two because it gives the appearance of reasonable, fair argument. It is only when we look more closely that the holes in the logical fiber show up. The following are some of the devices that make use of faulty logic to distort and mislead.

8. Faulty Cause and Effect

As the name suggests, this device sets up a cause-and-effect rela-   29 tionship that may not be true. The Latin name for this logical fallacy is *post hoc ergo propter hoc*, which means "after this, therefore because of this." But just because one thing happened after another doesn't mean that one *caused* the other.

An example of false cause-and-effect reasoning is offered by the story   30 (probably invented) of the woman aboard the ship *Titanic*. She woke up from a nap and, feeling seasick, looked around for a call button to summon the steward to bring her some medication. She finally located a small button on one of the walls of her cabin and pushed it. A split second later, the *Titanic* grazed an iceberg in the terrible crash that was to send the entire ship to its destruction. The woman screamed and said, "Oh, God, what have I done? What have I done?" The humor of that anecdote comes from the absurdity of the woman's assumption that pushing the small red button resulted in the destruction of a ship weighing several hundred tons: "It happened after I pushed it, therefore it must be *because* I pushed it"—*post hoc ergo propter hoc* reasoning. There is, of course, no cause-and-effect relationship there.

The false cause-and-effect fallacy is used very often by political can- 31
didates. "After I came to office, the rate of inflation dropped to 6 per-cent." But did the person do anything to cause the lower rate of inflation or was it the result of other conditions? Would the rate of inflation have dropped anyway, even if he hadn't come to office? Senator Yakalot uses false cause and effect when he says "our forefathers who made this country great never had free hot meal handouts! And look what they did for our country!" He does it again when he concludes that "driving full-sized cars means a better car safety record on our American roads today."

False cause-and-effect reasoning is terribly persuasive because it seems 32
so logical. Its appeal is apparently to experience. We swallowed X prod-uct—and the headache went away. We elected Y official and unemploy-ment went down. Many people think, "There *must* be a connection." But causality is an immensely complex phenomenon; you need a good deal of evidence to prove that an event that follows another in time was "therefore" caused by the first event.

Don't be taken in by false cause and effect; be sure to ask, "Is there 33
enough evidence to prove that this cause led to that effect? Could there have been any *other* causes?"

9. False Analogy

An analogy is a comparison between two ideas, events, or things. 34
But comparisons can be fairly made only when the things being compared are alike in significant ways. When they are not, false analogy is the result.

A famous example of this is the old proverb "Don't change horses 35
in the middle of a stream," often used as an analogy to convince voters not to change administrations in the middle of a war or other crisis. But the analogy is misleading because there are so many differences between the things compared. In what ways is a war or political crisis like a stream? Is the President or head of state really very much like a horse? And is a nation of millions of people comparable to a man trying to get across a

stream? Analogy is false and unfair when it compares two things that have little in common and assumes that they are identical. Senator Yakalot tries to hoodwink his listeners with false analogy when he says, "Trying to take Americans out of the kind of cars they love is as undemocratic as trying to deprive them of the right to vote."

Of course, analogies can be drawn that are reasonable and fair. It would be reasonable, for example, to compare the results of busing in one small Southern city with the possible results in another, *if* the towns have the same kind of history, population, and school policy. We can decide for ourselves whether an analogy is false or fair by asking, "Are the things being compared truly alike in significant ways? Do the differences between them affect the comparison?"

10. Begging the Question

Actually, the name of this device is rather misleading, because it does not appear in the form of a question. Begging the question occurs when, in discussing a questionable or debatable point, a person assumes as already established the very point that he is trying to prove. For example, "No thinking citizen could approve such a completely unacceptable policy as this one." But isn't the question of whether or not the policy *is* acceptable the very point to be established? Senator Yakalot begs the question when he announces that his opponent's plan won't work "because it is unworkable."

We can protect ourselves against this kind of faulty logic by asking, "What is assumed in this statement? Is the assumption reasonable, or does it need more proof?"

11. The Two Extremes Fallacy (False Dilemma)

Linguists have long noted that the English language tends to view reality in sets of two extremes or polar opposites. In English, things are either black or white, tall or short, up or down, front or back, left or right, good or bad, guilty or not guilty. We can ask for a "straightforward yes-or-no answer" to a question, the understanding being that we will not accept or consider anything in between. In fact, reality cannot always be dissected along such strict lines. There may be (usually are) *more* than just two possibilities or extremes to consider. We are often told to "listen to both sides of the argument." But who's to say that every argument has only two sides? Can't there be a third—even a fourth or fifth—point of view?

The two-extremes fallacy is at work in this statement by Lenin, the 40 great Marxist leader: "You cannot eliminate *one* basic assumption, one substantial part of this philosophy of Marxism (it is as if it were a block of steel), without abandoning truth, without falling into the arms of bourgeois-reactionary falsehood." In other words, if we don't agree 100 percent with every premise of Marxism, we must be placed at the opposite end of the political-economic spectrum—for Lenin, "bourgeois-reactionary falsehood." If we are not entirely *with* him, we must be against him; those are the only two possibilities open to us. Of course, this is a logical fallacy; in real life there are any number of political positions one can maintain *between* the two extremes of Marxism and capitalism. Senator Yakalot uses the two-extremes fallacy in the same way as Lenin when he tells his audience that "in this world a man's either for private enterprise or he's for socialism."

One of the most famous examples of the two-extremes fallacy in 41 recent history is the slogan, "America: Love it or leave it," with its implicit suggestion that we either accept everything just as it is in America today without complaint—or get out. Again, it should be obvious that there is a whole range of action and belief between those two extremes.

Don't be duped; stop and ask, "Are those really the only two options 42 I can choose from? Are there other alternatives not mentioned that deserve considerations?"

12. Card Stacking

Some questions are so multifaceted and complex that no one can 43 make an intelligent decision about them without considering a wide variety of evidence. One selection of facts could make us feel one way and another selection could make us feel just the opposite. Card stacking is a device of propaganda which selects only the facts that support the propagandist's point of view, and ignores all the others. For example, a candidate could be made to look like a legislative dynamo if you say, "Representative McNerd introduced more new bills than any other member of the Congress," and neglect to mention that most of them were so preposterous that they were laughed off the floor.

Senator Yakalot engages in card stacking when he talks about the 44 proposal to use smaller cars. He talks only about jobs without mentioning the cost to the taxpayers or the very real—though still denied—threat of depletion of resources. He says he wants to help his countrymen keep their jobs, but doesn't mention that the corporations that offer the jobs will also make large profits. He praises the "American chrome industry," overlooking the fact that most chrome is imported. And so on.

The best protection against card stacking is to take the "Yes, but . . ." attitude. This device of propaganda is not untrue, but then again it is not the *whole* truth. So ask yourself, "Is this person leaving something out that I should know about? Is there some other information that should be brought to bear on this question?" . . .

So far, we have considered three approaches that the propagandist can use to influence our thinking: appealing to our emotions, distracting our attention, and misleading us with logic that may appear to be reasonable but is in fact faulty and deceiving. But there is a fourth approach that is probably the most common propaganda trick of them all.

13. Testimonial

The testimonial device consists in having some loved or respected person give a statement of support (testimonial) for a given product or idea. The problem is that the person being quoted may *not* be an expert in the field; in fact, he may know nothing at all about it. Using the name of a man who is skilled and famous in one field to give a testimonial for something in another field is unfair and unreasonable.

Senator Yakalot tries to mislead his audience with testimonial when he tells them that "full-sized cars have been praised by great Americans like John Wayne and Jack Jones, as well as by leading experts on car safety and comfort."

Testimonial is used extensively in TV ads, where it often appears in such bizarre forms as Joe Namath's endorsement of a pantyhose brand. Here, of course, the "authority" giving the testimonial not only is no expert about pantyhose, but obviously stands to gain something (money!) by making the testimonial.

When celebrities endorse a political candidate, they may not be making money by doing so, but we should still question whether they are in any better position to judge than we ourselves. Too often we are willing to let others we like or respect make our decisions *for us*, while we follow along acquiescently. And this is the purpose of testimonial—to get us to agree and accept *without* stopping to think. Be sure to ask, "Is there any reason to believe that this person (or organization or publication or whatever) has any more knowledge or information than I do on this subject? What does the idea amount to on its own merits, without the benefit of testimonial?"

The cornerstone of democratic society is reliance upon an informed   51
and educated electorate. To be fully effective citizens we need to be able
to challenge and to question wisely. A dangerous feeling of indifference
toward our political processes exists today. We often abandon our right,
our duty, to criticize and evaluate by dismissing *all* politicians as "crooked,"
all new bills and proposals as "just more government bureaucracy." But
there are important distinctions to be made, and this kind of apathy can
be fatal to democracy.

If we are to be led, let us not be led blindly, but critically, intelli-   52
gently, with our eyes open. If we are to continue to be a government "by
the people," let us become informed about the methods and purposes of
propaganda, so we can be the masters, not the slaves of our destiny.

About the Essay

1. What are the four general types of propaganda devices that Cross discusses?

2. What, according to Cross, is the most common propaganda trick of them
all? Give some examples from your experience.

3. What organization does Cross use for each of her discussions of a propaganda device? Do you see any purpose for the order in which she presents the
thirteen devices?

4. Who is Senator Yakalot? What is his significance in Cross's essay?

5. Cross uses an analogy in her discussion of bandwagon appeal. How does
this analogy work? Is it a true or a false analogy, according to Cross's own
definitions? Explain.

Explorations

1. What propaganda devices do you recognize in present-day political speeches?
In advertising? Give examples of your own. When you recognize that you are
being propagandized, how does that affect you?

2. In her opening paragraph, Cross says that "propaganda is simply a means
of persuasion and so it can be put to work for good causes as well as bad."
Taking into account the rest of the essay as well as what you know about
propaganda, what are the implications of that statement? Consider the propaganda used by charitable organizations, for example. Do their "honorable"
goals justify possibly "dishonorable" methods? In other words, does the end
sometimes justify the means?

3. Assume that you are to speak for a position or a cause—say, a new law you favor, or an organization you belong to. Try to make your case without using any of the propaganda devices Cross discusses. As you work, keep track of the devices you wanted to use—that perhaps almost slipped in, despite your vigilance—but that you had to do without. How difficult is it to avoid propaganda in your writing? What devices come most easily to mind, or are hardest to do without?

Noel Perrin is a New Yorker by birth and has spent much of his life in the academic world, yet he is most widely known as an essayist on the demands and rewards of country life. He was born in 1927, attended Williams College, Duke University, and Cambridge University, England, and is now an English professor at Dartmouth College in New Hampshire. He lives in neighboring Vermont and wrote about his home state in *Vermont in All Weathers* (1973). His country pieces, which he calls "essays of a sometime farmer," have been collected in *First Person Rural* (1978) and *Second Person Rural* (1980).

Perrin's interest in ordinary things and his professional concern with language come together in "Tell Me, Pretty Billboard," from *First Person Rural*. Which of us hasn't sometimes wanted to talk back to the unhearing pitchmen on television and radio? Perrin goes even further: In this essay he not only talks to signs and packages but gets them to talk back to him.

Tell Me, Pretty Billboard

Drunks talk to lamp posts. Little girls in Victorian novels talk to imaginary playmates. I talk to the writing on packages and signs. [1]

It, of course, has been talking to me every since I learned to read, but it is only recently that I have started answering. Most of my life I have been a good consumer, like any other American, keeping my mouth shut and my ears open. Quietly I pushed my cart down supermarket aisles, listening to the mechanical music and being influenced by point-of-sale displays. Quietly I relaxed at home, watching teleshapes that couldn't see me, and hearing electronic voices that I could turn off but not answer. It was all perfectly normal and perfectly one-way. Never was I disturbed by my lack of I-thou relationships with vending machines, or by the fact that though a girl on a poster could stir me, there was no hope of my stirring her. [2]

About a year ago, though, I suddenly found myself wanting to ask a cigarette machine in Burlington, Vermont, why it charged more for cigarettes than the human beings in the drug store across the street. Hardly two weeks later I had an overwhelming urge to tell an electronic voice in my living room that the 'nei' of 'neither' may have been pronounced 'nigh' by the Electors of Hanover even after they moved to England and began speaking the king's English,[1] but the right way to say it is still 'knee.' Naturally I couldn't do either. [3]

---

[1]The British royal family is descended from the German royal house of Hanover. In German, *ei* is pronounced like *eye*.

The urge grew, though, and before I knew it I found myself writing 4
one letter to the company that owned the vending machine—you can
sometimes find the address on the side—and another to the network that
employed the rexophile announcer.

I promptly got answers from both, but the answers didn't tell me 5
much, except that public relations is a growing field. Both might have
been composed by the same man who handles correspondence for my
congressman. (I had happened to send him a thoughtful letter about Far
Eastern policy that same month.) All three replies had a kind of customized form letter quality that I assume is designed to give people like me
the illusion that we have gotten through when we haven't, except as
statistics, or what the network probably calls feedback. The congressman
said he valued my opinion, and would keep it in mind. The network said
it was delighted to hear from me, and its dictionary approved both the
pronunciations I mentioned. The vending machine company said vending machines were very expensive, and tobacco taxes very high. It also
said that as I was obviously a thoughtful person, it was sending me a
questionnaire to fill out on what kinds of products I would like to see
available in vending machines, and a quarter for my trouble.

It was at this point that I turned to fantasy. If dialogue with the 6
economy has to be an illusion, I decided, it might as well be illusion of
my own making. The answers would be more interesting. Since then I
have been holding frequent conversations with billboards and taped
messages and directions on razor-blade packages, and life is bearable
again.

I'll give an example. There is a highway sign I sometimes pass in 7
Connecticut which asserts that there are eight friendly inns on a body
of water called Lake Waramaug and urges me to stay at one of them. In
mere reality it would be difficult to ask that sign how friendliness can be
offered as a commodity, like clean towels or room service. For the dweller
in fantasy it's a snap. The last time by I had a chat with it which went
something like this:

ME: Hello, you friendly sign. 8
SIGN: (*friendlily*) Hello-alo. That's a nice car you're driving, Mister. I like 9
you. Why don't you take your next left and come on to Lake Waramaug?
ME: Maybe I will. Are all eight of the inns really friendly? 10
SIGN: Are they? Why, Mister, you don't know what friendship means 11
till you've stayed at Lake Waramaug.
ME: (*suddenly, at 39, struck by doubts*) By gosh, you're right, I don't know. 12
What does friendship mean?
SIGN: At our inns, it means that everybody from the bellhop to the 13

manager is sincerely glad to see you, that we have a relaxed, friendly atmosphere—

ME: Hold it. You can't define a word in terms of itself. 14

SIGN: Oops. I mean a relaxed, *casual* atmosphere where everything's very informal, where the bartender smiles as he mixes you a martini, where, well, where everybody from the bellhop to the manager is sincerely glad to see you. 15

ME: That's great! I love big welcomes. We'll all be real friends, right? 16

SIGN: (*after a second's hesitation*) Sure. Every guest is a friend. 17

ME: Sign, this is the best news I've had in a long time. It just happens that I'm dead tired, dead broke, and very hungry. A clean bed and a good dinner are just what I need. Which of my new friends shall I stay with? 18

SIGN: (*icy cold*) Listen, buddy, if you're looking for charity, why don't you try the Traveler's Aid? 19

ME: When I've got sincere friends all around Lake Waramaug? Why should I? 20

SIGN: OK, I walked into that one. So they're not your real friends. 21

ME: But they're still sincerely glad to see me? 22

SIGN: Well, yes, sure. What I meant was that provided you can pay your bill, everybody from the bellhop to the manager feels sincerely glad to see you, whether they personally like you or not; and any employee that can't feel that way gets fired. Fair enough? 23

ME: You mean you have to be a hypocrite to work at Lake Waramaug? 24

SIGN: Look, I'm just a sign, and I'm ten miles back on the road as it is. Why don't you go talk to the man that wrote me? 25

But I don't do that. Instead I drive on up to Vermont. A few miles from home I stop to buy some groceries. (I was lying when I told the sign I was broke. Unlike hotelkeepers, I'm naturally insincere.) The first thing I buy is a package of garden-fresh frozen vegetables. 26

ME: What does garden-fresh mean, Package? 27

PACKAGE: Just what it says. What's nicer and fresher than a garden? (*strikes an attitude*) 28

> A garden is a lovesome thing, Got wot!
> Rose plot . . .[2]

ME: Listen, I like gardens, too. I just want to know what garden-fresh means on a package of frozen peas. 29

---

[2]The package seems to have memorized "My Garden," by the nineteenth-century English poet Thomas Brown.

PACKAGE: If I have to spell it out, it means the peas inside me are as   30
fresh as if you'd gone into your own vegetable garden and picked them
right off the pea vines, ten minutes before dinner.

ME: When were the peas inside you picked?   31

PACKAGE: Oh, about six months ago. But they've been *frozen*, Mister.   32
They could just as well have been picked today.

ME: Were they frozen ten minutes after being picked?   33

PACKAGE: It was the same day. We rush them from the fields to the   34
plant—

ME: Ten minutes?   35

PACKAGE: All right, if you're going to be literal about it, the peas inside   36
me are as fresh as if you'd gone into your own vegetable garden and
picked them right off the pea vines within twelve hours before dinner.

ME: And there has been no deterioration at all during the six months?   37

PACKAGE: I said they were frozen.   38

ME: Biochemical change ceases entirely when peas are frozen?   39

PACKAGE: It goes a lot slower.   40

ME: But it does occur?   41

PACKAGE: Look, if you don't like frozen foods, grow your own damn   42
peas. *I* don't care.

ME: You are going to answer the question?   43

PACKAGE: (*in a fury*) Sure, there's a little deterioration. But it's well   44
within Department of Agriculture Standards, and—

But at this point the woman at the check-out counter shoves the   45
package in a freezer bag, and I drive on home. My next conversation
takes place about a month later, when I'm back in New York, about to
get a cup of coffee out of an automatic machine. There are no less than
five choices, with a button to push for each. I can have black, sugar
only, cream only, sugar and cream, or sugar and extra cream.

ME: Excuse me, but I was wondering why cream is spelled c-r-e-m-e?   46

MACHINE: Perfectly good spelling. The French use it, you know. *Voulez-*   47
vous un café-crème?

ME: *Oui. Avec sucre.*[3] But why French in New York City?   48

MACHINE: I didn't say it *was* French. I said the French use that spelling.   49
As a matter of fact, it has something to do with trademarks.

ME: I don't follow.   50

MACHINE: Come on, you haven't grown up in America without knowing   51
about trademarks. No company can get exclusive rights to a word unless
they figure out a new spelling. That's why there are so many. You don't

---

[3]"Would you like coffee with cream?" "Yes, with sugar."

think serious business executives *like* to name their stuff Wonda Winda or Tas-tee Bitz, do you?

ME: Do you have exclusive rights to c-r-e-m-e? I could swear I'd seen   52
that on some kind of make-up my wife uses.

MACHINE: Sure. That's so your wife won't think her make-up has cream   53
from cows in it. It means a creamy or cream-type preparation.

ME: But you do mean cream from cows, don't you?   54

MACHINE: I mean it's fresh-made hot coffee, served 24 hours a day, which   55
is quite a miracle, when you come to think of it.

ME: Cream from cows?   56

MACHINE: So it's from soybeans. You know there's a considerable body   57
of medical opinion that thinks cream from cows is pretty dangerous stuff.
Bad for the heart. You ought to be down on your knees thanking me.

ME: (*still upright*) I also know about that study of Irish twin brothers,   58
where one brother stayed in Ireland and the other came to the United
States. The ones back home used more butter and cream, but the mar-
garine-eaters over here had more heart attacks. What about that?

MACHINE: Easy. There's lots more stresses in American life.   59

ME: And therefore I've got to drink soybean juice in my coffee? Well,   60
why not say plainly that's what you serve, and why? Maybe you'd pull
the trade from the dairy restaurants.

MACHINE: Mister, you think we got room for health lectures on the panel   61
above a lousy pushbutton? C-r-e-m-e fits on the panel, everybody knows
what it means, everybody's happy.

ME: But—   62

MACHINE: (*going right on*) What else could we do? You've got to think   63
about customer recognition. Say we put your phrase—'soybean juice,'
was it?—on the panel. Does it sound like something to go in coffee? Or
does it confuse the hell out of everybody? Or maybe you want we should
put 'soy sauce'? Listen, the stoops we get would be coming with plates
and silverware, looking for the chow mein.

ME: But—   64

MACHINE: And if we put 'Cream substitute made from soybeans—better   65
for you,' I ask you, how are we going to get it all on?

ME: But what I've been trying to say is that space is plainly not the whole   66
problem. You've got room to help the customer recognize. Look at your
own panel. I see 'White Cross Dairy.' There, right above the c-r-e-m-e.
What about that?

MACHINE: (*blushing bright scarlet*) It's not very big type.   67

ME: Interesting phrase, though.   68

MACHINE: Don't say it, I know what you're thinking. To some extent   69
you have to compromise to succeed in business, and that's a fact.

ME: By the way, what's your sugar made of?
MACHINE: Sorry, Mister. You'll have to ask the Food and Drug Administration. I just went out of order.

About the Essay

1. What is the point of Perrin's essay? How did you decide what it is? How does Perrin present it?

2. What was lacking in the three letters Perrin describes in paragraph 5? Why was it lacking?

3. What is the tone of Perrin's fantasy dialogue? In what way does it continue the tone in his opening paragraph? In what way does this tone affect your reading of his criticisms? Cite passages from the essay in your response.

4. What advantages does Perrin gain by writing his essay as a series of imaginary dialogues? How else might he have presented his material?

5. Why might business executives want to invent silly names for their products? What reason does the vending machine give? What are trademarks for?

6. Why does the coffee machine blush at the label on its panel, above the buttons?

Explorations

1. Are there any ads today that you find especially irritating? What do you find wrong with each of them? Choose one and rewrite it to make it less objectionable—but no less interesting and effective.

2. Many students who have read Perrin's essay disagree with it, saying that advertising performs a useful service to consumers, and that most people know enough not to be taken in by half-truths and exaggerations. Do you agree? Why or why not? If you agree, what benefits do we receive either directly or indirectly from advertising?

3. In paragraph 5, Perrin says that all the replies to his correspondence had a "kind of customized form letter quality." Have you ever received such letters? How do you feel about them? Why do companies and public figures use them?

RON ROSENBAUM

Ron Rosenbaum was born in New York in 1946 and graduated from Yale University in 1968. He began his career as a writer by joining the staff of New York's weekly *Village Voice* and has contributed articles to magazines such as *Esquire* and *Harper's*. Some of these pieces have been collected in *Rebirth of a Salesman: Tales of the Song and Dance Seventies* (1978). He has also written a novel, *Murder at Elaine's* (1979).

Rosenbaum has arrived at the conclusion that advertising tells us more about ourselves and our times than does *Masterpiece Theatre* or "a week's worth of sit-coms." He has noticed that television advertising has begun to change with the onset of the 1980s, and in this essay, published in *Mother Jones* in 1981, he points out what is new—and why.

The Hard Sell

Too many viewers, I'm afraid, miss out on the most exciting intellectual challenge offered by television: the commercials. That's right. I said the intellectual challenge of TV commercials and I don't mean just the task of choosing between Stove Top stuffing and potatoes. I mean the pleasure to be found in pitting your intellect against some of the cleverest minds in the country, the Masterminds of Madison Avenue, and trying to figure out how they've figured *you* out. 1

Too many TV watchers still leave the room during TV commercials for some trivial reason. As a result, they miss some of the best-produced, most skillfully scripted and edited dramas on TV: more thought, more research into human nature and, in some cases, more dollars go into creating those 30- and 60-second ads than into the development of most 30- and 60-minute prime-time programs. 2

I never leave the room during the commercials. I sit spellbound watching them. I take notes. The highpoint of an evening before the set for me can be discovering a new wrinkle in Mr. Whipple's war on secretive Charmin squeezers, or catching the debut of one of the grand, soaring production numbers the airline or beer people put on to get us in the mood for getting high. I find more intrigue in trying to figure out the mysterious appeal of Mrs. Olsen and Robert Young, those continuing characters in coffee commercials, than in the predictable puzzles of *Masterpiece Theatre*. And I'm convinced that future archeologists will find more concentrated and reliable clues to the patterns of our culture in one Clorox ad than they could ever find in a week's worth of sit-coms. 3

301

Take a look at some of the key trends in TV ads of the 1980s, the   4
changes in tone and technique, and you can see what they tell us about
ourselves and consciousness of the new decade.

No More Nice Guys

The early '80s have witnessed the return of the Hard Sell, or what   5
might be called the "no more Mr. Nice Guy" school of commercial strategy. If you had been watching closely you could have picked up an advance warning, a seismic tremor of the shift to come, in the Buick slogan
change. In the fall of 1979 Buick abruptly yanked its confident slogan,
the one that told us "Make it Buick. After all, life is to enjoy." Then,
after that, everything changed.

The Buick ads of the '80s no longer take a firm position on the   6
meaning of life. Instead they give us hard numbers and initials: EPA est.
MPG.[1] Which leaves us to wonder; if life is no longer "to enjoy," what is
life to? In the world of the new no-nonsense ads, life is to *struggle*, life is
to fight for survival in a nasty brutish world. "Life got tougher," the makers of Excedrin tell us, so "we got stronger." And the airways are filled
with new, tougher, hard-edged combative spirit. Little old ladies are seen
savagely socking gas pumps in the midsections. Vicious tempers flare into
public displays of anger in Sanka commercials. For years, tough guy Robert Conrad postured pugnaciously and challenged the unsuspecting viewer:
"I dare you to call this an ordinary battery," threatening by implication
to step right out of the tube and commit some assault and battery right
there in our living rooms.

This aggressive stance is echoed by the take-it-or-leave-it approach   7
of the Italian food canner who declares, "Make it Progresso, or make it
yourself," and was heralded by the Japanese car maker who told us, "If
you can find a better-built small car than Toyota, buy it." This dismissive
imperative tone of voice is the new keynote of ads in the 1980s.

You could see the philosophy of the new no-nonsense school being   8
formulated by the deep-thinkers of Madison Avenue in the first year of
the new decade. The pages of *Advertising Age* were filled with speculations
by ad people about what to name the period. "The Aching '80s" was one
suggestion. "The Decade of Difficult Decisions," "The Era of Uncertainty," "The Return to Reality" were others. Each sage of the new era
wanted to distinguish the '80s from the previous decade, from what one
advertising agency commentator called "the self-centered, the self-indul-
gent, self-gratifying of the Me Decade."

---

[1]Environmental Protection Agency-estimated miles per gallon.

The battle between the old and the new is not confined to the pages   9
of *Ad Age.* If you want a quick tour of the combat zone, the best place to
start is with the big-money brokerage battle. You can usually catch the
clash on the Sunday interview shows (*Meet the Press* and the others).
Here you can see four brokerage houses go after their potential client
targets with two totally different advertising strategies. While Paine Webber and Dean Witter try to win hearts and minds with the Late-'70s-
Wish-Fulfillment approach, Merrill Lynch and Smith Barney assault the
viewer with the blasted landscape of Early '80s Angst.

To shift back and forth between the two worlds invites severe diso-   10
rientation. Start with Dean Witter's world, where ecstatic customers are
always getting calls and letters from their broker that cause them to burst
with joyful financial fulfillment as a heavenly-sounding choir croons:

"You look like you just heard from Dean Witter."   11

Contrast that with the lead character from another brokerage ad.   12
He's alone. He's lost. There is pain in his big sad eyes; he's cutting his
hooves on icy rocks and crusts of snow as he slowly picks his way in search
of shelter. This harsh winter scene is "today's investment climate," a
voice-over tells us, a time to "protect your assets." We watch the bull
finally find a dank cave in which to shelter his assets (a parable about tax
shelters,[2] it seems) just as a terrifying crack of thunder bursts over the
frozen wasteland outside. There hasn't been a storm more fraught with
the sheer terror of existence since the third act of *King Lear.* This is no
mere investment climate; this is all the cold and terror and loneliness of
modern life.

In his most recent appearances, we see the solitary bull wandering   13
a barren desert wasteland beset by the tormenting trickery of a mirage; in
another we see him stepping into a bewildering hedge maze, which conjures up the horror of the hedge maze chase in Stanley Kubrick's *The
Shining* as much as it does the subtle securities offered by hedge funds[3] on
the financial scene. Finally—it was inevitable—the poor beast becomes
the proverbial "bull in the china shop," making his way through a maze
of crystal and making us feel the frightening fragility of the most cloistered
of civilized interiors.

A Bull Apart

That lonely bull. He's lonelier than ever now, farther off than ever   14
from any hope of reunion with his herd. Faithful bull-watchers realize that

---

[2]Investments that permit one to "shelter" income from taxes.
[3]Investments that protect, or "hedge," against losses.

the '80s have introduced the third major phase in the bull's relation to the herd. In the original Merrill Lynch ads of the early '70s, when Merrill Lynch was still unabashedly "bullish on America," he was joyfully romping with the whole happy herd. In fact, we didn't even single out any particular bull, such was the togetherness of the big beasts. A late '70s series of Merrill Lynch ads would open on a lone bull majestically patrolling scenic outposts on his own but rejoining the herd in the final shot because, in the modified slogan, Merrill Lynch was "*still* bullish on America."

Then at the very beginning of the new decade the herd disappeared   15
from the ads completely. (What has become of the other bulls? PBB poisoning? Cattle mutilations?) Gone too is any attempt to further refurbish the "bullish on America" slogan. (What could they say—"We're *really, truly*, still bullish on America"?)

The new slogan, "Merrill Lynch—a breed apart," tells us there's no   16
time to worry about the herd; you have to look after your own assets in today's cold and nasty economic climate, in which the market falls more every day.

But wait—ten minutes later, on a break in *Issues and Answers*, for   17
instance, we're suddenly in a whole other America, the kind of place where everything goes right. We're back not just in civilization but at the summit of civilized achievements, where we hear the rattle of fine china teacups and the clink of crystal champagne glasses set to delicate waltz music. We're in the world of Paine Webber. Grateful clients are acquiring Renoirs, eating paté or otherwise comforting themselves with the satisfied obliviousness of the courtiers of Louis XVI.[4] The ad includes a sort of disclaimer to the effect that while Paine Webber cannot guarantee you wealth, if you bring your money to them, maybe someday "you might say, 'Thank you, Paine Webber' too."

Ah, yes . . . *maybe someday* . . . It's that old wish-fulfillment witch-   18
craft working.

Another quick flick of the remote control button and the spell of   19
such summery sophistries shatters under the frosty glare with which John Houseman fixes us in the Smith Barney ads. It is a shock, the shift from the plush carpeted Paine Webber world to the trashy, torn-ticker-tape litter on the floor of the stock exchange, from the soaring choirs of Dean Witter to the bare ruined choirs of the Big Board.[5]

---

[4]The shimmering impressionist paintings of Pierre Auguste Renoir (1841–1919) are occasionally auctioned at very high prices. King Louis XVI of France (1754–1793) ruled in splendor—until he was deposed in the French Revolution and later executed.

[5]A quotation board for securities listed on the New York Stock Exchange.

Houseman puts on a great performance. Smith Barney has invested 20
wisely in him. "The New York Stock Exchange. The day's trading is
over," he intones ominously in his classic debut spot. "Some tally their
profits," he says with a wintry, dismissive smile that implies: "Fat chance
that's you, fella." "Some," he concludes, impaling us with a veritable
icicle of a glance, "lick their wounds."

Wounds. Suffering. Pain. Insecurity. The tragic view of life. House- 21
man's debut for Smith Barney was the perfect harbinger of the New Hard
Sell. Unlike the old hard sell, with a fast-and-loud-talking salesperson
pitching a product, the new sell portrays the world as cold, brutally tough.
The product isn't pushed so much as the audience is impelled to reach—
reach *hard*—for the hope of security the product offers. The *hope* of security—that is what the '80s hard sell offers to those of us frozen out by
this brutal era.

The Tough Life

A recent editorial in *Ad Age* denounced the new Excedrin "Life got 22
tougher" ads for "overkill," for giving the impression that "life is now
akin to a forced march to the Gulag Archipelago[6] . . . a kind of doomsday
feeling."

Even if life is not getting *that* tough, *tough* is definitely the key word 23
in the world of today's TV commercials. Dodge trucks are "ram tough,"
and the Dodge ads feature hormone-crazed rams smashing horns against
each other. Ford trucks are "built tough," and their promo featured a
grueling tug of war with Toyota.

Then, too, the old-fashioned work ethic has returned to promi- 24
nence. "They make money the old-fashioned way. They earn it," John
Houseman says in a Smith Barney ad. Back to basics. Don't express yourself, protect yourself. Life is no longer to enjoy. Life is to avoid. The
essence of this new technique is to arouse anxiety and offer relief. It means
something, I think, that dollar for dollar Tylenol is the single most frequently purchased drugstore item in the United States today.

Certainly the older-type commercials, the softer, happier advertis- 25
ing pitches, continue to be the most popular with TV viewers. A look at
two years of polls by Video Storyboards Test Inc. (a market research outfit
that asks a cross section of people what they think is the most outstanding
TV commercial they have seen recently) consistently registers the popu-

---

[6]The system of Soviet prison camps where Stalin's political enemies were confined in
the 1940s.

larity of the spiritual, emotional, celebratory ad campaigns. The warmth and emotion of the "Mean Joe Greene and the Kid" Coke commercial made it the most popular in recent years. The stirring musical Americana of the soft drink spirituals, the lyrical beauty and hearty camaraderie of the beer ads and the blood-curdling cuteness of cat food commercials consistently push these upbeat celebrations of humanity, warmth and friendship into the Top 10 of such ad polls.

Whether or not they will continue to be popular with ad people as   26
selling tools is another question. There have been some interesting changes in the spiritual genre in the new season's ads.

Consider first the very popularity of the word. After a brief appear-   27
ance and quick death in 1976, the word *spirit* has arisen again. We have the "catch that Pepsi spirit" campaign; we have the cloud-level soaring "spirit of Hyatt" and the plucky American Motors gas-saving model, Spirit.

But, hovering over the grand, "Main Street parade" Pepsi spirit spot   28
is an aura of anxiety. We watch the little drum majorette drop her baton in practice at home. Now it's the Fourth of July parade, and we are treated to the anxious glances of the parents and friends as they wait to see if their child will suffer public humiliation. Of course, she catches it; but anxiety and suspense giving way to relief, and people gulping Pepsi to soothe throats dry from tension are not the unambiguous hallmarks of joy that once reigned in soft drink ads. Even they now bode harder times. . . .

Something More Than Feelings

Another technique of the late '70s school is the emphasis on feel-   29
ing. While this has been a good year for product feelings ("Feelin' 7-Up," "Oh, what a feeling . . . Toyota"), it has not been a particularly good season for feelings of love.

Why is love slighted? Why did AT&T cancel its love song theme,   30
"Feelings," and switch to the California hot-tub gestalt "Reach Out and Touch Someone" theme? What was the flaw for the ad people in "Feelings"?

Many to be sure would call it a criminally sentimental piece of   31
trash, but that never stopped other songs from making it. No, it is the fact that the Morris Albert classic is specifically a song about feelings of love. And with love there are always mixed feelings, touchy feelings, fiery feelings, not the comfortable nonthreatening warmth of reach-out-and-touch feelings. California closeness is a safer-selling feeling than those volatile feelings of love.

Increasingly, this year we find the notion of love ridiculed and   32
scorned. In one of those male-bonding, beer-bar get-togethers, a starry-
eyed man bursts in to announce "I've found *the* woman."

"*Again,*" some wise guy cracks scornfully to the roar of ridicule from   33
a crowd clearly disillusioned with the Western Romantic tradition.

While some wine commercials celebrate passion and *amore* between   34
men and women, the most conspicuous instance of love at first sight on
screen these days is between man and car (Mazda's "Just one look . . ."
theme), and the most conspicuous instance of erotic love is between a
woman and herself (the Rive Gauche[7] hard-driving, dawn-watching woman
who "goes it alone," whose "auto-eroticism" as Jeff Greenfield called it
before I got a chance to, is only thinly veiled—we even see the earth
move as she watches the sun also rise).

In fact, the one new ad that treated love uncynically celebrated   35
what is actually pubescent puppy love—the two shy kids in the 1980
"Love's Baby Soft" teenybopper fragrance ad. It's a brilliant and beguiling
piece of work, but nowhere do you find the equivalent for post-teen-
agers.

The only innovative use of love in the past few years is in the less-   36
than-romantic name of a cleansing product—"Love My Carpet." (The
most interesting new-product name on the market in recent years has
got to be "Gee, Your Hair Smells Terrific!" Look for more of these
exclamatory-sentence brand names in future TV commercials.)

Realm of Nightmare

In fact, there have been some vicious anti-Romance ads running   37
recently. The most insidious of the genre was the Longines spot that aired
last Christmastime. A cozy marital scene; the man has just given his wife
a watch he worked his heart out to afford. He's gazing at her, brimming
over with loving generosity as she announces, "I love it."

She pauses. Only a microsecond, but one of the most deadly micro-   38
seconds ever aired. "But?" he asks. "No, really," she replies with just a
fleeting smile.

The guy's heart is breaking. She's not even faking enthusiasm.   39
"C'mon, tell me," he pleads weakly.

"I guess I was hoping for a Longines," she says wistfully.   40

This is not Romance but a nasty little murder of it committed right   41
before our eyes.

---

[7]Left Bank; refers to the bohemian district of Paris on the left bank of the Seine River.

Here, we have entered the realm of nightmare. Here, other kinds   42
of feelings reign. We are working not with human potential but with
human paranoia. Anxiety. Loss. Fear of loss. Remember that nightmarish
classic, the American Express Lost Traveler's Cheques series. Who can
forget the smug sneer of the French concierge when the frantic young
American couple confess that the traveler's checks they have lost were
not American Express? "Ah," he says, as if gazing down from the frosty
remoteness of Mont Blanc at a particularly distasteful specimen of grape
blight. "Most people carry American Express."

What's shocking here is not the Gallic scorn but the supine re-   43
sponse of the American couple. Instead of grabbing the concierge by his
starched, stuffed shirt and reminding him that his mother hadn't asked
the Americans who liberated Paris what kind of bank checks they brought,
the couple turns away in humiliation and self-abasement: We *are* such
worms, we Americans, only good for our virtually worthless dollars, and
here we are too stupid even to do what Most People do and at least avoid
inconveniencing the concierge with our petty failures.

Certainly this abasement before foreigners must reflect more than   44
the lingering cringe of the colonials before continental civilization. It
suggests a kind of sickening national self-image that masochistically rel-
ishes affronts to our representatives abroad.

Consider the slogan for the ad: "American Express Traveler's   45
Cheques—don't leave home without them." Isn't the net effect of that
slogan—which follows portrait after panicked portrait of Americans robbed,
humiliated, traumatized, everything but taken hostage, generally in foreign lands—isn't the net effect to feed the voice inside our national psyche,
that fearful voice that simply says, "Don't leave home"?

The Humiliation Sell

Humiliation, embarrassment and slovenliness seem to be at the core   46
of not just Miller but Schlitz and other "lite" beer commercials. Ads for
full-bodied beers are still some of the most beautiful, most lyrical, glow-
ingly lit tributes to the romance of workingpeople, the dignity of the work
ethic and the nobility of adventure and athletic endeavor. But the Lite
ads give us symbols of humiliation, such as comedians Rodney Dangerfield
and malaprop-man Norm Crosby.

And there's Marv Throneberry, who has built a career out of two   47
humiliating seasons as last-place first baseman for the worst team in
baseball. It's marvelous that Miller beer has made him a national ce-
lebrity—anybody's better than Bruce Jenner—but what does his popu-

lar following suggest about our new notion of the heroic figure? Rodney Dangerfield, of course, is famous for "I don't get no respect," but the "lite" beer ethos seems to play upon our feelings that we don't *deserve* respect.

There are also the repeated small moments of defeat for the nonce-lebrity: the natural cereal eater who is constantly crestfallen at how many bowls of his brand it would take to equal the vitamins in Total; the shame-faced jerks ridiculed by their friends for forgetting the Prestone, failing to keep their guard up and stranding them all in the cold; the overachieving, overtime-working eager beavers who are constantly being whispered about because they "need a deodorant that works overtime"; the guy in the Yellow Pages ad who rips the bottom of his pants so embarrassingly that he has to wait in a telephone booth for a tailor to make him fit to appear in public again.

The Humiliation Sell goes hand in hand with what's happening in the "real people" genre of TV commercials. The real people being se-lected to appear in recent ads are, to put it bluntly, a much stupider, uglier breed than those of the late '70s. This is not the cute, stupid and ugly urban look of the late '60s "New York School" of filmic ad realists (the Alka-Seltzer "No Matter What Shape Your Stomach's In" campaign, for instance). No, this is a new kind of subhuman suburban subspecies. It is as if the ad people were saying to the public and the FTC: "You want honesty? You want truth and reality in ads? O.K. We'll rub your nose in realism! We'll show you 'real.' "

Someday, bits of this verité[8] material will be recognized as some of the most accurate journalism of our time. Nothing captures the bleak reality of the suburban teen-ager better than the picture of the "real kid" in a laundry detergent ad, staring vacantly with what looks like angel-dust-blasted eyes at two piles of white linen and grunting, "I'm not into wash, but like, that one's cleaner."

Not only do these real people look vacant, they seem totally cut off from the people closest to them; they exhibit not merely mistaken prod-uct identification responses but an almost pathological failure to know the world around them.

After all these years, how is it possible for a real person in a super-market aisle, approached by a man with a microphone, not to know that he or she ought to pick Stove Top stuffing instead of potatoes? And how could all those mothers in the Proctor & Gamble ads fail to know their sons and husbands prefer clean clothes to dingy? Are ad people trying to rub the noses of real people in their nitty-gritty griminess?

48

49

50

51

52

---

[8]Or *cinéma verité*, movies that present realistic slices of life.

And talk about rubbing it in: have you seen the latest Charmin   53
toilet paper ad with Mr. Whipple? It's a remarkable example of ad people
boasting shamelessly about their manipulative trickery to the very people
they have successfully hoodwinked.

This crown jewel of the epic Charmin campaign (first begun a dec-   54
ade ago, it transformed Charmin from a minor regional brand into the
No. 1 product of its kind) takes place outside Whipple's supermarket. He
has taken down his old Don't Squeeze the Charmin signs and is ushering
in a new era, during which there will be no more silly prohibitions on
squeezing. As he does so, he reflects on the whole "Don't Squeeze" theme
of the campaign and confides at last the true motive behind the gimmick.
"Squeezing the Charmin wasn't so bad after all," Whipple confesses. His
"Don't Squeeze" prissiness was just a trick to provoke and then co-opt
your rebelliousness. Hence, the brand-new Charmin slogan: "The squeezing gets you. The softness keeps you."

In other words, Whipple is virtually coming out and saying, "We   55
tricked you into buying it." You can almost hear the triumphant crowing
of the ad people—you laughed at us for putting on such a ridiculous campaign, but, Mr. and Mrs. America, the joke's on you: you bought it anyway.

Perhaps the final, most insulting touch to top off this trend was the   56
reappearance of ventriloquists' dummies in place of real people in some
campaigns. We have had one ventriloquist's dummy mouthing "ring around
the collar" in a Wisk ad and another saying "butter" in the Parkay mar-
garine spots. Real people are so malleable, so willing to say whatever the
ad people want them to, they might as well be ventriloquists' dummies as
far as the ad people are concerned. This explains, perhaps, the birth of
the dummy trend and the displacement of their flesh-and-blood counter-
parts.

One gets the feeling that these commercials are expressing a certain   57
impatience with the consumer on the part of ad people, perhaps even a
subconscious hostility. Industry has become tired of trying to persuade us,
seduce us, flatter us, indulge our fantasies. The Me Decade is over on
Madison Avenue, and from now on it's no more Mr. Nice Guy. Tough
times are here, even for advertising.

Advertising is going through a period during which precipitous   58
agency-client shifts have raised cries of disloyalty and betrayal in some
quarters. Product "positioning" wars and head-to-head comparison ad
conflicts grow more fierce, even vicious.[9] "ANOTHER ROUND IN COLA

---

[9]In advertising, "positioning" means tailoring a product and its advertising to appeal
to a specific group of consumers in a particular way.

WARS"; "GF SENDS 'MASTER BLEND' INTO BATTLE"—the images in the trade paper headlines are grimly warlike. Even in the sweet little candy world, big battles are erupting: "LIFE-SAVERS, CHICLE READY FOR CANDY ROLL MARKET CLASH" proclaimed one front page battle dispatch in *Ad Age.*

There are signs of even tougher times to come, both on the screen 59 and in the offices of Madison Avenue. The trade papers are reporting with increasing frequency the problems ad agencies are having with slow-paying buyers. Credit problems are cropping up and forcing the creation of a new get-tough policy toward debtors.

It was around the turn of the decade that I first spotted a notice in 60 *Ad Age* for an outfit that said it specialized in "advertising debt-collection problems." Their slogan: "We're gentlemen."

Were they hinting with that line that there are nongentlemen working 61 the suites of Madison Avenue, tough guys who specialize in more forceful, no-nonsense ways of dealing with advertising debt collection? One cannot help but imagine a *Rocky* type in a gray flannel suit visiting a Creative Director and delivering the ultimatum, "Pay up or we'll mangle the syntax of your slogan." Perhaps the only satisfaction we can get from all this is that if ads are getting tougher on life, life is certainly getting tougher on advertising.

About the Essay

1. What does Rosenbaum say is the difference between the ads of the 1970s and the 1980s? In what ways do his examples support his point?

2. Why do you think Rosenbaum devotes so much attention to stockbrokers' ads? Is there any reason why these ads, rather than some others, might be particularly good examples for him?

3. Why would a brokerage house feature bulls in its advertising? What is the meaning of the slogan, "Merrill Lynch is bullish on America"?

4. Why, in Rosenbaum's view, is the Longines commercial a drama of "human paranoia. Anxiety. Loss. Fear of loss"? If you have seen that commercial, how did you respond to it? What in the ad led to your response?

5. What, in your view, is the greatest strength of this essay? What do you regard as its greatest weakness? How do these judgments affect your response to the essay?

6. At the end of the essay, Rosenbaum turns from television ads to the advertising industry in general. What relevance do the last four paragraphs have to the rest of the essay? Can you think of another way to end the piece? Explain.

Explorations

1. The next time that you watch television pay special attention to the commercials. How would you characterize the tone and techniques of today's advertisements? Are they based upon a hard-sell approach? Cite one or two commercials as examples.

2. As Rosenbaum observes, advertisers and their agencies spend a great deal of money to find out how to persuade us to buy what they have to sell. How is this research done? (You will find books and articles on advertising research and television advertising in the college library.)

3. Imagine that you are responsible for preparing the first ad for a new product. Let the product be whatever you wish—a car, a soft drink, disposable paper socks, anything—and let it have whatever features you like. How would you advertise it? Write an ad that will *sell* your product. The ad could be for a newspaper or magazine, or it could be for a 30-second spot on TV. The important thing is to write *persuasive* copy.

ROBIN LAKOFF

One early expression of the contemporary feminist movement was the founding in 1972 of Ms magazine. Its purpose was to raise women's consciousness of their place in society, and its title symbolized that purpose: Ms was a new form of address for women, less prejudicial than Miss or Mrs., which indicate marital status in a way that Mr. does not. Robin Lakoff was an early contributor to Ms. She was born in 1942, earned her undergraduate and graduate degrees at Radcliffe College and Harvard University, and is now a professor of linguistics at the University of California at Berkeley. Her interest in the role of language in women's lives is reflected in her book, *Language and Women's Place* (1975). In "You Are What You Say," first published in Ms in 1974, Lakoff maintains that women are socially handicapped by the very language they are conditioned to speak.

You Are What You Say

"Women's language" is that pleasant (dainty?), euphemistic never-aggressive way of talking we learned as little girls. Cultural bias was built into the language we were allowed to speak, the subjects we were allowed to speak about, and the ways we were spoken of. Having learned our linguistic lesson well, we go out in the world, only to discover that we are communicative cripples—damned if we do, and damned if we don't.

If we refuse to talk "like a lady," we are ridiculed and criticized for being unfeminine. ("She thinks like a man" is, at best, a left-handed compliment.) If we do learn all the fuzzy-headed, unassertive language of our sex, we are ridiculed for being unable to think clearly, unable to take part in a serious discussion, and therefore unfit to hold a position of power.

It doesn't take much of this for a woman to begin feeling she deserves such treatment because of inadequacies in her own intelligence and education.

"Women's language" shows up in all levels of English. For example, women are encouraged and allowed to make far more precise discriminations in naming colors than men do. Words like *mauve, beige, ecru, aquamarine, lavender,* and so on, are unremarkable in a woman's active vocabulary, but largely absent from that of most men. I know of no evidence suggesting that women actually *see* a wider range of colors than men do. It is simply that fine discriminations of this sort are relevant to women's vocabularies, but not to men's; to men, who control most of

313

the interesting affairs of the world, such distinctions are trivial—irrelevant.

In the area of syntax, we find similar gender-related peculiarities of speech. There is one construction, in particular, that women use conversationally far more than men: the tag question. A tag is midway between an outright statement and a yes-no question; it is less assertive than the former, but more confident than the latter.

A *flat statement* indicates confidence in the speaker's knowledge and is fairly certain to be believed; a *question* indicates a lack of knowledge on some point and implies that the gap in the speaker's knowledge can and will be remedied by an answer. For example, if, at a Little League game, I have had my glasses off, I can legitimately ask someone else: "Was the player out at third?" A *tag question*, being intermediate between statement and question, is used when the speaker is stating a claim, but lacks full confidence in the truth of that claim. So if I say, "Is Joan here?" I will probably not be surprised if my respondent answers "no"; but if I say, "Joan is here, isn't she?" instead, chances are I am already biased in favor of a positive answer, wanting only confirmation. I still want a response, but I have enough knowledge (or think I have) to predict that response. A tag question, then, might be thought of as a statement that doesn't demand to be believed by anyone but the speaker, a way of giving leeway, of not forcing the addressee to go along with the views of the speaker.

Another common use of the tag question is in small talk when the speaker is trying to elicit conversation: "Sure is hot here, isn't it?"

But in discussing personal feelings or opinions, only the speaker normally has any way of knowing the correct answer. Sentences such as "I have a headache, don't I?" are clearly ridiculous. But there are other examples where it is the speaker's opinions, rather than perceptions, for which corroboration is sought, as in "The situation in Southeast Asia is terrible, isn't it?"

While there are, of course, other possible interpretations of a sentence like this, one possibility is that the speaker has a particular answer in mind—"yes" or "no"—but is reluctant to state it baldly. This sort of tag question is much more apt to be used by women than by men in conversation. Why is this the case?

The tag question allows a speaker to avoid commitment, and thereby avoid conflict with the addressee. The problem is that, by so doing, speakers may also give the impression of not really being sure of themselves, or looking to the addressee for confirmation of their views. This uncertainty is reinforced in more subliminal ways, too. There is a peculiar sentence-intonation pattern, used almost exclusively by women, as far as

I know, which changes a declarative answer into a question. The effect of using the rising inflection typical of a yes-no question is to imply that the speaker is seeking confirmation, even though the speaker is clearly the only one who has the requisite information, which is why the question was put to her in the first place:

(Q) When will dinner be ready?
(A) Oh . . . around six o'clock . . . ?

It is as though the second speaker were saying, "Six o'clock—if that's okay with you, if you agree." The person being addressed is put in the position of having to provide confirmation. One likely consequence of this sort of speech pattern in a woman is that, often unbeknownst to herself, the speaker builds a reputation of tentativeness, and others will refrain from taking her seriously or trusting her with any real responsibilities, since she "can't make up her mind," and "isn't sure of herself."

Such idiosyncrasies may explain why women's language sounds much more "polite" than men's. It is polite to leave a decision open, not impose your mind, or views, or claims, on anyone else. So a tag question is a kind of polite statement, in that it does not force agreement or belief on the addressee. In the same way a request is a polite command, in that it does not force obedience on the addressee, but rather suggests something be done as a favor to the speaker. A clearly stated order implies a threat of certain consequences if it is not followed, and—even more impolite— implies that the speaker is in a superior position and able to enforce the order. By couching wishes in the form of a request, on the other hand, a speaker implies that if the request is not carried out, only the speaker will suffer; noncompliance cannot harm the addressee. So the decision is really left up to the addressee. The distinction becomes clear in these examples:

Close the door.
Please close the door.
Will you close the door?
Will you please close the door?
Won't you close the door?

In the same ways as words and speech patterns used *by* women undermine her image, those used *to describe* women make matters even worse. Often a word may be used of both men and women (and perhaps of things as well); but when it is applied to women, it assumes a special meaning that, by implication rather than outright assertion, is derogatory to women as a group.

The use of euphemisms has this effect. A euphemism is a substitute   13
for a word that has acquired a bad connotation by association with something unpleasant or embarrassing. But almost as soon as the new word
comes into common usage, it takes on the same old bad connotations,
since feelings about the things or people referred to are not altered by a
change of name; thus new euphemisms must be constantly found.

There is one euphemism for *woman* still very much alive. The word,   14
of course, is *lady*. *Lady* has a masculine counterpart, namely *gentleman*,
occasionally shortened to *gent*. But for some reason *lady* is very much
commoner than *gent(leman)*.

The decision to use *lady* rather than *woman*, or vice versa, may   15
considerably alter the sense of a sentence, as the following examples
show:

(a) A woman (lady) I know is a dean at Berkeley.
(b) A woman (lady) I know makes amazing things out of shoelaces and
    old boxes.

The use of *lady* in (a) imparts a frivolous, or nonserious, tone to   16
the sentence: the matter under discussion is not one of great moment.
Similarly, in (b), using *lady* here would suggest that the speaker considered the "amazing things" not to be serious art, but merely a hobby or
an aberration. If *woman* is used, she might be a serious sculptor. To say
lady doctor is very condescending, since no one every says *gentleman doctor*
or even *man doctor*. For example, mention in the San Francisco *Chronicle*
of January 31, 1972, of Madalyn Murray O'Hair as the *lady atheist* reduces
her position to that of scatterbrained eccentric. Even *woman atheist* is
scarcely defensible: sex is irrelevant to her philosophical position.

Many women argue that, on the other hand, *lady* carries with it   17
overtones recalling the age of chivalry: conferring exalted stature on the
person so referred to. This makes the term seem polite at first, but we
must also remember that these implications are perilous: they suggest that
a "lady" is helpless, and cannot do things by herself.

Lady can also be used to infer frivolousness, as in titles of organi-   18
zations. Those that have a serious purpose (not merely that of enabling
"the ladies" to spend time with one another) cannot use the word *lady*
in their titles, but less serious ones may. Compare the *Ladies' Auxiliary*
of a men's group, or the *Thursday Evening Ladies' Browning and Garden
Society* with *Ladies' Liberation* or *Ladies' Strike for Peace*.

What is curious about this split is that *lady* is in origin a euphe-   19
mism—a substitute that puts a better face on something people find
uncomfortable—for *woman*. What kind of euphemism is it that subtly
denigrates the people to whom it refers? Perhaps *lady* functions as a

euphemism for *woman* because it does not contain the sexual implications present in *woman:* it is not "embarrassing" in that way. If this is so, we may expect that, in the future, *lady* will replace woman as the primary word for the human female, since *woman* will have become too blatantly sexual. That this distinction is already made in some contexts at least is shown in the following examples, where you can try replacing *woman* with *lady:*

> (a) She's only twelve, but she's already a woman.
> (b) After ten years in jail, Harry wanted to find a woman.
> (c) She's my woman, see, so don't mess around with her.

Another common substitute for *woman* is *girl.* One seldom hears a man past the age of adolescence referred to as a boy, save in expressions like "going out with the boys," which are meant to suggest an air of adolescent frivolity and irresponsibility. But women of all ages are "girls": one can have a man—not a boy—Friday, but only a girl—never a woman or even a lady—Friday; women have girlfriends, but men do not—in a nonsexual sense—have boyfriends. It may be that this use of *girl* is euphemistic in the same way the use of *lady* is: in stressing the idea of immaturity, it removes the sexual connotations lurking in *woman*. *Girl* brings to mind irresponsibility: you don't send a girl to do a woman's errand (or even, for that matter, a boy's errand). She is a person who is both too immature and too far from real life to be entrusted with responsibilities or with decisions of any serious or important nature.

Now let's take a pair of words which, in terms of the possible relationships in an earlier society, were simple male-female equivalents, analogous to *bull: cow*. Suppose we find that, for independent reasons, society has changed in such a way that the original meanings now are irrelevant. Yet the words have not been discarded, but have acquired new meanings, metaphorically related to their original senses. But suppose these new metaphorical uses are no longer parallel to each other. By seeing where the parallelism breaks down, we discover something about the different roles played by men and women in this culture. One good example of such a divergence through time is found in the pair, *master: mistress*. Once used with reference to one's power over servants, these words have become unusable today in their original master-servant sense as the relationship has become less prevalent in our society. But the words are still common.

Unless used with reference to animals, *master* now generally refers to a man who has acquired consummate ability in some field, normally nonsexual. But its feminine counterpart cannot be used this way. It is practically restricted to its sexual sense of "paramour." We start out with

20

21

22

two terms, both roughly paraphrasable as "one who has power over another." But the masculine form, once one person is no longer able to have absolute power over another, becomes usable metaphorically in the sense of "having power over *something*." *Master* requires as its object only the name of some activity, something inanimate and abstract. But *mistress* requires a masculine noun in the possessive to precede it. One cannot say: "Rhonda is a mistress." One must be *someone's* mistress. A man is defined by what he does, a woman by her sexuality, that is, in terms of one particular aspect of her relationship to men. It is one thing to be an *old master* like Hans Holbein,[1] and another to be an *old mistress*.

The same is true of the words *spinster* and *bachelor*—gender words   23
for "one who is not married." The resemblance ends with the definition. While *bachelor* is a neuter term, often used as a compliment, *spinster* normally is used pejoratively, with connotations of prissiness, fussiness, and so on. To be a bachelor implies that one has a choice of marrying or not, and this is what makes the idea of a bachelor existence attractive, in the popular literature. He has been pursued and has successfully eluded his pursuers. But a spinster is one who has not been pursued, or at least not seriously. She is old, unwanted goods. The metaphorical connotations of *bachelor* generally suggest sexual freedom; of *spinster*, puritanism or celibacy.

These examples could be multiplied. It is generally considered a   24
faux pas, in society, to congratulate a woman on her engagement, while it is correct to congratulate her fiancé. Why is this? The reason seems to be that it is impolite to remind people of things that may be uncomfortable to them. To congratulate a woman on her engagement is really to say, "Thank goodness! You had a close call!" For the man, on the other hand, there was no such danger. His choosing to marry is viewed as a good thing, but not something essential.

The linguistic double standard holds throughout the life of the   25
relationship. After marriage, bachelor and spinster become man and wife, not man and woman. The woman whose husband dies remains "John's widow;" John, however, is never "Mary's widower."

Finally, why is it that salesclerks and others are so quick to call   26
women customers "dear," "honey," and other terms of endearment they really have no business using? A male customer would never put up with it. But women, like children, are supposed to enjoy these endearments, rather than being offended by them.

In more ways than one, it's time to speak up.   27

---

[1]A German painter of the sixteenth century, famous for his portraits of English nobility at the court of Henry VIII.

About the Essay

1. In her first paragraph Lakoff says, "Cultural bias was built into the language we were allowed to speak, the subjects we were allowed to speak about, and the ways we were spoken of." How does she discuss and illustrate each of these three limitations in her essay? Which one receives the most attention, and which the least?

2. What does Lakoff mean by calling women "communicative cripples"? Does she convince you that this is so? If so, how? If not, why not?

3. What, in Lakoff's view, is the effect of referring to a woman as a *lady*? In what circumstances would you use the word *lady*? How does your use relate to Lakoff's view of this word?

4. Does Lakoff herself use women's language? If so, give some examples. If not, how would you classify the language she does use?

5. Was this essay written primarily to inform or to persuade? What leads you to your conclusion?

Explorations

1. Since 1974, when this essay was first published, many would say that women's legal status and attitudes towards themselves have significantly changed. Do women today still use "women's language"? Give examples from your own experience and observation.

2. What is "men's language"? Are there any disadvantages in talking "like a man"? In not doing so? Give a few representative examples of how men's talk differs from women's.

3. Lakoff says that women's language sounds much more polite than men's. Is politeness necessarily a sign of weakness or uncertainty? Explain. What is it good for? Is it ever desirable or necessary to be impolite? If so, when?

BARBARA LAWRENCE

Barbara Lawrence was born in Hanover, New Hampshire, and graduated from Connecticut College. Before becoming a professor of humanities at the State University of New York at Old Westbury, she worked as an editor at *McCall's, Redbook,* and the *New Yorker.* In the following essay, published in the *New York Times* in 1973, she defines obscenity and explains why she finds the obscene language some people use to be "implicitly sadistic or denigrating to women."

Four-Letter Words Can Hurt You

Why should any words be called obscene? Don't they all describe   1
natural human functions? Am I trying to tell them, my students demand,
that the "strong, earthy, gut-honest"—or, if they are fans of Norman
Mailer, the "rich, liberating, existential"—language they use to describe
sexual activity isn't preferable to "phony-sounding, middle-class words
like 'intercourse' and 'copulate'?" "Cop You Late!" they say with fancy
inflections and gagging grimaces. "Now, what is *that* supposed to mean?"

Well, what is it supposed to mean? And why indeed should one   2
group of words describing human functions and human organs be acceptable in ordinary conversation and another, describing presumably
the same organs and functions, be tabooed—so much so, in fact, that
some of these words still cannot appear in print in many parts of the
English-speaking world?

The argument that these taboos exist only because of "sexual hang-   3
ups" (middle-class, middle-age, feminist), or even that they are a result
of class oppression (the contempt of the Norman conquerors for the
language of their Anglo-Saxon serfs[1]), ignores a much more likely explanation, it seems to me, and that is the sources and functions of the
words themselves.

The best known of the tabooed sexual verbs, for example, comes   4
from the German *ficken*, meaning "to strike"; combined, according to
Partridge's etymological dictionary *Origins*, with the Latin sexual verb
futuere; associated in turn with the Latin *fustis*, "a staff or cudgel"; the
Celtic *buc*, "a point, hence to pierce"; the Irish *bot*, "the male member";

---

[1]In 1066 A.D. the French-speaking duchy of Normandy conquered England and replaced the Anglo-Saxon language with its own. Anglo-Saxon, also known as Old
English, was the native language of the conquered people. Modern English grew out
of a combination of Old French and Old English.

the Latin *battuere,* "to beat"; the Gaelic *batair,* "a cudgeller"; the Early Irish *bualaim,* "I strike"; and so forth. It is one of what etymologists sometimes call "the sadistic group of words for the man's part in copulation."

The brutality of this word, then, and its equivalents ("screw," "bang," etc.), is not an illusion of the middle class or a crotchet of Women's Liberation. In their origins and imagery these words carry undeniably painful, if not sadistic, implications, the object of which is almost always female. Consider, for example, what a "screw" actually does to the wood it penetrates; what a painful, even mutilating, activity this kind of analogy suggests. "Screw" is particularly interesting in this context, since the noun, according to Partridge, comes from words meaning "groove," "nut," "ditch," "breeding sow," "scrofula" and "swelling," while the verb, besides its explicit imagery, has antecedent associations to "write on," "scratch," "scarify," and so forth—a revealing fusion of a mechanical or painful action with an obviously denigrated object.

Not all obscene words, of course, are as implicitly sadistic or denigrating to women as these, but all that I know seem to serve a similar purpose: to reduce the human organism (especially the female organism) and human functions (especially sexual and procreative) to their least organic, most mechanical dimension; to substitute a trivializing or deforming resemblance for the complex human reality of what is being described.

Tabooed male descriptives, when they are not openly denigrating to women, often serve to divorce a male organ or function from any significant interaction with the female. Take the word "testes," for example, suggesting "witnesses" (from the Latin *testis*) to the sexual and procreative strengths of the male organ; and the obscene counterpart of this word, which suggests little more than a mechanical shape. Or compare almost any of the "rich," "liberating" sexual verbs, so fashionable today among male writers, with that much-derided Latin word "copulate" ("to bind or join together") or even that Anglo-Saxon phrase (which seems to have had no trouble surviving the Norman Conquest) "make love."

How arrogantly self-involved the tabooed words seem in comparison to either of the other terms, and how contemptuous of the female partner. Understandably so, of course, if she is only a "skirt," a "broad," a "chick," a "pussycat" or a "piece." If she is, in other words, no more than her skirt, or what her skirt conceals; no more than a breeder, or the broadest part of her; no more than a piece of a human being or a "piece of tail."

The most severely tabooed of all the female descriptives, incidentally, are those like a "piece of tail," which suggest (either explicitly or through antecedents) that there is no significant difference between the female channel through which we are all conceived and born and the anal outlet common to both sexes—a distinction that pornographers have always enjoyed obscuring.

This effort to deny women their biological identity, their individuality, their humanness, is such an important aspect of obscene language that one can only marvel at how seldom, in an era preoccupied with definitions of obscenity, this fact is brought to our attention. One problem, of course, is that many of the people in the best position to do this (critics, teachers, writers) are so reluctant today to admit that they are angered or shocked by obscenity. Bored, maybe, unimpressed, aesthetically displeased, but—no matter how brutal or denigrating the material—never angered, never shocked.

And yet how eloquently angered, how piously shocked many of these same people become if denigrating language is used about any minority group other than women; if the obscenities are racial or ethnic, that is, rather than sexual. Words like "coon," "kike," "spic," "wop," after all, deform identity, deny individuality and humanness in almost exactly the same way that sexual vulgarisms and obscenities do.

No one that I know, least of all my students, would fail to question the values of a society whose literature and entertainment rested heavily on racial or ethnic pejoratives. Are the values of a society whose literature and entertainment rest as heavily as ours on sexual pejoratives any less questionable?

About the Essay

1. Lawrence claims that sexual obscenity degrades women in particular, just as racial or ethnic obscenities degrade certain other groups. In your own words, what is her basic argument? How convincing is her argument? Explain your answer.

2. Why does Lawrence give so much detail in paragraph 4 about the origins of one tabooed word? How did you respond to this paragraph? Why?

3. In Lawrence's view, why are certain sexual words legitimately taboo? What other explanations does she mention and dismiss? What do you think of these other explanations for the taboos placed on certain words?

4. Lawrence begins her essay with two paragraphs of questions. How do these questions serve to introduce her topic? What advantage does she gain from having this introduction in the form of questions?

5. Do you know of any sexually tabooed words that Lawrence does not discuss? Do they confirm her argument, or not?

6. Lawrence concludes her essay with a question. How would you answer her question?

Explorations

1. Do you commonly use sexual obscenities and feel justified in doing so? Or do such words offend you? How would you describe your feelings, and defend your feelings to someone who does not share them?

2. Lawrence observes in paragraph 2 that "some of these words still cannot appear in print in many parts of the English-speaking world"—and books that contain these words, including some dictionaries, are banned from many school libraries and bookstores. What reasons can be given for and against censoring obscene words, or banning publications in which they appear? What is your position? How would you support it?

JOHN R. TRIMBLE

John R. Trimble not only teaches writing, he writes about it too. He was born 1940 in Canada and went to college in the United States, receiving degrees from Princeton and the University of California at Berkeley. Since 1970 he has taught composition, rhetoric, and eighteenth-century English literature at the University of Texas at Austin. His book, *Writing with Style: Conversations on the Art of Writing* (1975), is the source of this selection. For most people, writing is hard work. Trimble shows how we can make our writing fresh, perhaps even memorable—and thereby make our task, as writers and readers, more enjoyable.

The Case for Freshness

The difference between the almost right word and the right word is really a large matter—'tis the difference between the lightning-bug and the lightning.
MARK TWAIN

"There is no deodorant like success," writes Elizabeth Taylor. We read that and we stop in our tracks, smiling with amusement, perhaps even chuckling out loud. What captivates us? The answer is clear: the perfect freshness and whimsical aptness of the image.

Every time we write we have opportunities to delight our reader with arresting phrases like that one. Here's another, from the pen of critic John Aldridge, demolishing a piece of current fiction: "the drama, which develops at about the speed of creeping crab grass. . . ." And yet another, by novelist Kurt Vonnegut: "he had an upperclass Hoosier accent, which sounds like a bandsaw cutting galvanized tin." And one more, this one from T. S. Eliot as he reaches the end of several paragraphs of highly theoretical speculation: "Have I been toiling to weave a labored web of useless ingenuity?" Ah!

Each of these authors instinctively understands one of the chief secrets of artful writing: you must keep the reader in a state of near-perpetual surprise. Not suspense, but *surprise*. It's like baseball. A skilled pitcher mixes up his pitches. He'll throw a fast ball, then a curve, maybe a change-of-pace, then a knuckle ball. Skilled writers work much the same way. They're constantly feeding the reader's appetite for novelty, be it with a fresh idea, a fresh phrase, or a fresh image. And if they're naturally witty, they'll also serve him up the amusingly off-beat—the literary equivalent of a knuckle ball. Woody Allen's brilliant *New Yorker* pieces, now collected in his book *Getting Even,* provide classic examples of the latter.

I think you might find it instructive to listen to a few professionals   4 talk about their art. The agreement among them is remarkable. Here, first, is master storyteller Theodor Seuss Geisel (Dr. Seuss):

> We throw in as many fresh words as we can get away with. Simple, short sentences don't always work. You have to do tricks with pacing, alternate long sentences with short, to keep it alive and vital. Virtually every page is a cliff-hanger—you've got to force them to turn it.

Now, novelist Ford Madox Ford:

> Carefully examined, a good—an interesting—style will be found to consist in a constant succession of tiny, unobservable surprises.

An anonymous critic reviewing another writer's book:

> Best of all his style is laced with little surprises of diction or structure and the small shocks of well-made metaphors.

Science-fiction writer Ray Bradbury:

> Creativity is continual surprise.

To write creatively—to come up with "a constant succession of tiny   5 surprises"—we must *want* to. We all have imaginations; the trick is to use them. And it's in the using of them that writing suddenly becomes a labor of love—an intensely creative, pleasurable activity. Each time we set down a sentence we must ask ourselves: *"Now how can I express this more memorably?"* Occasionally, the mere addition of a choice adjective is all that is needed:

> He wrote with a *surgical* indifference to feelings.—WILLIAM NOLTE

More frequently, an adjustment of the verb—the engine of the sentence—will bring the desired effect:

> A prig is one who delights in demonstrating his superiority on small occasions, and it is precisely when he has a good case that he *rises* to the depths of prigocity.—DWIGHT MACDONALD

(Actually, this last sentence works its magic on us by two surprises, not one—first through the witty substitution of *rises* for *sinks,* and second through the wonderful nonce word *prigocity,* which converts mere priggishness into a complete and seemingly even fussier state of being.) But perhaps the best way, as the earlier examples showed, is through an image—a simile, say, or a metaphor.[1] Both are pictorial analogies which can explain and delight at the same time.

Unfortunately, memorable analogies seldom come unsought. Usu-   6
ally the writer must actively go out beating the bushes of his imagination to scare them up. A good tip is: *Always be thinking in terms of "like."* Such-and-such is like—like what? Challenge your imagination. What *is* it similar to? Do this with every sentence you write. Make it part of your writing habit. Charles Ferguson, in *Say It with Words*, offers another tip that will help you actually cultivate these metaphors and similes. I confess I was initially dubious as to its value, but after trying it (with some modifications) I found it to be wonderfully fruitful. Here is his recommendation:

> Let a person think, and as far as possible speak, for one day a week in the terms common to some particular profession or trade. In his reflections let him pick images from this vocabulary, and let him by this process see how many can be carried over into common speech and writing. On Monday it might be that he would choose his images from cooking; on Tuesday from engineering; on Wednesday from railroading; on Thursday from nuclear science; on Friday from agriculture; on Saturday from sport. And by Sunday he could certainly need a rest, but if he continued the process he might choose his terms from the wealth of language in the field of religion.

Sometimes, when an analogy suggests itself, you can simply tack it   7
right on to the end of your sentence—like this:

> A professor must have a theory, as a dog must have fleas.
> —H. L. MENCKEN

Sometimes you can even frame the entire thought in terms of the   8
comparison: you simply drop the explicit *like* or *as* and develop the analogy metaphorically. Here, for example, is an excerpt from John Mason Brown's review of *Death of a Salesman* which brilliantly illustrates the use—and effect—of a well-chosen metaphor:

> Mr. [Lee J.] Cobb's Willy Loman is irresistibly touching and wonderfully unsparing. He is a great shaggy bison of a man seen at that moment of defeat when he is deserted by the herd and can no longer run with it. Mr. Cobb makes clear the pathetic extent to which the herd has been Willy's life.

---

[1]A simile compares two things using *like* or *as* (e.g., "That apartment is like a zoo"); a metaphor makes the comparison without using *like* or *as* (e.g., "That apartment is a zoo"). [Trimble's note]

The beauty of that metaphor is that it allows us to *see* Cobb's portrayal of Willy Loman. We are given a visual—even an emotional—correlative of the bare abstract idea, and so that idea comes alive to us, and haunts our imagination with its poignance.

You can understand now, I think, why novelist Joseph Conrad could proclaim as his artistic mission: "My task which I am trying to achieve is, by the power of the written word to make you hear, to make you feel—it is, above all, to make you *see*. That—and no more, and it is everything." 9

Occasionally you run across a passage which seems the very quintessence of fresh, visual writing. Such a one, I believe, is the little vignette below, by novelist John Updike, appearing in his *Assorted Prose*. It makes a fitting conclusion to this chapter, for it says it all—by example. Read it twice, please: 10

> We recently had a carpenter build a few things in our house in the country. It's an old house, leaning away from the wind a little; its floors sag gently, like an old mattress. The carpenter turned his back on our tilting walls and took his vertical from a plumb line and his horizontal from a bubble level, and then went to work by the light of these absolutes. Fitting his planks into place took a lot of those long, irregular, oblique cuts with a ripsaw that break an amateur's heart. The bookcase and kitchen counter and cabinet he left behind stand perfectly up-and-down in a cockeyed house. Their rectitude is chastening. For minutes at a stretch, we study them, wondering if perhaps it isn't, after all, the wall that is true and the bookcase that leans. Eventually, we suppose, everything will settle into the comfortably crooked, but it will take years, barring earthquakes, and in the meantime we are annoyed at being made to live with impossible standards.

Note the seeming inevitability of the phrasing, so right is each word. Note, too, the originality of perception, the "small shocks of well-made metaphors," the fine wit (especially the pun on "rectitude"), and the sense of perfect wholeness it achieves. Updike knows how to break an amateur's heart himself.

About the Essay

1. What case does Trimble make for freshness in writing? How convincing do you find his argument? Explain your response.

2. In your own words, summarize Trimble's suggestions for bringing freshness to your writing.

3. Trimble opens his essay with an aphorism by Elizabeth Taylor. Why is it such an apt opening ?

4. Why do you think Trimble includes the remark by T. S. Eliot in paragraph 2? What is surprising about Eliot's comment?

5. Examine Trimble's own writing for examples of freshness. Has he followed his own advice? Explain, giving examples from the essay.

6. What is the pun on "rectitude" in the excerpt quoted in paragraph 10? Did you see it before Trimble pointed it out? If not, did you appreciate it when it was pointed out?

Explorations

1. Trimble suggests that to be creative we need only to use the imaginations all of us have. Do your own experiences bear this out, in your writing or in other things you do?

2. Try Charles Ferguson's technique for thinking of fresh images. Use one of the professions he lists, or choose another, if you prefer, and go through a day fitting images and expressions from that profession to whatever you do. Keep notes of the words and phrases you use. Did Ferguson's advice work?

ROBERT GRAVES

Most people know Robert Graves as the author of *I, Claudius* (1934) and *Claudius the God* (1934), two novels of Roman history that have been made into a popular television series. But Graves thinks of himself primarily as a poet. He was born in London in 1895, and graduated from St. John's College, Oxford, in 1925, his education having been interrupted by military service in World War I. He moved to the Mediterranean island of Majorca in 1929, and has lived there since. His poems, lucid and traditionally crafted but often surprising and stimulating in what they say, are available in *New Collected Poems* (1977). "The Cool Web" is a poem about language itself. In it Graves develops the idea that language insulates us from the full force of experience, and by his use of language he shows as well as tells us what he means.

The Cool Web

Children are dumb to say how hot the day is,
How hot the scent is of the summer rose,
How dreadful the black wastes of evening sky,
How dreadful the tall soldiers drumming by.

But we have speech, to chill the angry day,   5
And speech, to dull the rose's cruel scent.
We spell away the overhanging night,
We spell away the soldiers and the fright.

There's a cool web of language winds us in,
Retreat from too much joy or too much fear: 10
We grow sea-green at last and coldly die
In brininess and volubility.

But if we let our tongues lose self-possession,
Throwing off language and its watery clasp
Before our death, instead of when death comes,   15
Facing the wide glare of the children's day,
Facing the rose, the dark sky and the drums,
We shall go mad no doubt and die that way.

About the Poem

1. What does Graves mean by a "web of language," and by "language and its watery clasp"?

2. What contrast does Graves draw in stanzas 1 and 2? How does he make his contrast?

3. What contrast does Graves draw in stanzas 3 and 4? What does he mean by lines 11 and 12?

4. Why do you think Graves chose as his examples the heat of a summer day, the perfume of a rose, the black sky at night, and a troop of marching soldiers?

5. In Graves's opinion, what difference does language make to the way we live and die? Do you share his view? Explain.

Explorations

1. Write an account of an event—a class meeting, a football game, an afternoon at the beach, a brief conversation. What kinds of things did you find you could capture particularly well in language? What kinds of things evaded your attempts to put them into words, or seemed not even worth attempting? Knowing that you would write about the event, did you find yourself responding to it in an unusual way? What conclusions about the relation between language and experience can you draw from this experiment?

2. People often resort to euphemisms when they speak of unpleasant or unhappy circumstances—for example, they say "pass away" when they mean *die*. When other euphemisms can you think of? What kinds of experience do they refer to, and what is their function? Are euphemisms always a good or a bad thing, or sometimes one and sometimes the other? Discuss.

LEWIS CARROLL

Charles Lutwidge Dodgson was born in 1832 at Daresbury, England, in the country between the great northern cities of Manchester and Liverpool. He attended Oxford University, where he earned honors in classics and mathematics and remained as a teacher of mathematics. Like his father before him, he was ordained a minister in the Church of England, but he rarely preached. He is best known as the author of the two fantastic books he wrote under the pseudonym Lewis Carroll: *Alice's Adventures in Wonderland* (1865) and *Through the Looking-Glass* (1871). Originally written for a little girl Dodgson knew, these books stand among the most popular children's stories ever published. "Jabberwocky," from *Through the Looking Glass*, actually was written in 1855. Dodgson enjoyed creating puzzles and word games, and "Jabberwocky" has something in it of each.

Jabberwocky

'Twas brillig, and the slithy toves
   Did gyre and gimble in the wabe;
All mimsy were the borogoves,
   And the mome raths outgrabe.

"Beware the Jabberwock, my son!   5
   The jaws that bite, the claws that catch!
Beware the Jubjub bird, and shun
   The frumious Bandersnatch!"

He took his vorpal sword in hand;
   Long time the manxome foe he sought—   10
So rested he by the Tumtum tree,
   And stood awhile in thought.

And, as in uffish thought he stood,
   The Jabberwock, with eyes of flame,
Came whiffling through the tulgey wood,   15
   And burbled as it came!

One, two! One, two! And through and through
   The vorpal blade went snicker-snack!
He left it dead, and with its head
   He went galumphing back.   20

"And hast thou slain the Jabberwock?
  Come to my arms, my beamish boy!
O frabjous day! Callooh! Callay!"
  He chortled in his joy.

'Twas brillig, and the slithy toves
  Did gyre and gimble in the wabe;
All mimsy were the borogoves,
  And the mome raths outgrabe.

About the Poem

1. According to *Through the Looking-Glass*, toves are "something like badgers—they're something like lizards—and they're something like corkscrews. . . . also they make their nests under sundials—also they live on cheese." But other unusual words are variations on the familiar: *slithy*, for example, means "lithe and slimy." Find two or three such words and explain their derivations and meaning.

2. Find five words in "Jabberwocky" which you think are pure nonsense, and give your own definitions for them, explaining your definitions as best you can.

3. Since it contains nonsense words, is "Jabberwocky" a nonsense poem? Why or why not? What is it about?

Explorations

1. Write a short narrative using words you have invented for the purpose, some of them pure nonsense and others combining the sounds and meanings of familiar words. Or write a parody of "Jabberwocky" on an experience or subject of your choice—a meal in a fast food restaurant, perhaps, or a last-minute drive to score in a football game.

2. How are readers at all able to understand a nonsense poem like "Jabberwocky"? What would make the poem completely incomprehensible? What does this suggest about other problems of understanding—for example, reading on an unfamiliar subject or trying to follow a conversation in a foreign language?

LEO ROSTEN

Leo Rosten was born in Poland in 1908 and was brought to the United States by his parents in 1910. In 1930, armed with a bachelor's degree from the University of Chicago, he set out to teach English to garment workers at a Chicago night school. Out of these experiences came the stories that appeared first in *The New Yorker* and then in book form as *The Education of* H*Y*M*A*N   K*A*P*L*A*N (1937). Meanwhile he had resumed his studies in political science and sociology at the University of Chicago, earning his Ph.D. in 1937 with a thesis published that year as *The Washington Correspondents.* He published the K*A*P*L*A*N stories and his other early fiction under the name "Leonard Q. Ross," reserving his real name for what he expected to be his serious work. By 1941, however, after two more novels and several years in Hollywood, Rosten acknowledged that he was never going to be a sociologist. As he later said, "The only reason for being a professional writer is that you just can't help it."

Hyman Kaplan is "in his forties, a plump, red-faced gentleman, with wavy blond hair, *two* fountain pens in his outer pocket, and a perpetual smile." From his speech we gather he is a Jewish immigrant from eastern Europe who is trying his best to qualify for naturalization. In this selection, he runs afoul of the English language—and the English language runs afoul of Hyman Kaplan. In this strenuous contest between words and man, it is impossible to know the victor.

Mr. K★A★P★L★A★N, the Comparative, and the Superlative

For two weeks Mr. Parkhill had been delaying the inescapable: Mr. Kaplan, like the other students in the beginners' grade of the American Night Preparatory School for Adults, would have to present a composition for class analysis. All the students had had their turn writing the assignment on the board, a composition of one hundred words, entitled "My Job." Now only Mr. Kaplan's rendition remained.

It would be more accurate to say Mr. K★A★P★L★A★N's rendition of the assignment remained, for even in thinking of that distinguished student, Mr. Parkhill saw the image of his unmistakable signature, in all its red-blue-green glory.[1] The multicolored characters were more than a trademark; they were an assertion of individuality, a symbol of singularity,

---

[1]Mr. Kaplan always prints his name "in large, firm letters with red crayon. Each letter [is] outlined in blue. Between every two letters [is] a star, carefully drawn, in green."

333

a proud expression of Mr. Kaplan's Inner Self. To Mr. Parkhill, the signature took on added meaning because it was associated with the man who had said his youthful ambition had been to become "a physician and sergeant," the Titan who had declined the verb "to fail": "fail, failed, bankropt."

One night, after the two weeks' procrastination, Mr. Parkhill decided to face the worst. "Mr. Kaplan, I think it's your turn to—er—write your composition on the board."

Mr. Kaplan's great, buoyant smile grew more great and more buoyant. "My!" he exclaimed. He rose, looked around at the class proudly as if surveying the blessed who were to witness a linguistic *tour de force*, stumbled over Mrs. Moskowitz's feet with a polite "Vould you be so kindly?" and took his place at the blackboard. There he rejected several pieces of chalk critically, nodded to Mr. Parkhill—it was a nod of distinct reassurance—and then printed in firm letters:

My Job A Cotter In Dress Faktory
Comp. by
H★Y★

"You need not write your name on the board," interrupted Mr. Parkhill quickly. "Er—to save time . . ."

Mr. Kaplan's face expressed astonishment. "Podden me, Mr. Pockheel. But de name is by me *pot* of mine composition."

"Your name is *part* of the composition?" asked Mr. Parkhill in an anxious tone.

"Yassir!" said Mr. Kaplan with dignity. He printed the rest of H★Y★M★A★N K★A★P★L★A★N for all to see and admire. You could tell it was a disappointment for him not to have colored chalk for this performance. In pale white the elegance of his work was dissipated. The name, indeed, seemed unreal, the letters stark, anemic, almost denuded.

His brow wrinkled and perspiring, Mr. Kaplan wrote the saga of A Cotter In Dress Faktory on the board, with much scratching of the chalk and an undertone of sound. Mr. Kaplan repeated each word to himself softly, as if trying to give to its spelling some of the flavor and originality of his pronunciation. The smile on the face of Mr. Kaplan had taken on something beatific and imperishable: it was his first experience at the blackboard; it was his moment of glory. He seemed to be writing more slowly than necessary as if to prolong the ecstasy of his Hour. When he had finished he said "Hau Kay" with distinct regret in his voice, and sat down. Mr. Parkhill observed the composition in all its strange beauty:

My Job A Cotter In Dress Faktory
Comp. by
H★Y★M★A★N K★A★P★L★A★N

Shakspere is saying what fulls man is and I am feeling just the same way
when I am thinking about mine job a cotter in Dress Faktory on 38 st. by
7 av. For why should we slafing in dark place by laktric lights and all kinds
hot for $30 or maybe $36 with overtime, for Boss who is fat and driving
in fency automobil? I ask! Because we are the deprassed workers of world.
And are being exployted. By Bosses. In mine shop is no difference. Oh
how bad is laktric light, oh how is all kinds hot. And when I am telling
Foreman should be better conditions he hollers, Kaplan you redical!!

At this point a glazed look came into Mr. Parkhill's eyes, but he   10
read on.

So I keep still and work by bad light and always hot. But somday will the
workers making Bosses work! And then Kaplan will give to them bad
laktric and positively no windows for the air should come in! So they can
know what it means to slafe! Kaplan will make Foreman a cotter like he
is. And give the most bad dezigns to cot out. Justice.
   Mine job is cotting Dress dezigns.
                    T-H-E   E-N-D

Mr. Parkhill read the amazing document over again. His eyes, glazed   11
but a moment before, were haunted now. It was true: spelling, diction,
sentence structure, punctuation, capitalization, the use of the present
perfect for the present—all true.

"Is planty mistakes, I s'pose," suggested Mr. Kaplan modestly.   12

"Y-yes . . . yes, there are many mistakes."   13

"Dat's because I'm tryink to give *dip ideas*," said Mr. Kaplan with   14
the sigh of those who storm heaven.

Mr. Parkhill girded his mental loins. "Mr. Kaplan—er—your com-   15
position doesn't really meet the assignment. You haven't described your
job, what you *do*, what work is."

"Vell, it's not soch a interastink jop," said Mr. Kaplan.   16

"Your composition is not a simple exposition. It's more of a—well,   17
an *essay* on your *attitude*."

"Oh, fine!" cried Mr. Kaplan with enthusiasm.   18

"No, no," said Mr. Parkhill hastily. "The assignment was *meant* to   19
be a composition. You see, we must begin with simple exercises before
we try—er—more philosophical essays."

Mr. Kaplan nodded with resignation. "So naxt time should be no   20
ideas, like abot Shaksbeer? Should be only *fects*?"

"Y-yes. No ideas, only—er—facts."   21

You could see by Mr. Kaplan's martyred smile that his wings, like   22
those of an eagle, were being clipped.

"And Mr. Kaplan—er—why do you use 'Kaplan' in the body of   23
your composition? Why don't you say '*I* will make the foreman a cutter'
instead of '*Kaplan* will make the foreman a cutter'?"

Mr. Kaplan's response was instantaneous. "I'm so glad you eskink   24
me dis! Ha! I'm usink "Keplen' in de composition for plain and tsimple
rizzon: becawss I didn't vant de reader should tink I am *prajudiced* against
de foreman, so I said it more like abot a strenger: 'Keplen vil make de
foreman a cotter!' "

In the face of this subtle passion for objectivity, Mr. Parkhill was   25
silent. He called for corrections. A forest of hands went up. Miss Mitnick
pointed out errors in spelling, the use of capital letters, punctuation; Mr.
Norman Bloom corrected several more words, rearranged sentences, and
said, "Woikers is exployted with an 'i,' not 'y' as Kaplan makes"; Miss
Caravello changed "fulls" to "fools," and declared herself uncertain as to
the validity of the word "Justice" standing by itself in "da smalla da
sentence"; Mr. Sam Pinsky said he was sure Mr. Kaplan meant "*opprassed*
voikers of de voild, not *deprassed,* aldough dey are deprassed *too,*" to
which Mr. Kaplan replied, "So ve bote got right, no? Don' *chenge* 'deprassed,' only *add* 'opprassed.' "

Then Mr. Parkhill went ahead with his own corrections, changing   26
tenses, substituting prepositions, adding the definite article. Through the
whole barrage Mr. Kaplan kept shaking his head, murmuring "Mine
gootness!" each time a correction was made. But he smiled all the while.
He seemed to be proud of the very number of errors he had made; of the
labor to which the class was being forced in his service; of the fact that
his *ideas,* his creation, could survive so concerted an onslaught. And as
the composition took more respectable form, Mr. Kaplan's smile grew
more expansive.

"Now, class," said Mr. Parkhill, "I want to spend a few minutes   27
explaining something about adjectives. Mr. Kaplan uses the phrase—
er—'most bad.' That's wrong. There is a word for 'most bad.' It is what
we call the superlative form of 'bad.' " Mr. Parkhill explained the use of
the positive, comparative, and superlative forms of the adjective. "Tall,
taller, tallest.' 'Rich, richer, richest.' Is that clear? Well, then, let us try
a few others."

The class took up the game with enthusiasm. Miss Mitnick sub-   28
mitted "dark, darker, darkest"; Mr. Scymzak, "fat, fatter, fattest."

"But there are certain exceptions to this general form," Mr. Parkhill   29
went on. The class, which had long ago learned to respect that gamin,
The Exception to the Rule, nodded solemnly. "For instance, we don't
say 'good, gooder, goodest,' do we?"

"No, sir!" cried Mr. Kaplan impetuously. " 'Good, gooder, good*est?'*   30
Ha! It's to leff!"

"We say that X, for example, is good. Y, however, is—?" Mr.   31
Parkhill arched an eyebrow interrogatively.

"Batter!" said Mr. Kaplan.   32

"Right! And Z is—?"   33

"High-cless!"   34

Mr. Parkhill's eyebrow dropped. "No," he said sadly.   35

"*Not* high-cless?" asked Mr. Kaplan incredulously. For him there 36
was no word more superlative.

"No, Mr. Kaplan, the word is 'best.' And the word 'bad,' of which 37
you tried to use the superlative form . . . It isn't *bad, badder, baddest,*'
It's 'bad' . . . and what's the comparative? Anyone?"

"Worse," volunteered Mr. Bloom.   38

"Correct! And the superlative? Z is the—?"   39

" 'Worse' also?" asked Mr. Bloom hesitantly. It was evident he had 40
never distinguished the fine difference in sound between the comparative
and superlative forms of "bad."

"No, Mr. Bloom. It's not the *same* word, although it—er—sounds   41
a good deal like it. Anyone? Come, come. It isn't hard. X is *bad*, Y is
worse, and Z is the—?"

An embarrassed silence fell upon the class, which, apparently, had 42
been using "worse" for both the comparative and superlative all along.
Miss Mitnick blushed and played with her pencil. Mr. Bloom shrugged,
conscious that he had given his all. Mr. Kaplan stared at the board, his
mouth open, a desperate concentration in his eye.

"*Bad—worse.* What is the word you use when you mean 'most bad'?" 43

"Aha!" cried Mr. Kaplan suddenly. When Mr. Kaplan cried "Aha!"   44
it signified that a great light had fallen on him. "I know! De exect void!
So easy! *Ach!* I should know dat ven I vas wridink! *Bad—voise—*"

"Yes, Mr. Kaplan!" Mr. Parkhill was definitely excited.   45

"Rotten!"   46

Mr. Parkhill's eyes glazed once more, unmistakably. He shook his   47
head dolorously, as if he had suffered a personal hurt. And as he wrote
"W-O-R-S-T" on the blackboard there ran through his head, like a sad
refrain, this latest manifestation of Mr. Kaplan's peculiar genius: "bad—
worse—rotten; bad—worse . . ."

About the Story

1. How would you describe Hyman Kaplan? What is his attitude toward his
English class? How does he respond to the criticism of his composition?

2. How would you describe Mr. Parkhill?

3. What does Kaplan mean by "a physician and sergeant"? By "why should
we slafing in dark place by laktric lights and all kinds hot"?

4. Parkhill says that Kaplan's composition does not satisfy the assignment. Is Parkhill right? Does it matter, given the purpose of the course? Explain.

5. What is the author's attitude toward his characters and their situation? How do you know? Give some examples.

6. What did you find funniest about the story? Were there any parts or aspects of the story that Rosten obviously meant to be humorous that didn't amuse you? If so, what were they?

Explorations

1. How do you think Kaplan's composition read when his classmates and Mr. Parkhill were through with it? Write your own, corrected version. In what way is your version better? In what way is it not as good? What does this tell you about the peculiarities of language?

2. Until the mid-1920s, the United States accepted hundreds of thousands of immigrants every year from most parts of the world. Then Congress passed new laws restricting immigration to 150,000 people a year and setting quotas on where they could come from. Why? Who now may most freely immigrate and who is most restricted? What does this reveal about American social attitudes?

5 The Quality of Life

Men come together in cities in order to live; they remain together in order to live the good life.
ARISTOTLE

At a dinner party one should eat wisely but not too well, and talk well but not too wisely.
W. SOMERSET MAUGHAM

Fashion is that by which the fantastic becomes for a moment universal.
OSCAR WILDE

The art of medicine consists of amusing the patient while nature cures the disease.
VOLTAIRE

Work is a necessity for man. Man invented the alarm-clock.
PABLO PICASSO

A LMOST two hundred years ago, appalled by the dehumanizing effects of the Industrial Revolution on his countrymen, the English poet William Wordsworth wrote:

> *The world is too much with us; late and soon,*
> *Getting and spending, we lay waste our powers:*
> *Little we see in Nature that is ours;*
> *We have given our hearts away, a sordid boon!*

Not long afterward, Henry David Thoreau saw the same thing happening in America and retreated from his Concord home to a rough cabin at Walden Pond to begin his now famous experiment in living. As he said, "I went to the woods because I wished to live deliberately, to front only the essential facts of life, and see if I could not learn what it had to teach, and not, when I came to die, discover that I had not lived." Both men were protesting against what they saw as mediocrity in the quality of life—interestingly, at the very time when improved means of production and transportation were beginning to raise the economic standard for many people.

Today as then, ours is a world that is preoccupied with the

341

standard of living, yet gives little consideration to the actual quality of life. We use convenience foods to get us in and out of the kitchen faster but at the expense of both taste and nutrition. We place a high premium on rapid travel with little thought to how we can make valuable use of the time we save. We buy automobiles to get to work and then justify going to work as necessary to pay for our automobiles. We wear fashionable clothes not because they are comfortable and practical—often they are neither—but to show that we are up to date and can afford to be. Many of us go through life like this with little thought about what we are doing, and without questioning why we are doing it.

To ask such questions we need not retreat from civilization as Thoreau did, roughing it in the woods and growing our own food. Thoreau challenges us not to imitate his life but to examine our own, to discover for ourselves what we really need and what we can do without, and then to establish ways of life that give us the deepest satisfaction.

The selections that follow offer ways of beginning that examination. They are all concerned with the basic necessities of life—shelter, clothing, food, health, and work for our hands and minds. Each one, while exploring its particular subject, raises important questions about the ways we live.

HENRY DAVID THOREAU

In 1845, at the age of twenty-eight, Henry David Thoreau built a cabin in the woods near Walden Pond and moved in. He wanted to live alone with nature and hoped to simplify his life to be free of materialistic concerns. He stayed there for more than two years, an experience he later described in his greatest literary work, *Walden, or Life in the Woods* (1854).

Thoreau was born in 1817 in Concord, Massachusetts. After graduating from Harvard College, he worked as a schoolteacher, a house-painter, and a handyman—the latter for his mentor and friend, Ralph Waldo Emerson. Thoreau was always an activist, once going to jail rather than pay a poll tax to a government that made war with Mexico and supported slavery. This act of civil disobedience in protest of actions that he considered unjust is the subject of his essay "Civil Disobedience" (1849), which later inspired both Mahatma Gandhi and Martin Luther King, Jr., in their nonviolent protests. Thoreau died in 1862.

In the following selection from *Walden*, Thoreau begins by explaining his purpose in taking up a primitive life in the woods, but quickly turns to criticism of the way of life he left behind.

Simplicity

I went to the woods because I wished to live deliberately, to front only the essential facts of life, and see if I could not learn what it had to teach, and not, when I came to die, discover that I had not lived. I did not wish to live what was not life, living is so dear; nor did I wish to practice resignation, unless it was quite necessary. I wanted to live deep and suck out all the marrow of life, to live so sturdily and Spartan-like as to put to rout all that was not life, to cut a broad swath and shave close, to drive life into a corner, and reduce it to its lowest terms, and, if it proved to be mean, why then to get the whole and genuine meanness of it, and publish its meanness to the world; or if it were sublime, to know it by experience, and be able to give a true account of it in my next excursion. For most men, it appears to me, are in a strange uncertainty about it, whether it is of the devil or of God, and have *somewhat hastily* concluded that it is the chief end of man here to "glorify God and enjoy him forever."

Still we live meanly, like ants; though the fable tells us that we were long ago changed into men; like pygmies we fight with cranes;[1] it

---

[1] In an ancient Greek fable, the god Zeus transformed ants into men to populate a kingdom. In Homer's *Iliad*, he compares the Trojan army with cranes fighting against pygmies.

343

is error upon error, and clout upon clout, and our best virtue has for its occasion a superfluous and evitable wretchedness. Our life is frittered away by detail. An honest man has hardly need to count more than his ten fingers, or in extreme cases he may add his ten toes, and lump the rest. Simplicity, simplicity, simplicity! I say, let your affairs be as two or three, and not a hundred or a thousand; instead of a million count half a dozen, and keep your accounts on your thumb nail. In the midst of this chopping sea of civilized life, such are the clouds and storms and quicksands and thousand-and-one items to be allowed for, that a man has to live, if he would not founder and go to the bottom and not make his port at all, by dead reckoning, and he must be a great calculator indeed who succeeds. Simplify, simplify. Instead of three meals a day, if it be necessary eat but one; instead of a hundred dishes, five; and reduce other things in proportion. Our life is like a German Confederacy,[2] made up of petty states, with its boundary forever fluctuating, so that even a German cannot tell you how it is bounded at any moment. The nation itself, with all its so-called internal improvements, which, by the way are all external and superficial, is just such an unwieldy and overgrown establishment, cluttered with furniture and tripped up by its own traps, ruined by luxury and heedless expense, by want of calculation and a worthy aim, as the million households in the land; and the only cure for it as for them is in a rigid economy, a stern and more than Spartan simplicity of life and elevation of purpose. It lives too fast. Men think that it is essential that the *Nation* have commerce, and export ice, and talk through a telegraph, and ride thirty miles an hour, without a doubt, whether *they* do or not; but whether we should live like baboons or like men, is a little uncertain. If we do not get out sleepers, and forge rails, and devote days and nights to the work, but go to tinkering upon our *lives* to improve *them,* who will build railroads? And if railroads are not built, how shall we get to heaven in season? But if we stay at home and mind our business, who will want railroads? We do not ride on the railroad; it rides upon us. Did you ever think what those sleepers are that underlie the railroad? Each one is a man, an Irishman, or a Yankee man. The rails are laid on them, and they are covered with sand, and the cars run smoothly over them. They are sound sleepers, I assure you. And every few years a new lot is laid down and run over; so that, if some have the pleasure of riding on a rail, others have the misfortune to be ridden upon. And when they run over a man that is walking in his sleep, a supernumerary sleeper in the wrong position, and wake him up, they suddenly stop the cars, and make a hue and cry about it, as if this were

---

[2]At the time Germany consisted of more than a dozen independent kingdoms.

an exception. I am glad to know that it takes a gang of men for every five miles to keep the sleepers down and level in their beds as it is, for this is a sign that they may sometime get up again.

Why should we live with such hurry and waste of life? We are determined to be starved before we are hungry. Men say that a stitch in time saves nine, and so they take a thousand stitches to-day to save nine to-morrow. As for *work*, we haven't any of any consequence. We have the Saint Vitus' dance, and cannot possibly keep our heads still. If I should only give a few pulls at the parish bell-rope, as for a fire, that is, without setting the bell,[3] there is hardly a man on his farm in the outskirts of Concord, notwithstanding that press of engagements which was his excuse so many times this morning, nor a boy, nor a woman, I might almost say, but would forsake all and follow that sound, not mainly to save property from the flames, but, if we will confess the truth, much more to see it burn, since burn it must, and we, be it known, did not set it on fire,—or to see it put out, and have a hand in it, if that is done as handsomely; yes, even if it were the parish church itself. Hardly a man takes a half hour's nap after dinner, but when he wakes he holds up his head and asks, "What's the news?" as if the rest of mankind had stood his sentinels. Some give directions to be waked every half hour, doubtless for no other purpose; and then, to pay for it, they tell what they have dreamed. After a night's sleep the news is as indispensable as the breakfast. "Pray tell me anything new that has happened to a man anywhere on this globe,"—and he reads it over his coffee and rolls, that a man has had his eyes gouged out this morning on the Wachito River;[4] never dreaming the while that he lives in the dark unfathomed mammoth cave of this world, and has but the rudiment of an eye himself.

For my part, I could easily do without the post-office. I think that there are very few important communications made through it. To speak critically, I never received more than one or two letters in my life—I wrote this some years ago—that were worth the postage. The penny-post is, commonly, an institution through which you seriously offer a man that penny for his thoughts which is so often safely offered in jest. And I am sure that I never read any memorable news in a newspaper. If we read of one man robbed, or murdered, or killed by accident, or one house burned, or one vessel wrecked, or one steamboat blown up, or one cow run over on the Western Railroad, or one mad dog killed, or one lot of grasshoppers in the winter,—we never need read of another. One is enough. If you are acquainted with the principle, what do you care for

3

4

---

[3]Without standing the bell on its head.

[4]A river in southwest Arkansas.

a myriad instances and applications? To a philosopher all *news*, as it is called, is gossip, and they who edit and read it are old women over their tea. Yet not a few are greedy after this gossip. There was such a rush, as I hear, the other day at one of the offices to learn the foreign news by the last arrival, that several large squares of plate glass belonging to the establishment were broken by the pressure,—news which I seriously think a ready wit might write a twelvemonth or twelve years beforehand with sufficient accuracy. As for Spain, for instance, if you know how to throw in Don Carlos and the Infanta, and Don Pedro and Seville and Granada, from time to time in the right proportions,—they may have changed the names a little since I saw the papers,—and serve up a bull-fight when other entertainments fail, it will be true to the letter, and give us as good an idea of the exact state or ruin of things in Spain as the most succinct and lucid reports under this head in the newspapers: and as for England, almost the last significant scrap of news from that quarter was the revolution of 1649;[5] and if you have learned the history of her crops for an average year, you never need attend to that thing again, unless your speculations are of a merely pecuniary character. If one may judge who rarely looks into the newspapers, nothing new does ever happen in foreign parts, a French revolution not excepted.[6]

What news! how much more important to know what that is which   5
was never old! "Kieou-he-yu (great dignitary of the state of Wei) sent a man to Khoung-tseu to know his news. Khoung-tseu caused the messenger to be seated near him, and questioned him in these terms: What is your master doing? The messenger answered with respect: My master desires to diminish the number of his faults, but he cannot come to the end of them. The messenger being gone, the philosopher remarked: What a worthy messenger! What a worthy messenger!"[7] The preacher, instead of vexing the ears of drowsy farmers on their day of rest at the end of the week,—for Sunday is the fit conclusion of an ill-spent week, and not the fresh and brave beginning of a new one,—with this one other draggle-tail of a sermon, should shout with thundering voice,—"Pause! Avast! Why so seeming fast, but deadly slow?"

Shams and delusions are esteemed for soundest truths, while reality   6
is fabulous. If men would steadily observe realities only, and not allow themselves to be deluded, life, to compare it with such things as we

---

[5]When King Charles I was deposed and beheaded by a Puritan army commanded by Oliver Cromwell.

[6]There had been three, in 1789, 1830, and 1848, the latter while Thoreau was writing *Walden*.

[7]Quoted from Confucius, *Analects*, XIV.

know, would be like a fairy tale and the Arabian Nights' Entertainments.[8] If we respected only what is inevitable and has a right to be, music and poetry would resound along the streets. When we are unhurried and wise, we perceive that only great and worthy things have any permanent and absolute existence,—that petty fears and petty pleasures are but the shadow of the reality. This is always exhilarating and sublime. By closing the eyes and slumbering, and consenting to be deceived by shows, men establish and confirm their daily life of routine and habit everywhere, which still is built on purely illusory foundations. Children, who play life, discern its true law and relations more clearly than men, who fail to live it worthily, but who think that they are wiser by experience, that is, by failure. I have read in a Hindoo book, that "there was a king's son, who, being expelled in infancy from his native city, was brought up by a forester, and, growing up to maturity in that state, imagined himself to belong to the barbarous race with which he lived. One of his father's ministers having discovered him, revealed to him what he was, and the misconception of his character was removed, and he knew himself to be a prince. So soul," continues the Hindoo philosopher, "from the circumstances in which it is placed, mistakes its own character, until the truth is revealed to it by some holy teacher, and then it knows itself to be *Brahme.*"[9] I perceive that we inhabitants of New England live this mean life that we do because our vision does not penetrate the surface of things. We think that that *is* which *appears* to be. If a man should walk through this town and see only the reality, where, think you, would the "Mill-dam"[10] go to? If he should give us an account of the realities he beheld there, we should not recognize the place in his description. Look at a meeting-house, or a courthouse, or a jail, or a shop, or a dwelling-house, and say what that thing really is before a true gaze, and they would all go to pieces in your account of them. Men esteem truth remote, in the outskirts of the system, behind the farthest star, before Adam and after the last man. In eternity there is indeed something true and sublime. But all these times and places and occasions are now and here. God himself culminates in the present moment, and will never be more divine in the lapse of all the ages. And we are enabled to apprehend at all what is sublime and noble only by the perpetual instilling and drenching of the reality that surrounds us. The universe constantly and obediently

---

[8]The *Thousand and One Nights,* a collection of fabulous stories telling of such as Sindbad the Sailor and Ali Baba and the forty thieves.

[9]Brahma is the supreme creator in Hinduism. It can also refer to the individual soul identified with the supreme creator.

[10]The main street in Concord.

answers to our conceptions; whether we travel fast or slow, the track is laid for us. Let us spend our lives in conceiving then. The poet or the artist never yet had so fair and noble a design but some of his posterity at least could accomplish it.

Let us spend one day as deliberately as Nature, and not be thrown off the track by every nutshell and mosquito's wing that falls on the rails. Let us rise early and fast, or break fast, gently and without perturbation; let company come and let company go, let the bells ring and the children cry,—determined to make a day of it. Why should we knock under and go with the stream? Let us not be upset and overwhelmed in that terrible rapid and whirlpool called a dinner, situated in the meridian shallows. Weather this danger and you are safe, for the rest of the way is down hill. With unrelaxed nerves, with morning vigor, sail by it, looking another way, tied to the mast like Ulysses.[11] If the engine whistles, let it whistle till it is hoarse for its pains. If the bell rings, why should we run? We will consider what kind of music they are like. Let us settle ourselves, and work and wedge our feet downward through the mud and slush of opinion, and prejudice, and tradition, and delusion, and appearance, that alluvion which covers the globe, through Paris and London, through New York and Boston and Concord, through church and state, through poetry and philosophy and religion, till we come to a hard bottom and rocks in place, which we can call *reality*, and say, This is, and no mistake; and then begin, having a *point d'appui*,[12] below freshet and frost and fire, a place where you might found a wall or a state, or set a lamppost safely, or perhaps a gauge, not a Nilometer,[13] but a Realometer, that future ages might know how deep a freshet of shams and appearances had gathered from time to time. If you stand right fronting and face to face to a fact, you will see the sun glimmer on both its surfaces, as if it were a cimeter,[14] and feel its sweet edge dividing you through the heart and marrow, and so you will happily conclude your mortal career. Be it life or death, we crave only reality. If we are really dying, let us hear the rattle in our throats and feel cold in the extremities; if we are alive, let us go about our business.

7

---

[11]Thoreau compares dinner with the Sirens, whose ravishing song was said in ancient times to have lured sailors to their deaths. In Homer's *Odyssey*, the hero Odysseus, or in Latin Ulysses, wanted to hear the Sirens, but to prevent destruction of his vessel had himself tied to the mast of his ship.

[12]*Point d'appui*, French meaning literally "point of support," used often as a military expression meaning "base" or "foundation."

[13]A gauge used in ancient Egypt for measuring the depth of the Nile.

[14]A scimitar, a curved sword used in the Middle East.

Time is but the stream I go a-fishing in. I drink at it; but while I drink I see the sandy bottom and detect how shallow it is. Its thin current slides away, but eternity remains. I would drink deeper; fish in the sky, whose bottom is pebbly with stars. I cannot count one. I know not the first letter of the alphabet. I have always been regretting that I was not as wise as the day I was born. The intellect is a cleaver; it discerns and rifts its way into the secret of things. I do not wish to be any more busy with my hands than is necessary. My head is hands and feet. I feel all my best faculties concentrated in it. My instinct tells me that my head is an organ for burrowing, as some creatures use their snout and fore-paws, and with it I would mine and burrow my way through these hills. I think that the richest vein is somewhere hereabouts; so by the divining rod and thin rising vapors I judge; and here I will begin to mine.

About the Essay

1. What point, above all, does Thoreau want to make in this selection? How does he make his point?

2. What is Thoreau attacking in paragraph 2? What does he mean when he says "Our life is frittered away by detail"? What does his "simplicity" amount to? Why does he criticize the railroad?

3. In the paragraph 3, Thoreau says of work, "We haven't any of any consequence." What do you think he means by this? How does he support his statement?

4. Why does Thoreau feel he can do without the post office and without news? What point is he making? Do you think his view is a practical one for other people? Why or why not?

5. Thoreau quotes from Confucius and refers to Hindu scriptures. What do these materials add to his discussion? How do they affect your response to the essay?

6. Thoreau changes his tone and approach to his subject toward the end of the essay. Where does that change occur? How would you describe the change? Are you satisfied with the conclusion of "Simplicity"? Why or why not?

Explorations

1. Many people who read *Walden* get a strong sense of the kind of person Thoreau was. How would you characterize him? Imagine having a conversation with him. What would you talk about, and where would you agree—or disagree?

2. Thoreau says he wanted to live according to "the essential facts of life, and see if I could not learn what it had to teach, and not, when I came to die, discover that I had not lived." If that were your objective, how might you set about it? Where would you live, and how? What would you consider necessary, and what could you do without? Is such a life attainable, even if only for two years?

3. From time to time people have formed communities designed to "front only the essential facts of life." Indeed, one of them, Brook Farm, was founded near Boston in 1841 and had among its members the writers Nathaniel Hawthorne and Charles A. Dana. As a result of a fire and financial losses, it dissolved in 1847. More recently, many different kinds of communes were set up during the 1960s and 1970s by people "dropping out" of urban, industrial America. From your own research into Brook Farm or another such community, what were its successes and failures?

ADA LOUISE HUXTABLE

The last decade has seen the closing of many, perhaps most, five-and-ten-cent stores in America. To some, the passing of the five-and-ten kindles pure and simple nostalgia. To Ada Louise Huxtable, however, it symbolizes the end of an era of thrift and simple pleasures. Huxtable is an architectural historian and critic for the *New York Times*. She was born in New York City and studied at Hunter College and New York University. From 1946 to 1950 she was Assistant Curator of Architecture and Design at the Museum of Modern Art. Her books include *Classic New York* (1964) and *Kicked a Building Lately?* (1976). "Remnants of an Era: Two Silent Stores" appeared in 1980 in the *New York Times*. In it she chronicles the rise and decline of the five-and-ten, and discusses the significance of both.

Remnants of an Era: Two Silent Stores

It was not the marketing of opulence. It catered to anything except 1
expensive excess. It was an idea based on frugality and the most for the least. It was, in fact, a matter of nickels and dimes; it was that great American institution, the five-and-ten.

In theory and in folklore, it is still going strong. F.W. Woolworth 2
is celebrating its 100th anniversary this year. A number of Woolworth's competitors and copiers are around in one form or another. Kress's and Kresge's, Newberry's, Lamston's and Grant's, have engaged in the battle of bargains and novelties over the years as prices rose from a dime to a dollar.

But "The Great Five and Ten Cent Store," Woolworth's first suc- 3
cessful foray into the formula in Lancaster, Pa., in 1878, is a set of faded pictures now, and the "Woolworth idea" of selling an immense variety of goods at a fixed, low price is a thing of the past. The other essential part of the formula—arranging counterloads of merchandise so that customers could see and handle every item—has become a casualty of security and the packaging industry.

Corporate and marketing developments and changes in production, 4
distribution and life styles have turned the small-goods variety store into the discount supermarket that sells everything from brand-name clothing to major appliances.

The price tag can run in the hundreds and the tender is plastic 5
credit. But this is more than a revolution in selling styles. The rise and fall of the five-and-ten involves many themes: fashions in merchandising and morality, the development of trends and tastes, and a new scale and

351

set of standards for retail operations that have turned those who practiced a thrifty Yankee and pioneer ethic into a profligate consumer society.

To students of American business and culture, this is an instructive 6 chapter of socio-economic history. But for many of us the phasing out of the five-and-ten is a matter of pure, bathetic nostalgia. The mortal illness was not just creeping inflation. The death of the dime store is an all-too-appropriate story for our times.

The flagship stores of two of the largest competing chains—Wool- 7 worth and Kress—now stand empty at opposite corners of 39th Street on Fifth Avenue. Kress's was built in the popular Art Deco style as the crowning glory of "dimedom" in 1935. Woolworth's followed with an equally impressive Fifth Avenue store within a few years. The mode has been called Depression Modern by Martin Greif, and the Skyscraper Style by Cervin Robinson and Rosemarie Haag Bletter, in books of the same name that celebrate the architecture of the period. As Woolworth Modern, it continued to be the rather "retardataire" style of choice for the chain through the 1950's.[1]

The Kress Building closed in September 1977, and Woolworth's 8 followed last June. The two silent stores symbolized the end of an era. For millions of Americans, the climax and greatest joy of every downtown outing when they were young was the trip to the five-and-ten. For the boys it was the lure of unlimited gadgets and hardware counters that displayed every size and shape of shining hooks, nails and screws. For girls it was the clandestinely purchased Tangee lipstick and the dazzling array of forbidden costume jewelry.

In the fall, the back-to-school counter supplied the marbleized card- 9 board notebooks and cedar-scented pencils, the snap-ringed loose leaf binders and fresh sheaves of paper that signaled the season's start. There were after-school banana splits and tricolored ice cream sandwiches en-closed in square cookie covers with the flavor of pasteboard—a taste that became addictive.

The stores smelled of sweet candies and cosmetics and burned toast 10 from the luncheonette counters along the wall; they echoed to the sound of feet on hardwood floors, the ringing of old-fashioned cash registers and the clanging of bells for change.

And there was the absolute saturation of the eye with every con- 11 ceivable knickknack, arranged with a geometric precision based on the sales and esthetic theory that more is more. Show windows composed totally of fluted handkerchiefs, or enamel pots, or bars of soap, were an underappreciated art form.

---

[1]Outdated.

Rows of snap fasteners on cards and stacks of cups and saucers were 12
joined by new colored plastics of infinite uses and rampant kitsch that
are now collectors' items. No one had yet invented targeted promotions
or point-of-sale displays.[2] There was a simple cornucopia of counters.
"What the bazaar was to the Middle East," the anniversary literature tells
us, "Woolworth's was to America."

"Nothing over 10 cents" was the gilt-lettered message suspended 13
from the ceiling in early Woolworth stores and emblazoned in gold on
the carmine-red signs outside. The limit was held even as competitors
raised the ante in the search for more varied goods, to five, 10 and 15
cents, and then to five, 10 and 25 cents, and finally to a dollar top.

By 1919, when Frank Woolworth died, 600,000 American babies 14
were wearing his 10-cent gold-filled rings. European and Japanese imports
had become common. The Kress stores, with the declared aim of making
life better for everyone, introduced reproductions of art masterpieces for
a quarter, and "realistic" artificial flowers for a dime.

In 1932, Woolworth finally lifted its 10-cent limit to 20 cents, and 15
in 1935 all arbitrary price levels were removed. Dollar hats and 70-cent
turkey dinners were a far cry from the five-cent "Yankee notions" of the
first stores—the safety pins, thimbles, combs, button hooks, collar buttons, boot straps, pencils, baby bibs, harmonicas and napkins that were
the Yankee peddler's stock in trade.

Small change built both fortunes and monuments. In 1913, the 16
newly completed Woolworth Building in Lower Manhattan, the world's
tallest skyscraper at the time, was flooded with light from a switch in the
White House, and Cass Gilbert's Gothic extravaganza was immediately
dubbed the "cathedral of commerce."

The elaborate terra cotta traceries, the facade sculpture and glit- 17
tering mosaics, are said to have been paid for in cash by Frank Woolworth's nickels and dimes. The founder sat in an office that was a replica
of the Empire Room of Napoleon's palace at Compiègne, except that
marble was substituted for wood.[3]

Samuel H. Kress's Fifth Avenue store of 1935, by the architect 18
Edward F. Sibbert, featured granite, stainless steel, bronze and baked
enamel, and deco details that look like the tops of palm trees in the
sunrise. Critics were less enthusiastic about its style than its functional
plan, which included warehousing on the premises and fixed outlines on

---

[2]Ad campaigns directed at particular types of consumers and advertising displays, such
as posters or product racks, positioned at the place where consumers make their purchases.

[3]The Empire Room was a huge room designed in imitation of ancient Roman style.

the floor for ladders and other movable equipment. This concern with
the saving of time and energy harked back to Samuel Kress's Pennsylvania
Dutch belief in "the essential rightness of conservative frugality," which
also included the removal and saving of nails from crates.

It was hard work and hard bargains all the way. In the early years,   19
packages were wrapped in newspaper, and "chestnuts" and "stickers," or
items that did not move, were mixed with "plums" and "corkers": that
produced a good profit. The dimestore men could squeeze a buffalo nickel
until it bellowed. They knew, of course, what a nickel was worth in
those days.

The demise of the founders and the growth of the corporate struc-   20
ture ushered in decades of change. Woolworth acquired other companies
and expanded into fashion and foods; its Woolco Division entered the
discounting field. Kress was absorbed by the fashion conglomerate, Ge-
nesco, in the 1960's, and the S.S. Kresge Company was changed to the
K-Mart Corporation in 1977, with K-Marts accounting for 94.5 percent
of the company's domestic sales.

What had occurred was a total revolution in the American way of   21
living and buying. Stores grew to warehouse size, and aisles of goods
became acres of products. With the new mass merchandising of mass-
produced goods, locations shifted from Main Street to shopping centers.
Buying in quantity no longer meant saving up and splurging in one
glorious nickel and dime bash, or going in with $2 and coming out with
10 presents, from celluloid animals to unbelievable bric-a-brac.

Even in the remaining variety stores, costly plastic packs of multiple   22
items replaced the fun—and the economy—of being able to pick out
exactly what was wanted or needed. Sales policy and its handmaidens,
packaging and promotion, have a lot to answer for in the inflationary
spiral.

But not only the Yankee notions went the way of the 10-cent   23
bargain; thrift, frugality, and the time-honored concept of buying for
cash are equally obsolete. Overreaching and overpaying have become the
two sides of the coin that has no resemblance to small change. If I am
ever radicalized, it will be done by those advertisements for $150 shoes
and $90 jeans and $300 sets of cooking utensils with French names and
the implicit message that without them I might as well drop dead.

Kress sold a fine drip coffee pot for 50 cents, and I have gone to   24
wonderful parties in a pair of Woolworth "canary diamond" chandelier
earrings that are as close as I will ever get to the real Cartier thing. In
the dim light of a cocktail lounge dollar hats looked glamorous with a
10-cent veil. You can't buy happiness, of course, but there was a time
when you could get pretty close for a nickel or a dime.

About the Essay

1. According to Huxtable, what were the two essential features of the five-and-ten-cent store? What did these features give way to, and why?

2. What do you think Huxtable means when she says that "The death of the dime store is an all-too-appropriate story for our times"? In what way might students of American business and culture find the passing of the five-and-ten instructive?

3. What does Huxtable's essay gain from her description of the architectural styles of the Woolworth Building and Kress's Fifth Avenue store?

4. From Huxtable's brief references, what sort of men would you say Frank Woolworth and Samuel H. Kress may have been?

5. What is Huxtable's tone when she writes about the old five-and-tens? What does her tone tell you about her attitude?

6. What is the significance of Huxtable's closing sentence? Has she prepared for that conclusion earlier in the essay? Explain your answer.

Explorations

1. What is your favorite store? Try, simply by describing it and what you have bought there, to express your attitude toward it. Or, if you prefer, describe your least favorite store so as to make it clear why you can't stand the place.

2. Has any other American institution changed since your childhood so that it is no longer the way it used to be, or the way you remember it? What does the change represent? How do you feel about that change?

JOYCE MAYNARD

Joyce Maynard became a professional writer at an early age, publishing stories in *Seventeen* and *Women's Day* before she had graduated from high school. She was a sophomore at Yale when her first book appeared—*Looking Back: A Chronicle of Growing Up Old in the Sixties* (1973). Maynard was born in Durham, New Hampshire, in 1953, and now lives in New York City. In 1981 she published her first novel, *Baby Love*.

Some of us delight in shopping, especially shopping for clothes, but not Joyce Maynard. In "Clothes Anxiety," which first appeared in the weekly "Hers" column of the *New York Times*, she describes what happened when she tried, for once, to buy some fashionable clothes.

Clothes Anxiety

I love clothes. But sometimes I wish I had the kind of occupation that requires a uniform. As it is, I can spend 45 minutes getting dressed, change outfits a dozen times, and see myself reflected in a store window half an hour later, looking a mess. I have tried so hard to master this casual, thrown-together look I see in magazines. But my mascara smudges. My curls never last. Fashion eludes me.

One of my daughter's baby sitters solves the clothes problem by never getting out of her bathrobe. It's a nice bathrobe—there's nothing slovenly about this woman—and she always looks very neat, very attractive. I would take my hat off to her, if I had one.

But I have not mastered the art of accessorizing. I am still looking for the perfect pair of black pants, still making visits to the various branch stores of The Gap in search of the right blue jeans. My sister, who is an editor at a fashion magazine, and very fashionable herself, persists in giving me beautiful scarfs for my birthday every year. I put them in my drawer, thinking that soon I will get it all together and become the sort of person who wears beautiful, interestingly-knotted scarfs as color accents in my ensembles. But how to assemble the ensemble?

I have no expectation of becoming a fashion plate, but I would at least like my clothes not to work against my attempts to be taken seriously. And lately, I've been given a number of indications that, in the matter of fashion and general glamour, there is no such thing as remaining neutral. If a person isn't positively à la mode, she's déclassé.[1] Rental agents, observing my worn-out jeans and ancient red sweatshirt, have

---

[1] *à la mode:* in fashion. *déclassé:* loss of caste; fallen from one class to a lower one.

taken to asking me whether I realize how much the rent is. Salesladies, on the rare occasions when I venture, tentatively, toward the Better Dress racks, direct me to the sale items. The final blow came in a conversation with a friend the other day. I had just remarked that I would have had a harder time pursuing my career if I had weighed 300 pounds. "You know," he said, "you aren't exactly Catherine Deneuve."

I was really crushed. Never in my life have I imagined myself to be anything more in the looks department than a second-string Sally Fields. But no one needs to be reminded of the fact. For the rest of our discussion, I held up well, but when I put down the receiver I announced to my husband that I was going to give myself a five-day vacation, devote my time exclusively to improving how I look. I would get a good haircut. I would buy makeup at a place other than Woolworth's. I would become a fashionable person.

On the first day of my vacation, I dressed for Bloomingdale's as if for war. Walking uptown, I discovered a large spot on my dress, so I stopped at a store along the way, bought a cotton T-shirt and a denim skirt, put them on in the dressing room, stuffed my original outfit in my shopping bag before setting out again. Like one of those women who clean the house before the housekeeper comes.

Why—in all the years I spent in home economics classes, balancing books on my head—did no one ever give a lecture on how to deal with department stores? The minute I spin through the revolving doors, I feel lost. How do you choose among 100 silk blouses? How—even when you're about to get your hair cut short—do you stay away from the hand-painted hair combs and mother-of-pearl barrettes?

Actually, I did have a plan, I would get one pair of good pants, one neutral-colored skirt, one silk blouse, one classic black dress. I would find the perfect style of T-shirt and buy three in assorted colors. Then I would throw out just about everything else I own.

But there are five different floors in Bloomingdale's that carry T-shirts. The first pair of pants I tried on—viewed in a three-way-mirror—depressed me. I felt myself losing heart, brushing my hand along the racks the way children, walking home from school, idly drag their fingers along the pickets of a fence. I was drawn to a simple red dress, and was halfway to the fittimg room before it hit me that I had an almost identical one back in my closet.

I wandered into Designer Fashions then, and spent an hour trying on frilly voile party dresses I couldn't afford and couldn't use. I made my way to the infants' department, where I bought three new sleeper suits for the one member of our family who is already quite well dressed. I ended the afternoon in the shoe department and bought sandals that (I realized later) I have been seeing advertised on TV for weeks, with air bubbles trapped in the soles.

Days No. 2 and 3 didn't go a whole lot better. Humbled by 59th   11 Street, I spent an afternoon at Macy's, where—unable to decide between two pairs of pants I liked—I ended up buying nothing. On my way home I passed a sidewalk rack with a crudely lettered sign that said, "Any item on this rack, $3," and I bought two tops without trying them on.

My husband, who knows the trauma shopping expeditions represent   12 for me, and stands ready to applaud anything short of a gold lamé jump-suit, cheered my haphazardly chosen, ill-matched purchases at the end of each day of my make-over vacation. He thinks the denim skirt is great, and when he saw the sandals, he sang the jingle from the TV commercial. (Similarly, when I set out last year, after a month's delib-eration, to get a haircut, and then changed my mind just as the scissors were raised, he greeted my return from the hairdresser's with hearty ex-clamations of "What an improvement!")

On the fourth day, I returned to Bloomingdale's for a makeup anal-   13 ysis, and drifted through the aisles, wondering how a person knows whether she wants Revlon or Estée Lauder or Helena Rubinstein. In the end my choice was (as usual) totally arbitrary. My makeup consultant had, in fact, unusually bad skin and garishly applied lipstick and eyeshadow.

I filled out a form for her, all about my T-zone, which seems to be   14 another way of saying face. She told me my skin falls in the greenish category, and prescribed a four-step program involving cleanser, skin lotion, moisturizer and cleansing grains. The total cost of my program was $40. I said I would have to do without the cleansing grains and moisturizer. She looked shocked. I was repentant. A minute later she was applying green eyeshadow and bright pink lipstick. On that, at least, I held my ground. "I'll be back for those next week," I told her.

Tonight, on the eve of my haircut, I feel strangely calm—detached,   15 already, from my hair. On the table in front of me I have spread out my air-bubble shoes, my two $3 tops, my skin-care products and the outfit I bought to buy outfits in. I have decided, I think, to retire from being fashionable; this vacation has been too exhausting.

It isn't a lack of interest in clothes that makes me throw in the   16 towel—rather, an excessive one. I have no desire, I see, to own a *single* silk blouse, a *single* pair of pants. If I can't have every color of the rainbow, every flowered hat and frilly dress, I would just as soon not enter the game at all. I do own one good black suit—frayed just enough to render proof that it's a classic—and I think I will simply hold onto it and (like Lillie Langtry[2]) make the very lack of variety in my dress something of a trademark. My T-zone will be moisturized, in any case. And I am, after all, walking on air.

About the Essay

1. In her opening sentence Maynard says "I love clothes." Does she really? Considering this statement, why does she despair of being fashionable?

2. How do others respond to Maynard's style of dressing? What does she herself think of her clothes?

3. Maynard refers to various well-known actresses. What is your reaction to these references? How do the allusions express Maynard's attitude toward herself?

4. Which paragraph or sentence do you think is the funniest in the essay? What is so funny about it? Did anything in the essay cause you to stop and think seriously about it? If so, what was it?

5. Maynard uses a number of devices for ironic or satiric purposes in her writing. One such device is the use of hyperbole, as in "I dressed for Bloomingdale's as if for war." What other examples of exaggeration can you find in her essay? How do these affect your responses?

6. In your opinion, does Maynard end her essay satisfactorily? Why or why not? Has she prepared for her conclusion earlier in the essay? Explain.

Explorations

1. What kind of shopping makes you especially nervous? Is it for clothes, as with Maynard, or for something else? Describe what typically happens when you have to do this kind of shopping. Why do you think it makes you so anxious?

2. In paragraph 4 Maynard says, "I would at least like my clothes not to work against my attempts to be taken seriously." How should she have dressed for her meetings with rental agents, sales people, and others whom she wanted to respond to her seriously? Why might such clothes make much difference in how she is received?

3. Read Alison Lurie's "The Language of Clothes" (pages 360–368), and then analyze Maynard's sense of style.

[2]The English actress who, before she achieved fame, used to wear a simple black dress for all occasions, slightly modified each time.

ALISON LURIE

"The apparel oft proclaims the man," says old Polonius to his son in Shakespeare's *Hamlet*. "And the woman too," he might have added. Alison Lurie goes further in her book *The Language of Clothes* (1982). Not only do our clothes make statements about us, she asserts, but items of clothing are like a vocabulary, and an ensemble is like a sentence. The analogy brings together her interest in clothes and her concern with language. Lurie is the author of several novels, including *Love and Friendship* (1962) and *The War Between the Tates* (1974). She has also written books for children and edited a series of children's classics. She teaches a popular course in children's literature at Cornell University, where she has been lecturer in English since 1968. In the following selection from *The Language of Clothes*, Lurie discusses just what it is that clothes express and how they express it.

The Language of Clothes

For thousands of years human beings have communicated with one another first in the language of dress. Long before I am near enough to talk to you on the street, in a meeting or at a party, you announce your sex, age and class to me through what you are wearing—and very possibly give me important information (or misinformation) as to your occupation, origin, personality, opinions, tastes, sexual desires and current mood. I may not be able to put what I observe into words, but I register the information unconsciously; and you simultaneously do the same for me. By the time we meet and converse we have already spoken to each other in an older and more universal tongue.

• • • •

If clothing is a language, it must have a vocabulary and a grammar like other languages. Of course, as with human speech, there is not a single language of dress, but many: some (like Dutch and German) closely related and others (like Basque) almost unique. And within every language of clothes there are many different dialects and accents, some almost unintelligible to members of the mainstream culture. Moreover, as with speech, each individual has his own stock of words and employs personal variations of tone and meaning.

The Vocabulary of Fashion

The vocabulary of dress includes not only items of clothing but also hairstyles, accessories, jewelry, makeup and body decoration. Theoreti-

360

cally, at least, this vocabulary is as large as or larger than that of any spoken tongue, since it includes every garment, hairstyle and type of body decoration ever invented. In practice, of course, the sartorial resources of an individual may be very restricted. Those of a sharecropper, for instance, may be limited to five or ten "words" from which it is possible to create only a few "sentences" almost bare of decoration and expressing only the most basic concepts. A so-called fashion leader, on the other hand, may have several hundred "words" at his or her disposal, and thus be able to form thousands of different "sentences" that will express a wide range of meanings. Just as the average English-speaking person knows many more words than he or she will ever use in conversation, so all of us are able to understand the meaning of styles we will never wear.

To choose clothes, either in a store or at home, is to define and   4 describe ourselves. Occasionally, of course, practical considerations enter into these choices: considerations of comfort, durability, availability and price. Especially in the case of persons of limited wardrobe, an article may be worn because it is warm or rainproof or handy to cover up a wet bathing suit—in the same way that persons of limited vocabulary use the phrase "you know" or adjectives such as "great" or "fantastic." Yet, just as with spoken language, such choices usually give us some information, even if it is only equivalent to the statement "I don't give a damn what I look like today."

Archaic Words

Besides containing "words" that are taboo, the language of clothes,   5 like speech, also includes modern and ancient words, words of native and foreign origin, dialect words, colloquialisms, slang and vulgarities. Genuine articles of clothing from the past (or skillful imitations) are used in the same way a writer or speaker might use archaisms: to give an air of culture, erudition or wit. Just as in educated discourse, such "words" are usually employed sparingly, most often one at a time—a single Victorian cameo or a pair of 1940s platform shoes or an Edwardian velvet waistcoat,[1] never a complete costume. A whole outfit composed of archaic items from a single period, rather than projecting elegance and sophistication, will imply that one is on one's way to a masquerade, acting in a play or film or putting oneself on display for advertising purposes. Mixing garments from several different periods of the past, on the other hand,

---

[1]Queen Victoria reigned in England from 1837 to 1901. King Edward VII reigned from 1901 to 1910.

suggests a confused but intriguingly "original" theatrical personality. It is therefore often fashionable in those sections of the art and entertainment industry in which instant celebrities are manufactured and sold.

When using archaic words, it is essential to choose ones that are decently old. The sight of a white plastic Courrèges miniraincoat and boots (in 1963 the height of fashion) at a gallery opening or theater today would produce the same shiver of ridicule and revulsion as the use of words such as "groovy," "Negro" or "self-actualizing."

In *Taste and Fashion,* one of the best books ever written on costume, the late James Laver proposed a timetable to explain such reactions; this has come to be known as Laver's Law. According to him, the same costume will be:

Indecent	10 years before its time
Shameless	5 years before its time
Daring	1 year before its time
Smart	
Dowdy	1 year after its time
Hideous	10 years after its time
Ridiculous	20 years after its time
Amusing	30 years after its time
Quaint	50 years after its time
Charming	70 years after its time
Romantic	100 years after its time
Beautiful	150 years after its time

Laver possibly overemphasizes the shock value of incoming fashion, which today may be seen merely as weird or ugly. And, of course, he is speaking of the complete outfit, or "sentence." The speed with which a single "word" passes in and out of fashion can vary, just as in spoken and written languages.

Foreign Words

The appearance of foreign garments in an otherwise indigenous costume is similar in function to the use of foreign words or phrases in standard English speech. This phenomenon, which is common in certain circles, may have several different meanings.

First, of course, it can be a deliberate sign of national origin in someone who otherwise, sartorially or linguistically speaking, has no accent. Often this message is expressed through headgear. The Oxford-educated Arab who tops his Savile Row[2] suit with a turban is telling us graphically that he has not been psychologically assimilated, that his ideas and opinions remain those of an Asian. As a result, we tend to see the non-European in Western dress with native headgear or hairdo as dignified, even formidable, while the reverse outfit—the Oriental lady in a kimono and a plastic rain hat or the sheikh in native robes and a black bowler—appears comic. Such costumes seem to announce that their wearers, though not physically at ease in our country, have their heads full of half-baked Western ideas.

More often the wearing of a single foreign garment, like the dropping of a foreign word or phrase in conversation, is meant not to advertise foreign origin or allegiance but to indicate sophistication. It can also be a means of advertising wealth. When we see a fancy Swiss watch, we know that its owner either bought it at home for three times the price of a good English or American watch or else he or she spent even more money traveling to Switzerland.   10

Slang and Vulgar Words

Casual dress, like casual speech, tends to be loose, relaxed and colorful. It often contains what might be called "slang words": blue jeans, sneakers, baseball caps, aprons, flowered cotton housedresses and the like. These garments could not be worn on a formal occasion without causing disapproval, but in ordinary circumstances they pass without remark. "Vulgar words" in dress, on the other hand, give emphasis and get immediate attention in almost any circumstances, just as they do in speech. Only the skillful can employ them without some loss of face, and even then they must be used in the right way. A torn, unbuttoned shirt, or wildly uncombed hair, can signify strong emotions: passion, grief, rage, despair. They are most effective if people already think of you as being neatly dressed, just as the curses of well-spoken persons count for more than those of the customarily foulmouthed.   11

Items of dress that are the sartorial equivalent of forbidden words have more impact when they appear seldom and as if by accident. The Edwardian lady, lifting her heavy floor-length skirt to board a tram, appeared unaware that she was revealing a froth of lacy petticoats and embroidered black stockings. Similarly, today's braless executive woman, leaning over her desk at a conference, may affect not to know that her   12

---

[2]The street in London where the most expensive and conservative men's tailors have their shops.

nipples show through her silk blouse. Perhaps she does not know it consciously; we are here in the ambiguous region of intention versus interpretation which has given so much trouble to linguists.

Personal Fashion: Situation and Self

As with speech, the meaning of any costume depends on circumstances. It is not "spoken" in a vacuum but at a specific place and time, any change in which may alter its meaning. Like the remark "Let's get on with this damn business," the two-piece tan business suit and boldly striped shirt and tie that signify energy and determination in the office will have quite another resonance at a funeral or picnic. [13]

In language we distinguish between someone who speaks a sentence well—clearly, and with confidence and dignity—and someone who speaks it badly. In dress, too, manner is as important as matter, and in judging the meaning of any garment we will automatically consider whether it fits well or is too large or too small, whether it is old or new and especially whether it is in good condition, slightly rumpled and soiled or crushed and filthy. Cleanliness may not always be next to godliness, but it is usually regarded as a sign of respectability or at least of self-respect. It is also a sign of status, since to be clean and neat involves the expense of time and money. [14]

In a few circles, of course, disregard for cleanliness has been considered a virtue. Saint Jerome's remark that "the purity of the body and its garments means the impurity of the soul" inspired generations of unwashed and smelly hermits. In the '60s some hippies and mystics scorned overly clean and tidy dress as a sign of compromise with the establishment and too great an attachment to the things of this world. There is also a more widespread rural and small-town dislike of the person whose clothes are too clean, slick and smooth. He—or she—is suspected of being untrustworthy, a smoothy or a city slicker. [15]

In general, however, to wear dirty, rumpled or torn clothing is to invite scorn and condescension. This reaction is ancient; indeed, it goes back beyond the dawn of humanity. In most species, a strange animal in poor condition—mangy, or with matted and muddy fur—is more likely to be attacked by other animals. In the same way, shabbily dressed people are more apt to be treated shabbily. A man in a clean, well-pressed suit who falls down in a central London or Manhattan street is likely to be helped up sooner than one in filthy tatters. [16]

Eccentric and Conventional Speech

In dress as in language, there is a possible range of expression from   17
the most eccentric statement to the most conventional. At one end of
the spectrum is the outfit of which the individual parts or "words" are
highly incongruent, marking its wearer (if not on stage or involved in
some natural disaster) as very peculiar or possibly deranged. Imagine, for
instance, a transparent sequined evening blouse over a dirty Victorian
cotton petticoat and black rubber galoshes. (I have observed this getup
in real life; it was worn to a lunch party at a famous Irish country house.)
If the same costume were worn by a man, or if the usual grammatical
order of the sentence were altered—one of the galoshes placed upside
down on the head, for example—the effect of insanity would be even
greater.

At the opposite end of the spectrum is the costume that is the   18
equivalent of a cliché; it follows some established style in every particular
and instantly establishes its wearer as a doctor, a debutante, a hippie or a
whore. Such outfits are not uncommon, for as two British sociologists
have remarked, "Identification with and active participation in a social
group always involves the human body and its adornment and clothing."
The more significant any social role is for an individual, the more likely
he or she is to dress for it. When two roles conflict, the costume will
either reflect the more important one or it will combine them, sometimes
with incongruous effects, as in the case of the secretary whose sober, effi-
cient-looking dark suit only partly conceals a tight, bright low-cut blouse.

The cliché outfit may in some cases become so standardized that it   19
is spoken of as a "uniform": the pin-striped suit, bowler and black umbrella of the London City man, for instance, or the blue jeans and T-
shirts of high school students. Usually, however, these costumes only look
like uniforms to outsiders; peers will be aware of significant differences.
The London businessman's tie will tell his associates where he went to
school; the cut and fabric of his suit will allow them to guess at his income. High school students, in a single glance, can distinguish new jeans
from those that are fashionably worn, functionally or decoratively patched
or carelessly ragged; they grasp the fine distinctions of meaning conveyed
by straight-leg, flared, boot-cut and peg-top. When two pairs of jeans are
identical to the naked eye, a label handily affixed to the back pocket gives
useful information, identifying the garment as expensive (so-called designer jeans) or discount-department-store. And even within the latter
category there are distinctions: In our local junior high school according
to a native informant, "freaks always wear Lees, greasers wear Wranglers
and everyone else wears Levis."

Of course, all these students are identical only below the waist;   20
above it they may wear anything from a lumberjack shirt to a lace blouse.
Grammatically, this costume seems to be a sign that in their lower or
physical natures these persons are alike, however dissimilar they may be
socially, intellectually or esthetically. If this is so, the opposite statement
can be imagined—and was actually made by my own college classmates
30 years ago. During the daytime we wore identical baggy sweaters over a
wide variety of slacks, plaid kilts, full cotton or straight tweed or slinky
jersey skirts, ski pants and Bermuda shorts. "We're all nice coeds from
the waist up; we think and talk alike," this costume proclaimed, "but as
women we are infinitely various."

Dressing for "Success"

For over 100 years books and magazines have been busy translating   21
the correct language of fashion, telling men and women what they should
wear to seem genteel, rich, sophisticated and attractive to the other sex.
Journals addressed to what used to be called "the career girl" advised her
how to dress to attract "the right kind of man"—successful, marriage-
minded. Regardless of the current fashion, a discreet femininity was always recommended: soft fabrics and colors, flowers and ruffles in modest
profusion, hair slightly longer and curlier than that of the other girls in
the office. The costume must be neither too stylish (suggesting expense
to the future husband) nor dowdy (suggesting boredom). Above all, a
delicate balance must be struck between the prim and the seductive, one
tending not to attract men and the other to attract the wrong kind. Times
have changed somewhat, and the fashion pages of magazines such as *Cos-
mopolitan* now seem to specialize in telling the career girl what to wear to
charm the particular wrong type of man who reads *Playboy*, while the
editorial pages tell her how to cope with the resulting psychic damage.

Two recent paperbacks, *Dress for Success* and *The Woman's Dress for*   22
Success Book, by John T. Molloy, instruct businessmen and business-
women how to select their clothes so that they will look efficient, authoritative and reliable even when they are incompetent, weak and shifty.
Molloy, who is by no means unintelligent, claims that his "wardrobe engineering" is based on scientific research and opinion polls. Also, in a
departure from tradition, he is interested in telling women how to get
promoted, not how to get married. The secret, apparently, is to wear an
expensive but conventional "skirted suit" in medium-gray or navy wool
with a modestly cut blouse. No sweaters, no pants, no very bright colors,
no cleavage, no long or excessively curly hair.

Anyone interested in scenic variety must hope that Molloy is mistaken; but my own opinion polling, unfortunately, backs him up. A fast-rising lady executive in a local bank reports to me—reluctantly—that "suits do help separate the women from the girls—provided the women can tolerate the separation, which is another question altogether."   23

Malevolent Clothing

At the other extreme from clothing which brings good luck and success is the garment of ill-omen. The most common and harmless version of this is the dress, suit or shirt which (like some children) seems to attract or even to seek out dirt, grease, protruding nails, falling ketchup and other hazards. Enid Nemy, who has written perceptively about such clothes for *The New York Times*, suggests that they may be lazy: "They'd just as soon rest on a hanger, or in a box—and they revolt when they're hauled into action." Or, she adds, they may be snobs, unwilling to associate with ordinary people. Whatever the cause, such accident-prone garments rarely if ever reform, and once one has been identified it is best to break off relations with it immediately. Otherwise, like accident-prone persons, it is apt to involve you in much inconvenience and possibly actual disaster, turning some important interview or romantic tryst into a scene of farce or humiliation. More sinister, and fortunately more rare, is the garment which seems to attract disasters to you rather than to itself. Ms. Nemy mentions an orange linen dress that apparently took a dislike to its owner, Margaret Turner of Dover Publications. Orange clothes, as it happens, do occasionally arouse hostility in our culture, but this dress seems to have been a special case. "Women friends seemed cattier, men seemed more aloof and I'd get into bad situations with my boss," Ms. Turner reported. "And that wasn't all. I'd spill coffee, miss train connections and the car would break down."   24

For some people the daily task of choosing a costume is tedious, oppressive or even frightening. Occasionally such people tell us that fashion is unnecessary; that in the ideal world of the future we will all wear some sort of identical jump suit—washable, waterproof, stretchable, temperature-controlled, timeless, ageless and sexless. What a convenience, what a relief it will be, they say, never to worry about how to dress for a job interview, a romantic tryst or a funeral!   25

Convenient, perhaps, but not exactly a relief. Such a utopia would give most of us the same kind of chill we feel when a stadium full of Communist-bloc athletes in identical sports outfits, shouting slogans in unison, appears on TV. Most people do not want to be told what to wear   26 any more than they want to be told what to say. In Belfast recently, 400 Irish Republican prisoners "refused to wear any clothes at all, draping themselves day and night in blankets," rather than put on prison uniforms. Even the offer of civilian-style dress did not satisfy them; they insisted on wearing their own clothes brought from home or nothing. Fashion is free speech, and one of the privileges, if not always one of the pleasures, of a free world.

About the Essay

1. Why does Lurie draw an analogy between clothes and language? How convincing is that analogy? Are there areas of language or fashion in which the analogy does not apply? If so, what are they?

2. How does Lurie develop and support her central idea? How effective is her strategy? Support your answers with citations from the essay.

3. Lurie says, "To choose clothes, either in a store or at home, is to define and describe ourselves." What does she mean? Do you agree?

4. Give your own examples of archaic and foreign dress, slang dress, vulgar dress, eccentric dress, conventional dress. What do these ways of dressing communicate to you? Either hold to Lurie's definitions of these types or supply definitions of your own.

5. In paragraph 12, Lurie says: "We are here in the ambiguous region of intention versus interpretation." What do the words *intention* and *interpretation* mean when applied to clothing and language?

6. What is implied by the discussion of "malevolent clothing"? How is it relevant to Lurie's point?

Explorations

1. Using Lurie's analogy between clothing and language, how would you classify the "words" in your repertoire of things to wear? Are you aware of choosing particular articles of clothing to wear in order to make a specific impression on people? Give some examples.

2. What did the well-dressed woman or man wear in 1580? There are books on the history of dress and costume to help you write your description. Or, using Laver's Law, what will the well-dressed woman or man of ten years from now be wearing? Or what will people of 150 years from now find beautiful? Explain your opinion.

JONATHAN MILLER

Jonathan Miller was born in London in 1934. The son of a distinguished British psychiatrist, he planned to become a medical researcher and teacher. As often happens, however, events brought about an unexpected turn in his career. After taking his undergraduate degree at Cambridge, Miller graduated as a doctor of medicine from University College (London) Medical School in 1958, and interned at the university's hospital. But he had in the meantime gotten involved in college theater at Cambridge, and in 1959 some friends asked him to help write and perform a new comedy review at the Edinburgh Festival the next year. This was to be a summer's lark, ending in two weeks of performances after which Miller was to return to his medical studies. But the review, *Beyond the Fringe,* was a tremendous hit, running for more than three years in London and New York, and Miller to his surprise found himself with a career in the theater. Since then he has become one of the most inventive and sought-after stage directors of the day. He has also done much work on television, supervising the filming of twelve Shakespeare plays for public television, directing six of them himself, and planning, writing, and narrating a series on health and medicine, *The Body in Question* (1978), which has also been published as a book. That book is the source of this selection. Health and sickness are generally believed to be bodily states. Miller points out that they are also conclusions we draw about the way we feel, and performances we give to persuade others to agree with our conclusions.

Deciding to Be Ill

Almost invariably it is the sufferer who shapes the experience of illness into an intelligible situation. At some level or other suffering gives way to a personal diagnosis. In the end the victim becomes a patient because he guesses that something is wrong or odd about him and that he is the unwilling victim of this process.

From the instant when someone first recognises his symptoms to the moment when he eventually complains about them, there is always an interval, longer or shorter as the case may be, when he argues with himself about whether it is worth making his complaint known to an expert. Naturally, it varies from symptom to symptom: someone who recognises that he is steadily losing weight measures this by a different standard from the one he would apply to a headache; the thoughts aroused by a painless swelling on the cheek are not the same as the intense irritation caused by an itching rash on the hand; when someone even-

369

tually decides to complain about increasing breathlessness he has rated himself on a different scale from the one he would use if he had blood in his water.

There are four independent scales which can be applied to a symptom to decide whether or not it demands attention. First, there is the symptom's intrinsic nastiness. Pain is intrinsically nasty, and most people would agree that nausea is, as well. The straightforward feeling of having either of these symptoms is quite enough to make you wish you hadn't.

In contrast to these, there are symptoms whose nastiness has to be inferred. The painless appearance of blood in the urine is not obviously unpleasant as a thing in itself. It is unsettling not because it causes discomfort, but because it carries alarming implications. The same principle applies to a painless, invisible lump in the breast.

Symptoms are also complained about because they reduce efficiency or restrict freedom of action. A patient who becomes steadily more breathless when he exerts himself eventually complains because he is frustrated by the way in which this cuts down his movements. It is not the feeling of breathlessness as such, but the results of it which lead him to complain. This also applies to tremor or muscular weakness of one kind or another: unless they come on rapidly enough to cause immediate suffering or alarm, they excite complaint because of the frustration they cause.

Finally, there is the question of embarrassment or shame. Patients may complain about a symptom simply because they regard it as unseemly. A painless blemish on the mouth can bring a patient to the clinic much sooner than a large, painful lesion on the shin. This applies to any publicly noticeable anomaly—a squint, drooping eyelid, hairlip, rash, loud intestinal noises, hoarseness—which seems to threaten the patient's self-esteem and which might be regarded as a stigma.

Obviously, a symptom can appear on more than one scale—perhaps on all four. The pain associated with cystitis—infection of the bladder—is extremely unpleasant in its own right, so it scores quite high on the intrinsic nastiness scale. On the other hand, it poses no threat to life, so that although it may excruciate the patient it doesn't actually alarm her. However, patients who suffer from severe cystitis know only too well how much it limits their freedom of action: long journeys are almost inconceivable, and while the illness lasts the unfortunate patient tends to hover within easy reach of a lavatory. So it gets a high score on the incapacity scale, and since it alters the patient's behaviour in what she regards as a noticeable way, it also gets a substantial score in terms of stigma and shame.

Angina is a pain that is unquestionably nasty, and since most people have learnt to associate it with the heart they are often alarmed by it as well. But greater perhaps than the discomfort and alarm is the sheer frustration of being brought to a standstill after walking less than 100 yards. It may be exasperation that eventually drives the patient to a doctor. 8

Breathlessness is an even more interesting example. It is more or less unpleasant in itself, and if the patient associates the symptom with his heart or his lungs he may also be alarmed by it. But, as with angina, the sense of incapacity may weigh most heavily, and if the patient prides himself on being able-bodied he may experience an intolerable sense of shame when his friends or colleagues leave him panting on a short stroll. However, if it comes on very rapidly or very severely, the scale changes. Someone who is awakened at night by an attack of paroxysmal breathlessness finds the feeling almost insufferable in itself, so that it now hits the very top of the intrinsic nastiness scale. Since most people would 9

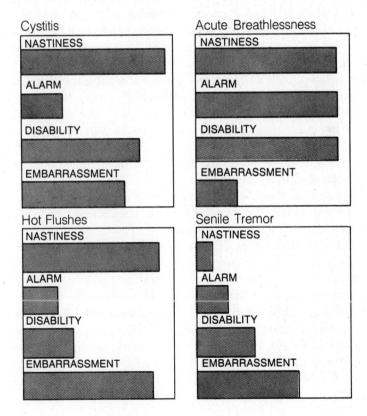

interpret it as a serious threat to life, it notches up a heavy score in terms of sheer alarm as well. And when breathlessness is extreme, the patient is often bed-ridden, so it also appears very high up on the incapacity scale. However, anyone preoccupied with drawing his next breath has very little time to feel ashamed of it, so that it doesn't even appear on the stigma scale, although a sense of shame and embarrassment can survive even the most fearful emergency—I can remember patients struggling for breath, waving a weak apology for what they obviously regarded as humiliating panic.

Elderly patients often expect to have shaky hands, and if they develop a tremor, as long as they have no reason to suspect a sinister cause, they are simply frustrated, since it makes it hard for them to dress and feed themselves. But even elderly patients may be embarrassed by their tremor: they are ashamed of not being able to help themselves and also imagine that people will think they are stupid or odd or even drunk. Once again the way in which this symptom is rated depends on other factors: its severity or the age of the victim at the onset. I can remember a patient who developed a spectacular tremor at the age of forty as the result of breathing in mercury fumes: this is the illness they used to call Hatter's Shakes, because of the mercury which was used to dress the felt. (I think it is probably the reason why the Mad Hatter in *Alice in Wonderland* is shown with a large chunk bitten out of his teacup.) My patient said that there was nothing intrinsically nasty about the shakes, and, since he had no reason to associate them with a dangerous industrial poison, he wasn't even alarmed by them. But he was seriously incapacitated by his tremor and what worried him most was the fact that it stopped him going to work—luckily for him, as it turned out. He was also embarrassed by his clumsiness.

To sum up, then. At one time or another we have all been irked by aches and pains. We have probably noticed alterations in weight, complexion and bodily function, changes in power, capability and will, unaccountable shifts of mood. But on the whole we treat these like changes in the weather: as part and parcel of living in an imperfect world. The changes they cause in our behaviour are barely noticeable—not inconvenient enough to interfere with our routine. We may retreat a little, fall silent, sigh, rub our heads, retire early, drink glasses of water, eat less, walk more, miss a meal here and there, avoid fried foods, and so on and so on. But sometimes the discomfort, alarm, embarrassment or inconvenience begin to obstruct the flow of ordinary life; in place of modest well-being, life becomes so intolerably awkward, strenuous or frightening that we fall ill.

Falling ill is not something that happens to us, it is a choice we make as a result of things happening to us. It is an action we take when we feel unacceptably odd. Obviously, there are times when this choice is taken out of the victim's hands: he may be so overwhelmed by events that he plays no active part in what happens next and is brought to the doctor by friends or relatives, stricken and helpless. But this is rare. Most people who fall ill have chosen to cast themselves in the role of patient. Viewing their unfortunate situation, they see themselves as sick people and begin to act differently.

. . . When someone falls ill but is not yet ready to summon expert help, he usually takes care to advertise his condition through the medium of a performance. In fact, such a performance is often demanded of him by those with whom he lives. Someone who takes to his bed when he has a sick headache, for instance, is not entirely prompted by the need for relief. It is a way of boosting his credibility as a sick person, and it may be the only way of getting the attention and concern which he thinks he deserves. In fact, the patient may have to abstain from activities he is quite capable of performing, if only to convince those around him that there is a good reason for his staying away from work.

A patient, then, is a special sort of person, rather like a recruit or a convert or a bride. By taking on the role of patient you change your social identity, turning yourself from someone who helps himself into someone who accepts the orders, routine and advice of qualified experts. You submit to the rules and recommendations of a profession, just as a novice submits to the rules and recommendations of his or her chosen order. Ordinary life is full of such voluntary transitions—changes of social role or status which are accompanied by corresponding changes in obligation and expectation. Whenever these take place, they are accompanied by rituals which mark the event and make it clearly recognisable to all who are involved. The anthropologists have called these 'rites of passage,' symbolic actions which represent and dramatise significant changes in social status: they include baptisms, immersions, confirmations, all sorts of melodramatic initiations and humiliating ordeals, such as strippings, shavings, scarrings. Whenever we cross a threshold from one social role to another we take pains to advertise the fact with ceremonies which represent it in terms of vivid and memorable images.

The idea of 'rites of passage' was first introduced by the French anthropologist Arnold Van Gennep in 1909. Van Gennep insisted that all rituals of 'passing through' occurred in three successive phases: a rite of separation, a rite of transition and a rite of aggregation. The person whose status is to be changed has to undergo a ritual which marks his

12

13

14

15

departure from the old version of himself: there has to be some act which symbolises the fact that he has rid himself of all his previous associations. He is washed, rinsed, sprinkled or immersed, and, in this way, all his previous obligations and attachments are symbolically untied and even annihilated. This stage is followed by a rite of transition, when the person is neither fish nor fowl; he has left his old status behind him but has not yet assumed his new one. This liminal condition is usually marked by rituals of isolation and segregation—a period of vigil, mockery perhaps, fear and trembling. There are often elaborate rites of humiliation—scourging, insults, and darkness. Finally, in the rite of aggregation, the new status is ritually conferred: the person is admitted, enrolled, confirmed and ordained.

This idea can be applied to the process of becoming a patient. The fact that most of the procedures involved have a rational and practical explanation doesn't prevent them from playing a very important symbolic role as well. Although one can readily understand most of what happens to someone on entering hospital in utilitarian terms, there is no doubt that both the patient and the doctor experience some of these manoeuvres as symbolic transformations. Once someone has chosen to fall ill he has to apply for the role of patient: he auditions for the part by reciting his complaint as vividly and as convincingly as he can. This can also be seen in terms of religious confirmation: the candidate submits himself to a formal questionnaire in order to satisfy the examiner that he is a suitable person to be enrolled. If he passes the preliminary test he has to undertake the initial rites of separation. He is undressed, washed, and until quite recently, he often had to submit himself to a cleansing enema. Then come the rites of transition. No longer a person in the ordinary world, he is not yet formally accepted by his fellow patients—anxious and isolated in his novice pyjamas, he awaits the formal act of aggregation. He is introduced to the ward sister, hands over his street clothes, submits to a questionnaire by the houseman and registrar.[1] Dressed with all the dignified credentials of a formally admitted patient, he awaits the forthcoming event.

About the Essay

1. What is Miller's thesis in this essay? Where is it stated?
2. According to Miller, people evaluate their symptoms by four criteria. In your own words, what are these criteria? Using Miller's criteria, how would

---

[1] A *houseman* is an intern. He would ask about the patient's symptoms and medical history, and the *registrar* would ask for the names of relatives, details of insurance coverage, and the like.

you evaluate an illness you have had—the flu, say, or a cold? What criteria would you normally use to evaluate an illness?

3. Miller finds elements of the theater in the way people behave when they think they are ill. What are those elements? What explanation does Miller offer for this behavior? How would you explain the same behavior?

4. Miller concludes with an analogy between a patient's admission to a hospital and a "rite of passage." What does this analogy contribute to the essay?

Explorations

1. Miller claims that we diagnose ourselves and, if we think we are ill, act out the part. Do you agree? Describe a recent illness you have had. How did you know you were ill, and what did you do about it?

2. Miller has observed elsewhere that we "perform" in many circumstances other than illness—for instance, we "act out" many other interactions with people, such as greetings and farewells. He cites the writings of sociologist Erving Goffman as the source of his insight. With or without consulting Goffman, pick out an occasion—a date, a meeting, a conversation—and discuss how much of the encounter is normally spontaneous and how much is acting. What, exactly, is meant by the word *acting* in this context? What actually determines your behavior?

NORMAN COUSINS

The great English surgeon William Osler once wrote, "One of the first duties of the physician is to educate the masses not to take medicine." Norman Cousins would agree. In 1964, at the age of forty-nine, he fell ill with a crippling and supposedly irreversible disease—the connective tissue in his spine was disintegrating. After doing some research, Cousins found that the pain-killing drugs given to him by the hospital were making his condition worse, so he stopped taking them, coping with the pain by a most unconventional method: watching old Marx Brothers movies. "I made the joyous discovery that ten minutes of genuine belly laughter had an anesthetic effect and would give me at least two hours of pain-free sleep," Cousins writes in *Anatomy of an Illness as Perceived by the Patient* (1979). Thanks to an understanding doctor, some novel ideas about treating his illness which Cousins himself suggested, and a powerful will to live, he recovered enough to go back to work at the *Saturday Review,* where he had served as editor for thirty-eight years, and has since regained much of his previous strength and mobility. Cousins therefore argues with special authority when he writes that most people know little about pain. His own experience supports his view that often we do better to deal directly with our pains than to mask them with drugs.

Pain Is Not the Ultimate Enemy

Americans are probably the most pain-conscious people on the face of the earth. For years we have had it drummed into us—in print, on radio, over television, in everyday conversation—that any hint of pain is to be banished as though it were the ultimate evil. As a result, we are becoming a nation of pill-grabbers and hypochondriacs, escalating the slightest ache into a searing ordeal.

We know very little about pain and what we don't know makes it hurt all the more. Indeed, no form of illiteracy in the United States is so widespread or costly as ignorance about pain—what it is, what causes it, how to deal with it without panic. Almost everyone can rattle off the names of at least a dozen drugs that can deaden pain from every conceivable cause—all the way from headaches to hemorrhoids. There is far less knowledge about the fact that about 90 percent of pain is self-limiting, that it is not always an indication of poor health, and that, most frequently, it is the result of tension, stress, worry, idleness, boredom, frustration, suppressed rage, insufficient sleep, overeating, poorly balanced diet, smoking, excessive drinking, inadequate exercise, stale air,

376

or any of the other abuses encountered by the human body in modern society.

The most ignored fact of all about pain is that the best way to 3 eliminate it is to eliminate the abuse. Instead, many people reach almost instinctively for the painkillers—aspirins, barbiturates, codeines, tranquilizers, sleeping pills, and dozens of other analgesics or desensitizing drugs.

Most doctors are profoundly troubled over the extent to which the 4 medical profession today is taking on the trappings of a pain-killing industry. Their offices are overloaded with people who are morbidly but mistakenly convinced that something dreadful is about to happen to them. It is all too evident that the campaign to get people to run to a doctor at the first sign of pain has boomeranged. Physicians find it difficult to give adequate attention to patients genuinely in need of expert diagnosis and treatment because their time is soaked up by people who have nothing wrong with them except a temporary indisposition or a psychogenic[1] ache.

Patients tend to feel indignant and insulted if the physician tells 5 them he can find no organic cause for the pain. They tend to interpret the term "psychogenic" to mean that they are complaining of nonexistent symptoms. They need to be educated about the fact that many forms of pain have no underlying physical cause but are the result, as mentioned earlier, of tension, stress, or hostile factors in the general environment. Sometimes a pain may be a manifestation of "conversion hysteria," . . . the name given by Jean Charcot to physical symptoms that have their origins in emotional disturbances.

Obviously, it is folly for an individual to ignore symptoms that could 6 be a warning of a potentially serious illness. Some people are so terrified of getting bad news from a doctor that they allow their malaise to worsen, sometimes past the point of no return. Total neglect is not the answer to hypochondria. The only answer has to be increased education about the way the human body works, so that more people will be able to steer an intelligent course between promiscuous pill-popping and irresponsible disregard of genuine symptoms.

Of all forms of pain, none is more important for the individual to 7 understand than the "threshold" variety. Almost everyone has a telltale ache that is triggered whenever tension or fatigue reaches a certain point. It can take the form of a migraine-type headache or a squeezing pain deep in the abdomen or cramps or a pain in the lower back or even pain in the joints. The individual who has learned how to make the corre-

---

[1]Originating in the mind, usually as the result of emotional disturbance.

lation between such threshold pains and their cause doesn't panic when they occur; he or she does something about relieving the stress and tension. Then, if the pain persists despite the absence of apparent cause, the individual will telephone the doctor.

If ignorance about the nature of pain is widespread, ignorance about the way pain-killing drugs work is even more so. What is not generally understood is that many of the vaunted pain-killing drugs conceal the pain without correcting the underlying condition. They deaden the mechanism in the body that alerts the brain to the fact that something may be wrong. The body can pay a high price for suppression of pain without regard to its basic cause.   8

Professional athletes are sometimes severely disadvantaged by trainers whose job it is to keep them in action. The more famous the athlete, the greater the risk that he or she may be subjected to extreme medical measures when injury strikes. The star baseball pitcher whose arm is sore because of a torn muscle or tissue damage may need sustained rest more than anything else. But his team is battling for a place in the World Series; so the trainer or team doctor, called upon to work his magic, reaches for a strong dose of butazolidine or other powerful pain suppressants. Presto, the pain disppears! The pitcher takes his place on the mound and does superbly. That could be the last game, however, in which he is able to throw a ball with full strength. The drugs didn't repair the torn muscle or cause the damaged tissue to heal. What they did was to mask the pain, enabling the pitcher to throw hard, further damaging the torn muscle. Little wonder that so many star athletes are cut down in their prime, more the victims of overzealous treatment of their injuries than of the injuries themselves.   9

The king of all painkillers, of course, is aspirin. The U.S. Food and Drug Administration permits aspirin to be sold without prescription, but the drug, contrary to popular belief, can be dangerous and, in sustained doses, potentially lethal. Aspirin is self-administered by more people than any other drug in the world. Some people are aspirin-poppers, taking ten or more a day. What they don't know is that the smallest dose can cause internal bleeding. Even more serious perhaps is the fact that aspirin is antagonistic to collagen, which has a key role in the formation of connective tissue.[2] Since many forms of arthritis involve disintegration of the connective tissue, the steady use of aspirin can actually intensify the underlying arthritic condition.   10

---

[2]*Collagen* is a protein; connective tissue is tissue composed of a particular cellular structure that binds together other tissue to form ligaments, tendons, etc.

The reason why aspirin is prescribed so widely for arthritic patients   11
is that it has an antiinflammatory effect, apart from its pain-deadening
characteristics. In recent years, however, medical researchers have suggested that the antiinflammatory value of aspirin may be offset by the
harm it causes to the body's vital chemistry. Doctors J. Hirsch, D. Street,
J.F. Cade, and H. Amy, in the March 1973 issue of the professional
journal *Blood*, showed that aspirin impedes the interaction between "platelet
release"[3] and connective tissue. In the *Annals of Rheumatic Diseases*, also
in March 1973, Dr. P.N. Sperryn reported a significant blood loss in
patients who were on heavy daily doses of aspirin. (It is not unusual for
patients suffering from serious rheumatoid arthritis to take as many as
twenty-four aspirin tablets a day.)

. . . I call attention to the article in the May 8, 1971 issue of   12
Lancet, the English medical journal. Dr. M. A. Sahud and Dr. R. J.
Cohen stated that the systematic use of aspirin by rheumatoid patients
produces abnormally low plasma-ascorbic-acid[4] levels. The authors reported that aspirin blocks the "uptake of ascorbic acid into the blood
platelets." Since vitamin C is essential in collagen formation, its depletion by aspirin would seem to run directly counter to the body's need to
combat connective tissue breakdown in arthritic conditions. The *Lancet*
article concludes that, at the very least, ascorbic acid should be admin-
istered along with aspirin to counteract its harmful effects.

Aspirin is not the only pain-killing drug, of course, that is known   13
to have dangerous side effects. Dr. Daphne A. Roe, of Cornell University, at a medical meeting in New York City in 1974, presented startling
evidence of a wide range of hazards associated with sedatives and other
pain suppressants. Some of these drugs seriously interfere with the ability
of the body to metabolize food properly, producing malnutrition. In some
instances, there is also the danger of bone-marrow depression, interfering
with the ability of the body to replenish its blood supply.

Pain-killing drugs are among the greatest advances in the history   14
of medicine. Properly used, they can be a boon in alleviating suffering
and in treating disease. But their indiscriminate and promiscuous use is
making psychological cripples and chronic ailers out of millions of people.
The unremitting barrage of advertising for pain-killing drugs, especially
over television, has set the stage for a mass anxiety neurosis. Almost
from the moment children are old enough to sit upright in front of a

---

[3]Small disks of blood that help in making an enzyme important in forming connective
tissue.

[4]Vitamin C in the blood.

television screen, they are being indoctrinated into the hypochondriac's clamorous and morbid world. Little wonder so many people fear pain more than death itself.

It might be a good idea if concerned physicians and educators could   15
get together to make knowledge about pain an important part of the regular school curriculum. As for the populace at large, perhaps some of the same techniques used by public-service agencies to make people cancer-conscious can be used to counteract the growing terror of pain and illness in general. People ought to know that nothing is more remarkable about the human body than its recuperative drive, given a modicum of respect. If our broadcasting stations cannot provide equal time for responses to the pain-killing advertisements, they might at least set aside a few minutes each day for common-sense remarks on the subject of pain. As for the Food and Drug Administration, it might be interesting to know why an agency that has so energetically warned the American people against taking vitamins without prescriptions is doing so little to control over-the-counter sales each year of billions of pain-killing pills, some of which can do more harm than the pain they are supposed to suppress.

About the Essay

1. What is Cousins's purpose in this essay? What does he want us to believe? What action does he want us to take?

2. If "pain is not the ultimate enemy," what, according to Cousins, is?

3. Why does Cousins give so much attention to aspirin? According to Cousins, what dangers are there from the sustained use of aspirin?

4. What does the example of the star baseball pitcher contribute to Cousins's argument? How does it make his essay more persuasive?

5. What in Cousins's tone contributes to the persuasiveness of his essay? Cite examples from the selection.

6. For what audience do you suppose Cousins wrote this essay? Do you think most readers would be convinced by what Cousins says about pain? Are you convinced? Why, or why not?

Explorations

1. Cousins believes that "the unremitting barrage of advertising for pain-killing drugs, especially over television, has set the stage for a mass anxiety neurosis. . . . Little wonder so many people fear pain more than death itself." What is your position on this issue? Write a persuasive essay in which

you support or refute his argument. Be sure to consider all forms of advertising.

2. In "Deciding to Be Ill" (pages 369–374), Jonathan Miller observes that we often diagnose our own ailments and decide whether they are serious enough that we should consider ourselves sick. How does his view relate to that of Norman Cousins?

LANCE MORROW

What are our attitudes toward our work, and toward work in general? What has become of the once-compelling American "work ethic"? Lance Morrow, writing in *Time* magazine for Labor Day, 1981, approaches these questions from the vantage point of our history as well as of our contemporary society. Morrow was born 1939 in Philadelphia and attended Harvard College, where he graduated in 1963. Shortly thereafter he joined the staff of *Time* and has been one of that magazine's regular contributors since 1965, writing on a wide range of topics of current interest.

The American work ethic had its origins in the beliefs of ascetic Protestants who held that God approves of strict discipline and hard work and shows His approval through worldly success and prosperity. Many non-Protestant immigrants also found justification for hard labor in an effort to make a better life for their families. But what is the value of work now, in the eighties? Morrow suggests some answers.

The Value of Working

During the 19th century industrialization of America, the idea of work's inherent virtue may have seemed temporarily implausible to generations who labored in the mines and mills and sweatshops. The century's huge machinery of production punished and stunned those who ran it. 1

And yet for generations of immigrants, work *was* ultimately availing: the numb toil of an illiterate grandfather got the father a foothold and a high school education, and the son wound up in college or even law school. A woman who died in the Triangle Shirtwaist Co. fire in lower Manhattan had a niece who made it to the halcyon Bronx, and another generation on, the family went to Westchester County.[1] So for millions of Americans, as they labored through the complexities of generations, work worked, and the immigrant work ethic came at last to merge with the Protestant work ethic. 2

The motive of work was all. To work for mere survival is desperate. To work for a better life for one's children and grandchildren lends the labor a fierce dignity. That dignity, an unconquerably hopeful energy and aspiration—driving, persisting like a life force—is the American quality that many find missing now. 3

---

[1] The Triangle Shirtwaist Company was a sweatshop employing European immigrants, mostly women, at very low wages. In a 1911 fire there 145 people were killed.

The work ethic is not dead, but it is weaker now. The psychology   4
of work is much changed in America. The acute, painful memory of the
Great Depression used to enforce a disciplined and occasionally docile
approach to work—in much the way that older citizens in the Soviet
Union do not complain about scarce food and overpopulated apartments,
because they remember how much more horrible everything was during
the war. But the generation of the Depression is retiring and dying off,
and today's younger workers, though sometimes laid off and kicked around
by recessions and inflation, still do not keep in dark storage that residual
apocalyptic memory of Hoovervilles and the Dust Bowl[2] and banks cap-
sizing.

Today elaborate financial cushions—unemployment insurance, union   5
benefits, welfare payments, food stamps and so on—have made it less
catastrophic to be out of a job for a while. Work is still a profoundly
respectable thing in America. Most Americans suffer a sense of loss, of
diminution, even of worthlessness if they are thrown out on the street.
But the blow seldom carries the life-and-death implications it once had,
the sense of personal ruin. Besides, the wild and notorious behavior of
the economy takes a certain amount of personal shame out of joblessness;
if Ford closes down a plant in New Jersey and throws 3,700 workers into
the unemployment lines, the guilt falls less on individuals than on Japanese imports or American car design or an extortionate OPEC.[3]

Because today's workers are better educated than those in the past,   6
their expectations are higher. Many younger Americans have rearranged
their ideas about what they want to get out of life. While their fathers
and grandfathers and great-grandfathers concentrated hard upon plow
and drill press and pressure gauge and tort, some younger workers now
ask previously unimaginable questions about the point of knocking themselves out. For the first time in the history of the world, masses of people
in industrially advanced countries no longer have to focus their minds
upon work as the central concern of their existence.

In the formulation of Psychologist Abraham Maslow, work func-   7
tions in a hierarchy of needs: first, work provides food and shelter, basic
human maintenance. After that, it can address the need for security and

---

[2]Hooverville was the name of any shantytown of unemployed, dispossessed people
during the early years of the Great Depression. The name came from President Herbert Hoover because it was during his administration that they existed. The Dust
Bowl was a region including Oklahoma and parts of neighboring states that was afflicted by severe drought and high winds.

[3]Organization of Petroleum-exporting Countries, the international price- and quota-
setting cartel.

then for friendship and "belongingness." Next, the demands of the ego arise, the need for respect. Finally, men and women assert a larger desire for "self-actualization." That seems a harmless and even worthy enterprise but sometimes degenerates into self-infatuation, a vaporously selfish discontent that dead-ends in isolation, the empty face that gazes back from the mirror.

Of course in patchwork, pluralistic America, different classes and   8
ethnic groups are perched at different stages in the work hierarchy. The immigrants—legal and illegal—who still flock densely to America are fighting for the foothold that the jogging tribes of self-actualizers achieved three generations ago. The zealously ambitious Koreans who run New York City's best vegetable markets, or boat people trying to open a restaurant, or Chicanos who struggle to start a small business in the *barrio* are still years away from est and the Sierra Club.[4] Working women, to the extent that they are new at it, now form a powerful source of ambition and energy. Feminism—and financial need—have made them, in effect, a sophisticated-immigrant wave upon the economy.

Having to work to stay alive, to build a future, gives one's exertions   9
a tough moral simplicity. The point of work in that case is so obvious that it need not be discussed. But apart from the sheer necessity of sustaining life, is there some inherent worth in work? Carlyle believed that "all work, even cotton spinning, is noble; work is alone noble." Was he right?

It is seigneurial cant to romanticize work that is truly detestable   10
and destructive to workers. But misery and drudgery are always comparative. Despite the sometimes nostalgic haze around their images, the preindustrial peasant and the 19th century American farmer did brutish work far harder than the assembly line. The untouchable who sweeps excrement in the streets of Bombay would react with blank incomprehension to the malaise of some $17-an-hour workers on a Chrysler assembly line. The Indian, after all, has passed from "alienation" into a degradation that is almost mystical. In Nicaragua, the average 19-year-old peasant has worked longer and harder than most Americans of middle age. Americans prone to restlessness about the spiritual disappointments of work should consult unemployed young men and women in their own ghettos: they know with painful clarity the importance of the personal dignity that a job brings.

---

[4]*Barrio*, Spanish for "neighborhood" and here used to refer to a Hispanic area. *Est*, Latin for "is," refers to a self-realization program and group founded by Werner Erhard. The Sierra Club is an organization for enjoying and protecting the wilderness of America.

Americans often fall into fallacies of misplaced sympathy. Psychol-   11
ogist Maslow, for example, once wrote that he found it difficult "to
conceive of feeling proud of myself, self-loving and self-respecting, if I
were working, for example, in some chewing-gum factory . . ." Well,
two weeks ago, Warner-Lambert announced that it would close down its
gum-manufacturing American Chicle factory in Long Island City, N.Y.:
the workers who had spent years there making Dentyne and Chiclets
were distraught. "It's a beautiful place to work," one feeder-catcher-
packer of chewing gum said sadly. "It's just like home." There is a peculiar
elitist arrogance in those who discourse on the brutalizations of work
simply because they cannot imagine themselves performing the job. Certainly workers often feel abstracted out, reduced sometimes to dreary
robotic functions. But almost everyone commands endlessly subtle systems of adaptation; people can make the work their own and even cherish
it against all academic expectations. Such adaptations are often more
important than the famous but theoretical alienation from the process
and product of labor.

Work is still the complicated and crucial core of most lives, the   12
occupation melded inseparably to the identity; Freud said that the successful psyche is one capable of love and of work. Work is the most
thorough and profound organizing principle in American life. If mobility
has weakened old blood ties, our co-workers often form our new family,
our tribe, our social world; we become almost citizens of our companies,
living under the protection of salaries, pensions and health insurance.
Sociologist Robert Schrank believes that people like jobs mainly because
they need other people; they need to gossip with them, hang out with
them, to schmooze. Says Schrank: "The workplace performs the function
of community."

Unless it is dishonest or destructive—the labor of a pimp or a hit   13
man, say—all work is intrinsically honorable in ways that are rarely
understood as they once were. Only the fortunate toil in ways that express
them directly. There is a Renaissance splendor in Leonardo's effusion:
"The works that the eye orders the hands to make are infinite."[5] But
most of us labor closer to the ground. Even there, all work expresses the
laborer in a deeper sense: all life must be worked at, protected, planted,
replanted, fashioned, cooked for, coaxed, diapered, formed, sustained.
Work is the way that we tend the world, the way that people connect.
It is the most vigorous, vivid sign of life—in individuals and in civili-
zations.

---

[5]Refers to Leonardo da Vinci (1452–1519), Italian artist and scientist.

About the Essay

1. In Morrow's view, what is the value of working? How does he support his view?

2. Morrow says, "The work ethic is not dead, but it is weaker now." How does he support that statement? In your own view, what reasons are there for believing or disbelieving his statement?

3. What kinds of workers does Morrow approve of? What workers does he disapprove of? How does he reveal his attitudes? What specific words reveal his attitudes?

4. What is "self-actualization"? What does Morrow think of it? How does his opinion relate to his views on the value of working?

5. In paragraph 10, what does Morrow mean by the statement, "It is seigneurial cant to romanticize work that is truly detestable and destructive to workers"? What does he mean by his statement, "The Indian, after all, has passed from 'alienation' into a degradation that is almost mystical"? What examples can you give of romanticizing "detestable" work and of "mystical" degradation?

6. Morrow says "Work is still a profoundly respectable thing in America." What reasons does Morrow give for believing this? How does he qualify his assertion?

7. Morrow asks, "is there some inherent worth in work?" How does he (not Carlyle) answer his question? How would you answer his question?

Explorations

1. What would you like your life's work to be? What are your expectations of such work? What satisfaction and rewards do you hope to get from your work? Is there any occupation that interests you but seems beyond your reach?

2. Morrow quotes the nineteenth-century British writer Thomas Carlyle as saying, "All work, even cotton-spinning, is noble; work is alone noble. . . ." How would you support or oppose Carlyle's view? If you consider work noble, how would you define *noble*? If not, how would you characterize work? What other pursuits might be as noble as work? more noble?

3. Read several accounts people have written about what they do and how they feel about their work. (One excellent source is Studs Terkel's *Working.*) Or, interview people you know personally who are working, such as teachers, grocery clerks, and the like. What conclusions can you draw about people's expectations and attitudes about their work?

MARILYN MACHLOWITZ

Most people want their work to be satisfying, and admire or envy those who are happy in their work. But what if work becomes an obsession? Marilyn Machlowitz, a management psychologist, has studied obsessive workers for some years and has published her findings in *Workaholics* (1980). She was born in 1952 and graduated from Princeton, then earning her doctorate in psychology at Yale. She is currently at work on a study of the consequences of succeeding at an early age.

The word *workaholics* was formed by analogy with *alcoholic*, and suggests that those who live for their work are victims of an unfortunate addiction. But are they? In this selection from her book, Machlowitz defines workaholism and describes how some typical over-achievers behave. Judgment of this behavior she leaves to her readers.

Workaholics

To rest is to rust.
LESTER LANIN

When I interviewed Dr. Stuart Berger, who is now an associate   1
professor of psychiatry at Harvard, he was 25 and wrapping up his final days at New York City's Bellevue Hospital. A tall, good-looking man with dark, curly hair, Berger was wearing jeans and Adidas, almost as much a part of the uniform of a young doctor as the beeper attached to his belt. We met in his small apartment, which was dominated by both its imposing view of the New York skyline and a large, well-stocked wine rack. The interview was interrupted by incessant phone calls, for which Berger apologized, explaining, "My life has been a bit busy."

And indeed it had. Besides seeing private patients, teaching psy-   2
chiatry and law, directing an institute for the study of law and medicine, consulting for a drug-free therapeutic community, seeing clinic patients, supervising medical students and junior residents, and writing a book, Berger had been flying around the country to lecture and appear on television talk shows.

"My average week is about 100 hours long and very fast-paced. I   3
get up about 6 A.M., shower, and have coffee; start reading journals at 6:30; see my first patients at 8:00; teach; never eat lunch—I just have garbage food all day. Three-quarters of the time I have a work-related dinner, and it's not uncommon on private days[1] to see patients until

---

[1]That is, days reserved for seeing patients in his office rather than at the hospital.

8:00, 8:30 at night. Of course, there's something very important to say about this horrendous-sounding schedule: I adore it!"

What makes him go and what keeps him going? "Give me a good   4
goal. Give me something I can get excited about, that I can fantasize about, that I can live. I don't need any thank you's. I don't need any appreciation. I just need something I can get excited about. . . . I absolutely crave psychiatry and love developing better systems for providing patient care. And these are things I can work on for months at a time at this pace. The goals are never accomplishable. There are always going to be more social problems. There'll never be an end. No matter how much I accomplish, it'll always be trivial compared to what's left to be done."

When asked what he does when he's not working, he paused and   5
was hard-pressed to come up with anything. "What kinds of things do I like? I have to think of them. I've given up collecting coins and I'd always been a great reader before I went to college." Having just bought a summer home, he was planning to spend time there. "I'm taking three-day weekends. People who know me don't believe it. I'll read the books that have been piling up for seven years, sail, lose some weight, jog, and make myself healthy before I go into hibernation again."

But even as he spoke, Berger began to doubt his words. Smiling   6
sheepishly, he said, "Call me up at the end of the summer and I'll tell you if I did it."

[Berger] has most of the earmarks of the workaholic: He is intense   7
and driven, he doesn't sleep much, he works almost all of his waking hours, and vacations and time off remain firmly in the realm of fantasy. Berger's workaholic tendencies seem to fit well with his job and with his single, busy life-style. He is what I call a fulfilled workaholic, one who gets great enjoyment from his work and who has successfully shaped the rest of his life around his central passion.

Others, especially those with families, have more difficulty accom-   8
plishing such a feat. Alex Loukides (a pseudonym) is a typical example. Brought up in a lower class Greek community in Connecticut, Loukides graduated from college and served in the Marines before he joined the Manhattan firm where he still works. Loukides is 41, his wife is a few years younger, and their two children are 12 and 14. Loukides is now a senior partner in the firm. Whereas most of his colleagues commute from lush suburbs, he still lives in the town where he grew up, despite his substantial six-figure income.

• • • •

His present position is, he says, more "unpredictable" and therefore   9
more "exhilarating" than any of the many he has held since his trainee
days. Still, he says, "I feel the same getting off the elevator as I did
twenty years ago. There's no sense of power or anything like that." He
cites his success in business as his main source of satisfaction, explaining,
"I don't think you can separate yourself from what you do. I don't think
your concept of yourself can be separated from what you do."

Loukides is frequently in his Manhattan office six days a week. He   10
arrives home around 8 P.M. His travel schedule is less time-consuming
than it could be, however, for when he travels, he resorts to turnaround
trips: "I've been to Paris thirteen times for a total of twelve days."

Nor are vacations a temptation. "Vacations bore me. I don't really   11
enjoy them. . . . In the past few years, I've made a real effort to take
them. We bought a house by the shore. This was an effort on my part
to force me to spend time with my family."

Not surprisingly, he feels guilty about "not having been as good a   12
husband and a father as I'd like to be. . . . I don't think the kids resent
my working [hard]. . . . I think my wife does. . . . she's a housewife and
she's going through the same thing every other woman's going through.
'Should I go back to school? Should I get a job?' I don't try to discourage
her, but I find it kind of threatening, too. It's sort of comfortable for me
to have her in the house."

• • • •

When I asked him if he was a workaholic, Loukides said, "I don't   13
know. If you asked my wife, she would say 'Definitely.' And probably a
lot of other people would, too. . . . If being a workaholic means you're
dependent on work and you have to work in order to function, well, I
think that's true for everybody."

Loukides seemed vaguely aware of some rumblings both in the office   14
(his "unpredictable" position) and at home. Yet he either doesn't see
clearly or chooses not to accept that some of these problems could be
tied to his addiction for work.

Both Loukides and Berger share six basic characteristics that set all   15
workaholics apart. These "traits" indicate that workaholism is considerably more paradoxical than the stereotype would lead us to believe. Still,
my research shows that these characteristics are common to each and
every workaholic that I interviewed. Let's take a look at them.

Workaholics are intense, energetic, competitive, and driven. The inten-   16
sity of a workaholic is inspiring. Eileen Ford, founder and head of the

New York modeling agency, skips much of the weekend social scene. "It's not the good life that interests me so much as the good job." She explains that she spends her weekends working. "I lock myself in my bedroom on Saturday and Sunday with shades drawn and work until I accomplish what I wish to accomplish."

Part of the ability to work so hard, finds Mrs. Ford, comes from working at what one enjoys. "If I'm working, that's just what I am doing, nothing else. I'm not thinking about what else I would like to do, only what I'm doing. My mind doesn't wander. I am capable of tremendous concentration. I am never tired." 17

Workaholics also have an overwhelming zest for life. They are people who wake up and can't wait to get going. A banker explained, "I have a tremendous amount of energy. . . . my father says Con Ed should have plugged into me during the energy crisis." Already energetic, workaholics are energized rather than enervated by their work—their energy paradoxically expands as it is expended. This relationship between energy and work is somewhat circular. As an advertising executive explained, "My energy contributes to my job and my job contributes to my energy." 18

Workaholics compete fiercely with others. However, the most stringent standards are internal and the strongest competition is with themselves. As one man explained, "I live on ten-year goals. . . . I set my own goals, make my own challenges, and compete with myself." They live life as a game—better yet, a race—to be won for fear that others will gain on them unless they keep getting ahead. One workaholic delighted in getting to work hours before anyone else because, "by 9:00 I had done a day's work. . . . I was already a day ahead of everybody." 19

Not surprisingly, the number one topic for comparison in this competition is hours of work. A young physician explained that the main obsession among his medical school classmates, the residents who supervised them in hospital wards, and the physicians who taught them the courses wasn't money, sex, or knowledge, but how hard they worked. Five-minute lunches never left much time for conversation, but this topic was always discussed. 20

Workaholics are driven. While waiting for the critical and commercial success that will permit him to move from Manhattan and television to Hollywood and the movies, a young screenwriter holds a full-time job as a staff writer for a mundane trade magazine. He considers himself a workaholic "because I totally define myself in terms of my work. . . . I'm so used to its directing my life. It's directing me. I'm not directing it. . . . But it's gone too far. I can't not do it. I get physically sick if I don't do something on a script each day. . . ." 21

His drive is not derived from a sense of self-discipline. Rather, his seeming self-discipline stems from his drive. "Writing gives me discipline. You have to be home at a certain time to write." He is not one to do nothing. "Intellectually, I realize there's a value to rest, [to] 'hanging out,' 'bumming around,' but emotionally, I can't."

Workaholics have strong self-doubts. Although they appear assured to the point of arrogance, they secretly suspect that they are inadequate. No matter how undeserved and/or suppressed these suspicions are, they still inspire insecurities. Working hard can be a way of concealing or compensating for such suspected shortcomings.

Shelly Gross is a producer, novelist, and co-founder of Music Fair Enterprises, Inc., an organization that produces shows and concerts throughout the United States and Canada. Gross' workweek typically includes commuting between suburban Philadelphia, where he lives and works, and Manhattan, where partner Lee Guber lives and works; catching new acts; and throwing cast suppers in each city. His strategy, like that of most workaholics, is to organize his time. "I try my best compulsively not to waste time." Gross feels uneasy when forced to waste time, so he makes sure that he's seldom put in that position: He fills his time with surf fishing and writing; he's finished five novels so far. What makes Shelly run? "Deep down inside, there's the feeling that I'm trading sweat for talent."

This concern is not uncommon. One man felt he wasn't quite the intellectual equal of his peers, despite his Harvard degrees. Therefore, he thought the only way to keep up would be by doing more. Others maintain that their work isn't just the thing they're best at, but the only thing they're even good at. Barbara Walters, for instance, squelches claims that she is an all-around Wonder Woman with an appealing combination of honesty and modesty. She told *Vogue* magazine, "I flunked gym, flunked home economics. I am not visual and can't draw. But I'm compulsive. Whatever it is, I must do it today. And must do it over until it's right."

Workaholics prefer labor to leisure. With respect to weekends and vacations, the ways of workaholics once again appear to be at odds with those of the rest of society. Either because of position or personality, they have blended or reversed the customary roles, preferring labor to leisure. What they do for a living has evolved into an endlessly fascinating endeavor. They have no use for and little need of free time. They find inactivity intolerable and pressure preferable. Workaholics never say

"Thank God it's Friday" for they prefer weekdays to weekends. Mondays, in fact, offer welcome relief from the "Sunday neurosis," a syndrome of anxiety and depression stimulated by weekend's tranquility.

Workaholics can—and do—work anytime and anywhere. They are [27] heedless of holidays, slow seasons, and weekends. Many maintain that they save time this way. Explains Senator William Proxmire "I find that by working on weekends or evenings or times when the phone is not ringing and others are not present, it is possible to accomplish a lot in a short time." Nor are they likely to turn off after hours. As a securities analyst said, "I'm forever thinking about new companies and new industries and, to a degree, this puts me in my office twenty-four hours a day."

As a result, their homes often become but branch offices of their [28] businesses and both airplanes and commuter trains are pressed into service as substitute offices. Mary Wells Lawrence, who heads Wells, Rich, Greene, a New York ad agency, was once asked by a reporter when she stops, slows down, turns off, tunes out. She replied, "Never. I am either digesting new material or looking for new solutions to a client's problem. When I'm on a plane, I don't waste a minute. I cover all the magazines— I demolish them. I see a picture of a yacht we could photograph, read about a restaurant to take clients to or a new take-out place for chili because there's a client who likes chili."

Workaholics make the most of their time. Their attitude toward time [29] and its use is their most telling trait: The quest to conquer time is constant. They glance at their watches continually, as though calculating how to fit the most work into the least amount of time. Saving time becomes a goal in itself as they put to good use the spare seconds others seem not to notice. As Stanley Marcus, the department store magnate, stated in *Minding the Store*, "Time is a precious possession and I attempt to make the most of it by not wasting it, for it is irreplaceable. One of the ways I cover so much ground is by using time judiciously. . . . we all have time to do everything we want to do if we organize our time properly."

For workaholics, "killing time" would seem tantamount to com- [30] miting suicide. . . . So they sleep six hours a night (at most) and get up and get going early. Their meals are typically functional (breakfast business meetings) or fast (lunch at the desk). They use lists, appointment books, and gadgets—the dictating devices, lighted pens for darkened rooms, and even car telephones that enable them to work wherever they are—to master every minute. Indeed, workaholics are so conscious of and compulsive about using every minute that they struggle to save seconds. They are the ones who continually punch the elevator button and then take the stairs because they don't want to wait. They rush through the day and into the night. As one harried woman reported, "I feel I even have to sleep fast."

They fill their Daytimers months in advance. And as Mary Wells 31 Lawrence told *Vogue*, "I run my life the way a lot of people run their businesses; I have to. I don't literally draw charts and graphs, but it's how I think. Everything is written down, planned in advance. I plan the year, I plan the month, I plan the week, I plan the day." Workaholics will win whenever being booked up becomes something of a status game. And a game it is. Jack Lenor Larsen, the New York fabric designer, cheerfully concedes that "to do ten things in one day would be too much, but to try for fifteen becomes an interesting game."

Workaholics blur the distinctions between business and pleasure. Louis 32 L'Amour, the prolific novelist, maintains that "the things I would do for fun are the things necessary to my work anyway. My work is also my hobby. I am happiest when working." One workaholic told me, "I don't think of work as any different from play. I mean, I do enjoy it—I'd rather do that than anything else. I'd rather do that than play—at anything else. I don't know why one has to draw the distinction."

As a result, the professional and personal lives of these work addicts 33 become intertwined. "Some of my best friends are people I've met over a conference table . . . and some of my clients are people I've met at parties," explained Laurel Cutler, senior vice-president for marketing planning at Leber Katz Partners in New York.

Although each and every workaholic exhibits these characteristics, 34 workaholics do differ from one another. The variation involves their attitude toward nonwork activities. Some workaholics, as the stereotype suggests, eschew these entirely. Others incorporate them into their work in one of several ways.

My research revealed four distinct types of workaholics. 35

The Dedicated Workaholic. The first type of workaholic is single- 36 minded and one-dimensional. These people fit the stereotype to a "T." They don't expand "job descriptions" to include their other interests because they simply have no other interests. They often seem humorless and brusque—and they are. As one executive recruiter confessed, "I'm so single-minded. I have to work very hard at not working twenty-four hours a day." Lew Wasserman, chairman of M.C.A., Inc., the enter-tainment conglomerate, has no hobbies. According to *Fortune*, "he ad-mits with seeming pride that he has never played a set of tennis or round of golf, and that in his forty-year career with M.C.A. he has taken but a single vacation." And Leda Sanford, a magazine editor, reportedly hates sports, spurns theatre and ballet, and is never without her briefcase.

Similarly, Revlon's Charles Revson was said to be particularly single-minded and exclusively devoted to his business. One of his associates once wished to interrupt a meeting momentarily to glance out the window as the Pope's motorcade passed by on Fifth Avenue. Revson was said to be indignant and totally uninterested in the historic procession below. The Vatican, after all, was not a prime purchaser of nail polish and lipstick.

The Integrated Workaholic. For the second type of workaholics, work is also "everything," but their work includes outside interests as well. By virtue of their job's purpose or their own personalities, they incorporate outside activities into the job itself. The president of one management consulting firm claimed to do little but work. Yet he reeled off trips and accomplishments ("I've published two books and have three more written in my head") that he merely considered to be part of his job.

David Rockefeller, chairman of The Chase Manhattan Bank, told *The New Yorker* "I can't imagine a more interesting job than mine. . . . The bank has dealings with everything. There is no field of activity it isn't involved in. It's a springboard for whatever interests one may have in any direction." And Barbara Walters once told a reporter, "I'm doing what I absolutely love. . . . I have the best job that anyone could have. . . . I have the opportunity to meet everyone, to interview everyone."

The Diffuse Workaholic. This third kind of workaholic is likely to have "fingers in lots of pies" and "several balls in the air" whether at work or not. These people may change jobs and fields fairly frequently. Their pursuits are more scattered than those of integrated workaholics. One Wall Street executive exemplified this approach particularly well. "I'm hyper during the day," he explained. "I have a kind of short attention span where a lot of things turn me on, and then, after a short period of time, I will drop them."

Similarly, one woman concedes "this job doesn't fill my time." So she resorts to filling her twenty-hour days with work for over a dozen committees, task forces, charitable organizations, civic groups, and community boards.

The Intense Workaholic. The fourth type of workaholic pursues leisure activities with the same passion, sense of purpose, and pace as he pursues work. A hobby just becomes "a job of a different kind." Recognizing this, one writer has warned that hobbies can be dangerous because workaholics will pursue them with "the same intensity and preoccupation as they do their work." As one woman workaholic told me, "I love sports. . . . I'm as avid about those as I am about working." She believes that "anybody who's very intense in business is also intense in their other pursuits." For example, more than one person in my sample was a marathoner, applying the same energy and exactitude toward training, clocking times, and completing difficult courses as toward their careers.

Alex Lewyt, who founded the vacuum cleaner company that bears his name, was profiled by *The New York Times*. Since Lewyt never took vacations, his doctor told him that he was a prime candidate for a heart attack and urged him to get a hobby. But he began collecting watches and clocks so obsessively that the doctor finally told him to lay off the timepieces, too.

43

About the Essay

1. What general definition of a workaholic does Machlowitz provide in this essay? How does she construct her definition?

2. Why do you think Machlowitz begins her essay with the anecdotes of Dr. Stuart Berger and Alex Loukides? How else might she have begun her essay?

3. Machlowitz is an authority on her subject. In what ways does she reveal the breadth and depth of her knowledge?

4. In what way is a workaholic different from other workers? What behavioral patterns characterize the workaholic? How does a workaholic relate to his or her job, family, friends, leisure time, and so forth?

5. Machlowitz divides workaholics into four types. What are they? What are the essential differences between these types? Do you know anyone you would call a workaholic? Which type is that person, and why?

6. Does any particular section of the essay strike you with unusual force? Which part? Why do you think you respond so strongly to it?

Explorations

1. Machlowitz's essay seems to imply that workaholics themselves may be very happy, but that those who live with them often suffer some deprivation. Do you think this is true or not? Why do you think so? To support your view, use examples and anecdotes from your own experiences and observations.

2. Machlowitz explains what workaholism is and what workaholics do, but she does not discuss how a person becomes addicted to work. What do you

think might be some reasons for such an addiction? How might workaholism be avoided? Or should it be?

3. In "The Value of Working" (pages 382–385), Lance Morrow discusses various needs that work can fill in people's lives. How does Morrow's essay contribute to an understanding of workaholism? What does Machlowitz's essay add to Morrow's discussion of the work ethic and the value of working?

DONALD HALL

Donald Hall, born in New Haven, Connecticut, in 1928, is a poet and a teacher of writing. After graduating from Harvard College and earning a degree at Oxford University, he became poetry editor of the *Paris Review* for nine years, and also joined the faculty of the University of Michigan, where he taught until 1975. Hall then left the university to devote his efforts wholly to writing. An acquaintance writes: "Donald Hall lives with his wife, the poet Jane Kenyon, in his ancestral farm house in New Hampshire. Through the zero winters they burn wood in ancestral woodstoves—eight cords, cut, split, delivered in the fall. Don rises in the night to stoke the fires. In the summers Jane grows a garden. . . . The barn is dilapidated now, the old buggy still inside which Don's grandfather drove to church three-quarters of a century ago. In New England no one throws much away."[1] A selection of his best poems is available as *A Blue Tit Tilts at the Edge of the Sea: Selected Poems 1964–1974* (1975), and his most recent book of poems is *Kicking the Leaves* (1979), from which "Ox Cart Man" is taken.

Ox Cart Man

In October of the year,
he counts potatoes dug from the brown field,
counting the seed, counting
the cellar's portion out,
and bags the rest on the cart's floor.   5

He packs wool sheared in April, honey
in combs, linen, leather
tanned from deerhide,
and vinegar in a barrel
hooped by hand at the forge's fire   10

He walks by ox's head, ten days
to Portsmouth Market, and sells potatoes,
and the bag that carried potatoes,
flaxseed, birch brooms, maple sugar, goose
feathers, yarn.   15

---

[1]Edward B. Germain, "Donald Hall," in *Contemporary Poets*, ed. James Vinson, 3rd ed. (New York: St. Martin's Press, 1980), p. 625.

When the cart is empty he sells the cart.
When the cart is sold he sells the ox,
harness and yoke, and walks
home, his pockets heavy
with the year's coin for salt and taxes,   2⊙

and at home by fire's light in November cold
stitches new harness
for next year's ox in the barn,
and carves the yoke, and saws planks
building the cart again.   2⊙

About the Poem

1. Why does the farmer sell the cart and the ox? How would you describe his philosophy of life?

2. In the first stanza (lines 1–5), what is the farmer doing with the potatoes?

3. How does Hall organize the events in the poem? What principle does he follow in dividing it into its five five-line stanzas?

4. Though the poem includes no rhymes, what evidence do you find that Hall has been careful to choose words for their sound as well as their meaning? How does the "sound" of the poem affect your response?

5. What point does Hall make in this poem? How does his choice of words enhance his point?

Explorations

1. Farmers like Hall's ox cart man are obliged to live in harmony with the seasons, but much of modern life is based on the conquest and exploitation of nature, rather than a respectful cooperation with it. What are some of the advantages of and dangers in our exploitation of nature? Is a simple life like the ox cart man's still possible—or desirable? Why or why not?

2. Would the ox cart man be an example of Henry David Thoreau's model of simplicity? (See "Simplicity," pages 343–349.) Why, or why not?

DIANE WAKOSKI

In her poetry, Diane Wakoski explores the difficulties of being a woman in late twentieth century America. She was born in Whittier, California, in 1937, and graduated from the University of California at Berkeley in 1960. She then went to New York City, where she worked as a bookstore clerk for three years and then taught English in the New York public school system. Meanwhile she had begun to publish some of her poems, and in 1966 her first major recognition came with the publication of *Discrepancies and Apparitions*. Since 1976 she has been on the faculty of Michigan State University. Her poems often reflect the emotional highs and lows of relationships between women and men; two of her books are *The Motorcycle Betrayal Poems* (1971) and *Dancing on the Grave of a Son of a Bitch* (1973). But her themes go beyond the personal to encompass, as she says, "the possibilities of magic, transformation, and the creation of beauty out of ugliness." "Ode to a Lebanese Crock of Olives," from *Waiting for the King of Spain* (1976), celebrates the pleasures of food and drink, both for their own sake and for what they can represent.

Ode to a Lebanese Crock of Olives

for Walter's Aunt Libby's diligence in making olives

As some women love jewels
and drape themselves with ropes of pearls, stud their ears
with diamonds, band themselves with heavy gold,
have emeralds on their fingers or
opals on white bosoms,   5
I live with the still life[1]
of grapes whose skins frost over with the sugar forming inside,
hard apples, and delicate pears;
cheeses,
from the sharp fontina, to icy bleu,   10
the aromatic chevres, boursault, boursin, a litany of
thick bread, dark wines,
pasta with garlic,
soups full of potato and onion;
and butter and cream,   15
like the skins of beautiful women, are on my sideboard.

---

[1]A still life is a painting of something inanimate, such as fruit or flowers. Wakoski's description of her "still life" sounds very much like a seventeenth-century Dutch painting.

These words are to say thank you
to
Walter's Aunt Libby
for her wonderful olives;   20
oily green knobs in lemon
that I add to the feast when they get here from Lebanon
(where men are fighting, as her sisters have been fighting
for years, over whose house the company stays in)
and whose recipes for kibbee or dolmas or houmas[2]   25
are passed along.

I often wonder,
had I been born beautiful,
a Venus on the California seashore,[3]
if I'd have learned to eat and drink so well?   30
For, with humming birds outside my kitchen window to remind of
    small elegance,
and mourning doves in the pines & cedar, speaking with grace,
and the beautiful bodies
of lean blond surfers,
dancing on terraces,   35
surely had I a beautiful face or elegant body,
surely I would not have found such pleasure
in food?
I often wonder why a poem to me
is so much more like a piece of bread and butter   40
than like a sapphire?
But with mockers flying in and out of orange groves,
and brown pelicans dipping into the Pacific,
looking at camelias and fuchsia,
an abundance of rose, and the brilliant purple ice plant   45
which lined the cliffs to the beach,
life was a "Still Life" for me.
And a feast.
I wish I'd known then
the paintings of Rubens or David,[4]   50
where beauty was not only
thin, tan, California girls,
but included all abundance.

---

[2]Kibbee, dolmas, and houmas are popular dishes from the Middle East.

[3]Venus, the classical goddess of love, was born in the sea.

[4]Peter Paul Rubens (1577–1640) painted voluptuous women; Jacques Louis David (1748–1825) painted elegant ladies of Napoleon's court.

As some women love jewels,
I love the jewels of life.   55
And were you,
the man I love,
to cover me (naked) with diamonds,
I would accept them too.

Beauty is everywhere,   60
in contrasts and unities.
But to you, I could not offer the thin tan fashionable body
of a California beach girl.
Instead, I could give the richness of burgundy,
dark brown gravies,   65
gleaming onions,
the gold of lemons,
and some of Walter's Aunt Libby's wonderful olives from Lebanon.

Thank you, Aunt Libby,
from a failed beach girl,   70
out of the West.

About the Poem

1. What delights the speaker most about food and drink? How does she express her delight?

2. Throughout, the poem compares jewels with food. What does this suggest about jewels? About food? What are the "jewels of life" for the speaker?

3. In lines 39–41 the speaker says, "I often wonder why a poem to me / is so much more like a piece of bread and butter / than like a sapphire?" What attitude toward poetry does this express? Do you agree with it? Why or why not?

4. In line 47 the speaker says, "life was a 'Still Life' for me." What do you think she means by this?

5. Lines 60–61 read, "Beauty is everywhere, / In contrasts and unities." How do these lines relate to the rest of the poem?

6. How would you describe the speaker of the poem? What image does she project? Why does she refer to herself as a "failed beach girl, / out of the West"?

Explorations

1. Do you, like Wakoski, get special pleasure out of the simple, basic things of life? Write about the source of your enjoyment, trying to make your readers gain as much pleasure from it as you do.

2. The great French chef Brillat-Savarin once described the perfect dinner as follows: "Let the number of guests not exceed twelve . . . so chosen that their occupations are varied, their tastes similar . . .; the dining room brilliantly lighted, the cloth pure white, the temperature between 60 and 68 degrees . . .; the dishes exquisite but few, the wines vintage . . .; the eating unhurried, dinner being the final business of the day . . .; the coffee hot . . .; the signal to leave not before eleven, and everyone in bed at midnight." How would you describe the perfect meal?

WILLIAM BUTLER YEATS

William Butler Yeats was not only one of the great poets of the modern age but also a figure in the movement to win his native Ireland independence from Great Britain. He was born near Dublin in 1865, and in his teens began to study painting. However, by the time he was twenty he had already published some poems, and his first book appeared when he was twenty-four. Soon he became conscious of the Irish nationalist movement, and sought to join in the creation of an indigenous Irish art. By 1915 he was so committed to the cause that he refused the honor of a knighthood from the King of England, and when Ireland did win independence Yeats was made a senator in the new national government. The next year, in 1923, he received the Nobel Prize for Literature. He continued to write poetry and many other various works until his death in 1939. His poetic work is available in a single volume as *Collected Poems*.

When he wrote "The Lake Isle of Innisfree," Yeats was twenty-five, living in London with his family, and deeply homesick for Ireland. Since his teens he had had the ambition of living on Innisfree, a lake in County Sligo, in imitation of Henry David Thoreau's life at Walden Pond (page 343), and that ambition provided the theme of his poem.

The Lake Isle of Innisfree

I will arise and go now, and go to Innisfree,
And a small cabin build there, of clay and wattles made:
Nine bean-rows will I have there, a hive for the honeybee,
And live alone in the bee-loud glade.

And I shall have some peace there, for peace comes dropping slow,   5
Dropping from the veils of the morning to where the cricket sings;
There midnight's all a glimmer, and noon a purple glow,
And evening full of the linnet's wings.

I will arise and go now, for always night and day
I hear lake water lapping with low sounds by the shore;   10
While I stand on the roadway, or on the pavements grey,
I hear it in the deep heart's core.

About the Poem

1. What is the mood of the speaker of the poem? How do you know?
2. What do you know about the speaker's plans for life on Innisfree?

3. What is peace compared with in lines 5 and 6? What does the comparison add to your sense of the atmosphere on Innisfree?

4. What contrast is drawn in the poem's last stanza? How does it affect the overall meaning of the poem?

5. How does Yeats achieve the patterned sound of the poem? Read the poem aloud to yourself, and listen carefully to the way the sound rises and falls. What effect does this have on your response to the poem?

Explorations

1. Yeats later called his plans for going to Innisfree a "daydream." Do you ever dream about doing something, even though you may never actually be able to do it? Do you really want to carry out your plan, or is the dream enough?

2. Is it possible in today's world to live alone and self-sufficiently as Thoreau did and Yeats dreamed of doing? What might be the advantages and disadvantages of such a way of life?

SHERWOOD ANDERSON

Sherwood Anderson (1876–1941) grew up in Clyde, Ohio, a small town like those he was later to picture in his novels and short stories. He had little formal education and at first drifted from job to job, soon achieving some success as an advertising copywriter and later as the president of a paint factory. He found emptiness in his success, however, and quite suddenly in 1912, at the age of thirty-six, he went to Chicago and began a career as a writer of fiction. He wrote several novels, including *Windy McPherson's Son* (1916) and *Dark Laughter* (1925), but is best known for his short stories, especially those in the collection *Winesburg, Ohio* (1919). Anderson's works all touch upon two themes: the loneliness and frustrations of life in a small town, and the alienation felt by people living and working in industrial society. Though his characters are often lonely and dissatisfied, his stories reflect a certain nostalgia for small-town America. The following story, taken from *The Triumph of the Egg* (1921), describes what happens to one family when it becomes possessed with "the American passion for getting up in the world."

The Egg

My father was, I am sure, intended by nature to be a cheerful, kindly man. Until he was thirty-four years old he worked as a farm hand for a man named Thomas Butterworth whose place lay near the town of Bidwell, Ohio. He had then a horse of his own and on Saturday evenings drove into town to spend a few hours in social intercourse with other farm hands. In town he drank several glasses of beer and stood about in Ben Head's saloon—crowded on Saturday evenings with visiting farm hands. Songs were sung and glasses thumped on the bar. At ten o'clock father drove home along a lonely country road, made his horse comfortable for the night and himself went to bed, quite happy in his position in life. He had at that time no notion of trying to rise in the world.

It was in the spring of his thirty-fifth year that father married my mother, then a country school teacher, and in the following spring I came wriggling and crying into the world. Something happened to the two people. They became ambitious. The American passion for getting up in the world took possession of them.

It may have been that mother was responsible. Being a school teacher she had no doubt read books and magazines. She had, I presume, read of how Garfield, Lincoln, and other Americans rose from poverty to fame and greatness and as I lay beside her—in the days of her lying-

405

in—she may have dreamed that I would some day rule men and cities. At any rate she induced father to give up his place as a farm hand, sell his horse and embark on an independent enterprise of his own. She was a tall silent woman with a long nose and troubled gray eyes. For herself she wanted nothing. For father and myself she was incurably ambitious.

The first venture into which the two people went turned out badly. Then rented ten acres of poor stony land on Griggs's Road, eight miles from Bidwell, and launched into chicken raising. I grew into boyhood on the place and got my first impressions of life there. From the beginning they were impressions of disaster and if, in my turn, I am a gloomy man inclined to see the darker side of life, I attribute it to the fact that what should have been for me the happy joyous days of childhood were spent on a chicken farm.

One unversed in such matters can have no notion of the many and tragic things that can happen to a chicken. It is born out of an egg, lives for a few weeks as a tiny fluffy thing such as you will see pictured on Easter cards, then becomes hideously naked, eats quantities of corn and meal bought by the sweat of your father's brow, gets diseases called pip, cholera, and other names, stands looking with stupid eyes at the sun, becomes sick and dies. A few hens and now and then a rooster, intended to serve God's mysterious ends, struggle through to maturity. The hens lay eggs out of which come other chickens and the dreadful cycle is thus made complete. It is all unbelievably complex. Most philosophers must have been raised on chicken farms. One hopes for so much from a chicken and is so dreadfully disillusioned. Small chickens, just setting out on the journey of life, look so bright and alert and they are in fact so dreadfully stupid. They are so much like people they mix one up in one's judgments of life. If disease does not kill them they wait until your expectations are thoroughly aroused and then walk under the wheels of a wagon—to go squashed and dead back to their maker. Vermin infest their youth, and fortunes must be spent for curative powders. In later life I have seen how a literature has been built up on the subject of fortunes to be made out of the raising of chickens. It is intended to be read by the gods who have just eaten of the tree of the knowledge of good and evil. It is a hopeful literature and declares that much may be done by simple ambitious people who own a few hens. Do not be led astray by it. It was not written for you. Go hunt for gold on the frozen hills of Alaska, put your faith in the honesty of a politician, believe if you will that the world is daily growing better and that good will triumph over evil, but do not read and believe the literature that is written concerning the hen. It was not written for you.

I, however, digress. My tale does not primarily concern itself with the hen. If correctly told it will center on the egg. For ten years my father and mother struggled to make our chicken farm pay and then they gave up that struggle and began another. They moved into the town of Bidwell, Ohio, and embarked in the restaurant business. After ten years of worry with incubators that did not hatch, and with tiny—and in their own way lovely—balls of fluff that passed on into seminaked pullethood and from that into dead henhood, we threw all aside and packing our belongings on a wagon drove down Griggs's Road toward Bidwell, a tiny caravan of hope looking for a new place from which to start on our upward journey through life.

We must have been a sad looking lot, not, I fancy, unlike refugees fleeing from a battlefield. Mother and I walked in the road. The wagon that contained our goods had been borrowed for the day from Mr. Albert Griggs, a neighbor. Out of its sides stuck the legs of cheap chairs and at the back of the pile of beds, tables, and boxes filled with kitchen utensils was a crate of live chickens, and on top of that the baby carriage in which I had been wheeled about in my infancy. Why we stuck to the baby carriage I don't know. It was unlikely other children would be born and the wheels were broken. People who have few possessions cling tightly to those they have. That is one of the facts that make life so discouraging.

Father rode on top of the wagon. He was then a bald-headed man of forty-five, a little fat and from long association with mother and the chickens he had become habitually silent and discouraged. All during our ten years on the chicken farm he had worked as a laborer on neighboring farms and most of the money he had earned had been spent for remedies to cure chicken diseases, on Wilmer's White Wonder Cholera Cure or Professor Bidlow's Egg Producer or some other preparations that mother found advertised in the poultry papers. There were two little patches of hair on father's head just above his ears. I remember that as a child I used to sit looking at him when he had gone to sleep in a chair before the stove on Sunday afternoons in the winter. I had at that time already begun to read books and have notions of my own and the bald path that led over the top of his head was, I fancied, something like a broad road, such a road as Caesar might have made on which to lead his legions out of Rome and into the wonders of an unknown world. The tufts of hair that grew above father's ears were, I thought, like forests. I fell into a half-sleeping, half-waking state and dreamed I was a tiny thing going along the road into a far beautiful place where there were no chicken farms and where life was a happy eggless affair.

6

7

8

One might write a book concerning our flight from the chicken 9
farm into town. Mother and I walked the entire eight miles—she to be
sure that nothing fell from the wagon and I to see the wonders of the
world. On the seat of the wagon beside father was his greatest treasure.
I will tell you of that.

On a chicken farm where hundreds and even thousands of chickens 10
come out of eggs surprising things sometimes happen. Grotesques are
born out of eggs as out of people. The accident does not often occur—
perhaps once in a thousand births. A chicken is, you see, born that has
four legs, two pairs of wings, two heads or what not. The things do not
live. They go quickly back to the hand of their maker that has for a
moment trembled. The fact that the poor little things could not live was
one of the tragedies of life to father. He had some sort of notion that if
he could but bring into henhood or roosterhood a five-legged hen or a
two-headed rooster his fortune would be made. He dreamed of taking
the wonder about to county fairs and of growing rich by exhibiting it to
other farm hands.

At any rate he saved all the little monstrous things that had been 11
born on our chicken farm. They were preserved in alcohol and put each
in its own glass bottle. These he had carefully put into a box and on our
journey into town it was carried on the wagon seat beside him. He drove
the horses with one hand and with the other clung to the box. When
we got to our destination the box was taken down at once and the bottles
removed. All during our days as keepers of a restaurant in the town of
Bidwell, Ohio, the grotesques in their little glass bottles sat on a shelf
back of the counter. Mother sometimes protested but father was a rock
on the subject of his treasure. The grotesques were, he declared, valuable.
People, he said, liked to look at strange and wonderful things.

Did I say that we embarked in the restaurant business in the town 12
of Bidwell, Ohio? I exaggerated a little. The town itself lay at the foot
of a low hill and on the shore of a small river. The railroad did not run
through the town and the station was a mile away to the north at a place
called Pickleville. There had been a cider mill and pickle factory at the
station, but before the time of our coming they had both gone out of
business. In the morning and in the evening busses came down to the
station along a road called Turner's Pike from the hotel on the main
street of Bidwell. Our going to the out-of-the-way place to embark in
the restaurant business was mother's idea. She talked of it for a year and
then one day went off and rented an empty store building opposite the
railroad station. It was her idea that the restaurant would be profitable.
Traveling men, she said, would be always waiting around to take trains
out of town and town people would come to the station to await incoming

trains. They would come to the restaurant to buy pieces of pie and drink coffee. Now that I am older I know that she had another motive in going. She was ambitious for me. She wanted me to rise in the world, to get into a town school and become a man of the towns.

At Pickleville father and mother worked hard as they always had done. At first there was the necessity of putting our place into shape to be a restaurant. That took a month. Father built a shelf on which he put tins of vegetables. He painted a sign on which he put his name in large red letters. Below his name was the sharp command—"EAT HERE"— that was so seldom obeyed. A showcase was bought and filled with cigars and tobacco. Mother scrubbed the floor and the walls of the room. I went to school in the town and was glad to be away from the farm and from the presence of the discouraged, sad-looking chickens. Still I was not very joyous. In the evening I walked home from school along Turner's Pike and remembered the children I had seen playing in the town school yard. A troop of little girls had gone hopping about and singing. I tried that. Down along the frozen road I went hopping solemnly on one leg. "Hippity Hop To The Barber Shop," I sang shrilly. Then I stopped and looked doubtfully about. I was afraid of being seen in my gay mood. It must have seemed to me that I was doing a thing that should not be done by one who, like myself, had been raised on a chicken farm where death was a daily visitor.

Mother decided that our restaurant should remain open at night. At ten in the evening a passenger train went north past our door followed by a local freight. The freight crew had switching to do in Pickleville and when the work was done they came to our restaurant for hot coffee and food. Sometimes one of them ordered a fried egg. In the morning at four they returned northbound and again visited us. A little trade began to grow up. Mother slept at night and during the day tended the restaurant and fed our boarders while father slept. He slept in the same bed mother had occupied during the night and I went off to the town of Bidwell and to school. During the long nights, while mother and I slept, father cooked meats that were to go into sandwiches for the lunch baskets of our boarders. Then an idea in regard to getting up in the world came into his head. The American spirit took hold of him. He also became ambitious.

In the long nights when there was little to do father had time to think. That was his undoing. He decided that he had in the past been an unsuccessful man because he had not been cheerful enough and that in the future he would adopt a cheerful outlook on life. In the early morning he came upstairs and got into bed with mother. She woke and the two talked. From my bed in the corner I listened.

13

14

15

It was father's idea that both he and mother should try to entertain   16
the people who came to eat at our restaurant. I cannot now remember
his words, but he gave the impression of one about to become in some
obscure way a kind of public entertainer. When people, particularly young
people from the town of Bidwell, came into our place, as on very rare
occasions they did, bright entertaining conversation was to be made.
From father's words I gathered that something of the jolly innkeeper effect
was to be sought. Mother must have been doubtful from the first, but
she said nothing discouraging. It was father's notion that a passion for
the company of himself and mother would spring up in the breasts of the
younger people of the town of Bidwell. In the evening bright happy
groups would come singing down Turner's Pike. They would troop shouting with joy and laughter into our place. There would be song and
festivity. I do not mean to give the impression that father spoke so
elaborately of the matter. He was as I have said an uncommunicative
man. "They want some place to go. I tell you they want some place to
go," he said over and over. That was as far as he got. My own imagination
has filled in the blanks.

For two or three weeks this notion of father's invaded our house.   17
We did not talk much, but in our daily lives tried earnestly to make
smiles take the place of glum looks. Mother smiled at the boarders and
I, catching the infection, smiled at our cat. Father became a little feverish
in his anxiety to please. There was no doubt, lurking somewhere in him,
a touch of the spirit of the showman. He did not waste much of his
ammunition on the railroad men he served at night but seemed to be
waiting for a young man or woman from Bidwell to come in to show
what he could do. On the counter in the restaurant there was a wire
basket kept always filled with eggs, and it must have been before his eyes
when the idea of being entertaining was born in his brain. There was
something pre-natal about the way eggs kept themselves connected with
the development of his idea. At any rate an egg ruined his new impulse
in life. Late one night I was awakened by a roar of anger coming from
father's throat. Both mother and I sat upright in our beds. With trembling
hands she lighted a lamp that stood on a table by her head. Downstairs
the front door of our restaurant went shut with a bang and in a few
minutes father tramped up the stairs. He held an egg in his hand and
his hand trembled as though he were having a chill. There was a half-
insane light in his eyes. As he stood glaring at us I was sure he intended
throwing the egg at either mother or me. Then he laid it gently on the
table beside the lamp and dropped on his knees beside mother's bed. He
began to cry like a boy and I, carried away by his grief, cried with him.
The two of us filled the little upstairs room with our wailing voices. It is

ridiculous, but of the picture we made I can remember only the fact that mother's hand continually stroked the bald path that ran across the top of his head. I have forgotten what mother said to him and how she induced him to tell her of what had happened downstairs. His explanation also has gone out of my mind. I remember only my own grief and fright and the shiny path over father's head glowing in the lamp as he knelt by the bed.

As to what happened downstairs. For some unexplainable reason I   18
know the story as well as though I had been a witness to my father's discomfiture. One in time gets to know many unexplainable things. On that evening young Joe Kane, son of a merchant of Bidwell, came to Pickleville to meet his father, who was expected on the ten o'clock evening train from the South. The train was three hours late and Joe came into our place to loaf about and to wait for its arrival. The local freight train came in and the freight crew were fed. Joe was left alone in the restaurant with father.

From the moment he came into our place the Bidwell young man   19
must have been puzzled by my father's actions. It was his notion that father was angry at him for hanging around. He noticed that the restaurant keeper was apparently disturbed by his presence and he thought of going out. However, it began to rain and he did not fancy the long walk to town and back. He bought a five-cent cigar and ordered a cup of coffee. He had a newspaper in his pocket and took it out and began to read. "I'm waiting for the evening train. It's late," he said apologetically.

For a long time father, whom Joe Kane had never seen before,   20
remained silently gazing at his visitor. He was no doubt suffering from an attack of stage fright. As so often happens in life he had thought so much and so often of the situation that now confronted him that he was somewhat nervous in its presence.

For one thing, he did not know what to do with his hands. He   21
thrust one of them nervously over the counter and shook hands with Joe Kane. "How-de-do," he said. Joe Kane put his newspaper down and stared at him. Father's eye lighted on the basket of eggs that sat on the counter and he began to talk. "Well," he began hesitatingly, "well, you have heard of Christopher Columbus, eh?" He seemed to be angry. "That Christopher Columbus was a cheat," he declared emphatically. "He talked of making an egg stand on its end. He talked, he did, and then he went and broke the end of the egg."

My father seemed to his visitor to be beside himself at the duplicity   22
of Christopher Columbus. He muttered and swore. He declared it was wrong to teach children that Christopher Columbus was a great man when, after all, he cheated at the critical moment. He had declared he

would make an egg stand on end and then when his bluff had been called he had done a trick. Still grumbling at Columbus, father took an egg from the basket on the counter and began to walk up and down. He rolled the egg between the palms of his hand. He smiled genially. He began to mumble words regarding the effect to be produced on an egg by the electricity that comes out of the human body. He declared that without breaking its shell and by virtue of rolling it back and forth in his hands he could stand an egg on its end. He explained that the warmth of his hands and the gentle rolling movement he gave the egg created a new center of gravity, and Joe Kane was mildly interested. "I have handled thousands of eggs," father said. "No one knows more about eggs than I do."

He stood the egg on the counter and it fell on its side. He tried the trick again and again, each time rolling the egg between the palms of his hands and saying the words regarding the wonders of electricity and the laws of gravity. When after a half hour's effort he did succeed in making the egg stand for a moment he looked up to find that his visitor was no longer watching. By the time he had succeeded in calling Joe Kane's attention to the success of his effort the egg had again rolled over and lay on its side.

Afire with the showman's passion and at the same time a good deal disconcerted by the failure of his first effort, father now took the bottles containing the poultry monstrosities down from their place on the shelf and began to show them to his visitor. "How would you like to have seven legs and two heads like this fellow?" he asked, exhibiting the most remarkable of his treasures. A cheerful smile played over his face. He reached over the counter and tried to slap Joe Kane on the shoulder as he had seen men do in Ben Head's saloon when he was a young farm hand and drove to town on Saturday evenings. His visitor was made a little ill by the sight of the body of the terribly deformed bird floating in the alcohol in the bottle and got up to go. Coming from behind the counter father took hold of the young man's arm and led him back to his seat. He grew a little angry and for a moment had to turn his face away and force himself to smile. Then he put the bottles back on the shelf. In an outburst of generosity he fairly compelled Joe Kane to have a fresh cup of coffee and another cigar at his expense. Then he took up a pan and filling it with vinegar, taken from a jug that sat beneath the counter, he declared himself about to do a new trick. "I will heat this egg in this pan of vinegar," he said. "Then I will put it through the neck of a bottle without breaking the shell. When the egg is inside the bottle it will resume its normal shape and the shell will become hard again. Then I will give the bottle with the egg in it to you. You can take it

about with you wherever you go. People will want to know how you got the egg in the bottle. Don't tell them. Keep them guessing. That is the way to have fun with this trick."

Father grinned and winked at his visitor. Joe Kane decided that the man who confronted him was mildly insane but harmless. He drank the cup of coffee that had been given him and began to read his paper again. When the egg had been heated in vinegar father carried it on a spoon to the counter and going into a back room got an empty bottle. He was angry because his visitor did not watch him as he began to do his trick, but nevertheless went cheerfully to work. For a long time he struggled, trying to get the egg to go through the neck of the bottle. He put the pan of vinegar back on the stove, intending to reheat the egg, then picked it up and burned his fingers. After a second bath in the hot vinegar the shell of the egg had softened a little but not enough for his purpose. He worked and worked and a spirit of desperate determination took possession of him. When he thought that at last the trick was about to be consummated the delayed train came in at the station and Joe Kane started to go nonchalantly out at the door. Father made a last desperate effort to conquer the egg and make it do the thing that would establish his reputation as one who knew how to entertain guests who came into his restaurant. He worried the egg. He attempted to be somewhat rough with it. He swore and the sweat stood out of his forehead. The egg broke under his hand. When the contents spurted over his clothes, Joe Kane, who had stopped at the door, turned and laughed.

A roar of anger rose from my father's throat. He danced and shouted a string of inarticulate words. Grabbing another egg from the basket on the counter, he threw it, just missing the head of the young man as he dodged through the door and escaped.

Father came upstairs to mother and me with an egg in his hand. I do not know what he intended to do. I imagine he had some idea of destroying it, of destroying all eggs, and that he intended to let mother and me see him begin. When, however, he got into the presence of mother something happened to him. He laid the egg gently on the table and dropped on his knees by the bed as I have already explained. He later decided to close the restaurant for the night and to come upstairs to get into bed. When he did so he blew out the light and after much muttered conversation both he and mother went to sleep. I suppose I went to sleep also, but my sleep was troubled. I awoke at dawn and for a long time looked at the egg that lay on the table. I wondered why eggs had to be and why from the egg came the hen who again laid the egg. The question got into my blood. It has stayed there, I imagine, because I am the son of my father. At any rate, the problem remains unsolved in my mind. And that, I conclude, is but another evidence of the complete and final triumph of the egg—at least as far as my family is concerned.

About the Story

1. What is the theme of this story? Why do you think so?

2. What kind of person was the father before he was married? How did he change with marriage? How does the narrator account for the change?

3. What does the father reveal about himself in setting up a display of dead, monstrously deformed chickens in his restaurant? By entertaining his customers with tricks involving eggs?

4. How does the narrator know what happened between his father and Joe Kane? Why do you think Anderson presents that incident as he does?

5. What is the emotional tone of the story the narrator tells? How did you respond to the story? What particular details affected the way you responded?

6. What does the egg symbolize? What is meant in the final sentence by "the complete and final triumph of the egg"?

Explorations

1. Tell a story concerning a friend or relative. It can be sad, funny, or whatever you choose, but tell the story in a way that reveals your own attitude toward the incident and that will make your readers respond to it in the same way you do.

2. In "The Egg," Anderson shows how ambition to succeed can instead lead to failure. What are the implications of this view? How might one go about directing his or her own ambitions so as to increase the chances of success?

6 The Lively Arts

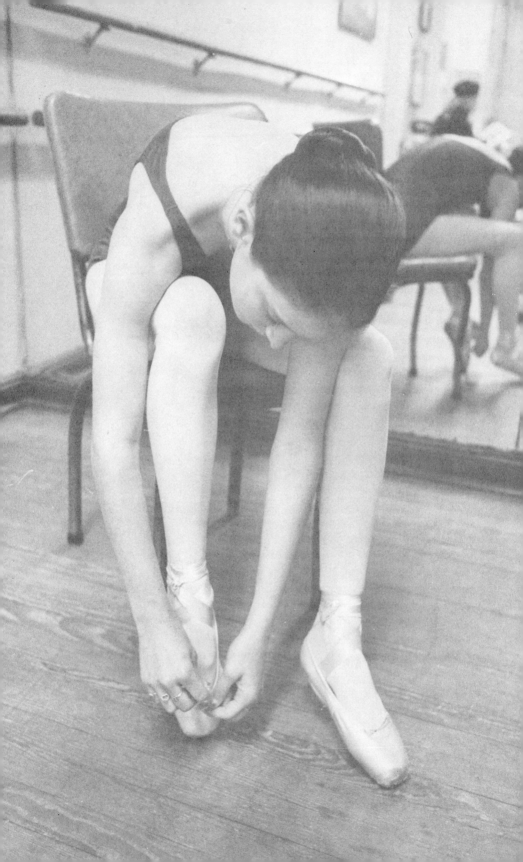

Life is very nice, but it lacks form. It's the aim of art to give it some.
JEAN ANOUILH

Every great and original writer, in proportion as he is great and original, must himself create the taste by which he is to be relished.
WILLIAM WORDSWORTH

The art of acting consists in keeping people from coughing.
SIR RALPH RICHARDSON

Painting is easy when you don't know how, but very difficult when you do.
EDGAR DÉGAS

A work of art has no importance whatever to society. It is only important to the individual.
VLADIMIR NABOKOV

THE arts reach far back into time, even beyond the record of written history. The ancient cave paintings in southern France tell us this, as do the figures of clay and bone still being discovered at archaeological sites. Old as they are, however, the arts are very much alive. They are woven into every culture, past and present, whether or not its people can write or read. Every nation, every tribe has its own repertoire of stories, songs, and dances, its own styles of visual art, and its own traditions of drama. The power of art is such that it enthralls even the very young. Indeed, Pablo Picasso once observed that "Every child is an artist. The problem is how to remain an artist once he grows up."

The arts offer us some of the most intense and profound pleasures we can know. Something deep in human nature finds expression in the creation and the experience of art. And the pleasure of art may be ours whether the work at hand is new or very old. The eighteenth-century music of Bach, the sixteenth-century paintings and sculptures of Michelangelo, the pre-Christian tragedies of Sophocles can still

417

excite and move us, just as does the latest novel by John Updike or the most recent ballet by Jerome Robbins.

As with so many things in life, what we get from art increases with the commitment we make to it. At first, a story may appeal to our taste for adventure or romance, certainly a genuine pleasure. But anyone who likes to read stories will fairly soon begin to accumulate some knowledge about different writers and their styles, and then about the form of the short story and how various writers use it. We may respond to a picture because it seems interesting or beautiful, but as we see more and more pictures—and possibly try our own hands at a little drawing or painting—we come to learn about the possibilities of paint on canvas, and can distinguish a masterpiece from the less special. In short, we develop critical standards. And though such standards may make us dissatisfied with the ordinary, they also deepen our appreciation of the very best and heighten our desire to experience more of it.

The pieces that follow touch upon several of the arts—literature, dance, theater, painting and sculpture, film—and of course the selections are all works of art themselves. Some explore the nature of art, others its purposes, and still others the artist's methods, intentions, and role in society. Taken together, they all testify to the vitality of the arts.

NORTHROP FRYE

"What good is the study of literature? . . . What difference does the study of literature make in our social or political or religious attitude?" Thus the distinguished Canadian scholar and critic Northrop Frye begins *The Educated Imagination* (1964), a published series of radio talks in which he discusses the relationship between literature and life. Such questions have been on his mind for many years, he says.

Born in Sherbrooke, Quebec, in 1912, Frye studied both English and philosophy at Victoria College, University of Toronto, before qualifying at Emanuel College to be ordained a minister. He then earned an M.A. in English at Oxford University and returned to Victoria College to teach literature, ultimately becoming its chancellor as well. He has published sixteen books, including the powerfully influential *Anatomy of Criticism* (1957), and hundreds of articles as well. Frye observes, "I have unconsciously arranged my life so that nothing has ever happened to me, and no biographer could possibly take the smallest interest in me." But he is so widely known and respected throughout his country that in 1979 he was named Canada's most distinguished citizen of the year.

Frye observes that we live not only according to our perceptions of the real world but according to our visions of a world we want to live in. Such visions are the product of our imaginations. Literature, too, is such a product, and in turn it can serve to educate the imagination. In this selection from *The Educated Imagination*, Frye suggests how this may be so.

The Keys to Dreamland

Suppose you're walking down the street of a North American city. 1 All around you is a highly artificial society, but you don't think of it as artificial: you're so accustomed to it that you think of it as natural. But suppose your imagination plays a little trick on you of a kind that it often does play, and you suddenly feel like a complete outsider, someone who's just blown in from Mars on a flying saucer. Instantly you see how conventionalized everything is: the clothes, the shop windows, the movement of the cars in traffic, the cropped hair and shaved faces of the men, the red lips and blue eyelids that women put on because they want to conventionalize their faces, or "look nice," as they say, which means the same thing. All this convention is pressing toward uniformity or likeness. To be outside the convention makes a person look queer, or, if he's driving a car, a menace to life and limb. The only exceptions are people who have decided to conform to different conventions, like nuns or beatniks. There's clearly a strong force making toward conformity in society, so strong that it seems to have something to do with the stability of society itself. In ordinary life even the most splendid things we can think of, like goodness and truth and beauty, all mean essentially what we're accustomed to. As I hinted just now in speaking of female make-up, most of our ideas of beauty are pure convention, and even truth has been defined as whatever doesn't disturb the pattern of what we already know.

When we move on to literature, we again find conventions, but this time we notice that they are conventions, because we're not so used to them. These conventions seem to have something to do with making literature as unlike life as possible. Chaucer represents people as making up stories in ten-syllable couplets. Shakespeare uses dramatic conventions, which means, for instance, that Iago has to smash Othello's marriage and dreams of future happiness and get him ready to murder his wife in a few minutes. Milton has two nudes in a garden haranguing each other in set speeches beginning with such lines as "Daughter of God and Man, immortal Eve"—Eve being Adam's daughter because she's just been extracted from his ribcase. Almost every story we read demands that we accept as fact something that we know to be nonsense: that good people always win, especially in love; that murders are complicated and ingenious puzzles to be solved by logic, and so on. It isn't only popular literature that demands this: more highbrow stories are apt to be more ironic, but irony has its conventions too. If we go further back into literature, we run into such conventions as the king's rash promise, the enraged cuckold, the cruel mistress of love poetry—never anything that we or any other time would recognize as the normal behavior of adult people, only the maddened ethics of fairyland.

Even the details of literature are equally perverse. Literature is a world where phoenixes and unicorns are quite as important as horses and dogs—and in literature some of the horses talk, like the ones in *Gulliver's Travels*. A random example is calling Shakespeare the "swan of Avon"— he was called that by Ben Jonson. The town of Stratford, Ontario, keeps swans in its river partly as a literary allusion.[1] Poets of Shakespeare's day hated to admit that they were writing words on a page: they always insisted that they were producing music. In pastoral poetry they might be playing a flute (or more accurately an oboe), but every other kind of poetic effort was called song, with a harp, a lyre or a lute in the background, depending on how highbrow the song was. Singing suggests birds,

---

[1]Shakespeare was born in the English town of Stratford on the river Avon. Stratford, Ontario, is the home of an annual Shakespearean festival.

and so for their typical songbird and emblem of themselves, the poets chose the swan, a bird that can't sing. Because it can't sing, they made up a legend that it sang once before death, when nobody was listening. But Shakespeare didn't burst into song before his death: he wrote two plays a year until he'd made enough money to retire, and spent the last five years of his life counting his take.

. . . Life and literature, then, are both conventionalized, and of the conventions of literature about all we can say is that they don't much resemble the conditions of life. It's when the two sets of conventions collide that we realize how different they are.   4

In fact, whenever literature gets too probable, too much like life, some self-defeating process, some mysterious law of diminishing returns, seems to set in. There's a vivid and expertly written novel by H. G. Wells called *Kipps*, about a lower-middle-class, inarticulate, very likeable Cockney, the kind of character we often find in Dickens. Kipps is carefully studied: he never says anything that a man like Kipps wouldn't say; he never sounds the "h" in *home* or *head*; nothing he does is out of line with what we expect such a person to be like. It's an admirable novel, well worth reading, and yet I have a nagging feeling that there's some inner secret in bringing him completely to life that Dickens would have and that Wells doesn't have. All right, then, what would Dickens have done? Well, one of the things that Dickens often does do is write *badly*. He might have given Kipps sentimental speeches and false heroics and all sorts of inappropriate verbiage to say; and some readers would have clucked and tut-tutted over these passages and explained to each other how bad Dicken's taste was and how uncertain his hold on character could be. Perhaps they'd be right too. But we'd have had Kipps a few times the way he'd look to himself or the way he'd sometimes wish he could be: that's part of his reality, and the effect would remain with us however much we disapproved of it. Whether I'm right about this book or not, and I'm not at all sure I am, I think my general principle is right. What we'd never see except in a book is often what we go to books to find. Whatever is completely lifelike is a bit of a laboratory specimen there. To bring anything really to life in literature we can't be lifelike: we have to be literaturelike.   5

The same thing is true even of the use of language. We're often taught that prose is the language of ordinary speech, which is usually true in literature. But in ordinary life prose is no more the language of ordinary speech than one's Sunday suit is a bathing suit. The people who actually speak prose are highly cultivated and articulate people, who've read a good many books, and even they can speak prose only to each other. If you read the beautiful sentences of Elizabeth Bennett's conversation in   6

Pride and Prejudice, you can see how in that book they give a powerfully convincing impression of a sensible and intelligent girl. But any girl who talked as coherently as that on a street car would be stared at as though she had green hair. It isn't only the difference between 1813 and 1962 that's involved either, as you'll see if you compare her speech with her mother's. The poet Emily Dickinson complained that everybody said "What?" to her, until finally she practically gave up trying to talk altogether, and confined herself to writing notes.

All this is involved with the principle I've touched on before: the difference between literary and other kinds of writing. If we're writing to convey information, or for any practical reason, our writing is an act of will and intention: we mean what we say, and the words we use represent that meaning directly. It's different in literature, not because the poet doesn't mean what he says too, but because his real effort is one of putting words together. What's important is not what he may have meant to say, but what the words themselves say when they get fitted together. With a novelist it's rather the incidents in the story he tells that get fitted together—as D.H. Lawrence says, don't trust the novelist; trust his story. That's why so much of a writer's best writing is or seems to be involuntary. It's involuntary because the forms of literature itself are taking control of it, and these forms are what are embodied in the conventions of literature. Conventions, we see, have the same role in literature that they have in life: they impose certain patterns of order and stability on the writer. Only, if they're such different conventions, it seems clear that the order of words, or the structure of literature, is different from the social order. . . .

So literature has no consistent connection with ordinary life, positive or negative. Here we touch on another important difference between structures of the imagination and structures of practical sense, which include the applied sciences. Imagination is certainly essential to science, applied or pure. Without a constructive power in the mind to make models of experience, get hunches and follow them out, play freely around with hypotheses, and so forth, no scientist could get anywhere. But all imaginative effort in practical fields has to meet the test of practicability, otherwise it's discarded. The imagination in literature has no such test to meet. You don't relate it directly to life or reality: you relate works of literature, as we've said earlier, to each other. Whatever value there is in studying literature, cultural or practical, comes from the total body of our reading, the castle of words we've built, and keep adding new wings to all the time.

So it's natural to swing to the opposite extreme and say that literature is really a refuge or escape from life, a self-contained world like the world of the dream, a world of play or make-believe to balance the world of work. Some literature is like that, and many people tell us that they only read to get away from reality for a bit. And I've suggested myself that the sense of escape, or at least detachment, does come into everybody's literary experience. But the real point of literature can hardly be that. Think of such writers as William Faulkner or François Mauriac, their great moral dignity, the intensity and compassion that they've studied the life around them with. Or think of James Joyce, spending seven years on one book and seventeen on another, and having them ridiculed or abused or banned by the customs when they did get published. Or of the poets Rilke and Valéry, waiting patiently for years in silence until what they had to say was ready to be said. There's a deadly seriousness in all this that even the most refined theories of fantasy or make-believe won't quite cover. Still, let's go along with the idea for a bit, because we're not getting on very fast with the relation of literature to life, or what we could call the horizontal perspective of literature. That seems to block us off on all sides.

The world of literature is a world where there is no reality except   10
that of the human imagination. We see a great deal in it that reminds us vividly of the life we know. But in that very vividness there's something unreal. We can understand this more clearly with pictures, perhaps. There are trick-pictures—*trompe l'oeil*,[2] the French call them—where the resemblance to life is very strong. An American painter of this school played a joke on his bitchy wife by painting one of her best napkins so expertly that she grabbed at the canvas trying to pull it off. But a painting as realistic as that isn't a reality but an illusion: it has the glittering unnatural clarity of a hallucination. The real realities, so to speak, are things that don't remind us directly of our own experience, but are such things as the wrath of Achilles or the jealousy of Othello, which are bigger and more intense experiences than anything we can reach—except in our imagination, which is what we're reaching with. Sometimes, as in the happy endings of comedies, or in the ideal world of romances, we seem to be looking at a pleasanter world than we ordinarily know. Sometimes, as in tragedy and satire, we seem to be looking at a world more devoted to suffering or absurdity than we ordinarily know. In literature we always seem to be looking either up or down. It's the vertical perspective that's important, not the horizontal one that looks out to life. Of course, in the greatest works of literature we get both the up and down views, often at the same time as different aspects of one event.

There are two halves to literary experience, then. Imagination gives   11
us both a better and a worse world than the one we usually live with, and demands that we keep looking steadily at them both. . . . Literature

---

[2]French, "deceive the eye," used as an art term to refer to a style of painting.

is not a world of dreams, but it would be if we had only one half without the other. If we had nothing but romances and comedies with happy endings, literature would express only a wish-fulfilment dream. Some people ask why poets want to write tragedies when the world's so full of them anyway, and suggest that enjoying such things has something morbid or gloating about it. It doesn't, but it might if there were nothing else in literature.

This point is worth spending another minute on. You recall that terrible scene in *King Lear* where Gloucester's eyes are put out on the stage. That's part of a play, and a play is supposed to be entertaining. Now in what sense can a scene like that be entertaining? The fact that it's not really happening is certainly important. It would be degrading to watch a real blinding scene, and far more so to get any pleasure out of watching it. Consequently, the entertainment doesn't consist in its reminding us of a real blinding scene. If it did, one of the great scenes of drama would turn into a piece of repulsive pornography. We couldn't stop anyone from reacting in this way, and it certainly wouldn't cure him, much less help the public, to start blaming or censoring Shakespeare for putting sadistic ideas in his head. But a reaction of that kind has nothing to do with drama. In a dramatic scene of cruelty and hatred we're seeing cruelty and hatred, which we know are permanently real things in human life, from the point of view of the imagination. What the imagination suggests is horror, not the paralyzing sickening horror of a real blinding scene, but an exuberant horror, full of the energy of repudiation. This is as powerful a rendering as we can ever get of life as we don't want it.

So we see that there are moral standards in literature after all, even though they have nothing to do with calling the police when we see a word in a book that's more familiar in sound than in print. . . . Literature keeps presenting the most vicious things to us as entertainment, but what it appeals to is not any pleasure in these things, but the exhilaration of standing apart from them and being able to see them for what they are because they aren't really happening. The more exposed we are to this, the less likely we are to find an unthinking pleasure in cruel or evil things. As the eighteenth century said in a fine mouth-filling phrase, literature refines our sensibilities.

The top half of literature is the world expressed by such words as sublime, inspiring, and the like, where what we feel is not detachment but absorption. This is the world of heroes and gods and titans and Rabelaisian giants,[3] a world of powers and passions and moments of

---

[3]Such as the hero of the great French writer François Rabelais' novel *Gargantua* (1534), a man of huge stature and appetites.

ecstasy far greater than anything we meet outside the imagination. Such forces would not only absorb but annihilate us if they entered ordinary life, but luckily the protecting wall of the imagination is here too. As the German poet Rilke says, we adore them because they disdain to destroy us. We seem to have got quite a long way from our emotions with their division of things into "I like this" and "I don't like this." Literature gives us an experience that stretches us vertically to the heights and depths of what the human mind can conceive, to what corresponds to the conceptions of heaven and hell in religion. In this perspective what I like or don't like disappears, because there's nothing left of me as a separate person: as a reader of literature I exist only as a representative of humanity as a whole. . . .

No matter how much experience we may gather in life, we can 15 never in life get the dimension of experience that the imagination gives us. Only the arts and sciences can do that, and of these, only literature gives us the whole sweep and range of human imagination as it sees itself. It seems to be very difficult for many people to understand the reality and intensity of literary experience. To give an example that you may think a bit irrelevant: why have so many people managed to convince themselves that Shakespeare did not write Shakespeare's plays, when there is not an atom of evidence that anybody else did? Apparently because they feel that poetry must be written out of personal experience, and that Shakespeare didn't have enough experience of the right kind. But Shakespeare's plays weren't produced by his experience: they were produced by his imagination, and the way to develop the imagination is to read a good book or two. As for us, we can't speak or think or comprehend even our own experience except within the limits of our own power over words, and those limits have been established for us by our great writers.

Literature, then, is not a dream-world: it's two dreams, a wish- 16 fulfillment dream and an anxiety dream, that are focused together, like a pair of glasses, and become a fully conscious vision. Art, according to Plato, is a dream for awakened minds, a work of imagination withdrawn from ordinary life, dominated by the same forces that dominate the dream, and yet giving us a perspective and dimension on reality that we don't get from any other approach to reality. So the poet and the dreamer are distinct, as Keats says. Ordinary life forms a community, and literature is among other things an art of communication, so it forms a community too. In ordinary life we fall into a private and separate subconscious every night, where we reshape the world according to a private and separate imagination. Underneath literature there's another kind of subconscious, which is social and not private, a need for forming a community around certain symbols, like the Queen and the flag, or around certain gods that represent order and stability, or becoming and change, or death and rebirth to a new life. This is the myth-making power of the human mind, which throws up and dissolves one civilization after another.

In all our literary experience there are two kinds of response. There is the direct experience of the work itself, while we're reading a book or seeing a play, especially for the first time. This experience is uncritical, or rather pre-critical, so it's not infallible. If our experience is limited, we can be roused to enthusiasm or carried away by something that we can later see to have been second-rate or even phony. Then there is the conscious, critical response we make after we've finished reading or left the theatre, where we compare what we've experienced with other things of the same kind, and form a judgment of value and proportion on it. This critical response, with practice, gradually makes our pre-critical responses more sensitive and accurate, or improves our taste, as we say. But behind our responses to individual works, there's a bigger response to our literary experience as a whole, as a total possession.

The critic has always been called a judge of literature, which means, not that he's in a superior position to the poet, but that he ought to know something about literature, just as a judge's right to be on a bench depends on his knowledge of law. If he's up against something the size of Shakespeare, he's the one being judged. The critic's function is to interpret every work of literature in the light of all the literature he knows, to keep constantly struggling to understand what literature as a whole is about. Literature as a whole is not an aggregate of exhibits with red and blue ribbons attached to them, like a cat-show, but the range of articulate human imagination as it extends from the height of imaginative heaven to the depth of imaginative hell. Literature is a human apocalypse, man's revelation to man, and criticism is not a body of adjudications, but the awareness of that revelation, the last judgment of mankind.

About the Essay

1. In the opening paragraphs of his essay, Frye discusses the relation between life and literature. What point about life and literature does he make by discussing conventions? How does he use literary examples to support his point? What examples of your own can you draw on from life or literature to support Frye's point?

2. What does Frye mean by the horizontal and vertical perspectives of literature? What, according to him, is the value of a scene like the blinding of Gloucester in *King Lear?*

3. Frye writes: "In this perspective what I like or don't like disappears, because there's nothing left of me as a separate person: as a reader of literature

I exist only as a representative of humanity as a whole." What exactly does he mean by this? How does the context affect your understanding of this statement? Do you agree or disagree with Frye? Why?

4. How is literature dreamlike? How does it differ from our dreams? What do you think the "keys to dreamland" are?

5. What is Frye's purpose in this essay? What does he want us to believe when we have finished reading it?

6. In his last sentence, Frye alludes to the Bible's Book of Revelation, with its prophecy of the end of the world and God's last judgment. What does this allusion tell us about Frye's view of literature? What, for example, does it suggest about the function of literature?

Explorations

1. What literary work or works have you most enjoyed reading? What works would you say are most important to you? In what way are they important? What, for you, is the value of literature?

2. Frye argues that violence on the stage or screen may have a positive moral influence on its viewers, whereas observing real violence would be degrading. Do you agree with this position? Consider comparable examples of real and dramatized violence, such as a movie about boxing like *Raging Bull* and an actual boxing match, or a television drama of the assassination of President Kennedy and a film of the actual event. What exactly is the effect each one has on you? Why do you think you respond as you do?

3. Consider a literary work you have read recently, perhaps one of the short stories in this book. What aspects of the work relate clearly to any of the points made by Frye in his discussion? In particular, what would you say is the moral significance of the work?

Writers of fiction tell their stories but rarely want to explain them. The short-story writer Eudora Welty once wrote: "I never saw, as reader or writer, that a finished story stood in need of any more from the author: for better or worse, there the story is." But Welty's story "A Worn Path" (included in this volume on page 102) brought her so many letters, all asking the same question, that she decided in 1974 to write an essay answering that question: "Is Phoenix Jackson's grandson really dead?" Even for those who would never have asked this question, the essay is absorbing and enlightening, for in it the writer allows us to look into her workshop to see how she came to write the story—what first gave her the idea for it and how she developed that idea. (For biographical information about Eudora Welty, see page 102.)

"Is Phoenix Jackson's Grandson Really Dead?"

A story writer is more than happy to be read by students; the fact   1
that these serious readers think and feel something in response to his work he finds life-giving. At the same time he may not always be able to reply to their specific questions in kind. I wondered if it might clarify something, for both the questioners and myself, if I set down a general reply to the question that comes to me most often in the mail, from both students and their teachers, after some classroom discussion. The unrivaled favorite is this: "Is Phoenix Jackson's grandson really *dead?*"

It refers to a short story I wrote years ago called "A Worn Path,"   2
which tells of a day's journey an old woman makes on foot from deep in the country into town and into a doctor's office on behalf of her little grandson; he is at home, periodically ill, and periodically she comes for his medicine; they give it to her as usual, she receives it and starts the journey back.

I had not meant to mystify readers by withholding any fact; it is   3
not a writer's business to tease. The story is told through Phoenix's mind as she undertakes her errand. As the author at one with the character as I tell it, I must assume that the boy is alive. As the reader, you are free to think as you like, of course: the story invites you to believe that no matter what happens, Phoenix for as long as she is able to walk and can hold to her purpose will make her journey. The *possibility* that she would keep on even if he were dead is there in her devotion and its single-minded, single-track errand. Certainly the *artistic* truth, which should be good enough for the fact, lies in Phoenix's own answer to that

question. When the nurse asks, "He isn't dead, is he?" she speaks for herself: "He still the same. He going to last."

· The grandchild is the incentive. But it is the journey, the going of the errand, that is the story, and the question is not whether the grandchild is in reality alive or dead. It doesn't affect the outcome of the story or its meaning from start to finish. But it is not the question itself that has struck me as much as the idea, almost without exception implied in the asking, that for Phoenix's grandson to be dead would somehow make the story "better."

It's *all right*, I want to say to the students who write to me, for things to be what they appear to be, and for words to mean what they say. It's all right, too, for words and appearances to mean more than one thing—ambiguity is a fact of life. A fiction writer's responsibility covers not only what he presents as the facts of a given story but what he chooses to stir up as their implications; in the end, these implications, too, become facts, in the larger, fictional sense. But it is not all right, not in good faith, for things *not* to mean what they say.

The grandson's plight was real and it made the truth of the story, which is the story of an errand of love carried out. If the child no longer lived, the truth would persist in the "wornness" of the path. But his being dead can't increase the truth of the story, can't affect it one way or the other. I think I signal this, because the end of the story has been reached before old Phoenix gets home again: she simply starts back. To the question "Is the grandson really dead?" I could reply that it doesn't make any difference. I could also say that I did not make him up in order to let him play a trick on Phoenix. But my best answer would be: "*Phoenix is alive.*"

The origin of a story is sometimes a trustworthy clue to the author— or can provide him with the clue—to its key image; maybe in this case it will do the same for the reader. One day I saw a solitary old woman like Phoenix. She was walking; I saw her, at middle distance, in a winter country landscape, and watched her slowly make her way across my line of vision. That sight of her made me write the story. I invented an errand for her, but that only seemed a living part of the figure she was herself: what errand other than for someone else could be making her go? And her going was the first thing, her persisting in her landscape was the real thing, and the first and the real were what I wanted and worked to keep. I brought her up close enough, by imagination, to describe her face, make her present to the eyes, but the full-length figure moving across the winter fields was the indelible one and the image to keep, and the perspective extending into the vanishing distance the true one to hold in mind.

I invented for my character, as I wrote, some passing adventures—   8
some dreams and harassments and a small triumph or two, some jolts to
her pride, some flights of fancy to console her, one or two encounters
to scare her, a moment that gave her cause to feel ashamed, a moment
to dance and preen—for it had to be a *journey,* and all these things
belonged to that, parts of life's uncertainty.

A narrative line is in its deeper sense, of course, the tracing out of   9
a meaning, and the real continuity of a story lies in this probing forward.
The real dramatic force of a story depends on the strength of the emotion
that has set it going. The emotional value is the measure of the reach
of the story. What gives any such content to "A Worn Path" is not its
circumstances but its *subject:* the deep-grained habit of love.

What I hoped would come clear was that in the whole surround of   10
this story, the world it threads through, the only certain thing at all is
the worn path. The habit of love cuts through confusion and stumbles
or contrives its way out of difficulty, it remembers the way even when it
forgets, for a dumbfounded moment, its reason for being. The path is
the thing that matters.

Her victory—old Phoenix's—is when she sees the diploma in the   11
doctor's office, when she finds "nailed up on the wall the document that
had been stamped with the gold seal and framed in the gold frame, which
matched the dream that was hung up in her head." The return with the
medicine is just a matter of retracing her own footsteps. It is the part of
the journey, and of the story, that can now go without saying.

In the matter of function, old Phoenix's way might even do as a   12
sort of parallel to your way of work if you are a writer of stories. The way
to get there is the all-important, all-absorbing problem, and this problem
is your reason for undertaking the story. Your only guide, too, is your
sureness about your subject, about what this subject is. Like Phoenix,
you work all your life to find your way, through all the obstructions and
the false appearances and the upsets you may have brought on yourself,
to reach a meaning—using inventions of your imagination, perhaps helped
out by your dreams and bits of good luck. And finally too, like Phoenix,
you have to assume that what you are working in aid of is life, not death.

But you would make the trip anyway—wouldn't you?—just on hope.   13

About the Essay

1. How does Welty answer the question that is her title? Why does she answer the question in that way? What do you learn from her answer?

2. Why might a reader think that "for Phoenix's grandson to be dead would

somehow make the story 'better' "? Does the story provide any basis for believing the boy may not be alive? Did the possibility occur to you?

3. In paragraph 6, Welty writes that the grandson's being dead "can't increase the truth of the story, can't affect it one way or the other. I think I signal this, because the end of the story has been reached before old Phoenix gets home again: she simply starts back." What does Welty mean by this statement? What is the "truth" of "A Worn Path"?

4. Have Welty's comments helped you to understand "A Worn Path" more fully than before? If so, how? For example, has your understanding of the story's title changed since reading her essay? Explain.

5. Welty says that "it is not a writer's business to tease." Is this a general truth, do you think? Do you know of any stories, or kinds of stories, which depend on the withholding of important facts?

6. Although Welty speaks mainly about writing, what does she say that applies to the *reading* of all fiction? Do you agree with what she says? Why or why not?

Explorations

1. Do you sometimes imagine a purpose and a past for some stranger whose appearance interests you? for some object you come across? Give an example or two of your inventions. What is the fascination of such imagining?

2. Discuss the difference between factual narrative and fictional stories. Can you as a reader always tell the difference? Does it matter to you? Why, or why not? Do you value one more than the other? Why?

GILBERT HIGHET

One of the reasons for writing about literature is to set a work in context. That is Gilbert Highet's purpose in the following discussion of Jonathan Swift's "A Modest Proposal." Highet was one of the great teachers of his time, and his writings likewise teach us much about the significance and value of our literary heritage.

Born 1906 in Scotland, Highet was educated at Glasgow University and Oxford University before coming to the United States in 1937. The next year he joined the faculty of Columbia University as a professor of Greek and Latin, and his affiliation with that school lasted until his death in 1978. Highet's influence spread beyond his classrooms through his lectures, his radio talks, and his many books, among them *The Classical Tradition: Greek and Roman Influences on Western Literature* (1949), *The Art of Teaching* (1954), and *The Powers of Poetry* (1960). In the following essay, taken from *An Anatomy of Satire* (1960), Highet discusses Swift's satire in the contexts of its original setting and purpose, of the relation between irony and truth, and of satire itself. If you have not already read Swift's "A Modest Proposal" (pages 695–702), you should do so before reading Highet's essay.

On Swift's "A Modest Proposal"

In [one] subtle variant of the satirical monologue, we hear . . . the voice of the satirist speaking out of a mask. Behind the mask his face may be dark with fury or writhing with contempt. But the voice is calm, sometimes soberly earnest, sometimes lightly amused. The lips of the mask and its features are persuasive, almost real, perfectly controlled. Some of those who hear the voice, and see the suave lips from which it issues, are persuaded that it is the utterance of truth and that the speaker believes everything he says.

This mask is Irony. The voice speaks a gross exaggeration or a falsehood, knowing it to be exaggerated or false, but announcing it as serious truth. Listening to it, intelligent men think, "That cannot be true. He cannot possibly mean that." They realize that he means the reverse of what he says. For the truth is sometimes so contemptible, sometimes so silly, sometimes so outrageous, and sometimes, unhappily, so familiar that people disregard it. Only when the reverse of such a truth is displayed as though it were veridical, can they be shocked into understanding it. Sometimes even then they are not convinced. They attack the satirist as a provocator, a liar. That is the penalty of being a satirist who uses irony.

432

Gentle irony and wounding sarcastic irony can be used as weapons 3
in all types of satire. They are, however, most effective in monologue,
where a skillful satirist can, now and then, allow the real truth to flash
through the mildly colored cloud of dissimulation. The finest example of
this in English is a prose pamphlet published by Jonathan Swift in 1729.
Even in its title we see the touch of the ironist: *A Modest Proposal for
Preventing the Children of Poor People in Ireland from Being a Burden to
Their Parents or Country, and for Making Them Beneficial to the Public*. It
did not purport to be by Swift himself, but by an anonymous Irish patriot,
whose motive in writing it was to benefit the kingdom of Ireland by
solving one of its chief problems. The problem was that, under English
domination, the population of Ireland was starving to death. One radical
solution, Irish independence, could not then be considered. Other measures
of complete social, financial, and moral reform were obviously right, and
therefore (Swift thought) would never be initiated. So, behind the ironic
mask of a philanthropist, he proposed a solution which was couched in
terms of blandly persuasive logic, but was so atrocious that no one could
possibly take it as serious.

This solution is that, since too many Irish babies are being born, 4
they should be treated, not as human beings, but as animals. They should
be slaughtered and eaten. The best age at which to eat them (from the
point of view of the consumers) would be one year, when, having been
nursed by their mothers, they would be healthiest, and their flesh ten-
derest. There is, Swift remarks, a supplementary suggestion, to let the
children grow to the age of twelve or thirteen and then serve them in
place of venison, which is becoming unhappily scarce; but to this proposal
he objects, on the ground that the meat would, at least in the males, be
lean and tough. "And besides, it is not improbable that some scrupulous
people might be apt to censure such a practice (although indeed very
unjustly) as a little bordering upon cruelty; which, I confess, has always
been with me the strongest objection against any project, how well soever
intended." Gravely, with a sweetly reasonable manner and an appearance
of earnest concern for a miserable down-trodden population, Swift enu-
merates the advantages of his modest proposal. It will diminish the number of papists, increase the annual income of the country, and raise the
general standard of living. Even in outline, this idea is horrible; the
supporting arguments are revolting; but Swift, who was long and deeply
lacerated by the restless ulcer of indignation, excels himself when he goes
into the practical details.

Cooking and serving. "A child will make two dishes [i.e. two separate 5
courses, for instance chops and a roast] at an entertainment for friends;
and when the family dines alone, the fore or hind quarter will make a

reasonable dish, and, seasoned with a little pepper or salt, will be very good boiled on the fourth day, especially in winter."

Other uses. "Those who are more thrifty (as I must confess the times require) may flay the carcase; the skin of which, artificially dressed, will make admirable gloves for ladies, and summer boots for fine gentlemen." 6

And the most difficult problem of all, *the method of slaughter.* "As to our city of Dublin, shambles may be appointed for this purpose in the most convenient parts of it, and butchers, we may be assured, will not be wanting; although I rather recommend buying the children alive and dressing them [i.e. cooking them] hot from the knife, as we do roasting pigs." 7

In a dozen pages, Swift has written a perfect satire. After going over the various advantages of this terrible scheme, he briefly considers and contemptuously dismisses other solutions for the Irish problem: what we should call sensible reforms, such as taxing absentee property-owners, cutting off expensive imports, and "teaching landlords to have at least one degree of mercy toward their tenants." "Let no man," he says with bitterness flashing out, "talk to me of these and the like expedients, till he has at least some glimpse of hope that there will ever be some hearty and sincere attempt to put them in practice." The irony, the scorn, and the despair of the satirist can go no further. He has attacked the demoralized Irish poor, the dishonest Irish middle-class, the luxurious and indifferent ruling group, the petty factionalism of all together, and the callous greedy English. "We can incur no danger," he says reassuringly, "in disobliging England. For this kind of commodity [infants' meat] will not bear exportation, the flesh being of too tender a consistence to admit a long continuance in salt; although perhaps I could name a country which would be glad to eat up our whole nation without it." Has satire ever had any immediate and visible effect? Certainly Swift's modest proposal had none. The rulers of Ireland did not think for a moment of eating the Irish children. They merely went on letting them starve to death. 8

Yet, fantastic as the proposal was, it could not be called wholly unthinkable. Another plan to solve the problem of Ireland, a plan which approached this in boldness and actually outdid it in finality, was seriously put forward by an Irish patriot. The unhappy Colonel Edward Despard (one of the last men to be hanged, drawn, and quartered for treason in England) told a friend that he had discovered an infallible remedy for the miseries of his country: "viz., a voluntary separation of the sexes, so as to leave no future generation obnoxious to oppression. This plan of cure would, he said, defy the machinations of the enemies of Ireland to interrupt its complete success." Swift proposed regulated cannibalism, which would have kept the Irish people alive although lowering their 9 rate of increase. Despard proposed racial suicide, which would have extinguished the suffering nation forever in three generations. Which was more extreme? If Swift, instead of recommending the sale, slaughter, cooking, and eating of babies, had written a Modest Proposal suggesting that the Irish should liberate themselves from servitude by refusing to have children altogether, would that pamphlet not have seemed to be a perfect satire on a hopeless situation?

We said that irony was stating the reverse of truth as though it   10
were clear truth. In Colonel Despard's suggestion, what had been irony in Swift became theoretical truth, for it was seriously intended. And in our own day, with Adolf Hitler's "final solution to the Jewish problem" we have seen Swift's outrageous fantasy almost rivaled by reality. The heaps of gold teeth extracted from the mouths of corpses, the hair clipped from cadavers to be used as stuffing, the lampshades made of human skin, the medical experiments on living victims—do these not seem like the crazy imaginings of some perverse satirist, rather than part of the history of our own times?

About the Essay

1. In your own words, define *irony*. According to Highet, why might Swift have thought irony a suitable way of making his point?

2. What does Highet mean when he says that Swift "excels himself when he goes into the practical details"? Are there any examples from "A Modest Proposal" that you might add to those Highet gives?

3. Irony, to be effective, depends on an audience's response. What does Highet say that response should be? What does he think is the relationship between the satirist who speaks ironically and his audience?

4. What is satiric monologue? What are its advantages and risks?

5. What is Highet's reason for telling us of Despard's proposal for solving the problem of Ireland? Why does he mention the Holocaust?

6. Has Highet contributed to your understanding and appreciation of Swift's "A Modest Proposal"? In what way?

Explorations

1. Find an essay, poem, or story that is ironic according to your own definition. (Some possible choices from this book include Russell Baker's "School vs. Education," Gwendolyn Brooks's "The Lovers of the Poor," and Isaac Bashevis Singer's "Gimpel the Fool.") Discuss the irony in the work you have chosen, explaining what the author achieves by using it.

2. Satire has been defined as the art of attacking someone or something by arousing people to derisive or scornful amusement. When and how may satire be effective? Is it ever reasoned or fair? Give examples to support your answer.

EDWARD HOAGLAND

Though he has written many short stories and three novels, Edward Hoagland is probably best known as an essayist. He is particularly interested in the North American wilderness and in the animals that live there; his books of essays include *The Courage of Turtles* (1970), *Walking the Dead Diamond River* (1973), and *Red Wolves and Black Bears* (1976). And yet he is a confirmed city dweller, born in 1932 in New York City and still a resident there. He graduated from Harvard College in 1954 (in the same class as John Updike) and then served in the Army for two years, meanwhile publishing *Cat Man* (1956), a novel of circus life. Since then he has taught writing occasionally at various colleges in the New York area and at the University of Iowa's famous creative writing program. A selection of his works is available as *The Edward Hoagland Reader* (1979). "On Essays" was first published in 1976 and is included in *The Tugman's Passage* (1982). In it Hoagland explores his own attitude towards the personal essay, offering at the same time an example of this form and an explanation of what it is.

On Essays

We sometimes hear that essays are an old-fashioned form, that so-and-so is the "last essayist," but the facts of the marketplace argue quite otherwise. Essays of nearly any kind are so much easier than short stories for a writer to sell, so many more see print, it's strange that though two fine anthologies remain that publish the year's best stories, no comparable collection exists for essays. Such changes in the reading public's taste aren't always to the good, needless to say. The art of telling stories predated even cave painting, surely; and if we ever find ourselves living in caves again, it (with painting and drumming) will be the only art left, after movies, novels, photography, essays, biography, and all the rest have gone down the drain—the art to build from.

One has the sense with the short story as a form that while everything may have been done, nothing has been overdone; it has a permanence. Essays, if a comparison is to be made, although they go back four hundred years to Montaigne,[1] seem a mercurial, newfangled, sometimes hokey affair that has lent itself to many of the excesses of the age, from spurious autobiography to spurious hallucination, as well as to the shabby careerism of traditional journalism. It's a greased pig. Essays are associated with the way young writers fashion a name—on plain, crowded

---

[1] Michel de Montaigne, the French essayist; see page 65.

newsprint in hybrid vehicles like the *Village Voice, Rolling Stone,* the *New York Review of Books,* instead of the thick paper stock and thin readership of *Partisan Review.*

Essays, however, hang somewhere on a line between two sturdy poles: this is what I think, and this is what I am. Autobiographies which aren't novels are generally extended essays, indeed. A personal essay is like the human voice talking, its order the mind's natural flow, instead of a systematized outline of ideas. Though more wayward or informal than an article or treatise, somewhere it contains a point which is its real center, even if the point couldn't be uttered in fewer words than the essayist has used. Essays don't usually boil down to a summary, as articles do, and the style of the writer has a "nap" to it, a combination of personality and originality and energetic loose ends that stand up like the nap on a piece of wool and can't be brushed flat. Essays belong to the animal kingdom, with a surface that generates sparks, like a coat of fur, compared with the flat, conventional cotton of the magazine article writer, who works in the vegetable kingdom, instead. But, essays, on the other hand, may have fewer "levels" than fiction, because we are not supposed to argue much about their meaning. In the old distinction between teaching and storytelling, the essayist, however cleverly he camouflages his intentions, is a bit of a teacher or reformer, and an essay is intended to convey the same point to each of us.

This emphasis upon mind speaking to mind is what makes essays less universal in their appeal than stories. They are addressed to an educated, perhaps a middle-class, reader, with certain presuppositions, a frame of reference, even a commitment to civility that is shared—not the grand and golden empathy inherent in every man or woman that a storyteller has a chance to tap.

Nevertheless, the artful "I" of an essay can be as chameleon as any narrator in fiction; and essays do tell a story quite as often as a short story stakes a claim to a particular viewpoint. Mark Twain's piece called "Corn-pone Opinions," for example, which is about public opinion, begins with a vignette as vivid as any in *Huckleberry Finn.* Twain says that when he was a boy of fifteen, he used to hang out a back window and listen to the sermons preached by a neighbor's slave standing on top of a woodpile: "He imitated the pulpit style of the several clergyman of the village, and did it well and with fine passion and energy. To me he was a wonder. I believed he was the greatest orator in the United States and would some day be heard from. But it did not happen; in the distribution of rewards he was overlooked. . . . He interrupted his preaching now and then to saw a stick of wood, but the sawing was a pretense—he did it with his mouth, exactly imitating the sound the bucksaw makes in shrieking its way through the wood. But it served its purpose, it kept his master from coming out to see how the work was getting along."

A novel would go on and tell us what happened next in the life of 6 the slave—and we miss that. But the extraordinary flexibility of essays is what has enabled them to ride out rough weather and hybridize into forms that suit the times. And just as one of the first things a fiction writer learns is that he needn't actually be writing fiction to write a short story—that he can tell his own history or anybody else's as exactly as he remembers it and it will be "fiction" if it remains primarily a story—an essayist soon discovers that he doesn't have to tell the whole truth and nothing but the truth; he can shape or shave his memories, as long as the purpose is served of elucidating a truthful point. A personal essay frequently is not autobiographical at all, but what it does keep in common with autobiography is that, through its tone and tumbling progression, it conveys the quality of the author's mind. Nothing gets in the way. Because essays are directly concerned with the mind and the mind's idiosyncrasy, the very freedom the mind possesses is bestowed on this branch of literature that does honor to it, and the fascination of the mind is the fascination of the essay.

About the Essay

1. In paragraph 3 Hoagland says, "Essays . . . hang somewhere on a line between two sturdy poles: this is what I think, and this is what I am." What does he mean by this statement?

2. Why does Hoagland say that essays usually can't be reduced to a summary, as in a single sentence? What distinction is he making here between an essay and a magazine article? To your mind, how valid is that distinction?

3. What central distinction does Hoagland make between essays and works of fiction? Why do you think Hoagland chooses these two forms to exemplify his main contrast? How do the main features of both forms serve his explanatory purpose?

4. How is this essay organized? What one structural feature runs throughout the essay? Why do you think Hoagland chooses this way of making his point?

5. What does Hoagland claim is the main purpose of all essays? Do you agree or disagree? Why?

Explorations

1. Hoagland's definition of the essay is based on his experience as a reader and writer. From what you have read, and from your own experiences writing compositions, how would you define the essay? In your opinion, what makes an essay good or bad?

2. In his closing paragraph Hoagland says, "An essayist soon discovers that he doesn't have to tell the whole truth and nothing but the truth; he can shape or shave his memories, as long as the purpose is served of elucidating a truthful point." Do you agree? Or would you regard such shaping and shaving as unjustifiable? Give reasons and examples to support your answer.

3. Hoagland says that "essays are directly concerned with the mind and the mind's idiosyncrasy." Choose an essay you have read and discuss what you can infer from it about the author's qualities of mind.

PETER BROOK

Bringing a play to life so that its performance excites and moves an audience is only partly the job of the actors on stage. Behind them, giving the production its pace, mood, and style, stands the director. One of the most innovative and brilliant directors in theater today is Peter Brook. Born in London in 1925, Brook directed his first play there at eighteen. In 1962 he was appointed co-director of the Royal Shakespeare Theatre, and there showed that he was equally at home in classic drama and the most experimental new work. His work with the RSC reached its climax in 1970 with his extraordinary production of A *Midsummer Night's Dream,* in which he avoided the traditional gossamer costumes, wings, and balletlike movements, instead putting Shakespeare's fairies on trapezes and stilts to juggle and spin plates on their wands, thus evoking the magic of the circus. Recently Brook has organized an experimental theater group in Paris, and in 1972 he took them on a meandering safari through north Africa, stopping at villages unannounced to perform for surprised but delighted tribespeople. He has also directed films, notably *Lord of the Flies* (1964). In the following selection, taken from *The Open Space* (1968), Brook's exposition of his dramatic theories, he explains how he uses exercises to bring his actors closer to each other and to the playtext and discusses what he thinks theater should do for its audiences.

Rehearsing a Play

The first rehearsal is always to a degree the blind leading the blind. On the first day a director may sometimes make a formal speech explaining the basic ideas behind the coming work. Or else he may show models or costume sketches, or books or photographs, or he may make jokes, or else get the actors to read the play. Having drinks or playing a game together or marching round the theatre or building a wall all work in the same way: no one is in a state to absorb what is said—the purpose of anything you do on the first day is to get you through to the second one. The second day is already different—a process is now at work, and after twenty-four hours every single factor and relationship has subtly changed. Everything you do in rehearsal affects this process: playing games together is a process that has certain results, like a greater feeling of confidence, friendliness and informality. One can play games at auditions just to bring about an easier atmosphere. The goal is never in the game alone—in the short time available for rehearsing a play, social ease is not enough. A harrowing collective experience—like the improvisations on madness we had to do for the *Marat/Sade*[1] brings about another result; the actors having shared difficulties are open to one another and to the play in a different way.

When Sir Barry Jackson asked me to direct [Shakespeare's] *Love's Labour's Lost* at Stratford in 1945, it was my first big production and I had already done enough work in smaller theatres to know that actors, and above all stage managers, had the greatest contempt for anyone who, as they always put it, 'did not know what he wanted'. So the night before the first rehearsal I sat agonized in front of a model of the set, aware that further hesitation would soon be fatal, fingering folded pieces of card-board—forty pieces representing the forty actors to whom the following morning I would have to give orders, definite and clear. Again and again, I staged the very first entry of the Court, recognizing that this was when all would be lost or won, numbering the figures, drawing charts, maneu-vering the scraps of cardboard to and fro, on and off the set, trying them in big batches, then in small, from the side, from the back, over grass mounds, down steps, knocking them all over with my sleeve, cursing and starting again. As I did so, I noted the moves, and with no one to notice my indecision, crossed them out, then made fresh notes. The next morning I arrived at rehearsal, a fat prompt book under my arm, and the stage management brought me a table, reacting to my volume, I observed, with respect.

I divided the cast into groups, gave them numbers and sent them to their starting places, then, reading out my orders in a loud confident way I let loose the first stage of the mass entrance. As the actors began to move I knew it was no good. These were not remotely like my card-board figures, these large human beings thrusting themselves forward, some too fast with lively steps I had not foreseen, bringing them suddenly on top of me—not stopping, but wanting to go on, staring me in the face: or else lingering, pausing, even turning back with elegant affecta-tions that took me by surprise—we had only done the first stage of the movement, letter A on my chart, but already no one was rightly placed and movement B could not follow—my heart sank and, despite all my preparation, I felt quite lost. Was I to start again, drilling these actors so that they conformed to my notes? One inner voice prompted me to do so, but another pointed out that my pattern was much less interesting than this new pattern that was unfolding in front of me—rich in energy, full of personal variations, shaped by individual enthusiasms and lazi-

2

3

---

[1] *The Persecution and Assassination of Jean-Paul Marat as Performed by the Inmates of the Asylum of Charenton under the Direction of the Marquis de Sade* (1964), a play by Peter Weiss, in which a group of mental patients act out events of the French Revolution. Brook directed this play in London in 1964 and in New York in 1966.

nesses, promising such different rhythms, opening so many unexpected possibilities. It was a moment of panic. I think, looking back, that my whole future work hung in the balance. I stopped, and walked away from my book, in amongst the actors, and I have never looked at a written plan since. I recognized once and for all the presumption and the folly of thinking that an inanimate model can stand for a man. . . .

Many exercises set out first to free the actor, so he may be allowed   4 to discover by himself what only exists in himself: next, to force him to accept blindly external directions, so that by cocking a sensitive enough ear he could hear in himself movements he would never have detected any other way. For instance a valuable exercise is dividing a Shakespeare soliloquy into three voices, like a canon, and then having the three actors recite at breakneck speed over and over again. At first, the technical difficulty absorbs all the actors' attention, then gradually as they master the difficulties they are asked to bring out the meaning of the words, without varying the inflexible form. Because of the speed and the mechanical rhythm this seems impossible: the actor is prevented from using any of his normal expressive equipment. Then suddenly he bursts a barrier and experiences how much freedom there can be within the tightest discipline.

Another variant is to take the two lines 'To be or not to be, That   5 is the question' and gives them to ten actors, one word each. The actors stand in a closed circle and endeavor to play the words one after the other, trying to produce a living phrase. This is so difficult that it instantly reveals even to the most unconvinced actor how closed and insensitive he is to his neighbour. When after long work the sentence suddenly flows, a thrilling freedom is experienced by everyone. They see in a flash the possibility of group playing, and the obstacles to it. This exercise can be developed by substituting other verbs for 'be', with the same effect of affirmation and denial—and eventually it is possible to put sounds or gestures in place of one or all of the words and still maintain a living dramatic flow between the ten participants.

The purpose of such exercises is to lead actors to the point where   6 if one actor does something unexpected but true, the others can take this up and respond on the same level. This is ensemble playing: in acting terms it means ensemble creation, an awesome thought. It is no use thinking that exercises belong to school and only apply to a certain period of the actor's development. An actor, like any artist, is like a garden and it is no help to pull out the weeds just once, for all time. The weeds always grow, this is quite natural, and they must be cleaned away, which is natural and necessary too.

An exercise we once developed involved taking a scene of Shakespeare's, such as Romeo's farewell to Juliet, and trying (artificially of course) to disentangle the different inter-twining styles of writing. The scene reads:

Juliet: Wilt thou be gone? It is not yet near day.
It was the nightingale, and not the lark,
That pierced the fearful hollow of thine ear.
Nightly she sing on yond pomegranate tree.
Believe me, love, it was the nightingale.

Romeo: It was the lark, the herald of the morn;
No nightingale. Look, love, what envious streaks
Do lace the severing clouds in yonder East.
Night's candles are burnt out, and jocund day
Stands tiptoe on the misty mountains tops.
I must be gone and live, or stay and die.

Juliet: Yond light is not daylight; I know it, I.
It is some meteor that the sun exhales
To be to thee this night a torchbearer
And light thee on thy way to Mantua.
Therefore stay yet. Thou needest not to be gone.

Romeo: Let me be ta'en, let me be put to death.
I am content, so thou wilt have it so.
I say yon grey is not the morning's eye;
'Tis but the pale reflex of Cynthia's brow.
Nor that is not the lark whose notes do beat
The vaulty heaven so high above our heads.
I have more care to stay than will to go.
Come, death, and welcome! Juliet wills it so.
How is't, my soul? Let's talk. It is not day.

The actors then were asked to select only those words that they could play in a realistic situation, the words that they could use unselfconsciously in a film. This produced:

Juliet: Wilt thou be gone? It is not yet near day. It was the nightingale [*pause*] not the lark [*pause*]

Romeo It was the lark [*pause*] no nightingale. Look love [*pause*] I must be gone and live, or stay and die.

Juliet: Yond light is no daylight; [*pause*] therefore stay yet. Thou needest not to be gone.

Romeo: Let me be ta'en, let me be put to death. I am content, so thou
wilt have it so. [*pause*] Come, death and welcome! Juliet wills
it so. How is't, my soul? Let's talk. It is not day.

Then the actors played this as a genuine scene from a modern play   8
full of living pauses—speaking the selected words out loud, but repeating
the missing words silently to themselves to find the uneven lengths of
the silences. The fragment of scene that emerged would have made good
cinema, for the moments of dialogue linked by a rhythm of silences of
unequal duration in a film would be sustained by close shots and other
silent, related images.

Once this crude separation had been made, it was then possible to   9
do the reverse: to play the erased passages with full recognition that they
had nothing whatsoever to do with normal speech. Then it was possible
to explore them in many different ways—turning them into sounds or
movements—until the actor saw more and more vividly how a single
line of speech can have certain pegs of natural speech round which twist
unspoken thoughts and feelings rendered apparent by words of another
order. . . .

. . . I hate letting people watch rehearsals because I believe that   10
the work is privileged, thus private: there must be no concern about
whether one is being foolish or making mistakes. Also a rehearsal may
be incomprehensible—often excesses can be left or encouraged even to
the amazement and dismay of the company until the moment is ripe to
call a halt. But even in rehearsal there is a time when one needs outside
people watching, when what always seem to be hostile faces can create
a good new tension and the tension a new focus: the work must all the
time set new demands. There is another point the director must sense.
He must sense the time when a group of actors intoxicated by their own
talent and the excitement of the work loses sight of the play. Suddenly
one morning the work must change: the result must become all important. Jokes and embroideries are then ruthlessly pared away and all the
attention put on to the function of the evening, on the narrating, the
presenting, the technique, the audibility, the communicating to the audience. So it is foolish for a director to take a doctrinaire view; either
talking technical language about pace, volume, etc.—or avoiding one
because it is inartistic. It is woefully easy for a director to get stuck in a
method. There comes a moment when talk about speed, precision, diction is all that counts. 'Speed up,' 'get on with it,' 'it's boring,' 'vary the
pace,' 'for Christ's sake,' is then the patter, yet a week before such old-
timer talk could have stultified all creativity.

The closer the actor approaches the task of performing, the more   11
requirements he is asked to separate, understand and fulfill simultane-

ously. He must bring into being an unconscious state of which he is completely in charge. The result is a whole, indivisible—but emotion is continually illuminated by intuitive intelligence so that the spectator, though wooed, assaulted, alienated and forced to reassess, ends by experiencing something equally indivisible. Catharsis can never have been simply an emotional purge:[2] it must have been an appeal to the whole man. . . .

. . . The only thing that all forms of theatre have in common is the need for an audience. This is more than a truism: in the theatre the audience completes the steps of creation. In the other arts, it is possible for the artist to use as his principle the idea that he works for himself. However great his sense of social responsibility, he will say that his best guide is his own instinct—and if he is satisfied when standing alone with his completed work, the chances are that other people will be satisfied too. In the theatre this is modifed by the fact that the last lonely look at the completed object is not possible—until an audience is present the object is not complete. No author, no director, even in a megalomaniac dream, would want a private performance, just for himself. No megalomaniac actor would want to play for himself, for his mirror. So for the author or the director to work for his own taste and his own judgment, he must work approximately for himself in rehearsal and only truly for himself when he is hemmed in by a dense bank of audience. I think any director will agree that his own view of his own work changes completely when he is sitting surrounded by people. . . .

I know of one acid test in the theatre. It is literally an acid test. When a performance is over, what remains? Fun can be forgotten, but powerful emotion also disappears and good arguments lose their thread. When emotion and argument are harnessed to a wish from the audience to see more clearly into itself—then something in the mind burns. The event scorches on to the memory an outline, a taste, a trace, a smell— a picture. It is the play's central image that remains, its silhouette, and if the elements are rightly blended this silhouette will be its meaning, this shape will be the essence of what it has to say. When years later I think of a striking theatrical experience I find a kernel engraved on my memory: two tramps under a tree, an old woman dragging a cart, a sergeant dancing, three people on a sofa in hell[3]—or occasionally a trace deeper than any imagery. I haven't a hope of remembering the meanings

12

13

---

[2] According to Aristotle's *Poetics*, the action in a tragedy arouses the emotions of pity and fear and by so doing purges them. The Greek word *katharsis* means "purgation."

[3] Brook refers successively to Samuel Beckett's *Waiting for Godot* (1952), Bertolt Brecht's *Mother Courage and Her Children* (1941), John Arden's *Serjeant Musgrave's Dance* (1959), and Jean-Paul Sartre's *No Exit* (1944).

precisely, but from the kernel I can reconstruct a set of meanings. Then a purpose will have been served. A few hours could amend my thinking for life. This is almost but not quite impossible to achieve.

About the Essay

1. From Brook's discussion, what does he seem to consider a director's responsibilities to be? Does his view surprise you in any way? If so, how?

2. Why did Brook's plan for the first scene of *Love's Labour's Lost* not work? What did he learn from this failure?

3. What do the performers gain from the exercise on *Romeo and Juliet*? How would the exercise improve their performance?

4. Brook says of rehearsal that there may come a time "when a group of actors intoxicated by their own talent and the excitement of the work loses sight of the play." How might this affect the actors' performances? What is the purpose of the "old-timer" talk the director may use to correct the situation?

5. In the last paragraph, Brook speaks of the "acid test" of a performance. What is that test?

6. Why does Brook say "in the theatre the audience completes the steps of creation"? In what way does a theater audience complete the creation of a play? What, do you think, are the "steps of creation" of a theatrical work?

Explorations

1. What dramatic performances—plays, movies, television—have you seen that pass Peter Brook's "acid test"? What is it that affected you most about each of these performances, and what was the effect? What conclusions can you draw about the value of the drama?

2. Have you ever taken part in any kind of performance that required rehearsal? Consider not only the theater but also music, dance, or public speaking. Describe your experience, considering the techniques and direction of the rehearsals as well as the way your attitudes developed toward the work and performance.

3. Discuss the art of the theater. How is it like other art forms, and how is it unique? What are its special risks and rewards?

AGNES DE MILLE

Born in New York City in 1908, Agnes De Mille is a celebrated dancer and choreographer. She was raised in the world of the theater; her father was a theatrical producer, and her uncle was the Hollywood film producer Cecil B. De Mille. In 1942 she created *Rodeo*, considered by many critics to be the first important American ballet. She has also made her mark on musical comedy, bringing ballet to such musicals as *Oklahoma!* (1943) and *Carousel* (1945). De Mille has written about her life in *Dance to the Piper* (1952) and *Reprieve: A Memoir* (1981). In the following selection from *Dance to the Piper* she describes a performance of the famed Russian ballerina Anna Pavlova and her own reactions to the performance.

Pavlova

Anna Pavlova! My life stops as I write that name. Across the daily 1 preoccupation of lessons, lunch boxes, tooth brushings and quarrelings with Margaret flashed this bright, unworldly experience and burned in a single afternoon a path over which I could never retrace my steps. I had witnessed the power of beauty, and in some chamber of my heart I lost forever my irresponsibility. I was as clearly marked as though she had looked me in the face and called my name. For generations my father's family had loved and served the theater. All my life I had seen actors and actresses and had heard theater jargon at the dinner table and business talk of box-office grosses. I had thrilled at Father's projects and watched fascinated his picturesque occupations. I took a proprietary pride in the profitable and hasty growth of "The Industry." But nothing in his world or my uncle's prepared me for theater as I saw it that Saturday afternoon.

Since that day I have gained some knowledge in my trade and I 2 recognize that her technique was limited; that her arabesques were not as pure or classically correct as Markova's, that her jumps and batterie were paltry, her turns not to be compared in strength and number with the strenuous durability of Baronova or Toumanova. I know that her scenery was designed by second-rate artists, her music was on a level with restaurant orchestrations, her company definitely inferior to all the standards we insist on today, and her choreography mostly hack. And yet I say that she was in her person the quintessence of theatrical excitement.

As her little bird body revealed itself on the scene, either immobile 3 in trembling mystery or tense in the incredible arc which was her lift, her instep stretched ahead in an arch never before seen, the tiny bones

447

of her hands in ceaseless vibration, her face radiant, diamonds glittering under her dark hair, her little waist encased in silk, the great tutu balancing, quickening and flashing over her beating, flashing, quivering legs, every man and woman sat forward, every pulse quickened. She never appeared to rest static, some part of her trembled, vibrated, beat like a heart. Before our dazzled eyes, she flashed with the sudden sweetness of a hummingbird in action too quick for understanding by our gross utilitarian standards, in action sensed rather than seen. The movie cameras of her day could not record her allegro. Her feet and hands photographed as a blur.

Bright little bird bones, delicate bird sinews! She was all fire and steel wire. There was not an ounce of spare flesh on her skeleton, and the life force used and used her body until she died of the fever of moving, gasping for breath, much too young.

She was small, about five feet. She wore a size one and a half slipper, but her feet and hands were large in proportion to her height. Her hand could cover her whole face. Her trunk was small and stripped of all anatomy but the ciphers of adolescence, her arms and legs relatively long, the neck extraordinarily long and mobile. All her gestures were liquid and possessed of an inner rhythm that flowed to inevitable completion with the finality of architecture or music. Her arms seemed to lift not from the elbow or the arm socket, but from the base of the spine. Her legs seemed to function from the waist. When she bent her head her whole spine moved and the motion was completed the length of the arm through the elongation of her slender hand and the quivering reaching fingers. I believe there has never been a foot like hers, slender, delicate and of such an astonishing aggressiveness when arched as to suggest the ultimate in human vitality. Without in any way being sensual, being, in fact, almost sexless, she suggested all exhilaration, gaiety and delight. She jumped, and we broke bonds with reality. We flew. We hung over the earth, spread in the air as we do in dreams, our hands turning in the air as in water—the strong forthright taut plunging leg balanced on the poised arc of the foot, the other leg stretched to the horizon like the wing of a bird. We lay balancing, quivering, turning, and all things were possible, even to us, the ordinary people.

I have seen two dancers as great or greater since, Alicia Markova and Margot Fonteyn, and many other women who have kicked higher, balanced longer or turned faster. These are poor substitutes for passion. In spite of her flimsy dances, the bald and blatant virtuosity, there was an intoxicated rapture, a focus of energy, Dionysian in its physical intensity, that I have never seen equaled by a performer in any theater of the world. Also she was the *first* of the truly great in our experience.

I sat with the blood beating in my throat. As I walked into the bright glare of the afternoon, my head ached and I could scarcely swallow. I didn't wish to cry. I certainly couldn't speak. I sat in a daze in the car oblivious to the grownups' ceaseless prattle. At home I climbed the stairs slowly to my bedroom and, shutting myself in, placed both hands on the brass rail at the foot of my bed, then rising laboriously to the tips of my white buttoned shoes I stumped the width of the bed and back again. My toes throbbed with pain, my knees shook, my legs quivered with weakness. I repeated the exercise. The blessed, relieving tears stuck at last on my lashes. Only by hurting my feet could I ease the pain in my throat.

Death came to Anna Pavlova in 1931, when she was fifty. She had not stopped touring for a single season. Her knees had sustained some damage, but she would not rest, and she was in a state of exhaustion when the train that was carrying her to Holland was wrecked. She ran out into the snow in her nightgown and insisted on helping the wounded. When she reached The Hague she had double pneumonia. Her last spoken words were, "Get the *Swan* dress ready."[1]

Standing on Ninth Avenue under the El, I saw the headlines on the front page of the *New York Times*. It did not seem possible. She was in essence the denial of death. My own life was rooted to her in a deep spiritual sense and had been during the whole of my growing up. It mattered not that I had only spoken to her once and that my work lay in a different direction. She was the vision and the impulse and the goal.

About the Essay

1. Why does De Mille hold Pavlova in such high esteem as a dancer, even though her technique was limited? What makes Pavlova so important to De Mille personally?

2. What is the central metaphor De Mille uses to describe Pavlova's appearance and way of dancing? How appropriate and effective is the metaphor in enabling you to visualize Pavlova dancing?

3. What does paragraph 8 contribute to our knowledge of Pavlova? What is its function in the essay?

4. What do we learn of De Mille herself from her essay?

5. A *dominant impression* is the atmosphere or mood that a writer creates in a description. What is the dominant impression that De Mille creates in her essay? How does she do it?

---

[1] One of Pavlova's most celebrated dances was as a dying swan, in a ballet created especially for her.

Explorations

1. Pavlova was a cultural hero for De Mille and the dancers of her generation. Name another such hero in one of the arts today. What is his or her influence on other artists? On the public? How can such influence be observed and measured?

2. De Mille says of Pavlova's performances that "her scenery was designed by second-rate artists, her music was on a level with restaurant orchestrations, her company definitely inferior to all standards we insist on today, and her choreography mostly hack." In the same period, the Ballet Russe under the director Serge Diaghilev featured scenery, music, and choreography by the great modern masters and had brilliant dancers as well. What, then, does the mediocrity around Pavlova reveal about her taste—or her financial backing? Consult library sources to support your answer.

KATHERINE KUH

Historians seek to discover and explain major movements and trends in human events of the past; art historians attempt to do the same for their subject. In her book *Break-up: The Core of Modern Art* (1965), from which the following selection is taken, Katherine Kuh offers her interpretation of what has been happening in painting and sculpture over the past hundred years. Kuh was born in 1904 in St. Louis and educated at Vassar College and the University of Chicago. She has been curator of modern painting and sculpture at the Chicago Art Institute, and in 1959 she became art editor for the *Saturday Review*. Her books include *Art Has Many Faces* (1951), *The Artist's Voice* (1962), and *The Open Eye* (1971). Her thesis in *Break-up*, and in this essay from that book, is that modern art is an art of fragmentation, and that the tendency to fragmentation has increased as time has passed.

Modern Art

The art of our century has been characterized by shattered surfaces, broken color, segmented compositions, dissolving forms and shredded images. Curiously insistent is this consistent emphasis on break-up. However, dissolution today does not necessarily mean lack of discipline. It can also mean a new kind of discipline, for disintegration is often followed by reconstruction, the artist deliberately smashing his material only to reassemble it in new and unexpected relationships. Moreover, the process of breaking up is quite different from the process of breaking down. And during the last hundred years, every aspect of art has been broken up—color, light, pigment, form, line, content, space, surface and design.

In the nineteenth century, easels were moved out-of-doors and color was broken into relatively minute areas in order to approximate the reality of sunlight and to preserve on canvas nature's own fleeting atmospheric effects. Known as Impressionism, this movement was the first step in a long sequence of experiments that finally banished the Renaissance emphasis on humanism, on three-dimensional form and on a traditional center of interest. Here was the beginning of a gradual but steady tendency toward diffusion in art. A few years later, Vincent Van Gogh transformed broken color into broken pigment. Less interested in realistic light than in his own highly charged emotions, he allowed smashing rhythmic brushstrokes to mirror his personal turbulence. In doing so he foretold twentieth-century Expressionism, that aptly named movement which relied on pitted surfaces, broken outlines, unpredictable color and scarred textures to intensify emotional expression. As the Impressionists

451

were bent on freeing nature from sham, so the Expressionists hoped to liberate their own feelings from all trace of artificiality.

Perhaps the most revolutionary break-up in modern art took place   3
a little more than fifty years ago with the advent of Cubism. It was the Cubists, Picasso, Braque, Duchamp, Picabia, Léger, Delaunay and Juan Gris, who responded to the inordinate multiplicity of present-day life by breaking up and arbitrarily rearranging transparent planes and surfaces so that all sides of an object could be seen at once. As the Cubists broke through the boundaries of conventional form to show multiple aspects simultaneously, their Italian colleagues, the Futurists, hoped to encompass the uninterrupted motion of an object at one time. This they tried to do by a series of overlapping transparent forms illustrating the path of an object as it moved through space.

With Surrealism came still another kind of break-up, the break-up   4
of chronology. Frankly influenced by Freudian discoveries, this movement splintered time sequence with an abandon borrowed from the world of fragmented dreams. Content was purposely unhinged in denial of all rational expression, allowing disconnected episodes to recreate the disturbing life of our unconscious. At the same time, perspective and distance often became severely dislocated. Denying the orderly naturalism of the Renaissance, painters today project space and distance from innumerable eye levels, intentionally segmenting their compositions into conflicting perspectives. We look from above, from below, from diverse angles, from near, from far—all at one and the same time (not an unfamiliar experience for eyes accustomed to air travel). Here again is the Cubist idea of simultaneity, the twentieth-century urge to approach a scene from many different directions in a single condensed encounter.

Finally we come to the total break-up of Abstract Expressionism, a   5
technique that celebrates the specific act of painting (sometimes appropriately called Action Painting). Now everything is shattered—line, light, color, form, pigment, surface and design. These canvases defy all the old rules as they reveal the immediate spontaneous feelings of the artist in the process of painting. There is no one central idea, no beginning, no end—only an incessant flow and flux where lightning brushstrokes report the artist's impulsive and compulsive reactions. The pigment actually develops a life of its own, almost strong enough to hypnotize the painter. Here break-up turns into both content and form, with the impetuous paint itself telling the full story. No naturalistic image is needed to describe these artists' volatile feelings.

As one looks back over the last hundred years, the history of break-   6
up becomes a key to the history of art. Why painters and sculptors of this period have been so involved with problems of dissolution is a ques-

tion only partly answered by the obvious impact of modern scientific methods of destruction. One cannot deny that the last two devastating wars and the possibility of a still more devastating one to come do affect our daily thinking. Since the discovery of the atom bomb, science has become almost synonymous with destruction. The influence of contemporary warfare with its colossal explosions and upheavals has unquestionably had much to do with the tendency toward fragmentation in art, but there have been other and earlier causes.

From the beginning, it was science in one form or another that affected modern painting and sculpture. In nineteenth-century Europe the interest in atmospheric phenomena was not an isolated expression limited to the Impressionists. At that time, numerous scientists were experimenting with all manner of optical color laws, writing widely on the subject as they investigated the relationship of color to the human eye. Artists like Monet and Seurat were familiar with these findings and not unnaturally applied them to their paintings. It would be a grave mistake to underestimate the influence of contemporary scientific research on the development of Impressionism. The wonders of natural light became a focus for nineteenth-century artists exactly as the magic of artificial light stimulated painters of the precentury. If the earlier men were more interested in rural landscapes seen out-of-doors in the sunlight, the later artists quite reasonably concentrated on city scenes, preferably at night when man-made luminosity tends to puncture both form and space.

Other scientific investigations also exerted considerable influence on present-day painters and sculptors. Inventions like the microscope and telescope, with their capacity to enlarge, isolate and probe, offer the artist provocative new worlds to explore. These instruments, which break up structures only to examine them more fully, demonstrate how details can be magnified and separated from the whole and operate as new experiences. Repeatedly artists in recent years have exploited this idea, allowing one isolated symbol to represent an entire complex organism. Miró often needs merely part of a woman's body to describe all women, or Léger, one magnified letter of the alphabet to conjure up the numberless printed words that daily bombard us.

As scientists smash the atom, so likewise artists smash traditional forms. For how, indeed, can anyone remain immune to the new mushroom shape that haunts us day and night? The American painter, Morris Graves, put it well recently, "You simply can't keep the world out any longer. Like everyone else, I've been caught in our scientific culture." This is not to say that painters are interested in reproducing realistic scenes of atomic explosions, but rather that they are concerned with the reactions accompanying these disasters. It is just possible that, with their extra-sensitized intuition, artists may have unconsciously predicted the discovery of atomic energy long before "the bomb" became a familiar household word, for the history of break-up in art antedates the history of nuclear break-up.

Even the invention of the X-ray machine has brought us closer to penetrating form. We no longer think of outer coverings as solid or final; we know they can be visually pierced merely by rendering them transparent. We have also learned from science that space penetrates everything. 10

The sculptor Gabo claims, "Space is a reality in all of our experiences and it is present in every object. . . . That's what I've tried to show in certain of my stone carvings. When they turn, observe how their curved forms seem interpenetrated by space." For the artist today, nothing is static or permanent. The new popular dances are no more potently kinetic than the new staccato art forms that everywhere confront us. 11

With the dramatic development of speedier transportation and swifter communication comes a visual overlapping responsible for much of contemporary art. In modern life one is simultaneously subjected to countless experiences that become fragmented, superimposed, and finally rebuilt into new experiences. Speed is a cogent part of our daily life. 12

How natural, then, that artists reflect this pressure by showing all sides of an object, its entire motion, its total psychological content in one concerted impact. It is almost as if the pressures of time had necessitated a visual speed-up not unlike the industrial one associated with the assembly line and mass production. Speed with its multiple overlays transforms our surroundings into jagged, interrupted images. 13

Modern technology and science have produced a wealth of new materials and new ways of using old materials. For the artist this means wider opportunities. There is no doubt that the limitations of materials and nature of tools both restrict and shape a man's work. Observe how the development of plastics and light metals along with new methods of welding and brazing have changed the direction of sculpture. Transparent plastic materials allow one to look through an object, to see its various sides superimposed on each other (as in Cubism or in an X ray). Today, welding is as prevalent as casting was in the past. This new method encourages open designs, often of great linear agility, where surrounding and intervening space becomes as important as form itself. In fact, it becomes a kind of negative form. While bronze casting and stone carving are techniques more readily adapted to solid volumes, welding permits perforated metal designs of extreme versatility that free sculpture from the static restrictions which for centuries have moored it to the floor. 14

More ambiguous than other scientific inventions familiar to modern 15 artists, but no less influential, are the psychoanalytic studies of Freud and his followers, discoveries that have infiltrated recent art, especially Surrealism. The Surrealists, in their struggle to escape the monotony and frustrations of everyday life, claimed that dreams were the only hope. Turning to the irrational world of their unconscious, they banished all time barriers and moral judgments to combine disconnected dream experiences from the past, present and intervening psychological states. The Surrealists were concerned with overlapping emotions more than with overlapping forms. Their paintings often become segmented capsules of associative experiences. For them, obsessive and often unrelated images replaced the direct emotional messages of Expressionism. They did not need to smash pigment and texture; they went beyond this to smash the whole continuity of logical thought.

There is little doubt that contemporary art has taken much from 16 contemporary life. In a period when science has made revolutionary strides, artists in their studios have not been unaware of scientists in their laboratories. But this has rarely been a one-way street. Painters and sculptors, though admittedly influenced by modern science, have also molded and changed our world. If break-up has been a vital part of their expression, it has not always been a symbol of destruction. Quite the contrary: it has been used to examine more fully, to penetrate more deeply, to analyze more thoroughly, to enlarge, isolate and make more familiar certain aspects of life that earlier we were apt to neglect. In addition, it sometimes provides rich multiple experiences so organized as not merely to reflect our world, but in fact to interpret it.

About the Essay

1. What does Kuh mean when she writes of "break-up" as the "core of modern art"? Briefly summarize her account of the progressive "break-up" of every aspect of art.

2. In paragraph 2, Kuh refers to "broken color" and "broken pigment." What do you think she means by this?

3. According to Kuh, what contemporary inventions, discoveries, or theories have influenced modern artists? How do they explain the trend toward dissolution?

4. What new materials and techniques mentioned by Kuh have influenced modern art? What specific art does she describe as being affected by modern technology?

5. What is Kuh's central thesis? Where does she state it? How does she develop it?

Explorations

1. Modern art, like modern music, dance, and literature, has proven extremely controversial, difficult for some people to enjoy while eliciting fierce partisanship from others. Think of the art that especially interests you—it can be rock music, film, comic strips as well as what is considered fine art—and describe your attitudes toward some works you know from the present and the past. Which do you prefer, past or present works? What kind of pleasure do you get from these works? In what ways are they similar and in what ways different? Do artists have an obligation to please anyone other than themselves? Why, or why not?

2. Choose an individual artist, group of artists, or art movement of the past hundred years, and write an essay in which you discuss the unity and variety in the body of work produced. If you like, begin your exploration by looking through an illustrated history of art, then follow it up with art books and reproductions in the library. Two good general histories of art are H. W. Janson's *History of Art* and Helen Gardner's *Art Through the Ages*. A few possible subjects are the Impressionist painter Claude Monet; Pablo Picasso; and the Surrealists, perhaps with special attention to René Magritte and Salvador Dalí.

BRUNO BETTELHEIM

Some people believe that art is understood and appreciated only by a minority with highly refined tastes, but history would suggest otherwise. The plays of Shakespeare, the operas of Giuseppe Verdi, and countless other masterpieces were enormously popular with all kinds of people right from the start and were not celebrated as works of art until that first popularity was past. The same thing has been happening with the movies, now that television has become the popular medium of entertainment; the films of Sergei Eisenstein, Orson Welles, Ingmar Bergman, and even Charlie Chaplin have come to be considered serious works of art. Bruno Bettelheim, however, is not interested in the status of the movies, but in what they communicate— how, like the drama of ancient Greece, the cathedrals of medieval Europe, and the paintings and sculpture of the Renaissance, they express our sense of community and offer us myths to live by.

Bettelheim was born in Vienna in 1903 and moved to the United States in 1939 after the Nazi annexation of Austria. From 1943 to 1973 he taught psychology at the University of Chicago and directed the Orthogenic School for Disturbed Children there. His books include many about the inner lives of children, including *The Informed Heart* (1960), but he has written on many subjects ranging from social change to fairy tales. A selection of Bettelheim's essays is available in *Surviving and Other Essays* (1979).

The Art of Moving Pictures

Whether we like it or not—and many may disagree with my thesis because painting, or music, or some other art is more important to them— the art of the moving image is the only art truly of our time, whether it is in the form of the film or television. The moving picture is our universal art, which comprises all others, literature and acting, stage design and music, dance and the beauty of nature, and, most of all, the use of light and of color. 1

It is always about us, because the medium is truly part of the message and the medium of the moving image is uniquely modern. Everybody can understand it, as everyone once understood religious art in church. And as people used to go to church on Sundays (and still do), so the majority today go to the movies on weekends. But while in the past most went to church only on some days, now everybody watches moving images every day. 2

All age groups watch moving pictures, and they watch them for 3

457

many more hours than people have ever spent in churches. Children and adults watch them separately or together; in many ways and for many people, it is the only experience common to parents and children. It is the only art today that appeals to all social and economic classes, in short, that appeals to everybody, as did religious art in times past. The moving picture is thus by far the most popular art of our time, and it is also the most authentically American of arts.

When I speak here of the moving picture as the authentic American   4
art of our time, I do not think of art with a capital A, nor of "high" art. Putting art on a pedestal robs it of its vitality. When the great medieval and Renaissance cathedrals were erected, and decorated outside and in with art, these were popular works, that meant something to everybody.

Some were great works of art, others not, but every piece was   5
significant and all took pride in each of them. Some gain their spiritual experience from the masterpiece, but many more gain it from the medi-ocre works that express the same vision as the masterpiece but in a more accessible form. This is as true for church music or the church itself as for paintings and sculptures. This diversity of art objects achieves a unity, and differences in quality are important, provided they all represent, each in its own way, the overarching vision and experience of a larger, im-portant cosmos. Such a vision confers meaning and dignity on our ex-istence, and is what forms the essence of art.

So among the worst detriments to the healthy development of the   6
art of the moving image are efforts by aesthetes and critics to isolate the art of film from popular movies and television. Nothing could be more contrary to the true spirit of art. Whenever art was vital, it was always equally popular with the ordinary man and the most refined person. Had Greek drama and comedy meant nothing to most citizens, the majority of the population would not have sat all day long entranced on hard stone slabs, watching the events on the stage; nor would the entire population have conferred prizes on the winning dramatist. The medieval pageants and mystery plays out of which modern drama grew were popular entertainments, as were the plays of Shakespeare. Michelangelo's David stood at the most public place in Florence, embodying the people's vision that tyranny must be overthrown, while it also related to their religious vision, as it represented the myth of David and Goliath. Everybody ad-mired the statue; it was simultaneously popular and great art, but one did not think of it in such disparate terms. Neither should we. To live well we need both: visions that lift us up, and entertainment that is down to earth, provided both art and entertainment, each in its different form

and way, are embodiments of the same visions of man. If art does not speak to all of us, common men and elites alike, it fails to address itself to that true humanity that is common to all of us. A different art for the elites and another one for average man tears society apart; it offends what we most need: visions that bind us together in common experiences that make life worth living.

When I speak of an affirmation of man, I do not mean the presentation of fake images of life as wonderfully pleasant. Life is best celebrated in the form of a battle against its inequities, of struggles, of dignity in defeat, of the greatness of discovering oneself and the other.

Quite a few moving pictures have conveyed such visions. In *Kagemusha*, the great beauty of the historical costumes, the cloak-and-dagger story with its beguiling Oriental settings, the stately proceedings, the pageantry of marching and fighting armies, the magnificent rendering of nature, the consummate acting—all these entrance us and convince us of the correctness of the vision here: the greatness of the most ordinary of men. The hero, a petty thief who turns impostor, grows before our eyes into greatness, although it costs him his life. The story takes place in sixteenth-century Japan, but the hero is of all times and places: he accepts a destiny into which he is projected by chance and turns a false existence into a real one. At the end, only because he wants to be true to his new self, he sacrifices his life and thus achieves the acme of suffering and human greatness. Nobody wants him to do so. Nobody but he will ever know that he did it. Nobody but the audience observes it. He does it only for himself; it has no consequences whatsoever for anybody or anything else. He does it out of conviction; this is his greatness. Life that permits the lowest of men to achieve such dignity is life worth living, even if in the end it defeats him, as it will defeat all who are mortal.

Two other films, very different, render parallel visions that celebrate life, a celebration in which we, as viewers, vicariously participate although we are saddened by the hero's defeat. The first was known in the United States by its English name, *The Last Laugh*, although its original title, *The Last Man*, was more appropriate. It is the story of the doorman of a hotel who is demoted to cleaning washrooms. The other movie is *Patton*. In one of these films the hero stands on the lowest rung of society and existence; in the other, he is on society's highest level. In both pictures we are led to admire a man's struggle to discover who he really is, for, in doing so, he achieves tragic greatness. These three films, as do many others, affirm man and life, and so inspire in us visions that can sustain us.

My choice of these three films out of many is arbitrary. What I want to illustrate is their celebration of life in forms appropriate to an age in which self-discovery may exact the highest possible price. Only through incorporating such visions can we achieve satisfaction with our own life, defeat and transcend existential despair.

What our society suffers from most today is the absence of consensus about what it and life in it ought to be. Such consensus cannot be gained from society's present stage, or from fantasies about what it ought to be. For that the present is too close and too diversified, and the future too uncertain, to make believable claims about it. A consensus in the present hence can be achieved only through a shared understanding of the past, as Homer's epics informed those who lived centuries later what it meant to be Greek, and by what images and ideals they were to live their lives and organize their societies.

Most societies derive consensus from a long history, a language all their own, a common religion, common ancestry. The myths by which they live are based on all of these. But the United States is a country of immigrants, coming from a great variety of nations. Lately, it has been emphasized that an asocial, narcissistic personality has become characteristic of Americans, and that it is this type of personality that makes for the malaise, because it prevents us from achieving a consensus that would counteract a tendency to withdraw into private worlds. In his study of narcissism, Christopher Lasch says that modern man, "tortured by self-consciousness, turns to new cults and therapies not to free himself of his personal obsessions but to find meaning and purpose in life, to find something to live for." There is widespread distress because national morale has declined, and we have lost an earlier sense of national vision and purpose.

Contrary to rigid religions or political beliefs, as are found in totalitarian societies, our culture is one of great individual differences, at least in principle and in theory. But this leads to disunity, even chaos. Americans believe in the value of diversity, but just because ours is a society based on individual diversity, it needs consensus about some overarching ideas more than societies based on the uniform origin of their citizens. Hence, if we are to have consensus, it must be based on a myth—a vision—about a common experience, a conquest that made us Americans, as the myth about the conquest of Troy formed the Greeks. Only a common myth can offer relief from the fear that life is without meaning or purpose. Myths permit us to examine our place in the world by comparing it to a shared idea. Myths are shared fantasies that form the tie that binds the individual to other members of his group. Such myths help to ward off feelings of isolation, guilt, anxiety, and purposelessness—in short, they combat isolation and anomie.

We used to have a myth that bound us together; in *The American* 14
Adam, R.W.B. Lewis summarizes the myth by which Americans used to live:

> God decided to give man another chance by opening up a new world across the sea. Practically vacant, this glorious land had almost inexhaustible natural resources. Many people came to this new world. They were people of special energy, self-reliance, intuitive intelligence, and purity of heart. . . . This nation's special mission in the world would be to serve as the moral guide for all other nations.

The movies used to transmit this myth, particularly the westerns, 15
which presented the challenge of bringing civilization to places where before there was none. The same movies also suggested the danger of that chaos; the wagon train symbolized the community men must form on such a perilous journey into the untamed wilderness, which in turn became a symbol for all that is untamed within ourselves. Thus the western gave us a vision of the need for cooperation and civilization, because without it man would perish. Another symbol often used in these westerns was the railroad, which formed the link between wilderness and civilization. The railroad was the symbol of man's role as civilizer.

Robert Warshow delineates in *The Immediate Experience* how the 16
hero of the western—the gunfighter—symbolizes man's potential: to become either an outlaw or a sheriff. In the latter role, the gunfighter was the hero of the past, and his opening of the West was our mythos, our equivalent of the Trojan War. Like all such heroes, the sheriff experienced victories and defeats, but, through these experiences, he grew wiser and learned to accept the limitations that civilization imposes.

This was a wonderful vision of man—or the United States—in the 17
New World; it was a myth by which one could live and grow, and it served as a consensus about what it meant to be an American. But although most of us continue to enjoy this myth, by now it has lost most of its vitality. We have become too aware of the destruction of nature and of the American Indian—part of the reality of opening the West— to be able to savor this myth fully; and, just as important, it is based on an open frontier that no longer exists. But the nostalgic infatuation with the western suggests how much we are in need of a myth about the past that cannot be invalidated by the realities of today. We want to share a vision, one that would enlighten us about what it means to be an Amer-

ican today, so that we can be proud not only of our heritage but also of
the world we are building together.

Unfortunately, we have no such myth, nor, by extension, any that
reflects what is involved in growing up. The child, like the society, needs
such myths to provide him with ideas of what difficulties are involved in
maturation. Fairy tales used to fill this need, and they would still do so,
if we would take them seriously. But sugar-sweet movies of the Disney
variety fail to take seriously the world of the child—the immense problems with which the child has to struggle as he grows up, to make himself
free from the bonds that tie him to his parents, and to test his own
strength. Instead of helping the child, who wants to understand the
difficulties ahead, these shows talk down to him, insult his intelligence,
and lower his aspirations.

While most of the popular shows for children fall short of what the
child needs most, others at least provide him with some of the fantasies
that relieve pressing anxieties, and this is the reason for their popularity.
Superman, Wonder Woman, and the Bionic Woman stimulate the child's
fantasies about being strong and invulnerable, and this offers some relief
from being overwhelmed by the powerful adults who control his existence. The Incredible Hulk affords a confrontation with destructive anger.
Watching the Hulk on one of his rampages permits a vicarious experience
of anger without having to feel guilty about it or anxious about the
consequences, because the Hulk attacks only bad people. As food for
fantasies that offer temporary relief, such shows have a certain value, but
they do not provide material leading to higher integration, as myths do.

Science-fiction movies can serve as myths about the future and thus
give us some assurance about it. Whether the film is *2001* or *Star Wars*,
such movies tell about progress that will expand man's powers and his
experiences beyond anything now believed possible, while they assure us
that all these advances will not obliterate man or life as we now know
it. Thus one great anxiety about the future—that it will have no place
for us as we now are—is allayed by such myths. They also promise that
even in the most distant future, and despite the progress that will have
occurred in the material world, man's basic concerns will be the same,
and the struggle of good against evil—the central moral problem of our
time—will not have lost its importance.

Past and future are the lasting dimensions of our lives; the present
is but a fleeting moment. So these visions about the future also contain
our past; in *Star Wars*, battles are fought around issues that also motivated
man in the past. There is good reason that Yoda appears in George Lucas's

film: he is but a reincarnation of the teddy bear of infancy, to which we turn for solace; and the Yedi Knight is the wise old man, or the helpful animal, of the fairy tale, the promise from our distant past that we shall be able to rise to meet the most difficult tasks life can present us with. Thus, any vision about the future is really based on visions of the past, because that is all we can know for certain.

As our religious myths about the future never went beyond Judgment Day, so our modern myths about the future cannot go beyond the search for life's deeper meaning. The reason is that only as long as the choice between good and evil remains man's paramount moral problem does life retain that special dignity that derives from our ability to choose between the two. A world in which this conflict has been permanently resolved eliminates man as we know him. It might be a universe peopled by angels, but it has no place for man.

What Americans need most is a consensus that includes the idea of individual freedom, as well as acceptance of the plurality of ethnic backgrounds and religious beliefs inherent in the population. Such consensus must rest on convictions about moral values and the validity of overarching ideas. Art can do this because a basic ingredient of the aesthetic experience is that it binds together diverse elements. But only the ruling art of a period is apt to provide such unity: for the Greeks, it was classical art; for the British, Elizabethan art; for the many petty German states, it was their classical art. Today, for the United States, it has to be the moving picture, the central art of our time, because no other art experience is so open and accessible to everyone.

The moving picture is a visual art, based on sight. Speaking to our vision, it ought to provide us with the visions enabling us to live the good life; it ought to give us insight into ourselves. About a hundred years ago, Tolstoy wrote, "Art is a human activity having for its purpose the transmission to others of the highest and best feelings to which men have risen." Later, Robert Frost defined poetry as "beginning in delight and ending in wisdom." Thus it might be said that the state of the art of the moving image can be assessed by the degree to which it meets the mythopoetic task of giving us myths suitable to live by in our time— visions that transmit to us the highest and best feelings to which men have risen—and by how well the moving images give us that delight which leads to wisdom. Let us hope that the art of the moving image, this most authentic American art, will soon meet the challenge of becoming truly the great art of our age.

About the Essay

1. According to Bettelheim, in what ways is the moving picture the art of our time? What does Bettelheim mean by "art" when he says this? Why does he consider the moving picture "the most authentically American of arts"?

2. What does Bettelheim mean by the word *myth*? What purpose do myths serve? Why does he say we no longer have myths? What has caused the decline of the myth of the American West?

3. Why, in Bettelheim's view, must Superman and Wonder Woman be considered less valuable than Michelangelo's statue of David? Do you agree? Why, or why not?

4. What does Bettelheim believe American society most lacks? In his view, what might movies do to supply that deficiency?

5. Bettelheim discusses three contemporary films: *Kagemusha, The Last Laugh*, and *Patton.* What is his point in that discussion? How is this point related to his overall argument?

6. In his last paragraph, Bettelheim quotes from Leo Tolstoy and Robert Frost about the meaning and purpose of art. How do these quotations relate to his thesis?

Explorations

1. Bettelheim says that movies are an art to the extent that they give us myths we can live by—"visions that transmit to us the highest and best feelings to which men have risen." Discuss a movie you have seen in recent months, showing how it meets or fails to meet Bettelheim's criterion. Do you consider the movie a true work of art, whether or not Bettelheim would? Why? What are your criteria, if they differ from his?

2. Bettelheim writes that "only as long as the choice between good and evil remains man's paramount moral problem does life retain that special dignity that derives from our ability to choose between the two." This thought, offered almost in passing, is meat enough in itself for much thought and discussion. Is choosing between good and evil humanity's greatest moral issue? Does our ability to make such a choice confer on our lives a special dignity, as Bettelheim says?

DYLAN THOMAS

What is poetry for? Why do poets write it? The English poet Shelley argued that poets are the unacknowledged legislators of mankind. Dylan Thomas, in the following poem, discloses a more modest ambition, and one which many readers would say he fulfills. He was born in Wales in 1914 and was educated at the local grammar school. Already greatly talented as a writer, he disregarded his father's advice to go on to a university, and at twenty published *Eighteen Poems*, a slender volume that contained several masterpieces. Thomas was a public man; he appeared regularly on the British Broadcasting Corporation radio broadcasts, reading poems in one of the great speaking voices of our times, and made several immensely popular lecture tours of America. Reckless living and heavy drinking brought him down during the last of those tours, and he died in New York at thirty-nine. His poetry is available as *Collected Poems* (1952); these poems along with his stories, essays, autobiographical reminiscences, and the verse play *Under Milk Wood* (1954) testify to the richness and diversity of his talent.

In My Craft or Sullen Art

In my craft or sullen art
Exercised in the still night
When only the moon rages
And the lovers lie abed
With all their griefs in their arms   5
I labour by singing light
Not for ambition or bread
Or the strut and trade of charms
On the ivory stages
But for the common wages   10
Of their most secret heart.

Not for the proud man apart
From the raging moon I write
On these spindrift pages
Nor for the towering dead   15
With their nightingales and psalms
But for the lovers, their arms
Round the griefs of the ages,
Who pay no praise or wages
Nor heed my craft or art.   20

About the Poem

1. What similarities and differences does Thomas see between himself and the lovers he writes for? Why does he write for them?

2. Why does Thomas refer to his writing as "my craft or sullen art"? What attitude does he express with the words "spindrift pages"?

3. Why does Thomas say that the lovers have "their arms/Round the griefs of the ages"?

4. What are the "wages" Thomas says he labors for?

5. What does Thomas mean by lines 12–16? Who do you think are "the towering dead/With their nightingales and psalms"?

Explorations

1. How does Thomas's view of his craft compare with that of Po Chü-i in "Madly Singing in the Mountains" (page 467)? How do the two poets' ways of expressing themselves relate to their views?

2. Compare Thomas's view of art to Bruno Bettelheim's (see pages 457–463). In what ways are they similar? How do they differ?

PO CHÜ-I

One of the greatest of all Chinese poets, Po Chü-i was born in Honan in 772. He served under the T'ang Dynasty as a civil servant, and like many other Chinese officials of the past and present, he also wrote verse. Some of these verses got him into trouble, for he dared to satirize the corruption of the government and its oppression of the people; what was worse, his poetry was widely popular. He was demoted and banished in 815, one year before he wrote the poem which follows. Ultimately he was recalled to service, and from 841 until his death in 846 served as president of the council of justice. In the course of his long life he wrote more than seventy books. A selection from them, including the poem printed here, has been accurately and sensitively translated by Arthur Waley. "Madly Singing in the Mountains" is anything but political, though it refers to Po Chü-i's banishment. In it he praises those things that give him joy, especially the making of poems.

Madly Singing in the Mountains

There is no one among men that has not a special failing:
And my failing consists in writing verses.
I have broken away from the thousand ties of life:
But this infirmity still remains behind.
Each time that I look at a fine landscape,   5
Each time that I meet a loved friend,
I raise my voice and recite a stanza of poetry
And am glad as though a God had crossed my path.
Ever since the day I was banished to Hsün-yang
Half my time I have lived among the hills.   10
And often, when I have finished a new poem,
Alone I climb the road to the Eastern Rock.
I lean my body on the banks of white stone:
I pull down with my hands a green cassia branch.
My mad singing startles the valleys and hills: 15
The apes and birds all come to peep.
Fearing to become a laughing-stock to the world,
I choose a place that is unfrequented by men.

About the Poem

1. Why does Po Chü-i consider writing verses, his "special failing," an "infirmity"?

2. What would you say is the poet's attitude toward himself and his art? What lines reveal this attitude?

3. Why, after finishing a new poem, does the poet feel the need to climb into the hills?

Explorations

1. Is your own "special failing" a delight in poetry, indifference to it, or active dislike? What is it in poetry—or your own attitudes—that causes you to respond to it as you do?

2. At the end of his poem, Po Chü-i writes:

> "Fearing to become a laughing-stock to the world,
> I choose a place that is unfrequented by men."

Earlier in the poem he writes:

> Each time that I look at a fine landscape,
> Each time that I meet a loved friend,
> I raise my voice and recite a stanza of poetry
> And am glad as though a God had crossed my path.

These sets of lines together express the character of poetry as both a private and public activity. In what way is a poem—or for that matter, any work of art—simultaneously a private and public object?

WILLIAM CARLOS WILLIAMS

The great Flemish artist Pieter Brueghel (1564–1638) was a special inspiration to William Carlos Williams, who wrote a sequence of poems called "Pictures from Brueghel" evoking ten of his paintings. Both men sought to capture the activities and character of ordinary people, and to present them plainly and without decorative flourishes. Williams was born in Rutherford, New Jersey, in 1883, and after attending the University of Pennsylvania and completing his medical training in Germany he returned to Rutherford to live out his years as a pediatrician. He died in 1963. His poems have been collected in several volumes, and he also wrote fiction, essays, and plays. For many his greatest work is the five-book epic *Paterson*, published from 1946 to 1958.

"The Dance" is an earlier poem than the "Pictures from Brueghel," but it too grows from a Brueghel painting, "Flemish Kermess." Williams gives us not only the sights but the imagined sounds of the picture, and above all its rollicking spirit.

The Dance

In Brueghel's great picture, The Kermess,
the dancers go round, they go round and
around, the squeal and the blare and the
tweedle of bagpipes, a bugle and fiddles
tipping their bellies (round as the thick-   5
sided glasses whose wash they impound)
their hips and their bellies off balance
to turn them. Kicking and rolling about
the Fair Grounds, swinging their butts, those
shanks must be sound to bear up under such   10
rollicking measures, prance as they dance
in Breughel's great picture, The Kermess.

About the Poem

1. Does this poem give you a detailed description of Brueghel's painting? If you were to try to reconstruct Brueghel's painting from the poem, what would you have to supply from your own imagination?

2. How does Williams capture the sounds of the dance?

3. What is the dominant impression—the atmosphere or mood that a writer

469

creates in a description—that Williams creates in "Flemish Kermess"? How does he achieve it?

4. Why do you think Williams begins and ends his poem with the same line?

Explorations

1. Write a description of a picture—or a dance—trying to capture the essence of what you see and hear.

2. Using art books and reproductions in the library, write about Pieter Brueghel's pictures of peasant life—his subjects, his characters, his way of representing them.

NATHANIEL HAWTHORNE

As a master American novelist and short-story writer, Nathaniel Hawthorne (1804–1864) devoted much of his life to perfecting—and contemplating—his craft. Accordingly, he wrote often on the theme of the artist's relation to society. In fact, Hawthorne began his own artistic career in almost total withdrawal from society. He was born to a prominent Puritan family in Salem, Massachusetts. After graduating in 1825 from Bowdoin College in Maine, he returned to his mother's home in Salem, where he lived in seclusion for twelve years, working at his craft. Apart from one or two short stories he published in magazines and a novel that he himself published but immediately withdrew, he produced little that he was willing to have others read. Finally, in 1837, he published *Twice-Told Tales,* a collection of short stories which brought him success as well as some fame, and in the same year he "reentered" society. In 1850 the first of his great novels appeared, *The Scarlet Letter,* followed by *The House of the Seven Gables* (1851) and *The Blithedale Romance* (1852). Hawthorne's works all deal with moral and spiritual conflicts, and his characters are often lonely or frustrated or frail. Many of them reflect his own conflict as an artist in society, torn between a desire to join the common reality and the pull of his own artistic, inner reality. Thus did he once say that he feared creating the "pale tint of flowers that blossom in too retired a shade." "The Artist of the Beautiful," from the 1846 collection *Mosses from an Old Manse,* explores this theme of the artist in society. In it Hawthorne tells of one man's struggle to create an object of exquisite beauty in a society that little understands the nature of his struggle or achievement.

The Artist of the Beautiful

An elderly man, with his pretty daughter on his arm, was passing 1 along the street, and emerged from the gloom of the cloudy evening into the light that fell across the pavement from the window of a small shop. It was a projecting window; and on the inside were suspended a variety of watches, pinchbeck, silver, and one or two of gold, all with their faces turned from the streets, as if churlishly disinclined to inform the wayfarers what o'clock it was. Seated within the shop, sidelong to the window, with his pale face bent earnestly over some delicate piece of mechanism on which was thrown the concentrated lustre of a shade lamp, appeared a young man.

"What can Owen Warland be about?" muttererd old Peter Hov- 2 enden, himself a retired watchmaker, and the former master of this same young man whose occupation he was now wondering at. "What can the fellow be about? These six months past I have never come by his shop without seeing him just as steadily at work as now. It would be a flight beyond his usual foolery to seek for the perpetual motion; and yet I know enough of my old business to be certain that what he is now so busy with is no part of the machinery of a watch."

"Perhaps, father," said Annie, without showing much interest in the question, "Owen is inventing a new kind of timekeeper. I am sure he has ingenuity enough."   3

"Poh, child! He has not the sort of ingenuity to invent anything better than a Dutch toy," answered her father, who had formerly been put to much vexation by Owen Warland's irregular genius. "A plague on such ingenuity! All the effect that ever I knew of it was to spoil the accuracy of some of the best watches in my shop. He would turn the sun out of its orbit and derange the whole course of time, if, as I said before, his ingenuity could grasp anything bigger than a child's toy!"   4

"Hush, father! He hears you!" whispered Annie, pressing the old man's arm. "His ears are as delicate as his feelings; and you know how easily disturbed they are. Do let us move on."   5

So Peter Hovenden and his daughter Annie plodded on without further conversation, until in a by-street of the town they found themselves passing the open door of a blacksmith's shop. Within was seen the forge, now blazing up and illuminating the high and dusky roof, and now confining its lustre to a narrow precinct of the coal-strewn floor, according as the breath of the bellows was puffed forth or again inhaled into its vast leathern lungs. In the intervals of brightness it was easy to distinguish objects in remote corners of the shop and the horseshoes that hung upon the wall; in the momentary gloom the fire seemed to be glimmering amidst the vagueness of unenclosed space. Moving about in this red glare and alternate dust was the figure of the blacksmith, well worthy to be viewed in so picturesque an aspect of light and shade, where the bright blaze struggled with the black night, as if each would have snatched his comely strength from the other. Anon he drew a white-hot bar of iron from the coals, laid it on the anvil, uplifted his arm of might, and was soon enveloped in the myriads of sparks which the strokes of his hammer scattered into the surrounding gloom.   6

"Now, that is a pleasant sight," said the old watchmaker. "I know what it is to work in gold; but give me the worker in iron after all is said and done. He spends his labor upon a reality. What say you, daughter Annie?"   7

"Pray don't speak so loud, father," whispered Annie, "Robert Danforth will hear you."   8

"And what if he should hear me?" said Peter Hovenden. "I say   9
again, it is a good and a wholesome thing to depend upon main strength
and reality, and to earn one's bread with the bare and brawny arm of a
blacksmith. A watchmaker gets his brain puzzled by his wheels within a
wheel, or loses his health or the nicety of his eyesight, as was my case,
and finds himself at middle age, or a little after, past labor at his own
trade and fit for nothing else, yet too poor to live at his ease. So I say
once again, give me main strength for my money. And then, how it
takes the nonsense out of a man! Did you ever hear of a blacksmith being
such a fool as Owen Warland yonder?"

"Well said, uncle Hovenden!" shouted Robert Danforth from the   10
forge, in a full, deep, merry voice, that made the roof reëcho. "And
what says Miss Annie to that doctrine? She, I suppose, will think it a
genteeler business to tinker up a lady's watch than to forge a horseshoe
or make a gridiron."

Annie drew her father onward without giving him time for reply.   11

But we must return to Owen Warland's shop, and spend more   12
meditation upon his history and character than either Peter Hovenden,
or probably his daughter Annie, or Owen's old schoolfellow, Robert
Danforth, would have thought due to so slight a subject. From the time
that his little fingers could grasp a penknife, Owen had been remarkable
for a delicate ingenuity, which sometimes produced pretty shapes in wood,
principally figures of flowers and birds, and sometimes seemed to aim at
the hidden mysteries of mechanism. But it was always for purposes of
grace, and never with any mockery of the useful. He did not, like the
crowd of school-boy artisans, construct little windmills on the angle of
a barn or watermills across the neighboring brook. Those who discovered
such peculiarity in the boy as to think it worth their while to observe
him closely, sometimes saw reason to suppose that he was attempting to
imitate the beautiful movements of Nature as exemplified in the flight of
birds or the activity of little animals. It seemed, in fact, a new development of the love of the beautiful, such as might have made him a
poet, a painter, or a sculptor, and which was as completely refined from
all utilitarian coarseness as it could have been in either of the fine arts.
He looked with singular distaste at the stiff and regular processes of
ordinary machinery. Being once carried to see a steam-engine, in the
expectation that his intuitive comprehension of mechanical principles
would be gratified, he turned pale and grew sick, as if something monstrous and unnatural had been presented to him. This horror was partly
owing to the size and terrible energy of the iron laborer; for the character
of Owen's mind was microscopic, and tended naturally to the minute,

in accordance with his diminutive frame and the marvellous smallness and delicate power of his fingers. Not that his sense of beauty was thereby diminished into a sense of prettiness. The beautiful idea has no relation to size, and may be as perfectly developed in a space too minute for any but microscopic investigation as within the ample verge that is measured by the arc of the rainbow. But, at all events, this characteristic minuteness in his objects and accomplishments made the world even more incapable than it might otherwise have been of appreciating Owen Warland's genius. The boy's relatives saw nothing better to be done—as perhaps there was not—than to bind him apprentice to a watchmaker, hoping that his strange ingenuity might thus be regulated and put to utilitarian purposes.

Peter Hovenden's opinion of his apprentice has already been expressed. He could make nothing of the lad. Owen's apprehension of the professional mysteries, it is true, was inconceivably quick; but he altogether forgot or despised the grand object of a watchmaker's business, and cared no more for the measurement of time than if it had been merged into eternity. So long, however, as he remained under his old master's care, Owen's lack of sturdiness made it possible, by strict injunctions and sharp oversight, to restrain his creative eccentricity within bounds; but when his apprenticeship was served out, and he had taken the little shop which Peter Hovenden's failing eyesight compelled him to relinquish, then did people recognize how unfit a person was Owen Warland to lead old blind Father Time along his daily course. One of his most rational projects was to connect a musical operation with the machinery of his watches, so that all the harsh dissonances of life might be rendered tuneful, and each flitting moment fall into the abyss of the past in golden drops of harmony. If a family clock was intrusted to him for repair,—one of those tall, ancient clocks that have grown nearly allied to human nature by measuring out the lifetime of many generations,—he would take upon himself to arrange a dance or funeral procession of figures across its venerable face, representing twelve mirthful or melancholy hours. Several freaks of this kind quite destroyed the young watchmaker's credit with that steady and matter-of-fact class of people who hold the opinion that time is not to be trifled with, whether considered as the medium of advancement and prosperity in this world or preparation for the next. His custom[1] rapidly diminished—a misfortune, however, that was probably reckoned among his better accidents by Owen Warland, who was becoming more and more absorbed in a secret occupation which drew all his science and manual dexterity into itself, and likewise

---

[1] Business.

gave full employment to the characteristic tendencies of his genius. This pursuit had already consumed many months.

After the old watchmaker and his pretty daughter had gazed at him out of the obscurity of the street, Owen Warland was seized with a fluttering of the nerves, which made his hand tremble too violently to proceed with such delicate labor as he was now engaged upon.

"It was Annie herself!" murmured he. "I should have known it, by this throbbing of my heart, before I heard her father's voice. Ah, how it throbs! I shall scarcely be able to work again on this exquisite mechanism to-night. Annie! dearest Annie! thou shouldst give firmness to my heart and hand, and not shake them thus; for if I strive to put the very spirit of beauty into form and give it motion, it is for thy sake alone. O throbbing heart, be quiet! If my labor be thus thwarted, there will come vague and unsatisfied dreams which will leave me spiritless to-morrow."

As he was endeavoring to settle himself again to his task, the shop door opened and gave admittance to no other than the stalwart figure which Peter Hovenden had paused to admire, as seen amid the light and shadow of the blacksmith's shop. Robert Danforth had brought a little anvil of his own manufacture, and peculiarly constructed, which the young artist had recently bespoken. Owen examined the article and pronounced it fashioned according to his wish.

"Why, yes," said Robert Danforth, his strong voice filling the shop as with the sound of a bass viol, "I consider myself equal to anything in the way of my own trade; though I should have made but a poor figure at yours with such a fist as this," added he, laughing, as he laid his vast hand beside the delicate one of Owen. "But what then? I put more main strength into one blow of my sledge hammer than all that you have expended since you were a 'prentice. Is not that the truth?"

"Very probably," answered the low and slender voice of Owen. "Strength is an earthly monster. I make no pretensions to it. My force, whatever there may be of it, is altogether spiritual."

"Well, but, Owen, what are you about?" asked his old schoolfellow, still in such a hearty volume of tone that it made the artist shrink, especially as the question related to a subject so sacred as the absorbing dream of his imagination. "Folks do say that you are trying to discover the perpetual motion."

"The perpetual motion? Nonsense!" replied Owen Warland, with a movement of disgust; for he was full of little petulances. "It can never be discovered. It is a dream that may delude men whose brains are mystified with matter, but not me. Besides, if such a discovery were possible, it would not be worth my while to make it only to have the secret turned to such purposes as are now effected by steam and water power. I am not ambitious to be honored with the paternity of a new kind of cotton machine."

"That would be droll enough!" cried the blacksmith, breaking out into such an uproar of laughter that Owen himself and the bell glasses on his work-board quivered in unison. "No, no, Owen! No child of yours will have iron joints and sinews. Well, I won't hinder you any more. Good night, Owen, and success, and if you need any assistance, so far as a downright blow of hammer upon anvil will answer the purpose, I'm your man." 21

And with another laugh the man of main strength left the shop. 22

"How strange it is," whispered Owen Warland to himself, leaning 23 his head upon his hand, "that all my musings, my purposes, my passion for the beautiful, my consciousness of power to create it,—a finer, more ethereal power, of which this earthly giant can have no conception,— all, all, look so vain and idle whenever my path is crossed by Robert Danforth! He would drive me mad were I to meet him often. His hard, brute force darkens and confuses the spiritual element within me; but, I, too, will be strong in my own way. I will not yield to him."

He took from beneath a glass a piece of minute machinery, which 24 he set in the condensed light of his lamp, and, looking intently at it through a magnifying glass, proceeded to operate with a delicate instrument of steel. In an instant, however, he fell back in his chair and clasped his hands, with a look of horror on his face that made its small features as impressive as those of a giant would have been.

"Heaven! What have I done?" exclaimed he. "The vapor, the in- 25 fluence of that brute force,—it has bewildered me and obscured my perception. I have made the very stroke—the fatal stroke—that I have dreaded from the first. It is all over—the toil of months, the object of my life. I am ruined!"

And there he sat, in strange despair, until his lamp flickered in the 26 socket and left the Artist of the Beautiful in darkness.

Thus it is that ideas, which grow up within the imagination and 27 appear so lovely to it and of a value beyond whatever men call valuable, are exposed to be shattered and annihilated by contact with the practical. It is requisite for the ideal artist to possess a force of character that seems hardly compatible with its delicacy; he must keep his faith in himself while the incredulous world assails him with its utter disbelief; he must stand up against mankind and be his own sole disciple, both as respects his genius and the objects to which it is directed.

For a time Owen Warland succumbed to this severe but inevitable 28 test. He spent a few sluggish weeks with his head so continually resting in his hands that the towns-people had scarcely an opportunity to see his countenance. When at last it was again uplifted to the light of day, a cold, dull, nameless change was perceptible upon it. In the opinion of Peter Hovenden, however, and that order of sagacious understandings who think that life should be regulated, like clockwork, with leaden weights, the alteration was entirely for the better. Owen now, indeed, applied himself to business with dogged industry. It was marvellous to witness the obtuse gravity with which he would inspect the wheels of a great old silver watch; thereby delighting the owner, in whose fob it had been worn till he deemed it a portion of his own life, and was accordingly jealous of its treatment. In consequence of the good report thus acquired, Owen Warland was invited by the proper authorities to regulate the clock in the church steeple. He succeeded so admirably in this matter of public interest that the merchants gruffly acknowledged his merits on 'Change; the nurse whispered his praises as she gave the potion in the sickchamber; the lover blessed him at the hour of appointed interview; and the town in general thanked Owen for the punctuality of dinner time. In a word, the heavy weight upon his spirits kept everything in order, not merely within his own system, but wheresoever the iron accents of the church clock were audible. It was a circumstance, though minute, yet characteristic of his present state, that, when employed to engrave names or initials on silver spoons, he now wrote the requisite letters in the plainest possible style, omitting a variety of fanciful flourishes that had heretofore distinguished his work in this kind.

One day, during the era of his happy transformation, old Peter   29
Hovenden came to visit his former apprentice.

"Well, Owen," said he, "I am glad to hear such good accounts of   30
you from all quarters, and especially from the town clock yonder, which speaks in your commendation every hour of the twenty-four. Only get rid altogether of your nonsensical trash about the beautiful, which I nor nobody else, nor yourself to boot, could ever understand,—only free yourself of that, and your success in life is as sure as daylight. Why, if you go on this way, I should even venture to let you doctor this precious old watch of mine; though, except my daughter Annie, I have nothing else so valuable in the world."

"I should hardly dare touch it, sir," replied Owen, in a depressed   31
tone; for he was weighted down by his old master's presence.

"In time," said the latter,—"in time, you will be capable of it."   32

The old watchmaker, with the freedom naturally consequent on   33
his former authority, went on inspecting the work which Owen had in hand at the moment, together with other matters that were in progress. The artist, meanwhile, could scarcely lift his head. There was nothing so antipodal to his nature as this man's cold, unimaginative sagacity, by

contact with which everything was converted into a dream except the densest matter of the physical world. Owen groaned in spirit and prayed fervently to be delivered from him.

"But what is this?" cried Peter Hovenden abruptly, taking up a dusty bell glass, beneath which appeared a mechanical something, as delicate and minute as the system of a butterfly's anatomy. "What have we here? Owen! Owen! there is witchcraft in these little chains, and wheels, and paddles. See! with one pinch of my finger and thumb I am going to deliver you from all future peril."

"For Heaven's sake," screamed Owen Warland, springing up with wonderful energy, "as you would not drive me mad, do not touch it! The slightest pressure of your finger would ruin me forever."

"Aha, young man! And is it so?" said the old watchmaker, looking at him with just enough penetration to torture Owen's soul with the bitterness of worldly criticism. "Well, take your own course; but I warn you again that in this small piece of mechanism lives your evil spirit. Shall I exorcise him?"

"You are my evil spirit," answered Owen, much excited,—"you and the hard, coarse world! The leaden thoughts and the despondency that you fling upon me are my clogs, else I should long ago have achieved the task that I was created for."

Peter Hovenden shook his head, with the mixture of contempt and indignation which mankind, of whom he was partly a representative, deem themselves entitled to feel towards all simpletons who seek other prizes than the dusty one along the highway. He then took his leave, with an uplifted finger and a sneer upon his face that haunted the artist's dreams for many a night afterwards. At the time of his old master's visit, Owen was probably on the point of taking up the relinquished task; but, by this sinister event, he was thrown back into the state whence he had been slowly emerging.

But the innate tendency of his soul had only been accumulating fresh vigor during its apparent sluggishness. As the summer advanced he almost totally relinquished his business and permitted Father Time, so far as the old gentleman was represented by the clocks and watches under his control, to stray at random through human life, making infinite confusion among the train of bewildered hours. He wasted the sunshine, as people said, in wandering through the woods and fields and along the banks of streams. There, like a child, he found amusement in chasing butterflies or watching the motions of water insects. There was something truly mysterious in the intentness with which he contemplated these living playthings as they sported on the breeze or examined the structure of an imperial insect whom he had imprisoned.

The chase of butterflies was an apt emblem of the ideal pursuit in which he had spent so many golden hours; but would the beautiful idea ever be yielded to his hand like the butterfly that symbolized it? Sweet, doubtless, were these days, and congenial to the artist's soul. They were full of bright conceptions, which gleamed through his intellectual world as the butterflies gleamed through the outward atmosphere, and were real to him, for the instant, without the toil, and perplexity, and many disappointments of attempting to make them visible to the sensual eye. Alas that the artist, whether in poetry, or whatever other material, may not content himself with the inward enjoyment of the beautiful, but must chase the flitting mystery beyond the verge of his ethereal domain, and crush its frail being in seizing it with a material grasp. Owen Warland felt the impulse to give external reality to his ideas as irresistibly as any of the poets or painters who have arrayed the world in a dimmer and fainter beauty, imperfectly copied from the richness of their visions.

The night was now his time for the slow progress of re-creating the one idea to which all his intellectual activity referred itself. Always at the approach of dusk he stole into the town, locked himself within his shop, and wrought with patient delicacy of touch for many hours. Sometimes he was startled by the rap of the watchman, who, when all the world should be asleep, had caught the gleam of lamplight through the crevices of Owen Warland's shutters. Daylight, to the morbid sensibility of his mind, seemed to have an intrusiveness that interfered with his pursuits. On cloudy and inclement days, therefore, he sat with his head upon his hands, muffling, as it were, his sensitive brain in a mist of indefinite musings; for it was a relief to escape from the sharp distinctness with which he was compelled to shape out his thoughts during his nightly toil. 40

From one of these fits of topor he was aroused by the entrance of Annie Hovenden, who came into the shop with the freedom of a customer, and also with something of the familiarity of a childish friend. She had worn a hole through her silver thimble, and wanted Owen to repair it. 41

"But I don't know whether you will condescend to such a task," said she, laughing, "now that you are so taken up with the notion of putting spirit into machinery." 42

"Where did you get that idea, Annie?" said Owen, starting in surprise. 43

"Oh, out of my own head," answered she, "and from something that I heard you say, long ago, when you were but a boy and I a little child. But come; will you mend this poor thimble of mine?" 44

"Anything for your sake, Annie," said Owen Warland,—"any-   45
thing, even were it to work at Robert Danforth's forge."

"And that would be a pretty sight!" retorted Annie, glancing with   46
imperceptible slightness at the artist's small and slender frame. "Well;
here is the thimble."

"But that is a strange idea of yours," said Owen, "about the spiri-   47
tualization of matter."

And then the thought stole into his mind that this young girl   48
possessed the gift to comprehend him better than all the world besides.
And what a help and strength would it be to him in his lonely toil if he
could gain the sympathy of the only being whom he loved! To persons
whose pursuits are insulated from the common business of life—who are
either in advance of mankind or apart from it—there often comes a
sensation of moral cold that makes the spirit shiver as if it had reached
the frozen solitudes around the pole. What the prophet, the poet, the
reformer, the criminal, or any other man with human yearnings, but
separated from the multitude by a peculiar lot, might feel, poor Owen
felt.

"Annie," cried he, growing pale as death at the thought, "how   49
gladly would I tell you the secret of my pursuit! You, methinks, would
estimate it rightly. You, I know, would hear it with a reverence that I
must not expect from the harsh, material world."

"Would I not? to be sure I would!" replied Annie Hovenden, lightly   50
laughing. "Come; explain to me quickly what is the meaning of this little
whirligig, so delicately wrought that it might be a plaything for Queen
Mab.[2] See! I will put it in motion."

"Hold!" exclaimed Owen, "hold!"   51

Annie had but given the slightest possible touch, with the point   52
of a needle, to the same minute portion of complicated machinery which
has been more than once mentioned, when the artist seized her by the
wrist with a force that made her scream aloud. She was affrighted at the
convulsion of intense rage and anguish that writhed across his features.
The next instant he let his head sink upon his hands.

"Go, Annie," murmured he; "I have deceived myself, and must   53
suffer for it. I yearned for sympathy, and thought, and fancied, and
dreamed that you might give it me; but you lack the talisman, Annie,
that should admit you into my secrets. That touch has undone the toil
of months and the thought of a lifetime! It was not your fault, Annie;
but you have ruined me!"

Poor Owen Warland! He had indeed erred, yet pardonably; for if   54
any human spirit could have sufficiently reverenced the processes so sa-

---

[2]Queen of the fairies.

cred in his eyes, it must have been a woman's. Even Annie Hovenden, possibly, might not have disappointed him had she been enlightened by the deep intelligence of love.

The artist spent the ensuing winter in a way that satisfied any   55
persons who had hitherto retained a hopeful opinion of him that he was, in truth, irrevocably doomed to unutility as regarded the world, and to an evil destiny on his own part. The decease of a relative had put him in possession of a small inheritance. Thus freed from the necessity of toil, and having lost the steadfast influence of a great purpose,—great, at least, to him,—he abandoned himself to habits from which it might have been supposed the mere delicacy of his organization would have availed to secure him. But when the ethereal portion of a man of genius is obscured, the earthly part assumes an influence the more uncontrollable, because the character is now thrown off the balance to which Providence had so nicely adjusted it, and which, in coarser natures, is adjusted by some other method. Owen Warland made proof of whatever show of bliss may be found in riot. He looked at the world through the golden medium of wine, and contemplated the visions that bubble up so gayly around the brim of the glass, and that people the air with shapes of pleasant madness, which so soon grow ghostly and forlorn. Even when this dismal and inevitable change had taken place, the young man might still have continued to quaff the cup of enchantments, though its vapor did but shroud life in gloom and fill the gloom with spectres that mocked at him. There was a certain irksomeness of spirit, which, being real, and the deepest sensation of which the artist was now conscious, was more intolerable than any fantastic miseries and horrors that the abuse of wine could summon up. In the latter case he could remember, even out of the midst of his trouble, that all was but a delusion; in the former, the heavy anguish was his actual life.

From this perilous state he was redeemed by an incident which   56
more than one person witnessed, but of which the shrewdest could not explain or conjecture the operation on Owen Warland's mind. It was very simple. On a warm afternoon of spring, as the artist sat among his riotous companions with a glass of wine before him, a splendid butterfly flew in at the open window and fluttered about his head.

"Ah," exclaimed Owen, who had drank freely, "are you alive again,   57
child of the sun and playmate of the summer breeze, after your dismal winter's nap? Then it is time for me to be at work!"

And, leaving his unemptied glass upon the table, he departed and   58
was never known to sip another drop of wine.

And now, again, he resumed his wanderings in the woods and   59
fields. It might be fancied that the bright butterfly, which had come so spirit-like into the window as Owen sat with the rude revellers, was

indeed a spirit commissioned to recall him to the pure, ideal life that had so etherealized him among men. It might be fancied that he went forth to seek this spirit in its sunny haunts; for still, as in the summer time gone by, he was seen to steal gently up wherever a butterfly had alighted, and lose himself in contemplation of it. When it took flight his eyes followed the winged vision, as if its airy track would show the path to heaven. But what could be the purpose of the unseasonable toil, which was again resumed, as the watchman knew by the lines of lamplight through the crevices of Owen Warland's shutters? The towns-people had one comprehensive explanation of all these singularities. Owen Warland had gone mad! How universally efficacious—how satisfactory, too, and soothing to the injured sensibility of narrowness and dulness—is this easy method of accounting for whatever lies beyond the world's most ordinary scope! From St. Paul's days down to our poor little Artist of the Beautiful, the same talisman had been applied to the elucidation of all mysteries in the words or deeds of men who spoke or acted too wisely or too well. In Owen Warland's case the judgment of his towns-people may have been correct. Perhaps he was mad. The lack of sympathy—that contrast between himself and his neighbors which took away the restraint of example—was enough to make him so. Or possibly he had caught just so much of ethereal radiance as served to bewilder him, in an earthly sense, by its intermixture with the common daylight.

One evening, when the artist had returned from a customary ramble 60 and had just thrown the lustre of his lamp on the delicate piece of work so often interrupted, but still taken up again, as if his fate were embodied in its mechanism, he was surprised by the entrance of old Peter Hovenden. Owen never met this man without a shrinking of the heart. Of all the world he was most terrible, by reason of a keen understanding which saw so distinctly what it did see, and disbelieved so uncompromisingly in what it could not see. On this occasion the old watchmaker had merely a gracious word or two to say.

"Owen, my lad," said he, "we must see you at my house to-morrow 61 night."

The artist began to mutter some excuse. 62

"Oh, but it must be so," quoth Peter Hovenden, "for the sake of 63 the days when you were one of the household. What, by boy! don't you know that my daughter Annie is engaged to Robert Danforth? We are making an entertainment, in our humble way, to celebrate the event."

"Ah!" said Owen. 64

That little monosyllable was all he uttered; its tone seemed cold 65 and unconcerned to an ear like Peter Hovenden's; and yet there was in it the stifled outcry of the poor artist's heart, which he compressed within him like a man holding down an evil spirit. One slight outbreak, however, imperceptible to the old watchmaker, he allowed himself. Raising the instrument with which he was about to begin his work, he let it fall upon the little system of machinery that had, anew, cost him months of thought and toil. It was shattered by the stroke!

Owen Warland's story would have been no tolerable representation of the troubled life of those who strive to create the beautiful, if, amid all other thwarting influences, love had not interposed to steal the cunning from his hand. Outwardly he had been no ardent or enterprising lover; the career of his passion had confined its tumults and vicissitudes so entirely within the artist's imagination that Annie herself had scarcely more than a woman's intuitive perception of it; but, in Owen's view, it covered the whole field of his life. Forgetful of the time when she had shown herself incapable of any deep response, he had persisted in connecting all his dreams of artistical success with Annie's image; she was the visible shape in which the spiritual power that he worshipped, and on whose altar he hoped to lay a not unworthy offering, was made manifest to him. Of course he had deceived himself; there were no such attributes in Annie Hovenden as his imagination had endowed her with. She, in the aspect which she wore to his inward vision, was as much a creature of his own as the mysterious piece of mechanism would be were it ever realized. Had he become convinced of his mistake through the medium of successful love,—had he won Annie to his bosom, and there beheld her fade from angel into ordinary woman,—the disappointment might have driven him back, with concentrated energy, upon his sole remaining object. On the other hand, had he found Annie what he fancied, his lot would have been so rich in beauty that out of its mere redundancy he might have wrought the beautiful into many a worthier type than he had toiled for; but the guise in which his sorrow came to him, the sense that the angel of his life had been snatched away and given to a rude man of earth and iron, who could neither need nor appreciate her ministrations,—this was the very perversity of fate that makes human existence appear too absurd and contradictory to be the scene of one other hope or one other fear. There was nothing left for Owen Warland but to sit down like a man that had been stunned.

He went through a fit of illness. After his recovery his small and slender frame assumed an obtuser garniture of flesh than it had ever before worn. His thin cheeks became round; his delicate little hand, so spiritually fashioned to achieve fairy task-work, grew plumper than the hand of a thriving infant. His aspect had a childishness such as might have induced a stranger to pat him on the head—pausing, however, in the act, to wonder what matter of child was here. It was as if the spirit had

66

67

484 *Nathaniel Hawthorne*

gone out of him, leaving the body to flourish in a sort of vegetable existence. Not that Owen Warland was idiotic. He could talk, and not irrationally. Somewhat of a babbler, indeed, did people begin to think him; for he was apt to discourse at wearisome length of marvels of mechanism that he had read about in books, but which he had learned to consider as absolutely fabulous. Among them he enumerated the Man of Brass, constructed by Albertus Magnus, and the Brazen Head of Friar Bacon;[3] and, coming down to later times, the automata of a little coach and horses, which it was pretended had been manufactured for the Dauphin of France; together with an insect that buzzed about the ear like a living fly, and yet was but a contrivance of minute steel springs. There was a story, too, of a duck that waddled, and quacked, and ate; though, had any honest citizen purchased it for dinner, he would have found himself cheated with the mere mechanical apparition of a duck.

"But all these accounts," said Owen Warland, "I am now satisfied are mere impositions."   68

Then, in a mysterious way, he would confess that he once thought differently. In his idle and dreamy days he had considered it possible, in a certain sense, to spiritualize machinery, and to combine with the new species of life and motion thus produced a beauty that should attain to the ideal which Nature has proposed to herself in all her creatures, but has never taken pains to realize. He seemed, however, to retain no very distinct perception either of the process of achieving this object or of the design itself.   69

"I have thrown it all aside now," he would say. "It was a dream such as young men are always mystifying themselves with. Now that I have acquired a little common sense, it makes me laugh to think of it."   70

Poor, poor and fallen Owen Warland! These were the symptoms that he had ceased to be an inhabitant of the better sphere that lies unseen around us. He had lost his faith in the invisible, and now prided himself, as such unfortunates invariably do, in the wisdom which rejected much that even his eye could see, and trusted confidently in nothing but what his hand could touch. This is the calamity of men whose spiritual part dies out of them and leaves the grosser understanding to assimilate them more and more to the things of which alone it can take cognizance; but in Owen Warland the spirit was not dead nor passed away; it only slept.   71

---

[3]Albertus Magnus (1193–1280) was a great medieval philosopher and teacher of St. Thomas Aquinas; Friar Bacon was Roger Bacon (1214–94), the great innovator of scientific method who was a Franciscan monk.

How it awoke again is not recorded. Perhaps the torpid slumber   72
was broken by a convulsive pain. Perhaps, as in a former instance, the
butterfly came and hovered about his head and reinspired him,—as indeed this creature of the sunshine had always a mysterious mission for
the artist,—reinspired him with the former purpose of his life. Whether
it were pain or happiness that thrilled through his veins, his first impulse
was to thank Heaven for rendering him again the being of thought,
imagination, and keenest sensibility that he had long ceased to be.

"Now for my task," said he. "Never did I feel such strength for it   73
as now."

Yet, strong as he felt himself, he was incited to toil the more   74
diligently by an anxiety lest death should surprise him in the midst of
his labors. The anxiety, perhaps, is common to all men who set their
hearts upon anything so high, in their own view of it, that life becomes
of importance only as conditional to its accomplishment. So long as we
love life for itself, we seldom dread the losing it. When we desire life for
the attainment of an object, we recognize the frailty of its texture. But,
side by side with this sense of insecurity, there is a vital faith in our
invulnerability to the shaft of death while engaged in any task that seems
assigned by Providence as our proper thing to do, and which the world
would have cause to mourn for should we leave it unaccomplished. Can
the philosopher, big with the inspiration of an idea that is to reform
mankind, believe that he is to be beckoned from this sensible existence
at the very instant when he is mustering his breath to speak the word of
light? Should he perish so, the weary ages may pass away—the world's,
whose life sand may fall, drop by drop—before another intellect is prepared to develop the truth that might have been uttered then. But history
affords many an example where the most precious spirit, at any particular
epoch manifested in human shape, has gone hence untimely, without
space allowed him, so far as mortal judgment could discern, to perform
his mission on the earth. The prophet dies, and the man of torpid heart
and sluggish brain lives on. The poet leaves his song half sung, or finishes
it, beyond the scope of mortal ears, in a celestial choir. The painter—
as Allston did[4]—leaves half his conception on the canvas to sadden us
with its imperfect beauty, and goes to picture forth the whole, if it be
no irreverence to say so, in the hues of heaven. But rather such incomplete designs of this life will be perfected nowhere. This so frequent
abortion of man's dearest projects must be taken as a proof that the deeds
of earth, however etherealized by piety or genius, are without value,

---

[4]Washington Allston (1779–1843), American landscape painter.

except as exercises and manifestations of the spirit. In heaven, all ordinary thought is higher and more melodious than Milton's song.[5] Then, would he add another verse to any strain that he had left unfinished here?

But to return to Owen Warland. It was his fortune, good or ill, to achieve the purpose of his life. Pass we over a long space of intense thought, yearning effort, minute toil, and wasting anxiety, succeeded by an instant of solitary triumph: let all this be imagined; and then behold the artist, on a winter evening, seeking admittance to Robert Danforth's fireside circle. There he found the man of iron, with his massive substance thoroughly warmed and attempered by domestic influences. And there was Annie, too, now transformed into a matron, with much of her husband's plain and sturdy nature, but imbued, as Owen Warland still believed, with a finer grace, that might enable her to be the interpreter between strength and beauty. It happened, likewise, that old Peter Hovenden was a guest this evening at his daughter's fireside, and it was his well-remembered expression of keen, cold criticism that first encountered the artist's glance.

"My old friend Owen!" cried Robert Danforth, starting up, and compressing the artist's delicate fingers within a hand that was accustomed to gripe bars of iron. "This is kind and neighborly to come to us at last. I was afraid your perpetual motion had bewitched you out of the remembrance of old times."

"We are glad to see you," said Annie, while a blush reddened her matronly cheek. "It was not like a friend to stay from us so long."

"Well, Owen," inquired the old watchmaker, as his first greeting, "how comes on the beautiful? Have you created it at last?"

The artist did not immediately reply, being startled by the apparition of a young child of strength that was tumbling about on the carpet,—a little personage who had come mysteriously out of the infinite, but with something so sturdy and real in his composition that he seemed moulded out of the densest substance which earth could supply. This hopeful infant crawled towards the new-comer, and setting himself on end, as Robert Danforth expressed the posture, stared at Owen with a look of such sagacious observation that the mother could not help exchanging a proud glance with her husband. But the artist was disturbed by the child's look, as imaging a resemblance between it and Peter Hovenden's habitual expression. He could have fancied that the old watchmaker was com-

---

[5]John Milton (1608–74), the great English poet.

pressed into this baby shape, and looking out of those baby eyes, and repeating, as he now did, the malicious question:—

"The beautiful, Owen! How comes on the beautiful? Have you   80
succeeded in creating the beautiful?"

"I have succeeded," replied the artist, with a momentary light of   81
triumph in his eyes and a smile of sunshine, yet steeped in such depth
of thought that it was almost sadness. "Yes, my friends, it is the truth.
I have succeeded."

"Indeed!" cried Annie, a look of a maiden mirthfulness peeping   82
out of her face again. "And is it lawful, now, to inquire what the secret
is?"

"Surely; it is to disclose it that I have come," answered Owen   83
Warland. "You shall know, and see, and touch, and possess the secret!
For, Annie,—if by that name I may still address the friend of my boyish
years,—Annie, it is for your bridal gift that I have wrought this spiri-
tualized mechanism, this harmony of motion, this mystery of beauty. It
comes late, indeed; but it is as we go onward in life, when objects begin
to lose their freshness of hue and our souls their delicacy of perception,
that the spirit of beauty is most needed. If,—forgive me, Annie,—if you
know how to value this gift, it can never come too late."

He produced, as he spoke, what seemed a jewel box. It was carved   84
richly out of ebony by his own hand, and inlaid with a fanciful tracery
of pearl, representing a boy in pursuit of a butterfly, which, elsewhere,
had become a winged spirit, and was flying heavenward; while the boy,
or youth, had found such efficacy in his strong desire that he ascended
from earth to cloud, and from cloud to celestial atmosphere, to win the
beautiful. This case of ebony the artist opened, and bade Annie place
her fingers on its edge. She did so, but almost screamed as a butterfly
fluttered forth, and, alighting on her finger's tip, sat waving the ample
magnificence of its purple and gold-speckled wings, as if in prelude to a
flight. It is impossible to express by words the glory, the splendor, the
delicate gorgeousness which were softened into the beauty of this object.
Nature's ideal butterfly was here realized in all its perfection; not in the
pattern of such faded insects as flit among earthly flowers, but of those
which hover across the meads of paradise for child-angels and the spirits
of departed infants to disport themselves with. The rich down was visible
upon its wings; the lustre of its eyes seemed instinct with spirit. The
firelight glimmered around this wonder—the candles gleamed upon it;
but it glistened apparently by its own radiance, and illuminated the finger
and outstretched hand on which it rested with a white gleam like that
of precious stones. In its perfect beauty, the consideration of size was

entirely lost. Had its wings overreached the firmament, the mind could not have been more filled or satisfied.

"Beautiful! beautiful!" exclaimed Annie. "Is it alive? Is it alive?"

"Alive? To be sure it is," answered her husband. "Do you suppose any mortal has skill enough to make a butterfly, or would put himself to the trouble of making one, when any child may catch a score of them in a summer's afternoon? Alive? Certainly! But this pretty box is undoubtedly of our friend Owen's manufacture; and really it does him credit."

At this moment the butterfly waved its wings anew, with a motion so absolutely lifelike that Annie was startled, and even awestricken; for, in spite of her husband's opinion, she could not satisfy herself whether it was indeed a living creature or a piece of wondrous mechanism.

"Is it alive?" she repeated, more earnestly than before.

"Judge for yourself," said Owen Warland, who stood gazing in her face with fixed attention.

The butterfly now flung itself upon the air, fluttered round Annie's head, and soared into a distant region of the parlor, still making itself perceptible to sight by the starry gleam in which the motion of its wings enveloped it. The infant on the floor followed its course with his sagacious little eyes. After flying about the room, it returned in a spiral curve and settled again on Annie's finger.

"But is it alive?" exclaimed she again; and the finger on which the gorgeous mystery had alighted was so tremulous that the butterfly was forced to balance himself with his wings. "Tell me if it be alive, or whether you created it."

"Wherefore ask who created it, so it be beautiful?" replied Owen Warland. "Alive? Yes, Annie; it may well be said to possess life, for it has absorbed my own being into itself; and in the secret of that butterfly, and in its beauty,—which is not merely outward, but deep as its whole system,—is represented the intellect, the imagination, the sensibility, the soul of an Artist of the Beautiful! Yes; I created it. But"— and here his countenance somewhat changed—"this butterfly is not now to me what it was when I beheld it afar off in the daydreams of my youth."

"Be it what it may, it is a pretty plaything," said the blacksmith, grinning with childlike delight. "I wonder whether it would condescend to alighten on such a great clumsy finger as mine? Hold it hither, Annie."

By the artist's direction, Annie touched her finger's tip to that of her husband; and, after a momentary delay, the butterfly fluttered from one to the other. It preluded a second flight by a similar, yet not precisely the same, waving of wings as in the first experiment; then, ascending from the blacksmith's stalwart finger, it rose in a gradually enlarging curve to the ceiling, made one wide sweep around the room, and returned with an undulating movement to the point whence it had started.

"Well, that does beat all nature!" cried Robert Danforth, bestowing the heartiest praise that he could find expression for; and, indeed, had he paused there, a man of finer words and nicer perception could not easily have said more. "That goes beyond me, I confess. But what then? There is more real use in one downright blow of my sledge hammer than in the whole five years' labor that our friend Owen has wasted on this butterfly."

Here the child clapped his hands and made a great babble of indistinct utterance, apparently demanding that the butterfly should be given him for a plaything.

Owen Warland, meanwhile, glanced sidelong at Annie, to discover whether she sympathized in her husband's estimate of the comparative value of the beautiful and the practical. There was, amid all her kindness towards himself, amid all the wonder and admiration with which she contemplated the marvellous work of his hands and incarnation of his ideas, a secret scorn—too secret, perhaps, for her own consciousness, and perceptible only to such intuitive discernment as that of the artist. But Owen, in the latter stages of his pursuit, had risen out of the region in which such a discovery might have been torture. He knew that the world, and Annie as the representative of the world, whatever praise might be bestowed, could never say the fitting word nor feel the fitting sentiment which should be the perfect recompense of an artist who, symbolizing a lofty moral by a material trifle,—converting what was earthly to spiritual gold,—had won the beautiful into his handiwork. Not at this latest moment was he to learn that the reward of all high performance must be sought within itself, or sought in vain. There was, however, a view of the matter which Annie and her husband, and even Peter Hovenden, might fully have understood, and which would have satisfied them that the toil of years had here been worthily bestowed. Owen Warland might have told them that this butterfly, this plaything, this bridal gift of a poor watchmaker to a blacksmith's wife, was, in truth, a gem of art that a monarch would have purchased with honors and abundant wealth, and have treasured it among the jewels of his kingdom as the most unique and wondrous of them all. But the artist smiled and kept the secret to himself.

"Father," said Annie, thinking that a word of praise from the old watchmaker might gratify his former apprentice, "do come and admire this pretty butterfly."

"Let us see," said Peter Hovenden, raising from his chair, with a sneer upon his face that always made people doubt, as he himself did, in

95

96

97

98

99

everything but a material existence. "Here is my finger for it to alight upon. I shall understand it better when once I have touched it."

But, to the increased astonishment of Annie, when the tip of her father's finger was pressed against that of her husband, on which the butterfly still rested, the insect drooped its wings and seemed on the point of falling to the floor. Even the bright spots of gold upon its wings and body, unless her eyes deceived her, grew dim, and the glowing purple took a dusky hue, and the starry lustre that gleamed around the black-smith's hand became faint and vanished.

"It is dying! it is dying!" cried Annie, in alarm.

"It has been delicately wrought," said the artist, calmly. "As I told you, it has imbibed a spiritual essence—call it magnetism, or what you will. In an atmosphere of doubt and mockery its exquisite susceptibility suffers torture, as does the soul of him who instilled his own life into it. It has already lost its beauty; in a few moments more its mechanism would be irreparably injured."

"Take away your hand, father!" entreated Annie turning pale. "Here is my child; let it rest on his innocent hand. There, perhaps, its life will revive and its colors grow brighter than ever."

Her father, with an acrid smile, withdrew his finger. The butterfly then appeared to recover the power of voluntary motion, while its hues assumed much of their original lustre, and the gleam of starlight, which was its most ethereal attribute, again formed a halo round about it. At first, when transferred from Robert Danforth's hand to the small finger of the child, this radiance grew so powerful that it positively threw the little fellow's shadow back against the wall. He, meanwhile, extended his plump hand as he had seen his father and mother do, and watched the waving of the insect's wings in infantine delight. Nevertheless, there was a certain odd expression of sagacity that made Owen Warland feel as if here were old Peter Hovenden, partially, and but partially, redeemed from his hard scepticism into childish faith.

"How wise the little monkey looks!" whispered Robert Danforth to his wife.

"I never saw such a look on a child's face," answered Annie, admiring her own infant, and with good reason, far more than the artistic butterfly. "The darling knows more of the mystery than we do."

As if the butterfly, like the artist, were conscious of something not entirely congenial in the child's nature, it alternately sparkled and grew dim. At length it arose from the small hand of the infant with an airy motion that seemed to bear it upward without an effort, as if the ethereal instincts with which its master's spirit had endowed it impelled this fair vision involuntarily to a higher sphere. Had there been no obstruction, it might have soared into the sky and grown immortal. But its lustre gleamed upon the ceiling; the exquisite texture of its wings brushed against that earthly medium; and a sparkle or two, as of stardust, floated downward and lay glimmering on the carpet. Then the butterfly came fluttering down, and, instead of returning to the infant, was apparently attracted towards the artist's hand.

"Not so! not so!" murmured Owen Warland, as if his handiwork could have understood him. "Thou hast gone forth out of thy master's heart. There is no return for thee." 108

With a wavering movement, and emitting a tremulous radiance, the butterfly struggled, as it were, towards the infant, and was about to alight upon his finger; but while it still hovered in the air, the little child of strength, with his grandsire's sharp and shrewd expression in his face, made a snatch at the marvellous insect and compressed it in his hand. Annie screamed. Old Peter Hovenden burst into a cold and scornful laugh. The blacksmith, by main force, unclosed the infant's hand, and found within the palm a small heap of glittering fragments, whence the mystery of beauty had fled forever. And as for Owen Warland, he looked placidly at what seemed the ruin of his life's labor, and which was yet no ruin. He had caught a far other butterfly than this. When the artist rose high enough to achieve the beautiful, the symbol by which he made it perceptible to mortal senses became of little value in his eyes while his spirit possessed itself in the enjoyment of the reality. 109

About the Essay

1. What social values do Warland, Danforth, Hovenden, and Annie each represent? In what ways is the conflict of those values at the heart of Hawthorne's story?

2. Why does Warland refuse to repair Hovenden's watch? What is the significance of his decision?

3. If Owen Warland loves Annie, why does he not profess his love to her? Would it have made any difference if he had? Why, or why not?

4. Warland seems to be able to create his masterpiece only after Annie and Danforth are married. Why is this so? What is the connection between the two events? Why do you think Warland gives the butterfly to Annie and Danforth as a wedding present?

5. Discuss the symbolism of the butterfly in "The Artist of the Beautiful." What does it mean to Warland? Why did he wish to create one, and why did he refuse to let it return to him at the end?

6. What is Hawthorne's view of the artist's role in society? Where in the story does he state this view directly? Do the events of the story reflect the

same view? Do you think that Hawthorne regards Warland with sympathy or with contempt? Why?

7. Why isn't the destruction of the butterfly at the end of the story a defeat for Warland? What does Hawthorne mean when he says in the last paragraph that Warland "had caught a far other butterfly than this"?

Explorations

1. Tension between the beautiful and the practical occurs not only in the world of Hawthorne's story but also in the world we live in. Why should something that is practical be beautiful as well? And must a beautiful thing also be practical? Apply this question to an aspect of society that particularly interests you—some possibilities are clothing, architecture, or transportation.

2. Every society has its artists, though it may respect or reward them no better than Hawthorne's townspeople did Owen Warland. Do you think a society should subsidize its artists, or should they have to earn their living as best they can? Why do you think so?

7 Pastimes

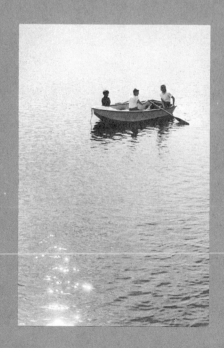

In our play we reveal what kind of people we are.
OVID

Man is so made that he can only find relaxation from one kind of labor by taking up another.
ANATOLE FRANCE

There is a function of a quasi-religious nature performed by a few experts but followed in spirit by the whole university world, serving indeed as a symbol to arouse in the students and in the alumni certain congregate and hieratic emotions. I refer, of course, to football.
CHARLES HORTON COOLEY

Most sorts of diversion in men, children, and other animals, are an imitation of fighting.
JONATHAN SWIFT

What the mass media offer is not popular art, but entertainment which is intended to be consumed like food, forgotten, and replaced by a new dish.
W. H. AUDEN

WHEN the day's work is done, there comes the time when we are free to do as we wish. Some of that time is consumed by the routine of living, of getting from one place to another, cooking meals, and doing laundry; some is devoted to personal business and projects, paying bills, practicing an instrument, or doing exercises. But for most of us, free time means time to have fun.

And how many kinds of fun there are! Some of our recreations are strenuous, like jogging or tennis; these not only help us to keep fit but also give us that sense of pleasant, relaxed exhaustion that comes after a good workout. Other recreations, such as chess or bridge, challenge our wits. Some people like nothing better than an afternoon's walk in the woods, with binoculars handy for bird-watching, while others delight in a good shopping trip to the city. Competitive

495

sports have their own special appeal, combining as they do the pleasures of play, competition, and reunion with our friends.

Americans and, no doubt, humans everywhere often prefer watching as much as doing. Indeed, more of us watch sporting events, especially on television, than take part in them. Television takes up much of our free time, dispensing entertainment to viewers at all times of the day and night. Movies, shows, and concerts draw us out of the house and into the theaters. Airlines even show movies in the air, so that we need never be at a loss to pass the time.

We spend a hundred billion dollars a year on our pastimes, and so there is an enormous industry whose business is our pleasure. We have made our leading entertainers and athletes into millionaires; more, we have made them into celebrities, even role models. As the 1980s began, there was a former basketball star in the Senate, a former championship quarterback in the House of Representatives, and a former film actor in the White House. Though other nations have elevated writers and musicians to high office, none has taken its popular entertainers quite so seriously.

Some of the selections that follow celebrate our pastimes, while others explore their implications for our values and our way of life. If, as seems likely, more and more work is to be done in automated factories and offices, then we will have more free time than ever to use in whatever way we wish, and recreation will occupy an even larger part of our lives than it does now. Then we may test the truth of Bertrand Russell's pronouncement: "To be able to fill leisure intelligently is the last product of civilization."

ROGER ANGELL

In a recent essay Roger Angell recalls a summer day when he was driving through New York City with his four-year-old daughter. They were listening to a ballgame on the car radio, and as they approached the Polo Grounds he pointed and explained, "Callie, the game we're listening to is being played right over there, right now. That's the game we're listening to, and this is the Polo Grounds, where the two teams are playing it, see? It's hard to explain, but—" She nodded, not much interested . . . but then she heard something on the radio and sat up suddenly and stared out at the great green ballpark beside the road. When she turned, her eyes were wide. "*Giants* are playing in there?" she asked. For Roger Angell, ballplayers are a special breed of giant. With eloquence and affection he has been covering baseball for *The New Yorker* for more than a decade. He was born in New York City in 1920, attended Harvard College, and now lives in New York, where he roots for the Yankees and the Mets but *cares* about the Boston Red Sox. His baseball essays have been collected in three volumes considered classics by fans and nonfans alike: *The Summer Game* (1972), *Five Seasons* (1977), and *Late Innings* (1982). The following piece is the concluding essay from *The Summer Game;* in it Angell considers the pleasure of watching baseball.

The Summer Game

Sports are too much with us. Late and soon, sitting and watching—   1
mostly watching on television—we lay waste our powers of identification and enthusiasm and, in time, attention as more and more closing rallies and crucial putts and late field goals and final playoffs and sudden deaths and world records and world championships unreel themselves ceaselessly before our half-lidded eyes. Professional leagues expand like bubble gum, ever larger and thinner, and the extended sporting seasons, now bunching and overlapping at the ends, conclude in exhaustion and the wrong weather. So, too, goes the secondary business of sports—the news or non-news off the field. Sports announcers (ex-halfbacks in Mod hairdos) bring us another live, exclusive interview in depth with the twitchy coach of some as yet undefeated basketball team, or with a weeping (for joy) fourteen-year-old champion female backstroker, and the sports pages, now almost the largest single part of the newspaper, brim with salary disputes, medical bulletins, franchise maneuverings, all-star ballots, drug scandals, close-up biogs, after-dinner tributes, union tactics, weekend wrapups, wire-service polls, draft-choice trades, clubhouse gossip, and the latest odds. The American obsession with sports is not a new phe-

nomenon, of course, except in its current dimensions, its excessive ex-
cessiveness. What *is* new, and what must at times unsettle even the most
devout and unselective fan, is a curious sense of loss. In the midst of all
these successive spectacles and instant replays and endless reportings and
recapitulations, we seem to have forgotten what we came for. More and
more, each sport resembles all sports; the flavor, the special joys of place
and season, the unique displays of courage and strength and style that
once isolated each game and fixed it in our affections have disappeared
somewhere in the noise and crush.

Of all sports, none has been so buffeted about by this unselective 2
proliferation, so maligned by contemporary cant, or so indifferently defended as baseball. Yet the game somehow remains the same, obdurately
unaltered and comparable only with itself. Baseball has one saving grace
that distinguishes it—for me, at any rate—from every other sport. Because of its pace, and thus the perfectly observed balance, both physical
and psychological, between opposing forces, its clean lines can be restored in retrospect. This inner game—baseball in the mind—has no
season, but it is best played in the winter, without the distraction of
other baseball news. At first, it is a game of recollections, recapturings,
and visions. Figures and occasions return, enormous sounds rise and swell,
and the interior stadium fills with light and yields up the sight of a young
ballplayer—some hero perfectly memorized—just completing his own
unique swing and now racing toward first. See the way he runs? Yes,
that's him! Unmistakable, he leans in, still following the distant flight
of the ball with his eyes, and takes his big turn at the base. Yet this is
only the beginning, for baseball in the mind is not a mere returning. In
time, this easy summoning up of restored players, winning hits, and
famous rallies gives way to reconsiderations and reflections about the sport
itself. By thinking about baseball like this—by playing it over, keeping
it warm in a cold season—we begin to make discoveries. With luck, we
may even penetrate some of its mysteries. One of those mysteries is its
vividness—the absolutely distinct inner vision we retain of that hitter,
that eager base-runner, of however long ago. My father was talking the
other day about some of the ballplayers he remembered. He grew up in
Cleveland, and the Indians were his team. Still are. "We had Nap Lajoie
at second," he said. "You've heard of him. A great big broad-shouldered
fellow, but a beautiful fielder. He was a rough customer. If he didn't like
an umpire's call, he'd give him a faceful of tobacco juice. The shortstop
was Terry Turner—a smaller man, and blond. I can still see Lajoie picking up a grounder and wheeling and floating the ball over to Turner.
Oh, he was quick on his feet! In right field we had Elmer Flick, now in
the Hall of Fame. I liked the center fielder, too. His name was Harry

Bay, and he wasn't a heavy hitter, but he was very fast and covered a lot of ground. They said he could circle the bases in twelve seconds flat. I saw him get a home run inside the park—the ball hit on the infield and went right past the second baseman and out to the wall, and Bay beat the relay. I remember Addie Joss, our great right-hander. Tall, and an elegant pitcher. I once saw him pitch a perfect game. He died young."

• • • •

I have watched many other sports, and I have followed some— football, hockey, tennis—with eagerness, but none of them yields these permanent interior pictures, these ancient and precise excitements. Baseball, I must conclude, is intensely remembered because only baseball is so intensely watched. The game forces intensity upon us. In the ballpark, scattered across an immense green, each player is isolated in our attention, utterly visible. Watch that fielder just below us. Little seems to be expected of him. He waits in easy composure, his hands on his knees; when the ball at last soars or bounces out to him, he seizes it and dispatches it with swift, haughty ease. It all looks easy, slow, and, above all, safe. Yet we know better, for what is certain in baseball is that someone, perhaps several people, will fail. They will be searched out, caught in the open, and defeated, and there will be no confusion about it or sharing of the blame. This is sure to happen, because what baseball requires of its athletes, of course, is nothing less than perfection, and perfection cannot be eased or divided. Every movement of every game, from first pitch to last out, is measured and recorded against an absolute standard, and thus each success is also a failure. Credit that strikeout to the pitcher, but also count it against the batter's average; mark his run unearned, because the left fielder bobbled the ball for an instant and a runner moved up. Yet, faced with this sudden and repeated presence of danger, the big-league player defends himself with such courage and skill that the illusion of safety is sustained. Tension is screwed tighter and tighter as the certain downfall is postponed again and again, so that when disaster does come—a half-topped infield hit, a walk on a close three-and-two call, a low drive up the middle that just eludes the diving shortstop—we rise and cry out. It is a spontaneous, inevitable, irresistible reaction.

Televised baseball, I must add, does not seem capable of transmitting this emotion. Most baseball is seen on the tube now, and it is presented faithfully and with great technical skill. But the medium is irrevocably two-dimensional; even with several cameras, television cannot bring us the essential distances of the game—the simultaneous flight of a batted ball and its pursuit by the racing, straining outfielders, the swift convergence of runner and ball at a base. Foreshortened on our screen, the players on the field appear to be squashed together, almost touching each other, and, watching them, we lose the sense of their separateness and lonesome waiting.

• • • •

Form is the imposition of a regular pattern upon varying and un- 5 predictable circumstances, but the patterns of baseball, for all the game's tautness and neatness, are never regular. Who can predict the winner and shape of today's game? Will it be a brisk, neat two-hour shutout? A languid, error-filled 12-3 laughter? A riveting three-hour, fourteen-inning deadlock? What other sport produces these manic swings? For the players, too, form often undergoes terrible reversals; in no other sport is a champion athlete so often humiliated or a journeyman so easily exalted. The surprise, the upset, the total turnabout of expectations and reputations— these are delightful commonplaces of baseball. Al Gionfriddo, a part-time Dodger outfielder, stole second base in the ninth inning of the fourth game of the 1947 World Series to help set up Lavagetto's game-winning double (and the only Dodger hit of the game) off the Yankees' Bill Bevens. Two days later, Gionfriddo robbed Joe DiMaggio with a famous game-saving catch of a four-hundred-and-fifteen-foot drive in deepest left field at Yankee Stadium. Gionfriddo never made it back to the big leagues after that season. Another irregular, the Mets' Al Weis, homered in the fifth and last game of the 1969 World Series, tying up the game that the Mets won in the next inning; it was Weis's third homer of the year and his first ever at Shea Stadium. And so forth. Who remembers the second game of the 1956 World Series—an appallingly bad afternoon of baseball in which the Yankees' starter, Don Larsen, was yanked after giving up a single and four walks in less than two innings? It was Larsen's *next* start, the fifth game, when he pitched his perfect game.

There is always a heavy splash of luck in these reversals. Luck, 6 indeed, plays an almost predictable part in the game; we have all seen the enormous enemy clout into the bleachers that just hooks foul at the last instant, and the half-checked swing that produces a game-winning blooper over second. Everyone complains about baseball luck, but I think it adds something to the game that is nearly essential. Without it, such a rigorous and unforgiving pastime would be almost too painful to enjoy.

• • • •

Always, it seems, there is something more to be discovered about 7 this game. Sit quietly in the upper stand and look at the field. Half close your eyes against the sun, so that the players recede a little, and watch the movements of baseball. The pitcher, immobile on the mound, holds the inert white ball, his little lump of physics. Now, with abrupt gestures, he gives it enormous speed and direction, converting it suddenly into a line, a moving line. The batter, wielding a plane, attempts to intercept the line and acutely alter it, but he fails; the ball, a line again, is redrawn to the pitcher, in the center of this square, the diamond. Again the pitcher studies his task—the projection of his next line through the smallest possible segment of an invisible seven-sided solid (the strike zone has depth as well as height and width) sixty feet and six inches away; again the batter considers his even more difficult proposition, which is to reverse this imminent white speck, to redirect its energy not in a soft parabola or a series of diminishing squiggles but into a beautiful and dangerous new force, of perfect straightness and immense distance. In time, these and other lines are drawn on the field; the batter and the fielders are also transformed into fluidity, moving and converging, and we see now that all movement in baseball is a convergence toward fixed points—the pitched ball toward the plate, the thrown ball toward the right angles of the bases, the batted ball toward the as yet undrawn but already visible point of congruence with either the ground or a glove. Simultaneously, the fielders hasten toward that same point of meeting with the ball, and both the base-runner and the ball, now redirected, toward their encounter at the base. From our perch, we can sometimes see three or four or more such geometries appearing at the same instant on the green board below us, and, mathematicians that we are, can sense their solution even before they are fully drawn. It is neat, it is pretty, it is satisfying. Scientists speak of the profoundly moving aesthetic beauty of mathematics, and perhaps the baseball field is one of the few places where the rest of us can glimpse this mystery.

The last dimension is time. Within the ballpark, time moves differently, marked by no clock except the events of the game. This is the unique, unchangeable feature of baseball, and perhaps explains why this sport, for all the enormous changes it has undergone in the past decade or two, remains somehow rustic, unviolent, and introspective. Baseball's time is seamless and invisible, a bubble within which players move at exactly the same pace and rhythms as all their predecessors. This is the way the game was played in our youth and in our fathers' youth, and even back then—back in the country days—there must have been the same feeling that time could be stopped. Since baseball time is measured only in outs, all you have to do is succeed utterly; keep hitting, keep the rally alive, and you have defeated time. You remain forever young. Sitting in the stands, we sense this, if only dimly. The players below us—Mays, DiMaggio, Ruth, Snodgrass—swim and blur in memory, the ball floats over to Terry Turner, and the end of this game may never come.

About the Essay

1. What, according to Angell, is wrong with sports in America today? What does he feel has been lost as a result?

2. What makes baseball different from all other sports, in Angell's view? Can you add any important distinctions of your own? What similarities do you find between baseball and other team sports?

3. What does Angell mean by the inner game of baseball? Why does he value it?

4. In paragraph 7 Angell uses terms from physics and geometry to characterize the movements of the game. What does this contribute to the essay?

5. What role does luck play in baseball? Give some examples of your own. What does Angell mean when he says that "without it, such a rigorous and unforgiving pastime would be almost too painful to enjoy"?

6. Several of Angell's paragraphs are quite long. How does this affect your response to the essay? Can you point to any paragraphs you think should be broken into shorter ones? If so, which ones, and where should they be divided?

Explorations

1. Angell does not play baseball and therefore writes about it from a spectator's point of view. Choose a sport that you play and write about it from a player's point of view. What is its essence—the quality or qualities that are needed to play it well, and that distinguish it from other sports?

2. Radio and TV broadcasters and newspaper reporters offer baseball fans numerous statistics about the game—batting averages, pitchers' earned run averages, and the like. What do such statistics contribute to the understanding and appreciation of this sport? What aspects of the sport do they *not* illuminate?

3. At the opening of his essay, Angell echoes some famous lines from a poem by William Wordsworth:

The world is too much with us; late and soon,
Getting and spending, we lay waste our powers:
Little we see in Nature that is ours;
We have given our hearts away, a sordid boon!

Apart from the verbal echo, what connections can you find between Angell's essay and the theme of these four lines?

JOHN McMURTRY

John McMurtry was a linebacker in both college and professional football, and until retiring in 1962 he suffered his share of serious injuries. He can therefore write from personal experience about that often violent sport. McMurtry was born in 1939 in Toronto, Canada, and received his B.A. at the University of Toronto, where he played college football. He then played briefly for the Calgary Stampeders of the Canadian Football League before completing a Ph.D. in philosophy at the University of London. Since 1970 he has taught social and political philosophy at the University of Guelph in Canada and has written *The Structure of Marx's World-View* (1978).

The following essay appeared in the Canadian news magazine *Maclean's* in 1971, a year in which the Vietnam War was still being fought and anti-war protests were at their peak. Accordingly, in his protest against the violence in football, McMurtry compares the sport to war.

Kill 'Em! Crush 'Em! Eat 'Em Raw!

A few months ago my neck got a hard crick in it. I couldn't turn   1
my head; to look left or right I'd have to turn my whole body. But I'd had cricks in my neck since I started playing grade-school football and hockey, so I just ignored it. Then I began to notice that when I reached for any sort of large book (which I do pretty often as a philosophy teacher at the University of Guelph) I had trouble lifting it with one hand. I was losing the strength in my left arm, and I had such a steady pain in my back I often had to stretch out on the floor of the room I was in to relieve the pressure.

A few weeks later I mentioned to my brother, an orthopedic sur-   2
geon, that I'd lost the power in my arm since my neck began to hurt. Twenty-four hours later I was in a Toronto hospital not sure whether I might end up with a wasted upper limb. Apparently the steady pounding I had received playing college and professional football in the late Fifties and early Sixties had drive my head into my backbone so that the discs had crumpled together at the neck—"acute herniation"—and had cut the nerves to my left arm like a pinched telephone wire (without nerve stimulation, of course, the muscles atrophy, leaving the arm crippled). So I spent my Christmas holidays in the hospital in heavy traction and much of the next three months with my neck in a brace. Today most of the pain has gone, and I've recovered most of the strength in my arm. But from time to time I still have to don the brace, and surgery remains a possibility.

503

Not much of this will surprise anyone who knows football. It is a   3
sport in which body wreckage is one of the leading conventions. A few
days after I went into hospital for that crick in my neck, another brother,
an outstanding football player in college, was undergoing spinal surgery
in the same hospital two floors above me. In his case it was a lower,
more massive herniation, which every now and again buckled him so
that he was unable to lift himself off his back for days at a time. By the
time he entered the hospital for surgery he had already spent several
months in bed. The operation was successful, but, as in all such cases,
it will take him a year to recover fully.

These aren't isolated experiences. Just about anybody who has ever   4
played football for any length of time, in high school, college or one of
the professional leagues, has suffered for it later physically.

Indeed, it is arguable that body shattering is the very *point* of foot-   5
ball, as killing and maiming are of war. (In the United States, for example, the game results in 15 to 20 deaths a year and about 50,000 major
operations on knees alone.) To grasp some of the more conspicuous
similarities between football and war, it is instructive to listen to the
imperatives most frequently issued to the players by their coaches, team-
mates and fans. "Hurt 'em!" "Level 'em!" "Kill 'em!" "Take 'em apart!"
Or watch for the plays that are most enthusiastically applauded by the
fans. Where someone is "smeared," "knocked silly," "creamed," "nailed,"
"broken in two," or even "crucified." (One of my coaches when I played
corner linebacker with the Calgary Stampeders in 1961 elaborated, often
very inventively, on this language of destruction: admonishing us to
"unjoin" the opponent, "make 'im remember you" and "stomp 'im like
a bug.") Just as in hockey, where a fight will bring fans to their feet more
often than a skillful play, so in football the mouth waters most of all for
the really crippling block or tackle. For the kill. Thus the good teams
are "hungry," the best players are "mean," and "casualties" are as much
a part of the game as they are of a war.

The family resemblance between football and war is, indeed, strik-   6
ing. Their languages are similar: "field general," "long bomb," "blitz,"
"take a shot," "front line," "pursuit," "good hit," "the draft" and so on.
Their principles and practices are alike: mass hysteria, the art of intim-
idation, absolute command and total obedience, territorial aggression,
censorship, inflated insignia and propaganda, blackboard manoeuvres and
strategies, drills, uniforms, formations, marching bands and training camps.
And the virtues they celebrate are almost identical: hyper-aggressiveness,
coolness under fire and suicidal bravery. All this has been implicitly
recognized by such jock-loving Americans as media stars General Patton
and President Nixon, who have talked about war as a football game.

Patton wanted to make his Second World War tank men look like football players. And Nixon, as we know, was fond of comparing attacks on Vietnam to football plays and drawing coachly diagrams on a blackboard for TV war fans.

One difference between war and football, though, is that there is 7 little or no protest against football. Perhaps the most extraordinary thing about the game is that the systematic infliction of injuries excites in people not concern, as would be the case if they were sustained at, say, a rock festival, but a collective rejoicing and euphoria. Players and fans alike revel in the spectacle of a combatant felled into semiconsciousness, "blindsided," "clotheslined" or "decapitated." I can remember, in fact, being chided by a coach in pro ball for not "getting my hat" injuriously into a player who was already lying helpless on the ground. (On another occasion, after the Stampeders had traded the celebrated Joe Kapp to BC, we were playing the Lions in Vancouver and Kapp was forced on one play to run with the ball. He was coming "down the chute," his bad knee wobbling uncertainly, so I simply dropped on him like a blanket. After I returned to the bench I was reproved for not exploiting the opportunity to unhinge his bad knee.)

After every game, of course, the papers are full of reports on the 8 day's injuries, a sort of post-battle "body count," and the respective teams go to work with doctors and trainers, tape, whirlpool baths, cortisone and morphine to patch and deaden the wounds before the next game. Then the whole drama is reenacted—injured athletes held together by adhesive, braces and drugs—and the days following it are filled with even more feverish activity to put on the show yet again at the end of the next week. (I remember being so taped up in college that I earned the nickname "mummy.") The team that survives this merry-go-round spectacle of skilled masochism with the fewest incapacitating injuries usually wins. It is a sort of victory by ordeal: "We hurt them more than they hurt us."

My own initiation into this brutal circus was typical. I loved the 9 game from the moment I could run with a ball. Played shoeless on a green open field with no one keeping score and in a spirit of reckless abandon and laughter, it's a very different sport. Almost no one gets hurt and it's rugged, open and exciting (it still is for me). But then, like everything else, it starts to be regulated and institutionalized by adult authorities. And the fun is over.

So it was as I began the long march through organized football. 10 Now there was a coach and elders to make it clear by their behavior that beating other people was the only thing to celebrate and that trying to shake someone up every play was the only thing to be really proud of.

Now there were severe rule enforcers, audiences, formally recorded victors and losers, and heavy equipment to permit crippling bodily moves and collisions (according to one American survey, more than 80% of all football injuries occur to fully equipped players). And now there was the official "given" that the only way to keep playing was to wear suffocating armor, to play to defeat, to follow orders silently and to renounce spontaneity for joyless drill. The game had been, in short, ruined. But because I loved to play and play skillfully, I stayed. And progressively and inexorably, as I moved through high school, college and pro leagues, my body was dismantled. Piece by piece.

I started off with torn ligaments in my knee at 13. Then, as the organization and the competition increased, the injuries came faster and harder. Broken nose (three times), broken jaw (fractured in the first half and dismissed as a "bad wisdom tooth," so I played with it for the rest of the game), ripped knee ligaments again. Torn ligaments in one ankle and a fracture in the other (which I remember feeling relieved about because it meant I could honorably stop drill-blocking a 270-pound defensive end). Repeated rib fractures and cartilage tears (usually carried, again, through the remainder of the game). More dislocations of the left shoulder than I can remember (the last one I played with because, as the Calgary Stampeder doctor said, it "couldn't be damaged any more"). Occasional broken or dislocated fingers and toes. Chronically hurt lower back (I still can't lift with it or change a tire without worrying about folding). Separated right shoulder (as with many other injuries, like badly bruised hips and legs, needled with morphine for the games). And so on. The last pro game I played—against Winnipeg Blue Bombers in the Western finals in 1961—I had a recently dislocated left shoulder, a more recently wrenched right shoulder and a chronic pain centre in one leg. I was so tied up with soreness I couldn't drive my car to the airport. But it never occurred to me or anyone else that I miss a play as a corner linebacker.

By the end of my football career, I had learned that physical injury—giving it and taking it—is the real currency of the sport. And that in the final analysis the "winner" is the man who can hit to kill even if only half his limbs are working. In brief, a warrior game with a warrior ethos into which (like almost everyone else I played with) my original boyish enthusiasm had been relentlessly taunted and conditioned.

In thinking back on how all this happened, though, I can pick out no villains. As with the social system as a whole, the game has a life of its own. Everyone grows up inside it, accepts it and fulfills its dictates as obediently as helots. Far from ever questioning the principles of the activity, people simply concentrate on executing these principles more aggressively than anybody around them. The result is a group of people who, as the leagues become of a higher and higher class, are progressively insensitive to the possibility that things could be otherwise. Thus, in football, anyone who might question the wisdom or enjoyment of putting on heavy equipment on a hot day and running full speed at someone else with the intention of knocking him senseless would be regarded simply as not really a devoted athlete and probably "chicken." The choice is made straightforward. Either you, too, do your very utmost to efficiently smash and be smashed, or you admit incompetence or cowardice and quit. Since neither of these admissions is very pleasant, people generally keep any doubts they have to themselves and carry on.

Of course, it would be a mistake to suppose that there is more blind acceptance of brutal practices in organized football than elsewhere. On the contrary, a recent Harvard study has approvingly argued that football's characteristics of "impersonal acceptance of inflicted injury," an overriding "organization goal," the "ability to turn oneself on and off" and being, above all, "out to win" are of "inestimable value" to big corporations. Clearly, our sort of football is no sicker than the rest of our society. Even its organized destruction of physical well-being is not anomalous. A very large part of our wealth, work and time is, after all, spent in systematically destroying and harming human life. Manufacturing, selling and using weapons that tear opponents to pieces. Making ever bigger and faster predator-named cars with which to kill and injure one another by the million every year. And devoting our very lives to outgunning one another for power in an ever more destructive rat race. Yet all these practices are accepted without question by most people, even zealously defended and honored. Competitive, organized injuring is integral to our way of life, and football is simply one of the more intelligible mirrors of the whole process: a sort of colorful morality play showing us how exciting and rewarding it is to Smash Thy Neighbor. 14

Now it is fashionable to rationalize our collaboration in all this by arguing that, well, man *likes* to fight and injure his fellows and such games as football should be encouraged to discharge this original-sin urge into less harmful channels than, say, war. Public-show football, this line goes, plays the same sort of cathartic role as Aristotle said stage tragedy does: without real blood (or not much), it releases players and audience from unhealthy feelings stored up inside them. 15

As an ex-player in this seasonal coast-to-coast drama, I see little to recommend such a view. What organized football did to me was make me *suppress* my natural urges and re-express them in an alienating, vicious form. Spontaneous desires for free bodily exuberance and fraternization with competitors were shamed and forced under ("If it ain't hurtin' it 16 ain't helpin' ") and in their place were demanded armored mechanical moves and cool hatred of all opposition. Endless authoritarian drill and dressing-room harangues (ever wonder why competing teams can't prepare for a game in the same dressing room?) were the kinds of mechanisms employed to reconstruct joyful energies into mean and alien shapes. I am quite certain that everyone else around me was being similarly forced into this heavily equipped military precision and angry antagonism, because there was always a mutinous attitude about full-dress practices, and everybody (the pros included) had to concentrate incredibly hard for days to whip themselves into just one hour's hostility a week against another club. The players never speak of these things, of course, because everyone is so anxious to appear tough.

    The claim that men like seriously to battle one another to some   17
sort of finish is a myth. It only endures because it wears one of the oldest and most propagandized of masks—the romantic combatant. I sometimes wonder whether the violence all around us doesn't depend for its survival on the existence and preservation of this tough-guy disguise.

    As for the effect of organized football on the spectator, the fan is   18
not released from supposed feelings of violent aggression by watching his athletic heroes perform it so much as encouraged in the view that people-smashing is an admirable mode of self-expression. The most savage attackers, after all, are, by general agreement, the most efficient and worthy players of all (the biggest applause I ever received as a football player occurred when I ran over people or slammed them so hard they couldn't get up). Such circumstances can hardly be said to lessen the spectators' martial tendencies. Indeed it seems likely that the whole show just further develops and titillates the North American addiction for violent self-assertion. . . . Perhaps, as well, it helps explain why the greater the zeal of U.S. political leaders as football fans (Johnson, Nixon, Agnew), the more enthusiastic the commitment to hard-line politics. At any rate there seems to be a strong correlation between people who relish tough football and people who relish intimidating and beating the hell out of commies, hippies, protest marchers and other opposition groups.

    Watching well-advertised strong men knock other people around,   19
make them hurt, is in the end like other tastes. It does not weaken with feeding and variation in form. It grows.

    I got out of football in 1962. I had asked to be traded after Calgary   20
had offered me a $25-a-week-plus-commissions off-season job as a clothing-store salesman. ("Dear Mr. Finks:" I wrote. [Jim Finks was then the Stampeders' general manager.] "Somehow I do not think the dialectical subtleties of Hegel, Marx and Plato would be suitably oriented amidst the environmental stimuli of jockey shorts and herringbone suits. I hope

you make a profitable sale or trade of my contract to the East.") So the Stampeders traded me to Montreal. In a preseason intersquad game with the Alouettes I ripped the cartilages in my ribs on the hardest block I'd ever thrown. I had trouble breathing and I had to shuffle-walk with my torso on a tilt. The doctor in the local hospital said three weeks rest, the coach said scrimmage in two days. Three days later I was back home reading philosophy.

About the Essay

1. What is McMurtry's thesis in this essay? How does he try to persuade you that he is right? What are the strengths and weaknesses of his central argument?

2. In his opening paragraph, McMurtry mentions that he is a teacher of philosophy at a university. How, if at all, did knowing this affect your reading of the essay?

3. Paragraphs 6–8 draw an extended analogy between football and war. According to McMurtry, what elements do football and war have in common? Are there any others that you would add? What are they? Are there differences that might make McMurtry's analogy less valid? What are they?

4. Why did McMurtry play football for so long, despite his many injuries? Why did he finally leave the game?

5. Why do you think McMurtry describes his football injuries in such great detail? What purpose do these descriptions serve? How do they affect your response to his essay?

6. What connection does McMurtry make between football and other areas of life? What conclusion does he draw? What conclusions would you draw? Why?

Explorations

1. Violence is inherent in some sports, such as football and boxing, but even in nonviolent sports, such as baseball, brawls erupt from time to time. Why do violent sports and fights appeal to spectators? How do you respond to them? What, if anything, do you think can and should be done to lessen the violence?

2. Should athletics be a part of college life? What do intercollegiate varsity sports do for a college? What do organized intramural sports contribute? What are the costs and dangers of each? Do the benefits outweigh the costs?

3. McMurtry suggests that organized football reflects, for better or worse, some widespread values of our culture. Choose another sport and consider how it relates to our cultural values.

ALISTAIR COOKE

Alistair Cooke is probably best known in the United States as the urbane host of public television's *Masterpiece Theater*, where he presents to Americans some of the best of British television. In England, however, he is known for the weekly fifteen-minute radio talks in which for more than thirty years he has been trying to explain America to the British. Cooke is well-equipped for both roles. He was born in 1908 in Manchester, England, and graduated from Cambridge University, then came to the United States as a Commonwealth Fellow to attend both Yale and Harvard. He became an American citizen in 1941, and during World War II he was the American correspondent for several British newspapers, but his true media have been radio and television. His most ambitious project was the television series *America*, which he wrote and narrated in 1972 and published in book form in 1973 as *Alistair Cooke's America*. A selection of his British broadcasts has been published as *The Americans* (1979). In the following piece, taken from that work and first broadcast in 1977, he discusses how big money in sports has affected the traditional virtues of courtesy and sportsmanship.

The Money Game

"Half the world," it says here, "will have watched or listened to Wimbledon before the hundredth anniversary of tennis is over." I fancy I hear the high protesting voice of Muhammad Ali crying: "No way, brother. Not one tenth, not one thousandth, of the world is gonna watch that tennis, but the whole world watches me, because I am the best, the prettiest."

Well, never mind the percentages. Let's hope that many more thousands saw Chris Evert correct the umpire's ruling in her favor than saw Connors snub the anniversary parade of champions and spend the time of the ceremony practicing fifty yards away with his partner in boorishness, the inimitable if not unspeakable Nastase. Miss Evert reached to lob a return of Miss Wade and was awarded the point. But she shook her head and pointed out that she had not reached the ball before its second bounce. It is a small thing and would have gone unremarked ten or twenty years ago. But today, in the money jungle of professional sports, it shone like a candle in a naughty world.

I remember the time when Bill Tilden, about fifty years ago, threw his racket at Wimbledon. The game was stopped. He was warned at once that one more tantrum like that and he would be thrown out of the tournament. He didn't do it again. But no more than two years ago I

510

saw one of the most famous women tennis players reel with shock at a linesman's call. She was the one who stopped play. She walked over to her chair, gathered the five or six rackets that are now required to play one game of tennis, tucked them under arm, and as she walked off she poked her forefinger up at the umpire at what the spectators applauded as an obscene invitation. (If the Supreme Court came to divide on the question of its obscenity, it would only be because the dissenters had led a sheltered life.)

She hadn't quit. She was just biding her time, and temper, till the officials came running, or kneeling, begging her to return. Which, about three minutes later, she graciously consented to do, as thousands of spectators came to their feet to pay tribute to an act of bravery in giving the umpire his comeuppance. The umpire had not taken her out and paddy-whacked her. He didn't fume or shout. He blushed. He cowered. He knew he had behaved badly. He seemed truly sorry. And the crowd cheered their heroine again and forgave him. The terrifying touch here was not the sluttishness of the—er—lady but the attitude of the crowd.

I am told by Mr. Herbert Warren Wind, one of the most distinguished of American sports writers, that a few years ago, when he was watching the Davis Cup matches being played in Rumania, he got the ghoulish impression that this reversal of values—this upside-down courtesy which George Orwell might have anticipated—was not only common among tennis crowds in Rumania but was organized by the state as a required exercise in patriotism. The crowd was expected to boo or hiss every point won by the Americans and to cheer every gesture—whether skillful or rude—of their idol, Nastase. Mr. Wind, who has been writing about tennis and golf for forty years or so, said the Rumanian experience was the most frightening thing he had seen in his professional life. He came away with the uncomfortable feeling that he had been brainwashed, or morally washed, or whatever.

It is this sort of thing that led an American political columnist at the end of last year to offer some pointed advice to Mr. Carter, who was then about to begin his term as President. The columnist laid down twenty numbered tips for the new President, most of them, of course, having to do with prudent political tactics. But the last three were about sports. Don't, he urged, use football lingo by way of encouraging your party. Don't talk about team play, or coming through in the last quarter, or giving it that old one-two. Don't invite athletes to the White House for dinner. Don't invite athletes ever. Have the courage to decide with Harry Truman that "sports is a lot of damn nonsense."

This attack of bile, I don't doubt, must have been brought on by unpleasant memories of Mr. Nixon's occupation of the White House, for nobody in American history, I dare say, has given the language of sport such a bad name by using it to recommend a strategy of deceit.

At the end of last year, too, Jim Murray, of the *Los Angeles Times*, the raciest, the most gifted of American sports writers, wrote a piece called "Whatever Happened to Frank Merriwell?" For the more tender members of the audience, may I say that a couple of generations ago Frank Merriwell was the fictional hero of all American small boys. Today he would provoke salvos of raucous laughter as a square and a sissy. Because—to use the quaint old phrases—he played fair, he gave his all and lost with a smile, he held to the naïve delusion that sport is synonymous with what we used to call sportsmanship.

I was mentioning these odious comparisons to a sports official the other day. He was not greatly moved. He said: "Well, sure. You're talking about the days before sports was a billion-dollar industry. Today we've got the Commies on our back. We teach the youngsters to develop competitive bite. We feed 'em money. The Russians draft 'em." It is true. Most nations now train a picked quota of their young to devote their lives exclusively to excelling in some single sport. In the so-called Free World we do this voluntarily or by the pressure of parents and the expectation of a million dollars. In the Communist world they do it by compulsion, isolating promising babies, like so many blood strains, from their fellows. In all countries the process intensifies, to the greater glory of the Fatherland, and no doubt also to the development of a ragged nervous system and a blank ignorance of the variety and values of human society.

This is nothing new. It happened more than two thousand years ago. But it was not looked on, by the generations that came after, as the high point of their civilization. The Greeks, when they developed competitive games, divided them into two categories. Neither offered money prizes. One, practiced by inferior athletes, rewarded the winners with gifts of olive oil. Which would be, I imagine, the equivalent of presenting the local tennis champion with a gallon of one of those "arthritic" rubs that don't cure anything but set up a secondary irritant to make you forget the first.

The great games, the spectator sports, were those competed for by the best, and to the victor went only a wreath. The Olympic Games, throughout their early history, were managed by officials whose title was a literal synonym for fairness. And the ground, the territory, on which the games were held was regarded as a holy place, so much so that it was held—even by the country's enemies—to be sacrosanct from invasion (Middle Eastern papers please copy). The great age of Greek sport was the fifth century B.C. After that, the most learned of their historians says all too cryptically: "Later, athletics degenerated into professionalism, and experts in various sports spent their whole time going from one contest to another, sometimes winning at them all and styling themselves *periodonikai* or 'leading money winners.'"

In Rome the decline from sport as an enjoyable end in itself to a   12
spectacle designed to satisfy the blood lust of the spectators was very much more rapid. In the early days Rome took over from her Etrurian invaders the practice of a gladiatorial combat as the last ceremony of a funeral. Pretty soon they added contests with wild beasts, bred and fattened for the purpose. By the time of the emperors the Romans were the supreme military power of the world, and though Augustus decided that enough foreign conquest was enough, the games were used as precautionary military exercises. To make the events at once more realistic and more satisfying to the mob's love of cruelty, the losers now faced defeat in the form of death. In the beginning, even in contests to the death, the contestants were the sons of noble families. To lose a son in the games was as honorable as losing him on a foreign battlefield. But when you have a large army permanently on hand whose military and naval games are much like the real thing, there is bound to develop a corps of performers who are better than others. They too, ordinary legionnaires, prisoners of war, even slaves, became an elite corps of gladiators and were trained severely and lavishly paid.

There is a passage in Robert Graves's *I, Claudius* in which the   13
gladiators are assembled in their underground locker room for a pep talk by Livia, the wife of Augustus and as wily an entrepreneur as the manager of any baseball club. She spent huge monies on the games, and at this point in the story she feels she is not getting her money's worth. At the end of her harangue she says: "These games are being degraded by more and more professional tricks to stay alive. I won't have it. So put on a good show, and there'll be plenty of money for the living, and a decent burial for the dead. If you let me down, I'll break this guild, and I'll send the lot of you to the mines in New Media. That's all I've got to say to you."

Well, we've not quite come to that. But the true tone of sports in   14
the 1970s is set by the elite corps, the best of the pros—that is to say, by the richest gamesmen: the baseball, basketball, football, and now tennis stars who have sweated their way up to prodigious salaries, are admiringly interviewed by cynical sycophants, and receive the same adoring space as rock stars about their lavish pads, their king-size beds with sable quilts, their hand-made automobiles, their sleek girls in every port.

Money has got to be the reason, a primary reason anyway, why the   15
insulted umpire sent his officials to beg the tennis star to return to the

court and go on with the game. She earns a fortune. The fans pay to subsidize that fortune. The fans come not merely to see a game superlatively played. They have learned to expect high jinks and low jinks as part of the show. Any sports promoter will tell you that a sports crowd spurned is a dangerous social animal. In other words, the officials, who sometimes seem so cowed, must have in mind the maintenance of public order, which has come to have little to do with public courtesy. In America we have much rough play and some furious spectators, but— for no good reason I can see—we do not yet have basketball and baseball crowds tearing up the grounds or breaking up trains and ripping underground stations apart. I don't know why this hasn't happened—it no doubt will—since those of us brought up on the legend of British courtesy read with dismay of the hooliganism, bordering on criminal assault, of British football crowds, and of such desperate proposals to meet it as building ten-foot concrete walls around the inner ring of the stadiums and surrounding each playing field with a hundred cops.

I may have seemed to be reacting so far in the old man's standard fashion to the disappearance of amateurism in first-class sport. And, of course, it is true that—in tennis, particularly—much of the genteel air of the sport in the old days has been drowned out by the roar of the cash register. But I must say that genteelism, with its pleasant manners, was due to the comfortable fact that most players at Wimbledon and Forest Hills were upper-middle-class offspring who didn't have to work for a living. The same, at one time, was true of international golf. But plainly— it ought to be plain today—it is not only absurd, it is unjust to expect people who earn a living at a game to have the same nonchalant code of behavior as the loitering heirs of company directors who could afford to travel to France or Britain or America to play a game while professionals (footballers as a gross example) were being paid at the going rate of plumbers' assistants. I applaud the fact that games can now be a career, and a profitable one, and that the expert should be considered like any other star entertainer and be paid accordingly.

But there has come a point where the impulse to take up a game is very often the impulse to earn a million dollars, and so far, in the rush of a whole generation to make the million, there has not yet evolved a decent ethic that can discipline the game for the audience that has its mind more on the game than the million.

Six figures, I suggest, is some sort of turning point in the career, and too often the character, of the very young. A twenty-year-old who earns a $100,000 or £100,000—and nowadays it's more likely to be half a million—is encouraged by the media to see himself/herself as a movie star entitled to adoration, the pamperings of luxury, and no questions asked about behavior on or off the course, the rink, the court, the field. I suppose the television satellite has had a world to do with it. The best boxers know that—by virtue of worldwide exposure—the organizers will take in twenty millions or more, so the boxer doesn't pause for long before saying, "Some of those millions should be mine." And if the difference between winning forty thousand and twenty thousand turns on a linesman's call, it takes considerable character not to blow up. I heard a young fan say it would take a superman.

Well, it doesn't take a superman. It takes simply a type of human being who was taught when young the definition of a brat. I like to think that in one sport, at least, the type is still extant. Golf remains an oasis in a desert of gold and scruffy manners. Maybe it's because it doesn't allow for team-play infighting. It's you and the ball and the course. And the rules. Even so, a man missing a three-foot putt today can lose in the instant $20,000. He looks wretched or very forlorn. He does not batter the marshals with his putter or refuse to play next week. A few years ago a single act of cheating—of slightly moving the ball into a better lie—caused a well-known pro to be suspended from the tour for good. Three years ago Jack Nicklaus, the reigning star of the game, and—it seemed then—his heir apparent, Johnny Miller, were offered one million dollars to the winner of a head-to-head eighteen-hole game. One million dollars in one afternoon. They promptly turned it down as being, in Nicklaus' words, "not in the best interests of the game." May their tribe increase.

19

About the Essay

1. What is Cooke's main point in this essay? Is he simply against athletes' making a great deal of money, or is he in favor of something positive?

2. What words does Cooke use to describe the athletes and the behavior he disapproves of? What do those words reveal about his attitude?

3. What reasons does Cooke give for the conditions he deplores? Do you find his reasons relevant? Why?

4. Cooke describes the behavior not only of professional athletes but of sports fans. What does he observe about the spectators? How does this connect with his main point?

5. In paragraphs 10–13, Cooke tells us about sports in ancient Greece and Rome. What is the purpose of these examples? How do they relate to his main point?

6. Do you agree with Cooke in his view that "golf remains an oasis in a desert of gold and scruffy manners"? Is golf comparable to big-time tennis in ways relevant to Cooke's point? Why, or why not?

Explorations

1. Think of some incidents of good and bad sportsmanship in games you have watched—or played. How did these incidents affect you? If there were other spectators, how did they react? What are the inducements toward sportsmanlike play, and toward its opposite?

2. Cooke says of Frank Merriwell that "He played fair, he gave his all and lost with a smile, he held to the naive delusion that sport is synonymous with what we used to call sportsmanship." What moral ideals and attitudes does sportsmanship involve? What relevance do they have beyond sport?

3. As Cooke and many others have observed, professional sports is a mammoth entertainment enterprise, competing with other forms of entertainment for our free time and spare dollars. Discuss what you see as the advantages and disadvantages of sports as commercial entertainment.

GRACE BUTCHER

Grace Butcher was born in 1934 in Rochester, New York, and graduated from Hiram College. From 1958 to 1960 she was the American national champion in the 880-yard run, and competed against the Soviet Union as a member of the American track and field team in 1959. She is also a writer, and since 1968 she has taught English at Kent State University. She has contributed to several anthologies on women and sports and published several books of poems, including *Before I Go Out on the Road* (1979).

"So Much Depends upon a Red Tent" first appeared in *Sports Illustrated* in 1975. In it Butcher writes of a 2500-mile biking trip she made one summer to New England and Canada, telling how she prepared for the trip, where she went, and what she saw and did. Her title is a play upon a famous poem by William Carlos Williams. Here is the Williams poem.

The Red Wheelbarrow

so much depends
upon

a red wheel
barrow

glazed with rain
water

beside the white
chickens.

Williams's poem is relevant, indirectly, to Butcher's account of her trip, but she leaves it to her readers to discover how.

So Much Depends upon a Red Tent

The best part? There were a lot of best parts. Depends on my mood   1
when I look back on the trip. But the very best part was being alone. I
don't quite understand that about myself—this lifelong love of being
alone. I suppose being an only child is a big part of it. I just grew up
doing things alone. Feels natural now, as if that's how it's supposed to
be. And besides, I get along with myself better than with anybody else
I know.

Joyously riding alone, never having to ask someone, "Shall we stop   2
here? Do you want to turn off up there? Are you ready to go now? Should
we camp here?"—that was the best part of all.

And the riding! That's all I had to do, day after glorious day, my white BMW R60/6 under me humming quietly through the blue and green and golden world. The bike was new. I'd had it only long enough to put 1,200 miles on it and have it checked over before I took off. It was my second bike (my third, really, if you count the 125 Suzuki Challenger that I'd started racing several months before). But my second street bike. 3

I'd had my first lesson on a full-dress BMW R75/5 and had fallen in love with it. "When I get good enough," I said, "I'm going to have a BMW." In about a year, I figured. And I rode my little Suzuki GT 250 thousands of miles through the northeastern Ohio winter while people kept asking, "Gee, isn't it a little cold to be out on that thing?" I had to ride. I had to get good enough. 4

Gradually I got better. I had to get better than I was that first day in the last week of October '73. That was when I went out to the garage alone the first time to start up my first bike and ride it after an hour or so of lessons the day before in first and second gear, stopping, starting and turning (or rather, lurching, stalling and wobbling). 5

After 20 minutes of fumbling with switches, frantic and clumsy kicking, a call to the dealer to find out why it stalled every time I tried to put it in first gear ("Rev it up a bit," his wife said. "It's new; everything's tight"), drenched with sweat I got the bike out of the garage. Only stalled it three or four times (between the garage and the end of the driveway, that is). From there I managed to avoid going in the ditch on the far side of the road as I swung out with what I hoped would be flair and what ended up as a gigantic, lopsided wobble. I made a mental note to write the highway commissioner about widening the county roads. My self-image was in jeopardy. 6

But I rode over a hundred miles that day. And the next day. And the next. A week later, shivering violently in pouring rain and 45° temperatures, I took my riding test, passed and sang at the top of my voice all the 15 miles back home. 7

Carefully, intensely, I piled up the mileage. Carefully one day I rode far out into the country and on a deserted road red-lined it through the gears[1] to learn what the bike could do. Carefully I puttered through shopping centers, got groceries, did errands, rode to class. Carefully I rode fast on the freeways and slowly in traffic, with interest over rain 8

---

[1] That is, took the bike through all the gears at the highest engine speeds it was designed to tolerate.

grooves and with fear over the open steel grillwork of bridges. I rode
thousands of miles alone and once in a while with a friend. Carefully
that following summer I learned to race motocross and won a couple of
trophies in powder-puff events. Gradually I was starting to feel good
enough.

And then one day I walked into the cycle shop and there stood a   9
brand-new white BMW. I'd never seen a white one. And I said to myself
(and to anyone else who would listen), "O.K., Grace, I think you're
ready for a BMW."

Two weeks later I took off on a 2,500-mile camping trip through   10
New England and Canada. And the best thing of all was being alone
with my bike the whole time. It just seemed as if that was how it was
supposed to be.

I had camped once but I'd just stood and watched while a friend   11
put up the tent, made the fire, cooked the meal and packed up afterward.
So before I left I put up a red nylon tent in the orchard and practiced
sleeping in it so it would seem like home on the road. Oh, I was far from
the house—at least 50 yards. The rustlings in the bushes at night! Apples
thunderously falling to the ground in the dark! Leaves crashing into the
tent and sliding and scratching down the sides! Good thing I practiced.
Zipping myself into the tent and then into the sleeping bag produced
claustrophobia of alarming proportions.

But within a few days I was sleeping well. Once, when I was told   12
it had rained the night before, I was incredulous. Hadn't heard a thing.
And so, another best part of the trip was going to sleep once all the
camp chores were done, feeling the earth under me. I used no mattress,
just let my body melt down around any unevenness of ground under the
tent. I'm Capricorn, an earth sign. If that means anything, maybe that's
why sleeping on the ground felt so good. I felt as if the whole planet was
under me, holding me. A secure feeling. And outside, the bike would
be parked and chained as close to the tent as I could get it. It looked
massive and comforting, white in the moonlight, wet with dew, chrome
gleaming quietly.

Everything I needed was in one compact roll and two small sad-   13
dlebags loaded up the night before I left. That morning when I came
bounding out of the house in new leathers, feeling rather self-conscious,
I got down to reality quickly enough when my first tug didn't even budge
the loaded bike off its center stand. "Oh Lord," I said out loud, with a
weak grin in case *Candid Camera* was watching.

But the second or third tug got the bike down, and I was ready to   14
leave. Even as I coasted backward down the slight slope of the driveway

into the turnaround spot, though, I realized that this bike, which was still unfamiliar and a hundred pounds heavier than my other one, would handle differently with the load it now carried.

As I rode through the town of Chardon on the way to the freeway I began to feel like a worldly biker—full leathers, a big bike and all my worldly goods (more or less) tied on behind. And when I reached Route 90 and swooped (yes, with flair even!) down the ramp, checking out traffic, sun and blue sky in one glance, I said (out loud to myself, of course), "Well, here I go!" Not an especially original line, but the situation was original enough to make up for it. I, who had never even put up a tent in all my 40 years till two weeks before—I, who had never gone on a long motorcycle trip—I, who hadn't even been riding a year—I was leaving on a 2,500-mile camping trip on my incredibly fine bike, alone. I sang Moody Blues' songs and was amazingly happy.

Like fragmented, colored pieces in a kaleidoscope, images of each day's ride turned, changed, fell through my mind as I sat those nights writing in my journal by the light of a candle lantern. I loved that piece of equipment. A candle burns with a most peaceful flame.

All the trip long, people in cars waved and smiled. Mostly kids and, strangely enough, old ladies. I wondered about that and finally decided that the gray-haired gadabouts had reached a point in their lives when they realized most strongly that what life is *for*, if it is for anything, is to find out what you do well, and then *do* it, for heaven's sake, before it's too late. One group of ladies passed me, giving me a real lift with their big smiles and their waves. And coincidentally, we happened to stop at the same restaurant farther down the road. As I was taking off my gloves and helmet and brushing out my wind-tangled hair, one came bustling over to where I still sat on the bike. "I just wanted to tell you that we think you're just the bravest thing!" she beamed. "I said to the girls, 'My, just think how the wind must be blowing in her face!' And here you are out here all by yourself. We think that's just wonderful!"

I smiled modestly accepting the Wonder Woman image, and made a long acceptance speech extolling the joys of being female and being alone, riding a motorcycle. I found myself giving the same speech many times during the following weeks, and I never tired of it.

And so it went. I'd wondered, frankly, if I'd get hassled along the way. Hell's Angels? Rape? But people were only friendly, curious, helpful, courteous, interested. The bike was such a conversation piece that I'd get into discussions at traffic lights about the virtues of a shaft-driven engine (very virtuous!); at stop signs about what those things were sticking out on the sides ("Those are the cylinders, sir"); about how ghostly quiet the bike was ("Hey, is that thing running?"), and why couldn't *all* motorcycles be that quiet.

Mostly I'd ride along not too fast, just murmuring "Oh!" and "Gee!" 20 as I'd top another hill and be wonderstruck by the next panoramic view. Is there any more striking combination of trees than clusters of white birch, stark and chalky against dense pine forests? One day, camping by a mountain lake in Maine, I found several pieces of birch bark and wrote letters. I'd always wanted to write a letter on a piece of birch bark. I felt like the Indian I used to pretend I was when I was seven.

Beauty everywhere. Even asbestos mines in Quebec were amazingly 21 beautiful. They looked almost like natural gray canyons, and the piled-up asbestos like white mountains. Posing themselves against the backdrop of one of these "mountains" were four boxcars—two brown, one red and one green—and before them a sweep of green and golden meadow. I just sat and looked. The beauty of the mining area was astonishing.

Sometimes I'd feel so full of the scenery that I'd stop looking at it 22 for a while and just get into the rhythm of the road. Hills and curves, curves, curves. No, I wasn't scraping the foot pegs or the valve covers. But even now I remember the rhythm of those curves as I'd climb and plunge and letter-S through mile after mile, enclosed on both sides by deep pine forests of unforgettable scent.

Truly, I felt as if I had ridden into the pages of every motorcycle 23 magazine I'd ever read. I could see myself—wine-red leathers, immaculate white bike, blue pack—against the pines, the startling silver-blue of lakes, red and brown and gray rock walls, the curves of flower-strewn meadows—moving through all the colors and textures.

What would I *do* with this trip, I wondered. How would I use it? 24 What would it eventually mean to me? I pondered sometimes as I rode, or as I sat writing by candlelight, or as I washed my face with dew in the early mornings. How would I be different after I got home?

"But weren't you afraid?" People always asked that later. 25

No. Except once. Once in Quebec the road went off in two different 26 directions. My way, or so I thought, went across a bridge. And the bridge was that biker's nightmare: an open metal grillwork, slippery as ice, that sends the front wheel of a bike off in every direction. There's nothing to do but do nothing—to sit there, muscles frozen in an attitude of relaxation, hands holding the handlebars with a gentleness born of terror, for you must let the bike find its own way across.

Finally on the other side, I began to glory once more in the coun- 27 tryside, the road curving along a river lined with birches. But I started to notice that either the sun was going in the wrong direction or I was.

After about 10 miles I stopped and checked my map. I had to go back over that damn bridge.

Quebec. How could I have forgotten that it is French-speaking? As I crossed the border I felt a combination of dismay, amusement and eagerness. I'd always thought I was pretty good in high school and college French. Now we'd see.   28

It was O.K. Vocabulary came rushing back. At one point, after I'd set up camp and walked away for a bit, I returned to find half a dozen adults around my bike. And I could talk to them with eagerness and enthusiasm (though probably sounding like a 6-year-old) about the mechanical wonders of the bike. *"Il n'y a pas de chaîne,"*[2] I could say, gesturing at the chainless rear wheel and pointing out the enclosed drive shaft. I could answer questions about mileage, comfort, my route, my own brave self. *"Seule? Vous êtes seule? Vous êtes si brave!"*[3] I liked to hear it in any language.   29

Once I chose a cabin instead of my tent. It was tiny, on the shore of the mighty St. Lawrence, 20 miles wide at that point and masquerading as the ocean, with tides and sea gulls and a fine driftwood tree washed up on the beach to lean against. I built a fireplace of stones, cooked, ate, then sat with a cup of my special mix of hot chocolate and coffee, watching the sun set and the tide come in.   30

I had been sitting in the dark, on the red-brown sand, my back against the water-washed smoothness of the tree trunk. But gradually I slumped farther and farther down till just my head was against the tree and my body relaxed in the sand. My fire was only embers, an orange crescent of moon had brightened with the approach of darkness, the tide had come to within a few yards of my feet. I lay there for a long time, scarcely moving. I could not have been more content.   31

There were times when I could escape my own observation. So often, perhaps because of my obsession with writing, I found myself mentally recording something I was in the process of doing as if I'd already done it, picturing myself telling someone about it in the future. It was hard sometimes not to feel as if I were constantly posing for some invisible photographer. It was hard to get away from *watching* myself at some beautiful spot, and simply *be* there.   32

But here, or on the night shore of a mountain lake listening to the loons, or wrapped in the sensuous golden day that seemed to pour itself down over the Vermont hills as I curved and flowed along the black and   33

---

[2]"There's no chain."

[3]"Alone? You are alone? You are so brave!"

gray roads—here, on this trip was a kind of spontaneity that I'd never experienced. And my contentment had no particular structure other than knowing that I'd camp somewhere late in the afternoon and leave again sometime in the morning. No structure. No telephone ringing. No papers to grade. Nothing to do but tend to my bike and myself. Nothing to do day after shining blue day but ride. Except for a few calls home to my teen-age son, no one knew where I was. And for once, I didn't care that no one knew where to find me or when I'd be back.

I'd look down at the great silver sunbursts of my cylinders, feel the   34
power waiting quietly under my right hand. Everything I could possibly need was in my blue pack, my black saddlebags. I could feel the sun through the leathers, smell the scent of pine for days.

My old aunt and uncle in their farmhouse on 150 acres in the   35
Adirondacks. Hadn't seen them for years. Eighty-five years old he is, and his big-game-hunting license was on the dresser in the room where I slept. My aunt cooked for me and reminisced about my parents and made me feel loved. I rode away feeling I'd found part of my family again.

"Hi! Nice bike," said the guy at the stoplight somewhere in New   36
Hampshire. "You should take those metal covers off your plugs because they'll short out in a rainstorm. Mine did when I took a trip back in '72."

"What part of Ohio you from? I'm from Cincinnati," said the boy   37
wearing the cross-country T-shirt in the restaurant parking lot somewhere in western New York. So we talked about cross-country running and cross-country riding and how neat they both were.

"By cracky," said the white-haired, pleasant gentleman in the tiny   38
post office in Somewhere, Maine (people *do* say "by cracky" in New England, by cracky). "I got me this son of a gun of a crick in my back yesterday morning—don't your back bother you on that machine?"

The people. That was another best part. One old couple outside   39
an old inn, standing, looking at my bike. I spoke to them as I was leaving, and they offered to tear some pages out of their where-to-camp book for me. ("I have my own, thanks, but I sure do appreciate. . . .")

And the gas-station attendant in Quebec who answered my ques-   40
tions about the white "mountains" and sent his son inside to get me a piece of asbestos—shiny black rock with what looks like cotton fibers sticking out of it—so I could show it to my friends back home.

And the two little boys, whose grandparents ran the campgrounds,   41
showing me the best, prettiest, most isolated spot by a stream to pitch my tent, and who ran along with me a mile or so as I jogged for a while that evening.

And the three adults who'd seen my bike in a restaurant parking lot and came in, looking for someone with a helmet who must belong to the bike so they could ask questions about how I liked it. "It's not your *husband's*? It's not your *boy friend's*? It's *yours*?"

How nicely tired I was each night after eight hours or so on the road. How early I went to bed, and how early I woke and with what eagerness! Moving carefully inside my red tent in the morning, drops of condensation clinging like rubies to the sides, gleaming in the morning light. Fold up the tent wet—it'd dry in my pack from the heat of the sun on that day's ride. I was glad the tent was red. Every morning started with a glow.

I washed and polished the bike when it needed it or when I felt the urge. Very soothing to rub and polish the long dazzling pipes, the plain clean lines of the tank and fenders. Changed plugs once. Changed the oil once. Had the steering-head bearings tightened once. Put air in the tires once or twice. The bike gave a lot and asked little.

I always had some what-ifs on my mind. What if the bike breaks down? New bikes don't break down. What if there are no gas stations? There are *always* gas stations. What if a runaway logging truck comes careening around a curve on the wrong side of the road up there in the middle of nowhere?

My long hair is always in pigtails when I ride, and sometimes they blow in my face because my windshield changes the airflow. I like motorists to know I am female, so I don't tuck my hair under my helmet. And as a result, I've never yet experienced any of the hostility that male bikers so often report. But one day I thought, "The heck with it. I'll just tie my hair back. It'll be out of the way." And shortly after that I stopped at a gas station to ask directions. Walked in without taking off my helmet and goggles as I nearly always do. And the station attendant said pleasantly enough, "Yes, sir, what can I do for you?" Back came the pigtails and my identity.

Some guy on a very noisy bike appeared alongside once and nodded and smiled as if he thought he'd found a traveling companion. I was annoyed. The noise of his engine compared to mine soon gave me a headache. And the last thing I wanted on my trip was company. Doing it alone was the whole point. Finally we rode in under the golden arches of that famous and ubiquitous restaurant, our first chance to talk since he'd joined me. "Hope you don't mind my boogieing along with you," he said. "Well," I answered, "as a matter of fact. . . ." And I just told him in a friendly way how it was with me. "Oh, O.K. That's cool," he said and went boogieing on his way. No problem.

As one man put it someplace where I stopped for gas, "To see a woman like you on a bike like that . . . well, you have all my respect.

I can't imagine any guy would ever hassle you." And none ever did. I'm 5 feet 6 inches, 115 pounds. It wasn't my size that kept anyone from bothering me. It was something else. It was just what I was doing, I guess.

Busy, I sometimes felt very busy on my trip, once I'd stopped for the day. Unloading the bike, setting up camp, making a fire if I chose to, cooking, eating, cleaning up, arranging stuff in the tent, writing after all was taken care of—there seemed to be a great deal to do, and darkness seemed to come quickly. I was seldom awake after 10 P.M., seldom slept past five or six.   49

Making a fire that would burn right gave me great pleasure. I had to scrounge wood, and then stones with which to confine it. I had to be patient and not try to cook over the first high flames.   50

Once, I cooked a mixture of hamburger, hot dog, olives, cucumbers, egg and a can of pea soup, because that's what I had. It was delicious.   51

Once, by a river I found a thin flat stone to turn the fried eggs since I had no spatula. And I scoured the utensils with sand and dirt. It all made sense.   52

One thing I did not care for was threatening weather, riding with frequent glances up and around, checking the ominous clouds, always wondering if I should stop or keep going. But the weather was, on the whole, quite fine. I was rained in only one day, and that happened to be the time along the St. Lawrence that I had chosen the cabin instead of my tent.   53

I was quite happy at being rained in. The previous day's ride had covered only about 100 miles, all against a huge, hot wind, and I was glad for a cool rainy day. I'd ridden in a little rain to the nearby town and brought back enough food for six people. I lay on the bed, which nearly filled the one-room cabin, gazed out at the great river, whose endless sound filled my head, quieting me.   54

> *Gray sky, gray water,*
> *Creating no horizon.*
> *Where does the world end?*

I remembered a haiku I'd written years back. Sensuously, I ate, dozed, ate, wrote postcards, dozed, ate, wrote and finally slept. Everyone needs such days.

Sometimes I was disappointed to see what tourists call "camping." Camping at some sites I saw would have been like living in apartments, only outside. Numbered cubbyholes with bushes instead of walls. TV. Radio. Women walking around in bathrobes with their hair in rollers. Electric razors. I didn't stop at those places.   55

One beautiful warm, clear morning I just got up, put on shorts and   5
a T-shirt and walked into the surprisingly warm water of a mountain lake
in Quebec. It was just sunrise; no one was around. Briefly the thought
entered my mind, "Should I go swimming here alone?" I answered myself,
"Yes, do it. For once, be different. Forget about the shoulds and shouldn'ts
for a while." I felt exhilarated and peaceful at the same time. I wish
there were more lakes at sunrise in life.

When I came back across the border, feeling tense and excited at   5
the crossing as if I were a spy, the friendly customs man talked bikes to
me a bit as if to disarm me, then sprang *the* question: "What did you
bring back with you that you didn't have when you came over?" I thought
hard, desperately wanting to be honest. "Uh, two apples, two peaches,
a can of chicken and a piece of asbestos." (Oh, Lord, I was transporting
minerals across the border!) He laughed. "Well, you didn't do much for
the Canadian economy," he said and motioned me on.

Wow! I was back in the States! I could speak English again. Ver-   5
mont, I love you. I was surprised at how good that simple crossing felt.
The lush small farms fit just right in the valleys of Vermont. It looked
differently immediately. It was the United States.

It was a fine thing, all told, to be riding all day, every day, to be   5
alone and silent, to lay a decent fire and cook a simple meal, to sit with
my back against a white birch looking out over water with a cup of coffee
in my hand as the sun went down, to be gently tired from the road and
comfortable on the ground under a red roof.

The big white bike was always patiently nearby, forgiving of some   6
of my early clumsiness, always starting at a touch, quietly humming over
the hills and puttering through the towns, making friends wherever we
went. I would look at it last thing at night before closing my tent and
first thing in the morning. This trip was only the beginning. As William
Carlos Williams might have put it,

> So much depends upon
>   a red tent
>   glazed with dew
>   beside the white
>   motorcycle.

About the Essay

1. What was Butcher's purpose in undertaking her 2500-mile trip? How did
she prepare for the trip? What preparations does she not describe that you
can be reasonably certain she made? What considerations might have governed her choice of which preparations to mention?

2. Where did Butcher begin her trip, and what places did she visit along the way? How does she use geography to structure her essay? What other elements in the essay contribute to its organization?

3. How do the people she meets respond to Butcher? Why do they respond this way? For example, why do you think no one made trouble for her? What role does the big, white motorcycle play in the responses of people?

4. What, for Butcher, were the best parts of her trip? What things that she must have done often does she mention only in passing, or not at all? How does this affect the dominant impression she gives?

5. In her descriptions, which senses does Butcher appeal to? Cite passages appealing to each sense you name. In that connection, what is the relevance of William Carlos Williams's "The Red Wheelbarrow"? (See the introduction to the essay, page 517.)

6. When she set off on her trip, Butcher wondered what it would mean to her ultimately. Does she answer that question directly, or by implication? If so, what is her answer? Why does she write in her conclusion, "This trip was only the beginning"?

Explorations

1. What outdoor activity do you particularly enjoy—hiking, biking, fishing, jogging? What do you most enjoy about that activity? What preparations would you advise others to make so as to get the most from it? Or, if the outdoor life does not appeal to you, why doesn't it?

2. Think of a memorable trip you have taken. Where did you go? Why did you go there? How did you travel? What did you see and do? What made the trip particularly memorable?

3. Americans, it has been said, have for sixty years been conducting a love affair with the internal combustion engine. At the end of the 1970s nearly 120 million motor vehicles were registered in the fifty states—about one vehicle for every two Americans. Choose an aspect of American road transportation that interests you and write about it, doing research as needed.

E. B. WHITE

When E. B. White was awarded the Gold Medal for Essays and Criticism by the American Academy of Arts and Letters, it included the following citation: "If we are remembered as a civilized era. . . . it will be partly because of E. B. White. The historians of the future will decide that a writer of such grace and control could not have been produced by a generation wholly lacking in such qualities, and we will shine by reflection in his gentle light." Master essayist, storyteller, and poet, Elwyn Brooks White was born in 1899 in Mount Vernon, New York, lived some years in New York City, and has for many years made his home on a salt-water farm in Maine. After studying at Cornell University, he joined the staff of *The New Yorker* in 1926, where he wrote essays, editorials, anonymous fillers, and even cartoon captions that helped to establish the magazine's and his own reputation for witty and graceful prose. For some years he also wrote a monthly column for *Harper's* with his observations and reflections on topics both humorous and serious, personal and political. A selection of his essays is available in *The Essays of E. B. White* (1977). He is the author of the classic children's stories *Stuart Little* (1945) and *Charlotte's Web* (1952) and has revised William Strunk's celebrated work, *The Elements of Style* (1979). "Once More to the Lake," first published in *Harper's* in 1941, is a loving account of a trip White took with his son to the site of his own childhood vacations.

Once More to the Lake

One summer, along about 1904, my father rented a camp on a lake in Maine and took us all there for the month of August. We all got ringworm from some kittens and had to rub Pond's Extract on our arms and legs night and morning, and my father rolled over in a canoe with all his clothes on; but outside of that the vacation was a success and from then on none of us ever thought there was any place in the world like that lake in Maine. We returned summer after summer—always on August 1st for one month. I have since become a salt-water man, but sometimes in summer there are days when the restlessness of the tides and the fearful cold of the sea water and the incessant wind which blows across the afternoon and into the evening make me wish for the placidity of a lake in the woods. A few weeks ago this feeling got so strong I bought myself a couple of bass hooks and a spinner and returned to the lake where we used to go, for a week's fishing and to revisit old haunts.

I took along my son, who had never had any fresh water up his nose and who had seen lily pads only from train windows. On the journey over to the lake I began to wonder what it would be like. I wondered how time would have marred this unique, this holy spot—the coves and streams, the hills that the sun set behind, the camps and the paths behind the camps. I was sure that the tarred road would have found it out and I wondered in what other ways it would be desolated. It is strange how much you can remember about places like that once you allow your mind to return into the grooves which lead back. You remember one thing, and that suddenly reminds you of another thing. I guess I remembered clearest of all the early mornings, when the lake was cool and motionless, remembered how the bedroom smelled of the lumber it was made of and of the wet woods whose scent entered through the screen. The partitions in the camp were thin and did not extend clear to the top of the rooms, and as I was always the first up I would dress softly so as not to wake the others, and sneak out into the sweet outdoors and start out in the canoe, keeping close along the shore in the long shadows of the pines. I remembered being very careful never to rub my paddle against the gunwale for fear of disturbing the stillness of the cathedral.

The lake had never been what you would call a wild lake. There   3 were cottages sprinkled around the shores, and it was in farming country although the shores of the lake were quite heavily wooded. Some of the cottages were owned by nearby farmers, and you would live at the shore and eat your meals at the farmhouse. That's what our family did. But although it wasn't wild, it was a fairly large and undisturbed lake and there were places in it which, to a child at least, seemed infinitely remote and primeval.

I was right about the tar: it led to within half a mile of the shore.   4 But when I got back there, with my boy, and we settled into a camp near a farmhouse and into the kind of summertime I had known, I could tell that it was going to be pretty much the same as it had been before— I knew it, lying in bed the first morning, smelling the bedroom, and hearing the boy sneak quietly out and go off along the shore in a boat. I began to sustain the illusion that he was I, and therefore, by simple transposition, that I was my father. This sensation persisted, kept cropping up all the time we were there. It was not an entirely new feeling, but in this setting it grew much stronger. I seemed to be living a dual existence. I would be in the middle of some simple act, I would be picking up a bait box or laying down a table fork, or I would be saying something, and suddenly it would be not I but my father who was saying the words or making the gesture. It gave me a creepy sensation.

We went fishing the first morning. I felt the same damp moss cov-   5 ering the worms in the bait can, and saw the dragonfly alight on the tip of my rod as it hovered a few inches from the surface of the water. It was the arrival of this fly that convinced me beyond any doubt that everything was as it always had been, that the years were a mirage and there had been no years. The small waves were the same, chucking the rowboat under the chin as we fished at anchor, and the boat was the same boat, the same color green and the ribs broken in the same places, and under the floor-boards the same freshwater leavings and débris—the dead helgramite, the wisps of moss, the rusty discarded fishhook, the dried blood from yesterday's catch. We stared silently at the tips of our rods, at the dragonflies that came and went. I lowered the tip of mine into the water, tentatively, pensively dislodging the fly, which darted two feet away, poised, darted two feet back, and came to rest again a little farther up the rod. There had been no years between the ducking of this dragonfly and the other one—the one that was part of memory. I looked at the boy, who was silently watching his fly, and it was my hands that held his rod, my eyes watching. I felt dizzy and didn't know which rod I was at the end of.

We caught two bass, hauling them in briskly as though they were mackerel, pulling them over the side of the boat in a businesslike manner without any landing net, and stunning them with a blow on the back of the head. When we got back for a swim before lunch, the lake was exactly where we had left it, the same number of inches from the dock, and there was only the merest suggestion of a breeze. This seemed an utterly enchanted sea, this lake you could leave to its own devices for a few hours and come back to, and find that it had not stirred, this constant and trustworthy body of water. In the shallows, the dark, water-soaked sticks and twigs, smooth and old, were undulating in clusters on the bottom against the clean ribbed sand, and the track of the mussel was plain. A school of minnows swam by, each minnow with its small individual shadow, doubling the attendance, so clear and sharp in the sunlight. Some of the other campers were in swimming, along the shore, one of them with a cake of soap, and the water felt thin and clear and unsubstantial. Over the years there had been this person with the cake of soap, this cultist, and here he was. There had been no years.

Up to the farmhouse to dinner through the teeming, dusty field, the road under our sneakers was only a two-track road. The middle track was missing, the one with the marks of the hooves and the splotches of dried, flaky manure. There had always been three tracks to choose from in choosing which track to walk in; now the choice was narrowed down to two. For a moment I missed terribly the middle alternative. But the way led past the tennis court, and something about the way it lay there in the sun reassured me; the tape had loosened along the backline, the alleys were green with plantains and other weeds, and the net (installed in June and removed in September) sagged in the dry noon, and the whole place steamed with midday heat and hunger and emptiness. There was a choice of pie for dessert, and one was blueberry and one was apple, and the waitresses were the same country girls, there having been no passage of time, only the illusion of it as in a dropped curtain—the waitresses were still fifteen; their hair had been washed, that was the only difference—they had been to the movies and seen the pretty girls with the clean hair.

Summertime, oh summertime, pattern of life indelible, the fade-proof lake, the woods unshatterable, the pasture with the sweetfern and the juniper forever and ever, summer without end; this was the background, and the life along the shore was the design, the cottages with their innocent and tranquil design, their tiny docks with the flagpole and the American flag floating against the white clouds in the blue sky, the little paths over the roots of the trees leading from camp to camp and the paths leading back to the outhouses and the can of lime for sprinkling, and at the souvenir counters at the store the miniature birch-bark canoes and the post cards that showed things looking a little better than they looked. This was the American family at play, escaping the city heat, wondering whether the newcomers in the camp at the head of the cove were "common" or "nice," wondering whether it was true that the people who drove up for Sunday dinner at the farmhouse were turned away because there wasn't enough chicken. 8

It seemed to me, as I kept remembering all this, that those times and those summers had been infinitely precious and worth saving. There had been jollity and peace and goodness. The arriving (at the beginning of August) had been so big a business in itself, at the railway station the farm wagon drawn up, the first smell of the pine-laden air, the first glimpse of the smiling farmer, and the great importance of the trunks and your father's enormous authority in such matters, and the feel of the wagon under you for the long ten-mile haul, and at the top of the last long hill catching the first view of the lake after eleven months of not seeing this cherished body of water. The shouts and cries of the other campers when they saw you, and the trunks to be unpacked, to give up their rich burden. (Arriving was less exciting nowadays, when you sneaked up in your car and parked it under a tree near the camp and took out the bags and in five minutes it was all over, no fuss, no loud wonderful fuss about trunks.) 9

Peace and goodness and jollity. The only thing that was wrong now, really, was the sound of the place, an unfamiliar nervous sound of the outboard motors. This was the note that jarred, the one thing that would sometimes break the illusion and set the years moving. In those 10 other summertimes all motors were inboard; and when they were at a little distance, the noise they made was a sedative, an ingredient of summer sleep. They were one-cylinder and two-cylinder engines, and some were make-and-break and some were jump-spark, but they all made a sleepy sound across the lake. The one-lungers throbbed and fluttered, and the twin-cylinder ones purred and purred, and that was a quiet sound too. But now the campers all had outboards. In the daytime, in the hot mornings, these motors made a petulant, irritable sound; at night, in the still evening when the afterglow lit the water, they whined about one's ears like mosquitoes. My boy loved our rented outboard, and his great desire was to achieve singlehanded mastery over it, and authority, and he soon learned the trick of choking it a little (but not too much), and the adjustment of the needle valve. Watching him I would remember the things you could do with the old one-cylinder engine with the heavy flywheel, how you could have it eating out of your hand if you got really close to it spiritually. Motor boats in those days didn't have clutches, and you would make a landing by shutting off the motor at the proper time and coasting in with a dead rudder. But there was a way of reversing them, if you learned the trick, by cutting the switch and putting it on again exactly on the final dying revolution of the flywheel, so that it would kick back against compression and begin reversing. Approaching a dock in a strong following breeze, it was difficult to slow up sufficiently by the ordinary coasting method, and if a boy felt he had complete mastery over his motor, he was tempted to keep it running beyond its time and then reverse it a few feet from the dock. It took a cool nerve, because if you threw the switch a twentieth of a second too soon you could catch the flywheel when it still had speed enough to go up past center, and the boat would leap ahead, charging bull-fashion at the dock.

We had a good week at the camp. The bass were biting well and the sun shone endlessly, day after day. We would be tired at night and lie down in the accumulated heat of the little bedrooms after the long hot day and the breeze would stir almost imperceptibly outside and the smell of the swamp drift in through the rusty screens. Sleep would come easily and in the morning the red squirrel would be on the roof tapping out his gay routine. I kept remembering everything, lying in bed in the mornings—the small steamboat that had a long rounded stern like the lip of a Ubangi,[1] and how quietly she ran on the moonlight sails, when the older boys played their mandolins and the girls sang and we ate doughnuts dipped in sugar, and how sweet the music was on the water

---

[1] A member of an African tribe whose lower lip is stretched around a wooden, plate-like disk.

in the shining night, and what it had felt like to think about girls then. After breakfast we would go up to the store and the things were in the same place—the minnows in a bottle, the plugs and spinners disarranged and pawed over by the youngsters from the boys' camp, the fig newtons and the Beeman's gum. Outside, the road was tarred and cars stood in front of the store. Inside, all was just as it had always been, except there was more Coca-Cola and not so much Moxie and root beer and birch beer and sarsaparilla. We would walk out with a bottle of pop apiece and sometimes the pop would backfire up our noses and hurt. We explored the streams, quietly, where the turtles slid off the sunny logs and dug their way into the soft bottom; and we lay on the town wharf and fed worms to the tame bass. Everywhere we went I had trouble making out which was I, the one walking at my side, the one walking in my pants.

One afternoon while we were there at that lake a thunderstorm came up. It was like the revival of an old melodrama that I had seen long ago with childish awe. The second-act climax of the drama of the electrical disturbance over a lake in America had not changed in any important respect. This was the big scene, still the big scene. The whole thing was so familiar, the first feeling of oppression and heat and a general air around camp of not wanting to go very far away. In midafternoon (it was all the same) a curious darkening of the sky, and a lull in everything that had made life tick; and then the way the boats suddenly swung the other way at their moorings with the coming of a breeze out of the new quarter, and the premonitory rumble. Then the kettle drum, then the snare, then the bass drum and cymbals, then crackling light against the dark, and the gods grinning and licking their chops in the hills. Afterward the calm, the rain steadily rustling in the calm lake, the return of light and hope and spirits, and the campers running out in joy and relief to go swimming in the rain, their bright cries perpetuating the deathless joke about how they were getting simply drenched, and the children screaming with delight at the new sensation of bathing in the rain, and the joke about getting drenched linking the generations in a strong indestructible chain. And the comedian who waded in carrying an umbrella. [12]

When the others went swimming my son said he was going in too. He pulled his dripping trunks from the line where they had hung all through the shower, and wrung them out. Languidly, and with no thought of going in, I watched him, his hard little body, skinny and bare, saw him wince slightly as he pulled up around his vitals the small, soggy, icy garment. As he buckled the swollen belt suddenly my groin felt the chill of death. [13]

On the Essay

1. The first three paragraphs serve as an introduction to White's essay. Taken together, how do they prepare for what follows? What does each paragraph contribute?

2. White returns to the lake wondering whether it will be as he remembers it from his childhood vacations. What remains the same? What significance does White attach to the changes in the road, the waitresses, and the out-board-motor boats?

3. In paragraph 4 White tells us, "I began to sustain the illusion that [my son] was I, and therefore, by simple transposition, that I was my father." What first prompts this "illusion"? Where else does White refer to it? How does it affect your understanding of what the week at the lake means to White?

4. In paragraph 12 White describes a late afternoon thunderstorm at the lake. How does White organize his description? What does the metaphor of the old melodrama contribute to that description?

5. What is the tone of this essay, and what does it reveal about White's attitude toward his experience? Give examples to support your answer.

6. The closing sentence takes many readers by surprise. Why did White feel the "chill of death"? Has he prepared for this surprise earlier in the essay? If so, where?

Explorations

1. What, for you, is the ideal vacation? Where would you go and what would you do? What do you hope and expect that a good vacation will do for you?

2. Have you ever returned to a place you once knew well but have not seen in years—a house or a city where you once lived, a school you once attended, a favorite vacation spot? What memories did the visit bring back? Did you, like White, find that little had changed and feel that time had stood still, or were there many changes? If possible, you might make such a visit, to reflect on what has happened to the place—and to you—since you were last there.

3. White and his family had a tradition of going off to summer camp together. Today, many parents stay home but send their children to summer camp. (See, for example, the opening of "Television and Free Time," page 550.) What are the advantages, and disadvantages, to the children and to their parents of sending children to camp? If you yourself have been sent to camp, describe what the experience was like and how you felt and feel about it.

JOHN McPHEE

Game arcades with their pinball machines and video games have long been frowned on by upright citizens. Indeed, they were once outlawed in New York City. But the games have their defenders too, and one of these is John McPhee. Born in 1931 in Princeton, New Jersey, McPhee attended the university there and moved to New York to work as a television writer, an assistant editor for *Time*, and finally as a staff writer for *The New Yorker*. Though a city man, he often writes on nature and the environment, including such books as *The Pine Barrens* (1968) and *Coming into the Country* (1977). In fact, his interests are numerous, and his many magazine pieces and books cover topics as varied as oranges, tennis, and open-air markets. A representative selection is available in *The John McPhee Reader* (1976).

"The Pinball Philosophy" is from *Giving Good Weight* (1979), but was first published in 1975, before pinball had been legalized in New York. In the essay McPhee describes a best-of-five pinball match between two world-class players, the journalists J. Anthony Lukas and Tom Buckley, and offers Lukas's thoughts on the relevance of pinball to life.

The Pinball Philosophy

J. Anthony Lukas is a world-class pinball player who, between tilts, does some free-lance writing. In our city, he is No. ½. That is to say, he is one of two players who share pinball preeminence—two players whose special skills within the sport are so multiple and varied that they defy comparative analysis. The other star is Tom Buckley, of the *Times*. Pinball people tend to gravitate toward Lukas or Buckley. Lukas is a Lukasite. He respects Buckley, but he sees himself as the whole figure, the number "1." His machine is a Bally. Public pinball has been illegal in New York for many decades, but private ownership is permitted, and Lukas plays, for the most part, at home.

Lukas lives in an old mansion, a city landmark, on West Seventy-sixth Street. The machine is in his living room, under a high, elegant ceiling, near an archway to rooms beyond. Bally is the Rolls-Royce of pinball, he explains as he snaps a ball into action. It rockets into the ellipse at the top of the playfield. It ricochets four times before beginning its descent. Lukas likes a four-bounce hold in the ellipse—to set things up for a long ball. There is something faintly, and perhaps consciously, nefarious about Lukas, who is an aristocratic, olive-skinned, Andalusian sort of man, with deep eyes in dark wells. As the butts of his hands pound the corners of his machine, one can imagine him cheating at polo. "It's

535

a wrist game," he says, tremoring the Bally, helping the steel ball to bounce six times off the top thumper-bumper and, each time, go back up a slot to the ellipse—an awesome economy of fresh beginnings. "Strong wrists are really all you want to use. The term for what I am doing is 'reinforcing.' " His voice, rich and dense, pours out like cigarette smoke filtered through a New England prep school. "There are certain basics to remember," he says. "Above all, don't flail with the flipper. You *carry* the ball in the direction you want it to go. You can almost cradle the ball on the flipper. And always hit the slingshot hard. That's the slingshot there—where the rubber is stretched between bumpers. Reinforce it hard. And never—never—drift toward the free-ball gate." Lukas reinforces the machine just as the ball hits the slingshot. The rebound comes off with blurring speed, striking bumpers, causing gongs to ring and lights to flash. Under his hands, the chrome on the frame has long since worn away.

Lukas points out that one of the beauties of his Bally is that it is asymmetrical. Early pinball machines had symmetrical playfields—symmetrical thumper-bumpers—but in time they became free-form, such as this one, with its field laid out not just for structure but also for surprise. Lukas works in this room—stacks of manuscript on shelves and tables. He has been working for many months on a book that will weigh five pounds. It will be called *Nightmare: The Dark Side of the Nixon Years*—a congenially chosen title, implying that there was a bright side.[1] The pinball machine is Lukas's collaborator. "When a paragraph just won't go," he says, "and I begin to say to myself, 'I can't make this work,' I get up and play the machine. I score in a high range. Then I go back to the typewriter a new man. I have beat the machine. Therefore I can beat the paragraph." He once won a Pulitzer Prize.

The steel ball rolls into the "death channel"—Lukas's term for a long alley down the left side—and drops out of sight off the low end of the playfield, finished.

"I have thought of analogies between Watergate and pinball. Everything is connected. Bumpers. Rebounds. You light lights and score. Chuck Colson is involved in almost every aspect of the Watergate story: the dirty tricks, the coverup, the laundered money—all connected. How hard you hit off the thumper-bumper depends on how hard you hit off the slingshot depends on how well you work the corners. In a sense, pinball is a reflection of the complexity of the subject I am writing about. Bear in mind, I take this with considerable tongue-in-cheek."

With another ball, he ignites an aurora on the scoreboard. During

---

[1]Lukas ultimately decided to be less congenial, and changed the title to *Nightmare: The Underside of the Nixon Years*, Viking Press, 1976 (author's note).

the ball's complex, prolonged descent, he continues to set forth the pinball philosophy. "More seriously, the game does give you a sense of controlling things in a way that in life you can't do. And there is risk in it, too. The ball flies into the ellipse, into the playfield—full of opportunities. But there's always the death channel—the run-out slot. There are rewards, prizes, coming off the thumper-bumper. The ball crazily bounces from danger to opportunity and back to danger. You need reassurance in life that in taking risks you will triumph, and pinball gives you that reaffirmation. Life is a risky game, but you can beat it."

Unfortunately, Lukas has a sick flipper. At the low end of the   7
playfield, two flippers guard the run-out slot, but one waggles like a broken wing, pathetic, unable to function, to fling the ball uphill for renewed rewards. The ball, instead, slides by the crippled flipper and drops from view.

Lukas opens the machine. He lifts the entire playfield, which is   8
hinged at the back, and props it up on a steel arm, like the lid of a grand piano. Revealed below is a neat, arresting world that includes spring-loaded hole kickers, contact switches, target switches, slingshot assemblies, the score-motor unit, the electric anti-cheat, three thumper-bumper relays, the top rebound relay, the key-gate assembly ("the key gate will keep you out of the death channel"), the free-ball-gate assembly, and— not least—the one-and-a-quarter-amp slo-blo. To one side, something that resembles a plumb bob hangs suspended within a metal ring. If the bob moves too far out of plumb, it touches the ring. Tilt. The game is dead.

Lukas is not an electrician. All he can do is massage the flipper's   9
switch assembly, which does not respond—not even with a shock. He has about had it with this machine. One cannot collaborate with a sick flipper. The queasy truth comes over him: no pinball, no paragraphs. So he hurries downstairs and into a taxi, telling the driver to go to Tenth Avenue in the low Forties—a pocket of the city known as Coin Row.

En route, Lukas reflects on his long history in the game—New   10
York, Cambridge, Paris—and his relationships with specific machines ("they're like wives"). When he was the *Times'* man in the Congo, in the early sixties, the post was considered a position of hardship, so he was periodically sent to Paris for rest and rehabilitation, which he got playing pinball in a Left Bank brasserie.[2] He had perfected his style as an undergraduate at Harvard, sharing a machine at the *Crimson* with David Halberstam ("Halberstam is aggressive at everything he does, and

---

[2] A tavern or bar.

he was very good"). Lukas's father was a Manhattan attorney. Lukas's mother died when he was eight. He grew up, for the most part, in a New England community—Putney, Vermont—where he went to pre-prep and prep school. Putney was "straitlaced," "very high-minded," "a life away from the maelstrom"—potters' wheels, no pinball. Lukas craved "liberation," and developed a yearning for what he imagined as low life, and so did his schoolmate Christopher Lehmann-Haupt.[3] Together, one weekend, they dipped as low as they knew how. They went to New York. And they went to two movies! They went to shooting galleries! They went to a flea circus! They played every coin-operated machine they could find—and they stayed up until after dawn! All this was pretty low, but not low enough, for that was the spring of 1951, and still beyond reach—out there past the fingertips of Tantalus[4]—was pinball, the ban on which had been emphatically reinforced a few years earlier by Fiorello H. LaGuardia,[5] who saw pinball as a gambling device corruptive of the city's youth. To Lukas, pinball symbolized all the time-wasting and ne'er-do-welling that puritan Putney did not. In result, he mastered the game. He says, "It puts me in touch with a world in which I never lived. I am attracted to pinball for its seediness, its slightly disreputable reputation."

On Coin Row, Lukas knows just where he is going, and without a sidewise glance passes storefronts bearing names like The World of Pinball Amusement ("SALES—REPAIR") and Manhattan Coin Machine ("PARTS—SUPPLIES"). He heads directly for the Mike Munves Corporation, 577 Tenth Avenue, the New York pinball exchange, oldest house (1912) on the row. Inside is Ralph Hotkins, in double-breasted blazer—broker in pinball machines. The place is more warehouse than store, and around Hotkins, and upstairs above him, are rank upon rank of Gottliebs, Williamses, Ballys, Playmatics—every name in the game, including forty-year-old antique completely mechanical machines, ten balls for a nickel, the type that Mayor LaGuardia himself destroyed with an axe. Hotkins—a prosperous man, touched with humor, not hurting for girth—got his start in cigarette machines in the thirties, moved up to jukeboxes, and then, in 1945, while LaGuardia was still mayor, to game machines. He had two daughters, and he brought them up on pinball. They were in the shop almost every afternoon after school, and all day Saturday. One daughter now has a Ph.D. in English literature and the other a Ph.D. in

---

[3]David Halberstam and Christopher Lehmann-Haupt are journalists.

[4]In Greek myth, a barbaric king condemned eternally to thirst and hunger for fruit above his head that perpetually bounce out of reach.

[5]Mayor of New York City, 1933–45.

political science. So much for the Little Flower.⁶ In this era of open massage and off-track betting, Hotkins has expected the ban to lift, but the courts, strangely, continue to uphold it.⁷ Meanwhile, his customers—most of whom are technically "private"—include Wall Street brokerage houses where investors shoot free pinball under the ticker, Seventh Avenue dress houses that wish to keep their buyers amused, the Circus Circus peepshow emporium on West Forty-second Street, many salesrooms, many showrooms, and J. Anthony Lukas.

"Yes, Mr. Lukas. What can we do for you?" 12

Lukas greets Hotkins and then runs balls through a few selected 13 machines. Lukas attempts to deal with Hotkins, but Hotkins wants Lukas's machine and a hundred and fifty dollars. Lukas would rather fix his flipper. He asks for George Cedeño, master technician, who makes house calls and often travels as far as Massachusetts to fix a pinball machine. Cedeño—blue work smock, white shoes, burgundy trousers, silver hair—makes a date with Lukas.

Lukas starts for home but, crossing Forty-second Street, decides on 14 pure whim to have a look at Circus Circus, where he has never been. Circus Circus is, after all, just four blocks away. The stroll is pleasant in the afternoon sunlight, to and through Times Square, under the marquees of pornographic movies—*Valley of the Nymphs, The Danish Sandwich, The Organ Trail.* Circus Circus ("GIRLS! GIRLS! GIRLS! LIVE EXOTIC MODELS") is close to Sixth Avenue and consists, principally, of a front room and a back room. Prices are a quarter a peep in the back room and a quarter to play (two games) in the front. The game room is dim, and Lukas, entering, sees little at first but the flashing scoreboards of five machines. Four of them—a Bally, a Williams, two Gottliebs—flash slowly, reporting inexperienced play, but the fifth, the one in the middle, is exploding with light and sound. The player causing all this is hunched over, concentrating—in his arms and his hands a choreography of talent. Lukas's eyes adjust to the light. Then he reaches for his holster. The man on the hot machine, busy keeping statistics of his practice, is Tom Buckley.

"Tom." 15

"Tone." 16

"How is the machine?" 17

"Better than yours, Tone. You don't realize what a lemon you 18 have."

---

⁶Nickname of LaGuardia, derived from his given name, which in Italian means "little flower."

⁷And they did so until 1976, when pinball at last became legal (author's note).

"I love my Bally."   19

"The Bally is the Corvair of pinball machines. I don't even care   20
for the art on the back-glass. Williams and Gottlieb are the best. Bally
is nowhere."

Buckley, slightly older than Lukas, has a spectacled and professorial 21
look. He wears a double-breasted blazer, a buff turtleneck. He lives on
York Avenue now. He came out of Beechhurst, Queens, and learned his
pinball in the Army—in Wrightstown, New Jersey; in Kansas City. He
was stationed in an office building in Kansas City, and he moved up
through the pinball ranks from beginner to virtuoso on a machine in a
Katz drugstore.

Lukas and Buckley begin to play. Best of five games. Five balls a   22
game. Alternate shots. The machine is a Williams Fun-Fest, and Buckley
points out that it is "classic," because it is symmetrical. Each kick-out
well and thumper-bumper is a mirror of another. The slingshots are dual.
On this machine, a level of forty thousand points is where the sun sets
and the stars come out. Buckley, describing his own style as "guts pinball," has a first-game score of forty-four thousand three hundred and
ten. While Lukas plays his fifth ball, Buckley becomes avuncular. "Careful, Tony. You might think you're in an up-post position, but if you let
it slide a little you're in a down-post position and you're finished." Buckley's advice is generous indeed. Lukas—forty-eight thousand eight hundred
and seventy—wins the first game.

It is Buckley's manner to lean into the machine from three feet   23
out. His whole body, steeply inclined, tics as he reinforces. In the second
game, he scores fifty thousand one hundred and sixty. Lukas's address is
like a fencer's *en garde.* He stands close to the machine, with one foot
projecting under it. His chin is high. Buckley tells him, "You're playing
nice, average pinball, Tony." And Lukas's response is fifty-seven thousand nine hundred and fifty points. He leads Buckley, two games to none.

"I'm ashamed," Buckley confesses. And as he leans—palms pound-   24
ing—into the third game, he reminds himself, "Concentration, Tom.
Concentration is everything."

Lukas notes aloud that Buckley is "full of empty rhetoric." But   25
Lukas, in Game 3, fires one ball straight into the death channel and can
deliver only thirty-five thousand points. Buckley wins with forty. Perhaps
Lukas feels rushed. He prefers to play a more deliberate, cogitative game.
At home, between shots, in the middle of a game, he will go to the
kitchen for a beer and return to study the situation. Buckley, for his part,
seems anxious, and with good reason: one mistake now and it's all over.
In the fourth game, Lukas lights up forty-three thousand and fifty points;
but Buckley's fifth ball, just before it dies, hits forty-four thousand two

hundred and sixty. Games are two all, with one to go. Buckley takes a deep breath, and says, "You're a competitor, Tony. Your flipper action is bad, but you're a real competitor."

Game 5 under way. They are pummelling the machine. They are heavy on the corners but light on the flippers, and the scoreboard is reacting like a storm at sea. With three balls down, both are in the thirty-thousand range. Buckley, going unorthodox, plays his fourth ball with one foot off the floor, and raises his score to forty-five thousand points—more than he scored in winning the two previous games. He smiles. He is on his way in, flaring, with still another ball to play. Now Lukas snaps his fourth ball into the ellipse. It moves down and around the board, hitting slingshots and flippers and rising again and again to high ground to begin additional scoring runs. It hits sunburst caps and hole kickers, swinging targets and bonus gates. Minute upon minute, it stays in play. It will not die. 26

When the ball finally slips between flippers and off the playfield, Lukas has registered eighty-three thousand two hundred points. And he still has one ball to go. 27

Buckley turns into a Lukasite. As Lukas plays his fifth ball, Buckley cheers. "Atta way! Atta way, babes!" He goes on cheering until Lukas peaks out at ninety-four thousand one hundred and seventy. 28

"That was superb. And there's no luck in it," Buckley says. "It's as good a score as I've seen." 29

Lukas takes a cool final look around Circus Circus. "Buckley has a way of tracking down the secret joys of the city," he says, and then he is gone. 30

Still shaking his head in wonder, Buckley starts a last, solo game. His arms move mechanically, groovedly, reinforcing. His flipper timing is offhandedly flawless. He scores a hundred thousand two hundred points. But Lukas is out of sight. 31

About the Essay

1. How does Anthony Lukas's pinball machine help him write? What does playing pinball do for him in difficult moments?

2. What is Lukas's pinball philosophy? What one sentence sums it up?

3. McPhee's descriptions are vivid and frequently off-beat—for example, Lukas's voice, "rich and dense, pours out like cigarette smoke filtered through a New England prep school." What figures of speech are being used here? What sense of Lukas do you get from this detail? Choose two or three other descriptive details; explain what they convey and how they contribute to your understanding of their subject.

4. What outraged Mayor LaGuardia about pinball? What attracted the young Lukas to it? What conclusion might you draw from this?

5. What comparisons and contrasts does McPhee draw between Lukas's and Buckley's styles of play? About the machines they like to play? What do these comparisons suggest about their personalities? How does each player respond to his victories and defeats?

6. The best-of-five match between Lukas and Buckley is the climax of the essay. How does McPhee's writing convey the tension and excitement of the contest?

Explorations

1. Choose a video game and consider its relation to other aspects of life. For example, what might be the Pac-Man philosophy?

2. Compare video games with pinball. Is the player up against the same challenges in each? What skills are essential in one but useless in the other if you are to score high?

3. There is much opposition, especially among parents, to video game arcades and to video games themselves. Why do so many people find arcades and games objectionable? Why do so many others find them attractive? Do the games serve any useful function, or are they just ways of killing time?

DANIEL J. BOORSTIN

Television, not baseball, is the American national pastime. Nearly every home has at least one television set, and by the best estimates each set is turned on about six and a half hours a day. What exactly is television doing to our lives? In the following essay, the social historian Daniel J. Boorstin offers some answers. He was born in 1914 in Atlanta, Georgia, and after growing up in Tulsa, Oklahoma, went to Harvard, graduating in 1934; he then went to Oxford University as a Rhodes Scholar, and took a law degree at Yale in 1940. His career as a teacher began at Harvard Law School and reached its culmination at the University of Chicago, where he taught American history from 1944 to 1969. He then went to Washington, D.C., first as director of the National Museum of History and Technology at the Smithsonian Institution and then as Librarian of Congress. Of his many books the centerpiece is his trilogy, *The Americans* (1958, 1965, 1973). "Television" was published in *Life* in 1971. In this essay Boorstin considers how TV has changed us all—perhaps even more than we know.

Television

Just as the printing press democratized learning, so the television set has democratized experience. But while our experience now is more equal than ever before, it is also more separate. And no Supreme Court ruling can correct this segregation, no federal commission can police it. It is built into our TV sets.

Segregation from One Another

When a colonial housewife went to the village to draw water for her family, she saw friends, gathered gossip, shared the laughs and laments of her neighbors. When her great-great-granddaughter was blessed with running water, and no longer had to go to the well, this made life easier, but also less interesting. Running electricity, mail delivery and the telephone removed more reasons for leaving the house. And now the climax of it all is Television.

For television gives the American housewife in her kitchen her own private theater, her window on the world. Every room with a set becomes a private room with a view—a TV booth. Television brings in a supply of information, knowledge, news, romance, and advertisements—without her having to set foot outside her door. The range and variety and vividness of these experiences of course excel anything she gets outside, even while she spends hours driving around in her automobile. At home she now has her own private faucet of hot and cold running images.

But always before, to see a performance was to share an experience   4
with a visible audience. At a concert, or a ball game, or a political rally, the audience was half the fun. What and whom you saw in the audience was at least as interesting, and often humanly more important, than what you saw on the stage. While watching TV, the lonely American is thrust back on herself. She can, of course, exclaim or applaud or hiss, but nobody hears except the family in the living room. The other people at the performance take the invisible forms of "canned" laughter and applause.

And while myriad island audiences gather nightly around their sets,   5
much as cave-dwelling ancestors gathered around the fire, for warmth and safety and a feeling of togetherness, now, with more and more two-TV families, a member of the family can actually withdraw and watch in complete privacy.

Segregation from the Source

In the 1920s, in the early days of radio, "broadcast" entered the   6
language with a new meaning. Before then it meant "to sow seeds over the whole surface, instead of in drills or rows," but now it meant to diffuse messages or images to unidentified people at unknown destinations. The mystery of the anonymous audience was what made sensible businessmen doubt whether radio would ever pay. They had seen the telegraph and the telephone prosper by delivering a message, composed by the sender, to a particular recipient. They thought the commercial future of radio might depend on devising ways to keep the radio message private so that it could be sent to only one specific person.

The essential novelty of wireless communication—that those who   7
received "broadcast" messages were no longer addressees, but a vast mysterious audience—was destined, in the long run, to create unforeseen new opportunities and new problems for Americans in the age of television, to create a new sense of isolation and confinement and frustration for those who saw the images. For television was a one-way window. Just as Americans were segregated from the millions of other Americans who were watching the same program, so each of them was segregated in a fantastic new way from those who put on the program and who, presumably, aimed to please. The viewer could see whatever they offered, but nobody (except the family in the living room) could know for sure how he reacted to what he saw.

While the American felt isolated from those who filled the TV screen, 8
he also felt a new isolation from his government, from those who collected his taxes, who provided his public services, and who made the
crucial decisions of peace or war. Of course, periodically he still had the
traditional opportunity to express his preference on the ballot. But now
there was a disturbing and frustrating new disproportion between how
often and how vividly his government and his political leaders could get
their message to him and how often and how vividly he could get his to
them. Even if elected representatives were no more inaccessible to him
than they had ever been before, in a strange new way he surely felt more
isolated from them. They could talk his ear off on TV and if he wanted
to respond, all he could do was write them a letter. Except indirectly
through the pollsters, Americans were offered no new modern avenue
comparable to television by which to get their message back. They were
left to rely on a venerable, almost obsolete 19th-century institution, the
post office.

Segregation from the Past

Of all the forces which have tempted us to lose our sense of history, 9
none has been more potent than television. While, of course, television
levels distance—puts us closer and more vividly present in Washington
than we are in our state capital and takes us all instantly to the moon—
it has had a less noticeable but equally potent effect on our sense of time.
Because television enables us to be there, anywhere, instantly, precisely
because it fills the instant present moment with experience so engrossing
and overwhelming, it dulls our sense of the past. If it had not been possible for us all to accompany Scott and Irwin on their voyage of exploration on the moon, we would have had to wait to be engrossed in retrospect by the vivid chronicle of some Francis Parkman or Samuel Eliot
Morison,[1] and there would then have been no possible doubt that the
moon journey was part of the stream of our history. But with television
we saw the historic event—as we now see more and more of whatever
goes on in our country—as only another vivid item in the present.

Almost everything about television tempts the medium to a time- 10
myopia—to focus our interest on the here-and-now, the exciting, disturbing, inspiring, or catastrophic instantaneous now. Meanwhile, the high
cost of network time and the need to offer something for everybody pro-

---

[1]Francis Parkman (1823–93) and Samuel Eliot Morison (1887–1976) were great
American historians.

duce a discontinuity of programming, a constant shifting from one thing to another, an emphasis on the staccato and motley character of experience—at the cost of our sense of unity with the past.

But history is a flowing stream. We are held together by its conti- 11 nuities, by people willing to sit there and do their jobs, by the unspoken faiths of people who still believe much of what their fathers believed. That makes a dull program. So the American begins to think of the outside world as if there too the program changed every half hour.

Segregation from Reality

Of all the miracles of television none is more remarkable than its 12 power to give to so many hours of our experience a new vagueness. Americans have become increasingly accustomed to see something-or-other, happening somewhere-or-other, at sometime-or-other. The common-sense hallmarks of authentic first-hand experience (the ordinary facts which a jury expects a witness to supply to prove he actually experienced what he says) now begin to be absent, or to be only ambiguously present, in our television-experience. For our TV-experience we don't need to go out to see anything in particular. We just turn the knob. Then we wonder while we watch. Is this program "live" or is it "taped"? Is it merely an animation or a "simulation"? Is this a rerun? Where does it originate? When (if ever) did it really occur? Is this happening to actors or to real people? Is this a commercial? A spoof of a commercial? A documentary? Or pure fiction?

Almost never do we see a TV event from what used to be the indi- 13 vidual human point of view. For TV is many-eyed, and alert to avoid the monotony of one person's limited vision. And each camera gives us a close-up that somehow dominates the screen. Dick Cavett or Zsa Zsa Gabor fills the screen just like Dave Scott or President Nixon. Everything becomes theater, any actor—or even a spectator—holds center stage. Our TV perspective makes us understandably reluctant to go back to the seats on the side and in the rear which are ours in real life.

The experience flowing through our television channels is a miscel- 14 laneous mix of entertainment, instruction, news, uplift, exhortation, and guess what. Old compartments of experience which separated going to church, or to a lecture, from going to a play or a movie or to a ball game, from going to a political rally or stopping to hear a patent-medicine salesman's pitch—on television, such compartments are dissolved. Here at last is a supermarket of surrogate experience. Successful programming offers entertainment (under the guise of instruction), instruction (under the guise of entertainment), political persuasion (with the appeal of advertising) and advertising (with the appeal of drama).

A new miasma—which no machine before could emit—enshrouds the world of TV. We begin to be so accustomed to this foggy world, so at home and solaced and comforted within and by its blurry edges, that reality itself becomes slightly irritating.   15

Here is a great, rich, literate, equalitarian nation suddenly fragmented into mysterious anonymous island-audiences, newly separated from one another, newly isolated from their entertainers and their educators and their political representatives, suddenly enshrouded in a fog of new ambiguities. Unlike other comparable changes in human experience, the new segregation came with rocket speed. Television conquered America in less than a generation. No wonder its powers are bewildering and hard to define. It took 500 years for the printing press to democratize learning. Then the people, who at last could know as much as their "betters," demanded the power to govern themselves. As late as 1671, the governor of colonial Virginia, Sir William Berkeley, thanked God that the printing press (breeder of heresy and disobedience) had not yet arrived in his colony, and prayed that printing would never come to Virginia. By the early 19th century, aristocrats and men of letters would record (with Thomas Carlyle) that movable type[2] had disbanded hired armies and cashiered kings, and somehow created "a whole new democratic world."   16

With dizzying speed television has democratized experience. Like the printing press, it threatens—and promises—a transformation. Is it any wonder that, like the printing press before it, television has met a cool reception from intellectuals and academics and the other custodians of traditional avenues of experience?   17

Can TV-democratized experience carry us to a new society, beyond the traditional democracy of learning and politics? The great test is whether somehow we can find ways in and through television itself to break down the walls of the new segregation—the walls which separate us from one another, from the sources of knowledge and power, from the past, from the real world outside. We see clues to our frustrations in the rise of endless dreary talk-shows, as much as in the sudden increase in mass demonstrations. We must find ways outside TV to restore the sense of per-   18

---

[2]Thomas Carlyle (1795–1881) was a British author and sometime historian who disapproved of much that happened after the twelfth century. Movable type, and with it the printing press, was invented in Europe in the middle of the fifteenth century.

sonal presence, the sense of neighborhood, of visible fellowship, of publicly shared enthusiasm and dismay. We must find ways within TV to allow the anonymous audience to express its views, not merely through sampling and statistical averages, but person-to-person. We must find ways to decentralize and define and separate TV audiences into smaller, more specific interest-groups, who have the competence to judge what they see, and then to give the audiences an opportunity to react and communicate their reactions. We must try every institutional and technological device—from more specialized stations to pay TV, to cable TV, and other devices still unimagined.

Over a century ago, Thoreau warned that men were becoming "the tools of their tools." While this new-world nation has thrived on change and on novelty, our prosperity and our survival have depended on our ability to adapt strange new tools to wise old purposes. We cannot allow ourselves to drift in the channels of television. Many admirable features of American life today—the new poignance of our conscience, the wondrous universalizing of our experiences, the sharing of the exotic, the remote, the unexpected—come from television. But they will come to little unless we find ways to overcome the new provincialism, the new isolation, the new frustrations and the new confusion which come from our new segregation. 19

About the Essay

1. Boorstin opens his essay with the observation that television has "democratized experience." What does this mean? What else does he have to say in praise of television, if anything?

2. According to Boorstin, television is a force for segregation. What kind or kinds of segregation does he mean? Why does he use the word *segregation*?

3. What are the specific differences Boorstin means to suggest between television and the post office as means of communication?

4. How, according to Boorstin, does television affect our sense of the past? Give some examples from your own experience to illustrate his point.

5. How does television affect our sense of reality? What are some implications of Boorstin's discussion of this point?

6. What solutions does Boorstin propose to the problem he presents? Do you agree with him? What solution or solutions would you suggest?

Explorations

1. What are the differences between watching a movie in a theater and watching it at home on television? Which experience do you prefer? Why?

2. Even before television, many Americans have had little sense of history, and, sometimes, considerable skepticism about its usefulness—in Henry Ford's memorable dismissal, "History is bunk." Do you think Ford's statement is true? Why or why not? What are some practical uses of history, or dangers of ignoring it? Or is it safe, or even preferable, to "segregate" ourselves (as Boorstin would say) from the past?

MARIE WINN

Many people consider television to be a way of passing free time. Marie Winn suggests that for children television *eliminates* free time. Winn was born in 1937 in Czechoslovakia and as a child came with her family to settle in New York City. She graduated from Radcliffe College and did graduate work at Columbia University, then embarked on a career as a writer for and about children. Her best-known work is *The Plug-In Drug* (1977), a study of the effects of television on children's personalities and family life. She has also edited a book of songs and singing games for young children, *What Shall We Do and Allee Galloo* (1972). In "Television and Free Time," a selection from *The Plug-In Drug,* Winn explains how television tends to interfere with many children's ability to invent their own pastimes and develop independence of mind.

Television and Free Time

The founder and director of an excellent children's camp in Vermont began to observe a curious increase in homesickness in the early sixties. There had always been a small number of campers afflicted with homesickness, but now an epidemic seemed to have struck. The camp had devised a number of successful strategies for combating homesickness, and these were now applied with equal success. Nevertheless the increased incidence of homesickness continued to be a problem year after year. When the director checked with counselors from other camps, he learned that they had not encountered a similar problem. It was a mystery. Perhaps the answer would be found in some aspect of life at his camp that differed from other camps.

There was indeed one great difference: while other camps filled every minute of the campers' day with programmed activities, rests, and meals, this particular camp interspersed its programmed activities with four half-hours during which the children were free to pursue their own interests. These were called "drifting" periods. The camp director had deliberately structured a program that combined planned activities with free periods, believing that the opportunities provided by the free-time periods were as important for the children as those planned for them. Whatever growth took place during the camp months, he felt, depended as much on the child's deployment of the drifting periods as on his success at the programmed activities. However, he and his staff could not fail to observe that homesickness was most acute during those free-time periods.

The camp had been running in very much the same way, with the   3
same sort of staff and the same population of middle- and upper-middle-
class children, for over twenty years. Why now, starting in the mid-
sixties, were the free-time periods making numbers of children sufficiently
uncomfortable to feel homesick?

Since the youngest children at the camp were aged nine, the first   4
television-bred children would have arrived in camp in the mid-sixties.
These were children who had far less experience of free time in their
lives than previous generations. When suddenly confronted with regular
doses of free time, they reacted with anxiety and homesickness.

For homesickness is always a cry against a surfeit of independence,   5
a cry to return to a more dependent situation in which the child need
not function as a separate self. It represents a longing to return to that
cozy family group of which the child was once an actual physical appen-
dage, and from which he must, someday, extricate himself emotionally
if he is to grow up successfully.

When a child's opportunities to experience free time are limited,   6
he is more likely to remain in a state of inner dependence. While his
life is completely filled with adult-devised programs on television, his
dependence will not be apparent, for he is spared the need to act independently. But when he is forced to confront unstructured time, as the
campers were, he will find himself resourceless. His dependence will be
exposed.

A New Gresham's Law of Child Activity

It is all very well to sing the apotheosis of free time for children and   7
exhort parents to turn off their television sets. It is the *reality* of free time
that makes it so difficult for parents to stick to their resolve to limit their
children's television consumption.

The situation modern parents face upon turning off the television   8
set frequently proves to be discouraging. After expecting their offspring
to suddenly metamorphose into Victorian children who pursue hobbies
and wholesome adventures, it is depressing to see them hanging around
doing nothing. In a variety of rude ways the children reject those fine,
creative activities with which they are supposed to fill the vacuum, challenging the parents to either amuse them themselves or relent and let
them watch television.

Is it partly or wholly because of their early television experiences   9
that children today are less capable of dealing with free time? Do they

have greater difficulties in combating boredom than children did in the pre-television era?

A sort of Gresham's Law of Child Activity[1] seems to operate here: 10 passive amusements will drive out active amusements. Since passive amusements require less effort than active ones, human nature dictates that, all other things being equal, doing something easier is preferable to doing something harder.

Observe a child playing with a simple wooden truck who is pre- 11 sented with a complicated mechanical locomotive. Whereas he had been obliged to amuse himself by pushing the symbolic vehicle around the floor, devising an imaginary route in and out and under furniture (providing his own sound effects), now he watches the new toy with fascination, amazed by the smoke spouting from the stack, charmed by the rhythmic toot-toot of the engine, delighted by its ability to propel itself backward and forward.

But after a while the child's pleasure in the new toy begins to dimin- 12 ish. The fascinating toy, after all, has a limited repertory of actions: it moves, blows smoke, and goes toot-toot. The child wrings a terminal bit of amusement from the toy by taking it apart to see how it works. And it is finished.

The child's play with the simple wooden truck does not lead to a 13 similar habituation because its range of activities is limited only by his own imagination.

But now the troublesome aspect of Gresham's Law of Child Activity 14 becomes apparent: for though the attractiveness of the mechanical plaything is brief, there is something so compelling about the passive pleasure it affords the child that the appeal of another toy requiring active participation is diminished. When the mechanical toy breaks down, the child is not likely to go back to his wooden truck. That sort of play seems a bit dull and tame, a bit *difficult* now. How silly it seems to push a truck around the house and pretend that it's real when a painted truck that moves on its own is so much *realer*!

Not only will the child choose this particular mechanical toy over 15 the more effort-demanding symbolic toy it was meant to replace, but in the future he will tend to choose a passive occupation over an active one. Passive play experiences inevitably make active play less appealing, and therefore less likely to occur spontaneously.

The television set is the one mechanical toy that does not lead 16

---

[1]An analogy to Gresham's law in economics, which says that money of lesser intrinsic worth will circulate more freely than money of greater intrinsic worth because the latter will be hoarded, as in the case of gold and paper money.

easily to habituation and boredom, though the child's involvement with it is as passive as with any other mechanical toy. It chugs and toots and produces movements, while the child watches with wonder. But its actions and sounds are far less repetitive than the toy train's, so the watching child can maintain wonder and fascination almost indefinitely.

But just as the ordinary mechanical toy changes a child's relationship to symbolic toys, so do the passive pleasures of television watching transform his relationship to his own time. The strong pleasures of that safe, effortless, ever-amusing experience make the pleasures afforded by active entertainments seem too much like *work*.

17

This is not to say that normal children will stay huddled before the television all day in preference to playing baseball or going to a game with their father or baking a chocolate cake or engaging in some other appealing activity. Certain activities will always confound Gresham's Law of Child Activity by dint of their special attractions: special trips and activities, particularly with parents, beloved sports and games, activities that dovetail with the child's special interests. But those activities have got to be *pretty good*. Otherwise there's always television.

18

"TV is a killer of time for my children," reports a mother. "I think they'd almost rather do *anything* than watch TV. If I find them something they like to do and do it with them, they're perfectly happy. They'd prefer that to watching TV. It's just so much less effort to watch TV than to have to think of something to do. So if they don't have something *special* to do, like getting a Halloween costume ready or even going to a friend's house, their first thought is to watch TV."

19

Another mother says: "What I find with my seven-year-old is that it's the *excuse* of television, the very *presence* of the television set when he doesn't know what to do with himself, or when he has a day when another child isn't coming over to play, that keeps him from looking to himself for something to do. Instead, he'll want to sit in front of the television set just to let something come out at him. That's been the hardest thing about television for me. If the television were not there, if it didn't exist, he wouldn't have that problem."

20

A mother of a five-year-old boy observes: "My child is not the kind of child who will make a scene or have a temper tantrum. He'll just mope around and be bored. And I find it very hard to take that. It bothers me to think that he can't do anything with his time. The presence of the television is the excuse. He knows in the back of his mind that when he really hits rock bottom he can go to that television set."

21

An educator and authority on early childhood with forty years of experience as teacher and principal has noted a change in children's behavior since the advent of television:

22

"Young children today have a sophistication that comes from all 23
their contacts with the outside world via television, but sophistication
and maturity are not the same thing.

"Children today are often *less* mature in their ability to endure small 24
frustrations, or to realize that something takes a longer time to do, that
it isn't *instant.* They're less tolerant of letting themselves become absorbed in something that seems a little hard at first, or in something that
is not immediately interesting. I spend a lot of time at school telling
children that they have to participate in activities and try things even if
something doesn't seem all that interesting right at the start."

Other teachers observe that young children today find it harder to 25
work by themselves than children did in the pre-television era, that there
is a constant need for adult supervision or entertainment.

Whether children are so used to immediate gratification via the 26
television set that their abilities to amuse themselves have atrophied, or
whether a simple lack of experience with free time has left them with
undeveloped abilities, it nevertheless seems clear that children today have
greater difficulty dealing with free time than children of past eras.

For when those favorite, special activities are not available (as often 27
is the case, which is what makes them so special), then children today
are not likely to enlarge their interests by trying something new. They
will not take the same desperate measures to combat boredom that children of the past had need to resort to: inventing games, playing make-
believe, reading, rereading, writing to pen pals, pursuing hobbies—activities that grow on a child and make him grow. With the presence of a
source of passive amusement in every home, readily available to the child
at the first sign of boredom, a child's time becomes more and more dominated by this single time-suspending activity.

• • • •

In the not too distant past children were expected to be passive 28
participants in their school experiences. The idea used to be that the
teacher had a body of material to teach that children were to soak in as
part of a process called "learning." In this one-way process any activity
on the children's part other than that specifically directed by the teacher
was considered inappropriate.

Much of the success of this educational system depended on the 29
personality of the teacher. If he was wise and kindly and graced with that
indefinable charisma characterizing gifted teachers and performers, then
children, like the audience at a good play, would try to conform to his
rigorous behavior requirements and thus manage to soak in the required
information. If the teacher possessed none of these gifts, very little learning occurred.

When school let out in the old days, children ran amok. Outside   30
the boundaries of the schoolroom they ran, played games, dreamed, plot-
ted, planned, yelled like Indians, skipped stones, started fires, made fences,
baked cookies, rolled in the mud—played freely. Once school was over,
children took charge of their own activity.

Within the last decade a change has been taking place in the class-   31
room. Children are being encouraged to initiate, to explore, to manipulate, and the one-way process of education has been shifting to an inter-
active situation between the teacher and the child. Children are no longer
bound by rigid codes of behavior, but are allowed to move freely, to talk
naturally to each other and to the teacher in the course of their school
activities. The success of this new style of education depends less on the
teacher's charismatic personality and more on his intelligence and intuition, as well as on the equipment available in the classroom for the children's manipulations and explorations. As in the past, some children learn
and some children resist. But in either case the children spend their school
day in a more natural state of activity.

The atmosphere at three o'clock is calmer today. When school lets   32
out, kids no longer behave like creatures let out of cages. In their child-
centered classrooms they seem to have released an adequate amount of
energy. But for many of these children activity is just about over for the
day. They head for home to settle down in front of their television sets.
They watch the screen and passively soak in images, words, and sounds
hour after hour, as if in a dream.

It might seem to even out. If school has become an active experi-   33
ence, then why shouldn't the child spend a few passive hours watching
television? The answer is that no matter how child-centered and "free" a
school situation may be, it is still organized and goal-centered. The child
hasn't the freedom of choice and freedom to control his own time that
he has after school, when he can play a game or not, throw stones or not,
daydream or not. Though the hours in a modern classroom may be more
active, more amusing, less punitive and repressive than in the old-fashioned classroom, the child is still being manipulated in certain directions,
by the teacher, by the equipment in the classroom, by the time organization of the day. If he spends his nonschool time watching television, *that*
time is also being effectively organized and programmed for him. When,
then, is he going to live his *real life*?

About the Essay

1. According to Winn, why is it so important that children learn to use free
time actively and independently? What might be the consequences if they
do not?

2. What is the Gresham's Law of Child Activity? How does it work? Why is television a particularly powerful instrument of this law? What other "mechanical toys" serve the purposes of Gresham's Law?

3. Limiting television viewing is an obvious solution to the problem Winn describes. Why do parents not adopt that solution? Supply an example or two from your own experience, if you can, to support or oppose Winn's conclusions.

4. How is the relation between in-school and after-school activities changing? How are these changes affecting children? Does your own experience agree with Winn's conclusions?

5. What is Winn's purpose in her essay—to inform, to persuade, or something else? Why do you think so? What audience is she writing for? How do you know?

6. Winn concludes her essay by asking when a child is going to live his or her "real life." What does she mean by this? What are the implications of the question and its answer?

Explorations

1. Marie Winn's essay is taken from her book *The Plug-In Drug.* Is television drug-like? In what way? If you have a television set in your room, how much of your free time do you spend watching it? What sort of satisfaction does it provide? Try not turning the set on for a week, and report what happens— how you react, what you do, and so forth. If you do not have a television set, what other means do you have of passively killing time? What do they do for you?

2. The elderly have more free time than most people. Usually they are retired from their jobs and have no children at home. How do the older people you know use their free time? What, according to current research in the social sciences, are the consequences for the elderly of having few activities and resources to fill their days?

BARBARA HOWES

Barbara Howes was born in New York City in 1914 and received her B.A. from Bennington College in 1937. Her first book of poetry, *The Undersea Farmer*, appeared in 1948, and since that time she has published five more collections, among them *The Blue Garden* (1972) and *A Private Signal* (1977).

Fishermen love to tell stories, especially about the big one that got away. "Out Fishing," from *Looking Up at Leaves* (1966), tells just such a story, but not to boast—rather, to convey something of the violent union that, for a brief time, bound Howes and her fish together.

Out Fishing

We went out, early one morning,
Over the loud marches of the sea,
In our walnut-shell boat,
Tip-tilting over that blue vacancy.

Combering, coming in,   5
The waves shellacked us, left us breathless, ill;
Hour on hour, out
Of this emptiness no fish rose, until

The great one struck that twine—
Wrapped flying-fish hard, turned and bolted   10
Off through the swelling sea
By a twist of his shoulder, with me tied fast; my rod

Held him, his hook held me,
In tug-of-war—sidesaddle on the ocean
I rode out the flaring waves,   15
Rode till the great fish sounded; by his submersion

He snapped the line, we lost
All contact; north, south, west, my adversary
Storms on through his world
Of water: I do not know him: he does not know me.   20

About the Poem

1. Like an essay, this poem can be divided into an introduction, a body, and a conclusion. Where do those divisions come? What other structural principle does Howes use?

2. Howes uses some rhyme in her poem. Where does she use it? Are any of the rhyming (or nearly rhyming) words linked in other ways than by sound? If so, what are the connections?

3. What kind of vessel would a "walnut-shell boat" be? What, in the context of this poem, do *marches* and *sounded* mean? Look for other unusual words, or words used in an unusual way, and explain what they mean.

4. What does Howes tell us about the fish? What does she leave out? What more about the fish can you infer from her account? What is the significance of the fish, and of the experience the speaker had with it?

Explorations

1. Many people like to watch wild animals, either outdoors or at the zoo; others like to hunt them with rod or gun. What motivates us to seek out wild creatures? To capture or kill them?

2. If you like to go fishing, you probably have stories to tell—whether about big ones that got away or bigger ones that came home for supper. Recount one such story, and compare it with the tales of other members of the class. What elements, if any, do the stories all have in common?

ROBERT FRANCIS

Not many poets write about sports, but Robert Francis is one who does. The poem presented here is about skiing; other poems celebrate basketball and baseball. Francis was born in 1901 in Upland, Pennsylvania, studied at Harvard, and since 1926 has made his home in Amherst, Massachusetts. The body of his poetic work has been published as *Collected Poems 1936–1976* (1976). He has also edited a book of Robert Frost's "conversations and indiscretions" called *A Time to Talk* (1972) and his own autobiography, *The Trouble with Francis* (1971). "Skier" is from *Come Out Into the Sun* (1965).

Skier

He swings down like the flourish of a pen
Signing a signature in white on white.

The silence of his skis reciprocates
The silence of the world around him.

Wind is his one competitor   5
In the cool winding and unwinding down.

On incandescent feet he falls
Unfalling, trailing white foam, white fire.

About the Poem

1. Explain the simile in the first stanza.

2. Why does the speaker describe the skier's feet as incandescent?

3. What does the speaker mean when he says that the skier "falls/Unfalling"? What other paradoxes do you find in the poem?

4. What is the relation of the speaker to the skier? Are the skier's emotions or appearance described in the poem?

Explorations

1. If you like downhill skiing, or some other sport, how would you convey the experience to someone who has never done it? When participating in the sport, as in skiing, tennis, hang-gliding, or fencing, are you ever aware

that you might be creating the kind of beauty that Francis describes? Choose a sport or recreation that you like and explore it in terms of questions like these.

2. Skiing, and other sports like automobile racing and sky-diving, can be dangerous and even deadly, yet many people find them exhilarating. Do you like to take part in such sports? How does your sense of the danger involved affect your enjoyment of a sport?

JOHN CHEEVER

Throughout his career John Cheever preferred to write about middle-class Americans, suburbanites living near the' great cities of the Northeast. Such people were his neighbors, and he presents them shrewdly, often satirically, but often also with sympathy. He himself was born in 1912 in the Boston suburb of Quincy and lived much of his life in Westchester County, just outside New York City. He studied at the Thayer Academy, but he was expelled from the school at seventeen. He had by then already found his vocation as a writer—indeed, his expulsion from Thayer provided the topic for a short story that was published that year in the *New Republic*—and so, instead of seeking to continue his education, he devoted himself to his craft. Cheever is a master of the short story; sixty-two of his own favorites were collected in 1978 as *The Stories of John Cheever*. He published four novels, including two that portray an Old Massachusetts family: *The Wapshot Chronicle* (1957) and *The Wapshot Scandal* (1964). He died in 1982. "The Golden Age" describes the Setons, an American family vacationing in a sixteenth-century castle in Italy. In spite of strong hopes and elaborate plans, Mr. Seton finds that he cannot really "get away from it all."

The Golden Age

Our ideas of castles, formed in childhood, are inflexible, and why try to reform them? Why point out that in a real castle thistles grow in the courtyard, and the threshold of the ruined throne room is guarded by a nest of green adders? Here are the keep, the drawbridge, the battlements and towers that we took with our lead soldiers when we were down with the chicken pox. The first castle was English, and this one was built by the King of Spain during an occupation of Tuscany, but the sense of imaginative supremacy—the heightened mystery of nobility—is the same. Nothing is inconsequential here. It is thrilling to drink Martinis on the battlements, it is thrilling to bathe in the fountain, it is even thrilling to climb down the stairs into the village after supper and buy a box of matches. The drawbridge is down, the double doors are open, and early one morning we see a family crossing the moat, carrying the paraphernalia of a picnic.

They are Americans. Nothing they can do will quite conceal the touching ridiculousness, the clumsiness of the traveler. The father is a tall young man, a little stooped, with curly hair and fine white teeth. His wife is pretty, and they have two sons. Both boys are armed with plastic machine guns, which were recently mailed to them by their grand-

561

parents. It is Sunday, bells are ringing, and who ever brought the bells into Italy? Not the *vaca*[1] in Florence but the harsh country bells that bing and bang over the olive groves and the cypress alleys in such an alien discord that they might have come in the carts of Attila the Hun. This urgent jangling sounds over the last of the antique fishing villages— really one of the last things of its kind. The stairs of the castle wind down into a place that is lovely and remote. There are no bus or train connections to this place, no *pensioni*[2] or hotels, no art schools, no tourists or souvenirs; there is not even a postcard for sale. The natives wear picturesque costumes, sing at their work, and haul up Greek vases in their fishing nets. It is one of the last places in the world where you can hear shepherds' pipes, where beautiful girls with loose bodices go unphotographed as they carry baskets of fish on their heads, and where serenades are sung after dark. Down the stairs come the Americans into the village.

The women in black, on their way to church, nod and wish them good morning. *"Il poeta,"* they say, to each other. Good morning to the poet, the wife of the poet, and the poet's sons. Their courtesy seems to embarrass the stranger. "Why do they call you a poet?" his older son asks, but Father doesn't reply. In the piazza there is some evidence of the fact that the village is not quite perfect. What has been kept out by its rough roads has come in on the air. The village boys roosting around the fountain have their straw hats canted over their foreheads, and matchsticks in their teeth, and when they walk they swagger as if they had been born in a saddle, although there is not a saddle horse in the place. The blue-green beam of the television set in the café has begun to transform them from sailors into cowboys, from fishermen into gangsters, from shepherds into juvenile delinquents and masters of ceremonies, their bladders awash with Coca-Cola, and this seems very sad to the Americans. *E colpa mia,*[3] thinks Seton, the so-called poet, as he leads his family through the piazza to the quays where their rowboat is moored.

The harbor is as round as a soup plate, the opening lies between two cliffs, and on the outermost, the seaward cliff, stands the castle, with its round towers, that the Setons have rented for the summer. Regarding the nearly perfect scene, Seton throws out his arms and exclaims, "Jesus, what a *spot!*" He raises an umbrella at the stern of the rowboat for his wife, and quarrels with the boys about where they will sit. "You sit where I tell you to sit, Tommy!" he shouts. "And I don't want to hear another

---

[1] Cowbells.

[2] Rented room in a boarding house or private home.

[3] It's my fault.

word *out* of you." The boys grumble, and there is a burst of machine-gun fire. They put out to sea in a loud but not an angry uproar. The bells are silent now, and they now hear the wheezing of the old church organ, its lungs rotted with sea fog. The inshore water is tepid and extraordinarily dirty, but out past the mole the water is so clear, so finely colored that it seems like a lighter element, and when Seton glimpses the shadow of their hull, drawn over the sand and rocks ten fathoms down, it seems that they float on blue air.

There are thongs for oarlocks, and Seton rows by standing in the waist and putting his weight against the oars. He thinks that he is quite adroit at this—even picturesque—but he would never, even at a great distance, be taken for an Italian. Indeed, there is an air of criminality, of shame about the poor man. The illusion of levitation, the charming tranquillity of the day—crenelated towers against the blueness of sky that seems to be a piece of our consciousness—are not enough to expunge his sense of guilt but only to hold it in suspense. He is a fraud, an impostor, an aesthetic criminal, and, sensing his feelings, his wife says gently, "Don't worry, darling, no one will know, and if they do know, they won't care." He is worried because he is not a poet, and because this perfect day is, in a sense, his day of reckoning. He is not a poet at all, and only hoped to be better understood in Italy if he introduced himself as one. It is a harmless imposture—really an aspiration. He is in Italy only because he wants to lead a more illustrious life, to at least broaden his powers of reflection. He has even thought of writing a poem—something about good and evil.

There are many other boats in the water, rounding the cliff. All the idlers and beach boys are out, bumping gunwales, pinching their girls, and loudly singing phrases of *canzone*.[4] They all salute *il poeta*. Around the cliff the shore is steep, terraced for vineyards, and packed with wild rosemary, and here the sea has beaten into the shore a chain of sandy coves. Seton heads for the largest of these, and his sons dive off the boat as he approaches the beach. He lands, and unloads the umbrella and the other gear.

Everyone speaks to them, everyone waves, and everyone in the village but the few churchgoers is on the beach. The Setons are the only strangers. The sand is a dark-golden color, and the sea shines like the curve of a rainbow—emerald, malachite, sapphire, and indigo. The striking absence of vulgarity and censoriousness in the scene moves Seton so that his chest seems to fill up with some fluid of appreciation. This is simplicity, he thinks, this is beauty, this is the raw grace of human nature!

---

[4]Songs.

He swims in the fresh and buoyant water, and when he has finished swimming he stretches out in the sun. But now he seems restless, as if he were troubled once more about the fact that he is not a poet. And if he is not a poet, then what is he?

He is a television writer. Lying on the sand of the cove, below the castle, is the form of a television writer. His crime is that he is the author of an odious situation comedy called "The Best Family." When it was revealed to him that in dealing with mediocrity he was dealing not with flesh and blood but with whole principalities and kingdoms of wrongdoing, he threw up his job and fled to Italy. But now "The Best Family" has been leased by Italian television—it is called "La Famiglia Tosta" over here—and the asininities he has written will ascend to the towers of Siena, will be heard in the ancient streets of Florence, and will drift out of the lobby of the Gritti Palace onto the Grand Canal. This Sunday is his début, and his sons, who are proud of him, have spread the word in the village. *Poeta!*

His sons have begun to skirmish with their machine guns. It is a harrowing reminder of his past. The taint of television is on their innocent shoulders. While the children of the village sing, dance, and gather wild flowers, his own sons advance from rock to rock, pretending to kill. It is a mistake, and a trivial one, but it flusters him, although he cannot bring himself to call them to him and try to explain that their adroitness at imitating the cries and the postures of the dying may deepen an international misunderstanding. They are misunderstood, and he can see the women wagging their heads at the thought of a country so barbarous that even little children are given guns as playthings. *Mamma mia!* One has seen it all in the movies. One would not dare walk on the streets of New York because of gang warfare, and once you step out of New York you are in a wilderness, full of naked savages.

The battle ends, they go swimming again, and Seton, who has brought along some spearfishing gear, for an hour explores a rocky ledge that sinks off the tip of the cove. He dives, and swims through a school of transparent fish, and farther down, where the water is dark and cold, he sees a large octopus eye him wickedly, gather up its members, and slip into a cave paved with white flowers. There at the edge of the cave he sees a Greek vase, an amphora. He dives for it, feels the rough clay on his fingers, and goes up for air. He dives again and again, and finally brings the vase triumphantly into the light. It is a plump form with a narrow neck and two small handles. The neck is looped with a scarf of darker clay. It is broken nearly in two. Such vases, and vases much finer, are often found along that coast, and if they are of no value they stand on the shelves of the café, the bakery, and the barbershop, but the value

8

9

10

of this one to Seton is inestimable—as if the fact that a television writer could reach into the Mediterranean and bring up a Greek vase were a hopeful cultural omen, proof of his own worthiness. He celebrates his find by drinking some wine, and then it is time to eat. He polishes off the bottle of wine with his lunch, and then, like everyone else on the beach, lies down in the shade and goes to sleep.

Just after Seton had waked and refreshed himself with a swim, he saw the strangers coming around the point in a boat—a Roman family, Seton guessed, who had come up to Tarlonia for the weekend. There were a father, a mother, and a son. Father fumbled clumsily with the oars. The pallor of all three of them, and their attitudes, set them apart from the people of the village. It was as if they had approached the cove from another continent. As they came nearer, the woman could be heard asking her husband to bring the boat up on the beach.   11

The father's replies were short-tempered and very loud. His patience was exhausted. It was not easy to row a boat, he said. It was not as easy as it looked. It was not easy to land in strange coves where, if a wind came up, the boat could be dashed to pieces and he would have to buy the owner a new boat. Boats were expensive. This tirade seemed to embarrass the mother and tire the son. They were both dressed for bathing and the father was not, and, in his white shirt, he seemed to fit that much less into the halcyon scene. The purple sea and the graceful swimmers only deepened his exasperation, and, red-faced with worry and discomfort, he called out excited and needless warnings to the swimmers, fired questions at the people on the shore (How deep was the water? How safe was the cove?), and finally brought his boat in safely. During this loud performance, the boy smiled slyly at his mother and she smiled slyly back. They had put up with this for so many years! Would it never end? Fuming and grunting, the father dropped anchor in two feet of water, and the mother and the son slipped over the gunwales and swam away.   12

Seton watched the father, who took a copy of *Il Tempo* out of his pocket and began to read, but the light was too bright. Then he felt anxiously in his pockets to see if the house keys and the car keys had taken wing and flown away. After this, he scraped a little bilge out of the boat with a can. Then he examined the worn oar throngs, looked at his watch, tested the anchor, looked at his watch again, and examined the sky, where there was a single cloud, for signs of a tempest. Finally, he sat down and lit a cigarette, and his worries, flying in from all points of the compass, could be seen to arrive on his brow. They had left the hot-water heater on in Rome! His apartment and all his valuables were   13 perhaps at that very moment being destroyed by the explosion. The left front tire on the car was thin and had probably gone flat, if the car itself had not been stolen by the brigands that you found in these remote fishing villages. The cloud in the west was small, to be sure, but it was the kind of cloud that heralded bad weather, and they would be tossed mercilessly by the high waves on their way back around the point, and would reach the *pensione* (where they had already paid for dinner) after all the best cutlets had been eaten and the wine had been drunk. For all he knew, the President might have been assassinated in his absence, the lira devalued. The government might have fallen. He suddenly got to his feet and began to roar at his wife and son. It was time to go, it was time to go. Night was falling. A storm was coming. They would be late for dinner. They would get caught in the heavy traffic near Fregene. They would miss all the good television programs. . . .

His wife and his son turned and swam back toward the boat, but they took their time. It was not late, they knew. Night was not falling, and there was no sign of a storm. They would not miss dinner at the *pensione.* They knew from experience that they would reach the *pensione* long before the tables were set, but they had no choice. They climbed aboard while the father weighed anchor, shouted warnings to the swimmers, and asked advice from the shore. He finally got the boat into the bay, and started around the point. 14

They had just disappeared when one of the beach boys climbed to the highest rock and waved a red shirt, shouting, "*Pesce cane! Pesce cane!*"[5] All the swimmers turned, howling with excitement and kicking up a heavy surf, and swam for the shore. Over the bar where they had been one could see the fin of a shark. The alarm had been given in time, and the shark seemed surly as he cruised through the malachite-colored water. The bathers lined the shore, pointing out the menace to one another, and a little child stood in the shallows shouting, "*Brutto! Brutto! Brutto!*"[6] Then everyone cheered as down the path came Mario, the best swimmer in the village, carrying a long spear gun. Mario worked as a stonemason and for some reason—perhaps his industriousness—had never fitted into the scene. His legs were too long or too far apart, his shoulders were too round or too square, his hair was too thin, and that luxuriance of the flesh that had been dealt out so generously to the other bucks had bypassed poor Mario. His nakedness seemed piteous and touching, like a stranger surprised in some intimacy. He was cheered and complimented as he came through the crowd, but he could not even muster a nervous 15

---

[5]Sand shark.

[6]Ugly! Ugly! Ugly!

smile and, setting his thin lips, he stroke into the water and swam to the bar. But the shark had gone, and so had most of the sunlight. The disenchantment of a dark beach moved the bathers to gather their things and start for home. No one waited for Mario; no one seemed to care. He stood in the dark water with his spear, ready to take on his shoulders the safety and welfare of the community, but they turned their backs on him and sang as they climbed the cliff.

To hell with "La Famiglia Tosta," Seton thought. To hell with it. 16 This was the loveliest hour of the whole day. All kinds of pleasure—food, drink, and love—lay ahead of him, and he seemed, by the gathering shadow, gently disengaged from his responsibility for television, from the charge of making sense of his life. Now everything lay in the dark and ample lap of night, and the discourse was suspended.

The stairs they took went past the ramparts they had rented, which 17 were festooned with flowers, and it was on this stretch from here up to the drawbridge and the portal, that the triumph of the King, the architect and the stonemasons was most imposing, for one was involved in the same breath with military impregnability, princeliness, and beauty. There was no point, no turning, no tower or battlement where these forces seemed separate. All the ramparts were finely corniced, and at every point where the enemy could have been expected to advance, the great, eight-ton crest of the Christian King of Spain proclaimed the blood, the faith, and the good taste of the defender. Over the main portal, the crest had fallen from its fine setting of sea gods with tridents and had crashed into the moat, but it had landed with its blazonings upward, and the quarterings, the cross, and the marble draperies could be seen in the water.

Then, on the wall, among the other legends, Seton saw the words, 18 "*Americani, go home, go home.*" The writing was faint; it might have been there since the war, or its faintness might be accounted for by the fact that it had been done in haste. Neither his wife nor his children saw it, and he stood aside while they crossed the drawbridge into the courtyard, and then he went back to rub the words out with his fingers. Oh, who could have written it? He felt mystified and desolate. He had been invited to come to this strange country. The invitations had been clamorous. Travel agencies, shipping firms, airlines, even the Italian government itself had besought him to give up his comfortable way of life and travel abroad. He had accepted the invitations, he had committed himself to their hospitality, and now he was told, by this ancient wall, that he was not wanted.

He had never before felt unwanted. It had never been said. He had 19 been wanted as a baby, wanted as a young man, wanted as a lover, a husband and father, wanted as a scriptwriter, a raconteur and companion. He had, if anything, been wanted excessively, and his only worry had been to spare himself, to spread his sought-after charms with prudence and discretion, so that they would do the most good. He had been wanted for golf, for tennis, for bridge, for charades, for cocktails, for boards of management—and yet this rude and ancient wall addressed him as if he were a pariah, a nameless beggar, an outcast. He was most deeply wounded.

Ice was stored in the castle dungeon, and Seton took his cocktail 20 shaker there, filled it, made some Martinis, and carried them up to the battlements of the highest tower, where his wife joined him to watch the light ring its changes. Darkness was filling in the honeycombed cliffs of Tarlonia, and while the hills along the shore bore only the most farfetched resemblance to the breasts of women, they calmed Seton's feelings and stirred in him the same deep tenderness.

"I might go down to the café after dinner," his wife said, "just to 21 see what sort of a job they did with the dubbing."

She did not understand the strength of his feelings about writing 22 for television; she had never understood. He said nothing. He supposed that, seen at a distance, on his battlement, he might have been taken for what he was not—a poet, a seasoned traveler, a friend of Elsa Maxwell's,[7] a prince or a duke—but this world lying all about him now did not really have the power to elevate and change him. It was only himself—the author of "The Best Family"—that he had carried at such inconvenience and expense across borders and over the sea. The flowery and massive setting had not changed the fact that he was sunburned, amorous, hungry, and stooped, and that the rock he sat on, set in its place by the great King of Spain, cut into his rump.

At dinner, Clementina, the cook, asked if she might go to the 23 village and see "La Famiglia Tosta." The boys, of course, were going with their mother. After dinner, Seton went back to his tower. The fishing fleet had begun to go out past the mole, their torches lighted. The moon rose and blazed so brightly on the sea that the water seemed to turn, to spin in the light. From the village he could hear the *bel canto*[8] of mothers calling their girls, and, from time to time, a squawk from the television set. It would all be over in twenty minutes, but the sense of wrongdoing *in absentia* made itself felt in his bones. Oh, how could one stop the advance of barbarism, vulgarity, and censoriousness? When he saw the lights his family carried coming up the stairs, he went down to

---

[7]A famous hostess.
[8]Beautiful singing.

the moat to meet them. They were not alone. Who was with them? Who were these figures ascending? The doctor? The Mayor? And a little girl carrying gladioli. It was a delegation—and a friendly one, he could tell by the lightness of their voices. They had come to praise him.

"It was so beautiful, so comical, so true to life!" the doctor said.   24

The little girl gave him the flowers, and the Mayor embraced him   25
lightly. "Oh, we thought, signore," he said, "that you were merely a poet."

About the Story

1. Why has Seton brought his family to Italy? What is he leaving behind? What does he hope to find in Italy? Does he find it? Explain.

2. Why does Seton pretend to be a poet? Is it likely that he might become a poet? Why do you think that?

3. Several objects in the story may have symbolic meaning—the castle that the Setons are renting, the amphora Seton brings up from the sea bottom, the shark that is spotted in the cove, and others as well. Which objects do you think are symbolic, and what do they symbolize? What does this use of symbolism add to the story?

4. The narrative focus of the story is on Seton, though he himself does not tell the story. What is the narrator's attitude toward him? What details in the story reveal that attitude?

5. What is the significance of the story's last sentence? How is it prepared for earlier in the story?

6. What is the theme of the story? Is there anything in Seton's attitude toward the townspeople that reciprocates their attitude toward him?

7. What does the story's title refer to? What does it mean?

Explorations

1. If you could travel abroad next summer, where would you go and what would you like to do there? Would you prefer to stay at home instead? In either case, why?

2. "A tourist," writes Emile Ganest, "is a fellow who drives thousands of miles so he can be photographed standing in front of his car." What is your definition of a tourist? What is the best kind of tourism—and the worst?

8 The State of the Union

The basic test of freedom is perhaps less in what we are free to do than in what we are free not to do.
ERIC HOFFER

Patriotism is your conviction that this country is superior to all other countries because you were born in it.
GEORGE BERNARD SHAW

America is a land of wonders, in which everything is in constant motion and every change seems an improvement. The idea of novelty is there indissolubly connected with the idea of amelioration. No natural boundary seems to be set to the efforts of man; and in his eyes what is not yet done is only what he has not yet attempted to do.
ALEXIS DE TOCQUEVILLE

A decent provision for the poor is the true test of civilization.
SAMUEL JOHNSON

What makes a nation great is not primarily its great men, but the stature of its innumerable mediocre ones.
JOSÉ ORTEGA Y GASSET

EVERY January the President gives us his assessment of the state of the Union. Every day, in our various ways, we make our own assessments. In part, these are based on self-interest. We want to live in reasonable comfort, to feel safe, to be happy, and we want our society to make all of this possible; if it does not, we are likely to conclude that the state of the Union is unsatisfactory and to demand changes. Yet Americans are also an idealistic people, with ethical standards of fairness and justice written into our history even before we became a nation, and we expect our society to embody these ethical ideals. When it does not, we again find that the state of the Union needs to be improved.

Individuals may and do disagree over national interests and even over what is fair and just. One person may argue that no rich nation that is just should have poor people within its borders; another, that

573

it is unjust to tax the successful in order to support the unsuccessful. Principles may be hard to reconcile with self-interest. We all believe in equality of opportunity—but how many of us are so unselfish as to surrender our own advantages in order to help the disadvantaged? And even when we agree in principle on a particular objective, we may disagree on the exact means to its achievement. Everyone wants to prevent nuclear war, but some argue for strengthening national defenses and others for complete disarmament. These and many other issues are not only difficult to deal with but often present real dilemmas—none of the possible solutions are wholly satisfactory, and perhaps none of them will even work. Yet few problems solve themselves, and so we continue striving to reach the best decisions and enact the most promising policies.

The selections that follow span two centuries and present many issues and viewpoints. Some are great statements of enduring principles and ideals, while others address major issues facing the country today. All invite us to ponder the state of the Union as it is now and as we wish it to be in the future.

THOMAS JEFFERSON

In June 1776 the Continental Congress chose a committee of five to draft a justification for revolution, with Benjamin Franklin, John Adams, and Thomas Jefferson among its members. The committee in turn asked Jefferson to write a first draft. Born in 1743 in Albemarle County, Virginia, Jefferson was the youngest delegate to the Congress. He was, in time, to become a governor, secretary of state, and President before he died on July 4, 1826, but in 1776 he was known only as a talented lawyer out of William and Mary College with a gift for words. His draft was lightly revised by Adams and Franklin and amended during the Congress's debate, but it remains essentially the work not of a committee but of one man with the political insight, the vision, and the rhetorical skill to speak for his people.

The Declaration of Independence

When in the course of human events, it becomes necessary for one people to dissolve the political bands which have connected them with another, and to assume among the Powers of the earth, the separate and equal station to which the Laws of Nature and of Nature's God entitle them, a decent respect to the opinions of mankind requires that they should declare the causes which impel them to the separation.   1

We hold these truths to be self-evident, that all men are created equal, that they are endowed by their Creator with certain unalienable Rights, that among these are Life, Liberty and the pursuit of Happiness. That to secure these rights, Governments are instituted among Men deriving their just powers from the consent of the governed. That whenever any Form of Government becomes destructive of these ends, it is the Right of the People to alter or to abolish it, and to institute new Government, laying its foundation on such principles and organizing its powers in such form, as to them shall seem most likely to effect their Safety and Happiness. Prudence, indeed, will dictate that Governments long established should not be changed for light and transient causes; and accordingly all experience hath shown, that mankind are more disposed to suffer, while evils are sufferable, than to right themselves by abolishing the forms to which they are accustomed. But when a long train of abuses and usurpations pursuing invariably the same Object evinces a design to reduce them under absolute Despotism, it is their right, it is their duty, to throw off such government, and to provide new Guards for their future security. Such has been the patient sufferance of these Colonies; and such is now the necessity which constrains them to alter   2 their former Systems of Government. The history of the present King of Great Britain is a history of repeated injuries and usurpations, all having in direct object the establishment of an absolute Tyranny over these States. To prove this, let Facts be submitted to a candid world.

He has refused his Assent to laws, the most wholesome and nec- 3 essary for the public good.

He has forbidden his Governors to pass Laws of immediate and 4 pressing importance, unless suspended in their operation till his Assent should be obtained; and when so suspended, he has utterly neglected to attend to them.

He has refused to pass other Laws for the accommodation of large 5 districts of people, unless those people would relinquish the right of Representation in the Legislature, a right inestimable to them and for- midable to tyrants only.

He has called together legislative bodies at places unusual, uncom- 6 fortable, and distant from the depository of their Public Records, for the sole purpose of fatiguing them into compliance with his measures.

He has dissolved Representative Houses repeatedly, for opposing 7 with manly firmness his invasions on the rights of the people.

He has refused for a long time, after such dissolutions, to cause 8 others to be elected; whereby the Legislative Powers, incapable of An- nihilation, have returned to the People at large for their exercise; the State remaining in the mean time exposed to all the dangers of invasion from without, and convulsions within.

He has endeavoured to prevent the population of these States; for 9 that purpose obstructing the Laws of Naturalization of Foreigners; refusing to pass others to encourage their migration hither, and raising the con- ditions of new Appropriations of Lands.

He has obstructed the Administration of Justice, by refusing his 10 Assent to Laws for establishing Judiciary Powers.

He has made Judges dependent on his Will alone, for the tenure 11 of their offices, and the amount and payment of their salaries.

He has erected a multitude of New Offices, and sent hither swarms 12 of Officers to harass our People, and eat out their substance.

He has kept among us, in time of peace, Standing Armies without 13 the Consent of our Legislature.

He has affected to render the Military independent of and superior 14 to the Civil Power.

He has combined with others to subject us to jurisdictions foreign 15 to our constitution, and unacknowledged by our laws; giving his Assent to their acts of pretended Legislation:

For quartering large bodies of armed troops among us: 16

For protecting them, by a mock Trial, from Punishment for any   17
Murders which they should commit on the Inhabitants of these States:

For cutting off our Trade with all parts of the world: 18

For imposing Taxes on us without our Consent: 19

For depriving us in many cases, of the benefits of Trial by Jury: 20

For transporting us beyond Seas to be tried for pretended offenses: 21

For abolishing the free System of English Laws in a Neighbouring   22
Province, establishing therein an Arbitrary government, and enlarging
its boundaries so as to render it at once an example and fit instrument
for introducing the same absolute rule into these Colonies:

For taking away our Charters, abolishing our most valuable Laws,   23
and altering fundamentally the Forms of our Governments:

For suspending our own Legislatures, and declaring themselves in-   24
vested with Power to legislate for us in all cases whatsoever.

He has abdicated Government here, by declaring us out of his   25
Protection and waging War against us.

He has plundered our seas, ravaged our Coasts, burnt our towns   26
and destroyed the Lives of our people.

He is at this time transporting large Armies of foreign Mercenaries   27
to compleat works of death, desolation and tyranny, already begun with
circumstances of Cruelty & perfidy scarcely paralleled in the most barbarous ages, and totally unworthy the Head of a civilized nation.

He has constrained our fellow Citizens taken Captive on the high   28
Seas to bear Arms against their Country, to become the executioners of
their friends and Brethren, or to fall themselves by their Hands.

He has excited domestic insurrections amongst us, and has endeav-   29
oured to bring on the inhabitants of our frontiers, the merciless Indian
Savages, whose known rule of warfare, is an undistinguished destruction
of all ages, sexes and conditions.

In every stage of these Oppressions We Have Petitioned for Redress   30
in the most humble terms: Our repeated petitions have been answered
only by repeated injury. A Prince, whose character is thus marked by
every act which may define a Tyrant, is unfit to be the ruler of a free
People.

Nor have We been wanting in attention to our British brethren.   31
We have warned them from time to time of attempts by their legislature
to extend an unwarrantable jurisdiction over us. We have reminded them
of the circumstances of our emigration and settlement here. We have
appealed to their native justice and magnanimity and we have conjured
them by the ties of our common kindred to disavow these usurpations,

which would inevitably interrupt our connections and correspondence. They too have been deaf to the voice of justice and of consanguinity. We must, therefore, acquiesce in the necessity, which denounces our Separation, and hold them, as we hold the rest of mankind, Enemies in War, in Peace Friends.

We, therefore, the Representatives of the United States of America, in General Congress, Assembled, appealing to the Supreme Judge of the world for the rectitude of our intentions, do, in the Name, and by Authority of the good People of these Colonies, solemnly publish and declare, That these United Colonies are, and of Right ought to be Free and Independent States; that they are Absolved from all Allegiance to the British Crown, and that all political connection between them and the State of Great Britain, is and ought to be totally dissolved; and that as Free and Independent States, they have full power to levy War, conclude Peace, contract Alliances, establish Commerce, and to do all other Acts and Things which Independent States may of right do. And for the support of this Declaration, with a firm reliance on the protection of Divine Providence, we mutually pledge to each other our lives, our Fortunes and our sacred Honor.

About the Selection

1. What, according to the Declaration of Independence, is the purpose of government? Are there other legitimate purposes that governments serve? If so, what are they?

2. What is the chief argument offered by the Declaration for "abolishing" English rule over the American colonies? How is that argument supported?

3. What argument does the Declaration make for overthrowing any unacceptable government? What assumptions underlie this argument? Where does sovereignty lie, according to the Declaration?

4. According to the Declaration, how did the colonists try to persuade the English king to rule more justly?

5. Is the language of the Declaration of Independence coolly reasonable or emotional, or does it change from one to the other? Give examples to support your answer.

Explorations

1. What purposes does a document like the Declaration of Independence serve? Who is meant to read it, and how are the readers expected to respond?

2. The adoption of the Declaration of Independence was, among other things,

a matter of practical politics. Using library sources, research the deliberations of the Continental Congress and explain how and why the final version of the Declaration differs from Jefferson's first draft.

3. To some people the Declaration of Independence still accurately reflects America's political philosophy and way of life; to others it does not. What is your own position? Discuss your view of the Declaration's contemporary relevance or lack of it.

ABRAHAM LINCOLN

The Battle of Gettysburg was fought in the rolling countryside of southeast Pennsylvania during the first three days of July 1863. We now know that it was the turning point of the American Civil War; that the Confederate Army, continually victorious until shortly before Gettysburg, would thereafter fight on within an ever-shrinking perimeter and finally surrender in April 1865; that there would be one nation, not two, between the Canadian and Mexican borders. But to President Abraham Lincoln at the time, Gettysburg was a lost military opportunity, for the Confederate Army, having lost nearly a third of its men, had escaped. The war went on bloodily and indecisively that summer and fall, and the bodies of the Gettysburg dead were left unburied where they fell. At last a national cemetery was constructed at the battlefield, and on November 19 Lincoln traveled there for the dedication.

His address is the best-known speech ever given by an American. Millions have memorized it, and countless Americans have quoted it or imitated its rhetoric for their own various purposes. But it is illuminating to look again at the familiar words with their original context in mind, to see how they served Lincoln's purpose, his sense of the occasion, and his larger sense of the nation's history and destiny.

The Gettysburg Address

Four score and seven years ago our fathers brought forth on this continent, a new nation, conceived in Liberty, and dedicated to the proposition that all men are created equal. 1

Now we are engaged in a great civil war, testing whether that nation, or any nation so conceived and so dedicated, can long endure. We are met on a great battle-field of that war. We have come to dedicate a portion of that field, as a final resting place for those who here gave their lives that that nation might live. It is altogether fitting and proper that we should do this. 2

But, in a larger sense, we can not dedicate—we can not consecrate—we can not hallow—this ground. The brave men, living and dead, who struggled here, have consecrated it, far above our poor power to add or detract. The world will little note, nor long remember what we say here, but it can never forget what they did here. It is for us the living, rather, to be dedicated here to the unfinished work which they who fought here have thus far so nobly advanced. It is rather for us to be here dedicated to the great task remaining before us—that from these honored dead we take increased devotion to that cause for which they gave the 3

580

last full measure of devotion—that we here highly resolve that these dead shall not have died in vain—that this nation, under God, shall have a new birth of freedom—and that government of the people, by the people, for the people, shall not perish from the earth.

About the Selection

1. To what issue of the Civil War is Lincoln referring in his two opening sentences? What specifically did the founding fathers do eighty-seven years before the Gettysburg Address? What purpose is served by linking the Civil War with the acts and intentions of the founders of the United States? Is the linkage justified?

2. A modern paraphrase of the opening sentence might read like this: "Eighty-seven years ago our ancestors created a new North American nation based on liberty and the idea that all men are created equal." How do the two versions differ in their effect?

3. In an early draft of the Address, the last sentence in paragraph 2 reads, "This we may, in all propriety, do." How does the earlier version differ from what Lincoln finally spoke? Why do you suppose Lincoln made the change?

4. At the opening of paragraph 3 Lincoln uses the words *dedicate, consecrate,* and *hallow.* What do these words mean in this context? Why do you think Lincoln placed them in this particular order?

5. What does Lincoln *not* say about the Battle of Gettysburg and the soldiers who fought and died there? What does his speech gain by this omission?

Explorations

1. Lincoln said at Gettysburg, "The world will little note, nor long remember what we say here, but it can never forget what they did here." He was wrong, of course; not many of us would remember the Battle of Gettysburg if not for Lincoln's commemoration of it. What about the Gettysburg Address makes it live on in the collective American memory? What relevance does it have for us in the 1980s?

2. Presidents often seek to influence national sentiment in their speeches. Woodrow Wilson, leading the nation to war, proclaimed in 1917, "The world must be made safe for democracy"; Franklin D. Roosevelt, at his first inauguration in the depths of the Great Depression, declared that "The only thing we have to fear is fear itself." One of the most famous of such statements is the close of Lincoln's Gettysburg Address: "That government of the people, by the people, for the people shall not perish from the earth." What makes statements like these memorable? Are they merely clever slogans or do they have greater significance? If the latter, what is that significance? If they are just slogans, how do you account for their staying power? Why do they still move us?

3. Imagine that you have been elected President of the United States and that your inauguration is a week away. Write an inaugural address in which you identify the chief problems and issues of the present and set forth your program for dealing with them. Consider first what approach to take—for example, you might write an inspirational address to the nation, or you may instead choose to describe in everyday language the problems that confront the nation and the actions you believe will solve those problems.

CHIEF SEATTLE

Born around 1786, Seattle was chief of the Suquamish Indians and leader of other tribes in the area around Puget Sound. He was an early and loyal friend of the white settlers who in the early nineteenth century were coming to the region in increasing numbers. In 1853, during the administration of President Franklin Pierce, the region was organized as the Washington Territory, with Isaac Stevens as governor. The next year Stevens, on behalf of the federal government, offered to buy two million acres of land from Seattle's people, and the Indians agreed. In later years, the settlers named their growing city after him, though Seattle consented to this reluctantly, believing that after death his spirit would be disturbed every time his name was mentioned. He died in 1866.

The following is Seattle's reply to Governor Stevens's offer. Though the great Indian relocations and massacres that were to begin in the 1860s were still in the future, and Indians were still the chief inhabitants of nearly half of the continent, Seattle clearly understood what was to come. His words are a prophecy—and a warning.

My People

Yonder sky that has wept tears upon my people for centuries untold,   1
and which to us appears changeless and eternal, may change. Today is fair. Tomorrow may be overcast with clouds. My words are like the stars that never change. Whatever Seattle says the great chief at Washington can rely upon with as much certainty as he can upon the return of the sun or the seasons. The White Chief says that Big Chief at Washington sends us greetings of friendship and goodwill. That is kind of him for we know he has little need of our friendship in return. His people are many. They are like the grass that covers vast prairies. My people are few. They resemble the scattering trees of a storm-swept plain. The great, and—I presume—good, White Chief sends us word that he wishes to buy our lands but is willing to allow us enough to live comfortably. This indeed appears just, even generous, for the Red Man no longer has rights that he need respect, and the offer may be wise also, as we are no longer in need of an extensive country. . . . I will not dwell on, nor mourn over, our untimely decay, nor reproach our paleface brothers with hastening it, as we too may have been somewhat to blame.

Youth is impulsive. When our young men grow angry at some real   2
or imaginary wrong, and disfigure their faces with black paint, it denotes that their hearts are black, and then they are often cruel and relentless,

and our old men and old women are unable to restrain them. Thus it has ever been. Thus it was when the white men first began to push our forefathers further westward. But let us hope that the hostilities between us may never return. We would have everything to lose and nothing to gain. Revenge by young men is considered gain, even at the cost of their own lives, but old men who stay at home in times of war, and mothers who have sons to lose, know better.

Our good father at Washington—for I presume he is now our father   3
as well as yours, since King George has moved his boundaries further north—our great good father, I say, sends us word that if we do as he desires he will protect us. His brave warriors will be to us a bristling wall of strength, and his wonderful ships of war will fill our harbors so that our ancient enemies far to the northward—the Hydas and Tsimpsians—will cease to frighten our women, children, and old men. Then in reality will he be our father and we his children. But can that ever be? Your God is not our God! Your God loves your people and hates mine. He folds his strong and protecting arms lovingly about the paleface and leads him by the hand as a father leads his infant son—but He has forsaken His red children—if they really are his. Our God, the Great Spirit, seems also to have forsaken us. Your God makes your people wax strong every day. Soon they will fill the land. Our people are ebbing away like a rapidly receding tide that will never return. The white man's God cannot love our people or He would protect them. They seem to be orphans who can look nowhere for help. How then can we be brothers? How can your God become our God and renew our prosperity and awaken in us dreams of returning greatness? If we have a common heavenly father He must be partial—for He came to his paleface children. We never saw Him. He gave you laws but He had no word for His red children whose teeming multitudes once filled this vast continent as stars fill the firmament. No; we are two distinct races with separate origins and separate destinies. There is little in common between us.

To us the ashes of our ancestors are sacred and their resting place   4
is hallowed ground. You wander far from the graves of your ancestors and seemingly without regret. Your religion was written upon tables of stone by the iron finger of your God so that you could not forget. The Red Man could never comprehend nor remember it. Our religion is the traditions of our ancestors—the dreams of our old men, given them in solemn hours of night by the Great Spirit; and the visions of our sachems;[1] and it is written in the hearts of our people.

---

[1]Indian chiefs.

Your dead cease to love you and the land of their nativity as soon   5
as they pass the portals of the tomb and wander way beyond the stars.
They are soon forgotten and never return. Our dead never forget the
beautiful world that gave them being.

Day and night cannot dwell together. The Red man has ever fled   6
the approach of the White Man, as the morning mist flees before the
morning sun. However, your proposition seems fair and I think that my
people will accept it and will retire to the reservation you offer them.
Then we will dwell apart in peace, for the words of the Great White
Chief seem to be the words of nature speaking to my people out of dense
darkness.

It matters little where we pass the remnant of our days. They will   7
not be many. A few more moons; a few more winters—and not one of
the descendants of the mighty hosts that once moved over this broad
land or lived in happy homes, protected by the Great Spirit, will remain
to mourn over the graves of a people once more powerful and hopeful
than yours. But why should I mourn at the untimely fate of my people?
Tribe follows tribe, and nation follows nation, like the waves of the sea.
It is the order of nature, and regret is useless. Your time of decay may
be distant, but it will surely come, for even the White Man whose God
walked and talked with him as friend with friend, cannot be exempt from
the common destiny. We may be brothers after all. We will see.

We will ponder your proposition, and when we decide we will let   8
you know. But should we accept it, I here and now make this condition
that we will not be denied the privilege without molestation of visiting
at any time the tombs of our ancestors, friends and children. Every part
of this soil is sacred in the estimation of my people. Every hillside, every
valley, every plain and grove, has been hallowed by some sad or happy
event in days long vanished. . . . The very dust upon which you now
stand responds more lovingly to their footsteps than to yours, because it
is rich with the blood of our ancestors and our bare feet are conscious of
the sympathetic touch. . . . Even the little children who lived here and
rejoiced here for a brief season will love these somber solitudes and at
eventide they greet shadowy returning spirits. And when the last Red
Man shall have perished, and the memory of my tribe shall have become
a myth among the White Men, these shores will swarm with the invisible
dead of my tribe, and when your children's children think themselves
alone in the field, the store, the shop, upon the highway, or in the
silence of the pathless woods, they will not be alone. . . . At night when
the streets of your cities and villages are silent and you think them
deserted, they will throng with the returning hosts that once filled and
still love this beautiful land. The White Man will never be alone.

Let him be just and deal kindly with my people, for the dead are   9
not powerless. Dead, did I say? There is not death, only a change of
worlds.

About the Selection

1. What are Chief Seattle's purposes in his speech? Whom is it addressed to?

2. What condition does Seattle demand before yielding the land to the U.S.
government? How does he prepare for this condition in his speech?

3. What is Seattle's attitude toward the white men, their president, and
their god? How do you know? Seattle refers to the president as the Indians'
"father." What does this signify? Why might Seattle presume that the White
Chief is good as well as great?

4. What, for you, is the most powerful part of the speech? What gives it its
power? What is the most surprising part, and why?

5. What differences between red men and white men does Seattle describe?
Why do you think he chooses to mention those particular differences? What
other differences might he have included, and why do you think he didn't?

6. Chief Seattle's address is rich in figures of speech, beginning with "My
words are like the stars that never change." What areas of knowledge and
experience does he continually draw on for his analogies and metaphors?
Give examples.

Explorations

1. Throughout his speech, Chief Seattle quietly registers a complaint that
was to become a battle cry in later years. This sentiment can be summed up
by his pessimistic view, "not one of the descendants of the mighty hosts that
once moved over this broad land or lived in happy homes, protected by the
Great Spirit, will remain to mourn over the graves of a people once more
powerful and hopeful than yours." What in the history of the American Indians may have led Chief Seattle to make this prediction, and what later
events seemed almost to fulfill it? Use library resources to support your answer.

2. Despite his obvious regret, Chief Seattle worked out an accommodation
with the more powerful forces of the United States. If you were in his position, would you have done the same or would you have led your people to
fight for its land and independence? Explain your choice.

MARTIN LUTHER KING, JR.

Martin Luther King, Jr., was born in 1929 in Atlanta, Georgia. The son of a Baptist minister, he was himself ordained at the age of eighteen and went on to study at Morehouse College, Crozer Theological Seminary, Boston University, and Chicago Theological Seminary. He first came to prominence in 1955, in Montgomery, Alabama, when he led a successful boycott against the city's segregated bus system. As the first president of the Southern Christian Leadership Conference, King promoted a policy of massive but nonviolent resistance to racial injustice, and in 1964 he was awarded the Nobel Peace Prize. He was assassinated in Memphis, Tennessee, in 1968.

"I Have a Dream" was spoken by King in 1963 from the steps of the Lincoln Memorial to more than 200,000 people who had come to Washington, D.C., to demonstrate for civil rights. In this mighty sermon, referring both to the great documents and speeches of our past and to the Bible, to patriotic song and to Negro spiritual, King presented his indictment of the present and his vision of the future.

I Have a Dream

I am happy to join with you today in what will go down in history as the greatest demonstration for freedom in the history of our nation. 1

Five score years ago, a great American, in whose symbolic shadow we stand today, signed the Emancipation Proclamation. This momentous decree came as a great beacon light of hope to millions of Negro slaves who had been seared in the flames of withering injustice. It came as a joyous daybreak to end the long night of their captivity. But one hundred years later, the Negro still is not free. One hundred years later, the life of the Negro is still sadly crippled by the manacles of segregation and the chains of discrimination. One hundred years later, the Negro lives on a lonely island of poverty in the midst of a vast ocean of material prosperity. One hundred years later, the Negro is still anguished in the corners of American society and finds himself in exile in his own land. And so we have come here today to dramatize a shameful condition. 2

In a sense we have come to our nation's capital to cash a check. When the architects of our republic wrote the magnificent words of the Constitution and the Declaration of Independence, they were signing a promissory note to which every American was to fall heir. This note was the promise that all men—yes, Black men as well as white men—would be guaranteed the inalienable rights of life, liberty, and the pursuit of happiness. 3

It is obvious today that America has defaulted on this promissory 4
note insofar as her citizens of color are concerned. Instead of honoring
this sacred obligation, America has given the Negro people a bad check,
a check which has come back marked "insufficient funds." But we refuse
to believe that the bank of justice is bankrupt. We refuse to believe that
there are insufficient funds in the great vaults of opportunity of this
nation; and so we have come to cash this check, a check that will give
us upon demand the riches of freedom and the security of justice.

We have also come to this hallowed spot to remind America of the 5
fierce urgency of *now*. This is no time to engage in the luxury of cooling
off or to take the tranquilizing drug of gradualism. *Now* is the time to
make real the promises of democracy. *Now* is the time to rise from the
dark and desolate valley of segregation to the sunlit path of racial justice.
Now is the time to lift our nation from the quicksands of racial injustice
to the solid rock of brotherhood. *Now* is the time to make justice a reality
for all of God's children.

It would be fatal for the nation to overlook the urgency of the 6
moment. This sweltering summer of the Negro's legitimate discontent
will not pass until there is an invigorating autumn of freedom and equality. Nineteen Sixty-three is not an end, but a beginning. And those who
hope that the Negro needed to blow off steam and will now be content
will have a rude awakening if the nation returns to business as usual.
There will be neither rest nor tranquility in America until the Negro is
granted his citizenship rights. The whirlwinds of revolt will continue to
shake the foundations of our nation until the bright day of justice emerges.

But there is something that I must say to my people who stand on 7
the warm threshold which leads into the palace of justice. In the process
of gaining our rightful place, we must not be guilty of wrongful deeds.
Let us not seek to satisfy our thirst for freedom by drinking from the cup
of bitterness and hatred. We must forever conduct our struggle on the
high plane of dignity and discipline. We must not allow our creative
protest to degenerate into physical violence. Again and again we must
rise to the majestic heights of meeting physical force with soul force.
And the marvelous new militancy which has engulfed the Negro community must not lead us to a distrust of all white people; for many of our
white brothers, as evidenced by their presence here today, have come to
realize that their destiny is tied up with our destiny, and they have come
to realize that their freedom is inextricably bound to our freedom.

We cannot walk alone. And as we walk we must make the pledge 8
that we shall always march ahead. We cannot turn back. There are
those who are asking the devotees of civil rights, "When will you be
satisfied?" We can never be satisfied as long as the Negro is the victim

of the unspeakable horrors of police brutality. We can never be satisfied as long as our bodies, heavy with the fatigue of travel, cannot gain lodging in the motels of the highways and the hotels of the cities. We cannot be satisfied as long as the Negro's basic mobility is from a smaller ghetto to a larger one. We can never be satisfied as long as our children are stripped of their selfhood and robbed of their dignity by signs stating "For Whites Only." We cannot be satisfied as long as the Negro in Mississippi cannot vote and a Negro in New York believes he has nothing for which to vote. No, no, we are not satisfied, and we will not be satisfied until justice rolls down like waters and righteousness like a mighty stream.

I am not unmindful that some of you have come here out of great trials and tribulations. Some of you have come fresh from narrow jail cells. Some of you have come from areas where your quest for freedom left you battered by the storms of persecution and staggered by the winds of police brutality. You have been the veterans of creative suffering. Continue to work with the faith that unearned suffering is redemptive.

Go back to Mississippi, and go back to Alabama. Go back to South Carolina. Go back to Georgia. Go back to Louisiana. Go back to the slums and ghettos of our Northern cities, knowing that somehow this situation can and will be changed. Let us not wallow in the valley of despair.

I say to you today, my friends, even though we face the difficulties of today and tomorrow, I still have a dream. It is a dream deeply rooted in the American dream. I have a dream that one day this nation will rise up and live out the true meaning of its creed: "We hold these truths to be self-evident, that all men are created equal." I have a dream that one day, on the red hills of Georgia, sons of former slaves and the sons of former slave owners will be able to sit down together at the table of brotherhood. I have a dream that one day even the state of Mississippi, a state sweltering with the heat of injustice, sweltering with the heat of oppression, will be transformed into an oasis of freedom and justice. I have a dream that my four little children will one day live in a nation where they will not be judged by the color of their skin, but by the content of their character.

I have a dream today. I have a dream that one day down in Alabama—with its vicious racists, with its governor's lips dripping with the words of interposition and nullification—one day right there in Alabama, little Black boys and Black girls will be able to join hands with little white boys and white girls as sisters and brothers.

I have a dream today. I have a dream that one day every valley shall be exalted and every hill and mountain shall be made low, the

9

10

11

12

13

rough places will be made plain and the crooked places will be made straight, and the glory of the Lord shall be revealed, and all flesh shall see it together.

This is our hope. This is the faith that I go back to the South with.   14
And with this faith we will be able to hew out of the mountain of despair a stone of hope. With this faith we will be able to transform the jangling discords of our nation into a beautiful symphony of brotherhood. With this faith we will be able to work together, to play together, to struggle together, to go to jail together, to stand up for freedom together, knowing that we will be free one day.

And this will be the day—this will be the day when all of God's   15
children will be able to sing with new meaning:

> My country, 'tis of thee,
> Sweet land of liberty,
>   Of thee I sing;
> Land where my fathers died,
> Land of the Pilgrims' pride,
> From every mountainside
>   Let freedom ring.

And if America is to be a great nation, this must become true.

And so let freedom ring from the prodigious hilltops of New Hamp-   16
shire. Let freedom ring from the mighty mountains of New York. Let freedom ring from the heightening Alleghenies of Pennsylvania. Let freedom ring from the snow-capped Rockies of Colorado. Let freedom ring from the curvaceous slopes of California.

But not only that. Let freedom ring from Stone Mountain of Geor-   17
gia. Let freedom ring from Lookout Mountain of Tennessee. Let freedom ring from every hill and molehill of Mississippi. "From every mountainside let freedom ring."

And when this happens—when we allow freedom to ring, when   18
we let it ring from every village and every hamlet, from every state and every city—we will be able to speed up that day when all of God's children, Black men and white men, Jews and Gentiles, Protestants and Catholics, will be able to join hands and sing in the words of the old Negro spiritual: "Free at last! Free at last! Thank God Almighty. We are free at last!"

About the Selection

1. To whom does King address his speech? In essence, what does he say to them?

2. King's speech can be divided into several sections, each serving a specific purpose. Where are those sections and what is the purpose of each?

3. What do you find in King's speech that reflects the particular time and place where it was given? Look beyond his specific reference to the occasion at the beginning of paragraph 2.

4. How appropriate and effective is King's analogy of the bad check? Why do you think so?

5. In his speech, King's range of reference is wide and varied. Which allusions do you recognize? What effect would you expect these references to have on King's audience? How did they affect you?

6. King's speech, like Lincoln's Gettysburg Address, has outlasted the occasion for which it was written. In your opinion, why is this so? What qualities of language and thought are the source of its power? What phrase or phrases do you consider most memorable? Why?

Explorations

1. What is your attitude toward this nation and its varied people? Do you see America as a nation that perpetuates injustice or as a nation struggling to realize an ideal of justice? Explain your view.

2. In the years since King's speech, how much of his dream for America has come true? What still needs to be done? What are the prospects for the future?

3. King says that his dream is "deeply rooted in the American dream." What is the American dream? Can that dream be realized? If so, how? If not, why does it persist?

BETTY FRIEDAN

Betty Friedan, a leader of the contemporary women's movement, was born in Peoria, Illinois, in 1921 and graduated from Smith College in 1942. As a housewife and a writer for women's magazines on "housewifely" subjects, she began in the 1950s to question the traditional roles imposed on American women, and after five years of thought and research she published *The Feminine Mystique* (1963). The book was an early catalyst of feminist thought and action, and Friedan followed it up in 1966 by founding the National Organization for Women and serving as its president until 1970. Her most recent book, *The Second Stage* (1981), reviews the progress women have made in the past decade and proposes new goals for the future.

In this selection from *The Second Stage*, Friedan suggests that the time has arrived for a reconciliation between feminism and the institution of the family. Here she looks beyond what she calls the feminist mystique to discuss the possibilities of progress—for women and men.

Feminism's Next Step

"The women's movement is over," said my friend, a usually confident executive, who is also a wife and feminist. "At least," she continued in a grim tone, "it is in my shop. The men are making jokes about bimbos again, and the other woman in the executive group and I just look at each other. It doesn't matter if we get mad; they act as if we aren't there. When a new job opens up, all they look for now is men. It's as if the word has gone out that we've lost our case; there won't be any equal rights amendment, so they don't need to worry anymore about lawsuits over sex discrimination, even though laws against it are still on the books. They figure they can do what they want about women now, like the old days."

The women's movement in some form will never be over. But the rights that women have struggled to win in the last decade are in deadly danger, with right-wing groups in Congress determined to gut laws against sex discrimination and to abolish legal abortion and a conservative Supreme Court already backtracking on equality. . . .

And there are other signs that we have reached, not the beginning of the end, but the end of the beginning.

Listening to my own daughter and others of her generation, I sense something off, out of focus, going wrong. From the daughters, working so hard at their new careers, determined not to be trapped as their mothers were, expecting so much and taking for granted the opportunities we fought for, I've begun to hear undertones of pain and puzzlement, almost a bitterness that they hardly dare admit. As if, with all those opportunities that we won for them, they are reluctant to speak out loud about certain other needs some of us rebelled against—needs for love, security, men, children, family, home.

I sense a frustration in women not so young, about those careers 5 they're lucky to have, facing agonizing conflicts over having children. Can they have it all? How?

I sense a desperation in divorced women and men and an unspoken 6 fear of divorce in those still married, which is being twisted into a backlash against equal rights that are more essential than ever for the divorced.

I sense a sullen impatience among some of those women who en- 7 tered the work force in unprecedented millions over the last 10 years, who are in fact earning 59 cents for every dollar men earn because the only jobs available to most women are still in the low-paying clerical and service fields. Even among the few who have broken through to the executive suite, I sense the exhilaration of trying to be superwomen giving way to disillusionment with the tokens of power.

What is going wrong? Why this uneasy sense of battles won, only 8 to be fought again, of battles that should have been won and yet are not, of battles that suddenly one does not really want to win, and the weariness of battle altogether—how many feel it?

I, and other feminists, dread to discuss these troubling symptoms 9 because the women's movement has been the source and focus of so much of our energy, strength and security for so long. We cannot conceive that it will not go on forever the same way it has for nearly 20 years. But we cannot go on denying these puzzling symptoms of distress. If they mean something is seriously wrong, we had better find out and change direction yet again, before it is too late.

I believe it is over, the first stage. We must now move into the 10 second stage of the sex-role revolution, which the women's movement set off.

In that first stage, our aim was full participation, power and voice 11 in the mainstream—inside the party, the political process, the professions, the business world. But we were diverted from our dream by a sexual politics that cast man as enemy and seemed to repudiate the traditional values of the family. In reaction against the feminine mystique, which defined women solely in terms of their relation to men as wives, mothers and homemakers, we insidiously fell into a feminist mystique, which denied that core of women's personhood that is fulfilled through love, nurture, home. We seemed to create a polarization between feminists and those women who still looked to the family for their very identity, not only among the dwindling numbers who were still full-time

housewives, but also among women who do not get as much sense of
worth or security from their jobs as they get—or wish they could get—
from being someone's wife or mother. The very terms in which we fought
for abortion, or against rape, or in opposition to pornography seemed to
express a hate for men and a lack of reverence for childbearing that
threatened those women profoundly. That focus on sexual battles also
took energy away from the fight for the equal rights amendment and kept
us from moving to restructure work and home so that women could have
real choices. We fought for equality in terms of male power, without
asking what equality really means between women and men.

I believe that we have to break through our own feminist mystique   12
now and move into the second stage—no longer against, but with men.
In the second stage we have to transcend that polarization between feminism and the family. We have to free ourselves from male power traps,
understand the limits of women's power as a separate interest group and
grasp the possibility of generating a new kind of power, which was the
real promise of the women's movement. For the second stage is not so
much a fixed agenda as it is a process, a mode that will put a new value
on qualities once considered—and denigrated as—special to women, feminine qualities that will be liberated in men as they share experiences
like child care. These qualities, used mainly in the private world of the
family until now, were previewed for the first time publicly in the wom-
en's movement; now they will be used in a larger political sphere by both
men and women.

• • • •

The true potential of women's power can be realized only by tran-   13
scending the false polarization between feminism and the family. It is an
abstract polarization that does not exist in real life.

For instead of the polarization that has plagued the women's move-   14
ment in the last few years and prevented the very possibility of political
solutions, new research shows that virtually all women today share a
basic core of commitment to the family and to their own equality within
and beyond it, as long as family and equality are not seen to be in conflict.

One such study, "Juggling Contradictions: Women's Ideas About   15
Families," was conducted by Nancy Bennett, Susan Harding, et al. of
the Social Science Research Community at the University of Michigan
in 1979. The 33 women in this study were between the ages of 28 and
45, white, with children, living in small and medium-size Michigan cities.
A third of the women had some college education, most of the families
had an income of between $15,000 and $30,000, and more than half

the women were employed, most of them part time, at jobs ranging from selling real estate to nursing, hairdressing, and cleaning houses.

The researchers admitted that their preconceptions and practically everything they had read had prepared them to put the women they interviewed into two categories—familial or individualistic. The "familial ideology" places a tremendous value on the family and on motherhood, both as an activity and as a source of identity. It holds that family—husband and children—should be the primary focus of a woman's life and that the needs of the family should be placed above all else. In contrast, the "individualistic ideology" places the individual on an equal level with the family—mothers have needs and goals to meet as persons apart from the family.

The researchers reported: "Instead of finding categories of women, we found categories of ideas . . . bits and pieces of two distinct belief systems—familial and individualistic ideologies. None of the women we spoke with subscribed completely to one ideology or the other; they all expressed some combination of the two, in their words and in their lives. The ideologies are opposed in the political arena. . . . The women we spoke with, however, did not present these ideas as contradictory."

The researchers stressed: "We were not surprised to find conflicting ideas or ideologies expressed by the women we interviewed, but to find them combined in the views and behavior of each woman."

The tension between the two ideologies—woman-as-individual and woman-serving-her-family—looked irreconcilable in the abstract, but was, in fact, reconciled in the women's lives. They worked, usually part time or on different shifts from their husbands, shared child care with husbands or grandmothers or others and approved of child-care centers, even if they were not yet ready to use them themselves.

Even those who themselves symbolize or preach one or the other ideology can be seen combining both in their own lives. When Rosabeth Moss Kanter, the eminent sociologist and author of "Men and Women in the Corporation," takes her 2-year-old son to a board meeting, her partner-husband, Barry, takes over with the child. They describe this arrangement in feminist terms. But when Marabel Morgan "saves" her marriage, not by decking her body in ostrich feathers but by enlisting her husband as partner-manager to keep track of and invest the money she earns lecturing on the "Total Woman," she describes this as "feminine," not feminist.

There are not two kinds of women in America. The political polarization between feminism and the family was preached and manipulated by extremists on the right—and colluded in, perhaps unconsciously, by feminist and liberal or radical leaders—to extend or defend their own political power. Now, as ideological polarization is being resolved in real life by juggling and rationalizing new necessities in traditional terms and old necessities in feminist terms, women will strengthen the family in evolving ways.

Politically, for the women's movement to continue to promote issues like E.R.A., abortion and child care solely in individualistic terms subverts our own moral majority. Economic necessity and the very survival of the family now force the increasing majority of women to work and to make painful choices about having more children. And women who merely tolerated, or even disapproved of, these concerns, will now face them as matters of concrete personal urgency and the survival of their families. The women's movement has appealed to women as individualists; the Moral Majority has played to and elicited an explosive, defensive reaction on behalf of women as upholders of the family. Perhaps the reactionary preachers of the Moral Majority who decry women's moves to equality as threats to the family are merely using the family to limit women's real political power. In a similar vein, feminists intent on mobilizing women's political power are, in fact, defeating their own purpose by denying the importance of the family.

That Michigan study showed something very important. All the women believed in equality and all of them believed in the family—from the same or converging needs for security, identity, and some control over their lives. Whether or not they supported a particular issue depended on how they perceived its affecting them. No appeal would be acceptable, even to the most individualistic, if it denied or conflicted with their commitment to the family, which they all shared.

"Family" is not just a buzz word for reactionaries; for women, as for men, it is the symbol of that last area where one has any hope of control over one's destiny, of meeting one's most basic human needs, of nourishing that core of personhood threatened now by vast impersonal institutions and uncontrollable corporate and government bureaucracies. Against these menaces, the family may be as crucial for survival as it used to be against the untamed wilderness and the raging elements, and the old, simple kinds of despotism.

For the family, all psychological science tells us, is the nutrient of our humanness, of all our individuality. The Michigan women, and all the others they exemplify, may show great political wisdom as well as personal survival skills in holding on to the family as the base of their identity and human control.

It is time to start thinking of the movement in new terms. It is very important indeed that the daughters—and the sons—hold on to the dream of equality in the years ahead and move consciously to the second stage of the sex-role revolution. If we cannot, at this moment, solve the new problems we can no longer deny, we must at least pass on the right questions. These second-stage questions reflect the most urgent problems now facing this nation.

There is a quiet movement of American men that is converging on   27
the women's movement, though it is masked at the moment by a re-surgence of *machismo*. This movement of men for self-fulfillment beyond the rat race for success and for a role in the family beyond breadwinner makes it seem that women are seeking power in terms men are leaving behind. Even those women who have made it on such terms are forfeiting the quality of life, exchanging their old martyred service of home and children for harassed, passive service of corporation.

In the second stage, women have to say "No" to standards of success   28
on the job set in terms of men who had wives to take care of all the details of life, and standards at home set in terms of women whose whole sense of worth and power had to come from that perfectly run house, those perfectly controlled children. Instead of accepting that double bur-den, women will realize that they can and must give up some of that power in the home and the family when they are carrying part of the breadwinning burden and some beginnings of power on the job. Instead of those rigid contracts that seemed the feminist ideal in the first stage, there will be in the second stage an easy flow as man and woman share the chores of home and children—sometimes 50–50, sometimes 20–80 or 60–40, according to their abilities and needs. In the second stage, the woman will find and use her own strength and style at work, instead of trying so hard to do it man's way, and she will not feel she has to be more independent than any man for fear that she will fall back into that abject dependence that she sometimes secretly yearns for.

Politically, instead of focusing on woman as victim and on sexual   29
battles that don't really change anything, like those marches against pornography, feminists in the second stage will forge new alliances with men from unions, church and corporation that are essential if we are to restructure jobs and home on a human basis.

Despite the recent Supreme Court decision, which ruled that women   30
may be excluded from the draft, I feel that in the second stage, questions like "Should women be drafted?" will be obsolete, for it will be under-stood that for the nation's survival, women simply will have to be drafted if a major war threatens. With the dangers of nuclear holocaust, new questions need to be asked about the defense of the nation that demand a sensitivity to human values and to life on the part of both male and female military leaders.

Above all, the second stage involves not a retreat to the family, but embracing the family in new terms of equality and diversity. The choice to have children—and the joys and burdens of raising them—will be so costly and precious that it will have to be shared more equally by mother, father and others from, or in place of, the larger family. The trade-offs will be seen more clearly as both men and women become realistic about the values and the price. It will probably not be possible economically for most women to have a real choice to be just a housewife, full-time or lifelong. But men as well as women will be demanding parental leave or reduced schedules for those few years—or in early, middle or later life for their own rebirth. A voucher system, such as Milton Friedman and other conservatives have already proposed for different purposes, could be used to provide a "child allowance," payable perhaps as a tax rebate, to every man or woman who takes primary responsibility for care of a child or dependent parent at home. She or he would get equal credit in the wage-earning spouse's pension and old-age Social Security vestment; this credit would not be lost in case of divorce. If both parents returned to work and shared child-care responsibilities, they could use those vouchers to help pay for child care in the community. Many advanced nations have such a child or family allowance.

And in the second stage, unions and companies will begin to give priority to restructuring hours of work—flextime and flexible benefit packages—not just to help women but because men will be demanding them and because improved quality of work will not only cost less but yield greater results in terms of reduced absenteeism, increased productivity and profit than the conventional package.

But in the second stage when we talk about "family" we will no longer mean just Mom and Dad and the kids. We will be more keenly aware of how the needs of both women and men for love and intimacy and emotional and economic sharing and support change over time and of the new shapes family can take. In the second stage we will need new forms of homes and apartments that don't depend on the full-time service of the housewife, and new shared housing for single parents and people living alone—widowed, married and divorced—who are the largest new group in the population.

The only bright spot in the housing market this past year was the great increase in sales of homes and condominiums to single women living alone. But since in fact it takes two incomes to buy housing today, banks and boards of condominiums and mortgage lending officers will increasingly be faced with requests for mortgages or leases by two, three or more persons unrelated by blood or marriage.

The common interests of all these kinds of families will create the 35
basis for a new political alliance for the second stage that may not be a
women's movement. Men may be—must be—at the cutting edge of the
second stage. Women were reborn, in effect, merely by moving across
into man's world. In the first stage, it almost seemed as if women and
men were moving in opposite directions, reversing roles or exchanging
one half-life for another. In the second stage, we will go beyond the
either-or of "superwoman" or "total woman" and "house husband" or
"urban cowboy" to a new wholeness: an integration, in our personal lives,
of the masculine and feminine in each of us in all our infinite personal
variety—not unisex but new human sex.

If we can move beyond the false polarities and single-issue battles, 36
and appreciate the limits and true potential of women's power, we will
be able to join with men—follow or lead—in the new human politics
that must emerge beyond reaction. It will be a new, passionate volun-
teerism, an activism that comes out of living these new problems for
which there may be no single answer. It must have the same kind of
relevance to the vital interests in life of both men and women and meet
the same needs for higher purpose and communality as did the women's
movement.

Now, those whose roots are in the service of life must have the 37
strength to ask, if no one else does, what should government be responsible for if not for the needs of people in life? And the strength to start
from those real needs of life to take back government, for the people.
The second stage may even now be evolving, out of or aside from what
we have thought of as our battle.

I know that equality, the personhood we fought for, is truly nec- 38
essary for women—and opens new life for men. But I hear now what I
could not hear before—the fears and feelings of some who have fought
against our movement. It is not just a conspiracy of reactionary forces,
though such forces surely play upon and manipulate those fears.

There is no going back. The women's movement was necessary. 39
But the liberation that began with the women's movement isn't finished.
The equality we fought for isn't livable, isn't workable, isn't comfortable
in the terms that structured our battle. The first stage, the women's
movement, was fought within and against and defined by that old structure of unequal, polarized male and female sex roles. But to continue
reacting against such structure is still to be defined and limited by its
terms. What's needed now is to transcend those terms and transform the
structure itself.

How do we surmount the reaction that threatens to destroy the   4
very gains we thought we had already won in the first stage of the women's
movement? How do we surmount our own reaction, which shadows our
feminism and our femininity (we blush even to use that word now)? How
do we transcend the polarization between women and women and between women and men to achieve the new human wholeness that is the
promise of feminism, and get on with solving the concrete, practical,
everyday problems of living, working and loving as equal persons? This
is the personal and political business of the second stage.

About the Essay

1. What, briefly, does Friedan mean by the "first stage" and "second stage"
of the women's movement? Why does she believe the movement is due for a
change? Considering her arguments, do you agree? Why or why not?

2. How does Friedan use a University of Michigan study, "Juggling Contradictions: Women's Ideas About Families"? What purpose does this study serve
in the essay?

3. What criticisms of the women's movement does Friedan make? What
contributions to new life-styles, social organization, and political arrangements does she believe women can make? What are your views on the matter?

4. According to Friedan, what had been the prevailing attitude toward men
in the first stage of the women's movement? What changes does she call for?

5. Friedan argues that the women's movement polarized women. Which types
of women were involved? What ideological camps did they fall into? What,
according to Friedan, is wrong with this polarization?

6. How does Friedan open her essay, and how does she close it? What are
the stylistic differences between the opening and closing? Comment on the
effectiveness of each one.

Explorations

1. What, in your view, should be feminism's next step? What should its chief
objectives be, and how might those be realized?

2. At the end of June 1982, after gaining ratification from thirty-five states,
the Equal Rights Amendment to the Constitution failed to be ratified by the
three states that would have made a three-fourths majority. It was obviously
highly controversial. Do you believe the ERA was needed or not? What were
the strongest arguments for and against it? In your opinion, why did it fail?

3. Both Friedan's essay and King's speech (pages 587–590) are calls to their followers to join with others to achieve their goals. Friedan's essay in effect repeats King's assertion: "We cannot walk alone." Why do you think these calls were felt to be necessary? Were King and Friedan right?

JOHN KENNETH GALBRAITH

One of the world's best-known economists, John Kenneth Galbraith was born in 1908 on a small farm near Iona Station, Ontario, Canada. He received a bachelor's degree from the University of Toronto and earned his master's and doctoral degrees in economics at the University of California at Berkeley. In 1934 he went to Harvard, where he was to teach economics for the next forty years. His academic career has occasionally been interrupted for periods of government service, notably from 1941 to 1943 when he was in Washington, D.C., helping to administer price controls and from 1961 to 1963 when he was John F. Kennedy's ambassador to India. His books include *The Affluent Society* (1958), *The New Industrial State* (1967), and *Economics and the Public Purpose* (1973). His memoirs, *A Life in Our Times*, were published in 1981.

We live, Galbraith says, in an affluent society, one in which most people are decently housed, clothed, and fed, and have some chance of becoming positively wealthy. Yet there stubbornly remains a minority of people who are truly poor, many of them through no fault of their own. An affluent society that is also, in Galbraith's words, compassionate and rational, would seek to alleviate that poverty. In this chapter from the 1975 edition of *The Affluent Society* Galbraith, himself both rational and compassionate, explains how that could be done.

The Position of Poverty

"The study of the causes of poverty," Alfred Marshall observed at the turn of the century, "is the study of the causes of the degradation of a large part of mankind." He spoke of contemporary England as well as of the world beyond. A vast number of people both in town and country, he noted, had insufficient food, clothing and houseroom; they were: "Overworked and undertaught, weary and careworn, without quiet and without leisure." The chance of their succor, he concluded, gave to economic studies, "their chief and their highest interest."

No contemporary economist would be likely to make such an observation about the United States. Conventional economic discourse makes obeisance to the continued existence of some poverty. "We must remember that we still have a great many poor people." In the nineteen-sixties, poverty promised, for a time, to become a subject of serious political concern. Then war came and the concern evaporated or was displaced.

• • • •

The privation of which Marshall spoke was, a half century ago, the common lot at least of all who worked without special skill. As a general affliction, it was ended by increased output which, however imperfectly it may have been distributed, nevertheless accrued in substantial amount to those who worked for a living. The result was to reduce poverty from the problem of a majority to that of a minority. It ceased to be a general case and became a special case. It is this which has put the problem of poverty into its peculiar modern form.

II

For poverty does survive. In part, it is a physical matter; those 4
afflicted have such limited and insufficient food, such poor clothing, such crowded, cold and dirty shelter that life is painful as well as comparatively brief. But just as it is far too tempting to say that, in matters of living standards, everything is relative, so it is wrong to rest everything on absolutes. People are poverty-stricken when their income, even if adequate for survival, falls radically behind that of the community. Then they cannot have what the larger community regards as the minimum necessary for decency; and they cannot wholly escape, therefore, the judgment of the larger community that they are indecent. They are degraded for, in the literal sense, they live outside the grades or categories which the community regards as acceptable.

• • • •

The degree of privation depends on the size of the family, the place 5
of residence—it will be less with given income in rural areas than in the cities—and will, of course, be affected by changes in living costs. The Department of Health, Education and Welfare[1] has established rough standards, appropriately graded to family size, location and changing prices, to separate the poor from the less poor and the affluent. In 1972, a non-farm family of four was deemed poor if it had an income of $4275; a couple living otherwise than on a farm was called poor if it had less than $2724 and an unattached individual if receiving less than $2109. A farm family of four was poor with less than $3639; of two with less than $2315.

By these modest standards, 24.5 million households, including in- 6
dividuals and families, were poor in 1972 as compared with 13.4 million in 1959. Because of the increase in population, and therewith in the number of households, in these years the reduction in the number of poor households, as a proportion of all households, was rather greater—from 24 percent in 1959 to 12 percent in 1972.

---

[1]Since 1979, the Department of Health and Human Services. In that year, Education was separated into its own department.

One can usefully think of the foregoing deprivation as falling into   7
two broad categories. First, there is what may be called *case* poverty.
This one encounters in every community, rural or urban, however prosperous that community or the times. Case poverty is the poor farm family
with the junk-filled yard and the dirty children playing in the bare dirt.
Or it is the gray-black hovel beside the railroad tracks. Or it is the
basement dwelling in the alley.

Case poverty is commonly and properly related to some character-   8
istic of the individuals so afflicted. Nearly everyone else has mastered his
environment; this proves that it is not intractable. But some quality
peculiar to the individual or family involved—mental deficiency, bad
health, inability to adapt to the discipline of industrial life, uncontrollable procreation, alcohol, discrimination involving a very limited minority, some educational handicap unrelated to community shortcoming,
or perhaps a combination of several of these handicaps—has kept these
individuals from participating in the general well-being.

Second, there is what may be called *insular* poverty—that which   9
manifests itself as an "island" of poverty. In the island, everyone or nearly
everyone is poor. Here, evidently, it is not easy to explain matters by
individual inadequacy. We may mark individuals down as intrinsically
deficient in social performance; it is not proper or even wise so to characterize an entire community. The people of the island have been frustrated by some factor common to their environment.

Case poverty exists. It has also been useful to those who have   10
needed a formula for keeping the suffering of others from causing suffering
to themselves. Since this poverty is the result of the deficiencies, including the moral shortcomings, of the persons concerned, it is possible
to shift the responsibility to those involved. They are worthless and, as
a simple manifestation of social justice, they suffer for it. Or, at a somewhat higher level of social perception and compassion, it means that the
problem of poverty is sufficiently solved by private and public charity.
This rescues those afflicted from the worst consequences of their inadequacy or misfortune; no larger social change or reorganization is suggested. Except as it may be insufficient in its generosity, the society is
not at fault.

Insular poverty yields to no such formulas. In earlier times, when   11
agriculture and extractive industries[2] were the dominant sources of livelihood, something could be accomplished by shifting the responsibility
for low income to a poor natural endowment and thus, in effect, to God.
The soil was thin and stony, other natural resources absent and hence

[2]Extractive industries are the various mining industries.

the people were poor. And, since it is the undoubted preference of many to remain in the vicinity of the place of their birth, a homing instinct that operates for people as well as pigeons, the people remained in the poverty which heaven had decreed for them. It is an explanation that is nearly devoid of empirical application. Connecticut is very barren and stony and incomes are very high. Similarly Wyoming. West Virginia is well watered with rich mines and forests and the people are very poor. The South is much favored in soil and climate and similarly poor and the very richest parts of the South, such as the Mississippi-Yazoo Delta, have long had a well-earned reputation for the greatest deprivation. Yet so strong is the tendency to associate poverty with natural causes that even individuals of some modest intelligence will still be heard, in explanation of insular poverty, to say, "It's basically a poor country." "It's a pretty barren region."

12 Most modern poverty is insular in character and the islands are the rural and urban slums. From the former, mainly in the South, the southern Appalachians and Puerto Rico, there has been until recent times a steady flow of migrants, some white but more black, to the latter. Grim as life is in the urban ghetto, it still offers more hope, income and interest than in the rural slum. Largely in consequence of this migration, the number of poor farm families—poor by the standards just mentioned—declined between 1959 and 1973 from 1.8 million to 295,000. The decline in the far larger number of poor non-farm households in these years was only from 6.5 million to 4.5 million.

13 This is not the place to provide a detailed profile of this poverty. More than half of the poor households are headed by a woman, although in total women head only 9 percent of families. Over 30 percent are black, another 10 percent are of Spanish origin. A very large proportion of all black households (31 percent in 1973 as compared with 8 percent of whites) fall below the poverty line. Especially on the farms, where the young have departed for the cities, a disproportionate number of the poor are old. More often than not, the head of the household is not in the labor force at all.

14 But the more important characteristic of insular poverty is forces, common to all members of the community, which restrain or prevent participation in economic life at going rates of return. These restraints are several. Race, which acts to locate people by their color rather than by the proximity to employment, is obviously one. So are poor educational facilities. (And this effect is further exaggerated when the poorly educated, endemically a drug on the labor market, are brought together in dense clusters by the common inadequacy of the schools available to blacks and the poor.) So is the disintegration of family life in the slum

which leaves households in the hands of women. (Family life itself is in some measure a manifestation of affluence.) And so, without doubt, is the shared sense of helplessness and rejection and the resulting demoralization which is the product of the common misfortune.

III

With the transition of the very poor from a majority to a comparative minority position, there has been a change in their political position. Any tendency of a politician to identify himself with those of the lowest estate usually brought the reproaches of the well-to-do. Political pandering and demagoguery were naturally suspected. But, for the man so reproached, there was the compensating advantage of alignment with a large majority. Now any politician who speaks for the very poor is speaking for a small and generally inarticulate minority. As a result, the modern liberal politician regularly aligns himself not with the poverty-ridden members of the community but with the far more numerous people who enjoy the far more affluent income of (say) the modern trade union member or the intellectual. Ambrose Bierce, in *The Devil's Dictionary*, called poverty "a file provided for the teeth of the rats of reform." It is so no longer. Reform now concerns itself with the needs of people who are relatively well-to-do—whether the comparison be with their own past or with those who are really at the bottom of the income ladder.

In consequence, a notable feature of efforts to help the very poor is their absence of any very great political appeal. Politicians have found it possible to be indifferent where they could not be derisory. And very few have been under a strong compulsion to support these efforts.

The concern for inequality and deprivation had vitality only so long as the many suffered while a few had much. It did not survive as a decisive political issue in a time when the many had much even though others had much more. It is our misfortune that when inequality declined as an issue, the slate was not left clean. A residual and in some ways rather more hopeless problem remained.

IV

An affluent society, that is also both compassionate and rational, would, no doubt, secure to all who needed it the minimum income essential for decency and comfort. The corrupting effect on the human spirit of unearned revenue has unquestionably been exaggerated as, indeed, have the character-building values of hunger and privation. To secure to each family a minimum income, as a normal function of the society, would help ensure that the misfortunes of parents, deserved or otherwise, were not visited on their children. It would help ensure that poverty was not self-perpetuating. Most of the reaction, which no doubt would be adverse, is based on obsolete attitudes. When poverty was a majority phenomenon, such action could not be afforded. A poor society, as this essay has previously shown, had to enforce the rule that the person who did not work could not eat. And possibly it was justified in the added cruelty of applying the rule to those who could not work or whose efficiency was far below par. An affluent society has no similar excuse for such rigor. It can use the forthright remedy of providing income for those without. Nothing requires such a society to be compassionate. But it no longer has a high philosophical justification for callousness.

. . . . In the past, we have suffered from the supposition that the   19
only remedy for poverty lies in remedies that allow people to look after themselves—to participate in the economy. Nothing has better served the conscience of people who wished to avoid inconvenient or expensive action than an appeal, on this issue, to Calvinist precept—"The only sound way to solve the problem of poverty is to help people help themselves." But this does not mean that steps to allow participation and to keep poverty from being self-perpetuating are unimportant. On the contrary. It requires that the investment in children from families presently afflicted be as little below normal as possible. If the children of poor families have first-rate schools and school attendance is properly enforced; if the children, though badly fed at home, are well nourished at school; if the community has sound health services, and the physical well-being of the children is vigilantly watched; if there is opportunity for advanced education for those who qualify regardless of means; and if, especially in the case of urban communities, housing is ample and housing standards are enforced, the streets are clean, the laws are kept, and recreation is adequate—then there is a chance that the children of the very poor will come to maturity without inhibiting disadvantage. In the case of insular poverty, this remedy requires that the services of the community be assisted from outside. Poverty is self-perpetuating partly because the poorest communities are poorest in the services which would eliminate it. To eliminate poverty efficiently, we must, indeed, invest more than proportionately in the children of the poor community. It is there that high quality schools, strong health services, special provision for nutrition and recreation are most needed to compensate for the very low investment which families are able to make in their own offspring.

The effect of education and related investment in individuals is to   20
help them overcome the restraints that are imposed by their environment. These need also to be attacked even more directly—by giving the

mobility that is associated with plentiful, good and readily available housing, by provision of comfortable, efficient and economical mass transport,
by making the environment pleasant and safe, and by eliminating the
special health handicaps that afflict the poor.

Nor is case poverty entirely resistant to such remedies. Much can   21
be done to treat those characteristics which cause people to reject or be
rejected by the modern industrial society. Educational deficiencies can
be overcome. Mental deficiencies can be treated. Physical handicaps
can be remedied. The limiting factor is not a lack of knowledge of what
can be done. Overwhelmingly, it is a shortage of money.

V

Poverty—grim, degrading and ineluctable—is not remarkable in   22
India. For few, the fate is otherwise. But in the United States, the
survival of poverty is remarkable. We ignore it because we share with all
societies at all times the capacity for not seeing what we do not wish to
see. Anciently this has enabled the nobleman to enjoy his dinner while
remaining oblivious to the beggars around his door. In our own day, it
enables us to travel in comfort by Harlem and into the lush precincts of
midtown Manhattan. But while our failure to notice can be explained,
it cannot be excused. "Poverty," Pitt exclaimed, "is no disgrace but it is
damned annoying." In the contemporary United States, it is not annoying but it is a disgrace.

About the Essay

1. What is the position of poverty now, as Galbraith describes it? How does
contemporary poverty differ from that of earlier periods? What are the political consequences of this difference?

2. What is poverty, according to Galbraith? How does he construct his definition? Why should he feel the need to define the term at all?

3. Look closely at paragraph 6. What, in your own words, is the trend Galbraith describes there? Why does he call the government poverty standards
"modest"?

4. How is "case poverty" distinguished from "insular poverty"? Of what use
is this distinction to Galbraith's argument? How does it relate to your attitude
toward the poor and unemployed?

5. What cures for poverty does Galbraith recommend? What role do they
require government to play in society? If the policies he proposes were put to
you one by one, how would you vote on each? Why?

6. As a speaker and writer Galbraith is famous for his ironic wit. What ex-

amples of irony are there in this essay? What is Galbraith really saying in these instances? How does his ironic tone affect your response to the essay as a whole?

Explorations

1. The federal government defines poverty in absolute terms of household income, while Galbraith defines it as relative to the standard of living considered decent by a community. How would you define poverty? Why would you choose that definition over others?

2. What is the "position of poverty" now? What is the federal government's current official definition of poverty? What government programs are now in place to help the poor? In your opinion, is the government doing enough? Too much? What should be added to its programs, or dropped from them? In relation to other government expenses, what priority should be given to helping the poor?

3. Toward the end of his essay, Galbraith says: "The corrupting effect on the human spirit of unearned revenue has unquestionably been exaggerated as, indeed, have the character-building values of hunger and privation." Do you agree or disagree? Why?

H. L. MENCKEN

Born to a Baltimore cigar manufacturer, Henry Louis Mencken (1880–1956) brought a boisterous irreverence to American letters in the early years of this century. As a newspaper and magazine journalist, he wrote sardonically of the American "booboisie." He was contemptuous of politics and highly skeptical of democracy, once saying that "Democracy is the theory that the common people know what they want, and deserve to get it good and hard." Mencken began right out of high school as a reporter for the Baltimore *Herald*; six years later, at twenty-five, he was its editor-in-chief. He achieved a national audience as columnist for the Baltimore *Sun*, literary critic for the *Smart Set*, and cofounder and editor of the *American Mercury*, for which he wrote on everything from politics to music. Many of his best articles are collected in the six-volume *Prejudices* (1919–1927), and his own favorite articles can be found in *A Mencken Chrestomathy* (1949). But his most ambitious work is undoubtedly *The American Language* (1919; revised and supplemented 1921–1945), a monumental and highly entertaining study of our language.

In the *American Mercury*, Mencken once asked himself, in print: "If you find so much that is unworthy of reverence in the United States, then why do you live here?" The answer: "Why do men go to zoos?" The following talk, originally given at Columbia University in 1940, shows the same savagely humorous spirit.

The Politician

After damning politicians up hill and down dale for many years, as rogues and vagabonds, frauds and scoundrels, I sometimes suspect that, like everyone else, I often expect too much of them. Though faith and confidence are surely more or less foreign to my nature, I not infrequently find myself looking to them to be able, diligent, candid, and even honest. Plainly enough, that is too large an order, as anyone must realize who reflects upon the manner in which they reach public office. They seldom if ever get there by merit alone, at least in democratic states. Sometimes, to be sure, it happens, but only by a kind of miracle. They are chosen normally for quite different reasons, the chief of which is simply their power to impress and enchant the intellectually underprivileged. It is a talent like any other, and when it is exercised by a radio crooner, a movie actor or a bishop, it even takes on a certain austere and sorry respectability. But it is obviously not identical with a capacity for the intricate problems of statecraft.

Those problems demand for their solution—when they are soluble at all, which is not often—a high degree of technical proficiency, and with it there should go an adamantine kind of integrity, for the temptations of a public official are almost as cruel as those of a glamor girl or a dipsomaniac. But we train a man for facing them, not be locking him up in a monastery and stuffing him with wisdom and virtue, but by turning him loose on the stump. If he is a smart and enterprising fellow, which he usually is, he quickly discovers there that hooey pleases the boobs a great deal more than sense. Indeed, he finds that sense really disquiets and alarms them—that it makes them, at best, intolerably uncomfortable, just as a tight collar makes them uncomfortable, or a speck of dust in the eye, or the thought of Hell. The truth, to the overwhelming majority of mankind, is indistinguishable from a headache. After trying a few shots of it on his customers, the larval statesman concludes sadly that it must hurt them, and after that he taps a more humane keg, and in a little while the whole audience is singing "Glory, glory, hallelujah," and when the returns come in the candidate is on his way to the White House.

I hope no one will mistake this brief account of the political process under democracy for exaggeration. It is almost literally true. I do not mean to argue, remember, that all politicians are villains in the sense that a burglar, a child-stealer, or a Darwinian are villains. Far from it. Many of them, in their private characters, are very charming persons, and I have known plenty that I'd trust with my diamonds, my daughter or my liberty, if I had any such things. I happen to be acquainted to some extent with nearly all the gentlemen, both Democrats and Republicans, who are currently itching for the Presidency, including the present incumbent, and I testify freely that they are all pleasant fellows, with qualities above rather than below the common. The worst of them is a great deal better company than most generals in the army, or writers of murder mysteries, or astrophysicists, and the best is a really superior and wholly delightful man—full of sound knowledge, competent and prudent, frank and enterprising, and quite as honest as any American can be without being clapped into a madhouse. Don't ask me what his name is, for I am not in politics. I can only tell you that he has been in public life a long while, and has not been caught yet.

But will this prodigy, or any of his rivals, ever unload any appreciable amount of sagacity on the stump? Will any of them venture to tell the plain truth, the whole truth and nothing but the truth about the situation of the country, foreign or domestic? Will any of them refrain from promises that he knows he can't fulfill—that no human being *could* fulfill? Will any of them utter a word, however obvious, that will alarm and alienate any of the huge packs of morons who now cluster at the public trough, wallowing in the pap that grows thinner and thinner, hoping against hope? Answer: maybe for a few weeks at the start. Maybe before the campaign really begins. Maybe behind the door. But not after the issue is fairly joined, and the struggle is on in earnest. From that moment they will all resort to demagogy, and by the middle of June of election year the only choice among them will be a choice between amateurs of that science and professionals.

They will all promise every man, woman and child in the country   5
whatever he, she or it wants. They'll all be roving the land looking for chances to make the rich poor, to remedy the irremediable, to succor the unsuccorable, to unscramble the unscrambleable, to dephlogisticate the undephlogisticable. They will all be curing warts by saying words over them, and paying off the national debt with money that no one will have to earn. When one of them demonstrates that twice two is five, another will prove that it is six, six and a half, ten, twenty, *n*. In brief, they will divest themselves of their character as sensible, candid and truthful men, and become simply candidates for office, bent only on collaring votes. They will all know by then, even supposing that some of them don't know it now, that votes are collared under democracy, not by talking sense but by talking nonsense, and they will apply themselves to the job with a hearty yo-heave-ho. Most of them, before the uproar is over, will actually convince themselves. The winner will be whoever promises the most with the least probability of delivering anything.

Some years ago I accompanied a candidate for the Presidency on   6
his campaign-tour. He was, like all such rascals, an amusing fellow, and I came to like him very much. His speeches, at the start, were full of fire. He was going to save the country from all the stupendous frauds and false pretenses of his rival. Every time that rival offered to rescue another million of poor fish from the neglects and oversights of God he howled his derision from the back platform of his train. I noticed at once that these blasts of common sense got very little applause, and after a while the candidate began to notice it too. Worse, he began to get word from his spies on the train of his rival that the rival was wowing them, panicking them, laying them in the aisles. They threw flowers, hot dogs and five-cent cigars at him. In places where the times were especially hard they tried to unhook the locomotive from his train, so that he'd have to stay with them awhile longer, and promise them some more. There were no Gallup polls in those innocent days, but the local politicians had ways of their own for finding out how the cat was jumping, and they began to join my candidate's train in the middle of the night, and wake him

up to tell him that all was lost, including honor. This had some effect upon him—in truth, an effect almost as powerful as that of sitting in the electric chair. He lost his intelligent manner, and became something you could hardly distinguish from an idealist. Instead of mocking he began to promise, and in a little while he was promising everything that his rival was promising, and a good deal more.

One night out in the Bible country, after the hullabaloo of the day was over, I went into his private car along with another newspaper reporter, and we sat down to gabble with him. This other reporter, a faithful member of the candidate's own party, began to upbraid him, at first very gently, for letting off so much hokum. What did he mean by making promises that no human being on this earth, and not many of the angels in Heaven, could ever hope to carry out? In particular, what was his idea in trying to work off all those preposterous bile-beans and snake-oils on the poor farmers, a class of men who had been fooled and rooked by every fresh wave of politicians since Apostolic times? Did he really believe that the Utopia he had begun so fervently to preach would ever come to pass? Did he honestly think that farmers, as a body, would ever see all their rosy dreams come true, or that the share-croppers in their lower ranks would ever be more than a hop, skip and jump from starvation? The candidate thought awhile, took a long swallow of the coffin-varnish he carried with him, and then replied that the answer in every case was no. He was well aware, he said, that the plight of the farmers was intrinsically hopeless, and would probably continue so, despite doles from the treasury, for centuries to come. He had no notion that anything could be done about it by merely human means, and certainly not by political means: it would take a new Moses, and a whole series of miracles. "But you forget, Mr. Blank," he concluded sadly, "that our agreement in the premises must remain purely personal. You are not a candidate for President of the United States. *I am.*" As we left him his interlocutor, a gentleman grown gray in Washington and long ago lost to every decency, pointed the moral of the episode. "In politics," he said, "man must learn to rise above principle." Then he drove it in with another: "When the water reaches the upper deck," he said, "follow the rats."

About the Essay

1. What, according to Mencken, is wrong with politicians? What makes them the way they are?

2. What is Mencken's attitude toward the American people? Is it justified, in your view? Was it justified in his day?

3. Mencken is clearly having a good time with his topic. Does he also have a serious point? If so, what is it?

4. Even those who disagreed with Mencken, and they were many, found him vastly entertaining. Choose some phrases or sentences that you find particularly lively or humorous. How do those passages achieve their effect?

5. What is the purpose, and the effect on you, of the anecdote with which Mencken closes his remarks? Do you believe the incident ever really happened? Does it matter whether it did?

Explorations

1. What qualities do you look for in a candidate for public office? What qualities turn you away from a candidate? What contemporary politicians seem to possess the qualities you require? Discuss.

2. An old saying has it that a people gets the leader it deserves. Do you think the saying is true or not? Develop an argument and give examples to support your view.

3. In 1940, when Mencken spoke, candidates for President were chosen mainly by party leaders, and primaries and polls had comparatively little influence. Today the situation is reversed. But if the nominating procedure is more open and more democratic now than before, has it resulted in the nomination of better candidates? Cite examples from history to support your view. What conclusions can you draw from this about voters and politicians?

JOAN DIDION

A novelist and essayist, Joan Didion is also our liveliest reporter from California, writing about that state's water system and wind patterns, about Hollywood and Alcatraz. In the following article written in 1976, Didion reports on the "Diamond Lane," a pilot project designed to get the citizens of Los Angeles out of their cars and into buses and car pools—a hopeless undertaking in that city of freeways and free spirits. In the process she gives us some insights into the bureaucratic frame of mind. (Biographical information about Joan Didion is on page 33.)

Bureaucrats

The closed door upstairs at 120 South Spring Street in downtown Los Angeles is marked OPERATIONS CENTER. In the windowless room beyond the closed door a reverential hush prevails. From six A.M. until seven P.M. in this windowless room men sit at consoles watching a huge board flash colored lights. "There's the heart attack," someone will murmur, or "we're getting the gawk effect." 120 South Spring is the Los Angeles office of Caltrans, or the California Department of Transportation, and the Operations Center is where Caltrans engineers monitor what they call "the 42-Mile Loop." The 42-Mile Loop is simply the rough triangle formed by the intersections of the Santa Monica, the San Diego and the Harbor freeways, and 42 miles represents less than ten per cent of freeway mileage in Los Angeles County alone, but these particular 42 miles are regarded around 120 South Spring with a special veneration. The Loop is a "demonstration system," a phrase much favored by everyone at Caltrans, and is part of a "pilot project," another two words carrying totemic weight on South Spring.

The Loop has electronic sensors embedded every half-mile out there in the pavement itself, each sensor counting the crossing cars every twenty seconds. The Loop has its own mind, a Xerox Sigma V computer which prints out, all day and night, twenty-second readings on what is and is not moving in each of the Loop's eight lanes. It is the Xerox Sigma V that makes the big board flash red when traffic out there drops below fifteen miles an hour. It is the Xerox Sigma V that tells the Operations crew when they have an "incident" out there. An "incident" is the heart attack on the San Diego, the jackknifed truck on the Harbor, the Camaro just now tearing out the Cyclone fence on the Santa Monica. "Out there" is where incidents happen. The windowless room at 120 South Spring is

1

2

615

where incidents get "verified." "Incident verification" is turning on the closed-circuit TV on the console and watching the traffic slow down to see (this is "the gawk effect") where the Camaro tore out the fence.

As a matter of fact there is a certain closed-circuit aspect to the   3
entire mood of the Operations Center. "Verifying" the incident does not after all "prevent" the incident, which lends the enterprise a kind of tranced distance, and on the day recently when I visited 120 South Spring it took considerable effort to remember what I had come to talk about, which was that particular part of the Loop called the Santa Monica Freeway. The Santa Monica Freeway is 16.2 miles long, runs from the Pacific Ocean to downtown Los Angeles through what is referred to at Caltrans as "the East-West Corridor," carries more traffic every day than any other freeway in California, has what connoisseurs of freeways concede to be the most beautiful access ramps in the world, and appeared to have been transformed by Caltrans, during the several weeks before I went downtown to talk about it, into a 16.2-mile parking lot.

The problem seemed to be another Caltrans "demonstration," or   4
"pilot," a foray into bureaucratic terrorism they were calling "The Diamond Lane" in their promotional literature and "The Project" among themselves. That the promotional literature consisted largely of schedules for buses (or "Diamond Lane Expresses") and invitations to join a car pool via computer ("Commuter Computer") made clear not only the putative point of The Project, which was to encourage travel by car pool and bus, but also the actual point, which was to eradicate a central Southern California illusion, that of individual mobility, without anyone really noticing. This had not exactly worked out. "FREEWAY FIASCO," the *Los Angeles Times* was headlining page-one stories. "THE DIAMOND LANE: ANOTHER BUST BY CALTRANS." "CALTRANS PILOT EFFORT ANOTHER IN LONG LIST OF FAILURES." "OFFICIAL DIAMOND LANE STANCE: LET THEM HOWL."

All "The Diamond Lane" theoretically involved was reserving the   5
fast inside lanes on the Santa Monica for vehicles carrying three or more people, but in practice this meant that 25 per cent of the freeway was reserved for 3 per cent of the cars, and there were other odd wrinkles here and there suggesting that Caltrans had dedicated itself to making all movement around Los Angeles as arduous as possible. There was for example the matter of surface streets. A "surface street" is anything around Los Angeles that is not a freeway ("going surface" from one part of town to another is generally regarded as idiosyncratic), and surface streets do not fall directly within the Caltrans domain, but now the engineer in charge of surface streets was accusing Caltrans of threatening and intimidating him. It appeared that Caltrans wanted him to create a "confused

and congested situation" on his surface streets, so as to force drivers back to the freeway, where they would meet a still more confused and congested situation and decide to stay home, or take a bus. "We are beginning a process of deliberately making it harder for drivers to use freeways," a Caltrans director had in fact said at a transit conference some months before. "We are prepared to endure considerable public outcry in order to pry John Q. Public out of his car. . . . I would emphasize that this is a political decision, and one that can be reversed if the public gets sufficiently enraged to throw us rascals out."

Of course this political decision was in the name of the greater good, was in the interests of "environmental improvement" and "conservation of resources," but even there the figures had about them a certain Caltrans opacity. The Santa Monica normally carried 240,000 cars and trucks every day. These 240,000 cars and trucks normally carried 260,000 people. What Caltrans described as its ultimate goal on the Santa Monica was to carry the same 260,000 people, "but in 7,800 fewer, or 232,200 vehicles." The figure "232,200" had a visionary precision to it that did not automatically create confidence, especially since the only effect so far had been to disrupt traffic throughout the Los Angeles basin, triple the number of daily accidents on the Santa Monica, prompt the initiation of two lawsuits against Caltrans, and cause large numbers of Los Angeles County residents to behave, most uncharacteristically, as an ignited and conscious proletariat. Citizen guerrillas splashed paint and scattered nails in the Diamond Lanes. Diamond Lane maintenance crews expressed fear of hurled objects. Down at 120 South Spring the architects of the Diamond Lane had taken to regarding "the media" as the architects of their embarrassment, and Caltrans statements in the press had been cryptic and contradictory, reminiscent only of old communiqués out of Vietnam.

To understand what was going on it is perhaps necessary to have participated in the freeway experience, which is the only secular communion Los Angeles has. Mere driving on the freeway is in no way the same as participating in it. Anyone can "drive" on the freeway, and many people with no vocation for it do, hesitating here and resisting there, losing the rhythm of the lane change, thinking about where they came from and where they are going. Actual participants think only about where they are. Actual participation requires a total surrender, a concentration so intense as to seem a kind of narcosis, a rapture-of-the-freeway. The mind goes clean. The rhythm takes over. A distortion of time occurs, the same distortion that characterizes the instant before an accident. It takes only a few seconds to get off the Santa Monica Freeway at National-Overland, which is a difficult exit requiring the driver to

6

7

cross two new lanes of traffic streamed in from the San Diego Freeway, but those few seconds always seem to me the longest part of the trip. The moment is dangerous. The exhilaration is in doing it. "As you acquire the special skills involved," Reyner Banham observed in an extraordinary chapter about the freeways in his 1971 *Los Angeles: The Architecture of Four Ecologies*, "the freeways become a special way of being alive . . . the extreme concentration required in Los Angeles seems to bring on a state of heightened awareness that some locals find mystical."

Indeed some locals do, and some nonlocals, too. Reducing the number of lone souls careering around the East-West Corridor in a state of mechanized rapture may or may not have seemed socially desirable, but what it was definitely not going to seem was easy. "We're only seeing an initial period of unfamiliarity," I was assured the day I visited Caltrans. I was talking to a woman named Eleanor Wood and she was thoroughly and professionally grounded in the diction of "planning" and it did not seem likely that I could interest her in considering the freeway as regional mystery. "Any time you try to rearrange people's daily habits, they're apt to react impetuously. All this project requires is a certain rearrangement of people's daily planning. That's really all we want." 8

It occurred to me that a certain rearrangement of people's daily planning might seem, in less rarified air than is breathed at 120 South Spring, rather a great deal to want, but so impenetrable was the sense of higher social purpose there in the Operations Center that I did not express this reservation. Instead I changed the subject, mentioned an earlier "pilot project" on the Santa Monica: the big electronic message boards that Caltrans had installed a year or two before. The idea was that traffic information transmitted from the Santa Monica to the Xerox Sigma V could be translated, here in the Operations Center, into suggestions to the driver, and flashed right back out to the Santa Monica. This operation, in that it involved telling drivers electronically what they already knew empirically, had the rather spectral circularity that seemed to mark a great many Caltrans schemes, and I was interested in how Caltrans thought it worked. 9

"Actually the message boards were part of a larger pilot project," Mrs. Wood said. "An ongoing project in incident management. With the message boards we hoped to learn if motorists would modify their behavior according to what we told them on the boards." 10

I asked if the motorists had. 11

"Actually no," Mrs. Wood said finally. "They didn't react to the signs exactly as we'd hypothesized they would, no. *But*. If we'd *known* what the motorist would do . . . then we wouldn't have needed a pilot project in the first place, would we." 12

The circle seemed intact. Mrs. Wood and I smiled, and shook   13
hands. I watched the big board until all lights turned green on the Santa
Monica and then I left and drove home on it, all 16.2 miles of it. All
the way I remembered that I was watched by the Xerox Sigma V. All
the way the message boards gave me the number to call for CAR POOL
INFO. As I left the freeway it occurred to me that they might have their
own rapture down at 120 South Spring, and it could be called Perpetuating the Department. Today the California Highway Patrol reported
that, during the first six weeks of the Diamond Lane, accidents on the
Santa Monica, which normally range between 49 and 72 during a six-
week period, totaled 204. Yesterday plans were announced to extend the
Diamond Lane to other freeways at a cost of $42,500,000.

About the Essay

1. Why do you think Didion wrote for a national audience about the California Department of Transportation and its doings? What does her essay
have to say to out-of-state readers? Is there evidence that she has such readers
in mind?

2. Why does Didion refer repeatedly to the "windowless room" in which the
Caltrans bureaucrats work? What is the effect of her frequent use, always in
quotation marks, of Caltrans jargon? What other details of the essay reveal
to you her attitude toward her subject? What is that attitude?

3. Consider Didion's description of the Santa Monica Freeway. What kinds
of information does she give? What does each detail contribute? What is the
effect of the order in which she presents her information?

4. What exactly was the "Diamond Lane" meant to accomplish? Why did it
fail? Who is to blame for the failure, and why?

5. Didion quotes a Caltrans official as saying, "All this project requires is a
certain rearrangement of people's daily planning." Why does Didion have
reservations about this remark? What is your response to it? Why?

6. Look again at the concluding paragraph, considering the effect of each
sentence in it. How does Didion use the information she has given us earlier
in the essay? What purposes does the paragraph serve, besides ending the
essay? Why did she withhold important information about the Diamond Lane
until the last two sentences, when she could have given it in the first paragraph or elsewhere in the essay?

Explorations

1. What is a bureaucrat? What do bureaucrats do, and why are they so often
criticized? What experiences have you had with bureaucrats that might support or contradict the general view?

2. The federal bureaucracy has been described as the fourth branch of government, influencing policy as well as carrying it out. How does it exercise that influence? Is this good or bad for the country? Why do you think so?

3. The Caltrans Operations Center has an unreal quality about it, almost as if it were a set for a movie on the absurdity of bureaucratic behavior. What films have you seen that show the absurdity of bureaucracies? Why are bureaucracies so often treated in popular art forms as monstrously menacing?

FRAN LEBOWITZ

At the height of the 1970s anti-war protests, an ironic question was making the rounds: "What if they gave a war and nobody came?" In the following essay Fran Lebowitz has the definitive solution to that problem. She was born in 1951 in Morristown, New Jersey, and worked as a taxi driver, a bulk mailer, an apartment cleaner, an advertising salesperson, and a poetry reader before becoming established as a writer. She now writes two columns, "I Cover the Waterfront" in Andy Warhol's tabloid *Interview* and "The Lebowitz Report" in *Mademoiselle,* in which she offers her views on contemporary urban life, especially in New York City. The best of these columns have been collected in *Metropolitan Life* (1978) and *Social Studies* (1981). "War Stories" is from *Social Studies.* In it she explains in detail how to raise an army without resorting to the draft, and in particular how to recruit and organize that most important of special forces, the Writers' Regiment.

War Stories

Despite my strenuous, not to say unparalleled, efforts to remain ill-informed, it has come to my attention that there has been, of late, some talk of war. Discussions concerning the drafting of women, the enrichment of the defense budget, and a certain unease on the part of older teenagers has led me to assume that what you people have in mind here is a regular war with soldiers, as opposed to a modern war with buttons.

Being classically inclined, I applaud this apparent return to the tried and true, yet cannot help but feel that contemporary life has taken its toll and we will thus be compelled to make certain allowances and institute practices that can only be called unorthodox. It is, therefore, in the national interests of a smooth transition and eventual victory that I offer the following:

Suppose They Gave a War and You Weren't Invited

The first step in having any successful war is getting people to fight it. You can have the biggest battlefields on your bloc, the best artillery money can buy and strategies galore, but without those all-important combat troops your war just won't get started. Numbers alone are not enough, however, and many a country has made the mistake of filling its armed forces with too many of the same type. A good mix is essential. Monotony is as dangerous on the battlefield as it is on the highway. The problem, then, is how to attract the sort of large and varied group that you are going to need.

The draft, of course, is traditional and always appropriate but it has, 4 in recent years, fallen somewhat out of favor, becoming in the process not only old hat but downright ineffective. Clearly, extreme measures are called for, and in no way could they be better served than by the implementation of just a touch of psychological warfare. By combining the aforementioned situation with the indisputable fact that the grass is always greener on the other side of the fence, I suggest that instead of drafting, the powers that be consider inviting. Inviting ensures attendance by all but the most conscientious of objectors, who are impossible to get for really big things anyway. And although inviting might, at first glance, appear to be rather a grand gesture, the actual invitations can and should be simple and functional. Engraved invitations are showy, unduly formal and altogether lacking in urgency. The desired effect can probably best be achieved by the prudent use of the Mailgram. With the invitee's name and address in the upper left-hand corner a personal salutation is unnecessary.

We then proceed to the body of the Mailgram, which might, for 5 example, read:

YOU ARE CORDIALLY INVITED TO
ATTEND THE ONLY PREDECLARATION
INDUCTION INTO THE ARMY FOR THE
UNITED STATES OF AMERICA'S
FORTHCOMING WAR. THE INDUCTION
WILL BEGIN PROMPTLY AT 8:00 A.M. AT
201 VARICK STREET, NEW YORK CITY ON
APRIL 15. WE REGRET THAT DUE TO
LIMITED SPACE ONLY ONE PERSON CAN
BE ADMITTED PER INVITATION.

R.S.V.P. TO OUR OFFICES ON OR BEFORE
MARCH 30. YOUR NAME ON OUR R.S.V.P.
LIST WILL EXPEDITE YOUR ADMISSION.

THIS INVITATION IS NOT TRANSFERABLE.

Only one person can be admitted per invitation? This invitation is 6 not transferable? Talk about impact. Imagine, if you will, the days immediately following the receipt of this missive. You are one of the lucky ones. There are others less fortunate. First casual inquiries, then pointed requests, finally desperate begging. On the eve of the induction the truly insecure go out of town while the aggressively defensive announce that they're exhausted and have decided to just stay in and order Chinese food. Yes, people will be hurt. Friendships will be dissolved. New, decidedly unappealing alliances will be formed. It's too bad, but it can't be helped. Blood, sweat and tears are no longer enough; nowadays you need a door policy. All is fair in love and war.

The Children's Crusade

The most recent official statements on the subject indicate that when   7
it comes to war, the powers that be are partial to eighteen- and nineteen-year-olds. The parents of these youths may understandably be disconcerted at having to send their children off to what is at best an unfamiliar environment. In an effort to assuage these fears, I suggest that they think of the army as simply another kind of summer camp, and keep in mind that their child may well be the one to return with that highest of honors: Best All-Around Soldier.

Camp Base

For Boys and Girls Ages 18–19
■   Our 102nd season as a friendly,
caring community   ■   Complete
facilities   ■   Hiking   ■   Riflery   ■
Overnight trips   ■   Backpacking
■   Radar

Extra Special Forces

Being in my absolute latest possible twenties, I am not myself of   8
draftable age. That does not mean, though, that I am entirely without patriotism and the attendant desire to serve my country.

Desire is not, however (at least in this instance), synonymous with   9
fanaticism, and I do feel that those of us who choose to go should receive certain privileges and considerations. The kinds of certain privileges and considerations I had in mind were these: either I go right from the start as a general or they establish, along guidelines set down by me, a Writers' Regiment.

GUIDELINES SET DOWN BY ME

a. War is, undoubtedly, hell, but there is no earthly reason why it   10
has to start so early in the morning. Writers, on the whole, find it difficult
to work during the day; it is far too distracting. The writer is an artist,
a creative person; he needs time to think, to read, to ruminate. Rumi-
nating in particular is not compatible with reveille. Instead, next to each
(double) bed in the Writers' Barracks (or suites, as they are sometimes
called) should be a night table minimally equipped with an ashtray, a
refreshing drink, a good reading lamp and a telephone. Promptly at 1:30
P.M. the phone may ring and a pleasant person with a soft voice may
transmit the wake-up call.

b. In the army, discipline must, of course, be maintained and gen-   11
erally this is accomplished by a chain of command. In a chain of command you have what is known as the superior officer. The superior officer
is fine for ordinary soldiers such as lighting designers and art directors,
but the Writers' Regiment would, by definition, require instead something a bit different: the superior prose stylist. Having a superior prose
stylist would, I am sure, be an acceptable, even welcome, policy, and
will without question be adopted just as soon as the first writer meets
one.

c. The members of the Writers' Regiment would, of course, like to   12
join the rest of you in dangerous armed combat, but unfortunately the
pen is mightier than the sword and we must serve where we are needed.

International Arrivals

Traditionally, former U.S. Air Force pilots have sought and at-   13
tained employment with the commercial airlines. Today we can look forward to a reversal of this custom, as the U.S. Air Force becomes the
recipient of commercially trained airline personnel:

"Hello, this is your captain, Skip Dietrich, speaking. It's nice to   14
have you aboard. We're going to be entering a little enemy fire up ahead
and you may experience some slight discomfort. The temperature in the
metro Moscow area is twenty below zero and it's snowing. We're a little
behind schedule on account of that last hit, so we should be arriving at
around two-thirty Their Time. Those of you in the tourist cabin seated
on the right-hand side of the plane might want to glance out the window
and catch what's left of the wing before it goes entirely. That's about all
for now, hope you have a pleasant flight and thank you for flying United
States Air Force."

About the Essay

1. Does "War Stories" have a point? If so, what is it? If not, what is the essay's purpose?

2. What do Lebowitz's paragraphs 4–6 suggest about the draft? About invitations?

3. Lebowitz continually refers to *you* and *we*. Whom does she claim to be speaking for, and whom is she addressing?

4. The ad for Camp Base plays with and against our expectations of the Army and of summer camp. How does it do this?

5. How does Lebowitz organize her essay? What crucial aspects of military service does she leave out? Why?

6. Why does Lebowitz give her essay the title, "War Stories"? What does that expression generally mean? How is it relevant to this essay?

7. What makes Lebowitz's essay funny? What is the object of her humor? How would you describe the quality of her humor?

Explorations

1. The Selective Service System ceased drafting people into the Armed Forces as long ago as 1973, but registration for the draft was reintroduced in 1980. What arguments can be made for and against draft registration, and the draft itself, in peacetime? What is your personal view of the issue?

2. When Lebowitz says that "contemporary life has taken its toll" of public acceptance of the draft, she is referring to the time of the Vietnam War when thousands of Americans refused to be inducted, many of them leaving the country in protest. Look into the history of draft resistance during that war. How many draftees actually refused to enter the military? What happened to them, both during the war and after it? How did the draft, in effect since 1940 in peace and war, come to be abolished in 1973?

JONATHAN SCHELL

Who would survive a nuclear war? What kind of world would be left for them to live in? Since no nuclear war has been fought since the atomic bombs were dropped on Japan in 1945, and since those bombs were small by modern standards, such questions can be answered only by careful research and reasoning. Jonathan Schell did just such work in preparing his important and powerful book, *The Fate of the Earth* (1982). Schell was born in 1943 in New York City and earned a B.A. in Far Eastern history at Harvard College. He has since then worked on the staff of *The New Yorker* and published three other books: *Village of Ben Suc* (1967), *The Military Half* (1969), and *The Time of Illusion* (1976).

The following selection is drawn from *The Fate of the Earth*. The thesis of the book is that full-scale nuclear war could lead to the extinction of life on earth, a view that has been highly controversial. Schell's description of what actually happens in a nuclear explosion, however, is fully substantiated and frightening to think about.

The Fate of the Earth

Since July 16, 1945, when the first atomic bomb was detonated, at the Trinity test site, near Alamogordo, New Mexico, mankind has lived with nuclear weapons in its midst. Each year, the number of bombs has grown, until now there are some fifty thousand warheads in the world, possessing the explosive yield of roughly twenty billion tons of TNT, or one million six hundred thousand times the yield of the bomb that was dropped by the United States on the city of Hiroshima, in Japan, less than a month after the Trinity explosion. These bombs were built as "weapons" for "war," but their significance greatly transcends war and all its causes and outcomes. They grew out of history, yet they threaten to end history. They were made by men, yet they threaten to annihilate man. They are a pit into which the whole world can fall—a nemesis of all human intentions, actions, and hopes. Only life itself, which they threaten to swallow up, can give the measure of their significance. Yet in spite of the immeasurable importance of nuclear weapons, the world has declined, on the whole, to think about them very much. We have thus far failed to fashion, or to discover within ourselves, an emotional or intellectual or political response to them. This peculiar failure of response, in which hundreds of millions of people acknowledge the presence of an immediate, unremitting threat to their existence and to the existence of the world they live in but do nothing about it—a failure in

1

which both self-interest and fellow-feeling seem to have died—has itself been such a striking phenomenon that it has to be regarded as an extremely important part of the nuclear predicament as this has existed so far. Only very recently have there been signs, in Europe and in the United States, that public opinion has been stirring awake, and that ordinary people may be beginning to ask themselves how they should respond to the nuclear peril. . . .

We have lived in the shadow of nuclear arms for more than thirty-six years, so it does not seem too soon for us to familiarize ourselves with them—to acquaint ourselves with such matters as the "thermal pulse," the "blast wave," and the "three stages of radiation sickness." A description of a full-scale holocaust seems to be made necessary by the simple but basic rule that in order to discuss something one should first know what it is. . . .

Whereas most conventional bombs produce only one destructive effect—the shock wave—nuclear weapons produce many destructive effects. At the moment of the explosion, when the temperature of the weapon material, instantly gasified, is at the superstellar level, the pressure is millions of times the normal atmospheric pressure. Immediately, radiation, consisting mainly of gamma rays, which are a very high-energy form of electromagnetic radiation, begins to stream outward into the environment. This is called the "initial nuclear radiation," and is the first of the destructive effects of a nuclear explosion. In an air burst of a one-megaton bomb—a bomb with the explosive yield of a million tons of TNT, which is a medium-sized weapon in present-day nuclear arsenals—the initial nuclear radiation can kill unprotected human beings in an area of some six square miles. Virtually simultaneously with the initial nuclear radiation, in a second destructive effect of the explosion, an electro-magnetic pulse is generated by the intense gamma radiation acting on the air. In a high-altitude detonation, the pulse can knock out electrical equipment over a wide area by inducing a powerful surge of voltage through various conductors, such as antennas, overhead power lines, pipes, and railroad tracks. The Defense Department's Civil Preparedness Agency reported in 1977 that a single multi-kiloton nuclear weapon detonated one hundred and twenty-five miles over Omaha, Nebraska, could generate an electromagnetic pulse strong enough to damage solid-state electrical circuits throughout the entire continental United States and in part of Canada and Mexico, and thus threaten to bring the economies of these countries to a halt. When the fusion and fission reactions have blown themselves out, a fireball takes shape. As it expands, energy is absorbed in the form of X rays by the surrounding air, and then the air re-radiates a portion of that energy into the environment in the form of the thermal pulse—a wave of blinding light and intense heat—which is the third of the destructive effects of a nuclear explosion. (If the burst is low enough, the fireball touches the ground, vaporizing or incinerating almost everything within it.) The thermal pulse of a one-megaton bomb lasts for about ten seconds and can cause second-degree burns in exposed human beings at a distance of nine and a half miles, or in an area of more than two hundred and eighty square miles, and that of a twenty-megaton bomb (a large weapon by modern standards) lasts for about twenty seconds and can produce the same consequences at a distance of twenty-eight miles, or in an area of two thousand four hundred and sixty square miles. As the fireball expands, it also sends out a blast wave in all directions, and this is the fourth destructive effect of the explosion. The blast wave of an air-burst one-megaton bomb can flatten or severely damage all but the strongest buildings within a radius of four and a half miles, and that of a twenty-megaton bomb can do the same within a radius of twelve miles. As the fireball burns, it rises, condensing water from the surrounding atmosphere to form the characteristic mushroom cloud. If the bomb has been set off on the ground or close enough to it so that the fireball touches the surface, in a so-called ground burst, a crater will be formed, and tons of dust and debris will be fused with the intensely radioactive fission products and sucked up into the mushroom cloud. This mixture will return to earth as radioactive fallout, most of it in the form of fine ash, in the fifth destructive effect of the explosion. Depending upon the composition of the surface, from forty to seventy per cent of this fallout—often called the "early" or "local" fallout— descends to earth within about a day of the explosion, in the vicinity of the blast and downwind from it, exposing human beings to radiation disease, an illness that is fatal when exposure is intense. Air bursts may also produce local fallout, but in much smaller quantities. The lethal range of the local fallout depends on a number of circumstances, including the weather, but under average conditions a one-megaton ground blast would, according to the report by the Office of Technology Assessment, lethally contaminate over a thousand square miles. (A lethal dose, by convention, is considered to be the amount of radiation that, if delivered over a short period of time, would kill half the able-bodied young adult population.)

The initial nuclear radiation, the electromagnetic pulse, the thermal pulse, the blast wave, and the local fallout may be described as the local primary effects of nuclear weapons. Naturally, when many bombs are exploded the scope of these effects is increased accordingly. But in addition these primary effects produce innumerable secondary effects on societies and natural environments, some of which may be even more harmful than the primary ones. To give just one example, nuclear weapons, by flattening and setting fire to huge, heavily built-up areas, generate mass fires, and in some cases these may kill more people than the original thermal pulses and blast waves. Moreover, there are—quite distinct from both the local primary effects of individual bombs and their secondary effects—global primary effects, which do not become significant unless thousands of bombs are detonated all around the earth. And these global primary effects produce innumerable secondary effects of their own throughout the ecosystem of the earth as a whole. For a full-scale holocaust is more than the sum of its local parts; it is also a powerful direct blow to the ecosphere. In that sense, a holocaust is to the earth what a single bomb is to a city. Three grave direct global effects have been discovered so far. The first is the "delayed," or "worldwide," fallout. In detonations greater than one hundred kilotons, part of the fallout does not fall to the ground in the vicinity of the explosion but rises high into the troposphere and into the stratosphere, circulates around the earth, and then, over months or years, descends, contaminating the whole surface of the globe—although with doses of radiation far weaker than those delivered by the local fallout. Nuclear-fission products comprise some three hundred radioactive isotopes, and though some of them decay to relatively harmless levels of radioactivity within a few hours, minutes, or even seconds, others persist to emit radiation for up to millions of years. . . .

The second of the global effects that have been discovered so far 5
is the lofting, from ground bursts, of millions of tons of dust into the stratosphere; this is likely to produce general cooling of the earth's surface. The third of the global effects is a predicted partial destruction of the layer of ozone that surrounds the entire earth in the stratosphere. A nuclear fireball, by burning nitrogen in the air, produces large quantities of oxides of nitrogen. These are carried by the heat of the blast into the stratosphere, where, through a series of chemical reactions, they bring about a depletion of the ozone layer. Such a depletion may persist for years. The 1975 N.A.S. report has estimated that in a holocaust in which ten thousand megatons were detonated in the Northern Hemisphere the reduction of ozone in this hemisphere could be as high as seventy per cent and in the Southern Hemisphere as high as forty per cent, and that it could take as long as thirty years for the ozone level to return to normal. The ozone layer is crucial to life on earth, because it shields the surface of the earth from lethal levels of ultraviolet radiation, which is present in sunlight. Glasstone remarks simply, "If it were not for the absorption of much of the solar ultraviolet radiation by the ozone, life as currently

known could not exist except possibly in the ocean." Without the ozone shield, sunlight, the life-giver, would become a life-extinguisher. In judging the global effects of a holocaust, therefore, the primary question is not how many people would be irradiated, burned, or crushed to death by the immediate effects of the bombs but how well the ecosphere, regarded as a single living entity, on which all forms of life depend for their continued existence, would hold up. The issue is the habitability of the earth, and it is in this context, not in the context of the direct slaughter of hundreds of millions of people by the local effects, that the question of human survival arises. . . .

I asked Dr. Kendall, who has done considerable research on the consequences of nuclear attacks, to sketch out in rough terms what the actual distribution of bombs might be in a ten-thousand-megaton Soviet attack in the early nineteen-eighties on all targets in the United States, military and civilian.

"Without serious distortion," he said, "we can begin by imagining that we would be dealing with ten thousand weapons of one megaton each, although in fact the yields would, of course, vary considerably. Let us also make the assumption, based on common knowledge of weapons design, that on average the yield would be one-half fission and one-half fusion. This proportion is important, because it is the fission products—a virtual museum of about three hundred radioactive isotopes, decaying at different rates—that give off radioactivity in fallout. Fusion can add to the total in ground bursts by radioactivation of ground material by neutrons, but the quantity added is comparatively small. Targets can be divided into two categories—hard and soft. Hard targets, of which there are about a thousand in the United States, are mostly missile silos. The majority of them can be destroyed only by huge, blunt overpressures, ranging anywhere from many hundreds to a few thousand pounds per square inch, and we can expect that two weapons might be devoted to each one to assure destruction. That would use up two thousand megatons. Because other strategic military targets—such as Strategic Air Command bases—are near centers of population, an attack on them as well, perhaps using another couple of hundred megatons, could cause a total of more than twenty million casualties, according to studies by the Arms Control and Disarmament Agency. If the nearly eight thousand weapons remaining were then devoted to the cities and towns of the United States in order of population, every community down to the level of fifteen hundred inhabitants would be hit with a megaton bomb—which is, of course, many, many times what would be necessary to annihilate a town that size. For obvious reasons, industry is highly correlated with population density, so an attack on the one necessarily hits the other, especially when an attack of this magnitude is considered. Ten thousand targets would include everything worth hitting in the country and much more; it would simply *be* the United States. The targeters would run out of targets and victims long before they ran out of bombs. If you imagine that the bombs were distributed according to population, then, allowing for the fact that the attack on the military installations would have already killed about twenty million people, you would have about forty megatons to devote to each remaining million people in the country. For the seven and a half million people in New York City, that would come to three hundred megatons. Bearing in mind what one megaton can do, you can see that this would be preposterous overkill. In practice, one might expect the New York metropolitan area to be hit with some dozens of one-megaton weapons."

In the first moments of a ten-thousand-megaton attack on the United States, I learned from Dr. Kendall and from other sources, flashes of white light would suddenly illumine large areas of the country as thousands of suns, each one brighter than the sun itself, blossomed over cities, suburbs, and towns. In those same moments, when the first wave of missiles arrived, the vast majority of the people in the regions first targeted would be irradiated, crushed, or burned to death. The thermal pulses could subject more than six hundred thousand square miles, or one-sixth of the total land mass of the nation, to a minimum level of forty calories per centimetre squared—a level of heat that chars human beings. (At Hiroshima, charred remains in the rough shape of human beings were a common sight.) Tens of millions of people would go up in smoke. As the attack proceeded, as much as three-quarters of the country could be subjected to incendiary levels of heat, and so, wherever there was inflammable material, could be set ablaze. In the ten seconds or so after each bomb hit, as blast waves swept outward from thousands of ground zeros, the physical plant of the United States would be swept away like leaves in a gust of wind. The six hundred thousand square miles already scorched by the forty or more calories of heat per centimetre squared would now be hit by blast waves of a minimum of five pounds per square inch, and virtually all the habitations, places of work, and other man-made things there—substantially the whole human construct in the United States—would be vaporized, blasted, or otherwise pulverized out of existence. Then, as clouds of dust rose from the earth, and mushroom clouds spread overhead, often linking to form vast canopies, day would turn to night. (These clouds could blanket as much as a third of the nation.) Shortly, fires would spring up in the debris of the cities and in every forest dry enough to burn. These fires would simply burn down the United States. When one pictures a full-scale attack on the

8

United States, or on any other country, therefore, the picture of a single city being flattened by a single bomb—an image firmly engraved in the public imagination, probably because of the bombings of Hiroshima and Nagasaki—must give way to a picture of substantial sections of the country being turned by a sort of nuclear carpet-bombing into immense infernal regions, literally tens of thousands of square miles in area, from which escape is impossible. In Hiroshima and Nagasaki, those who had not been killed or injured so severely that they could not move were able to flee to the undevastated world around them, where they found help, but in any city where three or four bombs had been used—not to mention fifty, or a hundred—flight from one blast would only be flight toward another, and no one could escape alive. Within these regions, each of three of the immediate effects of nuclear weapons—initial radiation, thermal pulse, and blast wave—would alone be enough to kill most people: the initial nuclear radiation would subject tens of thousands of square miles to lethal doses; the blast waves, coming from all sides, would nowhere fall below the overpressure necessary to destroy almost all buildings; and the thermal pulses, also coming from all sides, would always be great enough to kill exposed people and, in addition, to set on fire everything that would burn. The ease with which virtually the whole population of the country could be trapped in these zones of universal death is suggested by the fact that the sixty per cent of the population that lives in an area of eighteen thousand square miles could be annihilated with only three hundred one-megaton bombs—the number necessary to cover the area with a minimum of five pounds per square inch of overpressure and forty calories per centimetre squared of heat. That would leave nine thousand seven hundred megatons, or ninety-seven per cent of the megatonnage in the attacking force, available for other targets. (It is hard to imagine what a targeter would do with all his bombs in these circumstances. Above several thousand megatons, it would almost become a matter of trying to hunt down individual people with nuclear warheads.)

The statistics on the initial nuclear radiation, the thermal pulses, and the blast waves in a nuclear holocaust can be presented in any number of ways, but all of them would be only variations on a simple theme—the annihilation of the United States and its people. Yet while the immediate nuclear effects are great enough in a ten-thousand-megaton attack to destroy the country many times over, they are not the most powerfully lethal of the local effects of nuclear weapons. The killing power of the local fallout is far greater. Therefore, if the Soviet Union was bent on producing the maximum overkill—if, that is, its surviving leaders, whether out of calculation, rage, or madness, decided to eliminate the United States not merely as a political and social entity but as a biological one—they would burst their bombs on the ground rather than in the air. Although the scope of severe blast damage would then be reduced, the blast waves, fireballs, and thermal pulses would still be far more than enough to destroy the country, and, in addition, provided only that the bombs were dispersed widely enough, lethal fallout would spread throughout the nation.

It has sometimes been claimed that the United States could survive   10 a nuclear attack by the Soviet Union, but the bare figures on the extent of the blast waves, the thermal pulses, and the accumulated local fallout dash this hope irrevocably. They spell the doom of the United States. And if one imagines the reverse attack on the Soviet Union, its doom is spelled out in similar figures. (The greater land mass of the Soviet Union and the lower megatonnage of the American forces might reduce the factor of overkill somewhat.) Likewise, any country subjected to an attack of more than a few hundred megatons would be doomed. Japan, China, and the countries of Europe, where population densities are high, are especially vulnerable to damage, even at "low" levels of attack. There is no country in Europe in which survival of the population would be appreciable after the detonation of several hundred megatons; most European countries would be annihilated by tens of megatons. And these conclusions emerge even before one takes into account the global ecological consequences of a holocaust, which would be superimposed on the local consequences. As human life and the structure of human existence are seen in the light of each person's daily life and experience, they look impressively extensive and solid, but when human things are seen in the light of the universal power unleashed onto the earth by nuclear weapons they prove to be limited and fragile, as though they were nothing more than a mold or a lichen that appears in certain crevices of the landscape and can be burned off with relative ease by nuclear fire.

Many discussions of nuclear attacks on the United States devote   11 considerable attention to their effect on the nation's economy, but if the population has been largely killed off and the natural environment is in a state of collapse "the economy" becomes a meaningless concept; for example, it makes no difference what percentage of "the automobile industry" has survived if all the producers and drivers of automobiles have died. Estimates of economic survival after a full-scale holocaust are, in fact, doubly unreal, because, as a number of government reports have shown, the nation's economy is so much more vulnerable to attack than the population that even at most levels of "limited" attack a greater proportion of the economy than of the population would be destroyed. An intact economic plant that goes to waste because there aren't enough people left to run it is one absurdity that a nuclear holocaust does not present us with. At relatively low levels of attack, however, the more or less complete destruction of the economy, accompanied by the survival of as much as twenty or thirty per cent of the population, is conceivable. Since the notion of "limited nuclear war" has recently become attractive to the American leadership, it may not be digressive to discuss what the consequences of smaller attacks would be. Our knowledge of nuclear effects is too imprecise to permit us to know at exactly what level of attack a given percentage of the population would survive, but the fact that sixty per cent of the population lives in eighteen thousand square miles and could be eliminated by the thermal pulses, blast waves, and mass fires produced by about three hundred one-megaton bombs suggests some rough magnitudes. The fallout that would be produced by the bombs if they were ground-burst would very likely kill ten or fifteen per cent of the remaining population (it could lethally contaminate some three hundred thousand square miles), and if several hundred additional megatons were used the percentage of the entire population killed in the short term might rise to something like eighty-five. Or, to put it differently, if the level of attack on civilian targets did not rise above the low hundreds of megatons, tens of millions of people might survive in the short term. But that same level of attack would destroy so much of the physical plant of the economy, and, of course, so many of the laborers and managers who make it work, that in effect the economy would be nearly one hundred per cent destroyed. . . .

Strategists of nuclear conflict often speak of a period of "recovery" after a limited attack, but a likelier prospect is a long-term radical deterioration in the conditions of life. For a while, some supplies of food and clothing would be found in the rubble, but then these would give out. For a people, the economy—any kind of economy, whether primitive or modern—is the means of survival from day to day. So if you ruin the economy—if you suspend its functioning, even for a few months— you take away the means of survival. Eventually, if enough people do live, the economy will revive in one form or another, but in the meantime people will die: they will starve, because the supply of food has been cut off; they will freeze, because they have no fuel or shelter; they will perish of illness, because they have no medical care. If the economy in question is a modern technological one, the consequences will be particularly severe, for then the obstacles to restoring it will be greatest. Because a modern economy, like an ecosystem, is a single, interdependent whole, in which each part requires many other parts to keep func-

12

tioning, its wholesale breakdown will leave people unable to perform the simplest, most essential tasks. Even agriculture—the immediate means of subsistence—is caught up in the operations of the interdependent machine, and breaks down when it breaks down. Modern agriculture depends on fertilizers to make crops grow, on machines to cultivate the crops, on transportation to carry the produce thousands of miles to the consumers, on fuel to run the means of transportation and the agricultural machinery, and on pesticides and drugs to increase production. If fertilizers, machines, transportation, fuel, pesticides, and drugs are taken away, agriculture will come to a halt, and people will starve. Also, because of the interdependence of the system, no sector of the economy can be repaired unless many of the other sectors are in good order.

But in a nuclear attack, of course, all sectors of the economy would be devastated at once. The task facing the survivors, therefore, would be not to restore the old economy but to invent a new one, on a far more primitive level. But the invention of a primitive economy would not be a simple matter. Even economies we think of as primitive depend on considerable knowledge accumulated through long experience, and in modern times this knowledge has been largely lost. The economy of the Middle Ages, for example, was far less productive than our own, but it was exceedingly complex, and it would not be within the capacity of people in our time suddenly to establish a medieval economic system in the ruins of their twentieth-century one. After a limited nuclear attack, the typical predicament of a survivor would be that of, say, a bus driver in a city who was used to shopping at a supermarket and found himself facing the question of how to grow his own food, or of a bookkeeper in a suburb who found that he must make his own clothing, not to mention the cloth for the clothing. Innumerable things that we now take for granted would abruptly be lacking. In addition to food and clothing, they would include: heating, electric lights, running water, telephones, mail, transportation of all kinds, all household appliances powered by electricity or gas, information other than by word of mouth, medical facilities, sanitary facilities, and basic social services, such as fire departments and police. To restore these essentials of life takes time; but there would be no time. Hunger, illness, and possibly cold would press in on the dazed, bewildered, disorganized, injured remnant of the population on the very day of the attack. They would have to start foraging immediately for their next meal. Sitting among the debris of the Space Age, they would find that the pieces of a shattered modern economy around them—here an automobile, there a washing machine—were mismatched to their elemental needs. Nor would life be made easier for them by the fact that their first need, once they left any shelters they might have found, would

13

be to flee the heavily irradiated, burned-out territories where they used to live, and to start over in less irradiated, unburned territories, which would probably be in the wilderness. Facing these urgent requirements, they would not be worrying about rebuilding the automobile industry or the electronics industry; they would be worrying about how to find non-radioactive berries in the woods, or how to tell which trees had edible bark. . . .

When the existence of nuclear weapons was made known, thoughtful people everywhere in the world realized that if the great powers entered into a nuclear-arms race the human species would sooner or later face the possibility of extinction. They also realized that in the absence of international agreements preventing it an arms race would probably occur. They knew that the path of nuclear armament was a dead end for mankind. The discovery of the energy in mass—of "the basic power of the universe"—and of a means by which man could release that energy altered the relationship between man and the source of his life, the earth. In the shadow of this power, the earth became small and the life of the human species doubtful. In that sense, the question of human extinction has been on the political agenda of the world ever since the first nuclear weapon was detonated, and there was no need for the world to build up its present tremendous arsenals before starting to worry about it. At just what point the species crossed, or will have crossed, the boundary between merely having the technical knowledge to destroy itself and actually having the arsenals at hand, ready to be used at any second, is not precisely knowable. But it is clear that at present, with some twenty thousand megatons of nuclear explosive power in existence, and with more being added every day, we have entered into the zone of uncertainty, which is to say the zone of risk of extinction. But the mere risk of extinction has a significance that is categorically different from, and immeasurably greater than, that of any other risk, and as we make our decisions we have to take that significance into account. Up to now, every risk has been contained within the frame of life; extinction would shatter the frame. It represents not the defeat of some purpose but an abyss in which all human purposes would be drowned for all time. We have no right to place the possibility of this limitless, eternal defeat on the same footing as risks that we run in the ordinary conduct of our affairs in our particular transient moment of human history. To employ a mathematical analogy, we can say that although the risk of extinction may be fractional, the stake is, humanly speaking, infinite, and a fraction of infinity is still infinity. In other words, once we learn that a holocaust *might* lead to extinction we have no right to gamble, because if we lose, the game will be over, and neither we nor anyone else will ever get

14

another chance. Therefore, although, scientifically speaking, there is all the difference in the world between the mere possibility that a holocaust will bring about extinction and the certainty of it, morally they are the same, and we have no choice but to address the issue of nuclear weapons as though we knew for a certainty that their use would put an end to our species. In weighing the fate of the earth and, with it, our own fate, we stand before a mystery, and in tampering with the earth we tamper with a mystery. We are in deep ignorance. Our ignorance should dispose us to wonder, our wonder should make us humble, our humility should inspire us to reverence and caution, and our reverence and caution should lead us to act without delay to withdraw the threat we now pose to the earth and to ourselves.

About the Essay

1. According to Schell, what is the central issue involved when we consider the effects of nuclear war? What reasons does he give for this view?

2. A large part of the essay is devoted to a minutely detailed description of the destructive effects of nuclear weapons. How has Schell organized his description? Why has he gone into such detail in these descriptions? How do the detailed descriptions affect your intellectual and emotional understanding of what nuclear war involves?

3. Why, according to Schell, would the United States, the Soviet Union, or any other densely populated industrial country be "doomed" after a nuclear attack? What specific details does he use to convey the difficulties survivors would face?

4. What, for you, is the most powerful part of Schell's essay? What gives it its power? Are there any passages where he failed to hold your interest? If so, where, and why?

5. What tone does Schell adopt in this essay? Is it maintained consistently throughout? If not, where does it change?

Explorations

1. Why, after many years of nuclear stalemate, have Americans newly become alarmed that nuclear bombs may finally fall? Do you personally feel at risk? Why? What measures might serve to lessen the risk? What are the prospects that such measures will be taken?

2. Investigate the making of the atomic bomb and its first and only use in war. What were the arguments for and against the project at the time? What were the effects of the bomb's first use? The dropping of the A-bombs on Japan is still controversial; what is your view?

3. Many political leaders have argued that the only way to assure peace is to build up our war machine. Do you agree or disagree? Why?

ROBERT FROST

Some nations have a poet laureate, a bard to provide appropriate verses for public occasions, but the United States does not. When in 1961 John F. Kennedy sought a poet to take part in his inauguration, however, he could have made no better choice than Robert Frost (1874-1963), whose poetic voice and subject matter are so thoroughly American. Frost was born in San Francisco but moved with his family to Massachusetts when he was eleven, and he became a New Englander through and through. He attended Dartmouth and Harvard briefly, spent some time as a millworker and schoolteacher, and then in 1900 moved to a farm in New Hampshire, where he lived most of the time for the rest of his life. From 1912 to 1915 he lived in England, where he published two books of poems that brought him his first critical recognition. He returned to the United States a popular poet and soon became a highly influential one, to teach at Amherst, Dartmouth, Harvard, and the University of Michigan and to be awarded numerous prizes and honors. Among his most celebrated poems are "The Tuft of Flowers" (1913), "Birches" (1916), and "Fire and Ice" (1923); they can be found in *Complete Poems* (1949).

Frost composed "The Gift Outright" for the Phi Beta Kappa chapter of William and Mary College, but it is more likely to be remembered as the poem he read at the Kennedy inauguration. In it he celebrates the birth of American independence and of the American spirit.

The Gift Outright

The land was ours before we were the land's.
She was our land more than a hundred years
Before we were her people. She was ours
In Massachusetts, in Virginia,
But we were England's, still colonials,   5
Possessing what we still were unpossessed by,
Possessed by what we now no more possessed.
Something we were withholding made us weak
Until we found out that it was ourselves
We were withholding from our land of living,   10
And forthwith found salvation in surrender.
Such as we were we gave ourselves outright
(The deed of gift was many deeds of war)
To the land vaguely realizing westward,
But still unstoried, artless, unenhanced,   15
Such as she was, such as she would become.

638

About the Poem

1. What gift is Frost referring to in his title? How was the gift made?

2. The poem is grounded in American history. What allusions to the American past does Frost make in the poem? Which lines carry these allusions?

3. What do lines 6 and 7 mean? What is meant by line 11?

4. In the poem Frost deliberately uses a number of words that have multiple meanings—*land, deed, realizing,* and *artless,* for example. Can you find others? Which meanings of each word come into play in the poem? What effect do these puns have on your response to the poem?

5. Frost uses parallelism in a number of places, as in "Such as she was, such as she would become." What other parallelisms are there in the poem? What is the effect of so many parallel expressions?

6. What does Frost suggest must be the relationship between a people and the land on which they live?

Explorations

1. Throughout their history, Americans have had an especially strong feeling for the land they lived on. Patriotic songs such as "America the Beautiful" celebrate the land, and the national parks system and much of the environmentalist movement are devoted to preserving it. Does the land have special significance for you? If so, what is that significance and how does it affect your life?

2. Compare the sentiments expressed in Frost's 16-line poem to those expressed in Chief Seattle's speech (pages 583–586). In what ways are they similar; in what ways different?

GWENDOLYN BROOKS

Gwendolyn Brooks was born in Topeka, Kansas, in 1917, but she grew up in Chicago and still makes that city her home. She graduated from Wilson Junior College in 1936 and held a number of jobs, including secretary to a spiritual advisor and publicity director of Chicago's NAACP Youth Council, until the appearance of her first book of poems, *A Street in Bronzeville*, in 1945. She was awarded the Pulitzer Prize in 1949 for *Annie Allen*. Like many other American poets, Brooks was deeply affected by the events of the 1960s; her books after 1967 reveal new concerns and a more militant voice. She has written a number of poems for public occasions, and in 1969 she was named poet laureate of Illinois. A miscellany of her earlier work is available as *The World of Gwendolyn Brooks* (1971), and her more recent poetry has been published by the Broadside Press, as has her autobiography, *Report from Part One* (1972). "The Lovers of the Poor" is taken from *The Bean Eaters* (1960). It reflects a sharp social awareness in its satiric depiction of two upper-class matrons who visit a Chicago slum tenement with charity on their minds but no idea of what they will find there.

The Lovers of the Poor

arrive. The Ladies from the Ladies' Betterment League
Arrive in the afternoon, the late light slanting
In diluted gold bars across the boulevard brag
Of proud, seamed faces with mercy and murder hinting
Here, there, interrupting, all deep and debonair,   5
The pink paint on the innocence of fear;
Walk in a gingerly manner up the hall.
Cutting with knives served by their softest care,
Served by their love, so barbarously fair.
Whose mothers taught: You'd better not be cruel!   10
You had better not throw stones upon the wrens!
Herein they kiss and coddle and assault
Anew and dearly in the innocence
With which they baffle nature. Who are full,
Sleek, tender-clad, fit, fiftyish, a-glow, all   15
Sweetly abortive, hinting at fat fruit,
Judge it high time that fiftyish fingers felt

640

Beneath the lovelier planes of enterprise.
To resurrect. To moisten with milky chill.
To be a random hitching-post or plush.   20
To be, for wet eyes, random and handy hem.
      Their guild is giving money to the poor.
The worthy poor. The very very worthy
And beautiful poor. Perhaps just not too swarthy?
Perhaps just not too dirty nor too dim   25
Nor—passionate. In truth, what they could wish
Is—something less than derelict or dull.
Not staunch enough to stab, though, gaze for gaze!
God shield them sharply from the beggar-bold!
The noxious needy ones whose battle's bald   30
Nonetheless for being voiceless, hits one down.
      But it's all so bad! and entirely too much for them.
The stench; the urine, cabbage, and dead beans,
Dead porridges of assorted dusty grains,
The old smoke, *heavy* diapers, and, they're told,   35
Something called chitterlings. The darkness. Drawn
Darkness, or dirty light. The soil that stirs.
The soil that looks the soil of centuries.
And for that matter the *general* oldness. Old
Wood. Old marble. Old tile. Old old old.   40
Not homekind Oldness! Not Lake Forest, Glencoe.[1]
Nothing is sturdy, nothing is majestic,
There is no quiet drama, no rubbed glaze, no
Unkillable infirmity of such
A tasteful turn as lately they have left,   45
Glencoe, Lake Forest, and to which their cars
Must presently restore them. When they're done
With dullards and distortions of this fistic
Patience of the poor and put-upon.
      They've never seen such a make-do-ness as   50
Newspaper rugs before! In this, this "flat,"
Their hostess is gathering up the oozed, the rich
Rugs of the morning (tattered! the bespattered. . . .)
Readies to spread clean rugs for afternoon.
Here is a scene for you. The Ladies look,   55
In horror, behind a substantial citizeness

---

[1]Lake Forest and Glencoe are fashionable suburbs of Chicago with old, stately homes.

Whose trains clank out across her swollen heart.
Who, arms akimbo, almost fills a door.
All tumbling children, quilts dragged to the floor
And tortured thereover, potato peelings, soft-   6◦
Eyed kitten, hunched-up, haggard, to-be-hurt.
            Their League is allotting largesse to the Lost
But to put their clean, their pretty money, to put
Their money collected from delicate rose-fingers
Tipped with their hundred flawless rose-nails seems . . .   6
            They own Spode, Lowestoft, candelabra,
Mantels, and hostess gowns, and sunburst clocks,
Turtle soup, Chippendale, red satin "hangings,"
Aubussons and Hattie Carnegie. They Winter
In Palm Beach; cross the Water in June; attend,   7◦
When suitable, the nice Art Institute;[2]
Buy the right books in the best bindings; saunter
On Michigan, Easter mornings, in sun or wind.
Oh Squalor! This sick four-story hulk, this fibre
With fissures everywhere! Why, what are bringings   75
Of loathe-love largesse? What shall peril hungers
So old old, what shall flatter the desolate?
Tin can, blocked fire escape and chitterling
And swaggering seeking youth and the puzzled wreckage
Of the middle passage, and urine and stale shames   80
And, again, the porridges of the underslung
And children children children. Heavens! That
Was a rat, surely, off there, in the shadows? Long
And long-tailed? Gray? The Ladies from the Ladies'
Betterment League agree it will be better   85
To achieve the outer air that rights and steadies,
To hie to a house that does not holler, to ring
Bells elsetime, better presently to cater
To no more Possibilities, to get
Away. Perhaps the money can be posted.   90
Perhaps they two may choose another Slum!
Some serious sooty half-unhappy home!—

---

[2]The trappings of wealth: *Spode*, expensive, porcelain chinaware; *Lowestoft*, another
expensive type of china; *Chippendale*, expensive antique furniture; *Aubusson*, an expensive ornamental rug; *Hattie Carnegie*, exclusive designer clothing worn by movie
stars and society women; *Cross the Water in June*, go to Europe; *Art Institute*, museum
of fine art in Chicago.

Where loathe-love likelier may be invested.
      Keeping their scented bodies in the center
Of the hall as they walk down the hysterical hall,   95
They allow their lovely skirts to graze no wall,
Are off at what they manage of a canter,
And, resuming all the clues of what they were,
Try to avoid inhaling the laden air.

About the Poem

1. Why are the ladies visiting the slum? What do they expect to find? What do they find instead?

2. What do the ladies finally decide to do? Why?

3. What does Brooks mean by the following passages:
    a. "Cutting with knives served by their softest care, / Served by their love, so barbarously fair." (Lines 8–9)
    b. "Judge it high time that fiftyish fingers felt / Beneath the lovelier planes of enterprise." (Lines 17–18)
    c. "Not staunch enough to stab, though, gaze for gaze! / God shield them sharply from the beggar-bold!" (Lines 28–29)

4. What is Brooks's attitude toward the ladies? Toward the people they visit? How does she reveal her attitude?

5. Why did Brooks call her poem "The Lovers of the Poor"? What did Brooks mean to convey by the name of the ladies' organization?

Explorations

1. Have you ever done charitable work? If so, what was your experience? How did you feel about those who were the beneficiaries of your work? How do you think those who received the charity felt? Can you draw any conclusions about the motivations and effects of charity?

2. "The Lovers of the Poor" provides one kind of insight into poverty; John Kenneth Galbraith's "The Position of Poverty" (pages 602–608) provides another. How do these two pieces complement each other? What aspects of poverty does neither touch upon?

3. It has been said that satires are the revenge victims take on their oppressors. Consider Swift's "Modest Proposal" (pages 695–702) in comparison with Brooks's "The Lovers of the Poor." How do these two works fulfill that aphorism?

KURT VONNEGUT, JR.

Our Declaration of Independence states as a "self-evident truth" that all are created equal. But what does it mean to be "equal"? In the following story, Kurt Vonnegut, Jr., shows what it does *not* mean. Vonnegut was born in 1922 in Indianapolis, Indiana. While he was a student at Cornell University, he joined the Army to serve in World War II and was sent to Europe. Taken prisoner by the German Army, he witnessed the Allied fire-bombing of Dresden in 1945, a bloody and pointless incident that inspired his novel *Slaughterhouse-Five* (1969). After the war he completed his education at the University of Chicago, then from 1947 to 1950 worked in the public relations department of General Electric; since then, he has worked full-time as a writer. Probably his best known novels, besides *Slaughterhouse-Five*, are *Player Piano* (1952) and *Cat's Cradle* (1963), and some of his short stories have been collected in *Welcome to the Monkey House* (1968). "Harrison Bergeron," from this collection, is set in 2081, but like much science fiction it offers a critique of the present as much as a prediction of the future.

Harrison Bergeron

The year was 2081, and everybody was finally equal. They weren't only equal before God and the law. They were equal every which way. Nobody was smarter than anybody else. Nobody was better looking than anybody else. Nobody was stronger or quicker than anybody else. All this equality was due to the 211th, 212th, and 213th Amendments to the Constitution, and to the unceasing vigilance of agents of the United States Handicapper General.

Some things about living still weren't quite right, though. April, for instance, still drove people crazy by not being springtime. And it was in that clammy month that the H-G men took George and Hazel Bergeron's fourteen-year-old son, Harrison, away.

It was tragic, all right, but George and Hazel couldn't think about it very hard. Hazel had a perfectly average intelligence, which meant she couldn't think about anything except in short bursts. And George, while his intelligence was way above normal, had a little mental handicap radio in his ear. He was required by law to wear it at all times. It was tuned to a government transmitter. Every twenty seconds or so, the transmitter would send out some sharp noise to keep people like George from taking unfair advantage of their brains.

George and Hazel were watching television. There were tears on Hazel's cheeks, but she'd forgotten for the moment what they were about.

On the television screen were ballerinas. 5

A buzzer sounded in George's head. His thoughts fled in panic, like 6
bandits from a burglar alarm.

"That was a real pretty dance, that dance they just did," said 7
Hazel.

"Huh?" said George. 8

"That dance—it was nice," said Hazel. 9

"Yup," said George. He tried to think a little about the ballerinas. 10
They weren't really very good—no better than anybody else would have
been, anyway. They were burdened with sashweights and bags of birdshot,
and their faces were masked, so that no one, seeing a free and graceful
gesture or a pretty face, would feel like something the cat drug in. George
was toying with the vague notion that maybe dancers shouldn't be handicapped. But he didn't get very far with it before another noise in his ear
radio scattered his thoughts.

George winced. So did two out of the eight ballerinas. 11

Hazel saw him wince. Having no mental handicap herself, she had 12
to ask George what the latest sound had been.

"Sounded like somebody hitting a milk bottle with a ball peen 13
hammer," said George.

"I'd think it would be real interesting, hearing all the different 14
sounds," said Hazel, a little envious. "All the things they think up."

"Um," said George. 15

"Only, if I was Handicapper General, you know what I would do?" 16
said Hazel. Hazel, as a matter of fact, bore a strong resemblance to the
Handicapper General, a woman named Diana Moon Glampers. "If I was
Diana Moon Glampers," said Hazel, "I'd have chimes on Sunday—just
chimes. Kind of in honor of religion."

"I could think, if it was just chimes," said George. 17

"Well—maybe make 'em real loud," said Hazel. "I think I'd make 18
a good Handicapper General."

"Good as anybody else," said George. 19

"Who knows better'n I do what normal is?" said Hazel. 20

"Right," said George. He began to think glimmeringly about his 21
abnormal son who was now in jail, about Harrison, but a twenty-one
gun salute in his head stopped that.

"Boy!" said Hazel, "that was a doozy, wasn't it?" 22

It was such a doozy that George was white and trembling, and tears 23
stood on the rims of his red eyes. Two of the eight ballerinas had collapsed
to the studio floor, were holding their temples.

"All of a sudden you look so tired," said Hazel. "Why don't you 24
stretch out on the sofa, so's you can rest your handicap bag on the pillows,

honeybunch." She was referring to the forty-seven pounds of birdshot in a canvas bag, which was padlocked around George's neck. "Go on and rest the bag for a little while," she said. "I don't care if you're not equal to me for a while."

George weighed the bag with his hands. "I don't mind it," he said. "I don't notice it any more. It's just a part of me."   25

"You been so tired lately—kind of wore out," said Hazel. "If there was just some way we could make a little hole in the bottom of the bag, and just take out a few of them lead balls. Just a few."   26

"Two years in prison and two thousand dollars fine for every ball I took out," said George. "I don't call that a bargain."   27

"If you could just take a few out when you came home from work," said Hazel. "I mean—you don't compete with anybody around here. You just set around."   28

"If I tried to get away with it," said George, "then other people'd get away with it—and pretty soon we'd be right back to the dark ages again, with everybody competing against everybody else. You wouldn't like that, would you?"   29

"I'd hate it," said Hazel.   30

"There you are," said George. "The minute people start cheating on laws, what do you think happens to society?"   31

If Hazel hadn't been able to come up with an answer to this question, George couldn't have supplied one. A siren was going off in his head.   32

"Reckon it'd fall all apart," said Hazel.   33

"What would?" said George blankly.   34

"Society," said Hazel uncertainly. "Wasn't that what you just said?"   35

"Who knows?" said George.   36

The television program was suddenly interrupted for a news bulletin. It wasn't clear at first as to what the bulletin was about, since the announcer, like all announcers, had a serious speech impediment. For about half a minute, and in a state of high excitement, the announcer tried to say, "Ladies and gentlemen—"   37

He finally gave up, handed the bulletin to a ballerina to read.   38

"That's all right—" Hazel said of the announcer, "he tried. That's the big thing. He tried to do the best he could with what God gave him. He should get a nice raise for trying so hard."   39

"Ladies and gentlemen—" said the ballerina, reading the bulletin. She must have been extraordinarily beautiful, because the mask she wore was hideous. And it was easy to see that she was the strongest and most graceful of all the dancers, for her handicap bags were as big as those worn by two-hundred-pound men.   40

And she had to apologize at once for her voice, which was a very 41
unfair voice for a woman to use. Her voice was a warm, luminous, timeless
melody. "Excuse me—" she said, and she began again, making her voice
absolutely uncompetitive.

"Harrison Bergeron, age fourteen," she said in a grackle squawk, 42
"has just escaped from jail, where he was held on suspicion of plotting
to overthrow the government. He is a genius and an athlete, is under-
handicapped, and should be regarded as extremely dangerous."

A police photograph of Harrison Bergeron was flashed on the screen— 43
upside down, then sideways, upside down again, then right side up. The
picture showed the full length of Harrison against a background calibrated
in feet and inches. He was exactly seven feet tall.

The rest of Harrison's appearance was Halloween and hardware. 44
Nobody had ever born heavier handicaps. He had outgrown hindrances
faster than the H-G men could think them up. Instead of a little ear radio
for a mental handicap, he wore a tremendous pair of earphones, and
spectacles with thick wavy lenses. The spectacles were intended to make
him not only half blind, but to give him whanging headaches besides.

Scrap metal was hung all over him. Ordinarily, there was a certain 45
symmetry, a military neatness to the handicaps issued to strong people,
but Harrison looked like a walking junkyard. In the race of life, Harrison
carried three hundred pounds.

And to offset his good looks, the H-G men required that he wear 46
at all times a red rubber ball for a nose, keep his eyebrows shaved off,
and cover his even white teeth with black caps at snaggle-tooth random.

"If you see this boy," said the ballerina, "do not—I repeat, do not— 47
try to reason with him."

There was the shriek of a door being torn from its hinges. 48

Screams and barking cries of consternation came from the television 49
set. The photograph of Harrison Bergeron on the screen jumped again
and again, as though dancing to the tune of an earthquake.

George Bergeron correctly identified the earthquake, and well he 50
might have—for many was the time his own home had danced to the
same crashing tune. "My God—" said George, "that must be Harrison!"

The realization was blasted from his mind instantly by the sound 51
of an automobile collision in his head.

When George could open his eyes again, the photograph of Har- 52
rison was gone. A living, breathing Harrison filled the screen.

Clanking, clownish, and huge, Harrison stood in the center of the 53
studio. The knob of the uprooted studio door was still in his hand.
Ballerinas, technicians, musicians, and announcers cowered on their knees
before him, expecting to die.

"I am the Emperor!" cried Harrison. Do you hear? I am the Emperor! Everybody must do what I say at once!" He stamped his foot and the studio shook.

"Even as I stand here—" he bellowed, "crippled, hobbled, sickened—I am a greater ruler than any man who ever lived! Now watch me become what I *can* become!"

Harrison tore the straps of his handicap harness like wet tissue paper, tore straps guaranteed to support five thousand pounds.

Harrison's scrap-iron handicaps crashed to the floor.

Harrison thrust his thumbs under the bar of the padlock that secured his head harness. The bar snapped like celery. Harrison smashed his headphones and spectacles against the wall.

He flung away his rubber-ball nose, revealed a man that would have awed Thor, the god of thunder.

"I shall now select my Empress!" he said, looking down on the cowering people. "Let the first woman who dares rise to her feet claim her mate and her throne!"

A moment passed, and then a ballerina arose, swaying like a willow.

Harrison plucked the mental handicap from her ear, snapped off her physical handicaps with marvelous delicacy. Last of all, he removed her mask.

She was blindingly beautiful.

"Now—" said Harrison, taking her hand, "shall we show the people the meaning of the word dance? Music!" he commanded.

The musicians scrambled back into their chairs, and Harrison stripped them of their handicaps, too. "Play your best," he told them, "and I'll make you barons and dukes and earls."

The music began. It was normal at first—cheap, silly, false. But Harrison snatched two musicians from their chairs, waved them like batons as he sang the music as he wanted it played. He slammed them back into their chairs.

The music began again and was much improved.

Harrison and his Empress merely listened to the music for a while— listened gravely, as though synchronizing their heartbeats with it.

They shifted their weights to their toes.

Harrison placed his big hands on the girl's tiny waist, letting her sense the weightlessness that would soon be hers.

And then, in an explosion of joy and grace, into the air they sprang!

Not only were the laws of the land abandoned, but the law of gravity and the laws of motion as well.

They reeled, whirled, swiveled, flounced, capered, gamboled, and spun.

They leaped like deer on the moon. 74

The studio ceiling was thirty feet high, but each leap brought the 75
dancers nearer to it.

It became their obvious intention to kiss the ceiling. 76

They kissed it. 77

And then, neutralizing gravity with love and pure will, they re- 78
mained suspended in air inches below the ceiling, and they kissed each
other for a long, long time.

It was then that Diana Moon Glampers, the Handicapper General, 79
came into the studio with a double-barreled ten-gauge shotgun. She fired
twice, and the Emperor and the Empress were dead before they hit the
floor.

Diana Moon Glampers loaded the gun again. She aimed it at the 80
musicians and told them they had ten seconds to get their handicaps
back on.

It was then that the Bergerons' television tube burned out. 81

Hazel turned to comment about the blackout to George. But George 82
had gone out into the kitchen for a can of beer.

George came back in with the beer, paused while a handicap signal 83
shook him up. And then he sat down again. "You been crying?" he said
to Hazel.

"Yup," she said. 84

"What about?" he said. 85

"I forget," she said. "Something real sad on television." 86

"What was it?" he said. 87

"It's all kind of mixed up in my mind," said Hazel. 88

"Forget sad things," said George. 89

"I always do," said Hazel. 90

"That's my girl," said George. He winced. There was the sound of 91
a rivetting gun in his head.

"Gee—I could tell that one was a doozy," said Hazel. 92

"You can say that again," said George. 93

"Gee—" said Hazel, "I could tell that one was a doozy." 94

About the Story

1. In what ways is Vonnegut's world of 2081 little changed from the present?
What is different? What can you infer from this about Vonnegut's intention?

2. Why does George refer to the competitive past as the "dark ages"? What
solution does "handicapping" offer? In what ways does being under-handi-
capped make Harrison dangerous?

3. Consider the specific handicaps that above-average people have to wear

in the story. How do you respond to Vonnegut's descriptions? What do those handicaps suggest about the collective mentality of 2081 society?

4. Why does Vonnegut make Harrison a fourteen-year-old child? What childish qualities does Harrison display?

5. Vonnegut's story is plausible up to the point where Harrison and the ballerina "defy the law of gravity and the laws of motion. . . ." Why do you think Vonnegut shifts to fantasy at this point? Would the story have been better or worse if he had kept to the physically possible? Why do you think so?

6. What can you say about the Handicapper General, Diana Moon Glampers? What does the story tell you, or allow you to infer, about her position in 2081 society and her way of doing her job?

7. The words *equality* and *average* refer to similar but essentially different concepts. In what significant way do they differ? How does this difference relate to the theme of Vonnegut's story?

Explorations

1. Is there a typical American attitude toward people of exceptional talent or achievement? What is your attitude? Are there dangers in too much respect for such people—or too little?

2. Choose an area of contemporary society in which handicaps are imposed to achieve social ends, such as affirmative action in employment, open admissions in schools and colleges, or the progressive income tax. What social ends does the handicap serve? What are its benefits? What harm does it do?

3. Compare and contrast "Harrison Bergeron" with W. H. Auden's "The Unknown Citizen" (page 87) as depictions of society.

9 Ultimates

Act in such a way that your principle of action might safely be made a law for the entire world.
IMMANUEL KANT

Faith may be defined briefly as an illogical belief in the occurrence of the improbable.
H.L. MENCKEN

The only thing necessary for the triumph of evil is for good men to do nothing.
EDMUND BURKE

I speak truth, not as much as I would like to, but as much as I dare; and I dare a little more as I grow older.
MICHEL DE MONTAIGNE

Nobody knows, in fact, what death is, nor whether to man it is not perhaps the greatest of all blessings; yet people fear it as if they surely knew it to be the worst of evils.
SOCRATES

F ROM our earliest years we are confronted by questions that seem to have no solid, definitive answers. How should we live? How should we behave toward others? Later in life, more such questions come pressing in. What is the meaning of happiness, freedom, equality, justice? What, indeed, is the meaning of life? And finally: What is death, and how ought we to die? Some of these questions fall, at least partially, within the purview of the law, but laws differ from place to place and from time to time—and cannot always be assumed to be right. Those who seek their own answers must rely on the two great areas of thought and experience which take such matters as their province: philosophy and religion.

How should we behave toward others? Both philosophy and religion offer ethical guidance, though from different standpoints. Philosophy assumes that we want to live happily, and seeks through reason to discover what will most likely provide the greatest happiness to the greatest number. Religion, on the other hand, requires us to

653

believe that the world and we who live in it were created for a divine purpose, and that we can fulfill that purpose only by obeying God's commandments as revealed in prophecy. Yet both may agree on how we ought to act. Most of the great religions teach the Golden Rule— that we should treat others as we want them to treat us. And the German philosopher Immanuel Kant, in the statement that heads this chapter, states a similar principle: We should behave only as we want all other people to behave. Reason and faith, at odds in their methods, are here in harmony.

Death challenges our reason and our faith to the fullest. We know that we must all die, but may we choose the moment and means of our death? May a person in extreme pain be permitted to put an end to both pain and life, or may a doctor or a friend do so for him? And when we die, is our consciousness snuffed out or do we live on as disembodied or reincarnated souls? What we believe can make a great difference not only in the way we die but in the way we live.

The selections that follow explore some of these difficult questions from various perspectives. Some fall within the Judaic and Christian traditions and are concerned with matters of faith, while others take up ethical issues in other ways. Together they show that religious and philosophical questions, often shoved aside as irrelevant, may penetrate to the very heart of our lives.

RICHARD RODRIGUEZ

The *Credo*, in church ritual, is a public statement of faith, a creed. In this selection from his autobiography, *Hunger of Memory* (1982), Richard Rodriguez affirms his belief in the life-enhancing power of Catholic liturgy and tells how he was brought up in the church. For him religion was not, as some have told him, an evasion of life, but an education in its passages and its meaning. (Biographical information about Richard Rodriguez is on page 251.)

Credo

I never read the Bible alone. In fifth grade, when I told a teacher   1
that I intended to read the New Testament over the summer, I did not
get the praise I expected. Instead, the nun looked worried and said I
should delay my plan for a while. ('Wait until we read it in class.') In
the seventh and eighth grades, my class finally did read portions of the
Bible. We read together. And our readings were guided by the teachings
of Tradition—the continuous interpretation of the Word passing through
generations of Catholics. Thus, as a reader I never forgot the ancient
Catholic faith—that the Church serves to help solitary man comprehend
God's World.

Of all the institutions in their lives, only the Catholic Church has   2
seemed aware of the fact that my mother and father are thinkers—persons
aware of the experience of their lives. Other institutions—the nation's
political parties, the industries of mass entertainment and communications, the companies that employed them—have all treated my parents
with condescension. The Church too has treated them badly when it
attempted formal instruction. The homily at Sunday mass, intended to
give parishioners basic religious instruction, has often been poorly prepared and aimed at a childish listener. It has been the liturgical Church
that has excited my parents. In ceremonies of public worship, they have
been moved, assured that their lives—all aspects of their lives, from
waking to eating, from birth until death, all moments—possess great
significance. Only the liturgy has encouraged them to dwell on the meaning of their lives. To think.

What the Church gave to my mother and father, it gave to me.   3
During those years when the nuns warned me about the dangers of

655

intellectual pride and referred to Christ as Baby Jesus, they were enabling me to participate fully in the liturgical life of the Church. The nuns were not interested in constructing a temple of religious abstractions. God was more than an idea; He was person—white-bearded, with big arms. (Pictures could not show what He really was like, the nuns said, but one could be sure that He was Our Father.) He loved us and we were to respond, like children, in love. Our response would be prayer.

In my first-grade classroom I learned to make the sign of the cross   4
with English words. In addition to prayers said at home (prayers before dinner and before sleeping), there were prayers in the classroom. A school day was divided by prayer. First, the Morning Offering. At 10:15, before recess, the Prayer to My Guardian Angel. At noontime, the Angelus, in celebration of the Word: 'The angel of the Lord declared unto Mary . . .' After lunch came the Creed. And before going home the Act of Contrition. In first grade I was taught to make the sign of the cross when I entered the church. And how to genuflect (the right knee bending and touching all the way to the floor). And the nuns told us of the most perfect prayer (Christ's offering of His body and blood to the Father), the 'sacrifice' of the mass.

Alongside red, yellow, blue, green, Dick and Jane, was disclosed   5
to us the knowledge of our immortal souls. And that our souls (we were Catholics) needed the special nourishment of the Church—the mass and the sacraments.

In second grade, at the age of seven, we were considered by the   6
Church to have reached the age of reason; we were supposed capable of distinguishing good from evil. We were able to sin; able to ask forgiveness for sin. In second grade, I was prepared for my first Confession, which took place on a Saturday morning in May. With all my classmates, I went to the unlit church where the nun led us through the forms of an 'examination of conscience.' Then, one by one—as we would be summoned to judgment after death—we entered the airless confessional. The next day—spotless souls—we walked as a class up the aisle of church, the girls in white dresses and veils like small brides, the boys in white pants and white shirts. We walked to the altar rail where the *idea* of God assumed a shape and a scent and a taste.

As an eight-year-old Catholic, I learned the names and functions   7
of all seven sacraments. I knew why the priest put glistening oil on my grandmother's forehead the night she died. At the baptismal font I watched a baby cry out as the priest trickled a few drops of cold water on his tiny red forehead. At ten I knew the meaning of the many ritual gestures the priest makes during the mass. I knew (by heart) the drama of feastdays

and seasons—and could read the significance of changing altar cloth colors as the year slowly rounded.

• • • •

I went to the nine o'clock mass every Sunday with my family. At 8 that time in my life, when I was so struck by diminished family closeness and the necessity of public life, church was a place unlike any other. It mediated between my public and private lives. I would kneel beside my brother and sisters. On one side of us would be my mother. (I could hear her whispered Spanish Hail Mary.) On the other side, my father. In the pew directly in front of us were the Van Hoyts. And in front of them were the druggist and his family. Over to the side was a lady who wore fancy dresses, a widow who prayed a crystal rosary. She was alone, as was the old man in front who cupped his face in his hands while he prayed. It was this same gesture of privacy the nuns would teach me to use, especially after Communion when I thanked God for coming into my soul.

The mass mystified me for being a public and a private event. We 9 prayed here, each of us, much as we prayed on our pillows—most privately—all alone before God. And yet the great public prayer of the mass would go on. No one ever forgot where they were. People stood up together or they knelt at the right time in response to the progression of the liturgy. Every Sunday in summer someone fainted from heat, had to be carried out, but the mass went on.

I remember being puzzled very early by how different things were 10 for the Protestants. Evangelical Christians would ring the doorbell to ask bluntly whether or not I was 'saved.' They proceeded to tell me about their own conversions to Christ. From classmates I would hear about Holy Rollers who jumped up and down and even fell to the floor at their services. It was funny. Hard to believe. My religion—the true religion— was so different. On Sunday afternoons, for a guilty few minutes, I'd watch an Oral Roberts prayer meeting on television. Members of the congregation made public confessions of sin, while people off camera shouted, 'Hallelujah, sister! Hallelujah, brother, preach it!'

Sister and *Brother* were terms I used in speaking to my teachers for 11 twelve years. *Father* was the name for the priest at church. I never confused my teachers or the priests with actual family members; in fact they were most awesome for being without families. Yet I came to use these terms with ease. They implied that a deep bond existed between my teachers and me as fellow Catholics. At the same time, however, *Sister* and *Father* were highly formal terms of address—they were titles, marks of formality like a salute or a curtsey. (One would never have spoken to a nun without first calling her Sister.) It was possible consequently to use these terms and to feel at once a close bond, and the distance of formality. In a way, that is how I felt with all fellow Catholics in my world. We were close—somehow related—while also distanced by careful reserve.

Not once in all the years of my Catholic schooling did I hear a   12
classmate or teacher make a public confession. ('Public' confessions were whispered through darkness to the shadow of a priest sworn to secrecy.) Never once did I hear a classmate or teacher make an exclamation of religious joy. Religious feelings and faith were channeled through ritual. Thus it was that my classmates and I prayed easily throughout the school day. We recited sublime prayers and childish ones ('Angel of God, my guardian dear . . .'). And nobody snickered. Because the prayers were always the same and because they were said by the group, we had a way of praying together without being self-conscious.

Children of ceremony: My classmates and I would rehearse our roles   13
before major liturgical celebrations. Several days before a feastday we would learn the movements for a procession. In the half-darkened church one nun stood aside with a wooden clapper which she knocked to tell us when to rise, when to kneel, when to leave the pew, when to genuflect ('All together!'). We'd rehearse marching (the tallest last) up the aisle in straight, careful lines. Worship was managed as ceremony.

My sense of belonging in this ceremonial Church was dearest when   14
I turned twelve and became an altar boy. Dressed in a cassock like a priest's I assisted at the performance of mass on the altar. It was my responsibility to carry the heavy red missal back and forth from one side of the altar to the other; to pour water and sweet-scented wine into the priest's chalice; to alert the congregation with a handbell at the *Sanctus* and at the elevation of the Host. But by far the greatest responsibility was to respond to the priest in memorized Latin prayers. I served as the voice of the congregation, sounding, all told, perhaps a hundred responsorial lines.

Latin, the nuns taught us, was a universal language. One could go   15
into a Catholic church anywhere in the world and hear the very same mass. But Latin was also a dead language, a tongue foreign to most Catholics. As an altar boy, I memorized Latin in blank envelopes of sound: *Ad day um qui lay tee fee cat u ven tu tem may um.*[1] Many of the 'ordinary' prayers of the mass were generally recognizable to me. (Any Catholic who used a bilingual missal could, after a while, recognize the meaning of whole prayers like the *Credo.*) I had the advantage of being

---

[1]"To God who gives joy to my youth"; the altar boy's response to the priest at the altar.

able to hear in the shrouded gallery of Latin sounds echoes of Spanish words familiar to me. Listening to a priest I could often grasp the general sense of what he was saying—but I didn't always try to. In part, Latin permitted escape from the prosaic world. Latin's great theatrical charm, its sacred power, was that it could translate human aspiration to a holy tongue. The Latin mass, moreover, encouraged private reflection. The sounds of Latin would sometimes blur my attention to induce an aimless drift inward. But then I would be called back by the priest's voice (*'Oremus . . .'*)[2] to public prayer, the reminder that an individual has the aid of the Church in his life. I was relieved of the burden of being alone before God through my membership in the Church.

Parish priests recognized and encouraged my fascination with the liturgy. During the last three years of grammar school, I was regularly asked to 'serve' as an altar boy. In my busiest year, eighth grade, I served at over two hundred masses. I must have served at about thirty baptisms and about the same number of weddings and funerals. During the school year I was excused from class for an hour or two to serve at a funeral mass. In summertime I would abandon adolescence to put the black cassock of mourning over a light summer shirt. A spectator at so many funerals, I grew acquainted with the rhythms of grief. I knew at which moments, at which prayers in church and at gravesides, survivors were most likely to weep. I studied faces. I learned to trust the grief of persons who showed no emotion. With the finesse of a mortician, I would lead mourners to the grave. I helped carry coffins (their mysterious weight—neither heavy nor light) to burial sites when there were not mourners enough. And then I would return. To class or to summer. Resume my life as a boy of thirteen. 16

There are people who tell me today that they are not religious because they consider religion to be an evasion of life. I hear them, their assurance, and do not bother to challenge the arrogance of a secular world which hasn't courage enough to accept the fact of old age. And death. I know people who speak of death with timorous euphemisms of 'passing away.' I have friends who wouldn't think of allowing their children to attend a funeral for fear of inflicting traumatic scars. For my part, I will always be grateful to the Church that took me so seriously and exposed me so early, through the liturgy, to the experience of life. I will always be grateful to the parish priest who forced a mortician to remove an elaborate arrangement of flowers from a coffin: 'Don't hide it!' 17

I celebrate now a childhood lived through the forms of the liturgical Church. As the Church filled my life, I grew to the assurance that my life, my every action and thought, was important for good or for bad. 18

---

[2]"Let us pray," which appears at several places in the mass.

Bread and wine, water, oil, salt, and ash—through ceremonies of guilt and redemption, sorrow and rebirth, through the passing liturgical year, my boyhood assumed all significance. I marvel most at having so easily prayed with others—not simply alone. I recall standing at the altar at Easter, amid candles and gold vestments, hearing the Mozart high mass. These were impossible riches. I remember wanting to cry out with joy, to shout. I wanted to shout. But I didn't, of course. I worshipped in a ceremonial church, one in a group. I remained silent and remembered to genuflect exactly on cue. After the mass, I pulled off the surplice and cassock and rushed to meet my parents, waiting for me in front of the church. 'It was very nice today,' my mother said. Something like that. 'It makes you feel good, the beautiful music and everything.' That was all that she said. It was enough.

About the Essay

1. What aspects of the Catholic church does Rodriguez devote the most attention to? What other aspects does he discuss little or not at all? How does this selectivity relate to his theme?

2. What contrasts does Rodriguez draw between Catholicism and Protestantism? What other contrasts do you see? What do they have essentially in common?

3. Why does Rodriguez consider Catholic ritual so important to him and to others of his faith? What does he say that Catholics gain from ceremonial expressions of faith?

4. What does Rodriguez mean by saying, "We walked to the altar rail where the *idea* of God assumed a shape and a scent and a taste"? How does this relate to his observation that "the nuns were not interested in constructing a temple of religious abstractions"?

5. What insights did Rodriguez gain from his experiences as a student and altar boy?

6. What is Rodriguez's tone in this essay? Is it appropriate for his subject? Why or why not?

Explorations

1. Whether or not you were raised within a church, what have been your most significant experiences with religion? Have those experiences influenced your attitudes and your life? If so, in what way?

2. Not only religion but many other aspects of people's lives have their rituals. Identify some of these other rituals, and discuss the purpose and meaning of ritual in our lives. What do you gain from ritual? Why do we impose it on ourselves?

MATTHEW

Little is known about Saint Matthew, the tax collector called by Jesus to be one of his disciples. The Gospel attributed to him was probably written by one or more anonymous Christians toward the end of the first century A.D., but legend says that it contains many sayings of Jesus that were collected and preserved by Matthew, sayings that are missing from the other Gospels.

Modern scholarship is divided on whether the Sermon is a single utterance or an anthology of sayings from different times and occasions, for it is episodic rather than tightly organized, with sudden shifts in subject. Gilbert Highet suggests that it reflects Jesus's epigrammatic style, that instead of making a speech he would have delivered such sayings one at a time, with pauses in between so that his listeners could absorb and reflect on them.

The Sermon on the Mount

Blessed are the poor in spirit: for theirs is the kingdom of heaven. 1

Blessed are they that mourn: for they shall be comforted. 2

Blessed are the meek: for they shall inherit the earth. 3

Blessed are they which do hunger and thirst after righteousness: for they shall be filled. 4

Blessed are the merciful: for they shall obtain mercy. 5

Blessed are the pure in heart: for they shall see God. 6

Blessed are the peacemakers: for they shall be called the children of God. 7

Blessed are they which are persecuted for righteousness' sake: for theirs is the kingdom of heaven. 8

Blessed are ye, when men shall revile you, and persecute you, and shall say all manner of evil against you falsely, for my sake. Rejoice, and be exceeding glad: for great is your reward in heaven: for so persecuted they the prophets which were before you. 9

Ye are the salt of the earth: but if the salt have lost his savour, wherewith shall it be salted? it is thenceforth good for nothing, but to be cast out, and to be trodden under foot of men. 10

Ye are the light of the world. A city that is set on a hill cannot be hid. Neither do men light a candle, and put it under a bushel, but on a candlestick; and it giveth light unto all that are in the house. Let your light so shine before men, that they may see your good works, and glorify your Father which is in heaven. 11

Think not that I am come to destroy the law, or the prophets; I am not come to destroy, but to fulfil. For verily I say unto you, Till 12 heaven and earth pass, one jot or one tittle shall in no wise pass from the law, till all be fulfilled. Whosoever therefore shall break one of these least commandments, and shall teach men so, he shall be called the least in the kingdom of heaven: but whosoever shall do and teach them, the same shall be called great in the kingdom of heaven. For I say unto you, That except your righteousness shall exceed the righteousness of the scribes and Pharisees,[1] ye shall in no case enter into the kingdom of heaven.

Ye have heard that it was said by them of old time, Thou shalt not kill; and whosoever shall kill shall be in danger of the judgment: but I say unto you, That whosoever is angry with his brother without a cause shall be in danger of the judgment: and whosoever shall say to his brother, Raca,[2] shall be in danger of the council: but whosoever shall say, Thou fool, shall be in danger of hell fire. Therefore if thou bring thy gift to the altar, and there rememberest that thy brother hath ought against thee; leave there thy gift before the altar, and go thy way; first be reconciled to thy brother, and then come and offer thy gift. Agree with thine adversary quickly, while thou art in the way with him; lest at any time the adversary deliver thee to the judge, and the judge deliver thee to the officer, and thou be cast into prison. Verily I say unto thee, Thou shalt by no means come out thence, till thou hast paid the uttermost farthing.

Ye have heard that it was said by them of old time, Thou shalt not commit adultery; but I say unto you, That whosoever looketh on a woman to lust after her hath committed adultery with her already in his heart. And if thy right eye offend thee, pluck it out, and cast it from thee: for it is profitable for thee that one of thy members should perish, and not that thy whole body should be cast into hell. And if thy right hand offend thee, cut it off, and cast it from thee: for it is profitable for thee that one of thy members should perish, and not that thy whole body should be cast into hell.

It hath been said, Whosoever shall put away his wife, let him give her a writing of divorcement: but I say unto you, That whosoever shall put away his wife, saving for the cause of fornication, causeth her to commit adultery: and whosoever shall marry her that is divorced committeth adultery.

Again, ye have heard that it hath been said by them of old time, Thou shalt not forswear thyself, but shalt perform to the Lord thine oaths: but I say unto you, Swear not at all; neither by heaven; for it is God's

---

[1]The scribes among the ancient Jews were dedicated to copying their holy scriptures; the Pharisees were an extremely devout Jewish sect.

[2]Emptyhead; a term of hatred and contempt.

throne: nor by the earth; for it is his footstool: neither by Jerusalem; for it is the city of the great King. Neither shalt thou swear by thy head, because thou canst not make one hair white or black. But let your communication be, Yea, yea; Nay, nay: for whatsoever is more than these cometh of evil.

Ye have heard that it hath been said, An eye for an eye, and a tooth for a tooth: but I say unto you, That ye resist not evil: but whosoever shall smite thee on thy right cheek, turn to him the other also. And if any man will sue thee at the law, and take away thy coat, let him have thy cloak also. And whosoever shall compel thee to go a mile, go with him twain. Give to him that asketh thee, and from him that would borrow of thee turn not thou away. 17

Ye have heard that it hath been said, Thou shalt love thy neighbor, and hate thine enemy. But I say unto you, Love your enemies, bless them that curse you, do good to them that hate you, and pray for them which despitefully use you, and persecute you; that ye may be the children of your Father which is in heaven; for he maketh his sun to rise on the evil and on the good, and sendeth rain on the just and on the unjust. For if ye love them which love you, what reward have ye? do not even the publicans the same? And if ye salute your brethren only, what do ye more than others? do not even the publicans so? Be ye therefore perfect, even as your Father which is in heaven is perfect. 18

Take heed that ye do not your alms before men, to be seen of them: otherwise ye have no reward of your Father which is in heaven. 19

Therefore when thou doest thine alms, do not sound a trumpet before thee, as the hypocrites do in the synagogues and in the streets, that they may have glory of men. Verily I say unto you, They have their reward. But when thou doest alms, let not thy left hand know what thy right hand doeth: that thine alms may be in secret: and thy Father which seeth in secret himself shall reward thee openly. 20

And when thou prayest, thou shalt not be as the hypocrites are: for they love to pray standing in the synagogues and in the corners of the streets, that they may be seen of men. Verily I say until you, They have their reward. But thou, when thou prayest, enter into thy closet, and when thou hast shut thy door, pray to thy Father, which is in secret; and thy Father which seeth in secret shall reward thee openly. 21

But when ye pray, use not vain repetitions, as the heathen do: for they think that they shall be heard for their much speaking. Be not ye therefore like unto them: for your Father knoweth what things ye have need of, before ye ask him. After this manner therefore pray ye: 22

Our Father which art in heaven, Hallowed be thy name. Thy kingdom come. Thy will be done in earth, as it is in heaven. Give us this day our daily bread. And forgive us our debts, as we forgive our debtors. 23

And lead us not into temptation, but deliver us from evil: for thine is the kingdom, and the power, and the glory, for ever. Amen.

For if ye forgive men their trespasses, your heavenly Father will also forgive you: but if ye forgive not men their trespasses, neither will your Father forgive your trespasses. 24

Moreover when ye fast, be not, as the hypocrites, of a sad countenance: for they disfigure their faces, that they may appear unto men to fast. Verily I say unto you, They have their reward. But thou, when thou fastest, anoint thine head, and wash thy face; that thou appear not unto men to fast, but unto thy Father which is in secret; and thy Father, which seeth in secret, shall reward thee openly. 25

Lay up not for yourselves treasures upon earth, where moth and rust doth corrupt, and where thieves break through and steal: but lay up for yourselves treasures in heaven, where neither moth nor rust doth corrupt, and where thieves do not break through nor steal: for where your treasure is, there will your heart be also. 26

The light of the body is the eye: if therefore thine eye be single, thy whole body shall be full of light. But if thine eye be evil, thy whole body shall be full of darkness. If therefore the light that is in thee be darkness, how great is that darkness! 27

No man can serve two masters: for either he will hate the one, and love the other; or else he will hold to the one, and despise the other. Ye cannot serve God and mammon. 28

Therefore I say unto you, Take no thought for your life, what ye shall eat, or what ye shall drink; nor yet for your body, what ye shall put on. Is not the life more than meat, and the body than raiment? Behold the fowls of the air: for they sow not, neither do they reap, nor gather into barns; yet your heavenly Father feedeth them. Are ye not much better than they? Which of you by taking thought can add one cubit unto his stature? And why take ye thought for raiment? Consider the lilies of the field, how they grow; they toil not, neither do they spin: and yet I say unto you, That even Solomon in all his glory was not arrayed like one of these. Wherefore, if God so clothe the grass of the field, which to day is, and to morrow is cast into the oven, shall he not much more clothe you, O ye of little faith? Therefore taken no thought, saying, What shall we eat? or, What shall we drink? or, Wherewithal shall we be clothed? (For after all these things do the Gentiles seek:) for your heavenly Father knoweth that ye have need of all these things. But seek ye first the kingdom of God, and his righteousness; and all these things shall be added unto you. 29

Take therefore no thought for the morrow: for the morrow shall take thought for the things of itself. Sufficient unto the day is the evil thereof. 30

Judge not, that ye be not judged. For with what judgment ye judge,   31
ye shall be judged: and with what measure ye mete, it shall be measured
to you again. And why beholdest thou the mote that is in thy brother's
eye, but considerest not the beam that is in thine own eye? Or how wilt
thou say to thy brother, Let me pull out the mote out of thine eye; and
behold, a beam is in thine own eye? Thou hypocrite, first cast out the
beam out of thine own eye; and then shalt thou see clearly to cast out
the mote of thy brother's eye.

Give not that which is holy unto the dogs, neither cast ye your   32
pearls before swine, lest they trample them under their feet, and turn
again and rend you.

Ask, and it shall be given you; seek and ye shall find; knock, and   33
it shall be opened unto you: for every one that asketh receiveth; and he
that seeketh findeth; and to him that knocketh it shall be opened. Or
what man is there of you, whom if his son ask bread, will he give him a
stone? Or if he ask a fish, will he give him a serpent? If ye then, being
evil, know how to give good gifts unto your children, how much more
shall your Father which is in heaven give good things to them that ask
him? Therefore all things whatsoever ye would that men should do to
you, do ye even so to them: for this is the law and the prophets.

Enter ye in at the strait gate: for wide is the gate, and broad is the   34
way, that leadeth to destruction, and many there be which go in thereat:
because strait is the gate, and narrow is the way, which leadeth unto
life, and few there be that find it.

Beware of false prophets, which come to you in sheep's clothing,   35
but inwardly they are ravening wolves. Ye shall know them by their
fruits. Do men gather grapes of thorns, or figs of thistles? Even so every
good tree bringeth forth good fruit; but a corrupt tree bringeth forth evil
fruit. A good tree cannot bring forth evil fruit, neither can a corrupt tree
bring forth good fruit. Every tree that bringeth not forth good fruit is
hewn down, and cast into the fire. Wherefore by their fruits ye shall
know them.

Not every one that saith unto me, Lord, Lord, shall enter into the   36
kingdom of heaven; but he that doeth the will of my Father which is in
heaven. Many will say to me in that day, Lord, Lord, have we not
prophesied in thy name? And in thy name have cast out devils? and in
thy name done many wonderful works? And then will I profess unto
them, I never knew you: depart from me, ye that work iniquity.

Therefore whosoever heareth these sayings of mine, and doeth them,   37
I will liken him unto a wise man, which built his house upon a rock:
and the rain descended, and the floods came, and the winds blew, and
beat upon that house; and it fell not: for it was founded upon a rock.
And every one that heareth these sayings of mine, and doeth them not,

shall be likened unto a foolish man, which built his house upon the sand: and the rain descended, and the floods came, and the winds blew, and beat upon that house; and it fell: and great was the fall of it.

About the Sermon

1. What is the purpose of the Sermon on the Mount? To whom is it addressed? How do you know? Cite passages from the text to support your answer.

2. What is the essential message of the Sermon on the Mount?

3. Are there attitudes and practices mentioned in the Sermon that you think irrelevant to contemporary life? If so, what are they? How do such references affect your response to the Sermon?

4. The Sermon is much concerned with social ethics. According to Jesus, how should people behave toward one another? Given human nature, do you think the ethical prescriptions of the Sermon realistic or idealistic? What kind of society would result if everyone followed them?

5. What, according to the Sermon, is the relationship between individuals and God? How should this be reflected in religious observance? In our attitudes toward life?

6. In the Sermon on the Mount, Jesus often teaches through analogies and metaphors. Identify some of each, and explain what they mean and why they are appropriate.

Explorations

1. Whether or not one is a Christian, the Sermon on the Mount offers a challenge to lead a just and moral life. Which of its injunctions do you find relevant to your own life? Why?

2. How, if at all, do you think Christianity or any religion should influence American politics and government? Given the constitutional separation of church and state, are there any ways in which government properly may influence the practice of religion?

JOHN HICK

If God exists, and if He is both benevolent and all-powerful, why then is there evil in the world? For believers, such a paradox can be resolved through faith. But what of skeptics? John Hick, a Presbyterian minister and teacher of philosophy, seeks to offer a logical, reasonable answer. Hick was born in 1922 in Scarborough, England, and was educated at the University of Edinburgh, Oxford University, and Westminster Theological College. He came to the United States in 1956 to teach philosophy at Cornell University, and since 1959 he has been Professor of Christian Philosophy at the Princeton Theological Seminary. His books include *Faith and Knowledge* (1957), *Arguments for the Existence of God* (1971), and *Biology and the Soul* (1972), all aimed at reconciling modern knowledge and values with Christian belief. In "The Problem of Evil," taken from *Philosophy of Religion* (1963), Hick argues that the existence of sin and suffering in the world is not evidence of God's shortcomings, or indeed of His nonexistence, but rather is necessary to His purpose.

The Problem of Evil

To many, the most powerful positive objection to belief in God is the fact of evil. Probably for most agnostics it is the appalling depth and extent of human suffering, more than anything else, that makes the idea of a loving Creator seem so implausible and disposes them toward one or another of the various naturalistic theories of religion.   1

As a challenge to theism, the problem of evil has traditionally been posed in the form of a dilemma: if God is perfectly loving, he must wish to abolish evil; and if he is all-powerful, he must be able to abolish evil. But evil exists; therefore God cannot be both omnipotent and perfectly loving.   2

Certain solutions, which at once suggest themselves, have to be ruled out so far as the Judaic-Christian faith is concerned.   3

To say, for example (with contemporary Christian Science), that evil is an illusion of the human mind, is impossible within a religion based upon the stark realism of the Bible. Its pages faithfully reflect the characteristic mixture of good and evil in human experience. They record every kind of sorrow and suffering, every mode of man's inhumanity to man and of his painfully insecure existence in the world. There is no attempt to regard evil as anything but dark, menacingly ugly, heart-rending, and crushing. In the Christian scriptures, the climax of this   4

667

history of evil is the crucifixion of Jesus, which is presented not only as a case of utterly unjust suffering, but as the violent and murderous rejection of God's Messiah. There can be no doubt, then, that for biblical faith, evil is unambiguously evil, and stands in direct opposition to God's will.

Again, to solve the problem of evil by means of the theory (sponsored, for example, by the Boston "Personalist" School) of a finite deity who does the best he can with a material [that is] intractable and coeternal with himself, is to have abandoned the basic premise of Hebrew-Christian monotheism; for the theory amounts to rejecting belief in the infinity and sovereignty of God.

Indeed, any theory which would avoid the problem of the origin of evil by depicting it as an ultimate constituent of the universe, coordinate with good, has been repudiated in advance by the classic Christian teaching, first developed by Augustine, that evil represents the going wrong of something which in itself is good. Augustine holds firmly to the Hebrew-Christian conviction that the universe is *good*—that is to say, it is the creation of a good God for a good purpose. He completely rejects the ancient prejudice, widespread in his day, that matter is evil. There are, according to Augustine, higher and lower, greater and lesser goods in immense abundance and variety; but everything which has being is good in its own way and degree, except in so far as it may have become spoiled or corrupted. Evil—whether it be an evil will, an instance of pain, or some disorder or decay in nature—has not been set there by God, but represents the distortion of something that is inherently valuable. Whatever exists is, as such, and in its proper place, good; evil is essentially parasitic upon good, being disorder and perversion in a fundamentally good creation. This understanding of evil as something negative means that it is not willed and created by God; but it does not mean (as some have supposed) that evil is unreal and can be disregarded. On the contrary, the first effect of this doctrine is to accentuate even more the question of the origin of evil.

Theodicy,[1] as many modern Christian thinkers see it, is a modest enterprise, negative rather than positive in its conclusions. It does not claim to explain, nor to explain away, every instance of evil in human experience, but only to point to certain considerations which prevent the fact of evil (largely incomprehensible though it remains) from constituting a final and insuperable bar to rational belief in God.

In indicating these considerations it will be useful to follow the traditional division of the subject. There is the problem of *moral evil* or

5

6

7

8

---

[1]The word *theodicy*, from the Greek *theos* (God) and *dike* (righteous), means the justification of God's goodness in the face of the fact of evil. (Author's note.)

wickedness: why does an all-good and all-powerful God permit this? And there is the problem of the *non-moral evil* of suffering or pain, both physical and mental: why has an all-good and all-powerful God created a world in which this occurs?

Christian thought has always considered moral evil in its relation   9
to human freedom and responsibility. To be a person is to be a finite center of freedom, a (relatively) free and self-directing agent responsible for one's own decisions. This involves being free to act wrongly as well as to act rightly. The idea of a person who can be infallibly guaranteed always to act rightly is self-contradictory. There can be no guarantee in advance that a genuinely free moral agent will never choose amiss. Consequently, the possibility of wrongdoing or sin is logically inseparable from the creation of finite persons, and to say that God should not have created beings who might sin amounts to saying that he should not have created people.

This thesis has been challenged in some recent philosophical dis-   10
cussions of the problem of evil, in which it is claimed that no contradiction is involved in saying that God might have made people who would be genuinely free and who could yet be guaranteed always to act rightly. A quote from one of these discussions follows:

> If there is no logical impossibility in a man's freely choosing the good on one, or on several occasions, there cannot be a logical impossibility in his freely choosing the good on every occasion. God was not, then, faced with a choice between making innocent automata and making beings who, in acting freely, would sometimes go wrong: there was open to him the obviously better possibility of making beings who would act freely but always go right. Clearly, his failure to avail himself of this possibility is inconsistent with his being both omnipotent and wholly good.[2]

A reply to this argument is suggested in another recent contribution   11
to the discussion. If by a free action we mean an action which is not externally compelled but which flows from the nature of the agent as he reacts to the circumstances in which he finds himself, there is, indeed, no contradiction between our being free and our actions being "caused" (by our own nature) and therefore being in principle predictable. There is a contradiction, however, in saying that God is the cause of our acting as we do but that we are free beings in relation to God. There is, in other words, a contradiction in saying that God has made us so that we shall of necessity act in a certain way, and that we are genuinely independent persons in relation to him. If all our thoughts and actions are divinely predestined, however free and morally responsible we may seem

---

[2]J. L. Mackie, "Evil and Omnipotence," *Mind* (April 1955), 209. (Author's note.)

to be to ourselves, we cannot be free and morally responsible in the sight of God, but must instead be his helpless puppets. Such "freedom" is like that of a patient acting out a series of post-hypnotic suggestions: he appears, even to himself, to be free, but his volitions have actually been pre-determined by another will, that of the hypnotist, in relation to whom the patient is not a free agent.

A different objector might raise the question of whether or not we deny God's omnipotence if we admit that he is unable to create persons who are free from the risks inherent in personal freedom. The answer that has always been given is that to create such beings is logically impossible. It is no limitation upon God's power that he cannot accomplish the logically impossible, since there is nothing here to accomplish, but only a meaningless conjunction of words—in this case "person who is not a person." God is able to create beings of any and every conceivable kind; but creatures who lack moral freedom, however superior they might be to human beings in other respects, would not be what we mean by persons. They would constitute a different form of life which God might have brought into existence instead of persons. When we ask why God did not create such beings in place of persons, the traditional answer is that only persons could, in any meaningful sense, become "children of God," capable of entering into a personal relationship with their Creator by a free and uncompelled response to his love.

When we turn from the possibility of moral evil as a correlate of man's personal freedom to its actuality, we face something which must remain inexplicable even when it can be seen to be possible. For we can never provide a complete causal explanation of a free act; if we could, it would not be a free act. The origin of moral evil lies forever concealed within the mystery of human freedom.

The necessary connection between moral freedom and the possibility, now actualized, of sin throws light upon a great deal of the suffering which afflicts mankind. For an enormous amount of human pain arises either from the inhumanity or the culpable incompetence of mankind. This includes such major scourges as poverty, oppression and persecution, war, and all the injustice, indignity, and inequity which occur even in the most advanced societies. These evils are manifestations of human sin. Even disease is fostered to an extent, the limits of which have not yet been determined by psychosomatic medicine, by moral and emotional factors seated both in the individual and in his social environment. To the extent that all of these evils stem from human failures and wrong decisions, their possibility is inherent in the creation of free persons inhabiting a world which presents them with real choices which are followed by real consequences.

We may now turn more directly to the problem of suffering. Even though the major bulk of actual human pain is traceable to man's misused freedom as a sole or part cause, there remain other sources of pain which are entirely independent of the human will, for example, earthquake, hurricane, storm, flood, drought, and blight. In practice it is often impossible to trace a boundary between the suffering which results from human wickedness and folly and that which falls upon mankind from without. Both kinds of suffering are inextricably mingled together in human experience. For our present purpose, however, it is important to note that the latter category does exist and that it seems to be built into the very structure of our world. In response to it, theodicy, if it is wisely conducted, follows a negative path. It is not possible to show positively that each item of human pain serves the divine purpose of good; but, on the other hand, it does seem possible to show that the divine purpose as it is understood in Judaism and Christianity could not be forwarded in a world which was designed as a permanent hedonistic paradise.

An essential premise of this argument concerns the divine purpose in creating the world. The skeptic's assumption is that man is to be viewed as a completed creation and that God's purpose in making the world was to provide a suitable dwelling-place for this fully-formed creature. Since God is good and loving, the environment which he has created for human life to inhabit is naturally as pleasant and comfortable as possible. The problem is essentially similar to that of a man who builds a cage for some pet animal. Since our world, in fact, contains sources of hardship, inconvenience, and danger of innumerable kinds, the conclusion follows that this world cannot have been created by a perfectly benevolent and all-powerful deity.

Christianity, however, has never supposed that God's purpose in the creation of the world was to construct a paradise whose inhabitants would experience a maximum of pleasure and a minimum of pain. The world is seen, instead, as a place of "soul-making" in which free beings, grappling with the tasks and challenges of their existence in a common environment, may become "children of God" and "heirs of eternal life." A way of thinking theologically of God's continuing creative purpose for man was suggested by some of the early Hellenistic Fathers of the Christian Church, especially Irenaeus. Following hints from St. Paul, Irenaeus taught that man has been made as a person in the image of God but has not yet been brought as a free and responsible agent into the finite likeness of God, which is revealed in Christ. Our world, with all its rough edges, is the sphere in which this second and harder stage of the creative process is taking place.

This conception of the world (whether or not set in Irenaeus' theological framework) can be supported by the method of negative theodicy. Suppose, contrary to fact, that this world were a paradise from which all possibility of pain and suffering were excluded. The consequences would be very far-reaching. For example, no one could ever injure anyone else: the murderer's knife would turn to paper or his bullets to thin air; the bank safe, robbed of a million dollars, would miraculously become filled with another million dollars (without this device, on however large a scale, proving inflationary); fraud, deceit, conspiracy, and treason would somehow always leave the fabric of society undamaged. Again, no one would ever be injured by accident: the mountain-climber, steeplejack, or playing child falling from a height would float unharmed to the ground; the reckless driver would never meet with disaster. There would be no need to work, since no harm could result from avoiding work; there would be no call to be concerned for others in time of need or danger, for in such a world there could be no real needs or dangers. 18

To make possible this continual series of individual adjustments, nature would have to work by "special providences" instead of running according to general laws which men must learn to respect on penalty of pain or death. The laws of nature would have to be extremely flexible: sometimes gravity would operate, sometimes not; sometimes an object would be hard and solid, sometimes soft. There could be no sciences, for there would be no enduring world structure to investigate. In eliminating the problems and hardships of an objective environment, with its own laws, life would become like a dream in which, delightfully but aimlessly, we would float and drift at ease. 19

One can at least begin to imagine such a world. It is evident that our present ethical concepts would have no meaning in it. If, for example, the notion of harming someone is an essential element in the concept of a wrong action, in our hedonistic paradise there could be no wrong actions—nor any right actions in distinction from wrong. Courage and fortitude would have no point in an environment in which there is, by definition, no danger or difficulty. Generosity, kindness, the *agape*[3] aspect of love, prudence, unselfishness, and all other ethical notions which presuppose life in a stable environment, could not even be formed. Consequently, such a world, however well it might promote pleasure, would be very ill adapted for the development of the moral qualities of human personality. In relation to this purpose it would be the worst of all possible worlds. 20

---

[3]Unselfish, spiritual love.

It would seem, then, that an environment intended to make pos- 21
sible the growth in free beings of the finest characteristics of personal
life, must have a good deal in common with our present world. It must
operate according to general and dependable laws; and it must involve
real dangers, difficulties, problems, obstacles, and possibilities of pain,
failure, sorrow, frustration, and defeat. If it did not contain the particular
trials and perils which—subtracting man's own very considerable contribution—our world contains, it would have to contain others instead.

To realize this is not, by any means, to be in possession of a detailed 22
theodicy. It is to understand that this world, with all its "heartaches and
the thousand natural shocks that flesh is heir to," an environment so
manifestly not designed for the maximization of human pleasure and the
minimization of human pain, may be rather well adapted to the quite
different purpose of "soul-making."

About the Essay

1. In what sense does Hick consider evil a problem? For whom is it a problem, and why?
2. Hick divides evil into two categories. What are they, and what does he
say is the purpose of each?
3. What is Hick's purpose in this essay? Is he more interested in describing
or in persuading? To what kind of audience is the essay directed? How has
the expected readership influenced the means Hick has used to achieve his
purpose?
4. According to Hick, why are the conclusions of theodicy negative rather
than positive? What do they prevent?
5. Consider Hick's discussion of human potential. How does he deal with
the argument that God could have created people with free will yet incapable
of wickedness? Does his reasoning seem to you to settle the issue? Why, or
why not?
6. Do you find Hick's conclusions convincing? Why, or why not? If not, how
would you oppose them?

Explorations

1. How would you define evil? What is its nature, and how can it be distinguished from insanity or mere nastiness? Give examples from your personal
experience, from contemporary or past society, or from literature, if you wish.
2. Hick discusses evil from a Christian perspective, but other religions define
evil and its purpose differently. Using library sources, discuss what several
religions teach about the nature of evil. How do they differ? What do they
have in common?

In the early 1970s America saw first a Vice-President and then a President resign under suspicion of criminal conduct. Highly placed businessmen were charged and in some cases jailed for questionable campaign contributions at home and outright bribery abroad. The Vietnam War left a legacy of deception in high places. It was in this context that Derek C. Bok, president of Harvard University, began to urge American colleges to offer their students, the country's future political and business leaders, more instruction in ethical issues. Bok was born in 1930 in Bryn Mawr, Pennsylvania, and after graduating from Stanford he went to Harvard Law School, where he was appointed to the faculty. In 1968 he became dean. He was appointed president of the university in 1971. His books include *Cases and Materials on Labor Law* (with Archibald Cox; 1962), *Labor and the American Community* (with John T. Dunlop; 1970), and most recently *Beyond the Ivory Tower: Social Responsibilities of the Modern University* (1982). He is married to Sissela Bok, author of "Professional Lies" (page 682). "Can Ethics Be Taught?" appeared in 1976 in *Change* magazine, and in revised form in *Beyond the Ivory Tower*. Bok's answer to his question is yes, to a degree. He urges colleges to offer courses that will help students identify ethical issues, consider options, and make reasoned decisions.

Can Ethics Be Taught?

Americans have few rivals in their willingness to talk openly about   1
ethical standards. They are preached in our churches, proclaimed by public officials, debated in the press, and discussed by professional societies to a degree that arouses wonder abroad. Yet there has rarely been a time when we have been so dissatisfied with our moral behavior or so beset by ethical dilemmas of every kind. Some of these problems have arisen in the backwash of the scandals that have recently occurred in government, business, and other areas of national life. Others are the product of an age when many new groups are pressing claims of a distinctly moral nature—racial minorities, women, patients, consumers, environmentalists, and many more.

It will be difficult to make headway against these problems without   2
a determined effort by the leaders of our national institutions. But the public is scarcely optimistic over the prospects, for society's faith in its leaders has declined precipitously in recent years. From 1966 to 1975, the proportion of the public professing confidence in Congress dropped from 42 to 13 percent; in major corporate presidents from 55 to 19

percent; in doctors from 72 to 43 percent; and in leaders of the bar from 46 to 16 percent. Worse yet, 69 percent of the public agreed in 1975 that "over the past 10 years, this country's leaders have consistently lied to the people."

It is also widely believed that most of the sources that transmit 3 moral standards have declined in importance. Churches, families, and local communities no longer seem to have the influence they once enjoyed in a simpler, more rural society. While no one can be certain that ethical standards have declined as a result, most people seem to think that they have, and this belief in itself can erode trust and spread suspicion in ways that sap the willingness to behave morally toward others.

In struggling to overcome these problems, we will surely need help 4 from many quarters. Business organizations and professional associations will have to take more initiative in establishing stricter codes of ethics and providing for their enforcement. Public officials will need to use imagination in seeking ways of altering incentives in our legal and regulatory structure to encourage moral behavior.

But it is also important to look to our colleges and universities and 5 consider what role they can play. Professors are often reluctant even to talk about this subject because it is so easy to seem censorious or banal. Nevertheless, the issue should not be ignored if only because higher education occupies such strategic ground from which to make a contribution. Every businessman and lawyer, every public servant and doctor will pass through our colleges, and most will attend our professional schools as well. If other sources of ethical values have declined in influence, educators have a responsibility to contribute in any way they can to the moral development of their students.

• • • •

Attention is being given today to developing problem-oriented courses 6 in ethics. These classes are built around a series of contemporary moral dilemmas. In colleges, the courses tend to emphasize issues of deception, breach of promise, and other moral dilemmas that commonly arise in everyday life. In schools of law, public affairs, business, and medicine, the emphasis is on professional ethics. Medical students will grapple with abortion, euthanasia, and human experimentation, while students of public administration will discuss whether government officials are ever justified in lying to the public, or leaking confidential information, or refusing to carry out the orders of their superiors. In schools of business, such courses may take up any number of problems—corporate bribes abroad, deceptive advertising, use of potentially hazardous products and methods of production, or employment practices in South Africa.

Whatever the problem may be, the classes generally proceed by discussion rather than lecturing. Instructors may present their own views, if only to demonstrate that it is possible to make carefully reasoned choices about ethical dilemmas. But they will be less concerned with presenting solutions than with carrying on an active discussion in an effort to encourage students to perceive ethical issues, wrestle with the competing arguments, discover the weaknesses in their own position, and ultimately reach thoughtfully reasoned conclusions.

What can these courses accomplish? One objective is to help students become more alert in discovering the moral issues that arise in their own lives. Formal education will rarely improve the character of a scoundrel. But many individuals who are disposed to act morally will often fail to do so because they are simply unaware of the ethical problems that lie hidden in the situations they confront. Others will not discover a moral problem until they have gotten too deeply enmeshed to extricate themselves. By repeatedly asking students to identify moral problems and define the issues at stake, courses in applied ethics can sharpen and refine the moral perception of students so that they can avoid these pitfalls.

Another major objective is to teach students to reason carefully about ethical issues. Many people feel that moral problems are matters of personal opinion and that it is pointless even to argue about them since each person's views will turn on values that cannot be established or refuted on logical grounds. A well-taught course can demonstrate that this is simply not true, and that moral issues can be discussed as rigorously as many other problems considered in the classroom. With the help of carefully selected readings, students can then develop their capacity for moral reasoning by learning to sort out all of the arguments that bear upon moral problems and apply them to concrete situations.

A final objective of these courses is to help students clarify their moral aspirations. Whether in college or professional school, many students will be trying to define their identity and to establish the level of integrity at which they will lead their professional lives. By considering a series of ethical problems, they can be encouraged to consider these questions more fully. In making this effort, students will benefit from the opportunity to grapple with moral issues in a setting where no serious personal consequences are at stake. Prospective lawyers, doctors, or businessmen may set higher ethical standards for themselves if they first encounter the moral problems of their calling in the classroom instead of waiting to confront them at a point in their careers when they are short of time and feel great pressure to act in morally questionable ways.

Despite these apparent virtues, the problem-oriented courses in eth-   11
ics have hardly taken the curriculum by storm. A few experimental of-
ferings have been introduced, but they are still regarded with indifference
or outright skepticism by many members of the faculty. What accounts
for these attitudes? To begin with, many skeptics question the value of
trying to teach students to reason about moral issues. According to these
critics, such courses may bring students to perceive more of the arguments
and complexities that arise in moral issues, but this newfound sophistication will simply leave them more confused than ever and quite unable
to reach any satisfactory moral conclusions.

This attitude is puzzling. It may be impossible to arrive at answers   12
to certain ethical questions through analysis alone. Even so, it is surely
better for students to be aware of the nuance and complexity of important
human problems than to act on simplistic generalizations or unexamined
premises. Moreover, many ethical problems are not all that complicated
if students can only be taught to recognize them and reason about them
carefully. However complex the issue, analysis does have important uses,
as the following illustrations make clear:

- In one Harvard class, a majority of the students thought it proper for a   13
  government official to lie to a congressman in order to forestall a re-
  gressive piece of legislation. According to the instructor, "The students
  seem to see things essentially in cost-benefit terms. Will the lie serve a
  good policy? What are the chances of getting caught? If you get caught,
  how much will it hurt you?" This is a very narrow view of deception.
  Surely these students might revise their position if they were asked to
  consider seriously what would happen in a society that invited everyone
  to lie whenever they believed that it would help to avoid a result which
  they believed to be wrong.

- The *New York Times* reports that many young people consider it per-   14
  missible to steal merchandise because they feel that they are merely
  reducing the profits of large corporations. At the very least, analysis will
  be useful in pointing out that theft is not so likely to diminish profits as
  to increase the price to other consumers.

- Courses in moral reasoning can also help students to avoid moral diffi-   15
  culties by devising alternate methods of achieving their ends. This is a
  simple point, but it is often overlooked. For example, many researchers
  commonly mislead their human subjects in order to conduct an important experiment. Careful study can often bring these investigators to
  understand the dangers of deception more fully and exert more imagination in devising ways of conducting their experiments which do not
  require such questionable methods.

- Even in the most difficult cases—such as deciding who will have access   16
  to some scarce, life-sustaining medical technique—progress can be made

by learning to pay attention not only to the ultimate problem of who shall live, but to devising procedures for making such decisions in a manner that seems reasonable and fair to all concerned.

There are other skeptics who concede that courses can help students   17
reason more carefully about ethical problems. But these critics argue that
moral development has less to do with reasoning than with acquiring
proper moral values and achieving the strength of character to put these
values into practice. Since such matters are not easily taught in a classroom, they question whether a course on ethics can accomplish anything
of real importance. It is this point of view that accounts for the statement
of one business school spokesman in explaining why there were no courses
on ethics in the curriculum: "On the subject of ethics, we feel that either
you have them or you don't."

There is clearly some force to this argument. Professors who teach   18
the problem-oriented courses do not seek to persuade students to accept
some preferred set of moral values. In fact, we would be uneasy if they
did, since such an effort would have overtones of indoctrination that
conflict with our notions of intellectual freedom. As for building character, universities can only make a limited contribution, and what they
accomplish will probably depend more on what goes on outside the classroom than on the curriculum itself. For example, the moral aspirations
of Harvard students undoubtedly profited more from the example of Archibald Cox than from any regular course in ethics.[1] Moreover, if a
university expects to overcome the sense of moral cynicism among its
students, it must not merely offer courses; it will have to demonstrate its
own commitment to principled behavior by making a serious effort to
deal with the ethical aspects of its investment policies, its employment
practices, and the other moral dilemmas that inevitably confront every
educational institution.

But it is one thing to acknowledge the limitations of formal learning   19
and quite another to deny that reading and discussion can have any effect
in developing ethical principles and moral character. As I have already
pointed out, problem-oriented courses encourage students to define their
moral values more carefully and to understand more fully the reasons that
underlie and justify these precepts. Unless one is prepared to argue that
ethical values have no intellectual basis whatsoever, it seems likely that
this process of thought will play a useful role in helping students develop
a clearer, more consistent set of ethical principles that takes more careful

---

[1] In 1973, Professor Archibald Cox of Harvard University was appointed Special Pros-
ecutor in the Watergate investigation that finally led to President Nixon's resignation.
Cox refused to submit to pressures from the White House and was fired.

account of the needs and interests of others. And it is also probable that students who fully understand the reasons that support their ethical principles will be more inclined to put their principles into practice and more uncomfortable at the thought of sacrificing principle to serve their own private ends.

• • • •

Is the effort worth making? I firmly believe that it is. Even if courses in applied ethics turned out to have no effect whatsoever on the moral development of our students, they would still make a contribution. There is value to be gained from any course that forces students to think carefully and rigorously about complex human problems. The growth of such courses will also encourage professors to give more systematic study and thought to a wide range of contemporary moral issues. Now that society is expressing greater concern about ethics in the professions and in public life, work of this kind is badly needed, for it is surprising how little serious, informed writing has been devoted even to such pervasive moral issues as lying and deception. But beyond these advantages, one must certainly hope that courses on ethical problems will affect the lives and thought of students. We cannot be certain of the impact these courses will have. But certainty has never been the criterion for educational decisions. Every professor knows that much of the information conveyed in the classroom will soon be forgotten. The willingness to continue teaching rests on an act of faith that students will retain a useful conceptual framework, a helpful approach to the subject, a valuable method of analysis, or some other intangible residue of intellectual value. Much the same is true of courses on ethical problems. Although the point is still unproved, it does seem plausible to suppose that the students in these courses will become more alert in perceiving ethical issues, more aware of the reasons underlying moral principles, and more equipped to reason carefully in applying these principles to concrete cases. Will they behave more ethically? We may never know. But surely the experiment is worth trying, for the goal has never been more important to the quality of the society in which we live. 20

About the Essay

1. What is Bok arguing for in his essay? What counterarguments does he consider, and what answers does he make to them? Can you think of any counterarguments that Bok has not considered? If so, what are they?

2. What skill does Bok assert courses in ethics might teach? How is this skill

exhibited in the four examples Bok gives in paragraphs 13–16? Would you be inclined to enroll in such a course? Why, or why not?

3. How is Bok's essay organized? What are its chief elements, and what does Bok gain by presenting them in his chosen order?

4. Bok quotes one academic spokesman as saying, "On the subject of ethics, we feel that either you have them or you don't." What is the implication of this statement? How does Bok respond? What is his objection to a teacher attempting to persuade students of a particular set of moral values? What do you think?

5. In two instances, Bok suggests that students will learn as much from moral examples as they will from classroom discussion. What are those instances? Why will students "profit more" from such examples than from the curriculum itself?

6. Bok's essay was written while the nation was still reeling from the Watergate scandal. How is this political trauma reflected in the essay? In what way does knowledge of the historical context affect your response to the essay?

7. According to Bok, what should a university do to set a good ethical example? What specific moral dilemmas can you offer as examples of what he means?

Explorations

1. Who or what has had the greatest influence on the development of your ethical standards? Has it been an individual or one of the institutions Bok names—family, church, local community—or some other source?

2. Consider one of the following moral dilemmas. How would you resolve it? In your answer explain why you adopted one solution rather than another. Can you arrive at a general principle that would help you to decide other, similar cases?

   a. Five people have suffered kidney failure and will die if they do not receive treatment from a dialysis machine. However, there is only one such machine available and only two of the patients can be treated; the others must be left to die. The patients are: a fourteen-year-old girl; a brilliant law student; the founder and president of a town's chief business; a mother of three young children; and a retired man dying from lung cancer. You must decide who lives or dies. What should you do?

   b. You are the governor of one of the states. The legislature has passed a bill imposing capital punishment for murder. If you sign it into law, about fifteen prisoners a year will be executed; if you veto it, the legislature will not be able to override your veto and the same prisoners will be released from prison after serving an average term of fifteen years. What should you do?

   c. You are the chief executive officer of a cosmetics company whose only profitable product is a heavily-advertised facial cream. Several women in a single city have suffered acid burns from the cream, but the news has not gotten into the newspapers. Nobody knows whether the cream was contaminated in your plant or tampered with at a later point. If you recall the cream, or even if the news gets out and women stop buying it, your company will go bankrupt. What should you do?

3. Courses in applied ethics are now taught in the philosophy or religion departments of most colleges. Should all students be required to take such a course? Why or why not?

The Ten Commandments forbid perjury in a court of law but do not otherwise mention lying, and our contemporary laws generally do the same. Yet truthfulness is universally regarded as one of the chief moral virtues, and its absence as a defect not easily forgiven. In *Lying: Moral Choice in Public and Private Life* (1978), Sissela Bok considers many aspects of this topic, from white lies to those told "in the national interest," in an effort to discover when and why people deceive and whether it is ever morally right to do so. She was born in 1934 in Sweden and grew up in Switzerland, France, and the United States, where she earned degrees in psychology from George Washington University and in philosophy from Harvard University. She teaches courses in ethics and decision-making at the Harvard-MIT Division of Health Sciences and Technology and has served as an advisor to various hospitals as well as to the Department of Health and Human Services in Washington. She is married to Derek C. Bok, author of "Can Ethics Be Taught?" (page 674).

"Professional Lies" is an excerpt from *Lying*. When we go to a doctor or a lawyer for help, Bok observes, we expect confidentiality—otherwise, we could not speak freely about our problems. And doctors and lawyers are pledged to keep our secrets as a matter of professional ethics. But does professional responsibility extend to telling lies on our behalf? This is the question she seeks to answer.

Professional Lies

[. . .] it is obviously a most effective protection for legitimate secrets that it should be universally understood and expected that those who ask questions which they have no right to ask will have lies told to them.
—H. SIDGWICK, THE METHODS OF ETHICS

It is only the cynic who claims "to speak the truth" at all times and in all places to all men in the same way but who, in fact, develops nothing but a lifeless image of the truth. He dons the halo of the fanatical devotee of truth who can make no allowance for human weaknesses; but, in fact, he is destroying the living truth between men. He wounds shame, desecrates mystery, breaks confidence, betrays the community in which he lives.
—DIETRICH BONHOEFFER, "WHAT IS MEANT BY 'TELLING THE TRUTH'?"

I don't see why we should not come out roundly and say that one of the

functions of the lawyer is to lie for his client; and on rare occasions, as I think I have shown, I believe it is.
—CHARLES CURTIS, "THE ETHICS OF ADVOCACY"

Confidentiality

Here is a crime contemplated but not yet consummated, without   1
malice, it is true, but nonetheless wilful, and from the basest and most
sordid motives. The prospective victim is most often a pure young woman,
confiding in the love and honor of the man who is about to do her this
unspeakable wrong. [. . .] A single word [. . .] would save her from this
terrible fate, yet the physician is fettered hand and foot by his cast-iron
code, his tongue is silenced, he cannot lift a finger or utter a word to
prevent this catastrophe.

So wrote a physician in 1904, to whom a syphilitic patient had   2
announced his plan to marry without letting his fiancée know of his condition.[1] At a time when venereal disease could almost never be cured and
was a subject so sensitive that prospective spouses could not discuss it,
many a physician was confronted by an agonizing choice: whether to uphold his duty of honoring the confidences of patients, or to help an innocent future victim, whose health might otherwise be destroyed, and
whose children could be born malformed or retarded. Physicians still face
similar conflicts: Should they reveal the recurring mental illness of patients soon to be married? Severe sexual problems? Progressively incapacitating genetic disease? One doctor recently wrote that he had seen many
"impossible marriages" contracted because he could not violate his oath
of professional secrecy.[2] To keep silent regarding a patient's confidences
is to honor one of the oldest obligations in medicine. Lawyers do the same
for their clients, as do priests in hearing confessions.

Silence is often sufficient to uphold this obligation. But sometimes   3
the silence is so interpreted that the secret stands revealed thereby. What
if the parents of the young girl became suspicious and asked the physician
if there was anything to prevent their daughter's marriage to the young
man? For the doctor merely to stammer that he cannot reveal confidences
is to confirm their suspicions. A lie is the simplest way to protect the secret,
though some have worked out subtle forms of evasion in answering unau-

---

[1]Prince Albert Morrow, *Social Diseases and Marriage* (New York and Philadelphia: Lea
Brothers & Co., 1904), p. 51. (Author's note.)

[2]Marcel Eck, *Lies and Truth* (New York: Macmillan Co., 1970), p. 183. (Author's
note.)

thorized questions regarding a professional secret, such as: "I know nothing about it" (with the mental reservation "to communicate to others").[3]

Difficult choices arise for all those who have promised to keep secret   4
what they have learned from a client, a patient, or a penitent.[4] How to deflect irate fathers asking whether their daughters are pregnant and by whom; how to answer an employer inquiring about the psychiatric record of someone on his staff; how to cope with questions from the press about the health of a congressional candidate: such predicaments grow more common than ever. The line between appropriate and inappropriate requests for information may shift from one society to another and be revised over time; but wherever the line is drawn, those charged with secrets have to decide how best to protect them.

A similar loyalty also shields colleagues. Politicians, for instance, or   5
doctors or lawyers are reluctant to divulge the incompetence or dishonesty of their fellows. Once again, when silence would give the game away, lying is one alternative. Some choose it even when they know that innocent persons will thereby be injured—mutilated through a clumsy operation, or embroiled in a law suit that never should have begun.

Are there limits to this duty of secrecy? Was it ever meant to stretch   6
so as to require lying? Where does it come from and why is it so binding that it can protect those who have no right to impose their incompetence, their disease, their malevolence on ignorant victims?

At stake is fidelity, keeping faith with those who have confided their   7
secrets on condition that they not be revealed. Fidelity to clients and peers is rooted in the most primeval tribal emotions: the loyalty to self, kin, clansmen, guild members as against the more diffusely perceived rest of humanity—the unrelated, the outsiders, the barbarians. Defending one's own is the rule long before justice becomes an issue. It precedes law and morality itself. Allied to the drive for self-preservation, it helps assure collective survival in a hostile environment. To reveal the truth about a friend can then come to mean that one is a "false friend." And to be "true" to kin and clan can mean confronting the world on their behalf with every weapon at one's disposal, including every form of deceit.[5]

---

[3]Bernard Häring, *The Law of Christ: Moral Theology for Priests and Laity*, vol. 3, trans. Edwin G. Kaiser (Westminster, Md.: Newman Press, 1966), p. 575. (Author's note.)

[4]See, for example, Harvey Kuschner et al., "The Homosexual Husband and Physician Confidentiality," *Hastings Center Report*, April 1977, pp. 15–17. (Author's note.)

[5]See, for an empirical study of teen loyalty, Esther R. Greenglass, "Effects of Age and Prior Help on 'Altruistic Lying,'" *The Journal of Genetic Psychology* 121 (1972): 303–13. Twelve-year-olds were found more willing to lie for a peer who previously helped them than eight-year-olds. No differences were found between the eight-year-olds and twelve-year-olds who had been refused help by a peer. (Author's note.)

This drive to protect self and kin, friends and associates, persists 8
even where moral rules and laws are recognized. Certain limits are then
established: fraud and assault come to be circumscribed. But the limits
are uncertain where these strong personal and professional bonds are
present. And so lies to protect confidentiality come to be pitted against
the restrictions on harming innocent persons. Practices, some legitimate,
others shoddy, persist and grow behind the shield of confidentiality.

In order to distinguish between them, we have to ask: How is con- 9
fidentiality itself defended? On what principles does it rest? And when, if
ever, can those principles be stretched to justify lies in the protection of
confidences?

Three separate claims are advanced in support of keeping secrets 10
confidential. First, that we have a right to protect ourselves and those
close to us from the harm that might flow from disclosure; second, that
fairness requires respect for privacy; and third, that added respect is due
for that which one has *promised* to keep secret.

The first claim appeals to the principle of avoiding harm. The lie to 11
cover up for a friend, a client, a colleague may prevent injuries to their
lives, even their liberty. The pilot whose heart condition is revealed may
lose his job; the syphilitic fiancé may be jilted; the physician accused of
malpractice may be convicted. Yet this appeal to principle obviously has
its limits. To lie to avoid harm to the pilot or the fiancé can bring on
greater harm, or more undeserved harm, to the passengers or the young
woman about to marry. It is here that the perspective *within* a profession
can be limiting; the bond of confidentiality can dim the perception of the
suffering imposed on outsiders. This is especially true when it is not certain that any one person will be harmed—if a surgeon's addiction, say,
means that one out of ten patients who would otherwise have lived die
during operations.

The second claim invokes the right to privacy. Many requests for 12
information are unwarranted and inherently unjust. To respond to them
with silence or to turn them down is, then, to provide no more than what
is due; but many are so perplexed or so frightened that they lie instead.
Bonhoeffer relates such a case:

> [. . .] a teacher asks a child in front of the class whether it is true, that his
> father often comes home drunk. It is true, but the child denies it.[6]

In this category fall also all the illegitimate inquiries regarding po- 13
litical beliefs, sexual practices, or religious faith. In times of persecution,

---

[6]Dietrich Bonhoeffer, *Ethics*, trans. Neville H. Smith (New York: Macmillan Co.,
1955), p. 367. (Author's note.)

honest answers to such inquiries rob people of their freedom, their employment, respect in their communities. Refusing to give information that could blacklist a friend is then justified; and in cases where refusal is difficult or dangerous, lying may fall into the category of response to a crisis. One has a right to protect oneself and others from illegitimate inquiries, whether they come from intruders, from an oppressive government, or from an inquisitorial religious institution. A large area of each person's life is clearly his to keep as secret as he wishes. This is the region of *privacy,* of personal concerns and liberty not to be tampered with.

The delineation of this region of private concerns is today in considerable disarray. Should contraceptive choices, for example, or choices to abort, be protected? Should employers be able to give job seekers lie-detector tests? How can privacy be secured against unwarranted inroads? Each year, ever more records are kept by schools, psychiatrists, employers, probation officers, and by vast government and insurance computer systems. Investigators collect derogatory (or what happens to be thought derogatory at any one time) information, which is then sought by many more groups—prospective employers, the government, scholars doing research, and the press. Personal privacy is under constant pressure; and the lines between legitimate and illegitimate inquiries need continuous vigilance. 14

But is the young fiancé's syphilis properly in this region of his private concerns? Surely his future wife has a stake in learning about it. And surely a physician's drug addiction or alcoholism is more than his private affair, just as the guilt of the client on whose behalf the lawyer cooperates in perjury is not a matter of privacy alone. 15

The third claim in defense of confidentiality allows disclosure of secrets to prevent harm and to guard privacy, unless a promise has been made not to reveal the information in question. Even when confidentiality is not otherwise fair or beneficial, the argument runs, a promise can make it so. And even when ordinary promises might well be broken, professional ones to clients, to patients, or to those coming for confession, remain inviolate. When a confessor protects a secret, he may do what he would not do for those to whom he has made no promise of secrecy. This promise may exert such a strong pull as to override not only veracity alone and not only the desire to allow no harm to be done, but both together. 16

What is it, then, about promises, that endows them with such power? In the first place, in making a promise, I set up expectations, an equilibrium; should I break my promise, I upset that equilibrium and fail to live up to those expectations; I am unfair, given what I had promised and what I now owe to another. Second, in breaking faith, I am failing to 17 make my promise *come true.* If I make a promise, knowing I shall break it, I am lying. Third, professional promises to clients are granted special inviolability so that those who most need help will feel free to seek it. Without a social policy allowing the protection of such secrets, people might not confide in lawyers or clergy. In this way, many would fail to benefit from legitimate means to help them.

But even this appeal to the sanctity of promises must surely have its 18 limits. We can properly promise only what is ours to give or what it is right for us to do in the first place. Having made a promise adds no justification at all to an undertaking to do something that is in itself wrong. Here again, the question which must be asked of the deceptive practices shielded by confidentiality is what, exactly, *can* be thought of as rightly having been promised to clients and peers.

• • • •

Fidelity to Clients

The relationship between a lawyer and his client is one of the inti- 19 mate relations. You would lie for your wife. You would lie for your child. There are others with whom you are intimate enough, close enough, to lie for them when you would not lie for yourself. At what point do you stop lying for them? I don't know and you are not sure.

This statement by Charles Curtis, a well-known Boston lawyer, has 20 stirred up much discussion and some censure.[7] Are there persons for whom one would lie when one would not lie for oneself? And why should there be such a difference? The same questions have arisen for clergymen and physicians who protect the secrets of their parishioners or patients. At stake here is not the protection of colleagues; it is the defense, thought more legitimate, of information given by clients to professionals in strictest confidence.

Most would agree with Curtis that the relationship between profes- 21 sional and client, like that between husband and wife, requires that certain secrets be protected. But few have come out in public to stretch that privilege so far as to include lying. Curtis himself drew the line at lying in court. More recently, however, Monroe Freedman, Dean of Hofstra

---

[7]Charles Curtis, "The Ethics of Advocacy," *Stanford Law Review* 4 (1951): 3; Henry Drinker, "Some Remarks on Mr. Curtis' 'The Ethics of Advocacy,' " *Stanford Law Review* 4 (1952): 349, 350; Marvin Frankel, "The Search for Truth: An Umpireal View," *University of Pennsylvania Law Review* 123 (1975): 1031. (Author's note.)

Law School and author of a well-known book on legal ethics, has advocated some forms of deception even in the courtroom:

> . . . the criminal defense attorney, however unwillingly in terms of personal morality, has a professional responsibility as an advocate in an adversary system to examine the perjurious client in the ordinary way and to argue to the jury, as evidence in the case, the testimony presented by the defendant.[8]

If, that is, a lawyer has a client who lies to the court and thus ⟨22⟩ commits perjury, Professor Freedman holds that this defense lawyer has the professional responsibility to ask questions which do not contest this testimony and even to use the false testimony in making the best case for the client to the court officers and the jury. That this can involve lying is beyond doubt. Nor is there serious doubt that such instances are not rare in actual practice. Yet perjury has traditionally been more abhorred than other lying. How is it, then, that it has come to be thus defended, albeit by a minority of commentators? Defended, moreover, not just as a regrettable practice at times excusable, but actually as a *professional responsibility.*

One reason, once again, lies in the tribal ethic of avoiding harm to ⟨23⟩ oneself and one's own. But it is often supported by an argument upholding the overriding strength of the privilege of confidentiality whenever a client gives information in confidence. Such a privilege is often thought to need no justification. Lawyers see it as so manifestly different from the shadier privileges claimed through the ages, ranging from the feudal sexual privilege to the excesses of "executive privilege," as to require no defense.

And yet, if we are to understand whether it *should* absolve lying in ⟨24⟩ court, we must ask: What underlies the special claim of this privilege of confidentiality? Lawyers advance three arguments to support it. They argue, first, that even the most hardened criminal has a right to advice, help, and skilled advocacy; the right to a person loyal to him in particular. Fairness demands that his concerns be given a hearing; but he can convey his predicament honestly only if he is assured that his confidence will not be betrayed.

We can accept this argument and still not see why it should be ⟨25⟩ stretched to justify lies. The assumption that the privilege can be thus stretched goes counter to the long tradition barring false witness, and the very special proscription of perjury. In the Jewish and Christian

---

[8]Monroe H. Freedman, *Lawyers' Ethics in an Adversary System* (Indianapolis and New York: Bobbs-Merrill Co., 1975), pp. 40–41. (Author's note.)

traditions, for example, false witness and perjury are the most serious forms of deception, inviting the most dire punishment. And a number of distinctions relevant to the dilemmas for contemporary lawyers have been worked out in some detail. Look, for example, at the ninth-century Penitential of Cummean:

> 8. He who makes a false oath shall do penance for four years.
> 9. But he who leads another in ignorance to commit perjury shall do penance for seven years.
> 10. He who is led in ignorance to commit perjury and afterward finds it out, one year.
> 11. He who suspects that he is being led into perjury and nevertheless swears, shall do penance for two years, on account of his consent.[9]

A second argument for confidentiality goes beyond the individual client's rights. It holds that not only should we all be able to expect discretion from our lawyers, but that the social system as a whole will benefit if confidences can be kept. Otherwise, clients may not dare to reveal their secrets to their lawyers, who, in turn, will not be able to present their cases adequately. Even though injustice may result in individual cases when a zealous lawyer succeeds in concealing a client's misdeeds in court, the general level of justice will be raised, it is claimed, if clients can trust their lawyers to keep their secrets. For some, this argument stretches, once again, all the way to lying in court. And, once more, they adduce no further argument for so enlarging the principle.[10]

. . . .

Those who take up the question, in courses and textbooks on professional responsibility, of what lawyers in today's courts should do give no references to the debates on such issues in moral philosophy and in theology; nor do they refer students and practitioners to authors within the legal profession itself who have confronted these questions, such as Grotius and Pufendorf.[11] This, in turn, is perhaps not to be wondered at, since philosophers themselves have paid little attention to such issues in the last few centuries.

[9]"The Penitential of Cummean," in James McNeill and Helena M. Gamer, *Handbooks of Penance* (New York: Columbia University Press, 1938), p. 106. (Author's note.)

[10]For a criticism of this position, see John Noonan, "The Purposes of Advocacy and the Limits of Confidentiality," *Michigan Law Review* 64: 1485. (Author's note.)

[11]Hugo Grotius, *On the Law of War and Peace*, bk. 3, chap. 1; Samuel Pufendorf, *Of the Law of Nature and Nations*, trans. Basil Kennett (London, 1710), vol. 2. (Author's note.)

But historical and professional insularity has dangers. It impover- 28
ishes; it leads to a vacuum of genuine analysis. Thus, one recent textbook
on the professional responsibility of lawyers holds merely:

> There is simply no consensus, for example, as to the lawyer's duty
> to the court if he knows his client is lying. In that and other situations a
> lawyer can only be sensitive to the issues involved and resolve these dif-
> ficult cases as responsibly as he or she is able.[12]

Closer to throwing up one's hands one cannot get. To leave such 29
choice open to the sensitive and the responsible without giving them
criteria for choice is to leave it open as well to the insensitive and the
corrupt.[13] References to responsibility and sensitivity are made to take
the place of analysis and broader inquiry.

The problem here, as with many other deceptive professional prac- 30
tices, is that the questions are too often left up to the professionals
themselves, whereas the issues obviously touch the *public* welfare intimately. There is, then, a great need for a wider debate and analysis of
these issues. When does the privilege of confidentiality exceed the boundaries of the law? When does the promise on which confidentiality is
based turn out to be itself illegitimate? Do we want a society where
lawyers can implicitly promise to guard their clients' secrets through perjury and lies? Such a debate would have to go beyond the confines of
the American Bar Association and the teaching of professional responsibility in law schools.

If the public were to enter such a debate, it is much more likely 31
that we should see the concerns central to this book come to the fore-
ground: concerns for the consequences of a professional *practice* and on
those engaging in it, their peers, the system of justice and society at
large; concerns for the ways in which such practices spread, and for the
added institutional damage which then results.

• • • •

One effect of a public debate of these questions would inevitably 32
be increased knowledge about deceptive professional practices in the law.

---

[12]Thomas D. Morgan and Ronald D. Rotunda, *Problems and Materials on Professional Responsibility* (Mineola, N.Y.: Foundation Press, 1976), p. 2. (Author's note.)

[13]Lawyers are not at all alone in such an intuitive view of decision. See, for example, Nicolai Hartmann, *Ethics*, vol. 2 (Atlantic Highlands, N.J.: Humanities Press, 1967), p. 285. (Author's note.) "What a man ought to do, when he is confronted with a serious conflict that is fraught with responsibility, is this: to decide according to his best conscience; that is according to his own living sense of the relative height of the respective values, and to take upon himself the consequences, external as well as inward, ultimately the guilt involved in the one value."

And it can be argued that this knowledge ought then to be shared with all who participate in trials—most especially judges and juries. Should juries perhaps then be instructed to take into account the fact that a number of lawyers believe it their right to build upon perjured testimony?

It is clear that even those lawyers willing to support such a right   33
for themselves would not wish juries to be thus instructed. But if they ask themselves why, they may come to see their own behavior in a different perspective. The most important reasons they might advance showing why juries should not have such knowledge are that it should remain easy to mislead them, that their trust in the legal profession and in courtroom procedures should remain whole. More than that, once forewarned, any juror with even minimal sense would then have to be quite suspicious about every *other* possible form of deception on the part of lawyers.

Imagining such instructions to the jury shows, I believe, that those   34
who wish to tell lies in court, even for the best of motives, cannot expose these motives to the light of publicity. They want to participate in a practice but not have it generally known that they do.

Can it be argued that such lies are so common by now that they   35
form an accepted practice that everyone knows about—much like a game or bargaining in a bazaar? But in that case, why should lawyers feel so uncomfortable at the prospect of instructing the jury about the practice? The fact is that, even though lawyers may know about such a practice, it is not publicly known, especially to jurors, much less consented to.

I believe, therefore, that a public inquiry into the appropriateness   36
of lying in court on behalf of perjurious clients would lead to a perception that there are limits to acceptable advocacy in court. And these limits, moreover, are not different because of the lawyer-client relationship. That relationship, with its privilege of confidentiality, does not in itself justify lying for clients. At the very least, the limits set would have to exclude actual presentation of perjury by lawyers as well as the more circuitous ways of building upon a client's perjury. Lawyers themselves might well be grateful for the standards to be publicly discussed and openly established. They could then more easily resist pressure from clients and resolve to their own satisfaction what might otherwise seem to present them with a confusing conflict of personal and professional principle.

Once again, what is needed is the ability to shift perspectives and   37
to see not only the needs that press for perjury and lying, but the effect that such practices have upon the deceived and social trust. Judge Marvin E. Frankel describes thus such a shift:

[. . .] our adversary system rates truth too low among the values that institutions of justice are meant to serve. [. . .] [O]ur more or less typical lawyer selected as a trial judge experiences a dramatic change in perspective as he moves to the other side of the bench.[14]

About the Essay

1. What reasons does Bok give for keeping secrets? What harm can this practice cause? What limitations on confidentiality does she suggest?

2. According to Bok, why do people lie to keep secrets? What could they do instead? How effective are these alternatives?

3. Dietrich Bonhoeffer, a Roman Catholic priest, was imprisoned and killed by the Nazis because he opposed Hitler's regime and refused to pretend otherwise. What does he mean by the statement used as an epigraph for this essay? How does the epigraph influence your response to the essay?

4. Bok observes that colleagues are "reluctant to divulge the incompetence or dishonesty of their fellows." Why do you think professionals might be so averse to "blowing the whistle"?

5. What kinds of deception do some lawyers believe they may rightly practice on behalf of their clients? How do they justify this practice? What are the objections to it?

6. How has Bok organized her essay? What are its main divisions? How do they relate to each other?

Explorations

1. What people do you expect to keep your secrets for you? Why do you expect them to do so? Why should it be in their interest to keep your secrets? In what circumstances could you forgive a breach of confidence?

2. Consider one of the following situations. How far could you justify keeping someone else's secret? If you felt it necessary not to keep silent, what would you do? Why?

   a. After having been out of work for a long time and with a large family to feed, you have just been hired as a truck driver for a toxic waste disposal company. Before long you learn that the company is dumping the waste illegally, without the proper safeguards. State investigators have so far been unsuccessful in finding the companies that have been doing this. If you come forward with the information you will of course lose your job.

   b. A classmate who is a close friend tells you he intends to buy a term

---

[14]Frankel, "The Search for Truth," pp. 203–4. (Author's note.)

paper for a course the two of you are taking. You learn that he did so and received an A grade for the paper, while yours, on which you worked for three weeks, was graded B − .

3. Read Derek C. Bok's "Can Ethics Be Taught?" (pages 674–679). What can college courses teach that would help deal with the problems Sissela Bok discusses in her essay?

JONATHAN SWIFT

One of the world's great satirists, Jonathan Swift was born in 1667 to English parents in Dublin, Ireland. He was educated at Trinity College there, receiving his diploma only by "special grace" owing to his offenses against its discipline. When his early efforts at a literary career in England met no success, he returned to Ireland in 1694 and was ordained an Anglican clergyman. From 1713 until his death in 1745 he was dean of Dublin's St. Patrick's Cathedral. A tireless pamphleteer on political and religious issues, a highly individual poet, and a fertile correspondent, Swift is best known as the author of *The Battle of the Books* and *A Tale of a Tub* (both 1704), of *Gulliver's Travels* (1726), and of the work included here, "A Modest Proposal" (1729).

In the 1720s Ireland had suffered several famines, but the Englishmen who owned most of the land did nothing to alleviate the suffering of the tenant farmers and their families, nor would the English government intervene. Various people wrote pamphlets proposing solutions to the Irish problem; "A Modest Proposal," published anonymously, was Swift's contribution to the discussion.

A Modest Proposal

For Preventing the Children of Poor People in Ireland
from Being a Burden to Their Parents or Country,
and for Making Them Beneficial to the Public

It is a melancholy object to those who walk through this great town[1] or travel in the country, when they see the streets, the roads, and cabin doors, crowded with beggars of the female-sex, followed by three, four, or six children, all in rags and importuning every passenger for an alms. These mothers, instead of being able to work for their honest livelihood, are forced to employ all their time in strolling to beg sustenance for their helpless infants, who, as they grow up, either turn thieves for want of work, or leave their dear native country to fight for the Pretender in Spain, or sell themselves to the Barbadoes.[2]

---

[1]Dublin.

[2]The Pretender was James Francis Edward Stuart (1688–1766), son of the deposed James II, who laid claim to the English throne from exile, at this time in Spain. Many Irish Catholics had joined an army seeking to restore him to the English throne. Other poor Irish emigrated to the Barbadoes, an English colony in the Caribbean, financing their voyage by agreeing to work there for a number of years.

I think it is agreed by all parties that this prodigious number of 2
children in the arms, or on the backs, or at the heels of their mothers,
and frequently of their fathers, is in the present deplorable state of the
kingdom a very great additional grievance; and therefore whoever could
find out a fair, cheap, and easy method of making these children sound,
useful members of the commonwealth would deserve so well of the public
as to have his statue set up for a preserver of the nation.

But my intention is very far from being confined to provide only 3
for the children of professed beggars; it is of a much greater extent, and
shall take in the whole number of infants at a certain age who are born
of parents in effect as little able to support them as those who demand
our charity in the streets.

As to my own part, having turned my thoughts for many years upon 4
this important subject, and maturely weighed the several schemes of other
projectors,[3] I have always found them grossly mistaken in their compu-
tation. It is true, a child just dropped from its dam may be supported by
her milk for a solar year, with little other nourishment; at most not above
the value of two shillings,[4] which the mother may certainly get, or the
value in scraps, by her lawful occupation of begging; and it is exactly at
one year old that I propose to provide for them in such a manner as
instead of being a charge upon their parents or the parish, or wanting
food and raiment for the rest of their lives, they shall on the contrary
contribute to the feeding, and partly to the clothing, of many thousands.

There is likewise another great advantage in my scheme, that it 5
will prevent those voluntary abortions, and that horrid practice of women
murdering their bastard children, alas, too frequent among us, sacrificing
the poor innocent babes, I doubt, more to avoid the expense than the
shame, which would move tears and pity in the most savage and inhuman
breast.

The number of souls in this kingdom being usually reckoned one 6
million and a half, of these I calculate there may be about two hundred
thousand couple whose wives are breeders; from which number I subtract
thirty thousand couples who are able to maintain their own children,
although I apprehend there cannot be so many under the present dis-
tresses of the kingdom; but this being granted, there will remain an
hundred and seventy thousand breeders. I again subtract fifty thousand
for those women who miscarry, or whose children die by accident or
disease within the year. There only remain an hundred and twenty thousand children of poor parents annually born. The question therefore is,

---

[3]People who offered projects.
[4]A shilling was worth about twenty-five cents; hence, about fifty cents.

how this number shall be reared and provided for, which, as I have already said, under the present situation of affairs, is utterly impossible by all the methods hitherto proposed. For we can neither employ them in handicraft or agriculture; we neither build houses (I mean in the country) nor cultivate land. They can very seldom pick up a livelihood by stealing till they arrive at six years old, except where they are of towardly parts;[5] although I confess they learn the rudiments much earlier, during which time they can however be looked upon only as probationers, as I have been informed by a principal gentleman in the county of Cavan, who protested to me that he never knew above one or two instances under the age of six, even in a part of the kingdom so renowned for the quickest proficiency in that art.

I am assured by our merchants that a boy or a girl before twelve years old is no salable commodity; and even when they come to this age they will not yield above three pounds, or three pounds and half a crown[6] at most on the Exchange; which cannot turn to account either to the parents or the kingdom, the charge of nutriment and rags having been at least four times that value.   7

I shall now therefore humbly propose my own thoughts, which I hope will not be liable to the least objection.   8

I have been assured by a very knowing American of my acquaintance in London, that a young healthy child well nursed is at a year old a most delicious, nourishing, and wholesome food, whether stewed, roasted, baked, or boiled; and I make no doubt that it will equally serve in a fricassee or a ragout.   9

I do therefore humbly offer it to public consideration that of the hundred and twenty thousand children, already computed, twenty thousand may be reserved for breed, whereof only one fourth part to be males, which is more than we allow to sheep, black cattle, or swine; and my reason is that these children are seldom the fruits of marriage, a circumstance not much regarded by our savages, therefore one male will be sufficient to serve four females. That the remaining hundred thousand may at a year old be offered in sale to the persons of quality and fortune through the kingdom, always advising the mother to let them suck plentifully in the last month, so as to render them plump and fat for a good table. A child will make two dishes at an entertainment for friends; and when the family dines alone, the fore or hind quarter will make a rea-   10

---

[5]Precocious.

[6]A pound equalled twenty shillings; a crown, five shillings; hence, about $15 or $15.63 in American currency.

sonable dish, and seasoned with a little pepper or salt will be very good boiled on the fourth day, especially in winter.

I have reckoned upon a medium that a child just born will weigh   11 twelve pounds, and in a solar year if tolerably nursed increaseth to twenty-eight pounds.

I grant this food will be somewhat dear, and therefore very proper   12 for landlords, who, as they have already devoured most of the parents, seem to have the best title to the children.

Infant's flesh will be in season throughout the year, but more plen-   13 tiful in March, and a little before and after. For we are told by a grave author, an eminent French physician,[7] that fish being a prolific diet, there are more children born in Roman Catholic countries about nine months after Lent than at any other season; therefore, reckoning a year after Lent, the markets will be more glutted than usual, because the number of popish infants is at least three to one in this kingdom; and therefore it will have one other collateral advantage, by lessening the number of Papists among us.[8]

I have already computed the charge of nursing a beggar's child (in   14 which list I reckon all cottagers, laborers, and four fifths of the farmers) to be about two shillings per annum, rags included; and I believe no gentleman would repine to give ten shillings for the carcass of a good fat child, which, as I have said, will make four dishes of excellent nutritive meat, when he hath only some particular friend or his own family to dine with him. Thus the squire will learn to be a good landlord, and grow popular among the tenants; the mother will have eight shillings net profit, and be fit for work till she produces another child.

Those who are more thrifty (as I must confess the times require)   15 may flay the carcass; the skin of which artificially[8] dressed will make admirable gloves for ladies, and summer boots for fine gentlemen.

As to our city of Dublin, shambles[9] may be appointed for this   16 purpose in the most convenient parts of it, and butchers we may be assured will not be wanting; although I rather recommend buying the children alive, and dressing them hot from the knife as we do roasting pigs.

A very worthy person, a true lover of his country, and whose virtues   17 I highly esteem, was lately pleased in discoursing on this matter to offer a refinement upon my scheme. He said that many gentlemen of this

---

[7]The sixteenth-century comic writer François Rabelais.
[8]Skillfully.
[9]Slaughterhouses.

kingdom, having of late destroyed their deer, he conceived that the want of venison might be well supplied by the bodies of young lads and maidens, not exceeding fourteen years of age nor under twelve, so great a number of both sexes in every county being now ready to starve for want of work and service; and these to be disposed of by their parents, if alive, or otherwise by their nearest relations. But with due deference to so excellent a friend and so deserving a patriot, I cannot be altogether in his sentiments; for as to the males, my American acquaintance assured me from frequent experience that their flesh was generally tough and lean, like that of our schoolboys, by continual exercise, and their taste disagreeable; and to fatten them would not answer the charge. Then as to the females, it would, I think with humble submission, be a loss to the public, because they soon would become breeders themselves: and besides, it is not improbable that some scrupulous people might be apt to censure such a practice (although indeed very unjustly) as a little bordering upon cruelty; which, I confess, hath always been with me the strongest objection against any project, how well soever intended.

But in order to justify my friend, he confessed that this expedient was put into his head by the famous Psalmanazar, a native of the island Formosa,[10] who came from thence to London above twenty years ago, and in conversation told my friend that in his country when any young person happened to be put to death, the executioner sold the carcass to persons of quality as a prime dainty; and that in his time the body of a plump girl of fifteen, who was crucified for an attempt to poison the emperor, was sold to his Imperial Majesty's prime minister of state, and other great mandarins of the court, in joints from the gibbet, at four hundred crowns. Neither indeed can I deny that if the same use were made of several plump young girls in this town, who without one single groat to their fortunes cannot stir abroad without a chair,[11] and appear at the playhouse and assemblies in foreign fineries which they never will pay for, the kingdom would not be the worse.

Some persons of a desponding spirit are in great concern about that vast number of poor people who are aged, diseased, or maimed, and I have been desired to employ my thoughts what course may be taken to ease the nation of so grievous an encumbrance. But I am not in the least pain upon that matter, because it is very well known that they are every day dying and rotting by cold and famine, and filth and vermin, as fast

---

[10]A Frenchman, George Psalmanazar pretended to be from Formosa and had written about his fictitious "homeland."

[11]A groat was an English coin worth about four pennies; a chair was a sedan chair carried by two or four servants while one or two people are seated in it.

as can be reasonably expected. And as to the younger laborers, they are now in almost as hopeful a condition. They cannot get work, and consequently pine away for want of nourishment to a degree that if at any time they are accidentally hired to common labor, they have not strength to perform it; and thus the country and themselves are happily delivered from the evils to come.

I have too long digressed, and therefore shall return to my subject. 20 I think the advantages by the proposal which I have made are obvious and many, as well as of the highest importance.

For first, as I have already observed, it would greatly lessen the 21 number of Papists, with whom we are yearly overrun, being the principal breeders of the nation as well as our most dangerous enemies; and who stay at home on purpose to deliver the kingdom to the Pretender, hoping to take their advantage by the absence of so many good Protestants, who have chosen rather to leave their country than to stay at home and pay tithes against their conscience to an Episcopal curate.

Secondly, the poorer tenants will have something valuable of their 22 own, which by law may be made liable to distress,[12] and help to pay their landlord's rent, their corn and cattle being already seized and money a thing unknown.

Thirdly, whereas the maintenance of an hundred thousand children, from two years old and upwards, cannot be computed at less than 23 ten shillings a piece per annum, the nation's stock will be thereby increased fifty thousand pounds per annum, besides the profit of a new dish introduced to the tables of all gentlemen of fortune in the kingdom who have any refinement in taste. And the money will circulate among ourselves, the goods being entirely of our own growth and manufacture.

Fourthly, the constant breeders, besides the gain of eight shillings 24 sterling per annum by the sale of their children, will be rid of the charge of maintaining them after the first year.

Fifthly, this food would likewise bring great custom to taverns, 25 where the vintners will certainly be so prudent as to procure the best receipts for dressing it to perfection, and consequently have their houses frequented by all the fine gentlemen, who justly value themselves upon their knowledge in good eating; and a skillful cook, who understands how to oblige his guests, will contrive to make it as expensive as they please.

Sixthly, this would be a great inducement to marriage, which all 26 wise nations have either encouraged by rewards or enforced by laws and penalties. It would increase the care and tenderness of mothers toward

---

[12]Seizure for the payment of debts.

their children, when they were sure of a settlement for life to the poor babes, provided in some sort by the public, to their annual profit instead of expense. We should see an honest emulation among the married women, which of them could bring the fattest child to the market. Men would become as fond of their wives during the time of their pregnancy as they are now of their mares in foal, their cows in calf, or sows when they are ready to farrow; nor offer to beat or kick them (as is too frequent a practice) for fear of a miscarriage.

Many other advantages might be enumerated. For instance, the addition of some thousand carcasses in our exportation of barreled beef, the propagation of swine's flesh, and improvement in the art of making good bacon, so much wanted among us by the great destruction of pigs, too frequent at our tables, which are no way comparable in taste or magnificence to a well-grown, fat, yearling child, which roasted whole will make a considerable figure at a lord mayor's feast or any other public entertainment. But this and many others I omit, being studious of brevity.

Supposing that one thousand families in this city would be constant customers for infants' flesh, besides others who might have it at merry meetings, particularly weddings and christenings, I compute that Dublin would take off annually about twenty thousand carcasses, and the rest of the kingdom (where probably they will be sold somewhat cheaper) the remaining eighty thousand.

I can think of no one objection that will possibly be raised against this proposal, unless it should be urged that the number of people will be thereby much lessened in the kingdom. This I freely own, and it was indeed one principal design in offering it to the world. I desire the reader will observe, that I calculate my remedy for this one individual kingdom of Ireland and for no other that ever was, is, or I think ever can be upon earth. Therefore let no man talk to me of other expedients: of taxing our absentees at five shillings a pound: of using neither clothes nor household furniture except what is of our own growth and manufacture: of utterly rejecting the materials and instruments that promote foreign luxury: of curing the expensiveness of pride, vanity, idleness, and gaming in our women: of introducing a vein of parsimony, prudence, temperance: of learning to love our country, in the want of which we differ even from Laplanders and the inhabitants of Topinamboo[13]: of quitting our animosities and factions, nor acting any longer like the Jews, who were murdering one another at the very moment their city was taken: of being a little cautious not to sell our country and conscience for nothing: of teaching landlords to have at least one degree of mercy toward their

---

[13] A district in Brazil inhabited by primitive tribes.

tenants: lastly, of putting a spirit of honesty, industry, and skill into our shopkeepers; who, if a resolution could now be taken to buy only our native goods, would immediately unite to cheat and exact upon us in the price, the measure, and the goodness, nor could ever yet be brought to make one fair proposal of just dealing, though often and earnestly invited to it.

Therefore I repeat, let no man talk to me of these and the like expedients, till he hath at least some glimpse of hope that there will ever be some hearty and sincere attempt to put them in practice.   30

But as to myself, having been wearied out for many years with offering vain, idle visionary thoughts, and at length utterly despairing of success, I fortunately fell upon this proposal, which, as it is wholly new, so it hath something solid and real, of no expense and little trouble, full in our own power, and whereby we can incur no danger in disobliging England. For this kind of commodity will not bear exportation, the flesh being of too tender a consistence to admit a long continuance in salt, although perhaps I could name a country which would be glad to eat up our whole nation without it.   31

After all, I am not so violently bent upon my own opinion as to reject any offer proposed by wise men, which shall be found equally innocent, cheap, easy, and effectual. But before something of that kind shall be advanced in contradiction to my scheme, and offering a better, I desire the author or authors will be pleased maturely to consider two points. First, as things now stand, how they will be able to find food and raiment for an hundred thousand useless mouths and backs. And secondly, there being a round million of creatures in human figure throughout this kingdom, whose sole subsistence put into a common stock would leave them in debt two millions of pounds sterling, adding those who are beggars by profession to the bulk of farmers, cottagers, and laborers, with their wives and children who are beggars in effect; I desire those politicians who dislike my overture, and may perhaps be so bold to attempt an answer, that they will first ask the parents of these mortals whether they would not at this day think it a great happiness to have been sold for food at a year old in the manner I prescribe, and thereby have avoided such a perpetual scene of misfortunes as they have since gone through by the oppression of landlords, the impossibility of paying rent without money or trade, the want of common sustenance, with neither house nor clothes to cover them from the inclemencies of the weather, and the most inevitable prospect of entailing the like or greater miseries upon their breed forever.   32

I profess, in the sincerity of my heart, that I have not the least personal interest in endeavoring to promote this necessary work, having no other motive than the public good of my country, by advancing our   33 trade, providing for infants, relieving the poor, and giving some pleasure to the rich. I have no children by which I can propose to get a single penny; the youngest being nine years old, and my wife past childbearing.

About the Essay

1. What is Swift's main target in this essay? What is the problem that he addresses? What specific solution does the essay propose? What other solutions to the problem does the essay dismiss in favor of his proposed solution?

2. How would you characterize the speaker? Why has Swift chosen such a person to make this proposal? What strategies does Swift employ to give the speaker authority? Explain.

3. In paragraph 2 the speaker talks of making Ireland's "children sound, useful members of the commonwealth." In what way is this statement ironic? Cite several other examples of Swift's use of irony.

4. In paragraph 6 the speaker refers to the women as "breeders." In terms of his proposal, why is this an appropriate choice of words? Cite examples of other such diction in the essay—for example, consider words used to describe the poor people of Ireland.

5. In what ways is Swift's argument logical? What is the effect of the calculations in paragraph 6?

6. At what point in the essay does it become clear that Swift is writing ironically? Where does the speaker's "mask" slip?

7. What is the purpose of the essay's final sentence?

Explorations

1. Write a modest proposal of your own to solve a difficult social or political problem of the present day.

2. Ireland's troubles with England have persisted for centuries. After doing whatever research is necessary, write a paper on a particular aspect of the problem, past or present, that you find interesting.

3. Read Gilbert Highet's essay "On Swift's 'A Modest Proposal'" (pages 432–435). Why is irony such an effective strategy for discussing difficult social problems? What advantages does it offer the author? Does it present any disadvantages? If so, what?

JAMES RACHELS

Suppose that someone is dying and is experiencing great pain which no medicine can relieve. Is it better to keep that person alive as long as possible, despite the suffering, or to end the suffering quickly through euthanasia? Active euthanasia, or "mercy killing," is legally considered murder, but passive euthanasia—withholding treatment that would keep the patient alive—is not; indeed, it is even endorsed by the American Medical Association. James Rachels, a professor of philosophy who is particularly concerned with ethical issues, disputes this position. Born in 1941 in Columbus, Georgia, Rachels earned degrees at Mercer University and the University of California, and has taught at the University of Miami, Coral Gables, since 1972. He is the editor of *Moral Problems* (1969, 1974, 1979), a reader in the ethical dimensions of contemporary social issues.

"Active and Passive Euthanasia" was first published in *The New England Journal of Medicine* in 1975, and has since been often reprinted and widely discussed. Arguing that mercy killing is morally no worse than allowing people to die, Rachels challenges doctors—and indeed all of us—to reconsider some basic assumptions.

Active and Passive Euthanasia

The distinction between active and passive euthanasia is thought   1
to be crucial for medical ethics. The idea is that it is permissible, at least in some cases, to withhold treatment and allow a patient to die, but it is never permissible to take any direct action designed to kill the patient. This doctrine seems to be accepted by most doctors, and it is endorsed in a statement adopted by the House of Delegates of the American Medical Association on December 4, 1973:

> The intentional termination of the life of one human being by another—mercy killing—is contrary to that for which the medical profession stands and is contrary to the policy of the American Medical Association.
> The cessation of the employment of extraordinary means to prolong the life of the body when there is irrefutable evidence that biological death is imminent is the decision of the patient and/or his immediate family. The advice and judgment of the physician should be freely available to the patient and/or his immediate family.

However, a strong case can be made against this doctrine. In what follows I will set out some of the relevant arguments, and urge doctors to reconsider their views on this matter.

To begin with a familiar type of situation, a patient who is dying   2
of incurable cancer of the throat is in terrible pain, which can no longer
be satisfactorily alleviated. He is certain to die within a few days, even
if present treatment is continued, but he does not want to go on living
for those days since the pain is unbearable. So he asks the doctor for an
end to it, and his family joins in the request.

Suppose the doctor agrees to withhold treatment, as the conven-   3
tional doctrine says he may. The justification for his doing so is that the
patient is in terrible agony, and since he is going to die anyway, it would
be wrong to prolong his suffering needlessly. But now notice this. If one
simply withholds treatment, it may take the patient longer to die, and
so he may suffer more than he would if more direct action were taken
and a lethal injection given. This fact provides strong reason for thinking
that, once the initial decision not to prolong his agony has been made,
active euthanasia is actually preferable to passive euthanasia, rather than
the reverse. To say otherwise is to endorse the option that leads to more
suffering rather than less, and is contrary to the humanitarian impulse
that prompts the decision not to prolong his life in the first place.

Part of my point is that the process of being "allowed to die" can   4
be relatively slow and painful, whereas being given a lethal injection is
relatively quick and painless. Let me give a different sort of example. In
the United States about one in 600 babies is born with Down's syndrome.
Most of these babies are otherwise healthy—that is, with only the usual
pediatric care, they will proceed to an otherwise normal infancy. Some,
however, are born with congenital defects such as intestinal obstructions
that require operations if they are to live. Sometimes, the parents and
the doctor will decide not to operate, and let the infant die. Anthony
Shaw describes what happens then:

> . . . When surgery is denied [the doctor] must try to keep the infant
> from suffering while natural forces sap the baby's life away. As a surgeon
> whose natural inclination is to use the scalpel to fight off death, standing
> by and watching a salvageable baby die is the most emotionally exhausting
> experience I know. It is easy at a conference, in a theoretical discussion,
> to decide that such infants should be allowed to die. It is altogether dif-
> ferent to stand by in the nursery and watch as dehydration and infection
> wither a tiny being over hours and days. This is a terrible ordeal for me
> and the hospital staff—much more so than for the parents who never set
> foot in the nursery.[1]

I can understand why some people are opposed to all euthanasia, and

[1] A. Shaw, "Doctor, Do We Have a Choice?" *The New York Times Magazine*, January
30, 1972, p. 54. (Author's note.)

insist that such infants must be allowed to live. I think I can also understand why other people favor destroying these babies quickly and painlessly. But why should anyone favor letting "dehydration and infection wither a tiny being over hours and days?" The doctrine that says that a baby may be allowed to dehydrate and wither, but may not be given an injection that would end its life without suffering, seems so patently cruel as to require no further refutation. The strong language is not intended to offend, but only to put the point in the clearest possible way.

My second argument is that the conventional doctrine leads to decisions concerning life and death made on irrelevant grounds. 5

Consider again the case of the infants with Down's syndrome who need operations for congenital defects unrelated to the syndrome to live. Sometimes, there is no operation, and the baby dies, but when there is no such defect, the baby lives on. Now, an operation such as that to remove an intestinal obstruction is not prohibitively difficult. The reason why such operations are not performed in these cases is, clearly, that the child has Down's syndrome and the parents and doctor judge that because of that fact it is better for the child to die. 6

But notice that this situation is absurd, no matter what view one takes of the lives and potentials of such babies. If the life of such an infant is worth preserving, what does it matter if it needs a simple operation? Or, if one thinks it better that such a baby should not live on, what difference does it make that it happens to have an unobstructed intestinal tract? In either case, the matter of life and death is being decided on irrelevant grounds. It is the Down's syndrome, and not the intestines, that is the issue. The matter should be decided, if at all, on that basis, and not be allowed to depend on the essentially irrelevant question of whether the intestinal tract is blocked. 7

What makes this situation possible, of course, is the idea that when there is an intestinal blockage, one can "let the baby die," but when there is no such defect there is nothing that can be done, for one must not "kill" it. The fact that this idea leads to such results as deciding life or death on irrelevant grounds is another good reason why the doctrine should be rejected. 8

One reason why so many people think that there is an important moral difference between active and passive euthanasia is that they think killing someone is morally worse than letting someone die. But is it? Is killing, in itself, worse than letting die? To investigate this issue, two cases may be considered that are exactly alike except that one involves killing whereas the other involves letting someone die. Then, it can be asked whether this difference makes any difference to the moral assessments. It is important that the cases be exactly alike, except for this one 9 difference, since otherwise one cannot be confident that it is this differ-ence and not some other that accounts for any variation in the assess-ments of the two cases. So, let us consider this pair of cases:

In the first, Smith stands to gain a large inheritance if anything should happen to his six-year-old cousin. One evening while the child is taking his bath, Smith sneaks into the bathroom and drowns the child, and then arranges things so that it will look like an accident.

In the second, Jones also stands to gain if anything should happen to his six-year-old cousin. Like Smith, Jones sneaks in planning to drown the child in his bath. However, just as he enters the bathroom Jones sees the child slip and hit his head, and fall face down in the water. Jones is delighted; he stands by, ready to push the child's head back under if it is necessary, but it is not necessary. With only a little thrashing about, the child drowns all by himself, "accidentally," as Jones watches and does nothing.

Now Smith killed the child, whereas Jones "merely" let the child die. That is the only difference between them. Did either man behave better, from a moral point of view? If the difference between killing and letting die were in itself a morally important matter, one should say that Jones's behavior was less reprehensible than Smith's. But does one really want to say that? I think not. In the first place, both men acted from the same motive, personal gain, and both had exactly the same end in view when they acted. It may be inferred from Smith's conduct that he is a bad man, although that judgment may be withdrawn or modified if certain further facts are learned about him—for example, that he is men-tally deranged. But would not the very same thing be inferred about Jones from his conduct? And would not the same further considerations also be relevant to any modification of this judgment? Moreover, suppose Jones pleaded, in his own defense, "After all, I didn't do anything except just stand there and watch the child drown. I didn't kill him; I only let him die." Again, if letting die were in itself less bad than killing, this defense should have at least some weight. But it does not. Such a "de-fense" can only be regarded as a grotesque perversion of moral reasoning. Morally speaking, it is no defense at all.

Now, it may be pointed out, quite properly, that the cases of eu-thanasia with which doctors are concerned are not like this at all. They do not involve personal gain or the destruction of normal healthy chil-dren. Doctors are concerned only with cases in which the patient's life is of no further use to him, or in which the patient's life has become or will soon become a terrible burden. However, the point is the same in these cases: the bare difference between killing and letting die does not,

10

11

12

13

in itself, make a moral difference. If a doctor lets a patient die, for humane reasons, he is in the same moral position as if he had given the patient a lethal injection for humane reasons. If his decision was wrong— if, for example, the patient's illness was in fact curable—the decision would be equally regrettable no matter which method was used to carry it out. And if the doctor's decision was the right one, the method used is not in itself important.

The AMA policy statement isolates the crucial issue very well; the crucial issue is "the intentional termination of the life of one human being by another." But after identifying this issue, and forbidding "mercy killing," the statement goes on to deny that the cessation of treatment is the intentional termination of a life. This is where the mistake comes in, for what is the cessation of treatment, in these circumstances, if it is not "the intentional termination of the life of one human being by another"? Of course it is exactly that, and if it were not, there would be no point to it. 14

Many people will find this judgment hard to accept. One reason, I think, is that it is very easy to conflate the question of whether killing is, in itself, worse than letting die, with the very different question of whether most actual cases of killing are more reprehensible than most actual cases of letting die. Most actual cases of killing are clearly terrible (think, for example, of all the murders reported in the newspapers), and one hears of such cases every day. On the other hand, one hardly ever hears of a case of letting die, except for the actions of doctors who are motivated by humanitarian reasons. So one learns to think of killing in a much worse light than of letting die. But this does not mean that there is something about killing that makes it in itself worse than letting die, for it is not the bare difference between killing and letting die that makes the difference in these cases. Rather, the other factors—the murderer's motive of personal gain, for example, contrasted with the doctor's humanitarian motivation—account for different reactions to the different cases. 15

I have argued that killing is not in itself any worse than letting die; if my contention is right, it follows that active euthanasia is not any worse than passive euthanasia. What arguments can be given on the other side? The most common, I believe, is the following: 16

"The important difference between active and passive euthanasia is that, in passive euthanasia, the doctor does not do anything to bring about the patient's death. The doctor does nothing, and the patient dies of whatever ills already afflict him. In active euthanasia, however, the doctor does something to bring about the patient's death: he kills him. 17

The doctor who gives the patient with cancer a lethal injection has himself caused his patient's death; whereas if he merely ceases treatment, the cancer is the cause of the death."

A number of points need to be made here. The first is that it is not exactly correct to say that in passive euthanasia the doctor does nothing, for he does do one thing that is very important: he lets the patient die. "Letting someone die" is certainly different, in some respects, from other types of action—mainly in that it is a kind of action that one may perform by way of not performing certain other actions. For example, one may let a patient die by way of not giving medication, just as one may insult someone by way of not shaking his hand. But for any purpose of moral assessment, it is a type of action nonetheless. The decision to let a patient die is subject to moral appraisal in the same way that a decision to kill him would be subject to moral appraisal: it may be assessed as wise or unwise, compassionate or sadistic, right or wrong. If a doctor deliberately let a patient die who was suffering from a routinely curable illness, the doctor would certainly be to blame for what he had done, just as he would be to blame if he had needlessly killed the patient. Charges against him would then be appropriate. If so, it would be no defense at all for him to insist that he didn't "do anything." He would have done something very serious indeed, for he let his patient die. [18]

Fixing the cause of death may be very important from a legal point of view, for it may determine whether criminal charges are brought against the doctor. But I do not think that this notion can be used to show a moral difference between active and passive euthanasia. The reason why it is considered bad to be the cause of someone's death is that death is regarded as a great evil—and so it is. However, if it has been decided that euthanasia—even passive euthanasia—is desirable in a given case, it has also been decided that in this instance death is no greater an evil than the patient's continued existence. And if this is true, the usual reason for not wanting to be the cause of someone's death simply does not apply. [19]

Finally, doctors may think that all of this is only of academic interest—the sort of thing that philosophers may worry about but that has no practical bearing on their own work. After all, doctors must be concerned about the legal consequences of what they do, and active euthanasia is clearly forbidden by the law. But even so, doctors should also be concerned with the fact that the law is forcing upon them a moral doctrine that may well be indefensible, and has a considerable effect on their practices. Of course, most doctors are not now in the position of being coerced in this matter, for they do not regard themselves as merely going along with what the law requires. Rather, in statements such as [20] the AMA policy statement that I have quoted, they are endorsing this doctrine as a central point of medical ethics. In that statement, active euthanasia is condemned not merely as illegal but as "contrary to that for which the medical profession stands," whereas passive euthanasia is approved. However, the preceding considerations suggest that there is really no moral difference between the two, considered in themselves (there may be important moral differences in some cases in their *consequences*, but, as I pointed out, these differences may make active euthanasia, and not passive euthanasia, the morally preferable option). So, whereas doctors may have to discriminate between active and passive euthanasia to satisfy the law, they should not do any more than that. In particular, they should not give the distinction any added authority and weight by writing it into official statements of medical ethics.

About the Essay

1. What is Rachels' thesis? Is he in favor of euthanasia? Support your answer.

2. According to Rachels, what is the difference between active and passive euthanasia? Which is generally considered more ethical? Which is more humane in Rachels' view? What do you think?

3. Is the example in paragraph 4 and the following discussion relevant to Rachels' thesis? Why does he include it?

4. What is the purpose of the hypothetical case involving Smith and Jones? Why do you think Rachels invented an example instead of drawing it from real life? What are the example's advantages and its limitations?

5. What was Rachels' purpose in writing this article? Who are his expected readers? How can you tell? Why is the article relevant to other readers?

Explorations

1. Are there any circumstances in which you might wish for euthanasia? If so, what are the circumstances and what would be your reasons? If not, what are your objections to euthanasia?

2. As doctors have discovered means of prolonging the lives of terminally ill people, the debate over euthanasia has intensified. Some terminally ill people have taken their lives and their deaths into their own hands. This of course amounts to suicide and is prohibited by law. It is defended, however, under the banner of "death with dignity." Research the issues involved and discuss

the pros and cons of euthanasia, taking medical, legal, and moral considerations into account.

3. As Rachels' article shows, the law often intervenes in moral questions.
Do you think this is a proper function of the law? When, if ever, should we
seek to legislate morality? How effective is such legislation? How should we
respond when the law compels us to act against our moral sense?

NORMAN COUSINS

Self-preservation is such a powerful force that most of us regard suicide as unnatural and wrong. But though it is condemned in western countries by church and state alike, suicide was considered an honorable means of preserving one's dignity in ancient Greece and Rome, and until recently in some eastern countries as well. In "The Right to Die," first published in the *Saturday Review* in 1975, Norman Cousins considers the case of an American couple, wholly committed to Christian ethics but foreseeing increasing illness and dependency in their remaining years, who decided to end their lives. Cousins argues that the fundamental right to life is balanced by the right to die when life has lost its value. (Biographical information about Norman Cousins is on page 376.)

The Right to Die

The world of religion and philosophy was shocked recently when   1
Henry P. Van Dusen and his wife ended their lives by their own hands.
Dr. Van Dusen had been president of Union Theological Seminary; for
more than a quarter-century he had been one of the luminous names in
Protestant theology. He enjoyed world status as a spiritual leader. News
of the self-inflicted death of the Van Dusens, therefore, was profoundly
disturbing to all those who attach a moral stigma to suicide and regard
it as a violation of God's laws.

Dr. Van Dusen had anticipated this reaction. He and his wife left   2
behind a letter that may have historic significance. It was very brief, but
the essential point it made is now being widely discussed by theologians
and could represent the beginning of a reconsideration of traditional
religious attitudes toward self-inflicted death. The letter raised a moral
issue: does an individual have the obligation to go on living even when
the beauty and meaning and power of life are gone?

Henry and Elizabeth Van Dusen had lived full lives. In recent years,   3
they had become increasingly ill, requiring almost continual medical
care. Their infirmities were worsening, and they realized they would soon
become completely dependent for even the most elementary needs and
functions. Under these circumstances, little dignity would have been left
in life. They didn't like the idea of taking up space in a world with too
many mouths and too little food. They believed it was a misuse of medical
science to keep them technically alive.

They therefore believed they had the right to decide when to die.   4
In making that decision, they weren't turning against life as the highest

711

value; what they were turning against was the notion that there were no circumstances under which life should be discontinued.

An important aspect of human uniqueness is the power of free will. In his books and lectures, Dr. Van Dusen frequently spoke about the exercise of this uniqueness. The fact that he used his free will to prevent life from becoming a caricature of itself was completely in character. In their letter, the Van Dusens sought to convince family and friends that they were not acting solely out of despair or pain.   5

The use of free will to put an end to one's life finds no sanction in the theology to which Pitney Van Dusen was committed. Suicide symbolizes discontinuity; religion symbolizes continuity, represented at its quintessence by the concept of the immortal soul. Human logic finds it almost impossible to come to terms with the concept of nonexistence. In religion, the human mind finds a larger dimension and is relieved of the ordeal of a confrontation with nonexistence.   6

Even without respect to religion, the idea of suicide has been abhorrent throughout history. Some societies have imposed severe penalties on the families of suicides in the hope that the individual who sees no reason to continue his existence may be deterred by the stigma his self-destruction would inflict on loved ones. Other societies have enacted laws prohibiting suicide on the grounds that it is murder. The enforcement of such laws, of course, has been an exercise in futility.   7

Customs and attitudes, like individuals themselves, are largely shaped by the surrounding environment. In today's world, life can be prolonged by science far beyond meaning or sensibility. Under these circumstances, individuals who feel they have nothing more to give to life, or to receive from it, need not be applauded, but they can be spared our condemnation.   8

The general reaction to suicide is bound to change as people come to understand that it may be a denial, not an assertion, of moral or religious ethics to allow life to be extended without regard to decency or pride. What moral or religious purpose is celebrated by the annihilation of the human spirit in the triumphant act of keeping the body alive? Why are so many people more readily appalled by an unnatural form of dying than by an unnatural form of living?   9

"Nowadays," the Van Dusens wrote in their last letter, "it is difficult to die. We feel that this way we are taking will become more usual and acceptable as the years pass.   10

"Of course, the thought of our children and our grandchildren makes us sad, but we still feel that this is the best way and the right way to go. We are both increasingly weak and unwell and who would want to die in a nursing home?   11

"We are not afraid to die. . . ." 12

Pitney Van Dusen was admired and respected in life. He can be 13
admired and respected in death. "Suicide," said Goethe, "is an incident
in human life which, however much disputed and discussed, demands
the sympathy of every man, and in every age must be dealt with anew."

Death is not the greatest loss in life. The greatest loss is what dies 14
inside us while we live. The unbearable tragedy is to live without dignity
or sensitivity.

About the Essay

1. What basic issue does the Van Dusens' suicide letter raise? What is Cousins' position on this issue? Where does he state his position?

2. Why, according to Cousins, has the idea of suicide been so "abhorrent throughout history"? Do you agree with him? Do you agree with his statement that enforcing the laws against suicide has been an "exercise in futility"? Are there reasons other than those Cousins gives why the law concerns itself with suicide?

3. Cousins structures his essay as an inductive argument—that is, he presents his evidence first and then bases a concluding generalization on it. Where does he move from evidence to conclusion? Does his conclusion take into account all of his evidence—as well as relevant evidence he may not present but you can think of?

4. What are the connotations of the italicized words in each of the following brief excerpts? How do they affect the meaning of their contexts?

   a. one of the *luminous* names in Protestant theology
   b. to keep them *technically* alive
   c. to prevent life from becoming a *caricature* of itself
   d. what moral or religious purpose is *celebrated*

5. Cousins says "the general reaction to suicide is bound to change." What reasons does he offer for believing this? What is *your* reaction to suicide? Has Cousins' essay affected your opinion in any way? If so, how?

Explorations

1. Central to Cousins' views on suicide is the belief that a life lacking in dignity is not worth living. In your view, what does it mean to preserve one's dignity? What indignities are the worst? In what circumstances might you sacrifice your life to maintain your dignity?

2. In recent years there has been an alarming increase in the number of suicides, especially among children and teenagers. Do research into the scope

of the problem, its possible causes, and proposed solutions if any, and write a paper reporting what you have found.

3. Cousins refers in his essay to the traditional religious attitudes toward suicide. What are they? Why do religions object so strenuously and absolutely to suicide when they may approve of martyrdom for the faith or of fatal acts of heroism in war?

VIRGINIA WOOLF

Virginia Woolf was born in London in 1882 to the distinguished scholar Leslie Stephen. She was educated at home with the resources of her father's superb library, and after his death moved with her sister and brothers to London's Bloomsbury district. There they became friends with a circle of writers and artists that included the novelist E.M. Forster and the economist John Maynard Keynes. Woolf started her writing career as a literary critic for the *Times Literary Supplement,* and in 1917 founded with her husband Leonard the Hogarth Press, which published many of the writers associated with the Bloomsbury group, including Woolf herself. She is best known for her novels, including *Jacob's Room* (1922), *Mrs. Dalloway* (1925), *To the Lighthouse* (1927), and *The Waves* (1931). Her essays have been published in the four-volume *Collected Essays* (1966–1967). In her later life Woolf was subject to periods of depression and anxiety, and in 1941 she took her own life. In the following essay, first published in 1942, she tells how the death of a moth brought home to her the power of life and the enormity of death.

The Death of the Moth

Moths that fly by day are not properly to be called moths; they do not excite that pleasant sense of dark autumn nights and ivy-blossom which the commonest yellow underwing asleep in the shadow of the curtain never fails to rouse in us. They are hybrid creatures, neither gay like butterlies nor sombre like their own species. Nevertheless the present specimen, with his narrow hay-coloured wings, fringed with a tassel of the same colour, seemed to be content with life. It was a pleasant morning, mid-September, mild, benignant, yet with a keener breath than of the summer months. The plough was already scoring the field opposite the window, and where the share had been, the earth was pressed flat and gleamed with moisture. Such vigour came rolling in from the fields and the down beyond that it was difficult to keep the eyes strictly turned upon the book. The rooks too were keeping one of their annual festivities; soaring round the tree-tops until it looked as if a vast net with thousands of black knots in it has been cast up into the air; which, after a few moments sank slowly down upon the trees until every twig seemed to have a knot at the end of it. Then, suddenly, the net would be thrown into the air again in a wider circle this time, with the utmost clamour and vociferation, as though to be thrown into the air and settle slowly down upon the tree-tops were a tremendously exciting experience. 1

The same energy which inspired the rooks, the ploughmen, the   2
horses, and even, it seemed, the lean bare-backed downs, sent the moth
fluttering from side to side of his square of the window-pane. One could
not help watching him. One was, indeed, conscious of a queer feeling
of pity for him. The possibilities of pleasure seemed that morning so
enormous and so various that to have only a moth's part in life, and a
day moth's at that, appeared a hard fate, and his zest in enjoying his
meagre opportunities to the full, pathetic. He flew vigorously to one
corner of his compartment, and, after waiting there a second, flew across
to the other. What remained for him but to fly to a third corner and
then to a fourth? That was all he could do, in spite of the size of the
downs, the width of the sky, the far-off smoke of houses, and the romantic voice, now and then, of a steamer out at sea. What he could do
he did. Watching him, it seemed as if a fibre, very thin but pure, of the
enormous energy of the world had been thrust into his frail and diminutive body. As often as he crossed the pane, I could fancy that a thread
of vital light became visible. He was little or nothing but life.

Yet, because he was so small, and so simple a form of the energy   3
that was rolling in at the open window and driving its way through so
many narrow and intricate corridors in my own brain and in those of
other human beings, there was something marvellous as well as pathetic
about him. It was as if someone had taken a tiny bead of pure life and
decking it as lightly as possible with down and feathers, had set it dancing
and zigzagging to show us the true nature of life. Thus displayed one
could not get over the strangeness of it. One is apt to forget all about
life, seeing it humped and bossed and garnished and cumbered so that it
has to move with the greatest circumspection and dignity. Again, the
thought of all that life might have been had he been born in any other
shape caused one to view his simple activities with a kind of pity.

After a time, tired by his dancing apparently, he settled on the   4
window ledge in the sun, and the queer spectacle being at an end, I
forgot about him. Then, looking up, my eye was caught by him. He was
trying to resume his dancing, but seemed either so stiff or so awkward
that he could only flutter to the bottom of the window-pane; and when
he tried to fly across it he failed. Being intent on other matters I watched
these futile attempts for a time without thinking, unconsciously waiting
for him to resume his flight, as one waits for a machine, that has stopped
momentarily, to start again without considering the reason for its failure.
After perhaps a seventh attempt he slipped from the wooden ledge and
fell, fluttering his wings, on to his back on the window-sill. The helplessness of his attitude roused me. It flashed upon me that he was in
difficulties; he could no longer raise himself; his legs struggled vainly.

But, as I stretched out a pencil, meaning to help him to right himself, it came over me that the failure and awkwardness were the approach of death. I laid the pencil down again.

The legs agitated themselves once more. I looked as if for the enemy   5 against which he struggled. I looked out of doors. What had happened there? Presumably it was midday, and work in the fields had stopped. Stillness and quiet had replaced the previous animation. The birds had taken themselves off to feed in the brooks. The horses stood still. Yet the power was there all the same, massed outside indifferent, impersonal, not attending to anything in particular. Somehow it was opposed to the little hay-coloured moth. It was useless to try to do anything. One could only watch the extraordinary efforts made by those tiny legs against an oncoming doom which could, had it chosen, have submerged an entire city, not merely a city, but masses of human beings; nothing, I knew, had any chance against death. Nevertheless after a pause of exhaustion the legs fluttered again. It was superb this last protest, and so frantic that he succeeded at last in righting himself. One's sympathies, of course, were all on the side of life. Also, when there was nobody to care or to know, this gigantic effort on the part of an insignificant little moth, against a power of such magnitude, to retain what no one else valued or desired to keep, moved one strangely. Again, somehow, one saw life, a pure bead. I lifted the pencil again, useless though I knew it to be. But even as I did so, the unmistakable tokens of death showed themselves. The body relaxed, and instantly grew stiff. The struggle was over. The insignificant little creature now knew death. As I looked at the dead moth, this minute wayside triumph of so great a force over so mean an antagonist filled me with wonder. Just as life had been strange a few minutes before, so death was now as strange. The moth having righted himself now lay most decently and uncomplaining composed. O yes, he seemed to say, death is stronger than I am.

About the Essay

1. What does the moth represent in this essay? What does the scene outdoors represent? How are they parallel?

2. What happens outdoors during the moth's death throes? What is the tone of Woolf's descriptions of the moth and the outdoors? How does this tone contribute to the essay's meaning and effect?

3. Why does Woolf feel pity for the moth? Although the creature is obviously symbolic, how does Woolf convey its concrete reality? What visual details does she provide?

4. What figures of speech does Woolf use to describe the scene outdoors and

the moth's actions? How do these add to your understanding and enjoyment of the essay?

5. What does Woolf mean when she writes, "One is apt to forget all about life, seeing it humped and bossed and garnished and cumbered so that it has to move with the greatest circumspection and dignity"?

6. Why does Woolf say in conclusion, "Just as life had been strange a few minutes before, so death was now as strange"? What, in her description, was "strange" about both life and death?

Explorations

1. As the seventeenth-century English writer Sir Thomas Browne once wrote, "The long habit of living indisposeth us for dying"—yet we must all die, of course. Do thoughts of death come to you from time to time? Under what circumstances? How do they affect your attitude toward life, if they do?

2. Like Virginia Woolf, many writers have found in small, apparently insignificant things the occasion for reflection on large topics. (See also Whitman, "A Noiseless Patient Spider," page 719.) Choose an apparently trivial object or event, then meditate on it, allowing it to suggest deeper thoughts and associations. Write an essay in which you present not only the larger ideas at which you arrived but the little one with which you began.

WALT WHITMAN

Walt Whitman's poems are often on a grand scale, as, for instance, is the 1346-line "Song of Myself." In "A Noiseless Patient Spider," however, he contemplates the cosmos in fewer than a hundred words. Whitman was born in 1819 in Huntington, Long Island, and grew up in Brooklyn. He left school at age eleven to work in a printer's office, and by his twenties he had become a journalist and a worker for the Democratic Party. Around 1852, however, Whitman moved back in with his family, doing occasional carpentry, reading widely, loafing and strolling about, and writing the poems that were published in 1855 as *Leaves of Grass*. He then resumed his journalistic work in order to support his now fatherless family, and prepared newly expanded editions of *Leaves of Grass* in 1856 and 1860. After suffering a stroke in 1872, he retired to Camden, New Jersey, where he died twenty years later. "A Noiseless Patient Spider" dates from 1868. In it Whitman presents an analogy between a spider making its web and his own soul seeking to connect with the universe.

A Noiseless Patient Spider

A noiseless patient spider,
I mark'd where on a little promontory it stood isolated,
Mark'd how to explore the vacant vast surrounding,
It launch'd forth filament, filament, filament, out of itself,
Ever unreeling them, ever tirelessly speeding them.   5

And you O my soul where you stand,
Surrounded, detached, in measureless oceans of space,
Ceaselessly musing, venturing, throwing, seeking the spheres to
    connect them,
Till the bridge you will need be form'd, till the ductile anchor hold,
Till the gossamer thread you fling catch somewhere, O my soul.   10

About the Poem

1. What does Whitman's poem say about the soul's activity and purpose? Why does he draw an analogy with the web-spinning spider? How did you respond to this analogy?

2. One stanza of the poem is a sentence; the other is not. Which is which? What word or words would you introduce to complete the non-sentence? Why might Whitman have preferred the sentence fragment?

3. Whitman often chooses particular words because of their sounds—their consonants and vowels, their rhythms. Pick out some such words in this poem and discuss what their sounds contribute to the poem.

4. How do you interpret the following phrases:
   a. launch'd forth filament, filament, filament
   b. seeking the spheres to connect them
   c. till the ductile anchor hold

5. Is "A Noiseless Patient Spider" a particularly apt title for the poem? What would Whitman have gained or lost by calling the poem "The Spider"?

Explorations

1. Here is an earlier version of Whitman's poem:

The Soul, reaching, throwing out for love,
As the spider, from some little promontory, throwing out filament after
   filament, tirelessly out of itself, that one at least may catch and form a
   link, a bridge, a connection
O I saw one passing alone, saying hardly a word—yet full of love I detected him, by certain signs
O eyes wishfully turning! O silent eyes!

What differences do you notice between the two poems? What similarities? Are they both about the same subject? Which do you like better? Why?

2. Look closely at an insect, a flower, a leaf, or some other natural thing, recording your observations in detail. Now try to write the essence of what you observed.

JOHN DONNE

John Donne's writings encompass both worldly and religious concerns, as did his life. He was born in London in 1572 and, after attending Oxford, Cambridge, and the law school at Lincoln's Inn, he began his public career as an officer on a warship headed for action against Spain. After two years of service he returned to England and in 1598 became secretary to a leading statesman of the day, with excellent prospects for a career at court. Those prospects were ruined in 1601, however, when Donne eloped with a member of the statesman's family, for which he not only lost his position but was briefly imprisoned. For the next fifteen years he sought a position at court, but in vain; King James saw in him the makings of an excellent preacher and would offer him no other appointment. Finally Donne agreed to take holy orders and in 1615 was appointed Reader in Divinity at Lincoln's Inn. He distinguished himself as the most eloquent preacher of the day and became Dean of Saint Paul's Cathedral in 1621. His poetry dates almost entirely from before 1615, but little of it was published until after his death in 1631. His other writings include sermons and devotions that are among the finest in the English language. "Death, Be Not Proud," the tenth of a series of nineteen *Holy Sonnets*, was evidently written around 1609 though not published until 1633. In it Donne uses a lawyer's reasoning and a Christian's faith to refute Death's claim to power.

Death, Be Not Proud

Death, be not proud, though some have callèd thee
Mighty and dreadful, for thou are not so;
For those whom thou think'st thou dost overthrow
Die not, poor Death, nor yet canst thou kill me.
From rest and sleep, which but thy pictures be,   5
Much pleasure; then from thee much more must flow,
And soonest our best men with thee do go,
Rest of their bones, and soul's delivery.
Thou'art slave to fate, chance, kings, and desperate men,
And dost with poison, war, and sickness dwell,   10
And poppy'or charms can make us sleep as well
And better than thy stroke; why swell'st thou then?
One short sleep past, we wake eternally
And death shall be no more; Death, thou shalt die.

About the Poem

1. How does Donne characterize death? How does he contrive to turn death into an almost human figure?

2. Why does Donne say that death should not be proud? What is the underlying assumption of the poem?

3. What does Donne mean by these two paradoxes:

   a. For those whom thou think'st thou dost overthrow
   Die not, poor Death, nor yet canst thou kill me.

   b. One short sleep past, we wake eternally
   And death shall be no more; Death, thou shalt die.

4. Paraphrase lines 5 and 6 to make their meaning clear.

5. What is Donne's tone in this poem? How does it suit his theme and his point of view?

6. The poem is divisible into several sections. Where do the divisions come, and how are they marked? What does each part of the poem contribute?

Explorations

1. The immortality of the soul is one of the great promises of several religions. Do you believe the soul will exist in an afterlife? How does your belief, or lack of it, affect your outlook on life and your attitude toward death?

2. Though death lies ahead for all of us, it has long been an "unthinkable" topic. Americans generally avoid discussing the topic, and consequently have had much difficulty in dealing with friends and relatives they know to be dying. Recent books and articles on death and dying may be changing this, however. Do some research into the subject, and report on those analyses and proposals that interest you.

ISAAC BASHEVIS SINGER

Gimpel is so willing to believe what others tell him that his neighbors think him a fool. Yet trust, the willingness to accept things on faith, is no less important to our public and private lives than our inclination to question and suspect. In "Gimpel the Fool," first published in 1953 in Saul Bellow's translation from the Yiddish, Isaac Bashevis Singer explores the tension between faith and doubt. In the surprising conclusion, Gimpel completely changes his way of life, yet manages to maintain his trust of humankind. (For biographical information about Isaac Bashevis Singer see page 170.)

Gimpel the Fool

I am Gimpel the fool. I don't think myself a fool. On the contrary. But that's what folks call me. They gave me the name while I was still in school. I had seven names in all: imbecile, donkey, flax-head, dope, glump, ninny, and fool. The last name stuck. What did my foolishness consist of? I was easy to take in. They said, "Gimpel, you know the rabbi's wife has been brought to childbed?" So I skipped school. Well, it turned out to be a lie. How was I supposed to know? She hadn't had a big belly. But I never looked at her belly. Was that really so foolish? The gang laughed and hee-hawed, stomped and danced and chanted a good-night prayer. And instead of the raisins they give when a woman's lying in, they stuffed my hand full of goat turds. I was no weakling. If I slapped someone he'd see all the way to Cracow. But I'm really not a slugger by nature. I think to myself: Let it pass. So they take advantage of me.

I was coming home from school and heard a dog barking. I'm not afraid of dogs, but of course I never want to start up with them. One of them may be mad, and if he bites there's not a Tartar in the world who can help you. So I made tracks. Then I looked around and saw the whole market place wild with laughter. It was no dog at all but Wolf-Leib the Thief. How was I supposed to know it was he? It sounded like a howling bitch.

When the pranksters and leg-pullers found that I was easy to fool, every one of them tried his luck with me. "Gimpel, the Czar is coming to Frampol: Gimpel, the moon fell down in Turbeen;[1] Gimpel, little Hodel Furpiece found a treasure behind the bathhouse." And I like a

1

2

3

---

[1] Frampol and Turbeen are mythical towns in Singer's fiction.

golem[2] believed everyone. In the first place, everything is possible, as it is written in the Wisdom of the Fathers. I've forgotten just how: Second, I had to believe when the whole town came down on me! If I ever dared to say, "Ah, you're kidding!" there was trouble. People got angry. "What do you mean! You want to call everyone a liar?" What was I to do? I believed them, and I hope at least that did them some good.

I was an orphan. My grandfather who brought me up was already   4 bent toward the grave. So they turned me over to a baker, and what a time they gave me there! Every woman or girl who came to bake a batch of noodles had to fool me at least once. "Gimpel, there's a fair in heaven; Gimpel, the rabbi gave birth to a calf in the seventh month; Gimpel, a cow flew over the roof and laid brass eggs." A student from the yeshiva[3] came once to buy a roll, and he said, "You, Gimpel, while you stand here scraping with your baker's shovel the Messiah has come. The dead have arisen." "What do you mean?" I said. "I heard no one blowing the ram's horn!" He said, "Are you deaf?" And all began to cry, "We heard it, we heard!" Then in came Rietze the Candle-dipper and called out in her hoarse voice, "Gimpel, your father and mother have stood up from the grave. They're looking for you."

To tell the truth, I knew very well that nothing of the sort had   5 happened, but all the same, as folks were talking, I threw on my wool vest and went out. Maybe something had happened. What did I stand to lose by looking? Well, what a cat music went up! And then I took a vow to believe nothing more. But that was no go either. They confused me so that I didn't know the big end from the small.

I went to the rabbi to get some advice. He said, "It is written,   6 better to be a fool all your days than for one hour to be evil. You are not a fool. They are the fools. For he who causes his neighbor to feel shame loses Paradise himself." Nevertheless the rabbi's daughter took me in. As I left the rabbinical court she said, "Have you kissed the wall yet?" I said, "No; what for?" She answered, "It's the law; you've got to do it after every visit." Well, there didn't seem to be any harm in it. And she burst out laughing. It was a fine trick. She put one over on me, all right.

I wanted to go off to another town, but then everyone got busy   7 matchmaking, and they were after me so they nearly tore my coat tails off. They talked at me and talked until I got water on the ear. She was no chaste maiden, but they told me she was virgin pure. She had a limp, and they said it was deliberate, from coyness. She had a bastard, and

---

[2]A slow-witted simpleton.

[3]In Europe, a rabbinical seminary.

they told me the child was her little brother. I cried, "You're wasting your time. I'll never marry that whore." But they said indignantly, "What a way to talk! Aren't you ashamed of yourself? We can take you to the rabbi and have you fined for giving her a bad name." I saw then that I wouldn't escape them so easily and I thought: They're set on making me their butt. But when you're married the husband's the master, and if that's all right with her it's agreeable to me too. Besides, you can't pass through life unscathed, nor expect to.

I went to her clay house, which was built on the sand, and the whole gang, hollering and chorusing, came after me. They acted like bear-baiters. When we came to the well they stopped all the same. They were afraid to start anything with Elka. Her mouth would open as if it were on a hinge, and she had a fierce tongue. I entered the house. Lines were strung from wall to wall and clothes were drying. Barefoot she stood by the tub, doing the wash. She was dressed in a worn hand-me-down gown of plush. She had her hair put up in braids and pinned across her head. It took my breath away, almost, the reek of it all.

Evidently she knew who I was. She took a look at me and said, "Look who's here! He's come, the drip. Grab a seat."

I told her all; I denied nothing. "Tell me the truth," I said, "are you really a virgin, and is that mischievous Yechiel actually your little brother? Don't be deceitful with me, for I'm an orphan."

"I'm an orphan myself," she answered, "and whoever tries to twist you up, may the end of his nose take a twist. But don't let them think they can take advantage of me. I want a dowry of fifty guilders, and let them take up a collection besides. Otherwise they can kiss my you-know-what." She was very plainspoken. I said, "It's the bride and not the groom who gives a dowry." Then she said, "Don't bargain with me. Either a flat 'yes' or a flat 'no'—Go back where you came from."

I thought: No bread will ever be baked from *this* dough. But ours is not a poor town. They consented to everything and proceeded with the wedding. It so happened that there was a dysentery epidemic at the time. The ceremony was held at the cemetery gates, near the little corpse-washing hut. The fellows got drunk. While the marriage contract was being drawn up I heard the most pious high rabbi ask, "Is the bride a widow or a divorced woman?" And the sexton's wife answered for her, "Both a widow and divorced." It was a black moment for me. But what was I to do, run away from under the marriage canopy?

There was singing and dancing. An old granny danced opposite me, hugging a braided white *chalah*.[4] The master of revels made a "God'a

8

9

10

11

12

13

---

[4]Bread.

726 Isaac Bashevis Singer

mercy" in memory of the bride's parents. The schoolboys threw burrs, as on Tishe b'Av fast day.[5] There were a lot of gifts after the sermon: a noodle board, a kneading trough, a bucket, brooms, ladles, household articles galore. Then I took a look and saw two strapping young men carrying a crib. "What do we need this for?" I asked. So they said, "Don't rack your brains about it. It's all right, it'll come in handy." I realized I was going to be rooked. Take it another way though, what did I stand to lose? I reflected: I'll see what comes of it. A whole town can't go altogether crazy.

At night I came where my wife lay, but she wouldn't let me in. "Say, look here, is this what they married us for?" I said. And she said, "My monthly has come." "But yesterday they took you to the ritual bath, and that's afterward, isn't it supposed to be?" "Today isn't yesterday," said she, "and yesterday's not today. You can beat it if you don't like it." In short, I waited.   14

Not four months later she was in childbed. The townsfolk hid their laughter with their knuckles. But what could I do? She suffered intolerable pains and clawed at the walls. "Gimpel," she cried, "I'm going. Forgive me." The house filled with women. They were boiling pans of water. The screams rose to the welkin.   15

The thing to do was to go to the House of Prayer to repeat Psalms, and that was what I did.   16

The townsfolk liked that, all right. I stood in a corner saying Psalms and prayers, and they shook their heads at me. "Pray, pray!" they told me, "Prayer never made any woman pregnant." One of the congregation put a straw to my mouth and said, "Hay for the cows." There was something to that too, by God!   17

She gave birth to a boy, Friday at the synagogue the sexton stood up before the Ark, pounded on the reading table, and announced, "The wealthy Reb Gimpel invites the congregation to a feast in honor of the birth of a son." The whole House of Prayer rang with laughter. My face was flaming. But there was nothing I could do. After all, I *was* the one responsible for the circumcision honors and rituals.   18

Half the town came running. You couldn't wedge another soul in. Women brought peppered chick-peas, and there was a keg of beer from the tavern. I ate and drank as much as anyone, and they all congratulated me. Then there was a circumcision, and I named the boy after my father, may he rest in peace. When all were gone and I was left with my wife alone, she thrust her head through the bed-curtain and called me to her.   19

---

[5]A day of fasting and mourning commemorating the destruction of the Temple in Jerusalem.

"Gimpel," said she, "why are you silent? Has your ship gone and   20
sunk?"

"What shall I say?" I answered. "A fine thing you've done to me!   21
If my mother had known of it she'd have died a second time."

She said, "Are you crazy, or what?"   22

"How can you make such a fool," I said, "of one who should be   23
the lord and master?"

"What's the matter with you?" she said. "What have you taken it   24
into your head to imagine?"

I saw that I must speak bluntly and openly. "Do you think this is   25
the way to use an orphan?" I said. "You have borne a bastard."

She answered, "Drive this foolishness out of your head. The child   26
is yours."

"How can he be mine?" I argued. "He was born seventeen weeks   27
after the wedding."

She told me then that he was premature. I said, "Isn't he a little   28
too premature?" She said, she had had a grandmother who carried just
as short a time and she resembled this grandmother of hers as one drop
of water does another. She swore to it with such oaths that you would
have believed a peasant at the fair if he had used them. To tell the plain
truth, I didn't believe her; but when I talked it over next day with the
schoolmaster he told me that the very same thing had happened to Adam
and Eve. Two they went up to bed and four they descended.

"There isn't a woman in the world who is not the granddaughter   29
of Eve," he said.

That was how it was; they argued me dumb. But then, who really   30
knows how such things are?

I began to forget my sorrow. I loved the child madly, and he loved   31
me too. As soon as he saw me he'd wave his little hands and want me
to pick him up, and when he was colicky I was the only one who could
pacify him. I bought him a little bone teething ring and a little gilded
cap. He was forever catching the evil eye from someone, and then I had
to run to get one of those abracadabras for him that would get him out
of it. I worked like an ox. You know how expenses go up when there's
an infant in the house. I don't want to lie about it; I didn't dislike Elka
either, for that matter. She swore at me and cursed, and I couldn't get
enough of her. What strength she had! One of her looks could rob you
of the power of speech. And her orations! Pitch and sulphur, that's what
they were full of, and yet somehow also full of charm. I adored her every
word. She gave me bloody wounds though.

In the evening I brought her a white loaf as well as a dark one,   32
and also poppyseed rolls I baked myself. I thieved because of her and
swiped everything I could lay hands on: macaroons, raisins, almonds,

cakes. I hope I may be forgiven for stealing from the Saturday pots the women left to warm in the baker's oven. I would take out scraps of meat, a chunk of pudding, a chicken leg or head, a piece of tripe, whatever I could nip quickly. She ate and became fat and handsome.

I had to sleep away from home all during the week, at the bakery. On Friday nights when I got home she always made an excuse of some sort. Either she had heartburn, or a stitch in the side, or hiccups, or headaches. You know what women's excuses are. I had a bitter time of it. It was rough. To add to it, this little brother of hers, the bastard, was growing bigger. He'd put lumps on me, and when I wanted to hit back she'd open her mouth and curse so powerfully I saw a green haze floating before my eyes. Ten times a day she threatened to divorce me. Another man in my place would have taken French leave and disappeared. But I'm the type that bears it and says nothing. What's one to do? Shoulders are from God, and burdens too.

One night there was a calamity in the bakery; the oven burst, and we almost had a fire. There was nothing to do but go home, so I went home. Let me, I thought, also taste the joy of sleeping in bed in midweek. I didn't want to wake the sleeping mite and tiptoed into the house. Coming in, it seemed to me that I heard not the snoring of one but, as it were, a double snore, one a thin enough snore and the other like the snoring of a slaughtered ox. Oh, I didn't like that! I didn't like it at all. I went up to the bed, and things suddenly turned black. Next to Elka lay a man's form. Another in my place would have made an uproar, and enough noise to rouse the whole town, but the thought occurred to me that I might wake the child. A little thing like that—why frighten a little swallow, I thought. All right then, I went back to the bakery and stretched out on a sack of flour and till morning I never shut an eye. I shivered as if I had had malaria. "Enough of being a donkey," I said to myself. "Gimpel isn't going to be a sucker all his life. There's a limit even to the foolishness of a fool like Gimpel."

In the morning I went to the rabbi to get advice, and it made a great commotion in the town. They sent the beadle for Elka right away. She came, carrying the child. And what do you think she did? She denied it, denied everything, bone and stone! "He's out of his head," she said. "I know nothing of dreams or divinations." They yelled at her, warned her, hammered on the table, but she stuck to her guns: it was a false accusation, she said.

The butchers and the horse-traders took her part. One of the lads from the slaughterhouse came by and said to me, "We've got our eye on you, you're a marked man." Meanwhile the child started to bear down and soiled itself. In the rabbinical court there was an Ark of the Covenant, and they couldn't allow that, so they sent Elka away.

I said to the rabbi, "What shall I do?" 37

"You must divorce her at once," said he. 38

"And what if she refuses?" I asked. 39

He said, "You must serve the divorce. That's all you'll have to do." 40

I said, "Well, all right, Rabbi. Let me think about it." 41

"There's nothing to think about," said he. "You mustn't remain 42
under the same roof with her."

"And what if she refuses?" I asked. 43

"Let her go, the harlot," said he, "and her brood of bastards with 44
her."

The verdict he gave was that I mustn't even cross her threshold— 45
never again, as long as I should live.

During the day it didn't bother me so much. I thought: It was bound 46
to happen, the abscess had to burst. But at night when I stretched out
upon the sacks I felt it all very bitterly. A longing took me, for her and
for the child. I wanted to be angry, but that's my misfortune exactly, I
don't have it in me to be really angry. In the first place—this was how
my thoughts went—there's bound to be a slip sometimes. You can't live
without errors. Probably that lad who was with her led her on and gave
her presents and what not, and women are often long on hair and short
on sense, and so he got around her. And then since she denies it so,
maybe I was only seeing things? Hallucinations do happen. You see a
figure or a mannikin or something, but when you come up closer it's
nothing, there's not a thing there. And if that's so, I'm doing her an
injustice. And when I got so far in my thoughts I started to weep. I
sobbed so that I wet the flour where I lay. In the morning I went to the
rabbi and told him that I had made a mistake. The rabbi wrote on with
his quill, and he said that if that were so he would have to reconsider
the whole case. Until he had finished I wasn't to go near my wife, but I
might send her bread and money by messenger.

Nine months passed before all the rabbis could come to an agree- 47
ment. Letters went back and forth. I hadn't realized that there could be
so much erudition about a matter like this.

Meanwhile Elka gave birth to still another child, a girl this time. 48
On the Sabbath I went to the synagogue and invoked a blessing on her.
They called me up to the Torah,[6] and I named the child for my mother-
in-law—may she rest in peace. The louts and loudmouths of the town
who came into the bakery gave me a going over. All Frampol refreshed

---

[6]The holy scriptures of the Jews, usually in a scroll. On special occasions a member
of the congregation is called upon to read from the scroll. It is considered a great
honor.

its spirits because of my trouble and grief. However, I resolved that I would always believe what I was told. What's the good of *not* believing? Today it's your wife you don't believe; tomorrow it's God Himself you won't take stock in.

By an apprentice who was her neighbor I sent her daily a corn or a wheat loaf, or a piece of pastry, rolls or bagels, or, when I got the chance, a slab of pudding, a slice of honeycake, or wedding strudel—whatever came my way. The apprentice was a goodhearted lad, and more than once he added something on his own. He had formerly annoyed me a lot, plucking my nose and digging me in the ribs, but when he started to be a visitor to my house he became kind and friendly, "Hey, you, Gimpel," he said to me, "you have a very decent little wife and two fine kids. You don't deserve them."

"But the things people say about her," I said.

"Well, they have long tongues," he said, "and nothing to do with them but babble. Ignore it as you ignore the cold of last winter."

One day the rabbi sent for me and said, "Are you certain, Gimpel, that you were wrong about your wife?"

I said, "I'm certain."

"Why, but look here! You yourself saw it."

"It must have been a shadow," I said.

"The shadow of what?"

"Just of one of the beams, I think."

"You can go home then. You owe thanks to the Yanover rabbi. He found an obscure reference in Maimonides[7] that favored you."

I seized the rabbi's hand and kissed it.

I wanted to run home immediately. It's no small thing to be separated for so long a time from wife and child. Then I reflected: I'd better go back to work now, and go home in the evening. I said nothing to anyone, although as far as my heart was concerned it was like one of the Holy Days. The women teased and twitted me as they did every day, but my thought was: Go on, with your loose talk. The truth is out, like the oil upon the water. Maimonides says it's right, and therefore it is right!

At night, when I had covered the dough to let it rise, I took my share of bread and a little sack of flour and started homeward. The moon was full and the stars were glistening, something to terrify the soul. I hurried onward, and before me darted a long shadow. It was winter, and a fresh snow had fallen. I had a mind to sing, but it was growing late and I didn't want to wake the householders. Then I felt like whistling,

---

[7]Moses ben Maimon (1135–1204), Jewish philosopher and commentator on religious law.

but I remembered that you don't whistle at night because it brings the demons out. So I was silent and walked as fast as I could.

Dogs in the Christian yards barked at me when I passed, but I thought: Bark your teeth out! What are you but mere dogs? Whereas I am a man, the husband of a fine wife, the father of promising children. 62

As I approached the house my heart started to pound as though it were the heart of a criminal. I felt no fear, but my heart went thump! thump! Well, no drawing back. I quietly lifted the latch and went in. Elka was asleep. I looked at the infant's cradle. The shutter was closed, but the moon forced its way through the cracks. I saw the newborn child's face and loved it as soon as I saw it—immediately—each tiny bone. 63

Then I came nearer to the bed. And what did I see but the apprentice lying there beside Elka. The moon went out all at once. It was utterly black, and I trembled. My teeth chattered. The bread fell from my hands, and my wife waked and said, "Who is that, ah?" 64

I muttered, "It's me." 65

"Gimpel?" she asked. "How come you're here? I thought it was forbidden." 66

"The rabbi said," I answered and shook as with a fever. 67

"Listen to me, Gimpel," she said, "go out to the shed and see if the goat's all right. It seems she's been sick." I have forgotten to say that we had a goat. When I heard she was unwell I went into the yard. The nannygoat was a good little creature. I had a nearly human feeling for her. 68

With hesitant steps I went up to the shed and opened the door. The goat stood there on her four feet. I felt her everywhere, drew her by the horns, examined her udders, and found nothing wrong. She had probably eaten too much bark. "Good night, little goat," I said. "Keep well." And the little beast answered with a "Maa" as though to thank me for the good will. 69

I went back. The apprentice had vanished. 70

"Where," I asked, "is the lad?" 71

"What lad?" my wife answered. 72

"What do you mean?" I said. "The apprentice. You were sleeping with him." 73

"The things I have dreamed this night and the night before," she said, "may they come true and lay you low, body and soul! An evil spirit has taken root in you and dazzles your sight." She screamed out, "You hateful creature! You moon calf! You spook! You uncouth man! Get out, or I'll scream all Frampol out of bed!" 74

Before I could move, her brother sprang out from behind the oven and struck me a blow on the back of the head. I thought he had broken 75 my neck. I felt that something about me was deeply wrong, and I said, "Don't make a scandal. All that's needed now is that people should accuse me of raising spooks and *dybbuks.*"[8] For that was what she had meant. "No one will touch bread of my baking."

In short, I somehow calmed her.

"Well," she said, "that's enough. Lie down, and be shattered by wheels."

Next morning I called the apprentice aside. "Listen here, brother!" I said. And so on and so forth. "What do you say?" He stared at me as though I had dropped from the roof or something.

"I swear," he said, "you'd better go to an herb doctor or some healer. I'm afraid you have a screw loose, but I'll hush it up for you." And that's how the thing stood.

To make a long story short, I lived twenty years with my wife. She bore me six children, four daughters and two sons. All kinds of things happened, but I neither saw nor heard. I believed, and that's all. The rabbi recently said to me, "Belief in itself is beneficial. It is written that a good man lives by his faith."

Suddenly my wife took sick. It began with a trifle, a little growth upon the breast. But she evidently was not destined to live long; she had no years. I spent a fortune on her. I have forgotten to say that by this time I had a bakery of my own and in Frampol was considered to be something of a rich man. Daily the healer came, and every witch doctor in the neighborhood was brought. They decided to use leeches, and after that to try cupping. They even called a doctor from Lublin,[9] but it was too late. Before she died she called me to her bed and said, "Forgive me, Gimpel."

I said, "What is there to forgive? You have been a good and faithful wife."

"Woe, Gimpel!" she said. "It was ugly how I deceived you all these years. I want to go clean to my Maker, and so I have to tell you that the children are not yours."

If I had been clouted on the head with a piece of wood it couldn't have bewildered me more.

"Whose are they?" I asked.

"I don't know," she said. "There were a lot . . . but they're not yours." And as she spoke she tossed her head to the side, her eyes turned glassy, and it was all up with Elka. On her whitened lips there remained a smile.

---

[8]A demon.

[9]A town in Poland.

I imagined that, dead as she was, she was saying, "I deceived Gim- 87
pel. That was the meaning of my brief life."

One night, when the period of mourning was done, as I lay dream- 88
ing on the flour sacks, there came the Spirit of Evil himself and said to
me, "Gimpel, why do you sleep?"

I said, "What should I be doing? Eating *kreplach?*"[10] 89

"The whole world deceives you," he said, "and you ought to deceive 90
the world in your turn."

"How can I deceive all the world?" I asked him. 91

He answered, "You might accumulate a bucket of urine every 92
day and at night pour it into the dough. Let the sages of Frampol eat
filth."

"What about the judgment in the world to come?" I said. 93

"There is no world to come," he said. "They've sold you a bill of 94
goods and talked you into believing you carried a cat in your belly. What
nonsense!"

"Well then," I said, "and is there a God?" 95

He answered, "There is no God, either." 96

"What," I said, "*is* there, then?" 97

"A thick mire." 98

He stood before my eyes with a goatish beard and horn, long- 99
toothed, and with a tail. Hearing such words, I wanted to snatch him
by the tail, but I tumbled from the flour sacks and nearly broke a rib.
Then it happened that I had to answer the call of nature, and, passing,
I saw the risen dough, which seemed to say to me, "Do it!" In brief, I
let myself be persuaded.

At dawn the apprentice came. We kneaded the bread, scattered 100
caraway seeds on it, and set it to bake. Then the apprentice went away,
and I was left sitting in the little trench of the oven, on a pile of rags.
Well, Gimpel, I thought, you've revenged yourself on them for all the
shame they've put on you. Outside the frost glittered, but it was warm
beside the oven. The flames heated my face. I bent my head and fell
into a doze.

I saw in a dream, at once, Elka in her shroud. She called to me, 101
"What have you done, Gimpel?"

I said to her, "It's all your fault," and started to cry. 102

"You fool!" she said. "You fool! Because I was false is everything 103
false too? I never deceived anyone but myself. I'm paying for it all,
Gimpel. They spare you nothing here."

---

[10]A dumpling.

734 Isaac Bashevis Singer

I looked at her face. It was black; I was startled and waked, and
remained sitting dumb. I sensed that everything hung in the balance. A
false step now and I'd lose Eternal Life. But God gave me His help. I
seized the long shovel and took out the loaves, carried them into the
yard, and started to dig a hole in the frozen earth.

My apprentice came back as I was doing it. "What are you doing
boss?" he said, and grew pale as a corpse.

"I know what I'm doing," I said, and I buried it all before his very
eyes.

Then I went home, took my hoard from its hiding place, and divided it among the children. "I saw your mother tonight," I said. "She's
turning black, poor thing."

They were so astounded they couldn't speak a word.

"Be well," I said, "and forget that such a one as Gimpel ever existed." I put on my short coat, a pair of boots, took the bag that held
my prayer shawl in one hand, my stock in the other, and kissed the
mezzuzah.[11] When people saw me in the street they were greatly surprised.

"Where are you going?" they said.

I answered, "Into the world." And so I departed from Frampol.

I wandered over the land, and good people did not neglect me.
After many years I became old and white; I heard a great deal, many lies
and falsehoods, but the longer I lived the more I understood that there
were really no lies. Whatever doesn't really happen is dreamed at night.
It happens to one if it doesn't happen to another, tomorrow if not today,
or a century hence if not next year. What difference can it make? Often
I heard tales of which I said, "Now this is a thing that cannot happen."
But before a year had elapsed I heard that it actually had come to pass
somewhere.

Going from place to place, eating at strange tables, it often happens
that I spin yarns—improbable things that could never have happened—
about devils, magicians, windmills, and the like. The children run after
me, calling, "Grandfather, tell us a story." Sometimes they ask for particular stories, and I try to please them. A fat young boy once said to
me, "Grandfather, it's the same story you told us before." The little
rogue, he was right.

So it is with dreams too. It is many years since I left Frampol, but
as soon as I shut my eyes I am there again. And whom do you think I
see? Elka. She is standing by the washtub, as at our first encounter, but
her face is shining and her eyes are as radiant as the eyes of a saint, and

---

[11]A small oblong container affixed to the door jamb of devout Jews. It contains verses
from the Torah and is kissed each time a Jew passes through the door.

she speaks outlandish words to me, strange things. When I wake I have forgotten it all. But while the dream lasts I am comforted. She answers all my queries, and what comes out is that all is right. I weep and implore, "Let me be with you." And she consoles me and tells me to be patient. The time is nearer than it is far. Sometimes she strokes and kisses me and weeps upon my face. When I awaken I feel her lips and taste the salt of her tears.

No doubt the world is entirely an imaginary world, but it is only once removed from the true world. At the door of the hotel where I lie, there stands the plank on which the dead are taken away. The grave-digger Jew has his spade ready. The grave waits and the worms are hungry; the shrouds are prepared—I carry them in my beggar's sack. Another *schnorrer*[12] is waiting to inherit my bed of straw. When the time comes I will go joyfully. Whatever may be there, it will be real, without complication, without ridicule, without deception. God be praised: there even Gimpel cannot be deceived.

About the Story

1. Is Gimpel really a fool? What evidence do you find in the story that he is, or is not? If he is not, why does he let himself be made to seem foolish?

2. Are the lies people tell Gimpel all of the same kind, or are there differences? What pattern do you see in the order in which Gimpel tells of these deceptions?

3. What does Gimpel's confession of thievery reveal about his character? What of his decision to defile the villagers' bread, and his later decision not to do so?

4. Gimpel speaks of visions—of the devil, of his dead wife. How do you interpret these visions?

5. What is the turning point of the story? What does Gimpel give up, and why? What is his new purpose? How does his later life relate to his earlier life?

6. What is Singer's theme in this story? What does Gimpel mean in the last paragraph of the story when he talks about the imaginary world and the true world?

Explorations

1. Gimpel is often troubled by the relation between appearance and reality. Are things as they seem or is there an explanation which, though perhaps far from obvious, offers more of the truth? This question lies at the root of many

---

[12]A beggar.

personal, professional, and social dilemmas. Choose a topic that you think embodies the problem of appearance and reality and discuss it, drawing on your experience and your reading for examples.

2. "Gimpel the Fool" and "The Sermon on the Mount" (page 661) are both in the Judaic tradition and both are, at least in part, about how one should live. What do the two have in common? Where do they differ?

Glossary

Abstract: See *Concrete/Abstract.*

Action is the series of events in a narrative. It is also called the story line. See also *Plot.*

Alliteration: See *Sound.*

Allusion is a passing reference to a person, place, or thing. Often drawn from history, the Bible, mythology, or literature, allusions are an economical way for a writer to convey the essence of an idea, atmosphere, emotion, or historical era. Some examples of allusion are "The scandal was his Watergate," "He saw himself as a modern Job," and "The campaign ended not with a bang but a whimper." An allusion should be familiar to the reader; if it is not, it will neither add to the meaning of a text nor enrich an emotion.

Analogy is a special form of comparison in which the writer explains something unfamiliar by comparing it to something familiar: "A transmission line is simply a pipeline for electricity. In the case of a water pipeline, more water will flow through the pipe as water pressure increases. The same is true of electricity in a transmission line."

Analysis is a type of exposition in which the writer considers a subject in terms of its parts or elements. For example, one may analyze a movie by considering its subject, its plot, its dialogue, its acting, its camera work, and its set. See also *Cause and Effect, Classification, Process Analysis.*

Anecdote. An anecdote is a brief story told to illustrate a concept or support a point. Anecdotes are often used to open essays because of the inherent interest of a story.

Antagonist. An antagonist is a character who struggles against the central character, or protagonist, in a conflict. Chillingworth in *The Scarlet Letter* is a villainous antagonist; Jim in *The Adventures of Huckleberry Finn*, a virtuous antagonist. See also *Protagonist.*

Anticlimax: See *Organization.*

Aphorism. An aphorism is a short, concise statement embodying a general truth.

Appropriateness: See *Diction.*

Argument is one of the four basic forms of discourse. (Narration, description, and exposition are the other three.) To argue is to attempt to persuade a reader to agree with a point of view or to pursue a particular course of action by appealing to the reader's rational or intellectual faculties. See also *Deduction, Induction, Logical Fallacies,* and *Persuasion.*

Assonance: See *Sound.*

Assumptions are things one believes to be true, whether or not their truth can be proven. All writing includes many unstated assumptions as well as some that are stated, and an active reader seeks to discover what those assumptions are and decide whether they are acceptable.

Attitude is the view or opinion of a person; in writing, the author's attitude is reflected in its tone. See also *Tone.*

Audience is the expected readership for a piece of writing. For example, the readers of a national weekly newsmagazine come from all walks of life and have diverse interests, opinions, and educational backgrounds. In contrast, the readership for an organic chemistry journal is made up of people whose interests and education are quite specialized.

Body. The body is the main part of an essay, in which the author develops ideas and supports the thesis. See also *Introduction, Conclusion.*

Cause and Effect is a form of analysis that answers the question *why*. It explains the reasons for an occurrence or the consequences of an action. Determining causes and effects is usually thought-provoking and quite complex. One reason for this is that there are two types of causes: (1) *immediate causes*, which are readily apparent because they are closest to the effect, and (2) *ultimate causes*, which are somewhat removed, not so apparent, or perhaps even obscure. Furthermore, ultimate causes may bring about effects which themselves become causes, thus creating what is called a *causal chain*. For example, the immediate cause of a flood may be the collapse of a dam, and the ultimate cause might be an engineering error. An intermediate cause, however, might be faulty construction of the dam owing to corruption in the building trades.

Character. A character is a person in a story. Characters are generally regarded as being one of two types: flat or round. A flat character is one who exhibits a single trait, such as the devoted husband, the kind grandmother, or the shrewd businessman; such a character is stereotypic, unwavering, and thoroughly predictable. A round character, on the other hand, displays various traits and is complex and at times unpredictable—in short, very much like most of us. The chief character in a story is often called the *protagonist*, whereas the character or characters who oppose the protagonist are the *antagonists*.

Chronology: See *Organization, Plot.*

Classification, sometimes called classification and division, is a form of exposition. When classifying, the writer sorts and arranges people, places, or things into categories according to their differing characteristics. When dividing, the writer creates new, smaller categories within a large category, usually for purposes of classification. For example, a writer might divide the large category *books* into several smaller ones: textbooks, novels, biographies, reference books, and so on. Then specific books could be classified by assigning them to these categories.

Cliché. A cliché is a trite or hackneyed expression, common in everyday speech but avoided in most serious writing.

Climax. In a work of fiction or drama, the climax is the point of highest tension, sometimes identical with the turning point of the narrative.

Coherence is a quality of good writing that results when all sentences, paragraphs, and longer divisions of an essay are naturally connected. Coherent writing is achieved through (1) a logically organized sequence of ideas, (2) the repetition of key words and ideas, (3) a pace suitable for the topic and the reader, and (4) the use of transitional words and expressions. See also *Organization, Transitions.*

Colloquial Expressions: See *Diction.*

Comparison and Contrast is a form of exposition in which the writer points out the similarities and differences between two or more subjects in the same class or category. The function of any comparison and contrast is to clarify— to reach some conclusion about the items being compared and contrasted. The writer's purpose may be simply to inform, or to make readers aware of similarities or differences that are interesting and significant in themselves. Or, the writer may explain something unfamiliar by comparing it to something very familiar, perhaps explaining squash by comparing it to tennis. Finally, the writer can point out the superiority of one thing by contrasting it with another—for example, showing that one product is the best by contrasting it with all its competitors.

Conclusion. The conclusion of an essay is the sentences or paragraphs that sum up the main points and suggest their significance or in some other way bring the essay to a satisfying end. See also *Introduction, Body.*

Concrete/Abstract. A concrete word names a specific object, person, place, or action: *bicycle, milkshake, building, book, John F. Kennedy, Chicago,* or *hiking.* An abstract word, in contrast, refers to general qualities, conditions, ideas, actions, or relationships which cannot be directly perceived by the senses: *bravery, dedication, excellence, anxiety, stress, thinking,* or *hatred.* Although writers must use both concrete and abstract language, good writers avoid too many abstract words. Instead, they rely on concrete words to define and illustrate abstractions.

Conflict in a story is the clash of opposing characters, events, and ideas. A resolution of the conflict is necessary in order for the story to conclude.

Connotation/Denotation refer to the meanings of words. Denotation is the literal meaning of a word. Connotation, on the other hand, is the implied or suggested meaning of a word, including its emotional associations. For example, the denotation of *lamb* is "a young sheep." The connotations of lamb are numerous: *gentle, docile, weak, peaceful, blessed, sacrificial, blood, spring, frisky, pure, innocent,* and so on. Good writers are sensitive to both the denotations and connotations of words.

Consonance: See *Sound.*

Contrast: See *Comparison and Contrast.*

Deduction is a method of reasoning from the general to the particular. The most common form of deductive reasoning is the *syllogism,* a three-part argument that moves from a general statement (major premise) and a specific statement (minor premise) to a logical conclusion, as in the following example:
 a. All women are mortal. (major premise)
 b. Judy is a woman. (minor premise)
 c. Therefore, Judy is mortal. (conclusion)
The conclusion to a deductive argument is persuasive only when both premises are true and the form of the syllogism is correct. Then it is said that the argument is sound.

Definition is a statement of the meaning of a word, or of an idea or even an experience. A definition may be brief or extended, the latter requiring a paragraph of an essay or even an entire essay. There are two basic types of brief definitions, each useful in its own way. The first method is to give a *synonym,* a word that has nearly the same meaning as the word you wish to define: *dictionary* for *lexicon, nervousness* for *anxiety.* No two words ever have exactly the same meaning, but you can, nevertheless, pair a familiar word with an unfamiliar one and thereby clarify your meaning. The other way to define quickly, often with a single sentence, is to give a *formal definition;* that is, to place the term to be defined in a general class and then to distinguish it from other members of that class by describing its particular characteristics. For example:

WORD	CLASS	CHARACTERISTICS
A *canoe*	is a *small boat*	that has *curved sides* and *pointed ends* and is *narrow, made of light-weight materials,* and *propelled by paddles.*
A *rowboat*	is a *small boat*	that has a *shallow draft* and usually a *flat* or *rounded bottom,* a *squared-off* or *V-shaped stern,* and *oar locks* for the *oars with which it is propelled.*

Denotation: See *Connotation/Denotation.*

Denouement is the resolution or conclusion of a narrative.

Description is one of the four basic forms of discourse. (Narration, exposition, and argument are the other three.) To describe is to give a verbal picture of a person, a place, or a thing. Even an idea or a state of mind can be made vividly concrete, as in, "The old woman was as silent as a ghost." Although descriptive writing can stand alone, description is often used with other rhetorical strategies; for instance, description can make examples more interesting, explain the complexities of a process, or clarify a definition or comparison. A good writer selects and arranges descriptive details to create a *dominant impression* that reinforces the point or the atmosphere of a piece of writing.

   Objective description emphasizes the *object* itself and is factual without resorting to such scientific extremes that the reader cannot understand the facts. *Subjective* or *impressionistic description*, on the other hand, emphasizes the *observer* and gives a personal interpretation of the subject matter through language rich in modifiers and figures of speech.

Dialogue is the conversation that is recorded in a piece of writing. Through dialogue writers reveal important aspects of characters' personalities as well as events in the plot.

Diction refers to a writer's choice and use of words. Good diction is precise and appropriate—the words mean exactly what the writer intends and are well suited to the writer's subject, intended audience, and purpose in writing. There are three main levels of diction, each with its own uses: formal, for grand occasions; colloquial, or conversational, especially for dialogue; and informal, for most essay writing. See also *Connotation/Denotation, Abstract/Concrete, Specific/General.*

Digression. A digression is any part of a piece of writing that is not clearly relevant to its main point.

Discourse, Forms of. The four traditional forms of discourse are narration, description, exposition, and argument. Depending on the purpose, a writer may use one or more than one of these forms in a piece of writing. For more information see *Argument, Description, Exposition,* and *Narration.*

Division: See *Classification.*

Dominant Impression: See *Description.*

Effect: See *Cause and Effect.*

Emphasis is the placement of important ideas and words within sentences and longer units of writing so that they have the greatest impact. In general, the end has the most impact, and the beginning nearly as much; the middle has the least. See also *Organization*.

Essay. An essay, traditionally, is a piece of nonfiction prose, usually fairly brief, in which the writer explores his or her ideas on a subject. Essays come in many forms including personal narratives and scientific and theoretical inquiries, as well as critical, humorous, and argumentative pieces. The word *essay* presently is used fairly loosely to include not only personal writing but most short nonfiction prose pieces. For a discussion of the essay as a form, see Edward Hoagland's "On Essays" (p. 436).

Evaluation of a piece of writing is the assessment of its effectiveness or merit. In evaluating a piece of writing, one should ask the following questions: What does the writer have to say? Are the writer's ideas challenging or thought-provoking? What is the writer's purpose? Is it a worthwhile purpose? Does the writer achieve the purpose? Is the writer's information sufficient and accurate? What are the strengths of the essay? What are its weaknesses? Depending on the type of writing and the purpose, more specific questions can also be asked. For example, with an argument one could ask: Does the writer follow the principles of logical thinking? Is the writer's evidence convincing?

Evidence is the data on which a judgment or argument is based or by which proof or probability is established. Evidence usually takes the form of statistics, facts, names, examples, illustrations, and opinions of authorities, and always involves a clear indication of its relevance to the point at issue.

Example. An example is a person, place, or thing used to represent a group or explain a general statement. Many entries in this glossary contain examples used in both ways. Examples enable writers to show and not simply to tell readers what they mean. The terms *example* and *illustration* are sometimes used interchangeably. See also *Specific/General*.

Explanation: See *Exposition*.

Exposition is one of the four basic forms of discourse. (Narration, description, and argument are the other three.) The purpose of exposition is to clarify, explain, and inform. The methods of exposition are analysis, definition, classification, comparison and contrast, cause and effect, and process analysis. For a discussion of each of these methods of exposition, see *Analysis, Cause and Effect, Classification, Comparison and Contrast, Definition,* and *Process Analysis*.

Fallacy: See *Logical Fallacies.*

Figures of Speech are words and phrases that are used in an imaginative rather than literal way. Figurative language makes writing vivid and interesting and therefore more memorable. The most common figures of speech are:

Simile. An explicit comparison introduced by *like* or *as:* "The fighter's hands were like stone."

Metaphor. An implied comparison which uses one thing as the equivalent of another: "All the world's a stage."

Personification. The attributing of human traits to an inanimate object: "The engine coughed and then stopped."

Hyperbole. A deliberate exaggeration or overstatement: "I am so hungry I could eat a horse."

Metonymy. A type of comparison in which the name of one thing is used to represent another, as in the words *White House* used to represent the President of the United States.

Synecdoche. Another comparison in which a part stands for the whole, as in the word *crown* used to represent a king or the word *sail* to represent a ship.

See also *Symbol.*

General: See *Specific/General.*

Generalization. A generalization is a broad idea or statement. Generalizations usually require support or proof. See also *Thesis.*

Genre. A genre is a type or form of literary writing, such as poetry, fiction, or the essay; also used to refer to more specific literary forms, as to an epic poem, novel, or detective story.

Hyperbole: See *Figures of Speech.*

Illustration: See *Example.*

Imagery is the verbal representation of a sense experience: sight, hearing, touch, smell, taste, even the sensations one feels inside one's own body. Writers use imagery to create details in their descriptions. Effective images can make writing come alive and enable the reader to experience vicariously what is being described.

Induction is a method of reasoning that moves from particular examples to a general statement. In doing so, the writer makes what is known as an *inductive leap* from the evidence to the generalization, which can never offer the absolute certainty of deductive reasoning. For example, after examining enrollment statistics, we can conclude that students do not like to take courses offered early in the morning or late in the afternoon. See also *Argument*.

Inference is the drawing of a conclusion from evidence.

Intention: See *Purpose.*

Interpretation is the explanation of a written work. Literary interpretation can deal with the meaning and significance of either the whole or the parts of a work. Interpretation may also involve discovering the author's purpose and intended audience, and possibly the work's relation to others by the same author, or on the same subject, or of the same kind.

Introduction. The introduction of an essay consists of the sentences or paragraphs in which the author captures the reader's interest and prepares for what is to come. An introduction normally identifies the topic, indicates what purpose the essay is to serve, and often states or implies the thesis. See also *Body, Conclusion.*

Irony is the use of language to suggest other than its literal meaning. *Verbal irony* uses words to suggest something different from their literal meaning. For example, when Jonathan Swift writes in A *Modest Proposal* that Ireland's population problem should be solved through cannibalism, he means that almost any other solution would be preferable. *Dramatic irony*, in literature, presents words or actions that are appropriate in an unexpected way. For example, Oedipus promises to find and punish the wrongdoer who has brought disaster on Thebes, then discovers that the criminal is himself. *Irony of situation* involves a state of affairs the opposite of what one would expect: a pious man is revealed as a hypocrite, or an athlete dies young.

Issue: See *Thesis.*

Jargon refers to specialized terms associated with a particular field of knowledge. Also, it sometimes means pseudo-technical language used to impress readers.

Levels of Diction: See *Diction.*

Logic, in writing, is the orderly, coherent presentation of a subject. As a subdivision of philosophy, logic is both the study and the method of correct reasoning, using the techniques of deduction or induction to arrive at conclusions.

Logical Fallacies are errors in reasoning that render an argument invalid. Some of the more common logical fallacies are:

Oversimplification. The tendency to provide simple solutions to complex problems: "The reason we have inflation today is that OPEC has unreasonably raised the price of oil."

Non sequitur ("It does not follow"). An inference or conclusion that does not follow from the premises or evidence: "He was a brilliant basketball player; therefore, he will be an outstanding Supreme Court justice."

Post hoc, ergo propter hoc ("After this, therefore because of this"). Confusing chance or coincidence with causation. Because one event comes after another one, it does not necessarily mean that the first event caused the second: "I know I caught my cold at the hockey game, because I didn't have it before I went there."

Begging the question. Assuming in a premise that which needs to be proved: "Government management of a rail system is an economic evil because it is socialistic."

Either/or thinking. The tendency to see an issue as having only two sides: "America—love it or leave it."

Metaphor: See *Figures of Speech.*

Meter: See *Sound.*

Metonymy: See *Figures of Speech.*

Modes, Rhetorical: See *Discourse, Forms of.*

Mood is the emotional effect or feeling that a literary work evokes in the reader.

Narration is one of the four basic forms of discourse. (Description, exposition, and argument are the other three.) To narrate is to tell a story, to tell what happened. Whenever you relate an incident or use an anecdote to make a point, you use narration. In its broadest sense, narration includes all writing that provides an account of an event or a series of events.

Objective/Subjective. Objective writing is impersonal in tone and relies chiefly on facts and logical argument. Subjective writing refers to the author's personal feelings and may appeal not to reasons but to the reader's emotions. A writer may modulate between the two within the same essay, according to his or her purpose, but one or the other is usually made to dominate.

Organization is the plan or scheme by which the contents of a piece of writing are arranged. Some often-used plans of organization are *chronological order*, which relates people and events to each other in terms of time, for example, as one event coming before another, or two conditions existing simultaneously; *spatial order*, which relates objects and events in space, for example, from far to near or from top to bottom; *climactic order*, which presents ideas and evidence in order of increasing importance, power, or magnitude to heighten emphasis; and its opposite, *anticlimactic order*.

Paradox. A paradox is a self-contradictory statement that yet has truth in it, for example: "Less is more."

Paragraph. The paragraph, the single most important unit of thought in an essay, is a series of closely related sentences. These sentences adequately develop the central or controlling idea of the paragraph. This central or controlling idea, usually stated in a topic sentence, is necessarily related to the purpose of the whole composition. A well-written paragraph has several distinguishing characteristics: a clearly stated or implied topic sentence, adequate development, unity, coherence, and an appropriate organizational strategy.

Parallelism. Parallel structure is the repetition of word order or form either within a single sentence or in several sentences that develop the same central idea. As a rhetorical device, parallelism can aid coherence and add emphasis. Roosevelt's statement, "I see one third of the nation ill-housed, ill-clad, and ill-nourished," illustrates effective parallelism.

Persona, or speaker, is the "voice" you can imagine uttering the words of a piece of writing. Sometimes the speaker is recognizably the same as the author, especially in nonfiction prose. Often, however, the speaker is a partly or wholly fictional creation, as in Jonathan Swift's "A Modest Proposal" and in short stories, novels, and poems.

Personification: See *Figures of Speech*.

Persuasion is the effort to make one's audience agree with one's thesis or point of view and thus accept a belief or take a particular action. There are two main kinds of persuasion: the appeal to reason (see *Argument*) and the appeal to an audience's emotions; both kinds are often blended in the same piece of writing.

Plot is the sequence or pattern of events in a short story, novel, film, or play. The chief elements of plot are its *action*, the actual event or events;

conflict, the struggle between opposing characters or forces; the *climax,* the turning point of the story; and the *denouement,* the final resolution or outcome of the story.

Poetry is a rhythmical, imaginative, and intense form of expression. Poetry achieves its intensity by not only saying things in the fewest possible words but also in relying more heavily than other forms of literature on such language devices as metaphor, symbol, connotation, allusion, sound repetition, and imagery.

Point of View, as a technical term in writing, refers to the grammatical person of the speaker in a piece of writing. For example, a first-person point of view uses the pronoun *I* and is commonly found in autobiography and the personal essay; a third-person point of view uses the pronouns *he, she,* or *it* and is commonly found in objective writing. Both are used in the short story to characterize the narrator, the one who tells the story. The narrator may be *omniscient*—that is, telling the actions of all the characters whenever and wherever they take place, and reporting the characters' thoughts and attitudes as well. A less knowing narrator, such as a character in the story, is said to have a *limited,* or restricted, point of view.

Process Analysis answers the question *how* and explains how something works or gives step-by-step directions for doing something. There are two types of process analysis: directional and informational. The *directional* type provides instructions on how to do something. These instructions can be as brief as the directions for making instant coffee printed on a label or as complex as the directions in a manual for building your own home computer. The purpose of directional process analysis is simple: the reader can follow the directions and achieve the desired results. The *informational* type of process analysis, on the other hand, tells how something works, how something is made, or how something occurred. You would use informational process analysis if you wanted to explain to a reader how the human heart functions, how hailstones are formed, how an atomic bomb works, how iron ore is made into steel, how you selected the college you are attending, or how the Salk polio vaccine was developed. Rather than giving specific directions, the informational type of process analysis has the purpose of explaining and informing.

Protagonist. The protagonist is the central character in the conflict of a story. He or she may be either a sympathetic character (Hester Prynne in *The Scarlet Letter*) or an unsympathetic one (Captain Ahab in *Moby-Dick*).

Purpose. The writer's purpose is what he or she wants to accomplish in a particular piece of writing. Sometimes the writer may state the purpose openly, but sometimes the purpose must be inferred from the written work itself.

Reader: See *Audience.*

Rhetoric is the effective use of language, traditionally the art of persuasion, though the term is now generally applied to all purposes and kinds of writing.

Rhyme: See *Sound.*

Rhythm: See *Sound.*

Satire is a literary composition, in prose or poetry, in which human follies, vices, or institutions are held up to scorn. For a discussion of Jonathan Swift's use of satire see Gilbert Highet's "On Swift's 'A Modest Proposal' " (page 432).

Setting is the time and place in which the action of a narrative occurs. Many critics also include in their notion of setting such elements as the occupations and lifestyles of characters as well as the religious, moral, and social environment in which they live.

Short Story. The short story, as the name implies, is a brief fictional narrative in prose. Short stories range in length from about 500 words (a short short story) to about 15,000–20,000 words (a long short story or novella).

Simile: See *Figures of Speech.*

Sound. Writers of prose and especially of poetry pay careful attention to the sounds as well as the meanings of words. Whether we read a piece aloud or simply "hear" what we read in our mind's ear, we are most likely to notice the following sound features of the language:

Rhythm. In language, the *rhythm* is mainly a pattern of stressed and unstressed syllables. The rhythm of prose is irregular, but prose writers sometimes cluster stressed syllables for emphasis: "Théy sháll nót páss." Much poetry is written in highly regular rhythms called *meters,* in which a pattern of stressed and unstressed syllables is set and held to: "Th' ĕxpénse | ŏf spír | ĭt ĭń | ă wáste | ŏf sháme." Even nonmetrical poetry may sometimes use regular rhythms, as in this line by Walt Whitman: "Ĭ célĕbráte mўsélf ańd síng mўsélf."

Assonance, Consonance, and Rhyme. The repetition of a consonant is called *consonance,* and the repetition of a vowel is called *assonance.* The following line of poetry uses consonance of *l* and *d,* and assonance of *o:* "R<u>o</u>ll on, thou deep and dark blue ocean—roll!" When two nearby words begin with the same sound, like *deep* and *dark* above, that sound pattern is called *alliteration*. And when two words end with whole syllables that sound the same, and one of those syllables is stressed, the result is called *rhyme*, as in strong/along and station/gravitation.

Spatial Order: See *Organization*.

Specific/General. General words name groups or classes of objects, qualities, or actions. Specific words, on the other hand, name individual objects, qualities, or actions within a class or group. To some extent the terms *general* and *specific* are relative. For example, *dessert* is a class of things. *Pie*, however, is more specific than *dessert* but more general than *pecan pie* or *chocolate cream pie*. Good writing judiciously balances the general with the specific. Writing with too many general words is likely to be dull and lifeless. General words do not create vivid responses in the reader's mind as concrete specific words can. On the other hand, writing that relies exclusively on specific words may lack focus and direction, the control that more general statements provide. See also *Example*.

Style is the individual manner in which a writer expresses his or her ideas. Style is created by the author's particular selection of words, construction of sentences, and arrangement of ideas. A skillful writer adapts his or her style to the purpose and audience at hand. Some useful adjectives for describing styles include literary or journalistic, ornamental or economical, personal or impersonal, formal or chatty, among others. But these labels are very general, and an accurate stylistic description or analysis of a particular author or piece of writing requires consideration of sentence length and structure, diction, figures of speech, and the like.

Subjective: See *Objective/Subjective*.

Symbol. A symbol is a person, place, or thing that represents something beyond itself. For example, the eagle is a symbol of the United States, and the cross, a symbol of Christianity.

Synecdoche: See *Figures of Speech*.

Theme is the central idea in a piece of writing. In fiction, poetry, and drama, the theme may not be stated directly, but it is then presented through the characters, actions, and images of the work. In nonfiction prose the theme is often stated explicitly in a thesis statement. See also *Thesis*.

Thesis. The thesis of an essay is its main idea, the point it is trying to make.

The thesis is often expressed in a one- or two-sentence statement, although sometimes it is implied or suggested rather than stated directly. The thesis statement controls and directs the content of the essay: Everything that the writer says must be logically related to the thesis. Some therefore prefer to call the thesis the *controlling idea*.

Tone. Comparable to "tone of voice" in conversation, the tone of a written work reflects the author's attitude toward the subject and audience. For example, the tone of a work might be described by such terms as friendly, serious, distant, angry, cheerful, bitter, cynical, enthusiastic, morbid, resentful, warm, playful, and so forth.

Transitions are words or phrases that link sentences, paragraphs, and larger units of a composition in order to achieve coherence. These devices include connecting words and phrases like *moreover, therefore,* and *on the other hand,* and the repetition of key words and ideas.

Unity. A well-written essay should be unified; that is, everything in it should be related to its thesis, or main idea. The first requirement for unity is that the thesis itself be clear, either through a direct statement, called the thesis statement, or by implication. The second requirement is that there be no digressions, no discussion or information that is not shown to be logically related to the thesis. A unified essay stays within the limits of its thesis.

Acknowledgments (continued from page iv)

Sherwood Anderson, "The Egg." From *The Triumph of the Egg* by Sherwood Anderson. Reprinted by permission of Harold Ober Associates Incorporated. Copyright © 1921 by B. W. Huebsch, Inc. Renewed 1948 by Eleanor Copenhaver Anderson.

Roger Angell, "The Summer Game." Excerpt from *The Summer Game* by Roger Angell. Copyright © 1971 by Roger Angell. Originally published in *The New Yorker*. Reprinted by permission of Viking Penguin Inc.

W. H. Auden, "The Unknown Citizen." Copyright 1940 and renewed 1968 by W. H. Auden. Reprinted from *W. H. Auden: Collected Poems,* by W. H. Auden, edited by Edward Mendelson, by permission of Random House, Inc., and by permission of Faber and Faber Ltd. from *Collected Poems* by W. H. Auden.

Russell Baker, "School vs. Education." Copyright © 1981 by The New York Times Company. Reprinted by permission.

Bruno Bettelheim, "The Art of Moving Pictures." Copyright © 1981 by *Harper's* Magazine. All rights reserved. Reprinted from the October 1981 issue by special permission.

Derek C. Bok, "Can Ethics Be Taught?" Reprinted by permission of *Change* Magazine, Vol. 8, No. 9 (October 1976). Copyrighted by Council on Learning, P.O. Box 2023, New Rochelle, NY 10802.

Sissela Bok, "Professional Lies." From *Lying: Moral Choice in Public and Private Life,* by Sissela Bok. Copyright © 1978 by Sissela Bok. Reprinted by permission of Pantheon Books, a Division of Random House, Inc.

Daniel J. Boorstin, "Television." Daniel Boorstin, *Life* Magazine, © 1971 Time Inc., reprinted with permission.

Anthony Brandt, "Rite of Passage." Copyright © 1981, by The Atlantic Monthly Company, Boston, MA. Reprinted with permission.

Peter Brook, "Rehearsing a Play." From *The Empty Space* by Peter Brook. Copyright © 1968 by Peter Brook. Reprinted with the permission of Atheneum Publishers and Granada Publishing Limited.

Gwendolyn Brooks, "The Lovers of the Poor." From *The World of Gwendolyn Brooks*. Copyright © 1960 by Gwendolyn Brooks. Reprinted by permission of Harper & Row, Publishers, Inc.

William F. Buckley, Jr., "Up from Misery." Reprinted by permission of G.P. Putnam's Sons from *A Hymnal: The Controversial Arts* by William F. Buckley, Jr. Copyright © 1975–78 by William F. Buckley, Jr.

Grace Butcher, "So Much Depends Upon a Red Tent." Reprinted courtesy of *Sports Illustrated* from the February 3, 1975 issue. © 1975 Time Inc.

Alexander Calandra, "Angels on a Pin." From *Saturday Review*, Dec. 26, 1968. © A. Calandra, Washington University, St. Louis, Mo. 63011.

John Cheever, "The Golden Age." Copyright © 1959 by John Cheever. Reprinted from *The Stories of John Cheever,* by John Cheever, by permission of Alfred A. Knopf, Inc.

Arthur C. Clarke, "Electronic Tutors." Reprinted by permission of the author and the author's agents, Scott Meredith Literary Agency, Inc., 845 Third Avenue, New York, NY 10022.

Alistair Cooke, "The Money Game." From *The Americans*, by Alistair Cooke. Copyright © 1979 by Alistair Cooke. Reprinted by permission of Alfred A. Knopf, Inc.

Norman Cousins, "Pain Is Not the Ultimate Enemy." Reprinted from *Anatomy Of An Illness* by Norman Cousins, by permission of W. W. Norton & Company, Inc. Copyright © 1979 by W. W. Norton & Company, Inc.

Norman Cousins, "The Right to Die." From *Saturday Review*, June 14, 1975. Reprinted by permission of the author.

Donna Woolfolk Cross, "Propaganda: How Not to be Bamboozled." Reprinted in *Speaking of Words: A Language Reader*, 2e. Copyright by Donna Woolfolk Cross. Reprinted by permission of the author.

Agnes De Mille, "Pavlova." From *Dance to the Piper* by Agnes De Mille. Reprinted by permission of Harold Ober Associates Incorporated. Copyright © 1951, 1952, 1979, 1980 by Agnes De Mille.

Joan Didion, "Bureaucrats." From *The White Album* by Joan Didion. Copyright © 1979 by Joan Didion. Reprinted by permission of Simon & Schuster, a Division of Gulf & Western Corporation.

Joan Didion, "On Self-Respect." From *Slouching Towards Bethlehem* by Joan Didion. Copyright © 1961, 1968 by Joan Didion. Reprinted by permission of Farrar, Straus and Giroux, Inc.

Robert Francis, "The Skier." Copyright © 1959 by Robert Francis, reprinted from *Robert Francis: Collected Poems, 1936–1976* (University of Massachusetts Press, 1976).

Betty Friedan, "Feminism's Next Step." From *The Second Stage* by Betty Friedan. Copyright © 1981 by Betty Friedan. Reprinted by permission of Summit Books, a Simon & Schuster Division of Gulf & Western Corporation.

Robert Frost, "The Gift Outright." From *The Poetry of Robert Frost* edited by Edward Connery Lathem. Copyright 1942 by Robert Frost. Copyright © 1969 by Holt, Rinehart and Winston. Copyright © 1970 by Lesley Frost Ballantine. Reprinted by permission of Holt, Rinehart and Winston, Publishers.

Northrop Frye, "The Keys to Dreamland." From *The Educated Imagination* by Northrop Frye published by Indiana University Press. Reprinted by permission of the publisher and the author.

John Kenneth Galbraith, "The Position of Poverty." From *The Affluent Society* by John Kenneth Galbraith. Copyright © 1958, 1969, 1976 by John Kenneth Galbraith. Reprinted by permission of Houghton Mifflin Company.

William Gaylin, "What You See is the Real You." Copyright © 1977 by The New York Times Company. Reprinted by permission.

William Golding, "Thinking as a Hobby." Reprinted by permission of Curtis Brown, Ltd. Copyright © 1961 by William Golding. First published in *Holiday* Magazine.

Robert Graves, "The Cool Web." From *Collected Poems* by Robert Graves. Reprinted by permission of the author.

Dick Gregory, "Shame." From *Nigger: An Autobiography* by Dick Gregory with Robert Lipsyte. Copyright, © 1964 by Dick Gregory Enterprises, Inc. Reprinted by permission of the publisher, E.P. Dutton, Inc.

Donald Hall, "Ox Cart Man." From *Kicking the Leaves* by Donald Hall. Reprinted by permission; © 1977 The New Yorker Magazine, Inc.

S. I. Hayakawa, "Our Son Mark." From *Through the Communication Barrier* by S. I. Hayakawa. Copyright S. I. Hayakawa. Reprinted by permission of the author.

Robert Hayden, "Those Winter Sundays." Reprinted from *Angle of Ascent, New and Selected Poems,* by Robert Hayden, with the permission of Liveright Publishing Corporation.

James Herriot, "The Junkman and His Cat." From *The Lord God Made Them All* by James Herriot. Copyright © 1981 by James Herriot. Reprinted by permission of St. Martin's Press, New York, and Harold Ober Associates Incorporated.

John Hick, "The Problem of Evil." From *Philosophy of Religion,* 2nd ed., © 1973, pp. 36–43. Reprinted by permission of Prentice-Hall, Inc., Englewood Cliffs, NJ.

Gilbert Highet, "On Swift's 'A Modest Proposal.' " Copyright © 1962 by Gilbert Highet. Published by Princeton University Press. Excerpt, pp. 57–61, reprinted by permission of Princeton University Press.

Edward Hoagland, "On Essays." From *The Tugman's Passage,* by Edward Hoagland. Copyright © 1982 by Edward Hoagland. Reprinted by permission of Random House, Inc.

Jeanne Wakatsuki Houston, "Living in Two Cultures." Copyright by Jeanne Wakatsuki Houston. Reprinted by permission of the author.

Barbara Howes, "Out Fishing." From *Looking Up at Leaves* by Barbara Howes. Copyright © 1966 by Barbara Howes. Reprinted by permission of the author.

Langston Hughes, "Theme for English B." From *Montage for a Dream Deferred.* Reprinted by permission of Harold Ober Associates Incorporated. Copyright © 1949 by Langston Hughes. Renewed 1977 by George Bass as Executor for the Estate of Langston Hughes.

Ada Louise Huxtable, "Remnants of an Era: Two Silent Stores." © 1980 by The New York Times Company. Reprinted by permission.

Susan Jacoby, "Unfair Game." © 1978 by The New York Times Company. Reprinted by permission.

Martin Luther King, Jr., "I Have a Dream." Reprinted by permission of Joan Daves. Copyright © 1963 by Martin Luther King, Jr.

Katharine Kuh, "Modern Art." From *Breakup: The Core of Modern Art* by Katharine Kuh. Copyright 1965 by Cory, Adams and MacKay Ltd., London, England. By permission of New York Graphic Society Books/Little, Brown and Company, Boston.

Robin Lakoff, "You Are What You Say." From *Ms.* Magazine. Reprinted by permission of the author.

Barbara Lawrence, "Four-Letter Words Can Hurt You." © 1973 by The New York Times Company. Reprinted by permission.

Fran Lebowitz, "War Stories." From *Social Studies,* by Fran Lebowitz. Copyright © 1981 by Fran Lebowitz. Reprinted by permission of Random House, Inc.

Andrea Lee, "Russian Friends." Copyright © 1980 by Andrea Lee. Reprinted from *Russian Journal,* by Andrea Lee, by permission of Random House, Inc. First appeared in *The New Yorker.*

Alison Lurie, "The Language of Clothes." From *The Language of Clothes,* by Alison Lurie. Copyright © 1981 by Alison Lurie. Reprinted by permission of Alfred A. Knopf, Inc.

Marilyn Machlowitz, "Workaholics." Reprinted from *Workaholics* by Marilyn Machlowitz. Copyright © 1980, by permission of Addison-Wesley Publishing Co., Reading, MA.

Joyce Maynard, "Clothes Anxiety." © 1979 by The New York Times Company. Reprinted by permission.

John McMurtry, "Kill 'Em! Crush 'Em! Eat 'Em Raw!" From *Maclean's* Magazine. Reprinted by permission of the author.

John McPhee, "The Pinball Philosophy." From *Giving Good Weight* by John McPhee. Copyright © 1975, 1979 by John McPhee. This essay originally appeared in *The New Yorker.* Reprinted by permission of Farrar, Straus and Giroux, Inc.

H. L. Mencken, "The Politician." Copyright 1924 by Alfred A. Knopf, Inc. and renewed 1952 by H. L. Mencken. Reprinted from *A Mencken Chrestomathy,* by H. L. Mencken, by permission of Alfred A. Knopf, Inc.

Jonathan Miller, "Deciding to Be Ill." From *The Body In Question,* by Jonathan Miller. Copyright © 1978 by Jonathan Miller. Reprinted by permission of Random House, Inc. Reprinted from *Natural Shocks* and *The Body In Question* by Jonathan Miller by permission of the publisher Jonathan Cape Ltd., London.

N. Scott Momaday, "The Way to Rainy Mountain." From *The Way to Rainy Mountain* by N. Scott Momaday. Reprinted by permission of the author.

Michel de Montaigne, "Of the Inconsistency of Our Actions." Reprinted from *The Complete Works of Montaigne,* translated by Donald M. Frame with the permission of the publishers, Stanford University Press. Copyright 1943 by Donald Frame, © 1948, 1957.

Lance Morrow, "The Value of Working." Copyright 1981 Time Inc. All rights reserved. Reprinted by permission from *Time* Magazine.

Anais Nin, "My Turkish Grandmother." Copyright © 1976 by Anais Nin. Reprinted by permission of Harcourt Brace Jovanovich, Inc., from her volume titled *In Favor of the Sensitive Man and Other Essays.*

Joyce Carol Oates, "In the Region of Ice." Reprinted from *The Wheel of Love* by Joyce Carol Oates by permission of the publisher, Vanguard Press, Inc. Copyright © 1970, 1969, 1968, 1967, 1966, 1965 by Joyce Carol Oates.

George Orwell, "A Hanging." From *Shooting an Elephant and Other Essays* by George Orwell, copyright 1950 by Sonia Brownell Orwell; renewed 1978 by Sonia Orwell. Reprinted by permission of Harcourt Brace Jovanovich, Inc., the estate of the late Sonia Orwell, and Martin Secker & Warburg Ltd.

George Orwell, "Politics and the English Language." Copyright 1946 by Sonia Brownell Orwell; renewed 1974 by Sonia Orwell. Reprinted from *Shooting an Elephant and Other Essays* by George Orwell by permission of Harcourt Brace Jovanovich, Inc., the estate of the late Sonia Orwell, and Martin Secker & Warburg Ltd.

George Orwell, "Shooting an Elephant." From *Shooting an Elephant and Other Essays* by George Orwell, copyright 1950 by Sonia Brownell Orwell; renewed 1978 by Sonia Orwell. Reprinted by permission of Harcourt Brace Jovanovich, Inc., the estate of the late Sonia Orwell, and Martin Secker & Warburg Ltd.

Rhetorical Index

The selections in *Outlooks and Insights* are arranged in nine sections according to their themes. The following index, which is certainly not exhaustive, first classifies many of the essays according to the rhetorical strategies they exemplify. It then classifies selections by genre—poems, short stories, autobiographical and biographical writings, speeches, and so forth.

1. Rhetorical Strategies

Analogy

Argument

Cause and Effect

Comparison and Contrast

Definition

Description

Division and Classification

Illustration

Narration

Persuasion

Process Analysis

2. Genres

Autobiography and Biography

Humor, Irony, Satire

Personal Essays

Public Documents, Broadcasts, and Speeches

Poems

Short Stories